Topics Covered	Page #
Create **executable MP3 files**	7
Understand **fair use**	
Find **MP3 files on newsgroups**	
Find **MP3 files using search engines**	
Find **MP3 files using search utilities**	
Find **MP3 files via Web sites**	98
Play MP3 files with **FreeAmp** on Windows	368
Play MP3 files with **FreeAmp** on Linux	571
Use **Freenet** to find music and other files	275
Learn about the **future of MP3 and digital audio**	32
Use **gnutella** to find music	209
Encode with **GOGO-no-coda** on Linux	603
Play MP3 files with **GrayAMP** on the Macintosh	509
Rip and encode with **Grip** on Linux	579
Play MP3 files on a **hand-held PC**	639
Choose the right **hardware for MP3 and digital audio**	39
Choose **headphones**	55
Play MP3 files through your **home stereo system**	641
Understand **how Internet broadcasting works**	699
Understand **how MP3 works**	12
Broadcast with **icecast**	719
Edit **ID3 tags**	761
Use **iMesh** to find music and other files	258
Understand the basics of **intellectual property**	72
Understand the basics of **Internet broadcasting**	699
Get the right **Internet connection** for digital audio	62
Understand **Internet radio**	285
Encode with **LAME** on Windows	405
Understand the **law and Internet broadcasting**	694
Understand **what's legal and what's not legal** with MP3	70
Understand the **legal issues surrounding Napster**	90
Determine whether a digital-audio file is **legal or illegal**	87
Use the **Liquid Audio** digital-audio format	885
Play MP3 files with **MACAST** on the Macintosh	503

MP3 Complete

Guy Hart-Davis
and
Rhonda Holmes

SAN FRANCISCO ▸ PARIS ▸ DÜSSELDORF ▸ SOEST ▸ LONDON

Publisher: Jordan Gold

Contracts and Licensing Manager: Kristine O'Callaghan

Acquisitions and Developmental Editor: Diane Lowery

Editor: Sarah Lemaire

Production Editor: Kylie Johnston

Technical Editor: Eric Bell

Book Designer: Maureen Forys, Happenstance Type-O-Rama

Electronic Publishing Specialist: Kris Warrenburg, Cyan Design

Proofreaders: Andrea Fox, Ho Lin, Laurie O'Connell, Nancy Riddiough, Lindy Wolf

Indexer: Lynnzee Elze

Cover Designer: Design Site

Cover Photographer: VCG/FPG International

Copyright © 2001 SYBEX Inc., 1151 Marina Village Parkway, Alameda, CA 94501. World rights reserved. No part of this publication may be stored in a retrieval system, transmitted, or reproduced in any way, including but not limited to photocopy, photograph, magnetic, or other record, without the prior agreement and written permission of the publisher.

Library of Congress Card Number: 00-108685

ISBN: 0-7821-2899-8

SYBEX and the SYBEX logo are registered trademarks of SYBEX Inc. in the USA and other countries.

Screen reproductions produced with FullShot 99. FullShot 99 © 1991-1999 Inbit Incorporated. All rights reserved.
FullShot is a trademark of Inbit Incorporated.

Screen reproductions produced with Collage Complete.
Collage Complete is a trademark of Inner Media Inc.

TRADEMARKS: SYBEX has attempted throughout this book to distinguish proprietary trademarks from descriptive terms by following the capitalization style used by the manufacturer.

The author and publisher have made their best efforts to prepare this book, and the content is based upon final release software whenever possible. Portions of the manuscript may be based upon pre-release versions supplied by software manufacturer(s). The author and the publisher make no representation or warranties of any kind with regard to the completeness or accuracy of the contents herein and accept no liability of any kind including but not limited to performance, merchantability, fitness for any particular purpose, or any losses or damages of any kind caused or alleged to be caused directly or indirectly from this book.

Manufactured in the United States of America

10 9 8 7 6 5 4 3 2 1

This book is dedicated to the MP3 community.

Acknowledgments

We'd like to thank the following people for their help with this book:

- Gary Masters for frequent help and encouragement.
- Diane Lowery for developing the book.
- Sarah Lemaire for editing the book with patience and good humor.
- Eric "Howling Dog" Bell for reviewing the manuscript for technical accuracy.
- Kylie Johnston for coordinating the production of the book.
- Kris Warrenburg for laying out the manuscript.
- Andrea Fox, Ho Lin, Laurie O'Connell, and Lindy Wolf for proofreading the book.
- Lynnzee Elze for creating the index.

Contents at a Glance

	Introduction	xxiii
Part I	**MP3 Basics**	**1**
Chapter 1	MP3 and Digital Audio	3
Chapter 2	A Hardware Primer for MP3 and Digital Audio	39
Chapter 3	Digital Audio and the Law	69
Part II	**Finding Digital Music Online**	**95**
Chapter 4	Finding MP3 Files via the Web and Newsgroups	97
Chapter 5	Finding MP3 Files Using Napster and Its Friends	125
Chapter 6	Tuning In to Internet Radio	279
Part III	**MP3 on Windows**	**295**
Chapter 7	Windows Players	297
Chapter 8	Windows Rippers and Encoders	385
Chapter 9	Windows Jukeboxes	417
Part IV	**MP3 on the Macintosh**	**473**
Chapter 10	Macintosh MP3 Players	475
Chapter 11	Macintosh Rippers and Jukeboxes	515
Part V	**MP3 on Linux**	**565**
Chapter 12	Linux Players	567
Chapter 13	Linux Rippers and Encoders	577

Part VI	**Taking MP3 beyond the Computer**	**607**
Chapter 14	Choosing a Portable MP3 Player	609
Chapter 15	MP3 on Your PDA, on Your Home Stereo, and in Your Car	635
Part VII	**Publishing, Promoting, and Broadcasting Your Music on the Web**	**655**
Chapter 16	Grasping the Opportunities the Web Offers	657
Chapter 17	Getting Your Music Up on the Web	671
Chapter 18	Broadcasting Your Music across the Internet	693
Part VIII	**Advanced Digital-Audio Maneuvers**	**733**
Chapter 19	Recording Music Files onto CDs	735
Chapter 20	Working with MP3 Files	759
Chapter 21	Creating Skins for Winamp and RealJukebox	805
Chapter 22	Building a Serious Music Collection	855
Chapter 23	Other Digital-Audio Formats	873
Glossary		902
Index		*917*

Contents

Introduction ... xxiii

Part I ▶ MP3 Basics — 1

Chapter 1 □ MP3 and Digital Audio — 3

Digital Audio, Take 1: Studios and CDs ... 4
Digital Audio, Take 2: Compressed Digital Audio ... 8
What Does "MP3" Mean? ... 10
How Does MP3 Work? ... 12
Choosing an Appropriate Encoding Rate ... 16
Publish without Being Damned ... 19
MP3 Advantages and Disadvantages ... 20
    Advantages and Disadvantages for the Music Enthusiast ... 20
    Advantages and Disadvantages for the Artist ... 23
    Advantages and Disadvantages for the Record Company ... 25
The Future of MP3 ... 32
Other Digital-Audio Formats ... 33
Up Next ... 37

Chapter 2 □ A Hardware Primer for MP3 and Digital Audio — 39

The Chip: Pentium 200MMX or Better; Mac G3 ... 42
RAM: 32MB or More (Preferably Much More) ... 43
CD or DVD Drive ... 44
Sound Card ... 44
Speakers ... 49
    Beware of Cheap Speakers ... 50
    Speaker Components ... 50
    Passive or Amplified Speakers ... 51
    Measuring Speaker Loudness ... 51
    Suit Your Speakers to Your Sonic Needs ... 53
    Surround Sound and Home Theater ... 54
    Listen before You Buy ... 55
Headphones ... 55
Storage ... 58
Ports ... 60

Internet Connection	62
Security	62
Cable Modem	63
Digital Subscriber Line (DSL)	63
Integrated Services Digital Network (ISDN)	64
Satellite Solutions	65
Maximizing Your Modem Connection	65
Up Next	67

Chapter 3 □ Digital Audio and the Law   69

What's Legal and What's Not (Brief Summary)	70
Intellectual Property	72
Copyright	73
The Copyright Notice	75
Registering the Copyright	76
Granting Rights to Someone Else	77
Fair Use	77
Personal Use	79
The Protagonists in the Digital-Audio Scene	79
Music Consumers	80
Artists	80
Record Companies	81
The Recording Industry Association of America (RIAA)	81
Retail Industry	81
MP3 Files Are Legal	82
Creating Digital-Audio Files	83
Distributing Digital-Audio Files	83
How to Know If a Digital-Audio File Is Legal	87
What's Happening in the Real World	88
Legal Issues Surrounding Napster	90
Up Next	94

Part II ▶ Finding Digital Music Online   95

Chapter 4 □ Finding MP3 Files via the Web and Newsgroups   97

Finding MP3 Files on Web Sites	98
Major Sites	99

Contents

Pirate Sites	107
Finding MP3 Files Using Search Engines	111
Oth.Net	114
Lycos MP3 Search	114
Musicseek	114
Audiogalaxy	114
Scour	114
Finding MP3 Files Using Search Utilities	115
MP3 Star Search	115
Go!Zilla	117
Finding MP3 Files on Newsgroups	119
Up Next	122

Chapter 5 □ Finding MP3 Files Using Napster and Its Friends   125

Where We Stand Vis-à-Vis the Law	127
RIAA versus Napster, Metallica versus Napster	127
Overview of Napster	128
Using Napster on Windows	129
Getting and Installing Napster	129
Finding Music with Napster	146
Downloading a Track	151
Playing Music in Napster	156
Chatting on Napster	158
Maintaining a Hot List	164
Sharing Music with Napster	166
Using Macster—Napster for the Macintosh	168
Getting, Installing, and Configuring Macster	169
Choosing Preferences in Macster	175
Finding and Downloading Music with Macster	180
Browsing a User's Library	185
Getting User Information	186
Sending a Message to a User	187
Chatting with Macster	189
Using Napster on Linux	191
Using Gnapster	192

Using Wrapster	207
Using gnutella	209
Using audioGnome	217
Installing audioGnome	217
Configuring audioGnome	219
Connecting to a Server	224
Finding Music with audioGnome	225
Downloading Files with audioGnome	227
Browsing a User's Library	229
Sharing Files	230
CuteMX, iMesh, and SpinFrenzy	231
CuteMX	231
iMesh	233
Getting and Installing iMesh	234
Configuring iMesh	245
Searching with iMesh	258
Forwarding Information about a Track to a Friend	261
Downloading with iMesh	262
Sharing Files with iMesh	265
Uploading Files	266
Using Contacts	267
Exiting iMesh	271
Freenet	272
Downloading and Installing the Java 2 Runtime Environment	273
Downloading and Installing Freenet	274
Downloading and Installing a GUI for Freenet	274
Finding the Files You Want	275
SpinFrenzy	275
Up Next	277

Chapter 6 □ Tuning In to Internet Radio   279

Streaming Audio and Internet Radio	280
Getting, Installing, and Configuring RadioSpy	282
Understanding the RadioSpy Interface	285
Connecting to a Station	291
Using Favorites	293
Up Next	293

Part III ▶ MP3 on Windows — 295

Chapter 7 □ Windows Players — 297

- Choosing a Stand-Alone MP3 Player — 299
- Windows Media Player — 301
  - Windows Media Player Versions up to 7 — 302
  - Windows Media Player 7 — 304
- Winamp — 314
  - Getting and Installing Winamp — 314
  - Using Winamp — 318
  - Playing Music with Winamp — 321
  - Using Playlists — 324
  - Using Bookmarks to Access Tracks Quickly — 328
  - Using the Graphic Equalizer to Tweak the Sound — 329
  - Editing Tag Information — 333
  - Enjoying Visualizations — 334
  - Winamp Keyboard Commands — 335
  - Applying Skins — 339
  - Adding Functionality with Plug-Ins — 340
- Sonique — 349
  - Getting and Installing Sonique — 349
  - Navigating the Interface — 352
  - Playing MP3 Files and SHOUTcast Streams — 356
  - Creating a Playlist — 357
  - Using the Audio Enhancement Control — 359
  - Enjoying Visualizations — 361
  - Changing Sonique's Skin — 363
  - Using Plug-Ins — 365
  - Sonique Keyboard Commands — 365
- Other Windows MP3 Players — 367
  - FreeAmp — 368
  - XingMP3 Player — 370
  - Audioactive Player — 374
  - UltraPlayer — 377
  - Unreal Player MAX — 379
- Up Next — 383

Chapter 8 □ Windows Rippers and Encoders — 385

- Do You Need a Separate Ripper and Encoder? — 386
- AudioCatalyst — 389
  - Installing and Configuring AudioCatalyst — 389
  - Ripping and Encoding with AudioCatalyst — 396
  - Encoding MP3 Files from WAV Files — 398
- MP3Enc — 399
- MP3 Producer and MP3 Producer Professional — 400
  - Getting and Installing MP3 Producer — 401
  - Encoding with MP3 Producer — 402
  - Batch-Processing Files — 403
- LAME — 405
  - Running LAME from the Command Line — 405
  - Using a Front End with LAME — 406
- BladeEnc — 409
- Audioactive Production Studio — 409
- Up Next — 415

Chapter 9 □ Windows Jukeboxes — 417

- MusicMatch Jukebox — 418
  - Getting, Installing, and Configuring MusicMatch Jukebox — 419
  - Ripping — 429
  - Adding and Editing Tags — 430
  - Building Your Music Library or Libraries — 432
  - Playing Music with MusicMatch Jukebox — 438
  - Using the Graphic Equalizer — 440
  - Use the Net Music Feature to Access Music on the Internet — 441
  - Playing Net Radio — 442
  - Burning CDs — 443
- RealJukebox and Real Entertainment Center — 448
  - Why Some People Don't Like RealNetworks — 449
  - Installing and Configuring RealJukebox — 450
  - Getting around RealJukebox — 459
  - Ripping — 461
  - Playing Music — 462
  - Using RealJukebox with a Portable MP3 Player — 464
  - Changing RealJukebox's Skin — 467
  - Converting Tracks from One Format or Bitrate to Another — 468

Siren Jukebox and Visiosonic PCDJ	469
Sonic Foundry Siren Jukebox	470
Visiosonic PCDJ	471
Up Next	472

Part IV ▸ MP3 on the Macintosh   473

Chapter 10 ▫ Macintosh MP3 Players   475

Playing MP3 Files with QuickTime and RealPlayer Basic	476
Playing MP3 Files with QuickTime	477
Playing MP3 Files with RealPlayer Basic	478
SoundApp	478
Creating and Using Playlists	480
Viewing the Information for a File	481
Choosing Preferences in SoundApp	481
QuickAmp	491
Creating and Using Playlists in QuickAmp	492
Choosing Settings for QuickAmp	494
Adding Information to Tracks	499
Applying Skins to QuickAmp	500
MACAST	501
Playing Music	503
Creating and Using Playlists	504
Using the Equalizer	506
Applying Skins and Using Visualizations	507
Using the AutoSleep Feature	508
GrayAMP	509
MACAST Lite	513
Up Next	513

Chapter 11 ▫ Macintosh Rippers and Jukeboxes   515

AudioCatalyst	516
Installing and Configuring AudioCatalyst	517
Ripping and Encoding with AudioCatalyst	521
MPegger	522
SoundJam MP	527
Installing and Configuring SoundJam	527
General Page Preferences	529

　　　　Files Page Preferences　531
　　　　ID3 Tags Page Preferences　533
　　　　CD Lookup Page Preferences　534
　　　　Plugins Page Preferences　535
　　　　Converter Page　535
　　　　Advanced Page Preferences　537
　　　　Navigating the SoundJam Interface　538
　　　　Ripping and Encoding with SoundJam　539
　　　　Adding and Updating Track Information　541
　　　　Creating and Using Playlists　542
　　　　Using the Graphic Equalizer　542
　　　　Visualizations　544
　　　　Applying Skins　545
　　MusicMatch Jukebox for the Mac　545
　　　　Configuring MusicMatch Jukebox　549
　　　　Ripping and Encoding with MusicMatch Jukebox　555
　　　　Adding and Editing Tags　556
　　　　Building Your Music Library or Libraries　557
　　　　Playing Music with MusicMatch Jukebox　561
　　　　Applying Themes to MusicMatch Jukebox　563
　　Up Next　564

Part V ▶ MP3 on Linux　565

Chapter 12 □ Linux Players　567

　　xmms　568
　　FreeAmp　571
　　mpg123　574
　　Up Next　575

Chapter 13 □ Linux Rippers and Encoders　577

　　Grip　579
　　　　Ripping and Encoding　586
　　cdparanoia　587
　　ripperX　591
　　　　Configuring ripperX　592
　　　　Ripping and Encoding with ripperX　599
　　NotLame　601

Contents

GOGO-no-coda	603
BladeEnc	605
MP3Enc	605
Up Next	606

Part VI ▶ Taking MP3 beyond the Computer — 607

Chapter 14 □ Choosing a Portable MP3 Player — 609

MP3s beyond the PC: Five Categories	610
Portable MP3 Players: A Burgeoning Market	613
Choosing the Right Portable Player	615
How Much Storage Do You Need?	615
Does It Support Your Operating System?	618
Does It Have the Basic Controls You Need?	618
How Does It Sound?	619
Do You Need to Play Music Files Other Than MP3 on It?	620
Do You Need to Be Able to Record?	620
Do You Need a Tuner?	621
How Are the Size and Ease of Use?	621
Do You Need a Line-Out Jack?	621
What Battery Type, What Battery Life?	622
How Will You Carry It?	623
How Are the Headphones?	625
Does the Software Want to Manage Your Life?	626
Do You Need Equalization Controls?	632
Are Looks Important?	633
Up Next	633

Chapter 15 □ MP3 on Your PDA, on Your Home Stereo, and in Your Car — 635

Playing MP3 Files on a Pocket PC or Palm-Size PC	636
Using the Windows Media Player for Palm-Size PCs	637
Other Options for Playing Music on Palm-Size PCs	638
Playing MP3 Files on a Hand-Held PC	639
Playing MP3 Files on a Handspring Visor	641
Playing MP3 Files through Your Stereo System	641
Connecting Your PC to Your Stereo System	642

Choosing an MP3 Home Stereo Component	643
AudioReQuest	644
SongBank	645
Playing MP3 Files in Your Car	645
Connecting Your Portable Player to Your Car Stereo	646
Getting an In-Dash Player or In-Car Jukebox	647
empeg car	649
Up Next	653

Part VII ▸ Publishing, Promoting, and Broadcasting Your Music on the Web — 655

Chapter 16 ▫ Grasping the Opportunities the Web Offers — 657

Promises and Threats of Digital Audio	659
Advantages and Disadvantages of MP3	659
Advantages and Disadvantages of Other Digital-Audio Formats	661
Being Realistic about Piracy	662
Release Lo-Fi Versions of Tracks	662
Release Tracks in a Secure Format	663
Release No Music at All	663
If Piracy Is Inevitable, What Can You Do?	664
Encourage Bootlegs of Live Performances	664
Establishing Your Goals	665
Developing a Promotional Strategy	666
Choosing the Best Digital-Audio Format for Distribution	668
Up Next	669

Chapter 17 ▫ Getting Your Music Up on the Web — 671

Getting Your Music onto Online Music Sites	672
Signing Up As an Artist on Riffage.com	674
Signing Up As an Artist on MP3.com	674
Building Your Own Web Site	675
Choosing an ISP	678
Interactivity and Feedback	679

Contents

Proceed with Caution	680
What Are the Interactive Features For?	681
Collecting Information about Your Audience	681
Designing Your Web Site	684
Starting Your Own Electronic Newsletter	690
Up Next	691

Chapter 18 □ Broadcasting Your Music across the Internet — 693

The Law and Internet Broadcasting	694
The Basics of Internet Broadcasting	699
How Does It Work?	699
Which Computer Will You Use?	700
Buying a Microphone	700
Is Your Connection Macho Enough?	703
Broadcasting with SHOUTcast	704
Collecting the Software	705
Unpacking and Installing the NetShow Tools	706
Installing the Plug-Ins	707
Installing and Configuring the SHOUTcast Server	707
Starting the SHOUTcast Server	712
Configuring Winamp to SHOUTcast	713
Adding Your Voice to the Airwaves	716
Silencing Local Output	718
Bringing the Server Down	718
Broadcasting with icecast	719
Getting, Installing, and Configuring icecast	719
Starting icecast	723
Sending the icecast Server an Audio Stream from an Encoder	724
Using liveice to Downsample Files for Broadcast	727
Shutting Down icecast	731
Up Next	731

Part VIII ▸ Advanced Digital-Audio Maneuvers — 733

Chapter 19 ▫ Recording Music Files onto CDs — 735

- Why Burn CDs of Music Files? — 736
- Data CDs and Audio CDs — 737
- Choosing a CD Recorder or CD Rewriter — 739
  - Get a Fast Recorder — 739
  - Internal or External? — 740
  - EIDE, SCSI, Parallel Port, USB, or FireWire? — 741
  - CD-R or CD-RW? — 743
- CD-R and CD-RW Media — 745
- Choosing CD-Recording Software — 746
  - 1. Did You Get Any CD-Recording Software with Your Drive? — 746
  - 2. Can You Make Do with Your MP3 Player or Jukebox? — 747
  - 3. Do You Want a General-Purpose Package or an MP3-Specific Software Package? — 750
- An Example: Creating Audio CDs with Easy CD Creator — 752
- Up Next — 757

Chapter 20 ▫ Working with MP3 Files — 759

- Creating MP3 Files of Your Own Music (Windows, Mac, Linux) — 760
- Editing ID3 Tags (Windows, Mac, Linux) — 761
  - Editing ID3 Tags in Windows — 762
  - Editing ID3 Tags on the Mac — 763
  - Editing ID3 Tags on Linux — 768
- Renaming MP3 Files (Windows, Linux) — 771
  - Rename MP3 Files with MP3 Renamer (Windows) — 772
  - Rename MP3 Files with G6 Renamer (Windows) — 774
  - Renaming MP3 Files on Linux — 779
- Editing MP3 Files (Windows, Linux) — 779
  - MP3Cutter (Windows) — 780
  - mp3asm (Linux) — 783

Repairing Cooked Files (Windows, Linux)	783
Uncook 95 (Windows)	784
mp3asm (Linux)	786
Creating Playlists (Windows, Mac, Linux)	786
Creating Playlists on Windows	787
Creating Playlists on the Mac	794
Creating Playlists on Linux	797
Creating Executable MP3 Files with MP3 to EXE (Windows)	797
Entering Information in CDDB (Windows, Mac, Linux)	801
Up Next	803

Chapter 21 □ Creating Skins for Winamp and RealJukebox — 805

Why Create Skins?	806
Creating Skins for Winamp	807
Preparing for Skinning	809
The Golden Rules of Skinning	811
Creating a Skin	816
Creating the Bitmaps	819
Changing the Cursors	833
Editing the Text Files	834
Creating Skins for RealJukebox	840
The Graphics Files	841
Finding the Positions for Your Controls	844
Creating the Skin.ini File	844
Packaging and Distributing Your Skin	851
Converting Winamp Skins to RealJukebox Skins	852
Up Next	853

Chapter 22 □ Building a Serious Music Collection — 855

CDs and Bit-Rot	856
Getting the Best Music Quality	859
Picking a Naming Convention for Your MP3 Files	861
Building an MP3 Server	863
Storage	864
Connectivity	866

Reliability	867
Operating System	867
Backing Up Your Server	869
Up Next	871

Chapter 23 □ Other Digital-Audio Formats — 873

Why Consider Using Other Digital-Audio Formats?	874
Better Technology	874
Better Audio Quality	875
Better Security	875
Greater Compression Ratios	875
...and the Disadvantages	876
AAC	876
QDesign's QDMC and MVP	877
a2b	879
a2b Components	880
Advantages and Disadvantages of a2b	881
Getting and Installing the a2b music player	881
OpenMG and ATRAC3	884
Liquid Audio	885
Getting and Installing Liquid Player	886
Getting Liquid Audio Tracks	891
Windows Media Technologies	893
TwinVQ (VQF Format)	896
Playing VQF Files	897
Creating VQF Files	898
RealAudio	899
QuickTime	900
Up Next	900

Glossary — 902

Index — 917

Introduction

MP3 has been the leading topic of interest on the Internet since September 1999, when the term "MP3" took over from "sex" as the most-searched-for word on the Internet.

MP3 is hot because it's the most exciting audio technology to hit the market for at least ten years. MP3 compresses high-quality digital audio into computer files that are small enough to store and transfer easily. MP3 has given hundreds of millions of music lovers new and easier ways to enjoy music, and it has given independent artists a vital tool for distributing and promoting their own music online without needing the backing of a record company. Some established artists are using MP3 aggressively, too. For example, in September 2000, the Smashing Pumpkins released an entire album—25 tracks of new material—as MP3 files and vinyl records, skipping the conventional CD release because of a dispute with their record company. At the same time, MP3 offers new and existing record companies a powerful tool for promoting their artists and products.

This book provides all the information you need to know to become expert with MP3 and enjoy digital audio to the max.

What Can You Do with MP3?

With MP3, you can do the following—and much more:

- Play high-quality music on your computer using attractive, customizable players with full equalization capabilities.
- Download hundreds of thousands of tracks—many of them free—from the Internet to your computer.
- Listen to thousands of radio stations over the Internet.
- Turn your computer into a jukebox that contains and plays only the music you like.

- Play music on skip-proof portable players, such as the Diamond Rio, Samsung Yepp, and Sony VAIO Music Clip.
- Create a digital jukebox in your car so that you'll never have to change CDs on mountain roads again.
- E-mail music to your friends.
- Record MP3 files of your own music and distribute them with minimal effort and cost.
- Get your own music onto the Web for everyone to listen to.
- Share your own music, and find the music you want, using Napster and similar technologies.
- Broadcast your music over the Internet from your computer.

This book shows you how to do all these things. Whether you're a music lover or a musician, you'll find all the information you need to create and play MP3 files. You'll also learn how to get the right hardware and software to make and enjoy MP3 files.

Who Is This Book For?

This book is for anyone who has a computer and is interested in music, either as a fan or as a recording artist. MP3 is revolutionizing the music-distribution landscape in much the same way that the Web has revolutionized the distribution of information. Here's what that means in practice:

- If you're a music enthusiast, MP3 provides you with a way of creating and managing the ultimate personalized jukebox on your computer. MP3 also provides you with access to an inexhaustible source of new music via the Internet. And much of that music is free. Whatever your taste in music, chances are good that you'll find thousands of tracks to download and scores of Internet radio stations playing that type of music around the clock. If there's no Internet radio station broadcasting what you like, you can even set one up yourself without much difficulty.

▶ If you're a recording artist, MP3 provides an exciting new distribution channel for your music, allowing you to bypass the bottleneck of the record companies once and for all. By using MP3, you can distribute your music over the Internet and Web within minutes of recording it, allowing you to reach current and potential listeners all over the world immediately—and get feedback from them.

WHAT DOES THIS BOOK COVER?

This book covers all you need to know to enjoy MP3 and digital audio on a computer running Windows, MacOS, or Linux.

Here are the details:

Chapter 1, "MP3 and Digital Audio" This chapter discusses why digital audio is hot and why you should be interested in it. This chapter shows you the advantages and disadvantages of MP3, and explains why MP3 is currently dominating the digital-audio scene. This chapter then briefly reviews the competing digital-audio formats.

Chapter 2, "A Hardware Primer for MP3 and Digital Audio" This chapter outlines the hardware you need in order to enjoy MP3 and other digital audio—everything from CPU and RAM to speakers (or headphones) and an Internet connection. This chapter also visits the question of whether you should upgrade an older computer to add digital-audio capabilities or buy a new computer instead.

Chapter 3, "Digital Audio and the Law" This chapter explains how digital audio and the law relate to each other, and clears up some misconceptions about what's legal and what's not legal with digital audio. You need to read this chapter because it's all too easy to commit a felony with digital audio if you don't know the law.

Chapter 4, "Finding MP3 Files via the Web and Newsgroups" This chapter shows you how to find MP3 files by searching the Web and by trolling through newsgroups. This chapter presents some of the most durable MP3 Web sites to date and shows you how to use search engines and search utilities to find the music you want.

Chapter 5, "Finding MP3 Files Using Napster and Its Friends" This chapter discusses how to use Napster—one of the most powerful and most controversial software technologies released in the last five years—and related technologies. Napster and Napster-like technologies make it easy to find and to share the music you like, but they bring a host of legal issues to the party. Apart from Napster itself (which is covered in detail), this chapter discusses Macster, Gnapster, gnutella, audioGnome, Wrapster, iMesh, CuteMX, Freenet, and SpinFrenzy.

Chapter 6, "Tuning In to Internet Radio" This chapter explains what streaming audio is and shows you how to use RadioSpy to tune into Internet radio broadcasts.

Chapter 7, "Windows Players" This chapter presents a handful of the most popular, most prominent, and most promising MP3 players for Windows. You'll find in-depth treatment of Windows Media Player, Winamp, and Sonique, together with an introduction to other players, including FreeAmp, XingMP3 Player, Audioactive Player, and Unreal Player MAX.

Chapter 8, "Windows Rippers and Encoders" This chapter first considers the question of whether you need a separate ripper and encoder (rather than an all-in-one MP3 solution). It then discusses the rippers and encoders AudioCatalyst, MP3Enc, MP3 Production Studio, LAME, BladeEnc, and Audioactive Production Studio.

Chapter 9, "Windows Jukeboxes" This chapter discusses in detail the two leading ripper/player/jukeboxes for Windows, MusicMatch Jukebox and RealJukebox. It also discusses two alternative jukeboxes, Siren Jukebox and Visiosonic PCDJ.

Chapter 10, "Macintosh MP3 Players" This chapter discusses the best and most popular MP3 players for the Macintosh platform. The chapter starts by explaining how you can use the widely installed applications QuickTime and RealPlayer Basic to play MP3 files at a pinch. It then presents the dedicated MP3 players SoundApp, QuickAmp, and MACAST in detail, and discusses two other Mac MP3 players, GrayAMP and MACAST Lite.

Chapter 11, "Macintosh Rippers and Jukeboxes" This chapter shows you how to use two of the leading ripper/encoders of the Mac, AudioCatalyst and MPegger, and the two leading ripper/player/jukeboxes for the Mac, SoundJam MP and MusicMatch Jukebox.

Chapter 12, "Linux MP3 Players" This chapter explains how to use three of the most popular MP3 players for Linux: xmms (a port of Winamp), FreeAmp (another graphical player), and mpg123 (a command-line player).

Chapter 13, "Linux Rippers and Encoders" This chapter shows you a number of solutions for ripping and encoding on Linux. In this chapter, you'll find what you need to know to use the graphical ripper/encoders Grip and ripperX, the powerful ripper cdparanoia, and the command-line encoders NotLame and GOGO.

Chapter 14, "Choosing a Portable MP3 Player" This chapter advises you on the difficult choices that you'll face if you decide to buy a portable MP3 player. The chapter first outlines the five categories of product that allow you to take MP3 beyond the PC. It then provides you with criteria to use in evaluating the portable MP3 players that are clamoring for your dollars.

Chapter 15, "MP3 on Your PDA, on Your Home Stereo, and in Your Car"   This chapter continues Chapter 14's discussion of how to take MP3 beyond the PC. This chapter shows you how to play MP3 files on a Pocket PC or Palm-size PC, a hand-held PC, or a Handspring Visor; how to play MP3 files through your home stereo; and how to enjoy MP3 in your car.

Chapter 16, "Grasping the Opportunities the Web Offers"   This chapter reviews the advantages and disadvantages that MP3 and the other digital-audio formats offer to the artist. The chapter offers a realistic view of piracy and discusses how to establish your goals in promoting your music online, how to develop a promotional strategy, and how to choose the best audio format for your needs.

Chapter 17, "Getting Your Music Up on the Web"   This chapter discusses a three-pronged strategy for promoting your music via the Web: making tracks available on major online music sites, building your own Web site, and starting an e-mail newsletter to develop interest in your work.

Chapter 18, "Broadcasting Your Music across the Internet"   This chapter explains the basics and the legalities of Internet broadcasting and shows you how to get yourself on the air. In this chapter, you'll find a detailed example of implementing a SHOUTcast server on a Windows platform and a discussion of the icecast server for Linux.

Chapter 19, "Recording Music Files onto CDs"   This chapter covers the whys, wherefores, and hows of recording both audio CDs and data CDs. This chapter shows you how to choose a CD recorder or CD rewriter and suitable software, and explains the differences between CD-R and CD-RW media.

Chapter 20, "Working with MP3 Files" This chapter discusses how to perform a number of important operations with MP3 files, such as creating MP3 files of your own music, editing the ID3 tags on MP3 files, and repairing damaged MP3 files. This chapter also explains how to create executable MP3 files that you can share with people who don't have an MP3 player installed on their computer and how to supply information to CDDB, the online database of CD information.

Chapter 21, "Creating Skins for Winamp and RealJukebox" This chapter explains how to create custom skins (graphical looks) for the Winamp MP3 player and the RealJukebox jukebox application.

Chapter 22, "Building a Serious Music Collection" This chapter offers advice on building a serious music collection using MP3 or another digital-audio format. This chapter starts by pointing up the looming specter of bit-rot that threatens to consume your CD collection. It then moves on to consider how to get the best music quality possible with MP3 before discussing how to build an effective MP3 server and how to protect your music collection by backing it up.

Chapter 23, "Other Digital-Audio Formats" This chapter begins by discussing the reasons for (and against) using a digital-audio format other than MP3. It then gives you the information you need about these digital-audio formats: AAC, a2b, ATRAC3, Liquid Audio, QDesign, MS Audio and Windows Media Technologies, TwinVQ, RealAudio, and QuickTime.

At the end of the book, you'll find a glossary and a comprehensive index.

Terminology and Conventions Used in This Book

To keep this book down to a manageable size, we've used a number of conventions to represent information concisely and accurately:

- The menu arrow, ➤, indicates selecting a choice from a menu or submenu. For example, "choose Edit ➤ Preferences" means that you should pull down the Edit menu and select the Preferences item from it.

- \+ signs indicate key combinations. For example, "press Ctrl+P" means that you should hold down the Ctrl key and press the P key; and "press Apple+Q" means that you should hold the Apple-symbol key on your Macintosh and press the Q key. Likewise, "Ctrl+click" and "Shift+click" indicate that you should hold down the key involved and then click.

- *Italics* indicate new terms being introduced.

- **Boldface** indicates text that you may need to type letter for letter.

- Unless we're missing it, there's no really appropriate word in English for "chunk of audio." For example, a song is usually understood to have words, and a track is usually understood as meaning one piece of music (or speech) from a CD, a cassette, or a vinyl record. In the absence of a better word, we'll refer to a chunk of audio as a track, except where one of the applications chooses to refer to it as a song.

- While we're on the subject of words, the words *folder* and *directory* mean the same thing for Windows-based computers. We've used them interchangeably, trying to follow the terminology that the application being discussed uses.

- URLs: We've left off the `http://` from each URL for brevity (and to prevent bad line breaks). For example, the URL `http://sound.media.mit.edu/mpeg4/` appears in the book as `sound.media.mit.edu/mpeg4/`. So you'll need to add the `http://` to each URL you use.

MP3 Is a Moving Target...

You'll see the phrase "at this writing" appear frequently in this book. This book went to press in October 2000 and reflects the state of MP3 software and hardware at that time.

Because MP3 software and hardware is evolving more or less at Internet speed, you'll likely find that some things have changed by the time you read this book. For example, you may find that newer versions of software applications have more features than we describe in the book, or that those features are implemented in a somewhat different way. However, the descriptions in this book should give you a good idea of how the applications work; if they're not the same feature for feature, they should at least be similar in enough ways for you to figure them out easily.

Enjoy!

PART I

MP3 Basics

LEARN TO:

- **UNDERSTAND WHY DIGITAL AUDIO IS IMPORTANT**
- **UNDERSTAND THE ADVANTAGES AND DISADVANTAGES OF MP3**
- **CHOOSE THE RIGHT HARDWARE FOR ENJOYING QUALITY DIGITAL AUDIO**
- **KNOW WHAT'S LEGAL WITH DIGITAL AUDIO, AND WHAT'S NOT**

Chapter 1
MP3 and Digital Audio

FEATURING
- What is digital audio?
- Why digital audio is an exciting technology
- The short version of how MP3 works
- Advantages and disadvantages of MP3
- Competing digital-audio formats

In this chapter, we'll discuss why digital audio is such a hot topic and how it affects you. We'll start by talking about what digital audio is, what you can do with it, and why you should be interested in it if you're not already. Then we'll switch the focus to MP3 for a bit. We'll give you the short version of how MP3 works, its advantages and disadvantages, and why it's currently dominating the digital-audio scene. After that, toward the end of the chapter, we'll give you a quick heads-up on the other digital-audio formats, what's good and what's bad about them, and why we'll spend most of the book showing you how to make the most of MP3 before returning to the other formats to discuss them in more depth.

Digital Audio, Take 1: Studios and CDs

Digital audio is audio that is stored in a digitized format rather than in an analog format. An analog signal is a continuously variable waveform, while a digital signal is a numeric representation of that waveform. To create a digital version of an analog sound, you examine the analog sound, measure the waveform at many regular intervals, and then store these measurements as numbers. (We'll talk about this in more detail later in this chapter when we discuss how MP3 works.)

As with analog recordings, digital audio can be any sound at all that can be recorded—whale songs, the gentle strains of Marilyn Manson, or the noise of a ten-ton truck with a cargo of live pigs disagreeing with a mountain bend. But instead of being stored on an analog medium such as audio tape or vinyl, digital audio can be stored and manipulated on computers.

At this point, you're probably wondering what we're making such a big deal about. Most recording studios have been using digital audio and computers for many years now, because doing so lets them record and manipulate the sound more easily, more accurately, and more cheaply than using analog recording equipment. For example, with digital recording, you can much more easily separate the tracks of a recording; you can clean up stray noise, edit out particular sounds, change certain frequencies of sounds, or synchronize tracks perfectly.

So recording studios have been using computers for recording, processing, and mixing for a long time. But once the music is finished, it is typically copied to physical media for distribution to the target audience rather than being distributed electronically as a digital file. The physical media might be digital (CDs) rather than analog (records or cassettes), but CDs were designed as an audio-distribution format rather than as a computer-friendly format.

There were several good reasons why CDs were designed as an audio-distribution format, and not as a media that was particularly computer oriented:

▶ First, when CDs were first released, the personal-computer revolution was just starting to happen. Computers had no sound capabilities to speak of, beyond issuing peremptory bleeps in complicated sequences intended to indicate different degrees of unhappiness. For example, three short bleeps and one long bleep on booting might indicate that the computer thought its graphics card had taken a hike. In addition, the storage capacity of computers in those days was (by today's standards) laughably small—a powerful computer would have enough storage for about 30 seconds of CD-quality audio if you cleared everything else off the hard disk. The arrival of the Amiga computer solved the first problem—the Amiga had full multimedia capabilities—but the second problem, lack of storage space, remained until the late 1990s.

▶ Second, the recording industry needed a more compact format for distributing audio—and a format for which it could charge more money than for records or cassettes.

▶ Third, the recording industry was concerned about music piracy. (And today, its fears have mostly come true.)

As you'll remember if you were around at that time, it took more than a decade for CDs to rout vinyl records and cassette tapes. The first reason was the perennial chicken-and-egg problem that any new physical medium suffers when challenging an existing medium. At first, there wasn't enough music available on CDs to convince consumers to buy CD players, and there weren't enough people using CD players to provoke the record companies into a wholesale commitment to CDs. (At this writing, DVD is gradually breaking through a similar problem in its encroachment on videotapes.)

Second, the higher prices on CDs acted as a strong disincentive for consumers to buy them. (DVD is having the same problem now.)

And third, some early CDs and early CD players managed to sound worse than the analog recordings to which they were technically superior: The sound was so crisp that it sounded unpleasant, particularly to those who'd grown up loving the "warm" sound of records.

At this writing (July 2000), CDs dominate the music scene. According to the International Federation of Phonographic Industries (IFPI to its friends), 3.8 billion units of recorded music were sold worldwide in 1999. Of those 3.8 billion units, 2.4 billion (a shade over 62 percent) were CDs, and 1.4 billion were cassette tapes and singles. In 1999, the percentage of CDs was up by 3 percent over 1998, which also saw total global sales of 3.8 billion units; sales of music cassettes fell by 7 percent and sales of singles fell by 4 percent from 1998 to 1999.

Statistically, MiniDiscs are almost irrelevant in this picture, with a mere million units sold worldwide for the year—and half of those were sold in the U.K. (MiniDiscs are popular in the U.K. primarily because CDs are even more absurdly overpriced there than they are in most of the rest of the Western world.)

CDs contain uncompressed digital audio recorded at 44.1kHz, "CD quality," which takes up about 10.5MB per minute (see the following Note for the details). So the files are huge; a three-minute track takes up around 30MB, and a CD can hold up to 650MB of data or up to about 74 minutes' worth of audio. Just storing these files on a hard drive would take up a significant chunk of space—you can put about 30 full CDs' worth of music on a chunky 20GB hard drive, but 30 CDs is laughably few to your average music fan.

NOTE

Tech moment: Here are the details on CD-quality audio. 44,100 samples per second times 2 tracks (stereo) times 2 bytes per sample gives 10,584,000 bytes per minute. A real megabyte is 1,048,576 bytes. (You doubtless knew that, but we mention it here because most hard-disk manufacturers call one million bytes a megabyte, which is why the typical hard disk appears to have only about 95 percent of its nominal capacity.) So a CD uses 10.09MB per minute. On a CD, each second of audio takes 75 sectors of 2352 bytes each. (When the CD is used for data, only 2,048 bytes of the sector are used for data—the rest is for error correction and housekeeping.) So a 650MB data CD-R can hold 74 minutes of CD audio.

Transferring files of 30 to 50MB from one computer to another is a pain in the seat. Floppies are pathetically inadequate; you can fit a couple of tracks on a 100MB Zip disk or a couple of dozen on a 1GB Jaz drive, and they'll take ages to transfer over any but the sturdiest and most expensive Internet connection. Only if you're connected to a local area network (LAN) can you afford to heave around files of this size with anything approaching frequency, and even then, your coworkers may threaten to stone you with Twinkies for monopolizing the available bandwidth.

So by size alone, digital audio on CDs enjoys a sort of de facto copy protection—the tracks are too big for you to copy and distribute easily. But there's another wrinkle. If you put an audio CD into your computer's CD drive and open a Windows Explorer window, you'll see that the CD appears to contain 1K tracks in a format called CDA rather than the 20 to 80MB files that you'd expect to find. These CDA files aren't the tracks themselves—they're just pointers (called *handles*) to the audio. They essentially provide an index to the audio on the CD. You can copy the CDA files from the CD to another drive, but doing so won't do you much good, because the audio will still be on the CD. To extract the audio from the CD requires a more sophisticated program than your favorite file-management program. It needs a *ripper,* a program designed to extract the audio data from the CD. (More on this in a moment.)

So digital audio is here and has been for a while—but the way we've just described it, it probably doesn't strike you as being too exciting. Where the excitement comes in is when you can compress the digital audio so that it becomes small enough to store and manipulate easily via computer. That's the key behind MP3 and the other digital-audio formats.

Digital Audio, Take 2: Compressed Digital Audio

Uncompressed digital-audio files tend to be huge and locked firmly to CDs, at least in the realm of the consumer. To deal with these problems, you take the following steps:

- Use a ripper to extract the audio files from the CD.
- Encode and compress the files to a more manageable size without losing a significant amount of audio quality.

These two steps have led to the massive success of MP3. Most of the other digital-audio file formats provide similar capabilities, but they haven't yet enjoyed the same widespread acceptance as MP3.

MP3 is essentially just a file format for storing compressed digital audio on computers. By using compression, MP3 files take up only one-tenth of the space of uncompressed high-quality audio. Compressed to an MP3 file at 128 kilobits per second (kbps), a rate generally considered to provide near-CD quality, a three-minute track takes up about 3MB rather than the 31MB or so that the uncompressed track would need. Other digital-audio formats take up a similar amount of space, with some (such as Microsoft's Windows Media Architecture and the VQF format) claiming even better compression ratios with similar or better audio quality.

In the last few years, hard drives have grown dramatically in capacity while dropping gradually in price. As a result, storing MP3 files and other compressed digital-audio files isn't a problem. Even a 10GB drive (modest by mid-2000 standards) can store more than 150 CDs' worth of MP3 files, and at this writing, 60GB hard drives have fallen in price to around $350, so you can get serious storage space without having to pawn your family jewels. By ripping devotedly for a few days (or weeks), you can put your entire CD collection on your computer and manage it from there, turning your computer into a digital jukebox.

Once you've recorded a digital-audio file in the MP3 format, you can store it on a computer and play it back whenever you want by using widely available software You can also transfer the MP3 file from your computer to a portable player (such as the Diamond Rio or the Creative Labs Nomad), to a personal digital assistant (PDA) such as a Palm, a Visor, or a Palm-size PC, to a hand-held computer, to a car player, or to a home-stereo component, so you can enjoy the digital-audio tracks you like pretty much anywhere.

Better yet, you can easily transfer the file from one computer to another, either electronically (via the Internet or another network) or by using physical media such as Zip disks or recordable CDs. Modem speeds are adequate for downloading compressed digital-audio files; at 56k, a 4MB file will take you between 15 and 20 minutes to download if all goes well. But if you're in a community that has access to cable modems, digital subscriber lines (DSLs), or fiber-optic connections, or if you're in a dorm networked to your institution's campus, you'll be able to download a track of that size in a matter of seconds.

Typically, when you download a digital-audio track, you save it to your hard drive, from where you can play it back to your ears' content. But you don't have to do that. Many MP3 Web sites provide streaming downloads that let you play the music without saving it, which both spares the Web site any copyright problems (they're essentially broadcasting the track, not providing you with a copy of it that would require authorization) and saves you disk space.

What Does "MP3" Mean?

So MP3 is much easier to handle than larger forms of digital audio. But where does the name come from?

The MP3 format gets its name from having been created under the auspices of MPEG. MPEG (pronounced *em-peg*) is the acronym for the Moving Picture Experts Group, a working group of the International Standards Organization (ISO) and the International Engineering Consortium (IEC) in charge of developing "international standards for compression, decompression, processing, and coded representation of moving pictures, audio, and their combination."

MPEG splits its work into major classes, each of which contains a number of layers. For example, the MPEG-1 class covers storage and retrieval of moving pictures and audio. Within that class are a number of layers, each of which provides specifications for a practical, real-world application. The layer in the MPEG-1 class that we're interested in is Layer III, which covers audio encoding and is discussed in the document ISO/IEC 11172-3. As it happens, Layer III of the MPEG-2 class (the class that covers digital television) also covers audio encoding and is relevant to MP3; this layer is discussed in the document ISO/IEC 13818-3. Layer III of MPEG-1 covers sampling rates of 32kHz, 44.1kHz, and 48kHz, while Layer III of MPEG-2 covers sampling rates of 16kHz, 22.05kHz, and 24kHz. Most people sample at 44.1kHz, because that produces what people consider "CD-quality" audio—audio that is just about as good as it gets, or at least as complete as it gets. (We'll revisit the topic of "CD quality" in a couple of minutes, so damp down any questions that you can feel brewing on that front.)

> **NOTE**
>
> The third class that MPEG has developed so far is MPEG-4 versions 1 and 2, which cover multimedia applications. You'll notice that MPEG-3 (which would have covered high-quality video) is missing. That's because MPEG ended up folding it into MPEG-2. MPEG is currently working on MPEG-4 versions 3 and 4, MPEG-7 (a "content representation standard for multimedia information search, filtering, management, and processing"), and MPEG-21 (a multimedia framework). To find out more about MPEG, visit the MPEG home page at `drogo.cselt.it/mpeg/`.

You'll notice that we said "developed under the auspices of MPEG" rather than "developed by MPEG." That's because MPEG codified the standard—they didn't create it. The encoding method was developed by Dr. Karlheinz Brandenburg at the Fraunhofer Institute for Integrated Circuits IIS-A in Germany. As a result, Fraunhofer holds the patent on the MP3 codec and gets to charge licensing fees to anyone creating technology that can create an MP3-compliant bitstream. This probably won't matter to you unless you're planning to develop an MP3 encoder, in which case you'll need to pay licensing fees to Fraunhofer. Check Fraunhofer's Web site (`iis.fhg.de`) for details.

How Does MP3 Work?

How does MP3 retain high audio quality with file sizes as small as one-tenth the size of comparable CD audio files? The brief explanation is that MP3 works by stripping and compressing audio down to the minimum amount of information required for it to sound good to the human ear. That's about all you need to know in order to create and enjoy MP3 files, but in case you're curious, we'll provide some explanation and a little detail in this section. (If you're not curious, skip straight ahead to the next section.)

MP3 uses a technique called *sampling* to create its digital representations of audio. Sampling is the process of examining the patterns of a sound to determine its characteristics and to record it from an analog (continuously variable) format into a digital (binary) format. To simplify absurdly, when you sample, you create a pattern of data points for the audio and save those data points in a digital file. The more data points there are, the closer the audio sounds to its original.

The three key measurements that describe sampling are the sampling rate, the sampling precision, and the bitrate:

- ▶ The *sampling rate* is the frequency with which the sound is examined. The sampling rate is measured in kilohertz (kHz)—thousands of cycles per second. CDs sample audio at a sampling rate of 44.1 kilohertz (kHz).

- ▶ The *sampling precision* (also called the *sampling resolution*) is the amount of information about the individual sample that is saved to the audio file. CDs use a sampling precision of 16 bits (2 bytes) per second; most people recording MP3 files use this sampling precision as well.

- ▶ The *bitrate* is the number of bits per second used to store the encoded information. Bitrates are measured in kilobits per second (kbps). 128kbps is generally considered to provide almost–CD-quality sound. Most MP3 encoders can encode at either a constant bitrate (CBR) or a variable bitrate (VBR).

The higher the sampling rate and sampling precision of the original material, and the higher the sampling precision and the bitrate of the encoded MP3 file, the more faithful the sound in the MP3 file is to the original sound—but the more data has to be stored and the larger the resulting file will be.

CD-quality audio, which is recorded at a sampling rate of 44.1kHz and a sampling precision of 16 bits, is considered to provide perfect audio for the human ear. The sampling is frequent enough, and the sampling precision stores enough information about the sound that the human ear can't detect anything missing. But this isn't absolutely true. There are a number of people who say that music recorded on CDs doesn't sound right to them, and others who claim to be able to hear imperfections or incompletenesses in the sound. The first group tend to be die-hard vinyl enthusiasts; the second group tend to be classical musicians and audio maniacs with stereo systems costing more than a mid-sized Toyota.

NOTE

We're sure we don't have to tell you that you need a decent sound system to make CD-quality audio sound good. A cheap CD player, a wretched receiver, and shoddy speakers can make even the most perfectly recorded and produced music sound atrocious.

CD audio files—"raw" audio files—may be huge, but they're not exactly stuffed with unnecessary information. The reason that CD-quality audio uses the 44.1kHz sampling rate is that audio recorded at lesser rates (for example, 22.05kHz or 11.025kHz) doesn't sound complete. Not enough information is stored to accurately convey the waveforms in the sound, so it ends up sounding distorted or incomplete. Likewise, audio recorded with a sampling precision of less than 16 bits doesn't sound too great, either.

> **NOTE**
>
> We're primarily talking about music here, because it includes frequencies around (and beyond) the high and low ends of the human hearing spectrum. Spoken audio (plays, audio books, radio shows, poetry, and so on) sounds anywhere from okay to fine with a lower sampling rate and sampling precision because its sounds typically fall into a far narrower range than those in music. Telephone frequencies were designed to carry the human voice effectively, and generally they work well unless the person you're trying to listen to has a voice in the supra-alto or basso profundo range. On the other hand, you'll probably know from far too much direct experience that music played over the phone sounds horrible; you only get some frequencies, and the rest get mangled. (Tech moment: This is part of the reason that on-hold music stinks. The rest of the reason is the taste of the people who build the systems—they try to choose music that won't offend anybody too much, and end up selecting twangings and oozings that please few beyond their creators.)

MP3 and other digital-compression techniques exploit the techniques of psychoacoustics to find out which parts of the sound they can get rid of without the human ear noticing too much. *Psychoacoustics* is the study of what people can and can't hear—*hear* in the sense not of the ear's capacity to pick up the sound, but rather to the brain's capacity to identify it as a separate sound. As you probably know, the human ear mostly misses out on large sections of the sound spectrum, both at the high end (things like bat squeaks and dog whistles) and at the low end (for example, the infrasonic rumblings that presage earthquakes). Even in the ranges that the ear does hear, the brain can only pick out and make sense of some of the sounds—a couple of conversations from a roomful of jabber, for example, or the screeching of car brakes loud enough to drown out morning birdsong.

An MP3 encoder analyzes an audio stream, essentially comparing it to a map of the limitations of human hearing and how well the brain can interpret this data. The encoder keeps only the frequencies and sounds that a human will be able to hear and distinguish. Anything else, it discards. For example, in a rock track, when a thundering bass line drowns out the bass drum, the MP3 encoder trashes the frequencies and sounds that represent the bass drum, because although those frequencies and sounds are there in the full version of the music, you won't be able to hear them. When the bass drum beats its way back through the bass line so that you'll be able to hear it, the encoder will keep those frequencies and sounds. The resulting file should sound to the human ear like the original; how exactly the compressed file sounds like the original depends on the bitrate of the file.

Technically, MP3 is a *lossy* method of compression—it actually removes information from the source rather than just squashing the source down to its smallest possible size. (The opposite of lossy compression is *lossless* compression. Zip is an example of lossless compression. When you expand a file from a zip archive, you get a file that contains exactly the same information as the original file.) Because it's lossy, MP3 can compress audio to different degrees: The more you compress audio, the more information is removed and the worse the result sounds. But as mentioned earlier, MP3 files encoded at 128kbps produce audio close to CD quality at about one-tenth the file size. These files are small enough to play on minute portable players, store en masse on a hard drive, transfer by the dozen using a Zip drive, or transfer across the Internet using even a relatively slow modem connection.

MP3 files have an additional benefit: Each file has a *tag*—a container with various slots to hold important pieces of information about the MP3 files, such as the artist's name, the track title, the album title (if the track is from an album), the genre, the year, and an optional comment. You don't *have* to enter the tag information in the MP3 file, but if you do, you can then use the tag information to catalog and sort your MP3 files. Most MP3 jukeboxes let you sort your MP3 files by the tag information, enabling you to easily access all the tracks by a given artist, all the tracks in the specified genre, or anything to which you've appended a particular comment (for example, "blazing guitar solo!").

Because MP3 uses lossy compression, the key to getting the MP3 files of the size and quality you need is to choose the appropriate encoding rate—one that balances audio quality with file size.

Choosing an Appropriate Encoding Rate

Before you start creating MP3 files, you need to choose an appropriate bitrate (the encoding rate) at which to sample the files. The right bitrate for you will depend on what you typically listen to, how you listen to it, and how much storage space you have, but not necessarily in that order.

Most encoders support constant bitrates of 64kbps, 96kbps, 128kbps, 160kbps, and 320kbps. Other encoders support in-between bitrates (such as 112kbps, 144kbps, and 192kbps) and variable bitrates. Most people find music sampled at a rate below 128kbps to be unacceptable to listen to, but for spoken audio, higher capacity options such as 64kbps or lower can be a good choice. Not coincidentally, several MP3 encoders have free versions that top out at 96kbps in order to encourage you to reach for your wallet in the hope of being able to actually enjoy your music via MP3.

As mentioned earlier in this chapter, the equation is simple: The higher the sampling rate, the better the music will sound, and the larger the resulting file size will be. A five-minute track recorded at 128kbps takes up around 4.6MB; recorded at 160kbps, it takes up about 5.75MB; and recorded at 320kbps, it takes up more like 11.4MB. You're still saving a great deal of space over the raw audio version of the file (which is more like 50MB), but it's nothing like as portable as the 128kbps and 160kbps versions.

With huge hard drives now affordable to most consumers, you can afford to store 320kbps MP3 files on your PC without breaking a sweat, provided that you don't have a colossal number of them. But if you use an ultra-portable or portable player, size becomes an issue much more quickly. Most ultra-portables max out at 64MB or 96MB of storage, and some portables have only a little more storage, in which case you'll want to make each megabyte count with as much listenable music as possible.

If you need to transfer files either via physical media (Zip disks or CDs) or via the Internet, you'll want to keep file sizes down to the minimum that delivers the quality you want. Most people can't really afford to set their MP3 encoder to the highest bitrate it supports, leave it there, and damn the torpedoes.

For encoding music, you'll usually want to use a bitrate of 128kbps minimum. For the first few dozen MP3 files you encode, listen closely to the results, and see if you need to increase the bitrate in order to get a quality that you'll enjoy listening to in the long term. You might also want to encode at a rate higher than you currently need, in the event that you purchase audio equipment sometime in the future that's substantially better than what you currently have. Some people swear by 160kbps, and others by 192kbps; a few people declare you need 320kbps to produce anything worth listening to. (We think they're full of it.)

Most MP3 software players can handle all known bitrates, and most hardware players can handle a wide variety of bitrates (some can't play variable bitrate files), so you don't need to worry that you're locking yourself down to a given bitrate by choosing it from the start. But if you're planning to build a music collection on MP3, you should think seriously about picking a standard bitrate so that you'll enjoy uniformly acceptable (or better) quality across the range of MP3 files. There's no sense in recording at an unsatisfactorily low bitrate now and promising yourself that you'll re-record all the tracks at a higher bitrate in due course. Unless you have phenomenal discipline, you'll forget. In any case, you'll be wasting time you could be better spending enjoying music.

> **NOTE**
>
> Two quick notes: First, using the right software, you can decrease the bitrate of an MP3 file, but you can't increase it—the information that you discarded when encoding it is gone for good. So if you're not sure at which rate to record, err on the high side rather than the low. Second, logic would suggest that ripping at a higher bitrate might be quicker than ripping at a lower bitrate, as it might require less compression and so less processing power. That's elegant thinking, but it's not really true. The amount of *compression* required remains more or less the same, but at a higher bitrate, the encoder discards less information. And in our empirical tests with a couple of popular encoders, encoding at 64kbps and 320kbps took approximately the same amount of time—but this also depends on which encoder you're using.

We listen mostly to rock music (as opposed to classical music or jazz—not as opposed to Sino-goth, Pentecostal metal, and the myriad other subdivisions of the rock category) and find that an encoding rate of 128kbps sounds pretty good. Some music sounds just about okay at 112kbps but at that rate, some of the sounds start sounding a little thin. Typically, the treble frequencies are the first to show weakness: You'll hear a sort of thinness in hi-hat and cymbal sounds, as if the sound isn't all there. (That's because it isn't, and there's not enough left of the sound to fool your brain.) At 96kbps, this thinness extends to some of the other instruments; at 64kbps, it's all the way through the music. Below that, music becomes about as listenable as fingernails scraping across a chalkboard.

Of course, this is our personal experience. Quite a few people claim to hear weaknesses at 128kbps, and so they prefer to encode everything at a bitrate of 160kbps or higher. Others swear that

64kpbs sounds just fine. And some people—relatively few—claim that even music encoded at 320kbps (the maximum rate of most MP3 encoders) sounds so horrible as not to be worth listening to. If you choose to ratchet your encoder all the way up like this, you may also want to create lower-caliber MP3 files of those tracks you want to listen to on your portable—assuming you deign to use one.

How an MP3 file sounds also depends on the quality of the hardware and software with which you're playing it back. It's obvious that if you use tin cans instead of speakers, even Vivaldi's best efforts will sound like cats mating more slowly than they'd like to. But it's not so obvious that some sound cards and some MP3 software players are lame enough to make most music sound terrible. And it's even less obvious that some portable hardware MP3 players sound far inferior to others. So if you want your MP3 music to sound good, you need to make sure you have quality all the way down the line from ripping and encoding to playback.

PUBLISH WITHOUT BEING DAMNED

So far in this chapter, we've pointed out a couple of things that MP3 is good for—storing audio on computers and small portable players, and transferring audio files easily from A to B, either via physical media or over the wires (or airwaves, if you have a wireless connection).

Those audio files can be anything that you have permission to encode or distribute. (We'll discuss permissions and all the legal aspects of MP3 and other digital music formats in Chapter 3, "Digital Audio and the Law.") For example, you can download an MP3 file from the MP3.com Web site (mp3.com) and store it on your computer. From there, you can simply play it back, or you can download it to a portable player or a car player so that you can rock out to it while turning cartwheels on the beach or trying your luck with the traffic police on the freeway.

For any musician or poet, though, MP3 offers a far more exciting possibility: You can easily create and distribute MP3 files of your own audio. If you have a band, you can create MP3 files either from recorded and mixed tapes, or directly from a live session. Then you can either post them on the Web and/or newsgroups or distribute them directly via e-mail, FTP, or file-sharing technologies such as Napster—or even via physical media if you prefer. Getting your music or verse out to the world has never been easier—or less expensive.

Hold that thought. We'll rack it and wheel it a little in the next section, when we discuss the advantages of MP3.

MP3 Advantages and Disadvantages

MP3 has several key advantages over conventional methods of distributing and listening to audio. It also has a number of disadvantages. We've broken down the advantages and disadvantages by the three main groups who are being affected by MP3: music enthusiasts (consumers), artists, and record companies.

Advantages and Disadvantages for the Music Enthusiast

For the music enthusiast, the advantages of MP3 are many and clear. That's why MP3 has become popular so rapidly, and why, in mid-1999, the term *MP3* overtook the term *sex* as the most–searched-for item on the Web.

These are the main advantages of MP3:

MP3 makes music portable. By compressing digital audio down to a manageable size, MP3 lets you take music with you pretty much wherever you go, either on a portable player or on a car player.

MP3 turns your computer into a jukebox. By using MP3 (or other digital-audio formats), you can easily store music on your computer, manage it, and play it back. Many software MP3 players provide *visualizations*—graphical displays keyed to the music—turning your computer into an audio-visual jukebox.

MP3 lets you share music easily. You can transfer MP3 files easily, either via physical media or electronically. (Bear in mind that there is a whole stack of intellectual-property issues associated with sharing music; we'll touch on these in due course.)

MP3 makes it easy to create custom CDs. Once you've built a collection of MP3 files on your computer or network, you can easily burn custom audio CDs that contain only the tracks you think should be included. You can also burn custom data CDs that contain a huge amount of music—between 100 and 200 tracks will fit on a single CD, depending on the length of the tracks and the bitrate at which you encode the MP3 files.

MP3 makes it easy to transmit files over the Internet. Even with Internet access speeds getting faster all the time, it's still impractical for many users to transmit standard, uncompressed, CD-quality digital-audio files, especially if they are using a modem. MP3 removes this restriction, cutting download times to one-tenth. Suddenly, it's feasible for even the lowliest 14,400 baud modem user to grab music off the Internet.

For the music enthusiast, the disadvantages of MP3 are few and minor—but let's list them anyway:

You need a computer.   Generally speaking, you'll need to have a computer in order to create, download, manage, and play back MP3 files. We say "generally speaking" because at this writing, one of the big new trends is a stereo-component MP3 player designed to fit into your stereo system rather than clutter up your desk. (Two of the current crop of these players are the AudioReQuest and the SongBank, both of which we'll discuss in more depth in Chapter 15, "MP3 on Your PDA, on Your Home Stereo, and in Your Car.") These players have CD drives that do double duty as players for conventional CD audio and rippers and encoders to convert your CDs to MP3s that they store on one or more internal hard drives. Some of them have keyboard jacks and can use your television as a display—okay, okay, they're computers by another name. (Mind you, just about everything is a computer these days, from that watch on your wrist to the high-tech network keeping aloft and amused that airplane currently drowning out the high notes you're not quite hitting on "White Rabbit.")

The music quality is lower than CD quality.   However high you push the bitrate on your MP3 files, they're still compressed and they'll never sound quite as good as CD audio. But most people find they can easily get high-enough audio quality from MP3.

You need to know a little bit of law.   You don't need to be a legal expert, but before you download or distribute any MP3 files, you should know what you can and cannot legally do. You can break the law with just a couple of clicks of your mouse, either by downloading (or otherwise receiving) illegal MP3 files or by distributing MP3 files without the explicit permission of the copyright holder.

As you can see, on the whole, MP3 is great for the music enthusiast.

Advantages and Disadvantages for the Artist

For the artist as well, MP3 provides several huge advantages and one colossal disadvantage. Because this disadvantage is so great, the question of whether MP3 is a good thing or a bad thing for the artist is much more delicately balanced than for the consumer.

The advantages that MP3 offers for the artist are compelling. These are the four main advantages:

> **You can publish and distribute your own music instantly over the Internet.** You no longer need to find a record company prepared to spend many thousands of dollars signing, packaging, and promoting you and your music. You can simply record the music using a computer, mix it to your satisfaction (again, using a computer), convert some tracks to MP3 or another digital format, and post them on the Web so that people can download them instantly and listen to them. You can give them away or you can charge money for them.

> **NOTE**
> For artists, secure digital-audio formats such as a2b and WMA offer solutions to many of the problems that MP3 files pose.

> **Promote your work online.** You can do this in any or all of several ways, including placing MP3 files on Web

sites for distribution, posting them to MP3 newsgroups, distributing them as e-mail attachments, or sharing them via Napster (which provides instant sharing of tracks by all members logged into a loose online community) or a related technology.

Release as many tracks—or as many versions of a track—as you like. Instead of struggling to decide which track to release next, you can release a whole slew of tracks with minimal cost and effort. You can also release multiple versions of a track to broaden its appeal rather than needing to choose the most mainstream version of a track.

Get instant feedback from your audience. By releasing music electronically, you can get feedback from your audience within days, hours, or even minutes.

As you can see from this list, MP3 and other digital-audio formats greatly enable the artist, essentially freeing them from the chokehold of the record company. Because the record companies no longer necessarily decide which artists to promote and how the music will sound, the music scene has become much freer. And because electronic distribution is far faster, far less expensive, and more efficient than physical distribution, it no longer takes a huge investment of money to get an artist's music out to the world.

In the heyday of the record companies—say, from the 1960s to the late 1990s—it took weeks or months (in some cases, years) to produce, manufacture, and distribute an album. Now, an artist or a band can record high-fidelity sound with an affordable computer, mix it to professional quality, and then distribute it immediately and painlessly using MP3 files. If anyone likes the music, they can pay to download further songs or buy a CD directly from the artist.

As you can see, MP3 and the other digital-audio formats pose a threat to the record companies. But as we'll discuss shortly, they're also tools that the record companies can exploit themselves to grow their businesses.

MP3 offers the artist four great advantages. But it also has the massive disadvantage of enabling piracy. Consumers can create and distribute illegal copies of the artist's work, costing the artist money they would have earned on sales or as royalties on sales. Any CDs that an artist has released can be ripped (extracted) from the CD, encoded to MP3 files, and distributed either on physical media or electronically.

Not only does each copy of an MP3 file retain the same quality (unlike audio tapes, in which each successive generation of copies loses audio quality), but because the copies are electronic, they cost nothing to produce (again, unlike audio tapes). By using the Internet and software such as Napster, a pirate can distribute thousands of copies of a track overnight—and each recipient of one of those copies can spread them further.

Advantages and Disadvantages for the Record Company

By enabling artists to distribute music on their own, MP3 seems to pose a severe threat to record companies by bypassing first, their control of the selection and recording process and second, their expensively built production and distribution systems.

That said, MP3 and the other digital-audio formats can be a powerful tool for a record company to use in promoting its artists and its music. If it so chooses, a record company can make its Web site into a major venue for music fans and can reap the following benefits:

Reduced production and distribution costs The record company will save a huge amount of money by moving from creating, distributing, and selling music on physical media (CDs, cassettes) to selling electronic copies.

Simple promotion To promote its artists, all a record company needs to do is build a Web site that offers freely downloadable music in digital-audio formats. Secure digital-audio formats let the record company give away restricted copies of a track. For example, they can give away a copy that expires after being played a certain number of times, that expires after a certain date, or that can be played only on the computer used to download it. Like the artist, the record company can get feedback on the music it's providing—and it can do it on a grand scale. Where an artist may use the feedback to shape one track or an album in a particular direction, a record company can use feedback to determine new market directions and help it find the stuff of future hits.

Direct sales to customers via the Web With the customers coming to its Web site to find the latest music, the record company can start selling it to them. By selling the electronic copies at a discount, the record company can give its customers an incentive to buy the electronic copies instead of the physical copies—and it can still rake in more money than it would have received for the physical copies. In this scenario, the middlemen—the distribution network and the retail stores—take a severe beating, but both the record companies and the consumers come out smiling. The record company can sell multiple versions or mixes of a track. And if the customers want to buy physical copies of a track or an album, or they want to create custom CDs, the record company can sell it to them via mail order.

Cross-promotion The record company can present information about related bands to customers, offering them free tracks to try. Customers can sign up for news (via, say, e-mail newsletters) on bands they're interested in, upcoming releases, concerts, and so on.

The main disadvantage of MP3 for the record company is the same as that for the artist: The record company can lose money through the piracy of released material. Also, as mentioned earlier, MP3 and other digital-audio formats reduce or obviate artists' need for the record company.

When it comes to MP3, some record companies are in a more peculiar situation than others. For example, Sony is a top record label with big-name artists, such as Celine Dion and Fiona Apple, but it's also a major manufacturer of audio equipment. Sony's hardware division apparently spent late 1998 and most of 1999 champing at the bit to release a killer MP3 player in the hopes of locking up the market—a market that could be even more lucrative than the Walkman market Sony created in the 1970s. What held them back was the threat that MP3 posed to Sony's record label.

Toward the end of 1999, Sony finally released the VAIO Music Clip—on the outside, exactly the kind of innovative MP3 player that you'd have expected to see from it about a year earlier. Longer and much thinner than most portable hardware MP3 players, the VAIO Music Clip handles secure MP3 and ATRAC3 formats, is SDMI compliant, and is designed to be hung on a strap around the user's neck rather than being clipped to a belt like most portable players.

Unfortunately, the security features designed to protect artists' and record companies' intellectual property trample vigorously on the features the user needs to use the VAIO Music Clip effectively and enjoy music on it. You need to convert each track to a secure format before you can load it on the VAIO Music Clip, and the elaborate check-in/check-out system of permissions makes it possible to get into absurd situations such as having music on the VAIO Music Clip that you cannot remove, rendering it useless (unless you want to listen to the same tracks forever).

ACHIEVING A TOLERABLE LEVEL OF PIRACY WITH DIGITAL AUDIO

At this writing, it's clear that digital audio is here to stay. The technology is here, it's effective, and millions of people are using it (especially MP3). It's equally clear that because MP3 is an insecure technology, a lot of music piracy is taking place—more than the music industry feels it can tolerate. So the key question facing the music industry is how to get piracy down to a tolerable level and keep it there.

Shouldn't the music industry be aiming to eradicate music piracy? Sure, but they'll never be able to do that, and in fact, there are reasons for the music industry to encourage tolerable levels of piracy.

Tolerable is hard to define, but you'd think a good target would be a level analogous to the level of piracy tacitly accepted when people taped LPs and duped cassettes for their friends. The record companies benefited indirectly by more people hearing the music and deciding that they wanted to buy an original copy for themselves. They also benefited directly—and continue to benefit—from the levy on each audio cassette sold.

When blank audio cassettes were first sold, the recording industry collectively squawked loudly enough to get a levy implemented on each audio cassette sold. Each time you buy a blank audio cassette, some of the money goes into a fund to pay artists royalties for the rights you might infringe by recording their copyrighted music onto the cassette. No matter if you use the cassette to record music to which you hold the copyright, or you use it to dictate memos, you pay the levy. At first, many people were annoyed both by the levy and by the presumption of guilt it implied, but by now, most people have forgotten about it. In any case, the cost of a blank audio cassette is relatively trivial for anyone who buys music regularly.

CONTINUED ➡

When digital audio tape (DAT) was released, posing the threat of perfect digital copies rather than lower-fidelity analog copies, the recording industry squawked so loudly that it effectively prevented DAT from catching on in North America. DAT was a great technology for the time, delivering perfect copies and great sound quality in an easy-to-handle format. But there was enough industry pressure to stop it in its tracks. Today, DAT is still around, but it's used primarily by serious audiophiles and by recording studios. DAT was never allowed to make it into the mainstream.

But MP3 has—and piracy is vigorous, if not rampant. And there's little hope of stamping it out, much as law enforcement in the Western world can't realistically expect to stamp out speeding, even though everybody knows the law, and most people realize that driving at a very high speed is a bad idea. Law enforcement could take a number of measures, such as increasing the penalty for speeding to an absurd level (lifetime imprisonment, say, or immediate forfeiture of all assets); they could increase enforcement, putting thousands more Highway Patrol vehicles on the road; they could even require all cars to have regulating devices that prevent cars from exceeding the speed limit. But none of these measures would work because many people would still want to drive faster than the speed limit, and so would doctor the regulating devices, hide their assets, or perhaps arm themselves to the teeth. In any case, drivers would still so heavily outnumber law enforcement officers that the latter could catch only a tiny fraction of the speeders.

The previous paragraph perhaps seems far fetched, but in many ways, the situation with piracy of digital music is similar to speeding. Indulge us here for a moment:

- With existing, readily available technology, it's easy to speed, and it's easy to pirate music with MP3.

CONTINUED ➡

- There are immediate benefits to speeding and pirating music with MP3. You get to your destination faster if you speed, and you can get and enjoy the music you want via MP3.
- People know both speeding and music piracy are wrong, but they do them anyway.
- The likelihood of being caught in either activity is low.

Given the ease of MP3 piracy, the strength of the motivation for doing it, and the ease of the average pirate escaping detection, it's hard to see how to reduce it.

Before MP3 became firmly established, there was talk of banning the MP3 format. How do you ban a file format—by performing house-to-house searches? This was neither a great idea nor an effective one, but an indication of the level of consternation that MP3 was causing.

More recently, the RIAA has concentrated its attentions on big targets, presumably trying to get the most bang, publicity, and effect for its legal buck. It has successfully sued MP3.com, one of the leading MP3 Web sites, for its Beam-it feature, which lets a consumer put a CD in their CD drive to show MP3.com that they own a copy of it and then access ready-ripped copies of the tracks from the CD online instantly. The RIAA is also suing Napster for its eponymous software, which lets users share MP3 files easily from their computers and tap into the pool of MP3 files that other users currently logged into the same Napster server are sharing.

As we see it, even though the RIAA has clipped MP3.com's wings a bit and may be able to shut down Napster, it won't have much effect on music piracy. MP3.com is only one of a large number of Web sites that promote music in MP3 format. And Napster has already spawned a number of similar

CONTINUED →

file-sharing software applications (including gnutella and audioGnome), some of which do not use a central server and so would be as hard to stamp out as an underground resistance movement.

A better option would be to sideline the MP3 format by superseding it with a superior and secure digital-audio format. We'll investigate the limitations of the leading secure digital-audio formats a little later in this chapter, but here's a brief preview: Some other digital-audio formats work better than others, but none offers the consumer any compelling advantages over MP3.

Besides, the freeness of the MP3 format has a strong appeal to the average consumer, who wants to be able to do what he or she likes with the music he or she has purchased: make a cassette recording, make an MP3 recording, make a compilation CD, or whatever. Few if any consumers will welcome a music format that proscribes them from enjoying music they've purchased—especially when the wide-open MP3 format is available and has shown them the freedom they can enjoy.

That said, most consumers can see that wholesale music piracy is wrong, whether that piracy is performed by conventional or analog means (such as selling pirated CDs or cassettes without paying royalties to the artist) or by digital means (such as ripping 100 CDs and sharing the resulting tracks via Napster or gnutella). Creating a couple of MP3 tracks and sharing them with a friend, or receiving a couple of MP3 tracks from a friend—that barely seems like copyright infringement. After all, if you like the music, you might buy the CD yourself—and that would be good for the artist (unless you were to get a pirated copy). But downloading tracks by the dozens, or giving a friend more than a handful of tracks, is clearly wrong.

CONTINUED →

> If you were feeling cynical, you might say the problem is that there's no way to get back to the days of tolerable piracy that's condoned or at least accepted by most of the music companies and artists, the days in which home taping was accepted as a way of spreading an artist's music without cutting savagely into their revenue stream. Piracy was limited by the physical medium used. If you wanted to share an album with a dozen friends at the same time, you needed to buy, record, and distribute a dozen cassettes, which would cost you time, money, and effort. But now you can put MP3 files of the tracks from the album (or, more likely, the CD) up on the Internet or share them via Napster, so that anyone online can access them in an instant.
>
> Pretty much as soon as the atom bomb had been used, people started to wish it could be un-invented, but of course there's no way to do so. What do you bet many artists and record companies want MP3 to be un-invented and replaced with a secure digital-audio format that allows high quality and easy distribution while protecting their intellectual property? But given that MP3 is here to stay, the artists and record companies are struggling to find a way to live with it—to live and to make money.

The Future of MP3

At this writing, MP3 is firmly established in the marketplace as a popular format for audio, and it has caused huge changes in how music is published and distributed. It's hard to see MP3 either going away or being superseded by one of the competing digital-audio formats for quite some time. Music enthusiasts, artists, and record companies can all benefit from using MP3, although the latter two groups may be able to benefit more from using digital-audio formats that provide more security but that are still easily accessible by their target audience.

An MP4 Structured Audio Format is currently under development, but it's far from mainstream deployment. To learn about MP4, visit the MP4 Structured Audio home page at `sound.media.mit.edu/mpeg4/`.

> **NOTE**
>
> Sony's deceptively named OpenMG software uses a format named OpenMG MP3 that is in fact a secure file. Each file is locked to the computer on which it was created and can be used on portable players but not on other computers. This format has no detectable appeal to consumers beyond allowing them to listen to music on Sony hardware players such as the VAIO Music Clip and the Memory Stick Walkman.

Other Digital-Audio Formats

At the beginning of this chapter, we mentioned some of the other digital-audio formats that are competing for consumers' attention and money. In this section, we'll list those formats briefly, with some quick details on the capabilities they provide. Then we'll ignore these formats until Chapter 23, "Other Digital Music Formats," in which we'll discuss them in more depth.

Each of these formats faces three significant hurdles in getting established as the music format of choice:

- First, the only compelling appeal to the consumer that any of these technologies can muster comes if they can provide music that the consumer cannot get in any other way. For example, if the Rolling Stones, Metallica, or Christina Aguilera were to release a dozen tracks only in the a2b format, consumers would have a compelling reason to use that format. But if consumers can get the same music in MP3 format, chances are that they'll stick with MP3, because it gives them more freedom than the competing formats.

- Second, most of these formats are designed more for security and commerce than for ease or pleasure of use. From the consumer's point of view, this means that you usually have to pay for the music (unless the track is a promotional freebie) and accept restrictions on how you can use the music. For example, you might get an Mjuice track with an expiration date of the week after next, an ATRAC3 track that you can only play on the computer with which you download it, or a Liquid Audio track that you can play only three times. None of the three has much appeal compared to an MP3 file that you can play until the cows come home—and which you can pass along to your friends as well.

- Third, the only advantages that the other digital-audio formats can offer the consumer are almost insignificant. Most of the formats claim to provide higher audio quality. In some, the claim is believable, but because MP3 already offers high-enough audio quality for the overwhelming majority of consumers, it's not much of a selling point. Some of the other formats offer greater compression ratios, giving high audio quality at an even smaller file size than MP3. This too is nice, but usually the difference in size between the MP3 file and the file in the other format isn't enough to be significant—particularly in view of how much smaller the MP3 file is than the original file.

- Fourth, MP3 has such high market share among users of digital audio that it's hard for any other format to build up any significant momentum. It's like other browsers trying to take on Internet Explorer; they may have better features that appeal to some people, but the majority of Internet Explorer users find the current product more than adequate for their needs.

These are the key digital-audio formats at this writing:

a2b   Created by AT&T, the a2b format provides both compression and encryption. a2b claims better compression (2.25MB for a three-minute song) and sound quality than MP3 and can store text and art with the audio. At this writing, a2b music players are available for Windows (95, 98, NT 4, and 2000) and the Macintosh (PowerPC).

ATRAC3   Created by Sony for use with its oddly-named OpenMG copyright-protection technology (it's no more open than North Korea), ATRAC3 provides good compression and strong security. By default, ATRAC3 limits you to using encoded files on the computer on which you encoded them (or with which you downloaded them) and with portable players attached to that computer. At this writing, Sony's implementation of ATRAC3 runs on Windows 98 only and has severe disadvantages. Among them, you can't restore encoded files from a backup, so if your hard drive goes south, so does your entire digital-audio collection. (Sony is apparently "considering" fixing this problem.) Interestingly, RealNetworks is integrating ATRAC3 into its widely used RealJukebox ripper/player/jukebox, which should help bring ATRAC3 into the mainstream.

Liquid Audio   One of the older digital-audio formats, Liquid Audio has been used for a number of years on sites such as the Internet Underground Musical Archive ("the granddaddy of all music Web sites") but has not quite established itself as a major format. Liquid Audio made a splash in late 1999 by persuading Alanis Morissette to use Liquid Audio in the Internet marketing campaign for her CD *MTV Unplugged*. You can burn CDs of Liquid Audio files by using Liquid Audio's Liquifier software, although its capabilities are limited in comparison to most CD-burning software. Liquid Player is available for Windows and the Macintosh. It plays MP3 files as well as Liquid Audio files, making it a workable solution for anyone who already has a collection of MP3 files but is transitioning to Liquid Audio.

Windows Media Technologies and MS Audio   Developed by Microsoft, Windows Media Technologies 4 has a secure compression scheme called MS Audio that claims to surpass MP3 in both compression and music quality. Windows Media Player, which can play files in MS Audio formats as well as MP3 and several other formats, comes with virtually every current version of Windows, and with Microsoft's Internet Explorer Web browser, making it perhaps the most widely distributed audio player. Furthermore, an increasing number of MP3 software players, including the market-leading Winamp and Sonique, can play MS Audio files, so if you receive an MS Audio file, you shouldn't have any problem getting to hear it on any version of Windows. That said, as of this writing, Microsoft has managed to persuade relatively few artists to release music in the MS Audio format, so there's little reason for consumers to want to use MS Audio.

Mjuice An encrypted MP3 format, Mjuice provides the same audio quality as MP3, but it lets the artist or record company create a copy-protected version of a track that can be played back any number of times on a registered user's player but not at all on an unregistered player. Mjuice files can also contain an expiration date, making them useful for promoting forthcoming releases. A number of MP3 players (including Winamp) and jukeboxes (including RealJukebox) can play Mjuice files.

TwinVQ/VQF Formally known as Transform-domain Weighted Interleave Vector Quantization Format or TwinVQF but more popularly known as VQF, this format boasts better compression and higher sound quality than MP3 but very little market share in the wide world. The MP3 player K-jofol plays VQF files, and you can also get a plug-in to enable Winamp to do so.

QDesign The QDesign Music Codec (QDMC) is a powerful codec created by Canada-based QDesign Corporation. The QDMC creates custom audio filters on the fly for each signal encoded instead of using a standardized set of filters. This makes for a slower encoding process than MP3, but it produces more accurate results—even at low bitrates. The QDesign encoder can create both QDesign files and MP3 files, and stores its native files in QuickTime format.

QuickTime Universally thought of as a video format because of the success of QuickTime videos, QuickTime can also create audio-only files that sound good at a relatively small file size. Free QuickTime players are available for platforms including Windows and the Macintosh, and the QDesign encoder (mentioned in the previous paragraph) creates files in QuickTime format.

RealAudio Famous for streaming audio, RealAudio is also a viable music-storage format, delivering near–CD-quality sound at bitrates lower than MP3 requires. But despite the wide availability of RealJukebox, which can record in both RealAudio and MP3 formats, RealAudio is not widely used for music storage.

Up Next

In this chapter, you've learned why MP3 and digital audio are exciting and why MP3 is so popular compared to its competitors. You've learned a bit about how compressed digital audio works, and how to choose an appropriate encoding rate for MP3. You've also learned a little about the leading competitors to MP3—and why they're trailing MP3 in the digital-audio field by a long margin.

In the next chapter, we'll discuss the hardware you need to enjoy MP3 and other digital audio on your computer. If you already have a supercharged multimedia PC or if you're a hardware guru, you might want to skip ahead to Chapter 3. If not, read on.

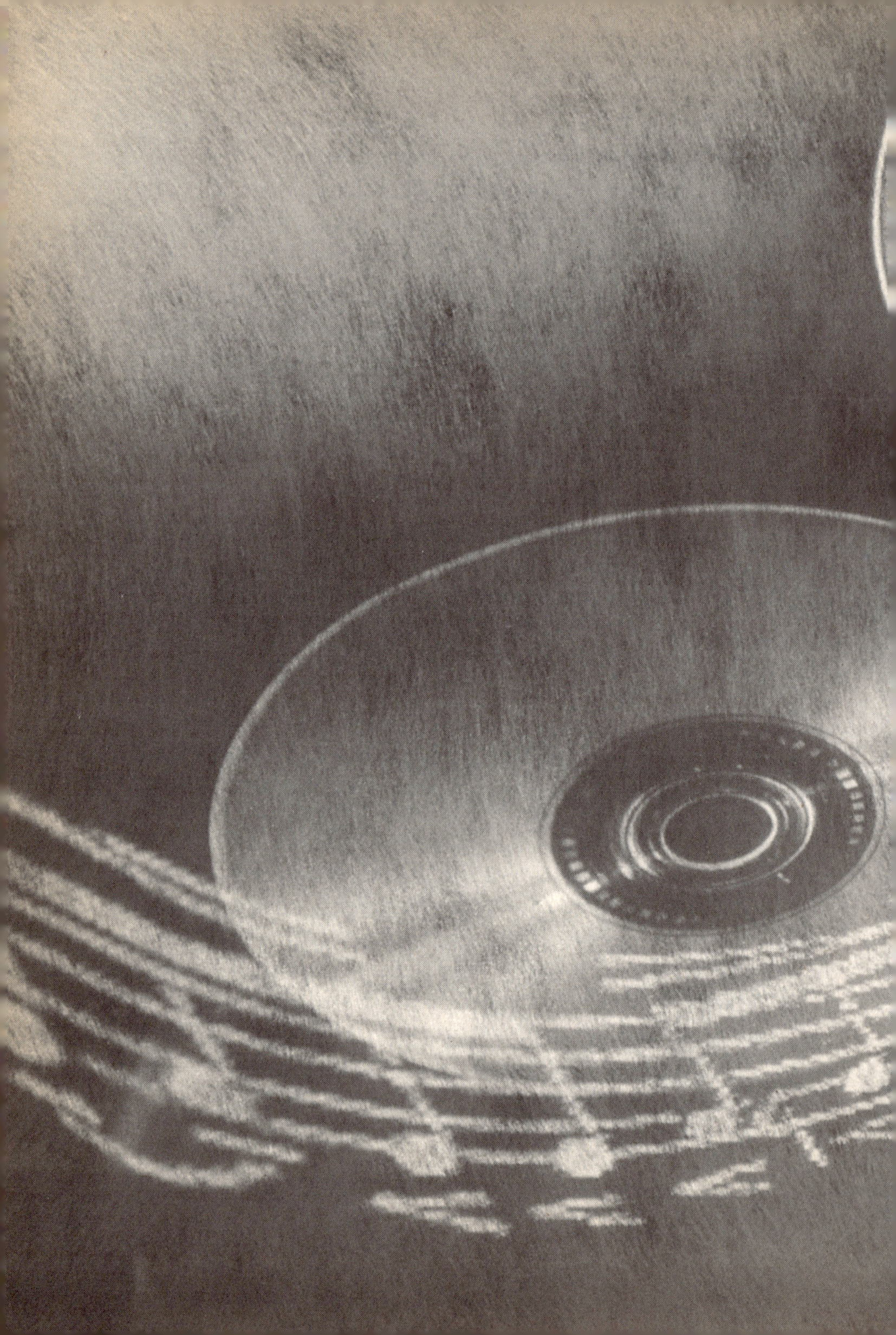

Chapter 2

A Hardware Primer for MP3 and Digital Audio

FEATURING

- Understanding the hardware requirements for digital audio
- Deciding whether to upgrade or buy a new computer
- Choosing speakers and headphones
- Getting a suitable Internet connection

Chapter Two

To record and play back MP3 and other digital-audio files, you need to have a moderately powerful computer (PC or Mac); you don't need the latest screamer with all the bells and whistles. The computer can be running just about any popular operating system—Windows, Mac OS, Linux, BeOS, Unix, and so on—that has MP3 tools available. It needs enough horsepower to encode the audio and play it back without faltering, enough storage to hold your music collection, and a fast enough Internet connection to enable you to upload and download multi-megabyte files without undue waiting.

In this chapter, we'll run you through the details of the hardware you need to enjoy MP3 and other forms of digital audio. Where appropriate, we'll suggest some upgrade options. We'll also offer some general advice on whether to upgrade an underpowered computer or simply replace it.

Before we get started, if you already have a fully functional multimedia PC and a speedy Internet connection, chances are you're already equipped for enjoying MP3, and you probably don't need to read this chapter.

SHOULD YOU UPGRADE OR SHOULD YOU BUY A NEW COMPUTER?

If your computer isn't quite up to recording and playing MP3, you'll need to either upgrade it or buy a new computer. Given the way that computer hardware prices have been falling over the last couple of years, whether to upgrade or buy a new computer can be a tough decision that often comes down to how much disposable income you have at the day of judgment.

If you'll need to upgrade several components of your computer in order to bring it up to scratch, consider seriously buying a

CONTINUED ➡

new computer. At this writing, retail computer prices have actually started to rise a little, for a number of reasons:

- First, the price wars of 1999 were vicious enough to take several companies out of the marketplace. For example, IBM and NEC Packard Bell have stopped selling desktop computers at retail, leaving companies such as Hewlett-Packard and Compaq in a better position to raise prices a bit. Even eMachines, the company that essentially defined the low-cost computer and helped drive prices lower, is selling more mid-priced computers than bargain-basement models.

- Second, many consumers have decided that they want a computer a little better than the minimally configured machines that sell for less than $500.

- Third, the economy is still going strong.

But even with the rise in computer prices, you can buy an effective multimedia computer for $600 or so—only a little more than it would cost to upgrade the processor, RAM, and hard drive of an older computer.

Whether you decide to upgrade or buy, be sure to weigh your options carefully before putting any money down. Use shop-bots (shopping robots) such as the Excite Shopping bot at www.jango.com to search for the lowest price available. The least you should do is cruise major online computer hardware sites, such as Computer Discount Warehouse (CDW; www.cdw.com), PC Connection (www.pcconnection.com), and Outpost.com (www.outpost.com) to make sure that you're not overpaying for a common piece of hardware. Watch for special offers, and if you qualify for any rebates, be sure to send them in within the required timeframe. (Did you know that an estimated 80 to 90 percent of computer-equipment rebates go unclaimed? That's why CompUSA and the OEMs love them.)

CONTINUED ➡

> One word of caution on special offers and rebates: Most of the hefty rebates that require you to sign up for three years of Internet connectivity with a particular ISP are a bad idea. Most of these offers leave you paying $600 or $700 in the long term in exchange for a $400 or $500 rebate in the short term—not a great deal by any standard, especially as they're for dial-up connectivity at a time when broadband access (cable, DSL, and wireless) is gradually spreading across North America.

The Chip: Pentium 200MMX or Better; Mac G3

Despite what Intel would have you believe, a super-fast chip isn't a vital component of your average computer today. You need a modest amount of speed for playing digital audio and considerably more speed for creating digital-audio files. But if you're planning a new computer, don't put your money into the chip at the expense of the other components.

Most ripping programs produce acceptable results with a processor as feeble (by year 2000 standards) as a Pentium 200MMX; some even can rip successfully with an ancient Pentium 133 (that's the "classic" Pentium without the MMX extensions). A faster chip will give you better performance, but even a mid-range chip such as a Celeron 500 will rip at a very acceptable rate. You probably don't need a supercooled gigahertz-plus Athlon unless you're running terrain-mapping software or editing digital video—or you're dangerously addicted to high-speed action games.

For playing back audio files, you may be able to stagger along with a Pentium 75 or so (or even a 486DX4 with a high clock speed), depending on the application you're using. Be warned that if your computer is around this performance level, you may hear interruptions in the audio as it struggles to keep up, and you may not be able to run other applications without interrupting playback. This won't be fun, but if it means you can squeeze a little more use out of your 1995 screamer, don't let us stop you.

If you're using a Macintosh, you'll want a PowerPC chip—preferably a G3. 233MHz or above will give you plenty of performance.

> **NOTE**
> One exception on the chip front is Sony's OpenMG Recorder software, which requires far more processing power than any other ripper we've used. If you're planning to use this software, consider a Pentium II 400 and 64MB RAM as a minimum.

RAM: 32MB or More (Preferably Much More)

For ripping, you need 32MB of RAM—absolute minimum. For playback, you need 16MB of RAM—absolute, absolute minimum. (Most modern operating systems need more than this, anyway.) As with almost any program, more RAM will make rippers and players run better. At this writing, RAM is once again nearing the historic low price it reached in mid-1999 (before an earthquake in Taiwan temporarily doubled prices). An extra 32MB or 64MB of RAM is a bargain that will give your computer a decent boost in performance.

If you're buying a new PC, get 128MB to start with; you won't regret it. Better yet, get that 128MB on a single module rather than on two modules so as to leave you as many memory sockets open as possible for future expansion. Also, we suggest not buying R-DRAM (Rambus memory) unless you have a compelling reason to do so. It provides better performance than regular SDRAM, but we don't feel that it justifies its price premium.

CD or DVD Drive

If you're going to rip and encode music from CDs, you'll need a CD drive or a DVD drive. That's no problem—it's hard to buy any computer except a subnotebook without a CD or DVD drive these days.

You'll be able to rip with just about any CD speed above 2x, but you'll get much better ripping speeds with a modern drive (say 40x or better). A SCSI drive minimizes the load on the processor, whereas ripping with an IDE drive imposes a significant load. If your processor is underpowered, a SCSI drive might help you out, but it'll be more expensive than an IDE drive, and it'll require an additional interface card (unless your motherboard has SCSI built in).

The CD drive needs to support digital-audio extraction in order to rip tracks digitally. (Most rippers offer an analog ripping option for CD drives that don't support digital extraction of audio, but the results aren't as good as digital ripping.) If your CD drive isn't up to ripping, get another one; it'll cost you anything from $35 and up.

If you have a DVD drive or are considering buying one, remember that DVD speeds refer to the speed at which the DVD drive works with DVDs, not with CDs; a DVD drive reads CDs at a much faster rate than DVDs. For example, a 12x DVD drive typically delivers more like 36x performance for CDs—not as fast as the latest CD drives but plenty fast enough to rip at a good speed.

Sound Card

You'll have a hard time buying a computer without a sound card these days, but if you want your digital music to be worth listening to, make sure that the sound card you get is adequate to your needs. All other things being equal, the better your sound card, the better the music will sound, both on playback and in the audio files that you create.

That's because some rippers extract audio from an audio CD in the conventional way: Circuitry in the drive converts the data to an analog signal, which is fed to the sound card, much as if you were listening to the CD through the sound card. At the sound card, the ripper samples the sound back to digital. These two steps add distortion and noise to the WAV file created (and in turn to the MP3 file created from the WAV file); the worse the sound card, the more distortion and noise you're apt to get. Better rippers (such as the Linux ripper cdparanoia) extract the digital data directly from the audio CD without using the sound circuitry, losing no data and adding no distortion or noise. If you use the latter type of ripper, you can rip CDs on a computer that has either a poor sound card or even no sound card at all.

Under almost all known circumstances, playback uses the sound card—it's the only way to get audio out of the computer without doing something strange. So you'll want to make sure that your playback machine has a good sound card.

As with many computer hardware items, sound cards have evolved greatly over the past few years. Five years ago, you just about had to buy the best sound card available in order to get decent sound on your computer. Nowadays, you can choose a sound card that's cheap and nasty, one that's merely adequate, one capable of producing monstrous surround sound, and one that aims to start composing digital music itself when it's just a little older.

Choosing a sound card is about as personal and revealing a decision as choosing a car or a stereo, so we won't try to influence you unduly. Instead, we'll content ourselves with giving you a few pointers, some of which you'll doubtless condemn as too obvious for you.

1. Make sure the sound card works with your computer and operating system. If your PC doesn't have a PCI slot free, a PCI sound card won't do you much good, and you may need to use ISA instead. If you *do* have PCI slots free, avoid ISA sound cards, because they draw much more heavily on the computer's processor than PCI cards do. If you have the option, get something better than the 16-bit Sound Blaster–compatible chips built into many modern ATX motherboards; they're enough

to handle routine noises and a little Doom or Unreal, but they'll spoil your enjoyment of digital music if you get seriously into it.

2. Go for a quality sound card if you can afford one. With the right driver and connections, any sound card can play back audio—but it doesn't necessarily make it sound good. A cheap card may produce muffled or distorted audio, and it may add noise to the signal.

The accuracy and clearness of the sound that a sound card produces depends on the quality of the digital-to-analog converter (DAC) that the card uses. When you play back an MP3 file, your sound card converts it from the digital data that the file is stored as to analog data that your ears can process. A basic sound card delivers a representation of the sound, but if its DAC isn't up to snuff, the sound is less accurate, and it may be noisy as well. Similarly, when you're encoding an MP3 file from an analog signal (such as a vinyl LP, a cassette, or a CD played into the line inputs of your sound card), the quality of the final result depends heavily on the analog-to-digital converter (ADC).

Furthermore, the more expensive sound cards include one or more digital signal processors (DSPs) that process some of the sound, which means that the CPU in your computer doesn't have to work as hard. For example, the EMU10K1 DSP used at this writing in the Sound Blaster Live! sound cards can process almost as many instructions per second as a Pentium 90—and it's dedicating all that processing power to audio.

Higher quality sound cards usually also have better quality connectors than cheap sound cards so that the signal passed from the sound card to your amplifier or speakers is more faithful. Higher quality cards may also offer other features, such as the ability to drive four or

A Hardware Primer for MP3 and Digital Audio   47

eight speakers (as opposed to the two that the typical low-end sound card can handle) and the ability to add environments to the sound—for example, altering the sound so that it sounds as if you're listening to it in a concert hall.

3. The quality of your sound card also affects the recordings you make through it. Even if you can tolerate some hiss and distortion in the music you play through your computer, you probably won't want any on the recordings you make on your computer from external sources. Again, high-quality connectors, good audio circuitry, and a high-quality ADC can help here. If you use a digital sound source, get a sound card that includes a digital input. Your digital sound source might be an external CD player (for example, one that produces a higher quality signal than your CD-ROM drive), a MiniDisc player, or a digital audio tape (DAT) player.

4. Make sure you have the appropriate cables and connectors for connecting your sound card to your speakers or your stereo. (Typically, you'll need different cables for your speakers than for feeding the output of your sound card into your receiver.) If you're buying connectors, make sure they're of suitable quality for your sound card—don't use cheap cables and connectors if you have a good sound card and a good stereo system.

5. If you're into MIDI, make sure that the sound card provides the connections you need and the number of voices you need. Practically every sound card has a built-in MIDI port, but you'll probably have to buy an external adapter cable to use it. (You should be able to find one for $20 to $30.) You'll want your sound card to support at least 64 voices at the same time (64-voice polyphony) from its wavetable synth section. Advanced sound cards support several hundred voices; some sound cards go up to 512 or even 1024 voices, which is probably more than

you need for any music. It's certainly more than your ear can likely distinguish, but you'll be able to win some of those "Who has more polyphony?" contests with your jealous friends.

> **NOTE**
>
> MP3 deals exclusively in mono and stereo formats—in other words, one (mono) or two (stereo) channels of music. Other digital-audio formats can use more channels. For example, the Advanced Audio Codec (AAC) is designed to work with up to 48 channels—enough to add surround-sound options, a dozen different languages, and more.

The following list mentions some sound cards that you may want to consider, with approximate prices as of this writing. But because hardware companies are constantly bringing out new models, you'll probably want to do some research on your own.

- The Sound Blaster Live! from Creative Labs is a PCI card that has built-in DSP effects such as reverb to help you customize how your MP3 tracks sound on playback. The Sound Blaster Live! MP3+ costs $99, comes with a bundle of MP3-oriented software, and is a good value. If you want bells and whistles, the Sound Blaster Live! Platinum costs $199 and includes a Live! Drive—a module that fits into a drive bay in the front of your computer like a CD-ROM drive and provides input and output jacks for S/PDIF (the Sony/Philips Digital Interface), headphones, line or microphone, and MIDI. Having the jacks right there is much handier than having them at the back of the PC, but you may not feel this feature is worth the extra expense.

- The Sound Blaster AWE64 from Creative Labs is a 64-voice ISA card that costs about $199. It's also available in a Value Edition that costs $99.

- The Turtle Beach Montego II Quadzilla costs $79 and supports four-speaker output for quadraphonic audio. If you want digital I/O, Voyetra Turtle Beach, Inc. also makes the Montego II Plus, a $149 board that provides lossless digital signal transfer and four-channel positional audio.
- The Diamond Monster Sound MX400 costs around $79.

> **WARNING**
>
> Before you buy a sound card for a Linux machine, make sure that drivers are available for it; otherwise, its voices will be silent. A good place to start looking for information on drivers is the sound card vendor's Web site, followed by the Linux distributor's site. For example, Red Hat Software keeps a list of supported hardware on its Web site at www.redhat.com. At this writing, leading sound cards such as the Sound Blaster Live! and Montego II Quadzilla do not have solid Linux drivers in all distributions, although the folks at Creative are working hard to deliver them for the Sound Blaster Live! sound card.

Speakers

The sound card is the first component for getting great sound out of your computer. The second is the speakers or headphones. In this section, we'll discuss speakers; in the next section, we'll discuss headphones.

Speakers come in a wide range of sizes, prices, and capabilities. This section discusses the important points that you need to keep in mind before opening your wallet.

Beware of Cheap Speakers

Beware of cheap speakers, and especially of the "multimedia speakers" thrown in to round out "complete" PC systems. Many of these speakers look unimpressive and sound even worse; don't rely on them to make your music sound good. Instead, plan to invest some money in better speakers right from the start. You can get worthwhile speakers starting at about $60, although if your budget runs to a few hundred dollars, you can get speakers that will really rock the house.

If you're buying a new PC, either get it with speakers that you know to be high quality rather than the echo chambers that the company may try to foist on you, or buy good speakers separately. For example, Dell offers a range of speakers, including some great models from Harman Kardon, while Gateway offers some powerful subwoofer sets from Boston Acoustics. If the manufacturer doesn't offer good speakers, buy them separately elsewhere.

Speaker Components

Most speakers are built around two or more *cones* or *drivers*. As you'd guess from the first name, cones have traditionally been conical, although recently manufacturers have started building flat speakers. In a two-way speaker, the *tweeter* plays the treble (high-frequency) sounds, and the *woofer* plays the bass sounds.

In a subwoofer system, the *subwoofer* plays the bass and very-low-frequency sounds—those bass rumbles that reverberate in your body more than in your ears. A subwoofer typically provides better bass than a non-subwoofer setup and is considered a must by most gamers and many audiophiles. The other advantage of a subwoofer system is that its satellite speakers can typically be quite small, allowing for discreet placement in your average office. Because it's difficult for humans to locate the positions of low-frequency sounds, the subwoofer is nondirectional, so it's typically designed to be placed on the floor and can be located just about anywhere in the room. That means you can hide it under your desk or behind another convenient piece of furniture if you like.

Passive or Amplified Speakers

Your next choice is between passive speakers—unpowered speakers—and amplified speakers. *Passive speakers* are typically used with an amplifier (which is often integrated into a receiver), as in your average home stereo system. The output from the CD, cassette deck, and radio goes into the amplifier, into which you plug the speakers. The amplifier runs on AC and provides the heavy-duty lifting; the speakers just reproduce the sound. When you plug passive speakers into a sound card that's designed to work with amplified speakers, you get minimal volume.

Amplified speakers contain their own amplifier or amplifiers. Usually there's one amplifier in one of the speakers, which makes it much heavier than the other one. That speaker is the one that receives the power—usually from AC because batteries won't get you far—and provides the boosting. In a subwoofer set, the subwoofer typically contains the amplifier, because there's more space in the subwoofer than in its satellites, and if the subwoofer is going to be on the floor, its weight is much less of an issue than if it's going to sit on a delicate piece of furniture.

Generally speaking, you'll want amplified speakers to connect to your computer unless you're in a cubicle environment and need to keep the volume level discreet, or unless you're going to connect your computer to your stereo system. For home, you'll usually want a subwoofer set; for the office, a subwoofer is probably overkill.

Measuring Speaker Loudness

The next thing you need to know about speakers is how their loudness and power handling are measured. The terminology is a little vague, and the manufacturers of less-wonderful speakers tend to exploit it to make their speakers appear more attractive.

Speaker volume is measured in decibels (dB), and sometimes referred to as *SPL* or *sound pressure level*. The power-handling capability of speakers is measured in watts. The way manufacturers measure the wattage of speakers varies wildly. You'll see measurements in RMS watts (*root mean square* watts), which measures the wattage that the amplifier or speaker can deliver continuously rather than the wattage volume at which it maxes out. The peak wattage is sometimes referred to as *peak output* or *peak power*. The peak is basically the point beyond which you're testing the speaker to destruction.

What manufacturers don't tell you is that the power-handling capability of a speaker doesn't necessarily directly reflect how loud the speaker will sound. Speakers that play loudly with just a little wattage are said to be "efficient." But efficiency isn't everything; it's much more important that the speaker deliver the sound accurately, without adding distortion. Unless your main motivation in choosing speakers is to get a shattering level of volume, we suggest putting quality of sound above quantity of sound.

Similarly, unless you live for distortion and feedback or are using audio as a weapon of terror against your housemates or neighbors, you'll seldom want to use your speakers at anywhere near their peak power handling level (let alone beyond it). The music will be distorted almost beyond recognition and will sound atrocious to most sentient beings. So when buying speakers, be aware that many manufacturers of less expensive speakers list the peak wattage rather than RMS wattage because the figure is higher and more impressive. If you see inexpensive speakers advertised as handling 100 watts, remember that that figure is almost certainly peak: They probably can't sustain that volume; and even if they can, they will probably produce ear-ripping distortion while doing so.

In general, if your speakers handle 50 watts RMS, have generally low distortion figures, reproduce sounds from 20 to 15,000Hz, and sound good to you, you're on the right track. (The best way to choose speakers is to read reviews for good candidates, canvass opinions from any friends or family members you've noticed appreciating quality sound, and then audition the speakers for yourself.)

For conventional use, consider a speaker system that handles something like 20 to 50 watts. For example, the Altec Lansing ADA880R subwoofer system ($299) is rated at 40 watts RMS through its satellites and 40 watts RMS through the subwoofer. The Creative Labs MicroWorks subwoofer system (built by Cambridge SoundWorks), which was one of the systems that we used for everything from the Sisters of Mercy to Filter while writing this book, delivers 13 watts per channel on the satellites and 45 watts on the subwoofers. This is enough to disturb the rest of the household. A nice feature of the MicroWorks system is that it accepts twin inputs, so you can hook in two computers at the same time and play them simultaneously for bizarre mixing effects when the urge strikes you.

Suit Your Speakers to Your Sonic Needs

Next, be sure that the speakers you get are suitable for the type of sounds that you want them to produce. Once you start looking into speakers, you'll find that some speakers are designed for general use, while others are designed primarily for use with specific types of music, with spoken audio, or with games. If you listen mostly to rock, get speakers designed for it. If you play a lot of games as well, get speakers that can punch out machine-gun fire and bellows without blowing a woofer. And if you listen to a bit of everything, get multipurpose speakers.

TIP

If your sonic needs are subservient to your spatial needs, consider a space-saving solution such as speakers built into your monitor or into your computer—for example, the "drive bay speakers" that some manufacturers build to fit into a spare drive bay in a desktop or tower case. Because it's usually placed smack in front of you, the monitor is usually a better bet than the computer, although many of the speakers that manufacturers build into their monitors are so poor that it's hard to imagine them being saleable without the monitor. Be aware that speakers built into flat-panel displays tend to lack wattage and punch in the interests of being sleek and trendy looking.

Surround Sound and Home Theater

If realistic sound is important to you and if you have plenty of money to burn, consider getting a surround sound or home theater system.

Surround sound uses four or five speakers to produce the effect of you being surrounded by the sound source. For example, when a car zips by in the background, you'll hear it go from left to right as you would with a normal stereo system, but you'll also hear that it's behind you rather than in front of you (or going straight through your head). Surround sound systems typically cost more than regular subwoofer systems, but if you like the effect, you may well find the expense justified. If you do opt for a system with extra speakers, make sure your sound card supports them. It should support 3D audio in games, too.

If you have a DVD drive or a sound card that supports positional audio, you may want to consider a *home theater system*. Home theater systems typically use *5.1* setups—five satellite speakers with a powered subwoofer—to deliver realistic sound effects; some home theater systems even use 7.1 setups. One example of a 5.1 setup is the DeskTop Theater 5.1 from Cambridge SoundWorks, which costs $299. DeskTop Theater is rated at 5 watts RMS to the main speakers and the surround speakers, 15 watts RMS to the center speaker, and 15 watts RMS to the subwoofer. The numbers may not seem impressive, but the sound is room filling. Other home theater systems cost upwards of $1000 and are designed to hook into your TV and stereo system—into which you can hook your PC.

Listen before You Buy

Before you buy a set of speakers, make sure to listen to them first. If your local store or superstore has a rack of speakers fed through a common control panel to let you test drive the speakers, make the most of it. Take along a few of your own CDs or a portable MP3 player (or CD player) if possible to make sure that the music you like sounds good through them. If your local store doesn't offer a test drive, ask your friends for a recommendation and listen to their speakers to make sure that they know what they're talking about.

HEADPHONES

If anything, headphones are even harder to choose than speakers, because they depend on the shape of your head and ears as well as the state of your brain. So one person's dream set can be another person's instrument of torture. We won't give specific recommendations beyond this one piece of advice: *Never buy headphones because they look good or because the price is right.* Life's too short to be stuck with uncomfortable headphones that'll whale the stuffing out of your ears just because they look cool.

There are several different styles of headphones:

Circumaural headphones or over-the-ear headphones
These are the headphones that completely enclose your ears. You can get either *open headphones* that expose the back of the diaphragm to the air, providing better sound, or *sealed headphones* that look and act more like a pair of

ear defenders, insulating you somewhat from outside sound. As you'd guess, sealed headphones are good for noisy environments such as music studios or busy family rooms, but they tend to be heavy. If you're looking for a recommendation, we can give you a couple to try. The Beyerdynamic DT831 headphones (about $200) score high marks for delivering quality music, but because they're closed, they tend to get hot (as Tony Hancock said in *The Radio Ham,* "Strewth! Pair of braised lamb chops under here."). The Sennheiser HD 565 Ovation headphones (about $220) are super-comfortable, open circumaural headphones that give a very civilized feel to all but the most raucous music while delivering exceptional punch and clarity.

Supra-aural headphones or on-the-ear headphones
These are the headphones that sit on your ears. They're lighter and smaller than circumaural headphones so they can be more comfortable to wear, provided they don't press too hard against your ears. Like circumaural headphones, most supra-aural headphones use a headband to keep them in place. Koss makes a style of supra-aural headphones that use ear clips (they call them "sportclips") to attach to your ears. This style frees you from a headband but makes you look like Mr. Spock using two old-fashioned hearing aids. If you're looking for standard supra-aural headphones for listening to rock, start by looking at the Grado 225s (about $200).

Ear-bud headphones These come in two styles: with a headband (buds that poke into your ears but don't wedge there) and without a headband (buds designed to wedge into your ear and stay there). Ear buds deliver an intense music experience but typically lower music quality, and they serve up less bass than circumaural or supra-aural headphones. Ear buds are considered by some to carry a higher threat of hearing damage than circumaural headphones or supra-aural headphones. (This is debatable—you can deafen yourself perfectly well with most circumaural and supra-aural headphones as well.) We don't have a recommendation for ear buds except to emphasize what you probably already know: Anything real cheap is probably a bad idea, and your priority should be getting a pair that sounds good, feels good, and remains in place for whatever activities you'll be performing while wearing the ear buds. Because ear-bud headphones actually sit in your ear, be especially alert for discomfort—it can indicate imminent damage, even if the volume is apparently low.

You don't have to pay a huge amount for headphones. A $20 set of ear buds can sound great, and a $75 set of supra-aural or circumaural headphones can sound better than a $300 set of speakers. If you'll be listening via headphones exclusively (or even just extensively), we doubt you'll regret paying for a decent pair.

On the mundane front, make sure that the headphone cord is long enough for your intended use and that the headphones come with the right kind of plug for the output jack you're planning to use. Many headphones use the $1/4$-inch plug that slides into the $1/4$-inch jacks on stereo equipment rather than the miniplug that most portable audio items use. You may need to get a $1/4$-inch plug-to-miniplug adapter. (The better headphones usually come with one.) Again, buy a quality adapter, or it'll cost you audio quality right where you don't need it to.

Big names in headphones include AKG, Beyerdynamic, Grado, Koss, and Sennheiser. (That's alphabetical order, not in order of recommendation.)

> **NOTE**
>
> If you'll always be using headphones rather than speakers, you may want to invest in a headphone amplifier to help power your headphones. For home use, you may also want to get wireless headphones that will let you roam further from your sound source. *Try these out before you buy them.* Cheaper wireless headphone sets can seriously clip the top and bottom end of the frequencies, and even better sets tend to suffer in comparison to wired headphones.

As with speakers, you'll want to listen to headphones before buying them. Besides the obvious—to hear the sound quality—you should make sure they fit your ears and are comfortable enough to wear for your typical listening session.

Storage

Once you get into digital audio, you'll probably want to store a large number of files. To do so, you'll need plenty of storage space, either on hard drives or on removable media.

For your most frequently used files, hard drives should be your primary storage for digital-audio files. Hard drives typically provide the least expensive means of mass storage apart from backup tapes (which are inconvenient to access), and with huge hard drives available at very affordable prices, you can pack a huge amount of storage into a desktop computer without breaking the bank. You can put up to four EIDE devices in most modern PCs. Most people will go for two or three hard drives and one CD-ROM drive, CD-R drive, CD-RW drive, or DVD drive, depending on their needs.

Encoded at 128kbps, each minute of compressed digital audio takes up about 1MB, so each gigabyte of disk space can store around 250 four-minute tracks. Put three 60GB drives in a desktop machine, and you've got plenty of space for a very serious music collection—even if you encode some of the tracks at a higher bitrate.

If you've filled your hard drives with music, or if you need portable storage, your next candidate should be removable media, such as Zip drives (either the 100MB Zip Classic or the 250MB Zip 250), Jaz drives (either the 1GB original Jaz or the Jaz 2GB), or the Orb from Castlewood Technologies (2.2GB). These all come in internal and external versions. You'll get the best performance from SCSI connection and the worst performance from parallel-port connections. You may also want to consider floppy-drive replacements such as the SuperDisk and LS-120. Forget about floppy disks unless you're using low-fidelity files (for example, spoken audio) or you're in desperate need to transfer a single file from one computer to another (in which case, use a zipping program that can create a zip file that spans multiple disks to divide up the file onto the floppies and then transfer it to the other computer and reconstitute it).

TIP

If you can't add any more hard drives to your computer (for example, if you have a laptop), consider attaching an external hard drive via the parallel port, a USB port, or a FireWire port, via SCSI, or via a PC card. External hard drives tend to be slower and more expensive than regular hard drives, but they're portable and effective.

If you have a CD-R or CD-RW drive, you can burn CDs for storage, transfer, or backup. CD-R and CD-RW media hold 650MB each (or 700MB for extended-capacity CDs), so you can fit a good amount of compressed digital audio onto them. For higher capacity, consider a DVD-RAM drive. Each side of a DVD-RAM disk holds 2.3GB, and you can get either single-sided disks or more expensive double-sided ones. At this writing, DVD-RAM is far more expensive than CD-R or

CD-RW as a storage medium, but if you need and can afford the capacity, it's a good alternative.

> **STORING MUSIC ON ONLINE DRIVES**
>
> One storage option that you may want to use from time to time is an online drive service such as FreeDrive or Visto. FreeDrive (www.freedrive.com) provides 50MB of space free. Visto (www.visto.com) provides 15MB of space for free for personal use and 25MB for each group that you create. (You can also pay FreeDrive or Visto for more space.) If you're a member of Yahoo!, you can store 10MB for free by using its Briefcase feature.
>
> Given that the space is either limited or expensive and that you'll be uploading and downloading files via the Internet, online drives are primarily useful for keeping backups of vital files or for transferring files from one computer to another. You don't want to try to store a large collection of digital-audio files on them.
>
> One online drive service that offers a huge amount of space is myplay.com, which gives you 3GB to use. The catch is that anything original you upload, they get to use "in whole or in part, on the Service itself and in connection with the advertising and promotion of the Service, throughout the world in any form, media, or technology now known or later developed." We don't like the sound of this and recommend that you read the terms and conditions carefully before signing up for myplay.com.

PORTS

Next, if you'll be using a portable hardware MP3 player, make sure that your computer has the right port or ports for it. If your computer and OS support USB, that'll usually mean a USB port.

A Hardware Primer for MP3 and Digital Audio

At this writing, most new hardware MP3 players use a USB port for two reasons:

- A USB port provides far greater speed across its 12Mbps bus than either of the two ubiquitous alternatives, the parallel port and the serial port.
- A USB port is now built into almost all new computers.

"Far greater speed" translates in practice to a more-or-less satisfactory speed for downloads. Some USB connections can transfer the best part of a megabyte a second, so it takes between one and two minutes to fill a 64MB player. When USB 2.0 is implemented, its 400Mbps or 800Mbps speed should enable you to fill a portable player in a few seconds. If FireWire (also known as i.LINK to Sony customers, or as IEEE1394, the number of its technical specification) ever takes off, it may become a viable method of loading portable players.

Earlier MP3 players relied on the parallel port, which was a good move in that almost every computer has one, but a bad move in that almost every computer is already using the parallel port for a printer, scanner, removable drive, or other device. Most parallel-port MP3 players came with pass-through ports that were supposed to pass through any data intended for devices other than the MP3 player. However, many of these ports disagreed with printers and scanners, and a better solution was to add another parallel port. (Most computers support up to two parallel ports. If you have a PCI slot free, you can easily add a PCI card that provides one or more additional parallel ports.)

If you need to add USB to your desktop computer and you have a PCI slot free, you can get a PCI card with two or more USB ports. Siig makes an interesting PCI card that has five USB ports, but it's hard to find at this writing. In general, you'll probably do better to get a two-port USB card and plug into it a hub that has the number of ports you require. Unless you keep your computer front and center on your desk, a hub is usually easier to plug USB devices into than the computer itself.

> **TIP**
>
> If you have a laptop and are planning to get an MP3 player that uses CompactFlash memory, consider loading it via a PC Card CompactFlash reader rather than via a parallel cable or USB cable—it'll be much quicker.

Internet Connection

If you're going to download digital-audio files (and perhaps also upload some), you'll want as fast an Internet connection as you can get and afford. We realize we're probably preaching to the choir on this topic, but this section provides a brief summary of the options you should be considering if your current Internet connection is a 90-pound weakling. In case you stop reading at the type of connection that seems most suitable to you, we'll start with a brief mention of security.

Security

Some Internet connections are less secure than others—but these days, whichever kind of Internet connection you have, consider securing it with a firewall. For a hardware firewall, evaluate products such as the Linksys Instant Broadband EtherFast Cable/DSL Router (less than $200) or the UMAX UGate series (which range from $180 to $350). For a software firewall, consider products such as BlackICE Defender from Network ICE ($39.95; www.networkice.com) or Zone Alarm from Zone Labs ($19.95; www.zonealarm.com).

Cable Modem

If cable modem access is available where you live, go for it. Cable provides the fastest affordable residential access—up to several megabits (millions of bits) per second.

Cable modem access has three main drawbacks:

- First, the bandwidth is shared with your neighbors, so if everyone gets online at the same time, the speed drops. Ask the cable company what the network's capacity is, how many people share that capacity, and what the minimum bandwidth they guarantee you is. (They may not guarantee any minimum bandwidth.) If you find the speed dropping to unacceptable levels, lobby the cable company vociferously to add bandwidth to your loop. Get your neighbors to lobby, too, if you can pry them away from their computers.

- Second, many cable companies implement an *upload speed cap*, which limits the amount of data you can upload, typically to prevent you from running a Web server. If you're not going to be running a server (or sharing many files via Napster or a similar technology), this shouldn't be a problem, but make sure that you know what the company's policy is before you sign up.

- Third, because the wire is shared, your computer is essentially networked with your neighborhood, so it's vital that you use a firewall to secure it. Also, be sure to turn off file-sharing on any computer that's connected to the Internet via a cable modem.

Digital Subscriber Line (DSL)

If digital subscriber line (DSL) access is available and affordable where you live, get it. DSL typically offers between 384kbps and 1.5Mbps downstream (to the consumer) and slower upstream (to the ISP) speeds. At this writing, the Baby Bells are vying with the cable companies for high-speed customers, so the cost of DSL is reasonable—from $35 to $50 per month for good service, including an account with their ISP.

Because DSL is always on, your computer is continuously connected to the Internet, so there's a threat of your computer being attacked across the wire. With DSL, the threat is significantly lower than with cable (because the wire isn't shared), but you'll still need a firewall.

Unlike with cable, you're not on the same local network as your neighbors, so the bandwidth isn't shared, and you should be able to get the minimum guaranteed rate (sometimes referred to as the *committed information rate* or *CIR*) any time of the day or night.

The main disadvantage of DSL is that it works only within a relatively short distance from the telephone company's central office, which means in effect that it's confined to urban locations. Some non-telco DSL providers are more aggressive with the distance than the telcos, but you'll typically have to pay more, and you'll get a lower speed connection. If you live out in the sticks, you're almost certainly beyond the range of DSL.

Integrated Services Digital Network (ISDN)

If you can't get cable or a DSL, your next choice should be ISDN (Integrated Services Digital Network). An ISDN is a digital line that's not as fast as a DSL but is more widely available, especially for people outside major metropolitan areas. ISDN's *basic rate interface (BRI)* provides two bearer channels that deliver 64kbps each, plus a 16kbps signaling channel, so it delivers decent speeds when both bearer channels are open. Check the prices before you order ISDN; it's traditionally been a business service, and it can be expensive, with most companies levying per-minute charges for each channel.

The good news about ISDN (apart from its wide availability) is that most implementations are symmetrical, so you get the same speed upstream as downstream.

Satellite Solutions

If you're too rural to get ISDN, or if ISDN is too slow for you, consider one of the satellite solutions available, such as DirecPC. These solutions typically offer speeds of around 400kbps downstream, so they can be good if you need to download large chunks of data (such as digital-audio files).

Satellite solutions have one major drawback: The satellite provides only downlink capabilities, so you have to use your phone line to send data to your ISP to tell them which information to deliver by satellite. But given that your only alternative is likely to be a modem connection, you may find this flaw quite sufferable. DirecPC currently offers plans starting at $19.99 a month for a truly miserable number of hours. Make sure that the plan you choose provides enough hours each month so that you don't start incurring expensive extra hours every month on your normal level of usage.

Here's another thing to watch for: Some satellite services have a *fair access policy (FAP)* by which they reserve the right to throttle back your download speed if you continuously run it full bore. In other words, you can have your 400kbps (or whatever speed), but you can't have it all the time. This can put a serious crimp into your ability to download a massive amount of music every day via a satellite hookup. So read your signup agreement carefully for details of the FAP, and be especially wary of clauses that allow the service provider to modify the terms of the contract without your explicit consent.

Maximizing Your Modem Connection

If you're stuck with modem access, here are four things worth trying to make the most of it:

- ▶ First, try to get 56K modem access—the fastest possible. As you doubtless know, 56K modems are limited by the FCC to downloading at a little over 53kbps and by line limitations to uploading at 33.6kbps.

- Second, consider getting a *dual-line modem* that bonds together two conventional modems (on two separate phone lines) to increase your speed. You need an ISP that supports modem bonding for this to succeed—and two phone lines, of course. (You'll also hear dual-line modems referred to as *shotgun modems*, after the hunting shotguns with two barrels side by side used in the days before the shotgun became a weapon of urban combat and pacification.) Alternatively, if your operating system and your ISP support multilink, get a second modem and phone line, activate multilink, and use both modems at once. (Windows 98, Windows Me, and Windows 2000 all support multilink.)

- Whatever speed modem you have, make sure you're getting maximum performance out of it. Use a utility such as TweakDUN (DUN is the acronym for *dial-up networking*) or MTU Speed Pro (MTU is the abbreviation for *maximum transfer unit*). Both TweakDUN and MTU Speed Pro tune your TCP/IP settings to make sure that your connection is as efficient as possible. TweakDUN and MTU Speed Pro are shareware and are available from many shareware archives. They're not infallible, but they're worth a try.

- If your connection is less speedy than you'd like, get a download-scheduling utility such as GetRight from Headlight Software (www.getright.com) or AutoFTP from PrimaSoft (www.primasoft.com) that will let you line up your downloads to perform at a time when you don't need to do other things on your computer. For example, you can arrange to download a hundred megabytes of music at an antisocial hour in the early morning, when your corner of the Internet is likely to be less busy.

Up Next

In this chapter, we've detailed the hardware you'll need in order to enjoy MP3 and other digital audio, from processor and RAM through Internet connection. We've discussed how to decide whether to upgrade or spring for a new computer; we've given you suggestions for how to choose intensely personal hardware such as sound cards, speakers, and headphones; and we've even harangued you briefly and moderately about security on your Internet connection

In the next chapter, we'll discuss the laws affecting digital audio and how you can enjoy music via MP3 and other formats while staying on the right side of the law.

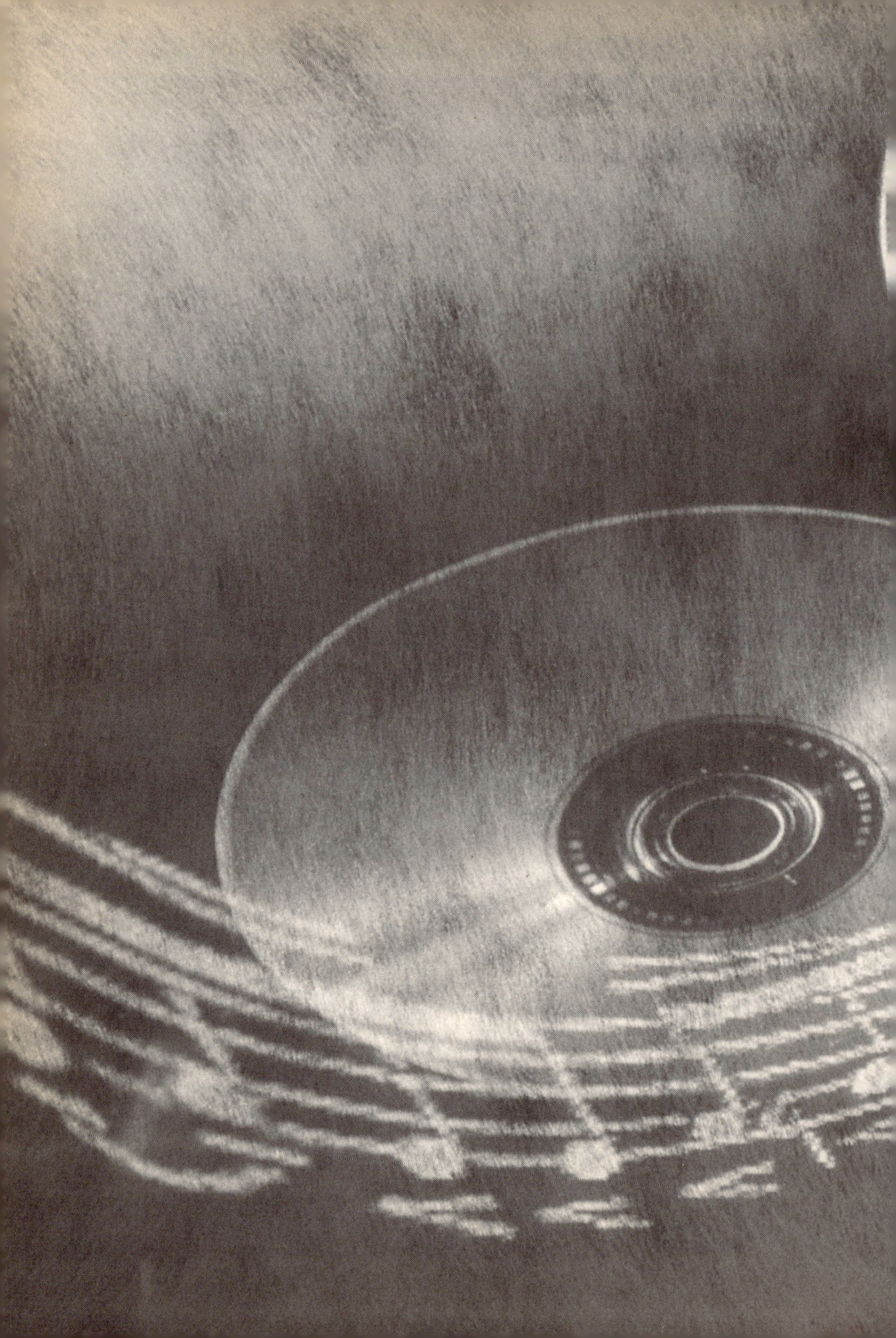

Chapter 3
Digital Audio and the Law

Featuring

- The short version of what's legal and what's not
- Intellectual property and copyright
- The protagonists in the digital-audio scene
- Fair use and personal use
- What's legal and what's not
- The legalities of creating and distributing digital-audio files
- How to tell whether a digital-audio file is legal or illegal
- Legal issues surrounding Napster

This chapter discusses how digital audio and the law relate to each other and how they get on. At this writing, there's a huge amount of confusion as to what's legal and what's not legal with digital audio, particularly in relation to creating, playing, and distributing MP3 files. The truth is straightforward and even logical, but it helps to know what you can and can't do with digital audio before you start breaking the law left, right, and center.

We'll start by visiting the idea of intellectual property, because it's central to copyright law, and copyright law is central to the issues surrounding digital audio. We'll discuss what copyright is, what it applies to, and how it works. We'll discuss who the major protagonists in the digital-audio business are, and we'll outline their main motivations. We'll tell you what you can do and can't do, and what most people are currently getting away with that they shouldn't be. We'll also look quickly at the specific legal issues that technologies such as Napster raise. Where appropriate, we'll touch on the relevant acts, such as the Audio Home Recording Act (AHRA) and the Digital Millennium Copyright Act (DMCA), but we won't delve into the details of those acts more than necessary.

First, though, for those who are in a hurry to start doing something other than read this chapter, here's a brief summary of what's legal and what's not.

What's Legal and What's Not (Brief Summary)

This section gives you the brief version of what's legal and what's not legal, without explaining why (or why not). It's for people who don't want (or can't be bothered) to read the whole chapter at this point.

Digital Audio and the Law 71

Legally, you can

- Listen to streaming audio from a Web site or an Internet radio station.
- Download a digital-audio file from a Web site or FTP site *provided that the copyright holder has granted the distributor permission to distribute it.*
- Download a digital-audio file from a computer via Napster or other similar file-sharing technologies *provided that the copyright holder has granted the distributor permission to distribute it.*
- Create digital-audio files of tracks on CDs you own for your personal use.
- Create and distribute digital-audio files of recordings for which you are the copyright holder.
- Burn CDs containing legal digital-audio files that you've recorded, either in their compressed format or expanded to CD-audio format.
- Download (or copy) MP3 files or other supported digital-audio files to portable audio devices (such as the Diamond Rio or the Creative Labs Nomad).

Legally, you cannot

- Lend a friend a CD so that she can create digital-audio files from it.
- Borrow a CD from a friend and create digital-audio files from it.
- Distribute digital-audio files that you've created from CDs or other recordings *unless you hold the copyright or the copyright holder has explicitly granted you permission to distribute them.*

- Post digital-audio files to a Web site *unless you hold the copyright or the copyright holder has explicitly granted you permission to distribute them.*

- Share digital-audio files via Napster or similar file-sharing technologies *unless you hold the copyright or the copyright holder has explicitly granted you permission to distribute them.*

- Sell digital-audio files *unless you hold the copyright or the copyright holder has explicitly granted you permission to distribute them.*

- Upload digital-audio files from a portable audio player that supports music uploading (such as the I-JAM or the eGo) to another computer. (In this scenario, you're essentially using the portable player to copy the files from one computer to another.)

If you want to know why you can and cannot legally do these things, read the rest of this chapter. If you're more interested in getting to the music, turn to Chapter 4, "Finding MP3 Files via the Web and Newsgroups."

Intellectual Property

Intellectual property is the cornerstone on which the system and concepts of copyright are based, so we'll discuss it briefly here.

> **NOTE**
>
> Intellectual property is sometimes abbreviated to IP, but because that abbreviation is more widely used to denote Internet Protocol, we won't use it here. Given that both abbreviations can be used in relation to computers and digital audio, it can become confusing. (Typically, "IP concerns" would refer to intellectual property, while "IP configuration" would refer to the Internet Protocol, but "IP security" might refer to either.)

Physical property is easy to understand because most everybody owns enough of it to want to object violently when some of it's taken away. Most moral codes and their related legal structures (we say "most" because we're neither anthropologists nor legal experts) classify the removal of property belonging to someone else as stealing and say it's a bad thing.

By its nature, intellectual property is much more slippery because it deals mostly with nonphysical objects. If Dick has a really nice Stratocaster, and Jane takes it away from him against his will, he won't have it any more. That's stealing, plain enough. But art such as a poem, a song, or a novel doesn't have a fixed physical format and can easily be copied. Intellectual property says that such art has a value and that the creator has the sole right to make and distribute copies of it, so that the creator can gain from creating the work in the first place. (In many cases, the creator assigns the right to make and distribute the copies to a third party, such as a publisher for a book or a record company for a song.) So if Jane writes the ultimate doom-rock dirge, and Dick records a version without her permission and makes it a hit, Dick has broken the law, and Jane can sue him for money putatively lost. (In practice, Jane probably won't sue Dick if he pays her enough money.)

Copyright

Most of the legalities surrounding digital-audio hinge on copyright, so it's helpful to know the basics of copyright. Copyright essentially works in the same way the world around, although its local implementations differ somewhat from each other. What we describe here is the U.S. implementation of copyright.

The basic idea behind copyright is straightforward, but the application of the idea is complex. In this section, we'll probably be guilty of oversimplification in the cause of getting the message across. So take this information as a starting point rather than gospel.

As defined in the Copyright Act of 1976, copyright protects expression in many forms including literary, dramatic, and musical works; sound recordings; audiovisual works (such as movies); performance expression such as pantomimes and choreography; architectural works (such as buildings); and graphic, pictorial, and sculptural works.

That probably seems like quite a comprehensive list, but there are a number of things that are not copyrightable:

- Ideas are not copyrightable—although the expression of an idea is.
- Facts are not copyrightable, because the information is not expression. For example, you couldn't copyright the fact that John Lennon was shot in 1980. But you could copyright the poem "John Lennon was shot today. I was surprised." (Actually, *you* can't copyright that poem, because *we* hold the copyright to it. But you get the idea.)
- Names and titles are not copyrightable—although you can trademark distinctive names and titles if you get to them before anybody else does.
- Short phrases are not copyrightable, although, again, you can trademark them if they're distinctive and haven't been trademarked yet. Just do it carefully.

As soon as you create an original work in a tangible format, you have the copyright on that work. For example, if you write a poem (however short, however bad—see the example in the second bullet point above), compose a melody (however short, however bad), or draw a picture of a miniature Stonehenge (however crude) on a napkin, you have a copyrighted work.

It's that simple—but there are several key points:

- First, the work needs to be original. If you write down a poem that somebody else has already written down, you're copying a copyrighted work, and you're infringing copyright. Similarly, if you compose a musical piece that consists entirely of sections lifted from other people's copyrighted works, chances are you're infringing copyright. (There are some exceptions, such as fair use—which we'll discuss in a minute or two—and parody.)

- Second, the work needs to be in a tangible format. What constitutes a tangible format is vague, but the work essentially needs to be detectable to the appropriate sense. For example, you could draw a logo on your computer and store it there or record a song onto a cassette, and each would be a copyrighted work: The work doesn't have to be stored on paper or in a visual medium. The main point is that you can't create an original work only in your head, because nobody else will be able to detect that it exists. So if you compose a poem, you need to write it down, but the medium doesn't matter—clay tablets, papyrus, lead type, and bits-'n'-bytes are all fine.

- Third, you don't even have to include a copyright notice on your work, though it's a good idea to do so. Because the copyright symbol (©) is displayed prominently on most published copyrighted works (such as this book), many people have gotten the idea that you need to include a copyright notice such as "Copyright © 2000 Kenny Cartman. All rights reserved" in order to claim copyright. You don't—the notice is just a formality identifying the copyright holder—but it's certainly a good idea to include a copyright notice.

The Copyright Notice

The example of a copyright notice that we just gave is redundant. You can use either the word "Copyright" or the © copyright symbol, but you may want to use both in cases where the symbol may not be correctly displayed. (For example, some Web browsers do not render the © character correctly.)

The copyright statement needs to include the year of publication. In many cases, you'll do well to include the full date (month, day, year) on the work in case your copyright is challenged by someone else claiming to have created the work before you.

The copyright notice needs to include the name of the owner of the copyright. In many cases, the owner of the copyright will not be the author or creator of the work. For example, if you create a work for your employer as part of your employment, your employer usually holds the copyright on it. On the other hand, if you write that novel you've always felt is in you, you hold the copyright on it.

In order to get copyright protection in Bolivia and Honduras, you need to include the reservation-of-rights phrase specified by the Buenos Aires Convention (*All rights reserved*) in the copyright notice. If you don't care about those two countries, you can skip the phrase.

Registering the Copyright

As we mentioned, simply creating an original work in a tangible form gets you the copyright for the work. You don't need to register the copyright in order to get it. But if you want to be able to sue anybody who infringes on your copyrighted work, or if you want to be able to get statutory damages in the event of an infringement, you need to register the copyright with the Copyright Office within three months of the date that you first published the work. If you don't register the work, you can only collect actual damages, which may be minimal or nominal (and these days, nominal is a kissing cousin of nothing).

Granting Rights to Someone Else

Once you've created an original work, you hold the copyright to it—and if you've registered the copyright, that goes in spades. But if you want to have somebody else publish the work, you'll typically need to grant them the rights to do so.

Which right or rights you grant depends on the relationship between you as the creator of the original work and your publisher. In some cases, the creator may grant a full suite of rights to the publisher, including rights for adaptations, derivative works, and translations. In other cases, the grant of rights may be limited. In either case, the rights remain in effect, although the holder of the rights may have changed.

FAIR USE

The next concept we need to throw at you is *fair use*. You'll need to know about fair use mostly if you sample or parody music or if you criticize music. Because a lot of people use the term wrongly to justify assorted law-twistings at the hands of digital-audio maniacs, you need to know approximately what it means, even if you're just interested in downloading music and playing it to amuse you and yours.

Fair use is a provision in the Copyright Act that essentially lets you use a portion of a copyrighted work "for purposes such as criticism, comment, news reporting, teaching (including multiple copies for classroom use), scholarship, or research" without infringing copyright.

Four factors are taken into account in determining what does or does not constitute fair use:

1. The "purpose and character" of the use: commercial, educational, reporting, scientific, and so on. Using a

portion of a copyrighted work in a commercial work isn't wrong, but usually works that are created for nonprofit purposes are more likely to qualify for fair use.

2. The type of the copyrighted work. Some works are deemed more worthy of copyright protection than others.

3. The amount of the copyrighted work used in relation to the whole work. Essentially, the amount of the copyrighted work used shouldn't be more than is necessary for the purpose of copying. That doesn't mean that there's a set maximum percentage of a work that you can use. It might well be fair use to include the whole of a haiku in an essay on Japanese poetry, where it might not be fair use to include a couple of paragraphs of *Finnegan's Wake* in an article on Joyce.

4. The effect that the use will have on the value of the copyrighted work or its potential market. For example, if you use a substantial and critical portion of a copyrighted work in such a way that nobody will be interested in that work (because of yours), it probably won't be regarded as fair use. The value and potential market for the copyrighted work include its derivative works—works derived from it.

As you can see, fair use is an extremely gray area of the law. If you bend the definition of fair use, you can claim that just about anything is fair use. But if you expect a judge and jury to agree with you, make sure you stay within the bounds of how a reasonable person (should some such person ever be found) could be expected to interpret the law.

Personal Use

Fair use, discussed in the previous section, is a key component of the Copyright Act. *Personal use,* a provision of the Audio Home Recording Act (AHRA) of 1992, is completely different and lets users of digital audio recording devices make copies of copyrighted works on other media. For example, if you buy a Korn CD, you can record it onto a cassette so that you can listen to it on your Walkman. As the name implies, that copy is for your personal use. If you give the cassette to a friend so that they can get the full Korn experience, that's illegal.

So far, so simple. But there's a twist: You'll notice that we said "digital audio recording devices" in the previous paragraph. Computers don't qualify as digital audio recording devices (although they can record audio digitally) but rather as "multipurpose devices." This means that, technically, audio copies you make on computers are not covered by the AHRA and personal use, but most authorities seem to agree that making digital-audio files of copies of music you own for your personal use is legal.

The Protagonists in the Digital-Audio Scene

Unless you're from Mars (or Venus), none of the major protagonists in the digital-audio scene should come as a surprise—music consumers, artists, record companies, and recording-industry associations. We'll summarize them and their primary motivations briefly in this section.

Music Consumers

Consumers, the biggest group, are the end users of the music—the people who buy copies of the music (on CD, cassette, or other media). Traditionally, music consumers have been able to vote only with their wallets—by buying music they like (and perhaps by buying related paraphernalia such as t-shirts and widgets), tickets to concerts, and so on. Music consumers have also been able to write to artists and record companies with suggestions and demands, but neither had any discernible effect unless it was part of a massive campaign of orchestrated letter-writing with a specific goal in mind (for example, getting music with offensive lyrics to bear a parental-advisory warning sticker).

The consumers' primary motivation is to get the music they like as inexpensively and with as little trouble as possible. Secondary motivations include promoting their favorite artists to family, friends, and the wide world, or simply worshipping at the shrine of the artist (so to speak).

Artists

Artists, a much smaller group, are the ones who invent and create the music, often with the help of a record company. An artist typically receives a royalty on each unit sold, either against gross receipts or against net receipts. An artist usually receives a percentage of ticket revenues for concerts.

Most artists' primary motivation is balanced between getting as many people as possible to hear (and, preferably, like) their music and making as much money as possible by selling copies of their music, concert tickets, and paraphernalia. Secondary motivations include expressing their philosophies and political views and saving everything from the rain forests to the whales, none of which need concern us here.

Record Companies

The record companies, an even smaller group, find, develop, produce, and promote artists. Almost all record companies' primary motivation is to make as much money as possible for their owners and shareholders by selling as many units of music as possible, and getting as much money as possible for each unit sold.

After the retailer's cut and the distributor's cut, the record company typically gets the bulk of the consumer's money and pays the artist royalties from this.

The Recording Industry Association of America (RIAA)

Next in the list of major protagonists in the digital-audio scene is the Recording Industry Association of America, Inc., known as the RIAA by its friends and by those who are short of time or ink. As its name suggests, the RIAA represents the recording industry. It directly represents the major record companies and indirectly represents the interests of the artists signed to the record companies.

Retail Industry

Last in the list of major protagonists in the digital-audio scene is the retail industry, which sells the bulk of the $38 billion worth of music sold worldwide in 1999.

As you'll know if you're a music consumer, music is sold pretty much everywhere in the U.S. these days, from airport kiosks and gas stations to Wal-Mart and Target to dedicated music stores to online retailers. At this writing, most music is sold on physical media such as CDs or cassettes; a tiny amount of music is sold as downloadable files over the Internet. (In 1999, 2.4 percent of U.S. consumers bought music using the Internet. This represents a meteoric rise from the 1.1 percent of consumers who bought music using the Internet in 1988, but it's still a very low number—and it includes the sales of physical media such as CDs via the Internet.)

Retailers' primary motivation is to make as much money by selling music as they can. This usually means selling as many units of music as possible at as much of a markup as their customers will accept. Secondary motivations vary and are not relevant here.

MP3 Files Are Legal

The first thing you need to know about MP3 is that there's nothing inherently legal or illegal in MP3. It's just a file format for compressed audio. MP3 is an ISO (International Organization for Standardization, sometimes called the International Standards Organization) standard, so it's not controlled by any one company in the way Microsoft controls, say, the Word document file format. Anybody can create an MP3 file, and anybody can use one.

Where the legal issues arise is with the content in the MP3 file. Just as a Word document can contain material that infringes copyright on a work (for example, if you type a published poem whose copyright is held by someone else into a Word document, chances are you've infringed their copyright), an MP3 file can contain music or other audio that infringes on a copyrighted work.

You can create MP3 files of audio whose copyright is held by other people for your own personal use (see the section titled "Personal Use" earlier in this chapter), but you cannot distribute those MP3 files. For an MP3 file to be distributed legally, the copyright holder for the music or other material in question needs to have granted permission for the music or material to be downloaded or played.

Creating Digital-Audio Files

This section discusses the issues you need to be aware of before you start creating digital-audio files for yourself.

Of the different types of digital-audio files, MP3 files are the easiest files to create because the software for creating them is not only widely available but also extremely simple to use. Set the software running, put a CD in your CD drive, and you're in business. VQF files are easy to make, and the encoder is widely available. Liquid Audio files are relatively easy to make, although the software involved, which is called the Liquifier, is picky about the hardware it runs on. Some other formats use encoders that have not been released to the public, so end users don't have an easy way of making files in those formats.

The legalities of whether you can or cannot create a digital-audio file of a copyrighted track are straightforward. If you own a legal copy of an audio item, you can legally make a copy of it for your personal use. For example, if you have a copy of Metallica's *S&M* concert recording, you can legally rip and encode the tracks on it for your personal use. You can download them to your portable MP3 player or to your car player, and play them as loud as you like. The moment you give one of these copies made for your personal use to someone else, you're breaking the law.

Distributing Digital-Audio Files

The legal position on distributing digital-audio files is very straightforward: You can do so if you hold the copyright or you have the copyright owner's explicit written permission to distribute the files. Otherwise, you can't. It makes no difference whether the distribution you're performing is free of charge or for profit, or whether you claim that you're promoting the copyright owner's interest by fostering interest in their material.

There's no way of getting around this legally. For example, the First Amendment guarantees you the right to free expression, but free expression does not allow you to violate copyright by stealing someone else's intellectual property. And because copyright is essentially the same worldwide, you can't circumvent U.S. copyright law by using, say, an offshore server to distribute digital-audio files. Under the Berne Convention, to which most major nations in the world are signatories, it's easy to prosecute copyright violations that occur in other countries.

The penalties for distributing copyrighted works illegally are severe. Under the No Electronic Theft Act (the NET Act) of 1997, reproducing or distributing "one or more copies of one or more copyrighted works with a total retail value of more than $1000" during any 180-day period is an infringement of copyright that can bring you three to five years in jail—and hefty fines. What's more, you don't have to profit directly from the piracy in order to be guilty.

Don't be fooled by that $1000 figure into thinking that you can distribute a few tracks illegally without fear because they're not worth that much. The courts may decide that because any track posted on a Web site can be downloaded by an almost infinite number of people, a single track is worth $1000 or more.

Just about the only exception to the law on distributing digital-audio files without the copyright owner's explicit written permission comes when you're selling a digital-audio file that you've purchased legally. (For example, sites such as EMusic.com sell individual tracks in MP3 format with the artist's or record company's blessing, because they get royalties from the transaction.) Under the First Sale Doctrine laid out in the Copyright Act, you can sell (or give) your copy of an audio recording to someone else in much the same way that you could sell them a (legal) CD.

The key to this provision is that when you've transferred your copy of the audio recording to the other person, you have to get rid of your own copy. Otherwise, you've simply copied it, and either you or the recipient has an illegal copy. Similarly, you can't legally copy a CD and then sell somebody else the original.

As you'll readily see, there are two problems with this, starting with enforcement. Until some monstrous and effective system for maintaining and tracking electronic copies is implemented, nobody's going to be able to tell whether you've really deleted your copy. And second, some of the current mechanisms for protecting copyright, such as Sony's SDMI-compliant OpenMG software, locks a legal audio file to a particular computer, preventing you from exercising your rights under the First Sale Doctrine. (You can sell someone your copy of the digital-audio file, but it won't work on any computer other than your own.) It's possible to argue that consumers might be justified in using hardware or software tools to circumvent such locking in order to preserve their rights under the First Sale Doctrine, but we wouldn't like to be the ones arguing the case.

SECURE DIGITAL MUSIC INITIATIVE (SDMI)

The Secure Digital Music Initiative (SDMI for short) is a forum of more than 180 companies and organizations interested in developing a framework for "a voluntary, open framework for playing, storing, and distributing digital music in a protected form." The companies and organizations involved come from a variety of industries and include the following:

- The recording industry, including the RIAA and Sony Music
- Agencies, including the powerful Harry Fox Agency

CONTINUED ➙

- Distributors and retailers, including Broadcast Music, Inc. (BMI)
- Consumer electronics companies, including Casio, Sony Electronics, JVC, Matsushita, and Motorola
- Information technology companies, including Microsoft and Sun Microsystems—and Fraunhofer
- Computer hardware manufacturers, including Compaq and Toshiba
- MP3 hardware and software companies, including MusicMatch, Audio Explosion/Mjuice, i2Go.com, Liquid Audio, and Napster

All in all, it's an impressive group of heavyweights and wannabe heavyweights.

SDMI aims to create a musical framework to please everybody by giving customers "convenient accessibility to quality digital music" while allowing artists to protect their copyrighted works against piracy, which would let the recording industry and information technology companies make money from selling music. What's good news for consumers is that SDMI recognizes that some people will want to distribute music in insecure formats, and the standards (specifications) it creates are designed to allow end users to play both secure and insecure music. So (at least in theory), you'll be able to play your utterly insecure MP3 files on SDMI-compliant devices.

To some extent, this has been borne out in the first SDMI-compliant devices that meet SDMI's first specification, which describes portable digital-audio devices. The Sony VAIO Music Clip and the Sony Memory Stick Walkman are players that comply with this specification, and they work with both

CONTINUED ➡

existing MP3 files (by converting them in a clumsy procedure to secure files) and with already secure files. Unfortunately, Sony's SDMI-compliant software for ripping, encoding, and managing your music is truly execrable, making both for a miserable user experience and for a bad impression of the SDMI standard.

To get the latest on SDMI, visit sdmi.org.

How to Know If a Digital-Audio File Is Legal

Given that it's illegal to download or to have illegal copies of digital-audio files, you may well be asking at this point how you can tell whether a digital-audio file is legal or not.

Sad to say, there's no clear-cut way of telling whether a digital-audio file is legal. This is true of any digital-audio file, though some of the copy-protected digital-audio file formats are difficult for the end user to create, meaning that the files are more likely to be legal. But it's doubly true of MP3 files, which anyone can create, either by ripping and encoding a CD or by encoding another sound stream.

You'll need to use your judgment as to whether a digital-audio file is legal or not. If the digital-audio file is posted on a big-name public site, such as EMusic.com, Riffage.com, or MP3.com, you're pretty safe to assume that it's a legal copy. Likewise, if the file is posted on a known record company's site or on the band's own official site, it should be legit. And in the rare cases in which the band has a publicly stated policy of encouraging bootleg tapes and audio files of their live performances (as the Grateful Dead did, and as Metallica has done), you probably don't need to worry.

Anywhere else, you need to be on your guard. Any digital-audio files of music by big-name artists posted on personal Web sites should be regarded as highly suspect, as should files posted on anything that identifies itself as an MP3z site or a warez site. (*Warez* is a term for pirated software, and *MP3z* is used to mean illegal MP3 files.)

WHAT'S HAPPENING IN THE REAL WORLD

Needless to say, what's legal is not necessarily what's happening in the real world. If the material so far in this chapter has seemed a little utopian, that's because it is.

Most people who are into both music and computers have started using their PCs as giant jukeboxes stuffed with MP3 files. These people are ripping and encoding all their CDs for personal use (which, you'll recall, is legal) and borrowing CDs from their friends and colleagues and ripping and encoding those (illegal). If they have LPs, they're recording them digitally and encoding the results (both legal) and sharing them with their friends (illegal). Some people are posting MP3 files to pirate Web sites and FTP sites for the world to download (illegal) or just sharing them on the fly via Napster and similar technologies (illegal).

Some people are dividing MP3 files up into smaller pieces that won't clog news servers and posting them to newsgroups (illegal), from which people can download them (illegal) and put them back together. Napster and its cohorts have put quite a crimp in this through their effectiveness and simplicity—there's little point in messing about with dozens of small files from newsgroups if you can get the same music (or a much better selection of it) in one-tenth the time via Napster.

Many people are e-mailing MP3 files to their friends and acquaintances. This is a poor idea, because despite their compression, most MP3 files are large enough (3 to 10MB) to make many mail servers choke, and people tend to get annoyed with their ISPs if the mail servers go belly-up time and again. (To prevent this happening, some ISPs program their mail servers to reject any attachments over a certain size, which prevents people from sending MP3 files of full tracks as attachments.)

Some commentators claim that people are using Napster to send a message to the recording industry that its prices are too high. These commentators affect to believe that if people could easily buy and download legal copies of the music they wanted, track by track (as opposed to album by album), for a fair price (unspecified, but usually on the order of 50 to 75 cents per track), they would be happy to buy it instead of getting it for free.

We don't entirely agree with this argument. Certainly, CD prices are higher than they should be, and the May 2000 agreement in which the Federal Trade Commission forced five major record companies (Sony, EMI, Universal, Time-Warner, and BMG) to stop using minimum-price programs for seven years should bring a welcome lowering of CD prices to the U.S. But we think that a lot of people will continue to take as much as they can for free even if a relatively low-priced and fully functional alternative is available. Even those people who end up buying tracks will most likely download illegal copies first (or perhaps free low-quality samples that the record companies may supply) to give the music a test drive and make sure they like it before opening their virtual wallets.

This leads us nicely to the topic of Napster, the music phenomenon of late 1999 and early 2000. We'll discuss the legal issues surrounding Napster in the next section, and then we'll discuss

Napster itself (and related technologies) in Chapter 5, "Finding MP3 Files Using Napster and Its Friends."

Legal Issues Surrounding Napster

Briefly, Napster provides an easy way for users to share MP3 files with each other. Each Napster user designates one or more shared folders on their computer and logs into a Napster server. (At this writing, there are many Napster servers, with a central server dynamically assigning each user who logs into the system to one of the available servers. Napster, Inc. plans to link all the servers together into one huge community at some unspecified date.) The user can then access any of the MP3 files that any of the other users logged into that server are sharing—and those other users can access the files that our protagonist is sharing. Once someone finds an MP3 file they're interested in, they can download it.

From the user's point of view, Napster is wonderful. With a bit of patience, you can find and download the music you want. And if the MP3 file is one that the person distributing it has the right to distribute, all is well. For example, a band might post a number of its tracks on Web sites such as Riffage.com and MP3.com for free download in order to get its name known, and might allow (or encourage) people to spread the MP3 files further afield. Alternatively, its members might choose to share those tracks directly via Napster; or it might take a Grateful Dead–style approach to bootleg recordings of live performances and encourage people to make them and distribute them. In these cases, where the band has given permission for the MP3 files to be distributed (or is providing the files themselves), there's no legal problem—anyone can download them, and that's fine. But if the MP3 files that people are distributing are ones they don't have the rights to distribute, there's a huge legal problem.

Once you look at Napster, you'll have little doubt that many of the MP3 files that people are sharing are ones that they don't have the rights to distribute. For example, Metallica hasn't given carte blanche to distribute its studio recordings—although it has for bootlegs of its live performances—and at this writing is suing Napster for encouraging copyright infringement. But if you search for Metallica tracks when logged into a Napster server, chances are you'll turn up a huge number of hits. Dr. Dre is likewise suing Napster.

At this writing, the RIAA is also suing Napster for encouraging copyright infringement. Legal experts are divided as to whether what Napster is doing is legal or not, and it'll be interesting (to say the least) to see how the case pans out.

In May 2000, Metallica delivered Napster a list of a third of a million names of Napster users who were offering MP3 files of copyrighted Metallica tracks (an estimated average of five tracks apiece) and forced Napster to remove these users from its system. This number is impressively large, especially given that the names were gathered over a two-day period at the end of April 2000, but they were probably substantially inflated by a bizarre design choice in Napster that shared the user's download directory as well as their chosen upload directories. So if you downloaded a Metallica track, Napster made you share it automatically without your choosing to do so. (We call this a bizarre design choice because it virtually guarantees that many Napster users will share files illegally. We thought this was a bug in Beta 5 of Napster 2, but subsequent betas make it clear that it's a deliberate design choice.) Many of these users, on finding themselves blocked from using Napster, uninstalled the software and reinstalled it, giving themselves a new screen name to change their identity.

Napster's position is that they're just making the software available—which is true, although Napster's Web site early on advertised the software as enabling the user to find just about any music they wanted and download it for free. Napster's license agreement makes the user acknowledge that they understand that it's illegal to distribute MP3 files without permission, and each time a user logs into a Napster server at the start of an Napster session, they see a message warning them about illegal MP3 files.

These are the arguments for Napster being legal:

- ▶ First, Napster doesn't control any of the music that is being shared. The music doesn't even pass through Napster's Web site; the Napster server builds and maintains a database of the users currently logged in and the tracks that they're making available, but the MP3 files are stored on the individual user's hard drive. When another user requests to download a track, it's transferred directly from user to user. However, in May 2000, a court ruled that Napster cannot claim to be an ISP to protect itself from lawsuits. (Briefly, ISPs are not responsible for the content they carry unless they seek to control or modify it.)

- ▶ Second, the plaintiff needs to prove that Napster is inducing illegal activity—not just that it's possible to use Napster to perform illegal activity.

- ▶ Third, some law experts say that the plaintiffs will have to prove that the Napster software is used almost exclusively for performing illegal activity. Because there's no question that some of the MP3 files that are being distributed via Napster are being distributed legally, that might be very hard to prove.

On the other side, some lawyers argue that because Napster, Inc. knows that some of its users are using Napster to infringe copyright, the company should be held responsible for their misconduct. This argument may be tough to make stick because of the wider implications it could have; with fair logic, you could say that car manufacturers know that some drivers use their vehicles to commit crimes, so the manufacturers should be held responsible. Clearly this would be absurd. But consider the recent lawsuits against gun manufacturers such as Smith & Wesson because some of the guns they made and sold (legally) were used to commit crimes.

At this writing, a number of universities have banned Napster, some because of intellectual-property concerns (including three that were named in Metallica's lawsuit against Napster), but more because of the massive amount of bandwidth that Napster users consume. Napster is working on adding features that allow administrators to allocate bandwidth effectively to reduce such problems. Students at some universities have registered enough discontent to make their universities un-ban Napster.

Napster's CEO, Eileen Richardson, has been quoted as calling Napster "the MTV of the Internet"—a catchy name but not an accurate one (as far as we can see). Napster claims to think that the recording industry should work with Napster in order to get its music and related paraphernalia to the artists' fans. This is clearly a self-serving point of view, but that Napster represents a new type of delivery mechanism that the recording industry might want to tap is undeniable.

Also undeniable is that there's no way to put the genie back in the bottle. Now that Napster has shown that user-to-user communities are a very viable way of distributing music, nobody will be able to get rid of them without an enormous amount of effort. Even if Napster itself is closed down, similar technologies, such as gnutella, audioGnome, CuteMX, and iMesh will continue to share files in this way. gnutella in particular will be difficult to stop, as unlike Napster, gnutella uses no central server that can be closed down. Instead, it's based on a loose user-to-user network that could only be shut down by determined filtering at many points throughout the Internet. (We'll discuss gnutella, audioGnome, CuteMX, and iMesh in more detail in Chapter 5.)

Up Next

In this chapter, we started off by looking briefly at what you can and cannot legally do with digital-audio files. We then looked at what intellectual property and copyright mean and what their implications are. We've discussed the legalities involved with downloading digital-audio files, creating your own digital-audio files, and distributing digital-audio files, and we've touched upon a couple of the laws governing them and a couple of the current lawsuits—the RIAA against MP3.com and the RIAA against Napster—that will help define the future of digital audio.

You're looking fidgety; it's high time we got into the music. Turn the page, and in the second part of the book we'll show you how to find digital-audio files—both legal and illegal ones—online.

PART II
FINDING DIGITAL MUSIC ONLINE

LEARN TO:

- **FIND MP3 FILES ON WEB SITES AND NEWSGROUPS**
- **FIND MP3 FILES USING SEARCH ENGINES**
- **FIND MP3 FILES USING SEARCH UTILITIES**
- **FIND MP3 FILES USING NAPSTER AND SIMILAR PROGRAMS**
- **TUNE INTO INTERNET RADIO**

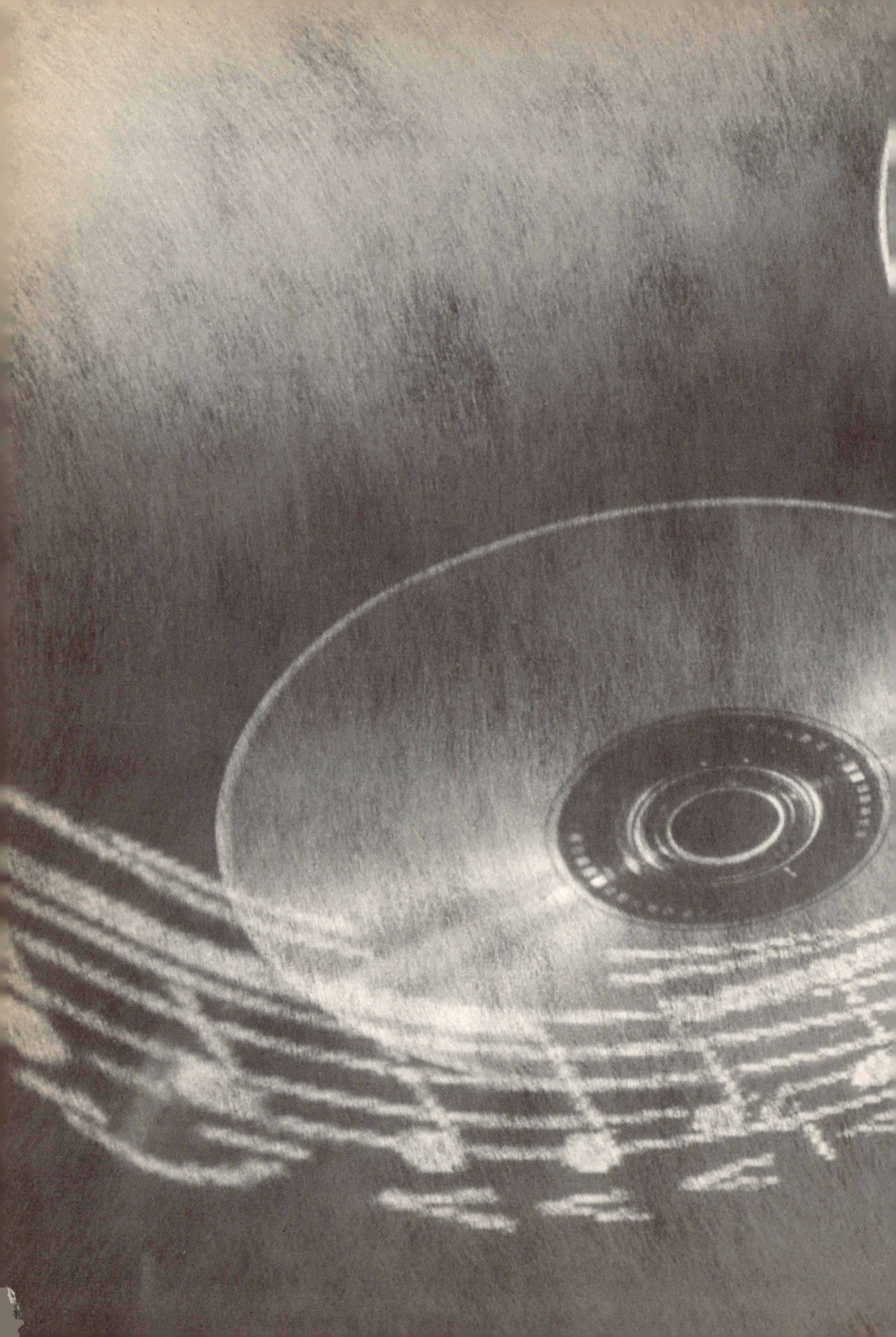

Chapter 4
Finding MP3 Files via the Web and Newsgroups

FEATURING

- Finding MP3 files on Web sites
- Finding MP3 files via search engines
- Finding MP3 files using search utilities
- Finding MP3 files on newsgroups

In this chapter, we'll discuss the first four ways of finding MP3 files online: looking on Web sites, using search engines, using search utilities, and visiting the right newsgroups.

In the next chapter, we'll show you the newer way of finding MP3 files online: using Napster and related technologies. Then, in the next part of the book, we'll show you how to create MP3 files yourself from recordings that you own.

Finding MP3 Files on Web Sites

If you've used the Web for more than even a few minutes, you'll know that it changes from day to day and grows dramatically every week. The number of Web sites that offer MP3 files seems to be growing even faster than the Web itself, so even if we wanted to provide you with a comprehensive list of such sites, we wouldn't be able to. Instead, this section lists a small number of specific sites that we've used and found helpful. (Beyond these, you'll undoubtedly find many sites on your own.) We'll also discuss some general principles for finding MP3 files on the Web so that you'll be able to find music even if all the sites mentioned in this section have mysteriously gone under.

Some of the sites you'll find are based on HTTP (Hypertext Transfer Protocol), but others use FTP, the file transfer protocol that has long been the workhorse for transferring information over the Internet. If you have a modern browser, you should be able to access most FTP sites seamlessly from it, but it'll look very Spartan compared to most Web sites—no graphics, just a text-based interface. Because FTP sites are relatively easy to set up with most server software and they're easy to maintain, they're popular with people whose primary interest is transferring files.

For the sites mentioned in this chapter, we'll give you a brief description and an overview of their features. Unless we have a very

Finding MP3 Files via the Web and Newsgroups

good reason to do so, we won't show you the sites, because their pages change even faster than U.S. foreign policy, and showing them to you is unlikely to be helpful.

> **TO DOWNLOAD OR NOT TO DOWNLOAD**
>
> Depending on the site, you may be able to download MP3 files to your computer and then play them from there, or play MP3 files directly across the Web using streaming audio, or both. Sites such as Riffage.com and MP3.com typically provide separate links for playing MP3 files from the Web and for downloading them. Some sites provide streaming music only, because they do not have the rights to distribute copies of the files. By using streaming audio, they allow you to listen to the music without being able to save it to disk. (That's in theory—in fact, you can save copies of streaming audio if you feel so bold.) Other sites, including FTP sites, are set up only for downloading and do not have streaming capabilities.
>
> Playing streaming compressed audio directly from Web sites requires a fast Internet connection—preferably a cable connection or a digital subscriber line (DSL). Playing audio over a modem link tends to deliver uneven, choppy sound and usually isn't worth doing unless this is the only way you can hear the files in question.

Major Sites

In this section, we'll look at some of the major MP3 sites. As mentioned earlier, things are changing quickly in the world of MP3, so don't be surprised if some of these sites have changed, merged, or consumed each other in the time between our writing this and your reading it.

Riffage.com

Riffage.com (www.riffage.com) provides one of the best collections of authorized files of cutting-edge music that you'll find on the Web. Riffage.com not only has a huge amount of music but also enables you to find it easily. The site has both a large number of free tracks and tracks that you have to pay for.

Riffage.com lets listeners post ratings and reviews of tracks, using these to maintain an average rating for the track so that you have some idea about how popular that track is with the people who have listened to it so far. You can also put together playlists that Riffage.com can then share with other people who appear to have similar tastes.

Riffage.com's features include a current featured artist, a list of new arrivals, a calendar of today's music releases, and a list of today's live events. You can browse the bands, the songs, and the labels by alphabetical lists and by featured artist in each genre. There's also a Top 40 list for each genre, which you can use to catch up with what other people are listening to.

Before you can do anything on Riffage.com, you need to register as a user (or "open an account," as Riffage.com terms it). You might want to register right away, but we think you'll probably want to wander around Riffage.com for a little while first to see what you find. The moment you try to download something, Riffage.com will ask you to register.

The registration process is simple, although you'll probably want to read the details of the My Riffage Agreement carefully. The key element is that anything you post to Riffage.com becomes the property of Riffage.com, so if you write and post the all-time classic review of a track or band, it's no longer yours.

Also on the registration front, know that the Type of Connection drop-down list controls the rate at which Riffage.com tries to stream music to you when you hit a streaming link—so don't

Finding MP3 Files via the Web and Newsgroups

choose a faster or slower connection than you have, because your listening will suffer either way.

As soon as you've registered, Riffage.com starts feeding you tracks and playlists to rate. If you're interested in having Riffage.com recommend music to you, rate these conscientiously so that Riffage.com can learn your taste in music and deliver taste matches instead of scattershot inappropriate picks.

MP3.com

MP3.com is one of the best-known MP3 sites on the Web. Its fame (or infamy) is justly derived from its name, the number of artists affiliated with it and the number of songs they provide on it, and the high-profile lawsuits that it has drawn down upon its head.

The MP3.com home page contains links to its various genres of music, to the main areas of MP3.com, to stories, and to news items.

MP3.com focuses on providing music from both known and unknown artists and provides a huge number of MP3 files for free download. Most artists who supply MP3 files to MP3.com supply at least two or three tracks, and many supply two or three tracks from each album. As a result, you may find up to 20 or more songs for some bands.

MP3.com sells CDs, both conventional ones and ones in its own DAM format. A DAM CD includes tracks in both CD-DA format (the regular format for CD tracks) and MP3 format, saving you the modest labor of ripping the tracks yourself. MP3.com sells DAM CDs off its own secure site. For sales of conventional CDs, MP3.com redirects you to online music vendors such as CDNOW and Amazon.com.

MP3.com provides plenty of ways to get to the music that interests you, including a search box on most of its pages, genre and subgenre pages, lists of featured songs and Top CDs, A–Z listings of artists, and not only a Top 40 list (for the whole site) but also a Bottom 40 list, which frequently contains a gem or two among the dross that you'd expect to find there.

MP3.com offers a feature named My.MP3.com that lets you round up the type of music you like into one convenient virtual area. You can add to My.MP3.com tracks that you find online, the contents of CDs that you buy online, and the contents of CDs that you have at home (by using the Beam-it feature). To use My.MP3.com, you need to sign up with MP3.com, which takes a couple of minutes and a minimum of probing into sensitive areas.

> **NOTE**
>
> At this writing, MP3.com's Beam-it feature is in jeopardy, as the RIAA has won a lawsuit claiming that it violates copyright laws. MP3.com is appealing the lawsuit, and in the interim, Beam-it is still up and running—but be aware it may not be there in the long term.

EMusic.com

EMusic.com is another great site for finding MP3 files. EMusic.com provides a few free songs, but mostly it sells individual MP3 files and whole albums for download. EMusic.com has more big (or at least medium-sized) names than sites such as MP3.com and Riffage.com. One of EMusic.com's more compelling features for music enthusiasts with eclectic tastes is the compilation CDs it offers, which give you a good introduction to a number of artists for a reasonable price.

If you're solely interested in free music, follow the Free Tracks links to get to the free tracks. You can also scan individual artists' listings for free tracks, which appear (marked "Free") along with the tracks for which you have to pay.

To buy music from EMusic.com, you create an account and enter your personal details, including your credit-card information. You can then add the tracks that you're interested in to your shopping cart (preferably after listening to the previews to make sure you're getting what you think you're getting) and check out in the usual manner for an e-commerce site.

songs.com

songs.com claims to have the largest group of successful (note the qualifier) independent artists on the Web, with more than 350 listed at this writing. Most of the artists provide only a few free tracks for download, but usually there's enough for you to get an idea of the artist's style. You'll need to supply an e-mail address for each track you download.

iCrunch

iCrunch bills itself as "essential U.K. music online," which sums up its contents well enough. From the iCrunch home page (www.crunch.co.uk—*not* www.crunch.com, which is a fitness site), you can access a wide variety of music. Most of the tracks have samples that you can play or download, but most of the full tracks you have to pay for.

Listen.com

Listen.com is a gateway site that provides access to a wide variety of music and audio, which it sorts into categories ranging from alternative and electronica to comedy and self-help. Using Listen.com, you drill down to find the music or audio you want and then choose a link to direct you to the site on which it is stored. For example, if you follow Listen.com's links for 10,000 Maniacs, you're directed to sites such as MP3.com, LAUNCH, and the Microsoft Network (MSN).

Spinfrenzy.com

Spinfrenzy.com is a Web site that enables user-to-user exchange of MP3 files, videos, photos, and audio files in formats other than MP3. To use Spinfrenzy.com, you need to download and install the Spinfrenzy Xchange software, which automatically searches your drives for files to share if you let it.

Once you have Spinfrenzy Xchange installed, you're ready to search for material and download it. The search functionality, implemented through a Web page, is effective and fast, but at this writing, Spinfrenzy.com's selection is limited, its download speeds are disappointing, and many of the files that you can access via this site appear to be shared illegally. Proceed with caution.

MP3Lit.com

MP3Lit.com bills itself "the source for free MP3 literature," which tells you much of what you need to know about this site. One thing that it doesn't tell you, but you should be able to guess, is that many of the bigger-name works offer only excerpts that are designed to lure you into buying the full work. That said, you'll find gems such as T.S. Eliot reading "The Love Song of J. Alfred Prufrock," J.R.R. Tolkien reading an excerpt from "The Two Towers" (from *The Lord of the Rings*), and Basil Rathbone reading from Edgar Allen Poe's "The Pit and the Pendulum."

MP3Lit.com offers various channels for topics including fiction, nonfiction, biography, poetry, and self-help, and has a LoudMouth area where you get to post your own spoken-word recordings.

eatsleepmusic.com

eatsleepmusic.com, originally a straightforward music site with eclectic tastes ranging from alternative and metal through rap and hip-hop, has undergone a conversion to karaoke and now bills itself "the Net's Koolest Karaoke Community." If you're into karaoke, this is a great site to check out, as it provides many karaoke tracks for $1 a pop (some for download, some only on CDs), together with karaoke rooms and a recording studio. So if you're ready to do the definitive karaoke cover of "Girls Just Wanna Have Fun" or "Stairway to Heaven," this is the place to be.

To use eatsleepmusic.com, you need to register, after which the site is easy to navigate. To buy karaoke tracks, you'll need plastic.

The Free Music Archive

The Free Music Archive (`www.free-music.com`) provides a ton of free music, mostly from lesser-known artists (and we say that kindly). Make sure you enter the hyphen in the URL, because `freemusic.com` is a different site that concentrates on music in MOD format. (MOD is another digital-audio format.)

The Free Music Archive has music in a good variety of formats, including MP3, VQF, MIDI, RealAudio, MOD, and ASF/WMA. As you'd guess, MP3 files make up the bulk of the offerings, with files in formats such as VQF in very short supply. You can browse by artist name or search by artist or track name. There's also a Top 50 and a Bottom 50.

The MP3 Place

The MP3 Place (`www.mp3place.com`) specializes in alternative, techno and dance, hip-hop, and punk and ska music. If these genres interest you, browse this site for music that appeals to you. If not, you may still want to stop by for the news, skins (different looks that you can apply to players and jukeboxes), and forums that this site also provides.

RioPort

RioPort (www.rioport.com) provides enough MP3 files to make it worth visiting—and to make you ignore the relentless ads for the Rio MP3 player.

WorldWideBands

WorldWideBands (www.worldwidebands.com) provides an eclectic selection of MP3 files from a wide variety of bands. You won't find bands from *every* corner of the earth, but WorldWideBands appears to be working toward that goal. WorldWideBands provides featured artists, lets you browse by genre or browse alphabetically, and lets you search by keyword.

Record Company Sites

As we mentioned in Chapter 1, "MP3 and Digital Audio," record companies are starting to use MP3 and other digital-audio formats to promote their artists. Very generally speaking, the smaller record companies are more aggressive than the major record companies in giving away MP3 files and promotional copies of tracks in other formats.

At this writing, Columbia Records, Sony Music, and some other big record companies offer RealAudio tracks that you can play on their Web sites. This is a step in the right direction—it lets consumers get to know the music without exposing the record company or artist to losing too much music. Another step in the right direction is that Sony has started selling individual tracks via download—but it has simultaneously taken a smart step in the wrong direction by pricing them absurdly high at $2.49 each. If the tracks are more expensive to get via download than on physical media and if they're locked to the computer on which you download them, we see no reason for people to buy them except for instant gratification.

We can't claim to understand the inner workings of the record companies, but it seems to us that they'd do well to provide low-fidelity versions of just about everything they have for free on the Web, with the goal of making the music accessible to the many people who haven't heard it but who might like some of it. People would then have the option to buy the music on physical media (such as CDs or cassettes) as usual, but they could also choose to pay for higher fidelity versions of the tracks—presumably in one of the secure digital-audio formats.

Pirate Sites

If you search for even a few seconds, you'll also find plenty of sites offering pirated MP3 files—often accompanied by warez (pirated software) and pornography, making up the three most sought clandestine categories on the Internet. Some pirates refer to pirated MP3 files as *MP3z*.

Should you choose to download pirated files, keep the following firmly in mind:

It's illegal to have pirated MP3 files. The odds against the FBI conducting a house-to-house search of your neighborhood for pirated MP3 files seem high, but the penalties can be severe.

Anyone supplying pirated (or ostensibly pirated) MP3 files doesn't have much respect for the law. Do you think they respect your computer—or your wallet? Be very careful what buttons you click when exploring or downloading files from these sites. In particular, *never* run any EXE files. Use an up-to-date virus scanner to check the files that you download before you try to use them, however harmless they may sound. Remember that file extensions under Windows are *not* an accurate indication of the file's contents. A file with an MP3 extension could be an executable file waiting to damage your computer. DOC files and XLS files can contain macro viruses that can do anything from wiping out your documents and crucial files to attempting to format your hard drive.

Watch out for any suspicious signs on your computer. If the hard drive starts thrashing unexpectedly or the processor gets stuck in overdrive when you're putting minimal demands on it, you may have a problem. If you suspect that someone is trying to access your computer—or has succeeded in doing so—drop the connection immediately. If dial-up networking is locked, disconnect the phone line from the modem. If you're using a network connection to connect to the Internet, pull the cable out of the back of the computer.

ESCAPE FROM PIRATES AND PORN SITES

Because of the popularity of MP3 music, it's become an even more favored decoy of Web predators than top-name stars such as Jennifer Lopez, Ricky Martin, or Calista Flockhart. If you click the wrong link after searching for MP3 files (or for Ricky, Jennifer, or Calista), you may find yourself caught surfing a porn site rather than an MP3 site (or star site). Caught?

Yes—by using a number of HTML and scripting tricks, a Web site can effectively capture your PC. Every time you close a browser window, it automatically opens another one; every time you give it a moment, it opens another window to tempt you with more of its wares.

The following illustration shows us the type of site from which you may get in trouble. Here, 40best.com is offering us links to "25000 illegal MP3 downloads" and "100% illegal fast MP3 downloads." At this point, we would advise you to back out before you hit anything unpleasant.

CONTINUED →

Finding MP3 Files via the Web and Newsgroups

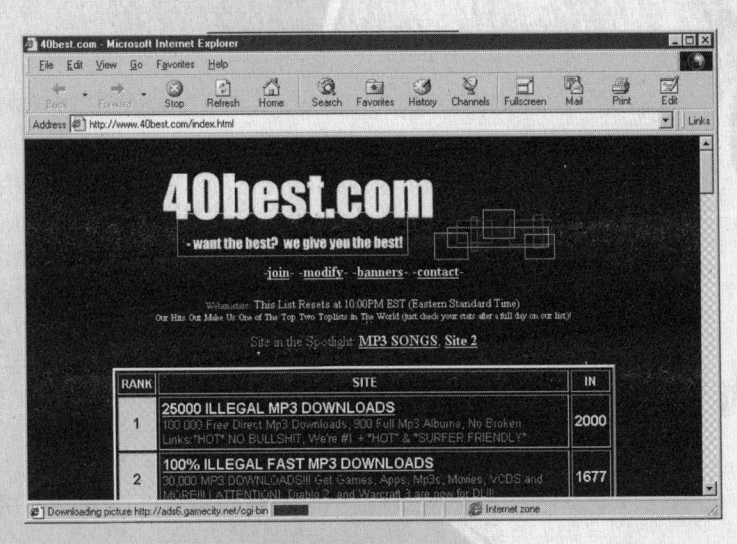

[Screenshot of 40best.com website in Microsoft Internet Explorer, showing "want the best? we give you the best!" with links to join, modify, banners, contact, and a ranking table listing "25000 ILLEGAL MP3 DOWNLOADS" at rank 1 with 2000 in, and "100% ILLEGAL FAST MP3 DOWNLOADS" at rank 2 with 1677 in.]

If you get caught by a porn site (or indeed, by any other site—anybody can do this, although in our experience, nobody but porn merchants, pirates, and angry teenagers seems to think this is a good idea), these are your best shots at escape, in order of preference:

- Use the Alt+F4 key combination to try to kill all the browser windows. Using the keyboard like this is usually faster than trying to click the Close button on a multitude of windows of varying sizes.

- If you have work open in any other application, switch to it (by using the Taskbar or by pressing Alt+Tab), save the work, and close the application. Doing so may well seem like preparation for craven surrender—but believe us, you'll regret it if you don't. Close any other applications you can, even if they're not doing anything useful.

- Unplug your modem line (if you're using a modem) or your network connection (if you're connecting to the Internet

CONTINUED →

via a network, a cable modem, or a DSL). If you're using an external modem, you can just switch it off instead, or unplug its power supply if it has no on/off switch.

▶ Press Ctrl+Alt+Del to display the Close Program dialog box (in Windows 9x or Windows Me), the Windows NT Security dialog box (in Windows NT 4), or the Windows Security dialog box (in Windows 2000). Then (in Windows 9x or Windows Me), from the Close Program dialog box (shown below), select the offending instance of the browser and click the End Task button. Repeat as necessary. If that doesn't do the trick, click the Shut Down button to shut down your computer. From the Windows NT Security dialog box in Windows NT 4 or from the Windows Security dialog box in Windows 2000, click the Task Manager button to display the Task Manager dialog box. Display the Applications page if it's not already displayed, then select the offending instance of Internet Explorer in the Tasks list box, and click the End Task button. If Windows NT or Windows 2000 displays the Ending Task dialog box, click the End Now button. Repeat until each instance of Internet Explorer controlled by the site is closed.

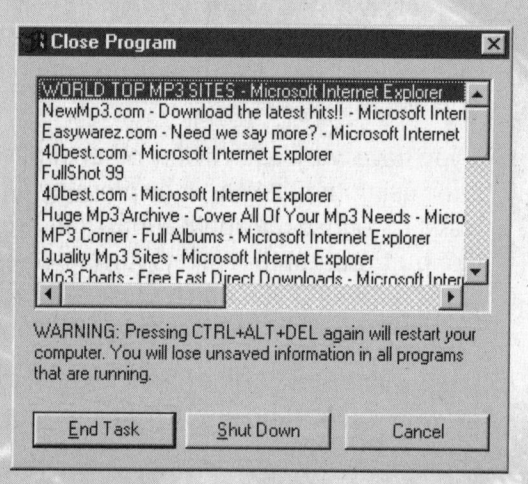

CONTINUED ➞

> If all else fails, reboot your computer. You may lose any configuration changes you've made in this Windows session, but if you suspect that the porn site is raiding your hard drive for information or attempting to damage it, the pain of a hard reboot pales in comparison.

TIP

If you're desperate not to run into porn (or want to keep your children away from it), you may want to start at the Pure MP3 site (`www.puremp3.org`), which guarantees that the sites it's linked to do not have porn themselves and do not link to any sites that have porn.

Finding MP3 Files Using Search Engines

The problem with the MP3 sites discussed so far in this chapter is that, although most of them provide an interesting selection of music in their own right, none is anywhere near comprehensive. So to find a particular track, you'll probably need to visit multiple sites in turn, and even after searching each, you may still be disappointed.

In this section, we'll look briefly at several search engines that attempt to solve this problem for you. In the next section, we'll look at a search utility that can automatically scour a number of sites for music.

Many of the sites to which these search engines direct you are FTP sites. Read the following sidebar for a warning about certain FTP sites that demand that you upload files before letting you download files.

BEWARE RATIO SITES

Beware any *ratio site*—a site that lets you download files only after you've uploaded some files to the site. Ratio sites get their name because they typically allow you to download at some ratio to what you upload. For example, a ratio site might allow you to download 3MB for every 1MB you upload.

If you're using an FTP client such as CuteFTP, you may see a message such as the one shown in the Login Messages dialog box below (which is demanding music with menace), when you run into a ratio site.

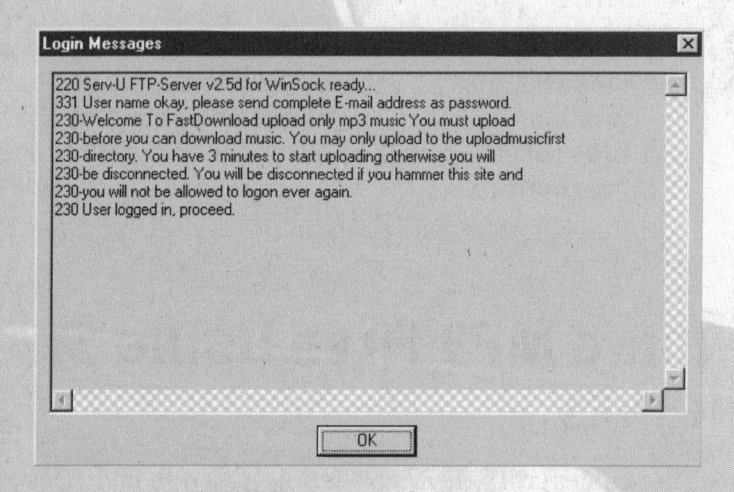

```
Login Messages                                              X
220 Serv-U FTP-Server v2.5d for WinSock ready...
331 User name okay, please send complete E-mail address as password.
230-Welcome To FastDownload upload only mp3 music You must upload
230-before you can download music. You may only upload to the uploadmusicfirst
230-directory. You have 3 minutes to start uploading otherwise you will
230-be disconnected. You will be disconnected if you hammer this site and
230-you will not be allowed to logon ever again.
230 User logged in, proceed.

                          [    OK    ]
```

If you're trying to download from a Web browser, you may see messages such as the one shown on the next page in Internet Explorer, saying that "the server returned extended information." This doesn't necessarily mean that the site is demanding an upload, but when you're trying to access an MP3 FTP site, it's very likely.

CONTINUED →

Finding MP3 Files via the Web and Newsgroups

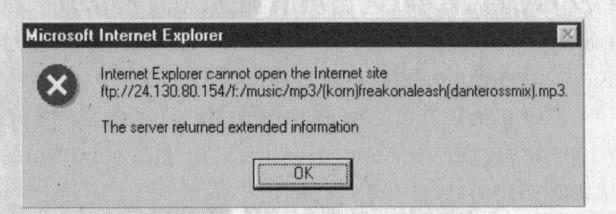

> **Microsoft Internet Explorer**
> Internet Explorer cannot open the Internet site
> ftp://24.130.80.154/f:/music/mp3/(korn)freakonaleash(danterossmix).mp3.
>
> The server returned extended information
>
> [OK]

Netscape gives a different message when it runs into this problem, as shown in the message box below. The message is perhaps a little misleading in that we know the file is there—we're just not allowed to get at it.

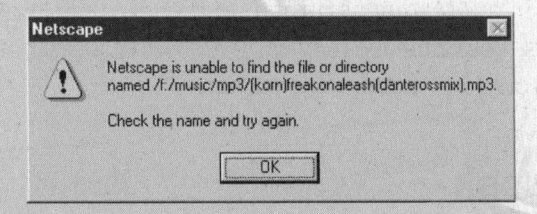

> **Netscape**
> Netscape is unable to find the file or directory named /f:/music/mp3/(korn)freakonaleash(danterossmix).mp3.
>
> Check the name and try again.
>
> [OK]

If you have music that you can legally distribute, feel free to go ahead and upload some. But keep in mind that because most people do not have music that they can legally distribute, these sites are pushing many people into uploading music illegally so that they can download music—which too might be illegal.

Oth.Net

One of the best places to start searching for music is Oth.Net (www.oth.net), which (at least at this writing) delivers some of the most accurate results and is one of the easiest search sites to use. Oth.Net's search engine is minimalist, yet fast and accurate, and (depending on the sites returned) you can sometimes download directly from its results page.

Lycos MP3 Search

Lycos MP3 Search (mp3.lycos.com) provides easy searching for MP3 files and claims to have more than one million files indexed. But in our testing, it turned up distressingly large numbers of dead links. Your mileage may vary; it's worth a try, but it may not reward anything but extreme persistence.

Musicseek

Musicseek (www.musicseek.net) lets you search for files in MP3, VQF, AAC, and RA (RealAudio) formats. It allows you to specify a minimum reliability rating for the results so that you avoid lame and flaky sites.

Audiogalaxy

Audiogalaxy (www.audiogalaxy.com) provides a rich searching environment and makes downloading very easy for users of GlobalSCAPE's CuteFTP FTP client application.

Scour

Scour (www.scour.com) is a gateway site that includes an MP3 search engine and an überdirectory of downloadable music. Scour is a tool for finding the music you want. Most of the music is actually stored on other sites, including MP3.com, EMusic.com, songs.com, and musicmatch.com. Scour is great for getting an overview of what's out there for downloading, but if you find yourself constantly hitting the same site (say, MP3.com) when following links from Scour, take the hint and go straight to that site in the future.

FINDING MP3 FILES USING SEARCH UTILITIES

This section will discuss a couple of the more popular search utilities for finding and downloading MP3 files: MP3 Star Search and Go!Zilla.

MP3 Star Search

MP3 Star Search is a powerful freeware utility that dredges through a plethora of search engines and integrates the results into an easy-to-use interface. MP3 Star Search is designed to integrate with CuteFTP, an easy-to-use shareware FTP utility from GlobalSCAPE. If you have CuteFTP (you can get it from www.cuteftp.com), you can download files directly from the MP3 Star Search interface.

At this writing, you can download MP3 Star Search from www.pcworld.com/r/shw/1%2C2087%2C6403%2C00.html. Unzip the contents of the distribution file to a temporary folder and run the resulting setup.exe file to start the installation routine, which is more or less standardized.

Here's how to use MP3 Star Search:

1. Run MP3 Star Search from the Start menu (or from wherever you put it).

Chapter Four

2. Select the Get Queued Pages check box to make sure that MP3 Star Search returns all pages of search results from each server it checks.

3. In the Search box, enter the name of the artist or track for which to search and click the Let the Search Begin button. MP3 Star Search builds a list of results in the Search Results box, showing the number of results for each search engine contacted.

4. Double-click a nonzero result to display the results for that search engine.

5. Click the + signs to expand a list. In Figure 4.1, note that our search for **Rollins Band** has returned hits from the 2LOOK4, search.mp3.de, and MP3.BOX search engines. Most of the results we're looking at are on target. A check mark means that MP3 Star Search has tested the FTP server as being active; a cross in a red circle means it's not active; and a question mark in a green circle means that MP3 Star Search is still testing it.

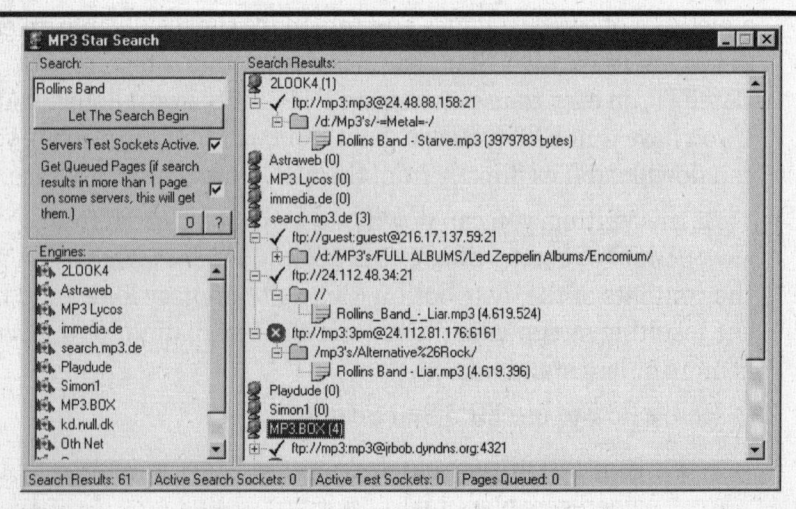

FIGURE 4.1: MP3 Star Search showing the results of a successful search for the Rollins Band

6. Download the MP3 file that appeals to you by doing one of the following:

   ▶ If you have CuteFTP and it's running, right-click the listing for the file you want and choose Get File from the context menu. CuteFTP logs into the FTP server and downloads the file.

   ▶ If you don't have CuteFTP, right-click the listing and choose Copy Location from the context menu. Switch to your Web browser, right-click in the address box, choose Paste from the context menu, and then press Enter to access the site. From there, you should be able to download the file as usual.

NOTE

Another MP3 metasearch utility you might want to try is MP3 Fiend, which you can download from www.mp3fiend.com.

Go!Zilla

Go!Zilla is a download and search utility that can come in handy when you're trying to download many MP3 files. Go!Zilla's talents include finding the fastest FTP site available for a given download, resuming broken downloads, and grabbing all the links out of a given page.

Download the latest version of Go!Zilla from the Go!Zilla Web site, www.gozilla.com, and run the distribution file to install the application.

You'll find Go!Zilla easy to use. Here are some tips to get you started:

- You can drag the link to a file to Go!Zilla to have it downloaded. For best results, keep Go!Zilla on top of all other windows by choosing Window ➢ Always on Top, or display the Go!Zilla drop target (a small icon) by choosing Window ➢ Drop Target.

- To find a file, choose File List ➢ Find File or press Ctrl+F to display the Find File on Net dialog box. Then specify the details and click the Search button.

- Use the Super Link Leecher to grab all the links from a page. With Netscape, the Super Link Leecher automatically grabs the links from the current page. With other browsers, you have to specify the Web page from which you want to grab the links. You can then select the links that you want to download.

- Go!Zilla automatically intercepts download links that you click in your browser. To stop Go!Zilla from automatically intercepting a link, hold down the Alt key as you click the link. To turn the automatic interception of links on and off, choose Auto ➢ Browser Integration.

> **WARNING**
>
> Go!Zilla has trouble dealing with some of the download links used by MP3.com and other sites—Go!Zilla interprets these links as pointing to text/HTML files and is unable to download the tracks they point to. If you find this happening, bypass the automatic interception of downloads and perform these downloads manually.

FINDING MP3 FILES ON NEWSGROUPS

The last source of MP3 files that we'll mention in this chapter is newsgroups.

At this writing, newsgroups are declining as a source of MP3 files, for several reasons:

- ▶ Newsgroups are much more difficult to use than newer technologies such as Napster.

- ▶ The selection of MP3 files on newsgroups is poor (and, in a vicious circle, it's getting poorer as fewer people transfer MP3 files via newsgroups).

- ▶ Newsgroups are traditionally a noisy place, with lots of spam, cluelessness, and flaming, so hanging around them looking for music can be more of a chore than a pleasure.

- ▶ Many of the tracks that you'll find in newsgroups are illegal copies.

That said, you can still find a good number of tracks in newsgroups. Moreover, newsgroups offer a couple of advantages over file-sharing technologies such as Napster:

- ▶ You can browse through a listing of what's available rather than searching for something specific. This is like going to a music store to buy a particular CD and seeing a half-dozen others that you'd forgotten you were wanting—only when you're downloading, the strain on your pocket is eliminated.

- ▶ If a file is listed in your newsreader, it will most likely be available for long enough for you to download it. By contrast, with Napster and similar technologies, files become unavailable the moment the user providing them goes offline—which they can do at any moment.

Current versions of the three main browsers—Netscape Communicator, Microsoft Internet Explorer, and Opera from Opera Software—provide a full-featured newsreader application, so chances are you already have one available to you. If not, consider getting a specialized newsreader, such as Forté's Free Agent (www.forteinc.com).

Here's an example of finding MP3 files via MP3 newsgroups. We'll use Internet Explorer's Outlook Express newsreader, but you can follow similar techniques with the other newsreaders.

1. Start your newsreader.

2. Display the Newsgroup Subscriptions dialog box by clicking the Newsgroups button or by choosing Tools ➢ Newsgroups.

3. Enter **mp3** in the Display Newsgroups Which Contain text box in Internet Explorer.

4. Select the Also Search Descriptions check box to have Outlook Express search the descriptions of the newsgroups as well as the names. Figure 4.2 shows the current selection of newsgroups devoted to MP3 files.

5. To subscribe to a newsgroup, double-click its name, or select it and click the Subscribe button. But first you'll probably want to examine it by selecting it and clicking the Go To button. If you find it useful, then subscribe to it.

When you visit one of the newsgroups, you'll find all sorts of files, as you see in Figure 4.3, which shows the `alt.binaries.sounds.mp3.1980s` newsgroup we visited. Odds are that all these files are illegal—but if you search the right places, you'll be able to turn up legal files as well.

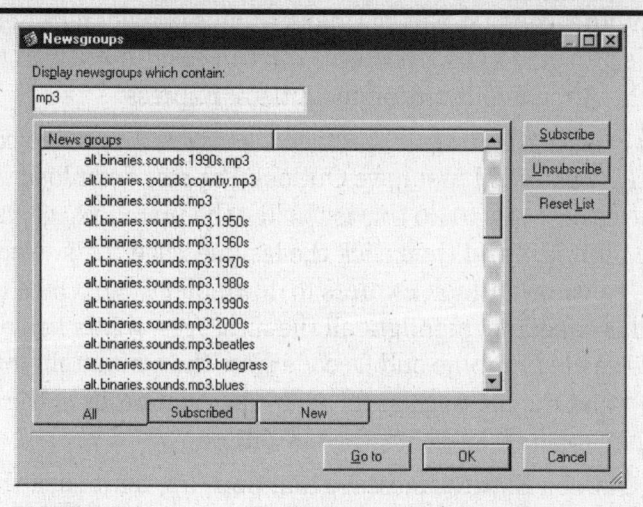

Finding MP3 Files via the Web and Newsgroups   121

FIGURE 4.2: Search for MP3 to find the newsgroups devoted to MP3 files.

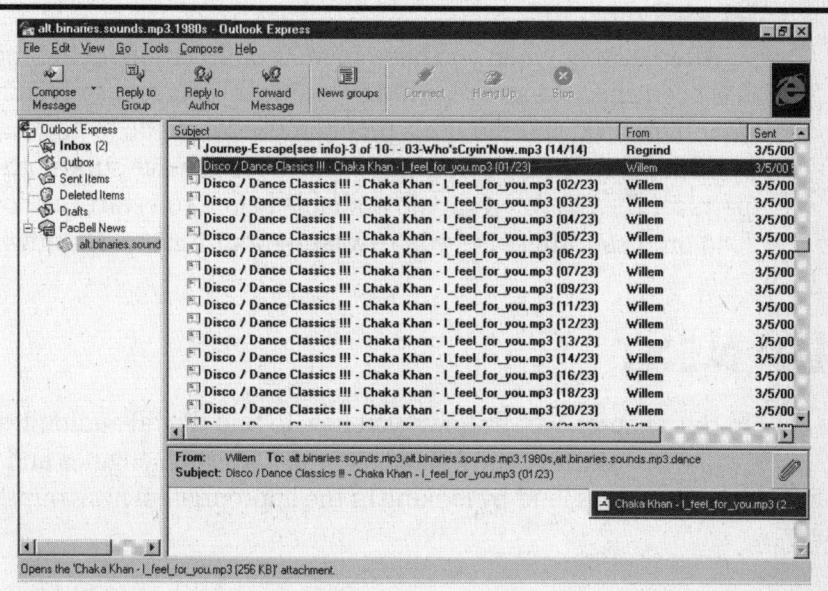

FIGURE 4.3: Many of the MP3 files that you'll find in newsgroups are illegal.

In the figure, the first part of Chaka Khan's classic track "I Feel for You" is attached to the message. You can easily download it by clicking the Attachment button in Outlook Express.

As you can see, there are 23 parts to this track. To get the complete track, you should first have Outlook Express download all 23 parts. The easiest way to do this is to click the first message, hold down the Shift key, and then click the last message. This selects all the parts, causing Outlook Express to download them. Once the download is complete, highlight all the messages, right-click one of them, and select Combine and Decode from the context menu. Make sure that the message parts are in the right order in the dialog box that appears, and click the OK button.

In the Outlook Express message that pops up, right-click the filename listed in the Attach field to save it to your hard disk. Choose the location provided or use the Browse button and the resulting dialog box to browse to another location. Then click the Save button.

Alternatively, when you have an MP3 or other binary file that has been encoded and received as multiple parts and stored on your hard disk, you can use a program like WinCode to perform the combine and decode operation. Remember to make sure all the parts for the file you want are available before you start the download process—otherwise, you're wasting your time and bandwidth.

Up Next

In this chapter, we've shown you how to find digital-audio files online by searching on Web sites, by using search engines and search utilities, and by looking in the appropriate newsgroups.

But we've been saving the best until last: At this writing, the best way of finding a wide variety of music is to use Napster, the hot freeware product that lets users join ad-hoc communities and share MP3 files, or related software. We'll show you how to do this in the next chapter.

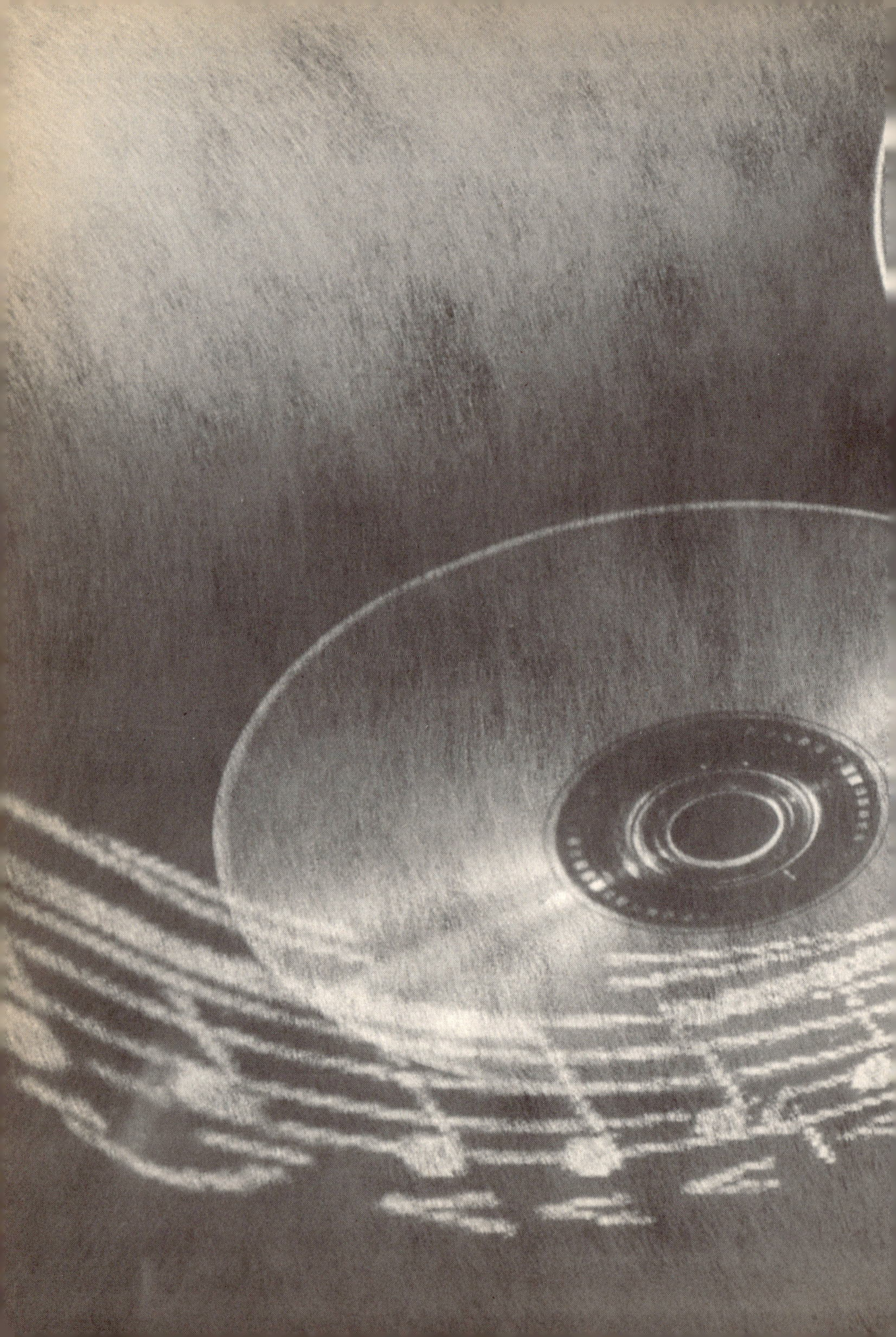

Chapter 5
Finding MP3 Files Using Napster and Its Friends

FEATURING

- An overview of Napster
- Using Napster on Windows
- Using Macster
- Using Gnapster
- Using Wrapster
- Using gnutella
- Using AudioGnome
- Using iMesh
- Using Freenet
- Using CuteMX and SpinFrenzy

Chapter Five

In this chapter, we'll show you how to use Napster, a wildly popular application that allows you to both find MP3 files online and share your own MP3 files online for others to download. We'll also show you some Napster-like technologies that stand ready to step in should Napster be closed down by legal challenges.

Napster creates MP3 communities on the fly from the users who log in to a server, enabling them to share MP3 files with one another. At this writing, Napster works only with MP3 and WMA files, although Napster itself plans to support other file formats, including graphics formats, in the future. Other Napster-like applications such as Wrapster and gnutella support other file formats as well.

Napster was originally developed for Windows, but it's rapidly proved such a hit that it's been implemented on most currently used operating systems and graphical environments. In this chapter, we'll discuss Napster itself (for Windows), Macster (for the Mac), and Gnapster (for Linux systems running the GNOME graphical environment). We'll start by discussing what Napster does and the issues it raises. We'll move on to the individual software implementations and look at each briefly in turn.

Other Napster clones, implementations, and related software include amster (for the Amiga); benapster and napster for beos (both for BeOS); jnap, jnapster, and java napster, multiplatform Java clients; and Napster/2 (for OS/2). For the latest URLs for these and other Napster-related software, check out the Napster FAQ at `faq.napster.com`.

At the end of this chapter, we'll discuss several Napster-related technologies:

- ▶ Wrapster, which lets you disguise other files as MP3 files so that you can exchange them via Napster
- ▶ gnutella, audioGnome, CuteMX, iMesh, Freenet, and SpinFrenzy, six user-to-user file-sharing technologies

Where We Stand Vis-à-Vis the Law

In this chapter, we'll assume that you're a law-abiding citizen who wants to enjoy music via MP3, so we'll warn you where you may run into problems with the law. If you're not concerned with staying on the right side of the law, feel free to disregard these warnings. We have no problem with your breaking the law (for example, by sharing files illegally), provided that you know that you're breaking the law, you know what the consequences are, and you're doing so of your own free will.

RIAA versus Napster, Metallica versus Napster

We visited the legal issues surrounding Napster briefly in the previous chapter, in which we discussed why some legal experts think that Napster has a good defense against accusations of inducing copyright infringement and why other experts think the opposite.

Before you start reading this chapter, we should point out that Napster is currently being sued by the Recording Industry Association of America (RIAA) and (separately) by Metallica, for copyright infringement. In July 2000, a San Francisco judge granted the RIAA an injunction shutting down Napster, but Napster almost immediately won a reprieve, allowing it to keep running pending appeal. If Napster loses either lawsuit (or both), it's possible that all Napster servers might be shut down—in which case, you'll want to try software such as Wrapster and gnutella instead of Napster. So we suggest checking the Napster Web site (www.napster.com) before reading this chapter.

Overview of Napster

In this section, we'll discuss briefly what Napster is, what it does, and what you can do with it.

Napster's inventor, Shawn Fanning (who gave the software the nickname he received for his nap of short hair), created Napster to solve the two key problems of getting MP3 files online:

- There's no central way to search for a particular MP3 file (although sites such as Scour and the Lycos Music MP3 Search site do their best), so you may not be able to find what you want, even if it exists.

- There's no easy way for artists to distribute their own music online other than signing up with sites such as Riffage.com or MP3.com.

Napster solves these problems by creating an ad hoc virtual community for sharing MP3 files. Each user designates one or more folders on his or her computer to be shared for uploads and, in turn, can search through and download any files that other people currently logged in have shared.

When you start Napster, it contacts the central Napster server, which maintains a database of the available Napster member servers and hands your connection off to one of them. Typically, the handoff is automatic, with the central server performing load-balancing for the member servers and sending you to an available and convenient server. Some Napster clients and add-on programs let you specify a particular server to log in to, which can be useful if you want to hang out with your friends at a particular virtual water cooler rather than being assigned to a server at the whim (so to speak) of the central server. Napster intends to tie together all the servers eventually, creating one immense community.

Once you're logged in to the member server, Napster adds any MP3 files that you're sharing to its current list of what's available. Other people logged in can then download the files that you're sharing, and you can download any of the files that everyone else is sharing. You can search through the list of files for ones that match specific criteria, and you can download multiple files at once if you feel so inclined. You can even chat with any of the other people who are logged on. When someone logs off, Napster removes their files from the list, so that they no longer appear to be available.

> **WARNING**
>
> As mentioned in the previous chapter, the legal problem with Napster is that many of the files that people are sharing are ones that they cannot legally share. So if you use Napster to find music, be careful not to download any illegal MP3 files unwittingly. If you look in the right places, you should be able to find a good number of legal MP3 files.

At this writing, a number of universities have banned Napster, some for intellectual-property concerns, but more of them for the massive amount of bandwidth that it devours. Napster is working on adding features that allow administrators to allocate bandwidth effectively to reduce such problems.

Using Napster on Windows

This section discusses how to get, install, and use Napster itself, the young granddaddy of the Napster clan. At this writing, Napster runs only on Windows, though a Macintosh client is under development.

Getting and Installing Napster

Start by downloading the latest version of Napster from www.napster.com. Once the download is complete, double-click the Napster distribution file to start the Setup routine, and then follow it as usual. You'll notice that the Software License Agreement that you have to accept warns you that "MP3 files may have been created or distributed without copyright owner authorization" and points out that "you are responsible for complying with all applicable federal and state laws applicable to such content, including copyright laws." If you read on (as you should), you'll also see that you consent to Napster automatically upgrading itself—and to Napster changing the terms and conditions of its software agreement by posting them on its Web site.

When Napster starts (which it does automatically by default at the end of the setup routine), you'll get to agree to the Software License Agreement and Disclaimer. Then you'll see the Connection Information dialog box, shown in Figure 5.1.

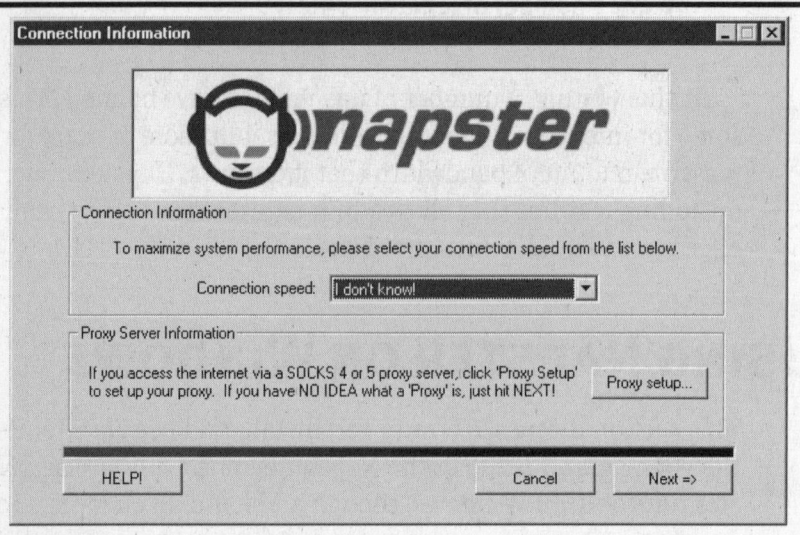

FIGURE 5.1: Specify the details of your connection in the Connection Information dialog box.

Specify the speed of your Internet or network connection in the Connection Speed drop-down list. The choices go from 14.4K Modem to T3 or Greater. A T1 line is a fast dedicated line typically used for business; it delivers a constant 1.5 million bits per second (Mbps)—about the same as a DSL on a good day. A T3 line is a *very*

Finding MP3 files Using Napster and Its Friends 131

fast line. If you're at a college, you may have a T1 or T3 connection. If you're at home, you're more likely to have a modem, cable, or a DSL.

> **NOTE**
>
> The speed you choose in the Connection Speed drop-down list controls the line speed that Napster displays in the information it lists about you, not the line speed that Napster uses for uploading and download files. (It uploads and downloads files as fast as it can.) The information Napster displays for you influences how other users interact with you—so you may choose to display misinformation rather than the truth. For example, if you have a 128K ISDN line, you'll get hit for downloads frequently because people will assume you'll deliver speedy downloads, whereas if you seem to have a slow modem connection, people may well shun you. But if you choose to declare a slower connection than you have, don't claim a 14.4K modem—hardly anyone uses them anymore, so people will assume that you're hiding a fast connection and will try downloading files from you to find out if they're right.

If your computer connects to the Internet through a proxy server, click the Proxy Setup button to display the Proxy Setup dialog box (shown in Figure 5.2). (You're most likely to be behind a proxy server in a company or campus environment, in which case you may need to ask your network administrator for this information.) Select the type of proxy server—SOCKS 4 or SOCKS 5—in the Proxy Type drop-down list, then fill in the server name in the Proxy Server text box and the port in the Proxy Port text box. If you're using a SOCKS 5 proxy server, fill in your username in the Proxy Username text box and your password in the Proxy Password text box. In the File Transfer drop-down list, choose the Download Files through Proxy item or the Download Files Directly from Source item as appropriate. Then click the OK button to close the Proxy Setup dialog box and return to the Connection Information dialog box.

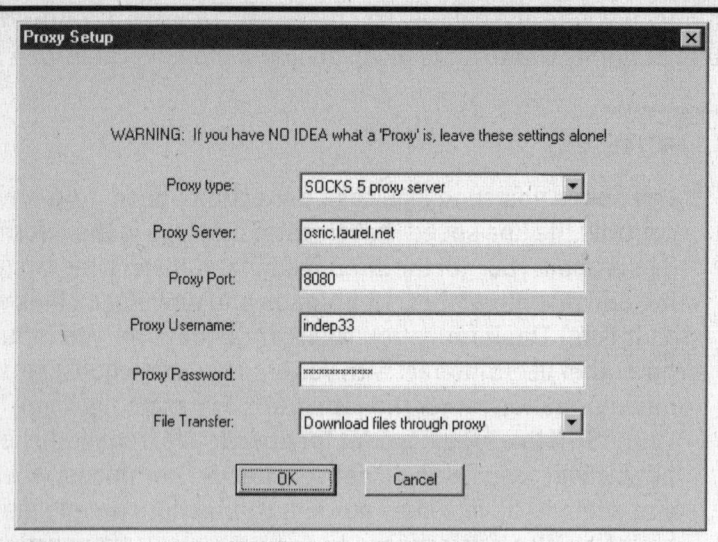

FIGURE 5.2: If your computer connects to the Internet through a proxy server, choose the appropriate settings in the Proxy Setup dialog box.

> **NOTE**
>
> A *proxy server* is a computer that relays information, stores frequently accessed information in its cache, and applies filters to requests. For example, a proxy server on a company network might store parts of the critical Web sites accessed by company personnel but prevent anyone from accessing a smut site.

The next dialog box you'll see is the Napster Configuration dialog box, shown in Figure 5.3, in which you get to enter the username you want, password, and e-mail address. Try to choose a unique username (all the obvious ones have been taken by now), and be sure to choose a password that'll be hard to hack. (If the username is already in use, Napster displays first a dialog box warning you of the problem and then a dialog box explaining that you got the password wrong, before returning you to the Napster Configuration dialog box so that you can try again.)

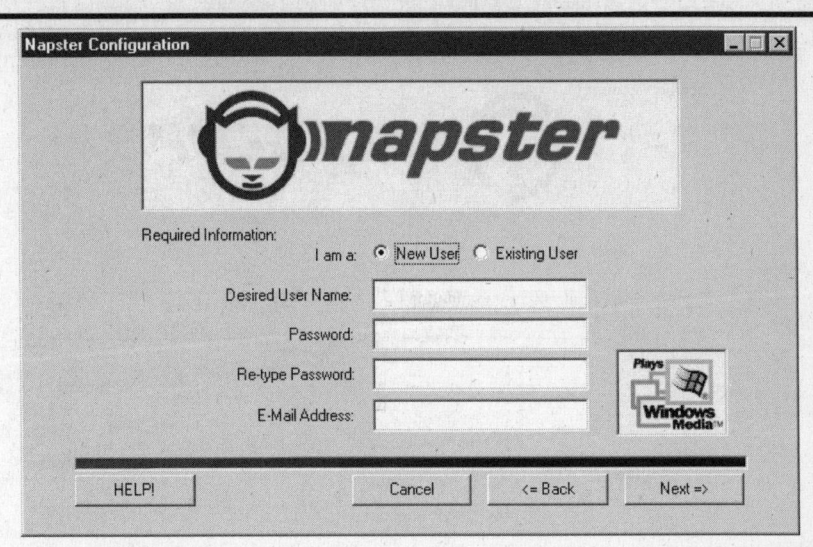

Finding MP3 files Using Napster and Its Friends

FIGURE 5.3: Enter your username and details in the Napster Configuration dialog box.

Once you've successfully chosen a username, Napster registers the name with the Napster servers and displays the Optional Information dialog box (shown in Figure 5.4), inviting you to supply your name, address, sex, age, income, and education. We suggest that you don't give out this information.

Next, you'll see the Scan for Files dialog box (shown in Figure 5.5), offering to scan your hard disks for MP3 and WMA files to share. *Unless you have no MP3 files or WMA files on your computer except for files that you have the rights to distribute, click the No button—otherwise, Napster sets up all the MP3 files and WMA files on your computer for sharing.*

FIGURE 5.4: Supply your demographics in the Optional Information dialog box only if you really want to.

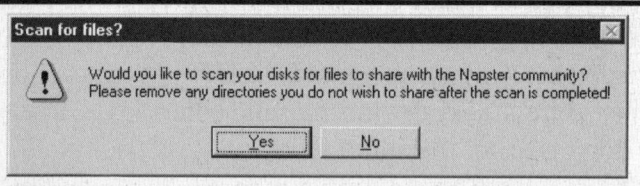

FIGURE 5.5: Don't let Napster scan your hard disks for audio files to share unless you have permission to share every audio file that's on your computer.

You can designate the appropriate folders for sharing when you dismiss the Scan for Files dialog box. Napster displays the Shared Folders dialog box (shown in Figure 5.6), which lets you designate the folders you want to share. Make sure you understand the legend and that you expand the tree so that you can see which folders are shared and which aren't. Be especially careful of folders shared by recursion—folders that are shared because their parent folder is shared—and be aware that you don't need to share any folders.

Finding MP3 files Using Napster and Its Friends   135

FIGURE 5.6: In the Shared Folders dialog box, make sure you're sharing only folders that contain MP3 and WMA files that you have the rights to distribute.

The next dialog box you'll see is the New File Repository dialog box (shown in Figure 5.7), in which you get to choose your download folder. *Be warned that this folder is shared with the Napster network.* It certainly shouldn't be, because there's no reason to assume that files that other people can legally distribute are ones that you can legally distribute as well—but shared it is. So make sure that this folder doesn't contain any subfolders that you don't want Napster to share—and as soon as you've downloaded some files, move them out of the download folder into a folder that is not shared.

Next, if Napster experiences an error in determining your data port, it concludes that your computer is behind a firewall and displays the File Server Settings dialog box, shown in Figure 5.8.

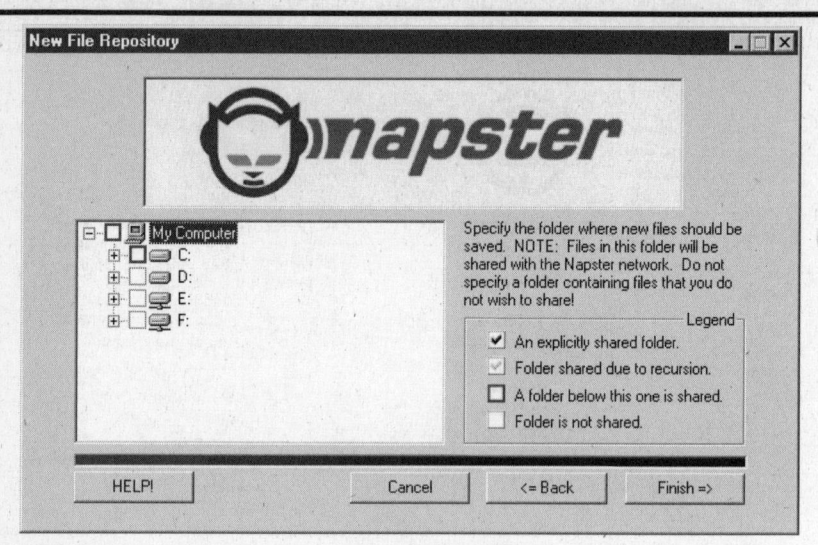

FIGURE 5.7: Designate your download folder in the New File Repository dialog box. This folder is shared, so make sure it doesn't contain any folders that you don't want shared recursively.

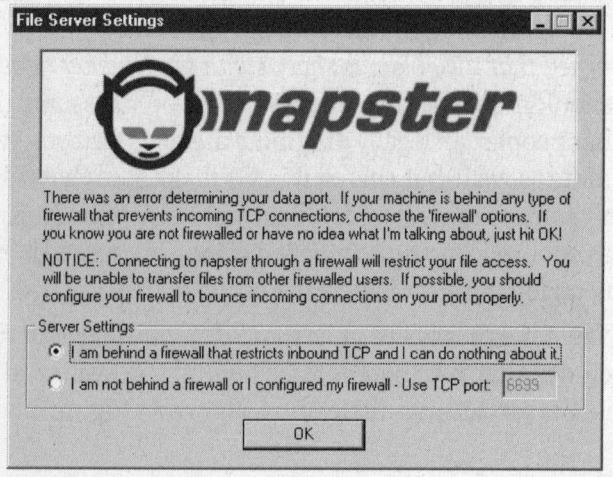

FIGURE 5.8: Specify your firewall settings in the File Server Settings dialog box.

Finding MP3 files Using Napster and Its Friends

If you have no control over your firewall, select the I Am Behind a Firewall That Restricts Inbound TCP and I Can Do Nothing About It option button. (TCP is the Transmission Control Protocol, part of the TCP/IP protocol suite.) Napster cannot transfer files from other users whose computers are behind firewalls, but files from computers not behind firewalls transfer fine. If you have control over your firewall or are able to specify a TCP port for data use, select the I Am Not Behind a Firewall or I Configured My Firewall – Use TCP Port option button and specify the TCP port in the text box.

> **NOTE**
>
> At this writing, Napster sometimes displays the File Server Settings dialog box even when you're connecting via an ISP and no firewall is involved. If this happens to you, try selecting the I Am Not Behind a Firewall or I Configured My Firewall – Use TCP Port option button and using the default port, 6699.

After that, Napster starts, displaying its Home page (shown in Figure 5.9).

Before you start using Napster, you should probably choose a few more settings ones that do not appear in the current setup routine. To set these settings or to change any of the Napster settings you chose during setup, choose File ➤ Preferences to display the Napster Preferences dialog box, which gathers together all the changeable information that you entered during setup. (You cannot change your username without reinstalling Napster.)

The Napster Preferences dialog box contains six pages: Personal, Chat, Schemes, Sharing, Downloading, and Proxy. The following sections discuss the extra options that you'll probably want to set.

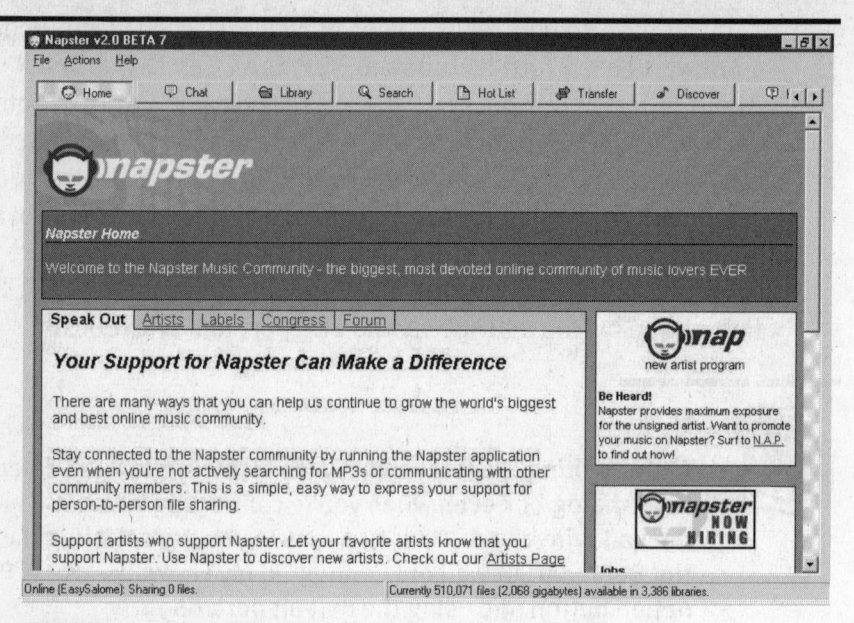

FIGURE 5.9: When Napster starts, it displays its Home page.

Personal Page

The Personal page of the Napster Preferences dialog box (shown in Figure 5.10) contains text boxes for your username (which you cannot change) and your e-mail address and password (which you can change). You can change your ostensible connection speed in the Connection Type drop-down list, and you can choose between the Napster Internal Player and your Default Media Player in the Media Player drop-down list.

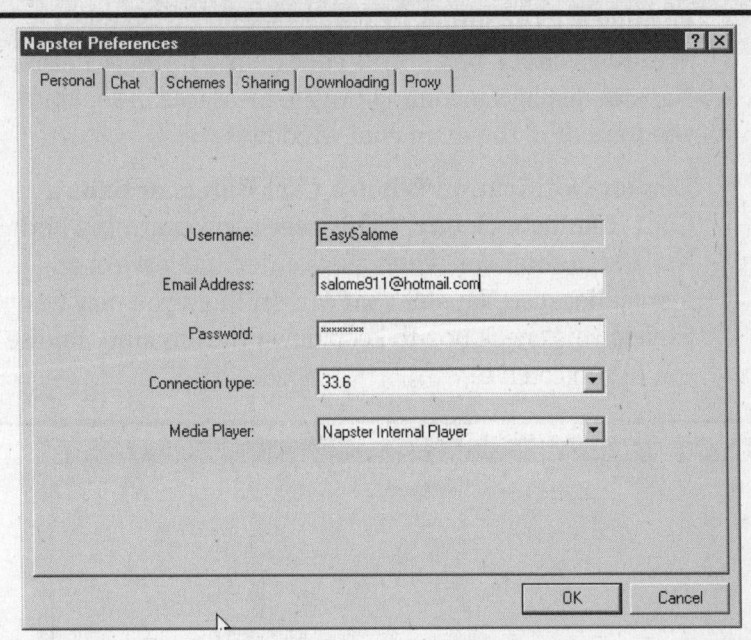

Finding MP3 files Using Napster and Its Friends   139

FIGURE 5.10: You can change your e-mail address, password, connection type, and media player on the Personal page of the Napster Preferences dialog box.

Chat Page

The Chat page of the Napster Preferences dialog box (shown in Figure 5.11) has four options that you'll probably want to set:

> **Automatically Join My Previous Channels When Signing On to Napster check box**   This check box lets you automatically join the chat channels you were using at the end of your last Napster session.

> **Do Not Display Offensive Words in Private Messages or Public Chat Rooms check box**   This check box switches on and off the "swear filter"—whether Napster bleeps out any offending words (starting with "suck" and escalating through "bitch" into the Seven Deadly Words Not Allowed on Television), substituting symbols instead.

Display My Incoming Private Messages in Separate Windows check box   This check box controls whether Napster displays incoming private messages in separate windows or in the main chat window.

Display Notification When a User Enters or Exits a Chat Room check box   This check box controls whether Napster notifies you when users enter and leave chat rooms. Because Napster chat can get busy, you may want to clear this check box to keep down the amount of noise you're subjected to.

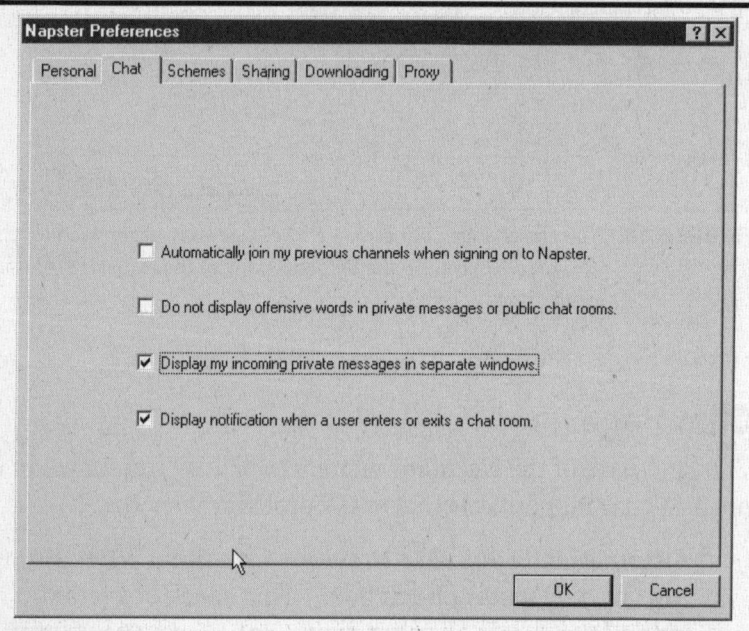

FIGURE 5.11:   Choose chat options on the Chat page of the Napster Preferences dialog box.

Schemes Page

The Schemes page of the Napster Preferences dialog box (shown in Figure 5.12) lets you use different color schemes for Napster. (The screen shots we show in this chapter use the default color scheme.)

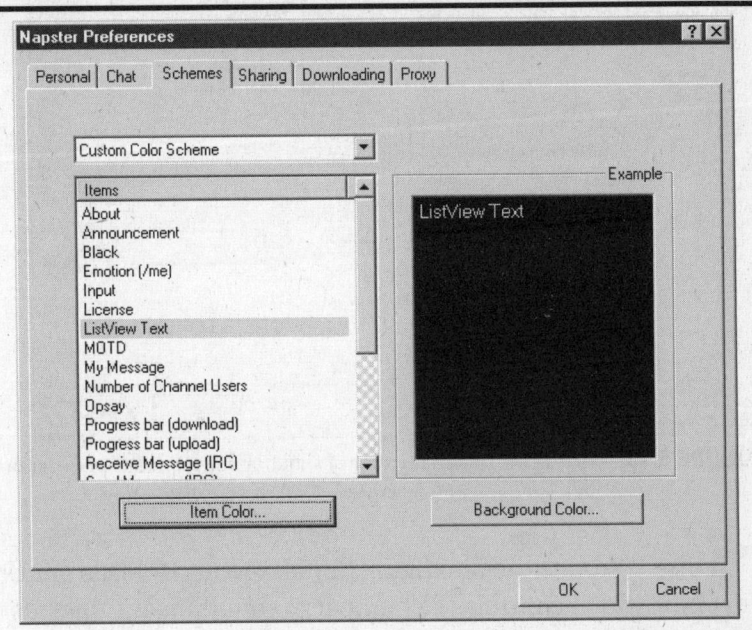

FIGURE 5.12: Choose color schemes for Napster on the Schemes page of the Napster Preferences dialog box.

Sharing Page

The Sharing page of the Napster Preferences dialog box (shown in Figure 5.13) lets you change the folder or folders you're sharing with the Napster community, change the TCP port you're using, and force Napster to search your hard disks for MP3 and WMA files to share via Napster.

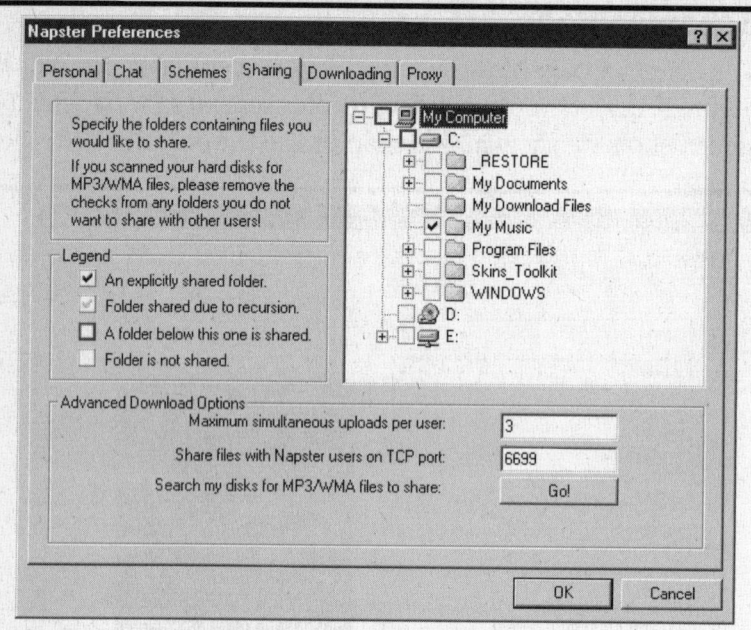

FIGURE 5.13: Set the maximum number of simultaneous uploads per user on the Sharing page of the Napster Preferences dialog box.

It also contains the Maximum Simultaneous Uploads Per User text box, which controls the number of simultaneous uploads. Make sure this setting is appropriate for your line speed: If you have a modem connection, reduce the upload number to 1 in order to give visitors the maximum speed possible. (If multiple visitors connect at the same time, they'll still get slow speeds.) If you have a heavy-duty connection such as a T1, choose a larger number.

Downloading Page

The Downloading page of the Napster Preferences dialog box (shown in Figure 5.14) lets you change your download folder and offers these three options:

> **Max Simultaneous Downloads text box** This text box controls the number of simultaneous downloads that Napster performs (if you've selected multiple files). If you have a fast connection, enter a number between 5 and 10

Finding MP3 files Using Napster and Its Friends

(or between 5 and 25) so that you can pull down a number of songs at the same time from lower-bandwidth sites. If you have a modem, keep the number low—perhaps 2 or 3—so that each song you're downloading gets a significant chunk of your bandwidth and none takes too long to download. Also, the longer a download takes, the greater the chance is that the Napster user you are downloading it from will go offline, leaving you stuck with an incomplete file.

> **TIP**
>
> If you have a modem connection, you'll often want to change your Max Simultaneous Downloads number to find the connections you need and maximize your download speed. When searching for files you want, set a value of around 5 so that Napster tests multiple connections at once and you can quickly see which users you can download from and which you can't. Once you get a couple of downloads running, lower the Max Simultaneous Downloads number to the number of connections, so that they go faster. And if you hit a user who's the mother lode of files you're after and from whom you can download files successfully, drop the Max Simultaneous Downloads number to 1 so that you get each track as quickly as possible, in case the user goes offline. Then queue all the tracks you want to download from the user, and Napster will download them one by one at your top speed.

Delete Partial Files When Download Fails drop-down list Select Yes in this drop-down list if you want Napster to automatically delete any file that isn't fully downloaded. The default setting is No, and there's also a Prompt Me setting that's useful if you'll be monitoring your Napster sessions closely. (We'd like to see a partial setting, where you could automatically delete anything of which you got, say, less than a third or a half, but keep anything of which you got more than that.)

Remove Successful Downloads from Transfer Window drop-down list Select Yes in this drop-down list instead of the default No if you want Napster to automatically remove the entries for successfully downloaded tracks from the Download page. This option is useful for heavy downloading sessions on a fast line.

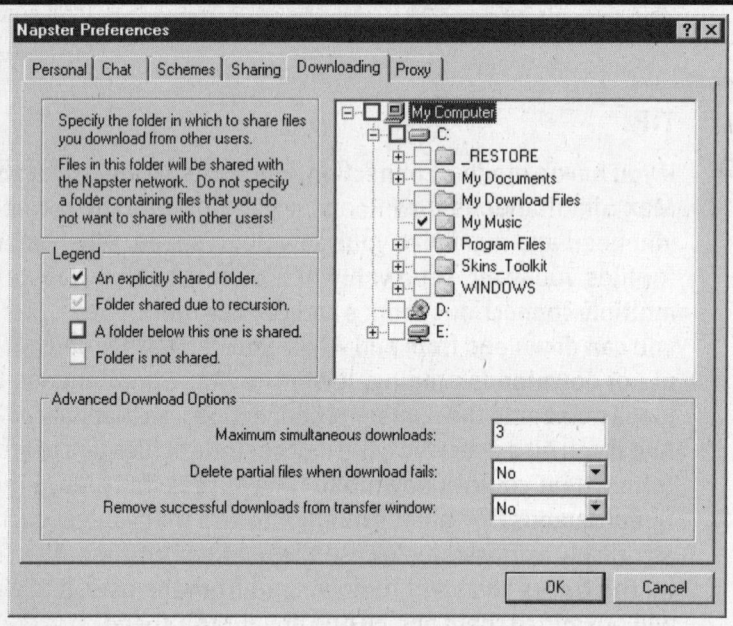

FIGURE 5.14: Choose download preferences on the Downloading page of the Napster Preferences dialog box.

Proxy Page

The Proxy page of the Napster Preferences dialog box (shown in Figure 5.15) offers a half-dozen settings for people connecting to the Internet through a proxy server. You'll recognize these settings as those that appear in the Proxy Setup dialog box, which we described earlier in the chapter.

If you don't use a proxy server, you don't need to mess with these settings; if you do use a proxy server, you need to get them right. If you don't know the details of your proxy server, ask your

Finding MP3 files Using Napster and Its Friends 145

network administrator—but if yours is a business setting, make sure you have a valid business reason for needing to know the proxy server information.

TIP

If you don't have a good reason, check to see if the information you need is residing in the bowels of your browser. In Internet Explorer, choose Tools ➣ Internet Options to display the Internet Options dialog box, click the Connections tab to display the Connections page, and click the LAN Settings button to display the Local Area Network (LAN) Settings dialog box, whose Proxy Server group box may be able help you. In Netscape Navigator, choose Edit ➣ Preferences to display the Preferences dialog box, expand the Advanced category, click the Proxies entry, and see what you find. This information won't necessarily be exactly what you need, but it may put you on the right track.

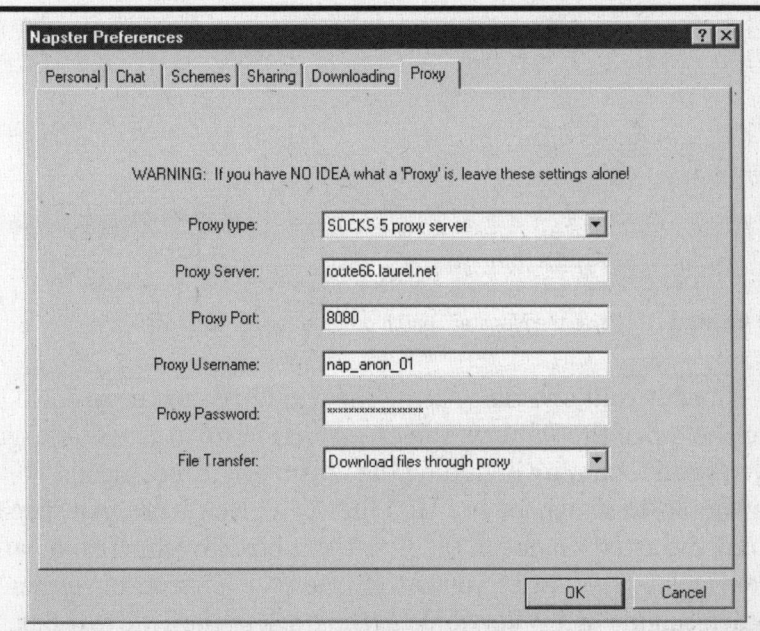

FIGURE 5.15: If you're connecting through a proxy server, you can tweak the settings on the Proxy page of the Napster Preferences dialog box.

Finding Music with Napster

The Napster interface consists of eight pages—Home, Chat, Library, Search, Hot List, Transfer, Discover, and Help—which you navigate between by clicking the eight corresponding buttons at the top of the Napster window or by pressing Ctrl+Tab (to move from left to right). As you'd guess, you use the Search page (shown in Figure 5.16) to find music. Click the Advanced button to display the advanced search fields.

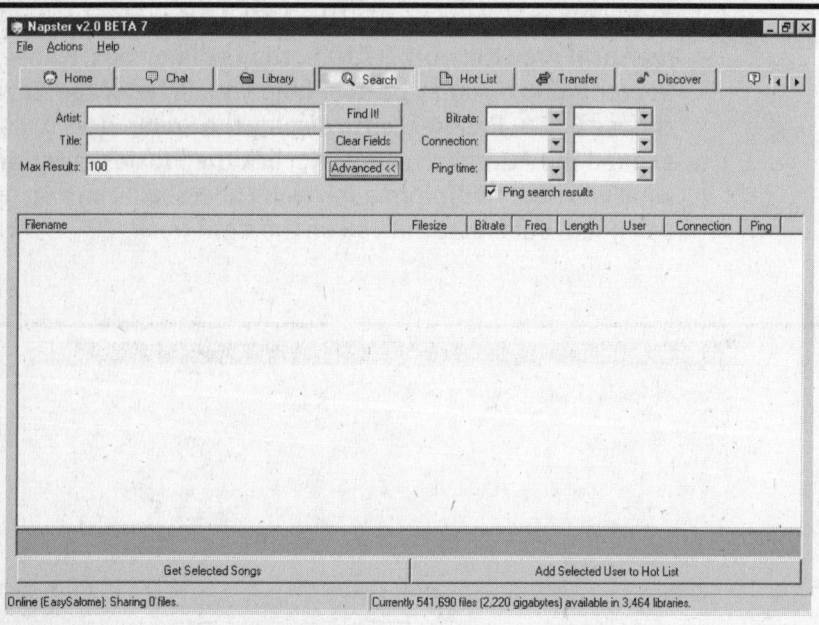

FIGURE 5.16: Use the Napster Search page to search for music.

Specify your criteria by using the text boxes and drop-down lists at the top of the window. You can search by up to six criteria, giving you good flexibility in finding the music you're looking for. For example, to search for any MP3 files by a given artist, you specify only the artist's name in the Artist text box. To search for a particular track by that artist, you specify the artist's name and either the track's name or any keywords in the track in the Title text box. To search for only copies at or above a certain bitrate (say, 128K) and available on ISDN or faster connections, click the Advanced button to display the Bitrate, Connection, and Ping Time fields, and then specify those criteria as well.

> **NOTE**
>
> At this writing, Napster only supports returning a maximum of 100 results, so there's no point in changing the number in the Max Results text box.

Use the three advanced fields to restrict the search as much as you want. Each of the drop-down lists in the left-hand column offers four settings: the default blank setting (meaning that the field is not used), AT LEAST, EQUAL TO, and AT BEST.

If you want to get MP3 files of only good quality or better, set the Bitrate row's first drop-down list to AT LEAST and the second to the minimum quality you want—for example, 128kbps. (If you have a slow connection and don't want to download any files of a bitrate higher than your chosen acceptable bitrate, select the EQUAL TO item instead of the AT LEAST item.)

Use the Connection row and the Ping Time row to make sure you only get hits that should download at a decent speed:

- You can specify a minimum, exact, or maximum line speed in the Connection row. If you use this field, you'll usually want to specify a minimum connection speed. For example, you might choose AT LEAST ISDN-128K to get hosts with two-channel ISDN or better. It seldom makes sense to specify an exact connection speed unless you feel you must have T3 connections only. And there's no sense in specifying a *maximum* connection speed—unless you're very strange, you'll want the fastest connection you can find.

- *Ping time* is the time it takes for a packet of information to get from your computer to the host computer and back. A longer ping time usually means there are more *hops* (stages) in the connection between your computer and the host, which translates to a greater burden on the Internet and a potentially longer download time. Usually you won't need to specify a ping time. Instead, you can sort your search results by ping time (provided you keep the Ping Search Results check box selected) and take the fastest relevant result. (If you do want to try setting a ping time, you might choose AT BEST 500 ms to avoid ultra-slow connections.)

> **TIP**
>
> Remember that 56K modems, DSLs, and cable connections have much slower upstream speeds than downstream speeds. A 56K modem delivers a maximum of 33.6K upstream, and many DSL and cable connections (depending on the carrier and the service plan) deliver only 128K maximum upstream. In particular, don't scorn ISDN connections—they deliver the data rate advertised, and an ISDN-128K connection often outperforms a DSL or cable on the upload. And if you're prepared to use modem connections, set a minimum of 33.6K or even 28.8K rather than 56K—33.6K is the maximum speed you'll get when downloading from a 56K modem, so there's no sense in excluding 33.6K modems, which will deliver the same speed. 28.8K is only about 15 percent slower than 33.6K, so it's still worth using. Also, remember that a number of Napster users will be deliberately hiding speedy connections in order to avoid downloads—so you may want to try downloading from some ostensible 14.4K connections or Unknown speed connections to see if they're really faster than they claim.

Often, you'll do best to start by performing a search with only one or two criteria, to see if you get some results. If you get plenty of results, apply further criteria and search again until you get a smaller number of results that more closely match your needs.

In particular, you may want to leave the Bitrate field open on your first search so that you see all the available copies of tracks. If

Finding MP3 files Using Napster and Its Friends 149

there are plenty of copies, you can then add in the bitrate criterion to narrow the field to your chosen bitrates. If not, you will at least be aware of low-bitrate versions of the tracks you're looking for rather than missing them altogether.

> **TIP**
>
> Keep an eye on the track length of the songs returned in your Napster searches. Some of the songs listed may be incomplete, because Napster downloads get broken off if the host goes offline. If you can figure out by consensus what the track length is for the song you're interested in, you'll be able to avoid wasting your time and bandwidth on downloading someone else's incomplete version.

When you've set your search criteria, click the Find It! button. Napster searches through the songs available in the libraries and returns a list of what it has found. Figure 5.17 shows Napster having found 100 tracks that match the search criterion "Cure." Most are tracks by the band The Cure (as you'd expect), but others are tracks with the word "Cure" in them (including tracks from Metallica, Morphine, and Denis Leary). The tracks are being supplied by a number of different users.

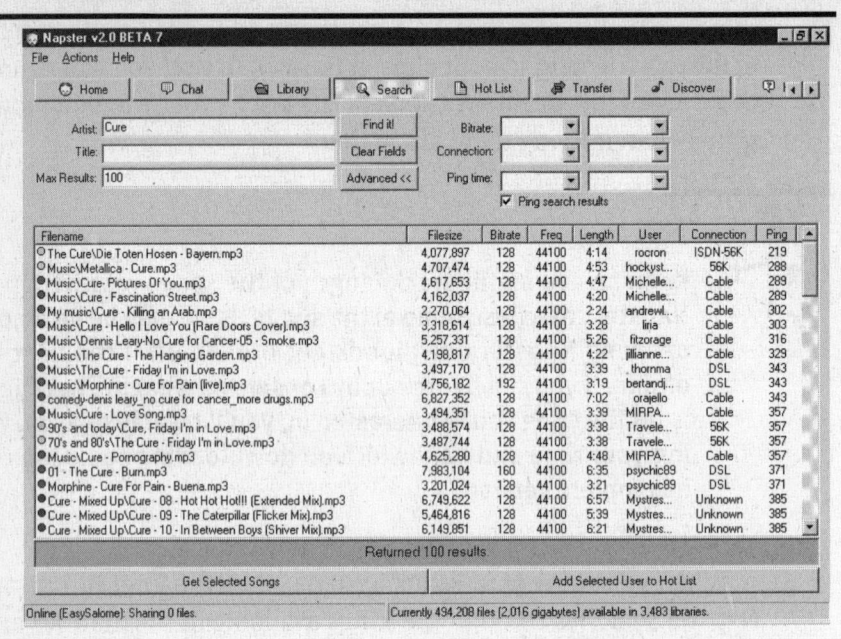

FIGURE 5.17: The Search page lists all matching songs found, with colored circles indicating the connection speed.

Most of the fields in the results list on the Search page are easy enough to understand: Filename, Filesize, Bitrate, Freq (frequency), Length (time in minutes and seconds), User (the host's name), Connection, and Ping (the ping time). The colored circles next to the filenames provide a quick guide to the line speed:

- A red circle denotes a 33.6K or slower modem, or an unknown speed. Remember that unknown speeds can be high—as can lines that the users have chosen to hide as low-speed modems.

- A yellow circle denotes anything from a 56K modem to a 128K ISDN line.

- A green circle denotes anything faster than a 128K line—a cable modem, a DSL, a T1, or a T3.

TIP

Something else to try—instead of searching for particular titles by the artists you're interested in, search for words like "rare," "bootleg," and "live." Doing so may turn up some true treasures—along with more Grateful Dead tracks than the average human can handle.

The Napster community is not only dynamic (with people logging on and off all the time) but also (as mentioned earlier) split across multiple servers. So the pool of available tracks changes constantly. If you don't find what you're looking for, disconnect from your current server (File ➢ Disconnect) and immediately connect again (File ➢ Connect) until you get a different server. Alternatively, try the same search later on the same server. Different people may be logged on by then, and the selection of tracks available is likely to be different.

Downloading a Track

To download one or more tracks that you've located, select it or them on the Search page. Then click the Get Selected Songs button at the bottom of the page, or right-click one of the tracks and choose Download from the context menu. Napster displays the Transfer page, as shown in Figure 5.18 with multiple Cure tracks being downloaded. Note that at this point we're almost certainly breaking the law—last we heard, The Cure hadn't granted all these people permission to shunt their copyrighted material around on the Internet, so they're illegal copies: illegal to share and illegal to download.

152   Chapter Five

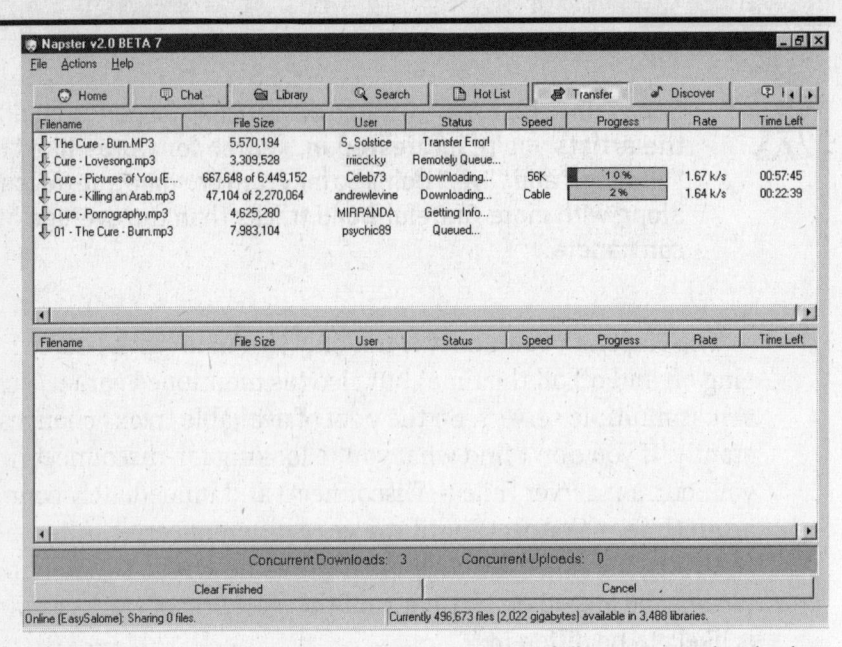

FIGURE 5.18: The Transfer page shows you the status of all your current downloads.

As each download runs, Napster shows you its status (Getting Info, Queued, Remotely Queued, Downloading, File Complete, Canceled, Unavailable, or Transfer Error), the line speed, a progress bar for it, the download rate (as in Figure 5.18), and the time left on the download. Here's what the status terms mean:

Getting Info   This means that Napster is contacting the host offering the file for download. If there's a problem with transferring the file, the transfer may get stuck at the Getting Info stage, in which case you'll need to cancel it. The transfer will eventually time out, but if you're at your computer, you'll probably nuke it for non-performance long before Napster times it out.

Downloading   This indicates that Napster has established a satisfactory connection to the host and is downloading the file. The bar in the Progress column shows you the progress of the download visually.

Finding MP3 files Using Napster and Its Friends 153

Unavailable This typically indicates that the download has failed, either because of firewalling problems or because the host has gone offline. It may also mean that the host has deliberately killed the download.

Transfer Error This typically indicates that the host has disconnected from or exited Napster.

Queued This indicates that you're currently downloading your maximum number of tracks (set in the Max Simultaneous Downloads text box on the Downloading page of the Napster Preferences dialog box), so the track is waiting for one of the current downloads to finish. If you want to download more tracks at once, increase the Max Simultaneous Downloads number—but remember that the more tracks you download at once, the more thinly your bandwidth is spread, and the longer each download will take.

Remotely Queued This indicates that the host is currently uploading its maximum number of tracks to you and other Napster users (as set in their Max Simultaneous Uploads Per User text box on the Sharing page of the Napster Preferences dialog box), so the track is waiting for one of those uploads to finish.

File Complete This indicates that Napster has finished downloading the file from the host and has saved it to the designated folder on your hard drive.

Canceled This indicates that you have canceled the download.

Timed Out This indicates that Napster has given up on trying to get a response from a host. Napster then moves on to the next download that you have queued.

Chapter Five

> **NOTE**
>
> When downloading, try to spread the load as much as possible: Don't try to download multiple files from the same host at the same time unless both you and the host have fast connections. For example, if you try to download ten tracks at once from a host that has a 56K modem, you'll get a miserable transfer rate of a few hundred bytes a second and each track will take several hours to download (assuming that the host allows each user to download that many tracks at once). Instead, hit multiple 56K hosts for a track apiece, and you'll get them much quicker (provided you have the bandwidth yourself). This strategy of not overburdening a host may be foiled by other people hitting the same host and downloading files, but at a minimum, make sure that you don't throttle any host by yourself.

When you try to download a file that has the same name as a file that's currently in your library, Napster displays the File Exists! dialog box (shown in Figure 5.19), which lets you overwrite the existing file or (if you can access the remote machine) rename the remote file. Usually, you won't be able to rename the file on the remote machine, so you'll do better to open an Explorer window, rename the existing file with that name, and then tell Napster to overwrite the existing file (which won't be there anymore, but Napster won't notice).

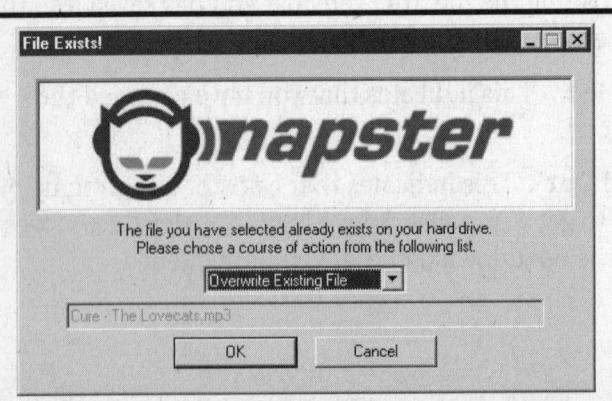

FIGURE 5.19: The File Exists! dialog box warns you that you're downloading a track with the same name as one already in your download directory and lets you decide how to solve the problem.

Finding MP3 files Using Napster and Its Friends

While downloading, you can use the two buttons at the bottom of the Transfer page to cancel or clear finished transfers:

- Click the Cancel button, or right-click the transfer and choose Cancel from the context menu, to cancel a transfer.

- Click the Clear Finished button to remove completed transfers from the Transfer page. Clearing finished transfers also removes from the Transfer page files that were unavailable or that were canceled.

The context menu for the downloads list box on the Transfer page gives you several more options:

- Choose the Play Song! item to play the track even as you're downloading it. You'll be able to hear only as much of the track as you've downloaded. This feature can help you identify tracks that you don't want to continue downloading (for example, if you're getting a different track than you thought, or if the track is low quality or damaged).

- Choose the Force Transfer item to force the transfer of a queued item. Forcing a transfer temporarily overrides your Maximum Simultaneous Downloads setting.

- Use the Prioritize submenu (which has items for Move Up, Move Down, Move to Top, and Move to Bottom) to improve the order in which you're downloading tracks. First, promote the tracks you're most interested in to the top of the list so that you get them before the hosts who are providing them go offline. Second, if you're downloading a number of tracks from a couple of hosts at about the same speed, you might want to alternate queued tracks so as to balance your demands on each host.

- Choose the Cancel Transfer item to cancel a transfer but keep it on the Transfer page, and the Delete/Abort Transfer item to cancel a transfer and remove it from the Transfer page.

- Choose the Clear Finished item to remove completed or impossible transfers from the Transfer page.

TIP

Napster stores the files for incomplete transfers in the \Napster\Incomplete\ folder. Visit this folder from time to time to retrieve lost partial gems and to clear out the residue.

Playing Music in Napster

Any MP3 files in the folders you've designated for sharing via Napster and in your download folder are listed in the library, which you access through the Library page (shown in Figure 5.20). You can play these files directly or add them to your playlist.

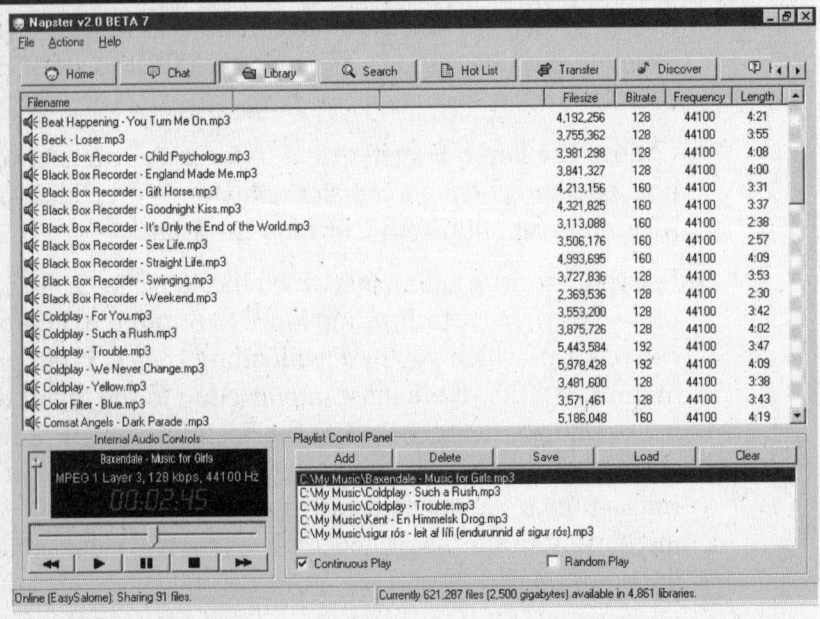

FIGURE 5.20: The Library page contains all the files you've shared and those you've downloaded.

Finding MP3 files Using Napster and Its Friends

> **WARNING**
>
> Remember that Napster shares your download folder, and you can't prevent it from doing so. This bizarre design decision makes it dangerous to keep in your download folder any MP3 files that you don't have the rights to distribute. If you download an MP3 file from a host that can legally distribute it, you're on the right side of the law; but if you share that file (or if Napster shares it for you), you're breaking the law. Because of this quirk, it's a good idea to move downloaded files out of your download folder immediately—but doing so prevents you from using Napster's player and playlist features to listen to the tracks.

The lower-left corner of the Library page contains the controls for Napster's internal audio player: a volume control, a position slider, and the standard buttons—Play, Pause, Stop, Previous, and Next. If you chose to use your default MP3 player instead of Napster's internal audio player, clicking the Play button launches (or switches to) your default player.

To play a song quickly, double-click it in the library. Otherwise, create a playlist by using the Add button to add tracks selected on the Library page to the playlist and then rearranging them into the order you want. Use the Save button and the resulting Save As dialog box to save a playlist you want to keep, and the Load button and resulting Open dialog box to open a saved playlist.

To delete a track from your library, right-click it and choose Delete (From Disk) from the context menu, and then choose the Yes button in the resulting Delete File dialog box.

To refresh your library when you've made changes to it by using Explorer, right-click in it and choose Refresh Library from the context menu. (Napster automatically adds to the library any tracks that you download.)

Chatting on Napster

To keep you entertained while searching for the MP3 files you want or letting people download the MP3 files you can legally share, Napster supports multiple chat channels that you can join and leave at will. The chat channels allow both public and private messaging—although at this writing, relatively few Napster users seem to spend much time chatting, presumably because they're there primarily for the music.

The Chat page, shown in Figure 5.21, is easy to navigate. You start off with a Private channel that remains open the whole time. The Private channel displays the Napster message of the day when you log on and also displays any private messages that are sent to you. (Private messages are also displayed on the current Chat page.)

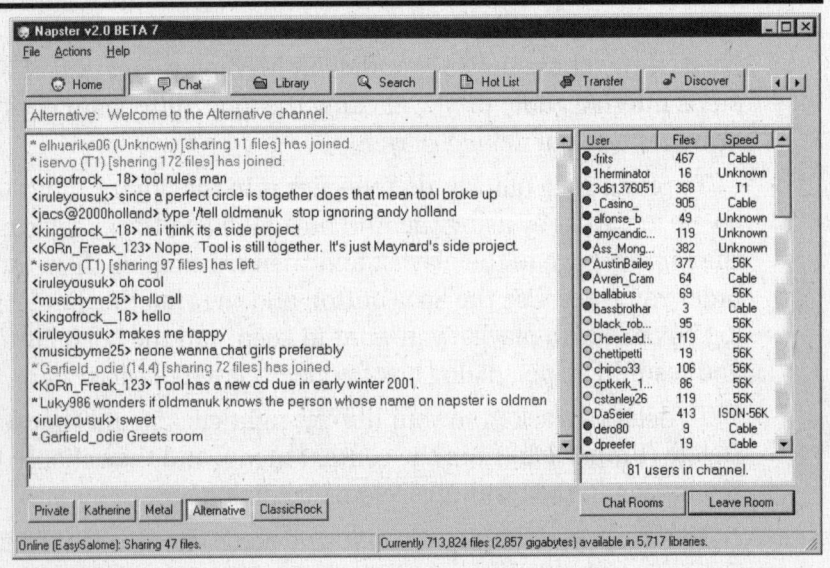

FIGURE 5.21: Napster's Chat page provides multiple chat channels and both public and private messaging.

Finding MP3 files Using Napster and Its Friends

To join another channel, click the Chat Rooms button. (If you joined any chat channels after running Napster the first time, you may already have other channels available.) Napster displays the Channel List dialog box with the root list of channels selected (shown in Figure 5.22). To display the full list of channels available on the server, including user-created channels, click the View All button. (To restore the view to the root list, click the resulting View Root button.)

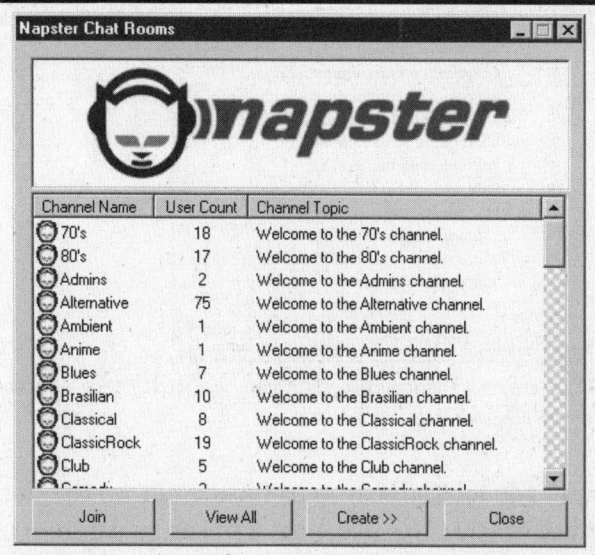

FIGURE 5.22: Use the Napster Chat Rooms dialog box to join and create chat rooms.

Select the channel or channels you want to join (Shift+clicking and Ctrl+clicking work for multiple selections), and then click the Join button to join them. You can join up to five channels at a time (on top of the Private channel).

You can create your own chat channel by clicking the Create >> button to display an extra part of the Napster Chat Rooms dialog box, entering the name in the Channel to Create text box, and clicking the Create button. This channel is then available to other users connected to the same server as you. To view the channel, users need to click the View All button to display the full list of channels. User-created channels appear with a smiley-face icon next to them, like the GreenRoom and IndustroGoth channels shown in Figure 5.23.

FIGURE 5.23: User-created channels are identified by a smiley-face icon instead of the Napster icon.

Each channel you join appears as a button across the bottom of the screen below the Chat text box. You can move from one chat channel to another by clicking the appropriate button, or you can move from one channel to the next (from left to right) by pressing Ctrl+X.

You can view the information available about a user by right-clicking their entry in the user list and choosing View Information from the context menu. Napster displays the Finger Information dialog box for the user, as shown in Figure 5.24.

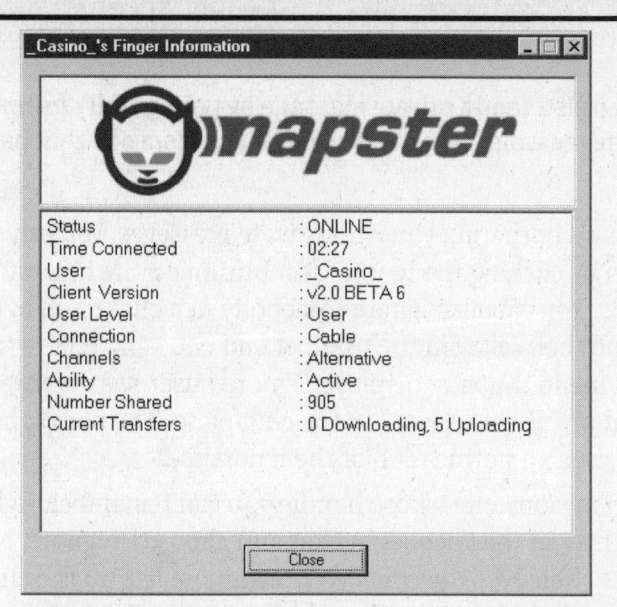

Finding MP3 files Using Napster and Its Friends 161

FIGURE 5.24: Use the View Information command and the resulting Finger dialog box to get information about another Napster user.

To send a private message to someone, right-click their entry in the user list and choose Private Message from the context menu. Napster displays the Instant Message window (shown in Figure 5.25). Type the message and press Enter to send it.

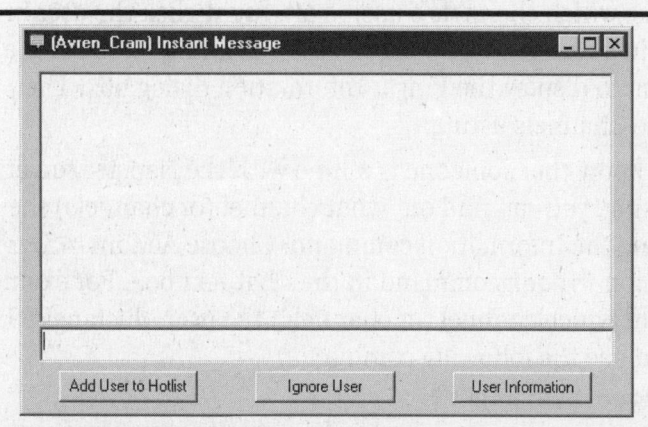

FIGURE 5.25: Sending an instant message

> **TIP**
>
> You can also send a private message by typing **/tell <*username*>** and the message in the text box at the bottom of a chat page.

If someone's bothering you with private messages, you can ignore them by clicking the Ignore User button on the Instant Message window. You can also ignore somebody in a chat room by right-clicking their entry in the user list and choosing Ignore from the context menu. Napster displays "Ignored user <*username*>'s channel and private messages" in the chat pane. The person being ignored receives no notification of the ignorance.

To un-ignore someone whose handle you can remember, right-click their entry in the user list in chat and choose Unignore. Napster displays "Removed <*username*> from ignore list" in the chat pane. If you've been ignoring a bunch of people and have forgotten who they all are, choose Action ➤ View Ignore List to display the Ignore List dialog box (shown in Figure 5.26). Use the Remove button to remove selected users from your ignore list, or use the Clear button to forgive everyone their trespasses in one fell swoop. Then click the Close button to close the Ignore List dialog box.

To find out information about a user, use the Information feature to see which channels a user is on. Right-click the user in the user list in a chat pane and choose View Information from the context menu to display the Finger Information dialog box. Then check the Channels listing.

If you know that someone is online with the Napster server you're using, you can find out what channel (or channels) they're in by using the Information command. Choose Actions ➤ Get User Information `finger` command in the Chat text box. For example, to find out which channel (or channels) the user Mustang999 is in, you could use the following command:

```
/finger Mustang999
```

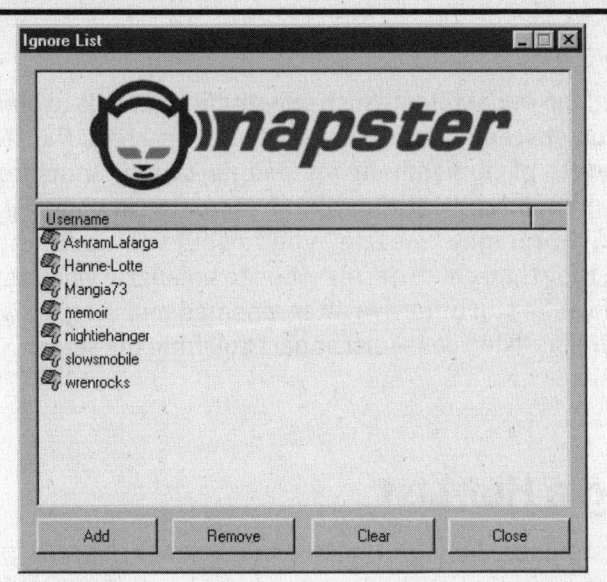

FIGURE 5.26: Use the Ignore List dialog box to un-ignore people whose names you've forgotten.

If the user is online with this server, you'll see the Finger Information dialog box for the user; this dialog box includes the user's current channel or channels. If the user is not currently online with this server, Napster doesn't display the Finger Information dialog box, but instead displays the message "user <*username*> is not a known user" in your chat pane. (This message is not visible to other participants in the chat room.)

TIP

Even if you care nothing for chat, you can use it to find out who's online and interested in the same types of music as you, the number of songs they're sharing, and the speed of their connection. Then check out interesting people by using the Hot List feature as described in the next section.

> **NOTE**
>
> Beyond the swear filter (which substitutes symbols to bleep out common obscenities and offensive words in chat), Napster has two levels of punishment for people caught transgressing against community standards of etiquette in chat. First, an administrator may "muzzle" you to shut you up for the time being; they then get to decide when to unmuzzle you later. Second, if you're still offensive after repeated muzzling, an administrator may "kill" you—disconnect you from the server.

Maintaining a Hot List

Apart from searching for a particular artist or track, Napster provides a great way to find out what music people are sharing: the hot list. This feature lets you browse through all the files that a particular user is offering, which lets you discover little-known music that people are sharing.

At this writing, with the Napster pool of music split across many servers, the hot list is not as compelling a feature as it will become once Napster integrates all servers into a common pool. You can add to the hot list any user whose name you encounter online or whose name you happen to know, but there's no guarantee that any person you add to your hot list in one session will log in to the same Napster server as you the next session—or that they'll even be online in the first place. Napster, Inc. has of course no control over who is online when, but they've been working on the server problem, and you can now see hot-list users across servers and exchange messages with them. But you cannot yet see the files they're sharing unless you're both connected to the same server.

One easy way to add a user to the hot list is from the Chat page, whose right-hand pane lists the users in your current chat channel, together with the number of songs they're sharing and their connection speed. (There's no list of users for the Private channel, of course.) By default, this pane is sorted alphabetically by user, but you

Finding MP3 files Using Napster and Its Friends 165

can sort by the Songs column or by the Speed column by clicking the column heading. Click a column heading a second time to sort the column in reverse alphabetical order.

You can add a user to the hot list from the Chat page, the Search page, or the Transfer page by either right-clicking a listing featuring them and choosing Add to Hot List from the context menu or by selecting the user and choosing Actions ➤ Add User to Hot List. On the Hot List page, you can add a user by clicking the Add User to Hot List button, entering the user's name in the User to Add text box, and clicking the OK button.

When you add a user to the hot list from the Chat page or the Search page, Napster displays the Hot List page. Figure 5.27 shows a hot list with seven of the members online (in the Online pane) and rather more offline (in the Offline pane).

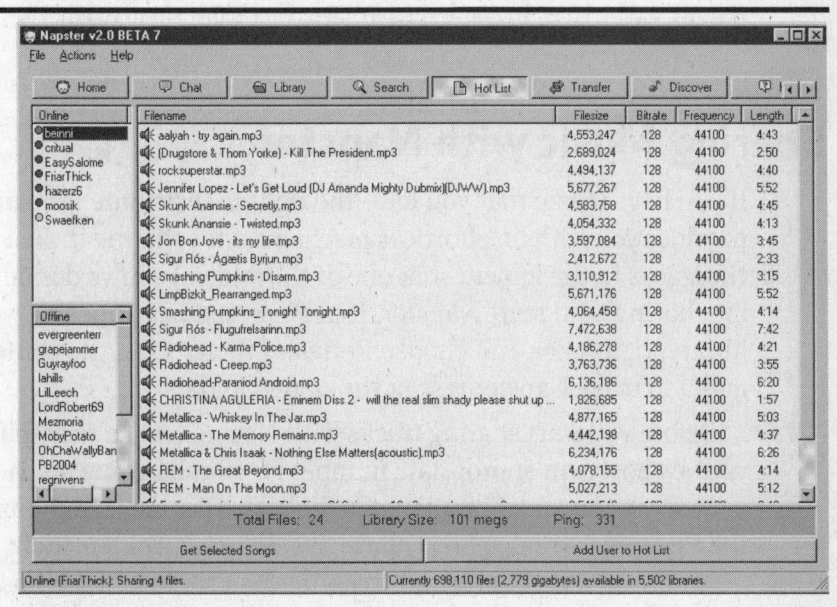

FIGURE 5.27: Use the Hot List page to browse through the list of MP3 files that another user is sharing.

To see what one of the users on your hot list is currently offering, click their entry in the Online box. If Napster is slow to show the user's list of files, right-click the entry and choose Refresh File List from the context menu. If you see the Napster Notification dialog box telling you that Napster is unable to transfer the file because both users are firewalled, you need to find another host or change your configuration so that incoming TCP packets can get through the firewall to your computer.

To remove a user from your hot list, right-click their entry in the Online pane or the Offline pane and choose Delete User from the context menu. Napster displays the Remove User dialog box (shown in Figure 5.28). Click the Yes button to complete the eviction.

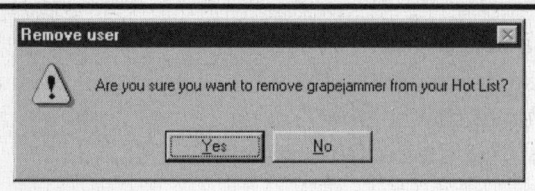

FIGURE 5.28: When you sicken of someone, remove them from your hot list.

Sharing Music with Napster

If you have music that you have the right to distribute, Napster provides you with an effortless mechanism for sharing it. Just place the tracks in the folder (or in one of the folders) you've designated for sharing, and start Napster. If the tracks don't appear in your library, right-click and choose Refresh Library from the context menu to make Napster rescan the shared folders.

Before you start sharing tracks with Napster, make sure that you've chosen an appropriate number for simultaneous uploads per user in the Max Simultaneous Uploads (Per User) text box in the Preferences dialog box (File ≻ Preferences). For a modem connection, you'll probably want to limit each user to 1 or 2 uploads at a time. Any more than that will deliver a lame data rate that will make the tracks take hours to transfer—and that's if only one user is downloading from your computer at a time. For a 64K ISDN connection, 2 or 3 is a reasonable number; 4 to 6 for a 128K ISDN line, a DSL, or a cable connection; and 10 to 50 for a T1, depending on whether you have the whole line to yourself (unlikely). If you have a

Finding MP3 files Using Napster and Its Friends 167

T3 to yourself, you'll be able to enter much higher numbers and still deliver a good data rate to a number of people.

Once you've shared the files, anybody logged on to the same Napster server as you can access them, either by turning them up in a search or by adding you to their hot list and explicitly scanning your shared files.

When someone is downloading a file from your computer, you'll see the entry appear in the Upload pane on the Transfer page, marked *Uploading*, as shown in Figure 5.29. If tracks are queued for upload from your computer, these do not appear in the Upload pane until they become active.

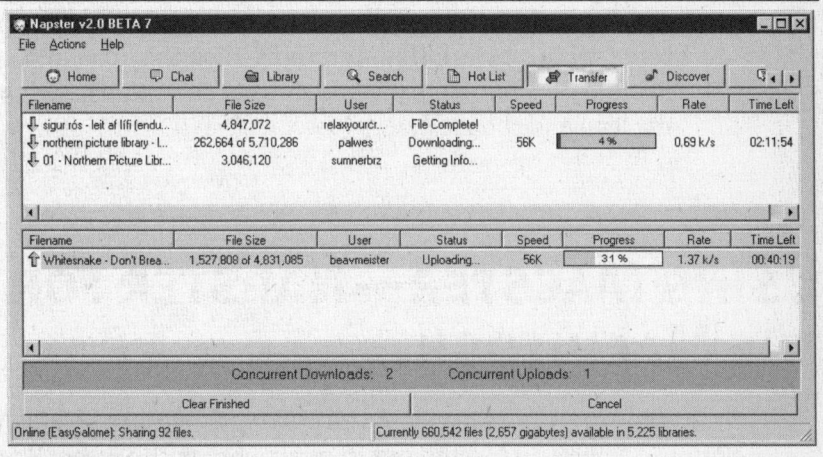

FIGURE 5.29: Tracks being uploaded from your computer appear in the lower pane on the Transfer page.

You can cancel a transfer by selecting it and clicking the Cancel button. Alternatively, right-click the transfer and choose Cancel Transfer from the context menu to cancel the transfer, or choose Delete/Abort Transfer to delete it and remove it from the Transfer page. In either case, the track is listed as Unavailable to the would-be downloader.

If you exit Napster while someone is downloading a track from your computer, the downloader gets a Transfer Error message for the track. If you disconnect from Napster but keep your Internet connection open, Napster can usually continue uploads that are in progress. (This is because Napster establishes a one-to-one connection between users rather than connecting them through the Napster server.)

> **WARNING**
>
> When exiting Napster, use the File ➢ Exit command rather than clicking the Close button in the upper right-hand corner of the window or using the control menu. Exit ends your Napster session. Clicking the Close button gets rid of the Napster window but leaves Napster running in the background, so people can continue downloading files that you're sharing. While Napster is running in the background, you'll see a Napster icon in your system tray. To restore Napster, right-click this icon and choose Restore from the context menu. To shut down Napster, right-click the icon and choose Exit.

Using Macster—Napster for the Macintosh

At this writing, the Mac community is implementing several Mac clones of Napster. Macster and Rapster work with System 8 and System 9, while Napster for the MacOS X—as its name implies—is for System X. And as mentioned earlier in the chapter, Napster, Inc. is working on a Mac port of Napster itself.

In this section, we'll discuss Macster. Macster and Rapster are currently more or less neck and neck in the race to implement a full and satisfactory version of Napster on the Mac, but on the whole we've had fewer crashes and better experiences with Macster. That said, we encourage you to investigate Rapster as well; like Macster, it has strong features and is free.

At this writing, the current version of Macster isn't final and doesn't support all of Napster's features, so the version that you download is likely to be substantially different than that we describe here.

Getting, Installing, and Configuring Macster

Download the latest version of Macster from the Macster Web site, `www.blackholemedia.com/macster`, and any support software required. (At this writing, Macster requires the Carbon Library Installer from Apple Computer.) Unstuff what you download if it doesn't unstuff itself automatically, and then double-click the Macster item in the distribution folder to start the setup routine running.

The Macster Setup Assistant walks you through the steps of the setup routine. First, the Account Type dialog box (shown in Figure 5.30) lets you create a new account or use an existing account (for example, an account you've set up with Napster or one of its clones).

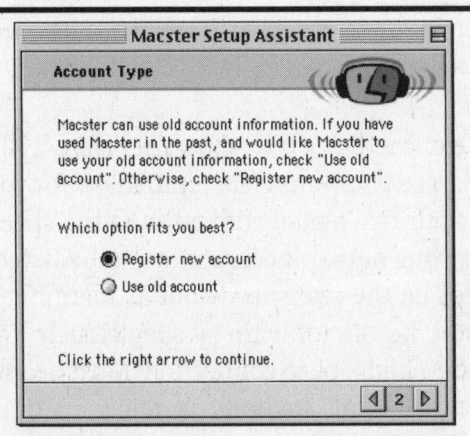

FIGURE 5.30: Macster lets you either register a new Napster account or set up an existing Napster account.

If you choose to set up a new account, you'll follow these steps:

▶ In the Account Information dialog box (shown in Figure 5.31), enter a login name and the password you want to use. The login name needs to be unique within the Napster system, which means you'll need to be creative. Consider using symbols or multiple underscores to make a unique version of a name that has already been taken. Make sure that your password is creative enough that it can't be cracked easily.

FIGURE 5.31: In the Account Information dialog box, enter a unique username and an unguessable password.

▶ In the Personal Preferences dialog box (shown in Figure 5.32), enter the e-mail address you want Napster to know for you (this might not be your real e-mail address) and the speed at which you want your network connection to be listed. (Again, this may not be the real speed—but as mentioned earlier in the chapter, beware of listing a suspiciously low modem speed to hide a high-speed connection: Most people —rightly—don't believe that anybody is really using a 14.4kbps modem anymore.)

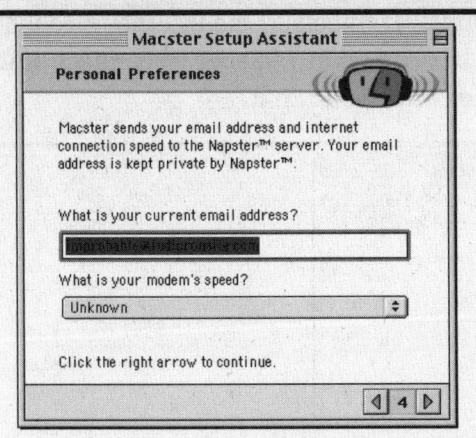

Finding MP3 files Using Napster and Its Friends 171

FIGURE 5.32: In the Personal Preferences dialog box, enter the e-mail address you want to share with Napster, and specify the speed as which you want your network connection to be listed.

▶ In the MP3 Download Folder dialog box, click the Choose Download Folder button. Use the resulting Choose a Folder dialog box (shown in Figure 5.33) to select the folder you want to store downloaded MP3 files in, and then click the Choose button.

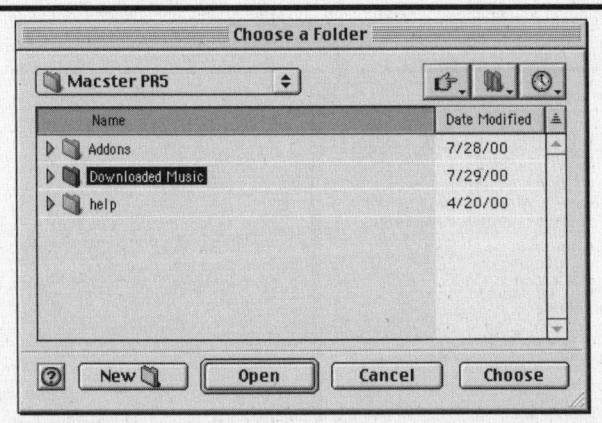

FIGURE 5.33: In the Choose a Folder dialog box, specify the folder in which you want Macster to store MP3 files you download.

▶ In the Network Options dialog box (shown in Figure 5.34), use the Yes and No option buttons to let Macster know whether your computer connects to the Internet through a firewall and whether you want Macster to connect automatically to Napster when you run it.

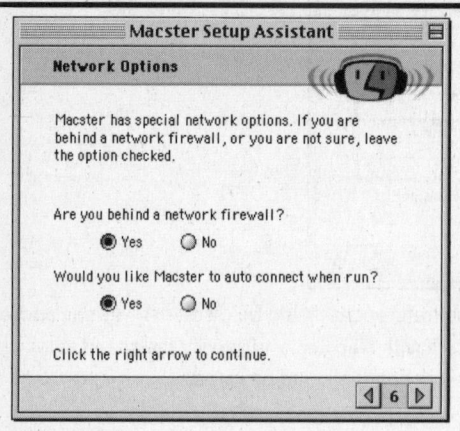

FIGURE 5.34: In the Network Options dialog box, specify whether your computer connects to the Internet through a firewall.

▶ In the Proxy Server dialog box (shown in Figure 5.35), choose proxy server settings if your network uses a proxy server. If you don't connect to the Internet through a firewall, you probably don't use a proxy server.

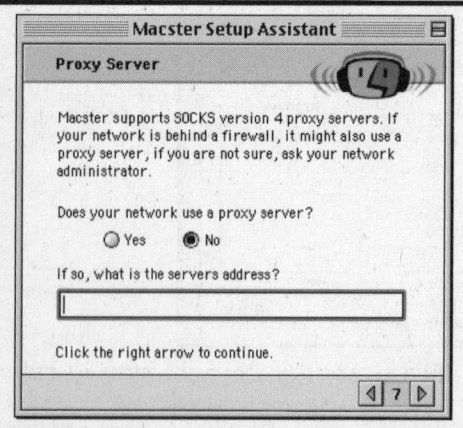

FIGURE 5.35: If your computer does connect to the Internet through a firewall, you might also need to specify proxy server settings in the Proxy Server dialog box.

Finding MP3 files Using Napster and Its Friends

▶ In the Registration dialog box (shown in Figure 5.36), click the Register Account button and wait while Macster registers your account and logs you in to it.

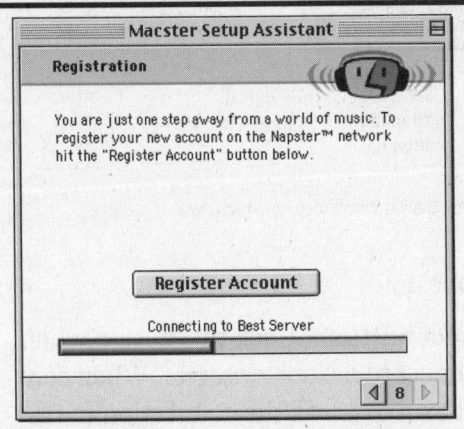

FIGURE 5.36: The Registration dialog box

TIP

Beta tip: If the setup routine crashes when you try to create an account, it probably means that your username wasn't unique. Delete the Macster Prefs file in the Preferences folder under your System folder, run Macster again, and try a different name.

Once you've successfully created a unique username and logged in, Macster displays the Macster panel, shown in Figure 5.37, and the Console window, which shows current messages.

Chapter Five

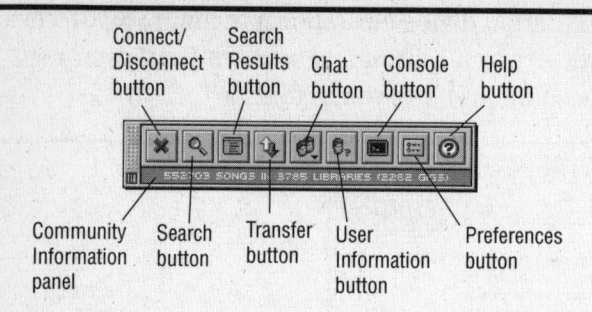

FIGURE 5.37: Use the Macster panel to navigate Macster.

Here's what the buttons do:

Connect/Disconnect button   Click this button when disconnected to connect to a Napster server. When connected, click this button to break the connection to the Napster server.

Search button   Click this button to display the Music Search dialog box.

Search Results button   Click this button to display the Search Results window.

Transfer button   Click this button to display the Transfer Manager window.

Chat button   Click this button to display a menu containing a Join item and a list of the chat windows you're currently in.

User Information button   Click this button to display the User Information dialog box.

Console button   Click this button to display the Console window.

Preferences button   Click this button to display the Preferences dialog box.

Help button   Click this button to access Macster's online help.

Community Information panel This panel displays three pieces of information about the Napster server you're currently connected to:

- The total number of tracks available
- The number of libraries available (in other words, the number of users)
- The data size (in gigabytes) of those tracks

Choosing Preferences in Macster

Before you start searching for and downloading music, set your preferences in Macster. Click the Preferences button on the Macster panel, or choose Edit ≻ Preferences, to display the Preferences dialog box, then set preferences as described in the following subsections.

General Page Preferences

The General page of the Preferences dialog box (shown in Figure 5.38) in Macster contains the following options:

MP3 Player group box Use the controls in this group box to identify to Macster the MP3 player you want to use. In the Default Players drop-down list, either select one of the players listed by name (for example, MACAST or GrayAMP) or select the Other option, use the resulting Choose a File dialog box to identify the player, and click the Choose button.

Filter Mature Language check box Select this check box (which is selected by default) if you want Macster to bowdlerize "mature" (in other words, adult) language in chat channels.

Show Join/Leave in Chat check box Select this check box (which is selected by default) if you want Macster to indicate when users join and leave the chat channels you're in.

Connect on Startup check box Select this check box if you want Macster to automatically connect to a Napster server when you run it. (Most people find this feature useful.)

Show Tooltips check box Select this check box (which is selected by default) if you want Macster to display ToolTips when you hover the mouse over its buttons.

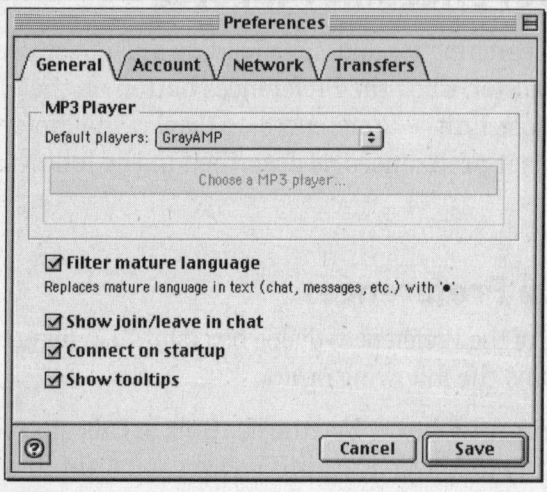

FIGURE 5.38: Identify your MP3 player on the General page of the Preferences dialog box.

Account Page Preferences

The Account page of the Preferences dialog box (shown in Figure 5.39) contains the following options:

User Account ID text box This text box contains your user ID for Napster. You shouldn't need to change this.

Password text box This text box contains your password for Napster. You shouldn't need to change this, either.

Email Address text box This text box contains the e-mail address that Macster supplies to Napster. You may want to use a secondary e-mail address or a fictional e-mail address instead of your primary e-mail address.

Connection Speed drop-down list Use this drop-down list to set the connection speed Napster lists for you. This is the speed that other users see when viewing search results and that Napster uses for searches that specify a connection speed. This speed need bear no relation to your actual connection speed and does not affect the speed at which you can download or upload information.

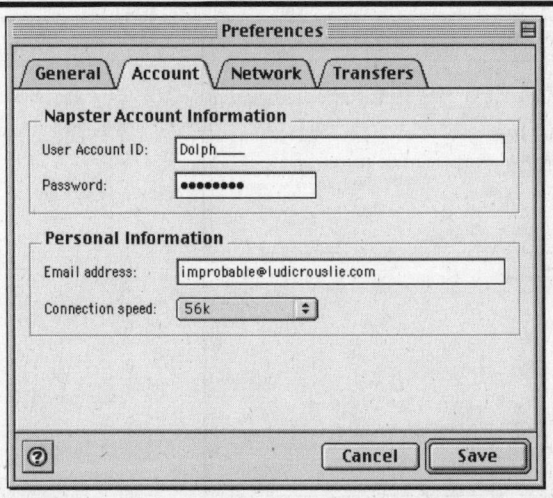

FIGURE 5.39: On the Account page of the Preferences dialog box, check the e-mail address and connection speed that Napster lists for you.

Network Page Preferences

The Network page of the Preferences dialog box (shown in Figure 5.40) contains the following options:

I Am Behind a Firewall check box   Select this check box if your Mac connects to the Internet through a firewall, or if you're not sure whether it does. If you chose the correct setting while configuring Macster, you shouldn't need to change it.

SOCKS v4 Proxy check box   If your Mac connects to the Internet through a proxy server, select this check box and enter the address of the proxy server in the Address text box. As with the previous check box, if you set this option correctly while configuring Macster, you shouldn't need to change it (unless your proxy server changes).

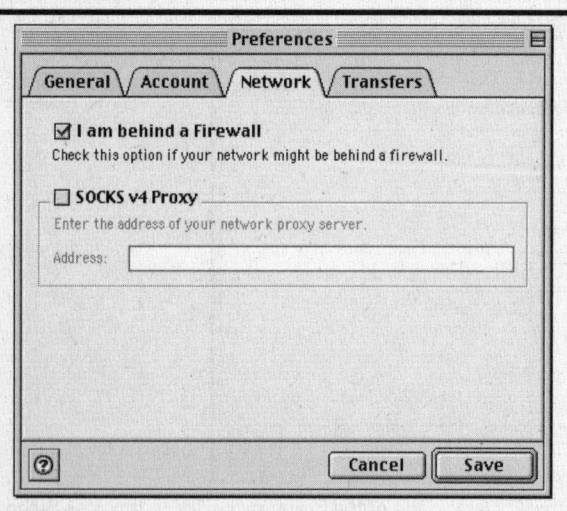

FIGURE 5.40:   If necessary, specify firewall and proxy settings on the Network page of the Preferences dialog box.

Transfers Page Preferences

The Transfers page of the Preferences dialog box (shown in Figure 5.41) contains the following options:

Max Simultaneous Downloads drop-down list Use this drop-down list to specify the largest number of files that you want Macster to download at once. The default setting is 1, which works well for modem connections but which you'll want to increase if you have a broadband connection. Macster offers settings from 1 to 10 files and a No Limit setting that's best kept for very fast connections.

Choose a Download Folder button Use this button and the resulting Choose a Folder dialog box to specify the folder in which you want Macster to store downloaded files.

Allow Sharing check box This check box controls whether Macster shares any files on your computer. *Select this check box only if you have files that you have the right to distribute.*

Max Simultaneous Uploads drop-down list If you're sharing files, use this drop-down list to specify the maximum number of files that Macster should try to upload at once. If you have a modem connection, keep the default setting, 1, so that your computer uploads files at a decent clip. If you have a broadband connection, specify a higher number. As with the Max Simultaneous Downloads drop-down list, Macster offers upload settings from 1 to 10 files and a No Limit setting that's best kept for very fast connections.

Choose a Folder to Share button If you're sharing files, use this button and the resulting Choose a Folder dialog box to specify the folder you want Macster to share with Napster users. By default, Macster shares your downloads folder, so you will almost certainly want to change this setting.

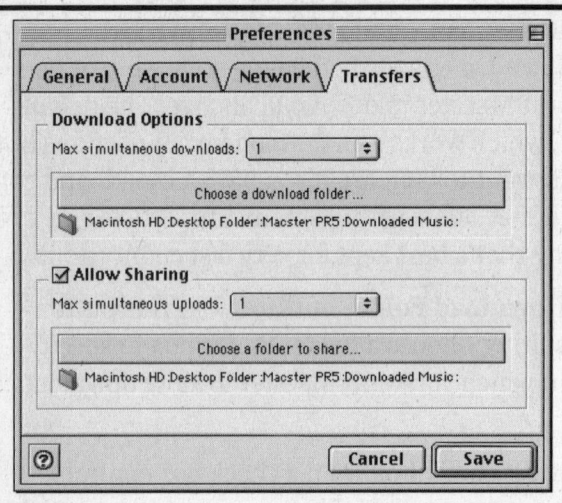

FIGURE 5.41: Choose downloading and file-sharing options on the Transfers page of the Preferences dialog box.

Finding and Downloading Music with Macster

To search for music with Macster, display the Music Search dialog box by clicking the Search for Music button on the Macster panel, pressing Apple+F, or choosing Find ➤ Find Music. Figure 5.42 shows the Music Search dialog box with a search item entered.

Finding MP3 files Using Napster and Its Friends

FIGURE 5.42: Use the Music Search dialog box to find the music you're interested in.

Specify criteria for the search as necessary. If you want to specify a bitrate, frequency, or line speed, click the Show Extended Search arrow. Macster displays the hidden bottom section of the Music Search dialog box, shown in Figure 5.43.

FIGURE 5.43: The Music Search dialog box hides Macster's extended-search features until you click the Show Extended Search button.

Click the Search button to set the search running. Macster searches the Napster server and displays the results in the Search Results window, as shown in Figure 5.44. Here, we've sorted the results by the Ping column, putting the closest connections at the top of the list.

182   Chapter Five

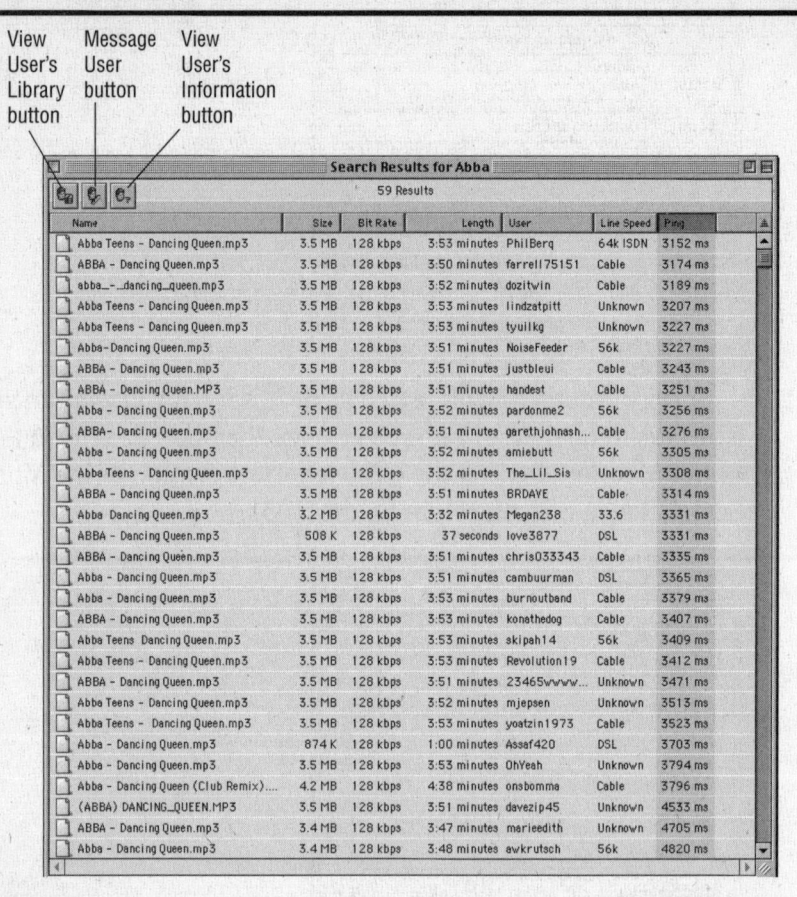

View User's Library button — **Message User button** — **View User's Information button**

Name	Size	Bit Rate	Length	User	Line Speed	Ping
Abba Teens - Dancing Queen.mp3	3.5 MB	128 kbps	3:53 minutes	PhilBerq	64k ISDN	3152 ms
ABBA - Dancing Queen.mp3	3.5 MB	128 kbps	3:50 minutes	farrell75151	Cable	3174 ms
abba_-_dancing_queen.mp3	3.5 MB	128 kbps	3:52 minutes	dozitvin	Cable	3189 ms
Abba Teens - Dancing Queen.mp3	3.5 MB	128 kbps	3:53 minutes	lindzatpitt	Unknown	3207 ms
Abba Teens - Dancing Queen.mp3	3.5 MB	128 kbps	3:53 minutes	tyuilkg	Unknown	3227 ms
Abba-Dancing Queen.mp3	3.5 MB	128 kbps	3:51 minutes	NoiseFeeder	56k	3227 ms
ABBA - Dancing Queen.mp3	3.5 MB	128 kbps	3:51 minutes	justbleui	Cable	3243 ms
ABBA - Dancing Queen.MP3	3.5 MB	128 kbps	3:51 minutes	handest	Cable	3251 ms
Abba - Dancing Queen.mp3	3.5 MB	128 kbps	3:52 minutes	pardonme2	56k	3256 ms
ABBA- Dancing Queen.mp3	3.5 MB	128 kbps	3:51 minutes	garethjohnash...	Cable	3276 ms
Abba - Dancing Queen.mp3	3.5 MB	128 kbps	3:52 minutes	amiebutt	56k	3305 ms
Abba Teens - Dancing Queen.mp3	3.5 MB	128 kbps	3:52 minutes	The_Lil_Sis	Unknown	3308 ms
ABBA - Dancing Queen.mp3	3.5 MB	128 kbps	3:51 minutes	BRDAYE	Cable	3314 ms
Abba Dancing Queen.mp3	3.2 MB	128 kbps	3:32 minutes	Megan238	33.6	3331 ms
ABBA - Dancing Queen.mp3	508 K	128 kbps	37 seconds	love3877	DSL	3331 ms
ABBA - Dancing Queen.mp3	3.5 MB	128 kbps	3:51 minutes	chris033343	Cable	3335 ms
Abba - Dancing Queen.mp3	3.5 MB	128 kbps	3:51 minutes	cambuurman	DSL	3365 ms
Abba - Dancing Queen.mp3	3.5 MB	128 kbps	3:53 minutes	burnoutband	Cable	3379 ms
ABBA - Dancing Queen.mp3	3.5 MB	128 kbps	3:53 minutes	konathedog	Cable	3407 ms
Abba Teens Dancing Queen.mp3	3.5 MB	128 kbps	3:53 minutes	skipah14	56k	3409 ms
Abba Teens - Dancing Queen.mp3	3.5 MB	128 kbps	3:53 minutes	Revolution19	Cable	3412 ms
ABBA - Dancing Queen.mp3	3.5 MB	128 kbps	3:51 minutes	23465vwww...	Unknown	3471 ms
Abba Teens - Dancing Queen.mp3	3.5 MB	128 kbps	3:52 minutes	mjepsen	Unknown	3513 ms
Abba Teens - Dancing Queen.mp3	3.5 MB	128 kbps	3:53 minutes	yoatzin1973	Cable	3523 ms
Abba - Dancing Queen.mp3	874 K	128 kbps	1:00 minutes	Assaf420	DSL	3703 ms
Abba - Dancing Queen.mp3	3.5 MB	128 kbps	3:53 minutes	OhYeah	Unknown	3794 ms
Abba - Dancing Queen (Club Remix)....	4.2 MB	128 kbps	4:38 minutes	onsbomma	Cable	3796 ms
(ABBA) DANCING_QUEEN.MP3	3.5 MB	128 kbps	3:51 minutes	davezip45	Unknown	4533 ms
ABBA - Dancing Queen.mp3	3.4 MB	128 kbps	3:47 minutes	marieedith	Unknown	4705 ms
Abba - Dancing Queen.mp3	3.4 MB	128 kbps	3:48 minutes	awkrutsch	56k	4820 ms

FIGURE 5.44: You can sort the results in the Search Results window by any of its columns by clicking the column heading.

> **TIP**
>
> If you don't find the track you're looking for, try disconnecting from your current Napster server and connecting to another server. The easiest way to do this is to double-click the Connect/Disconnect button on the Macster toolbar. The first click disconnects you from the current server, and the second click requests a new connection. But you can also press Apple+D (or choose File ➤ Disconnect) to disconnect, and press Apple+K (or choose File ➤ Connect) to reconnect.

Finding MP3 files Using Napster and Its Friends 183

To download a track, double-click it. (Alternatively, Shift+click to select multiple tracks, and then press the Return key.) Macster displays the Transfer Manager dialog box (shown in Figure 5.45) listing the downloads, the progress, the file size, the download speed, and the time remaining.

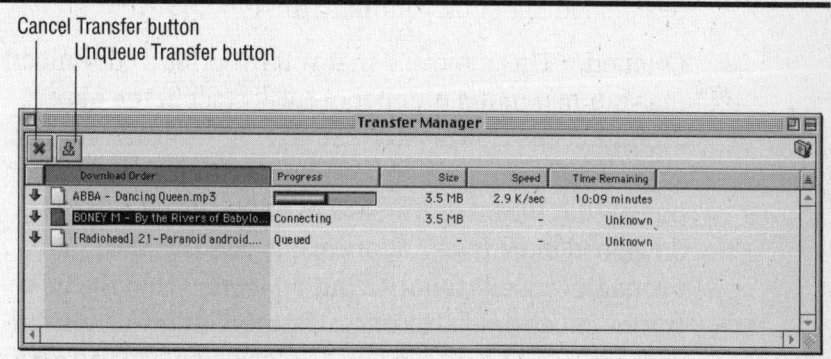

Cancel Transfer button
Unqueue Transfer button

Download Order	Progress	Size	Speed	Time Remaining
ABBA - Dancing Queen.mp3		3.5 MB	2.9 K/sec	10:09 minutes
BONEY M - By the Rivers of Babylo...	Connecting	3.5 MB	-	Unknown
[Radiohead] 21 - Paranoid android...	Queued	-	-	Unknown

FIGURE 5.45: The Transfer Manager dialog box lists your downloads and shows their progress.

When you're downloading tracks, Macster displays status information in the Progress column. These are the terms used and their meanings:

Waiting for Info This status means that Macster is getting information from the Napster server about the host offering the file for download.

Connecting This status means that Macster is contacting the host, offering the file for download. If there's a problem with transferring the file, the transfer may get stuck at the Waiting Connection stage, in which case you can either cancel it manually or wait for it to time out.

Waiting Connection This status means that Macster is trying to establish a connection with the host offering the file.

Timed Out   This status indicates that Macster has given up on trying to get a response from a host. Macster then moves on to the next download that you have queued.

File Complete   This indicates that Macster has finished downloading the file from the host and has saved it to the designated folder on your hard drive.

Queued   This indicates that you're currently downloading your maximum number of tracks (set in the Max Simultaneous Downloads text box on the Transfers page of the Preferences dialog box), so the track is waiting for one of the current downloads to finish. If you want to download more tracks at once, increase the Max Simultaneous Downloads number, but remember that the more tracks you download at once, the more thinly your bandwidth is spread, and the longer each download will take.

Remotely Queued   This indicates that the host is currently uploading its maximum number of tracks to you and other Napster users (as set in their Max Simultaneous Uploads text box on the Transfers page of the Preferences dialog box), so the track is waiting for one of those uploads to finish.

Failed   This typically indicates that the download has failed, either because of firewalling problems, because the host has deliberately canceled the download, or because the host has gone offline.

The progress bar appears when a download is running and shows you the progress of the download.

To kill a download, select it in the list and click the Cancel Transfer button. Macster removes it from the list in the Transfer Manager window.

To force a queued download to start right away, select it and click the Unqueue Transfer button. Forcing a download like this overrides the Max Simultaneous Downloads setting.

Browsing a User's Library

As does Napster, Macster lets you browse another user's library to find files that interest you. To browse a user's library, select the user in the Search Results window and click the View User's Library button. Figure 5.46 shows an example of browsing a library.

As in the Search Results window, you can double-click a file to download it. Click the Message User button to start an instant message to the user, or click the View User's Information button to view information about the user.

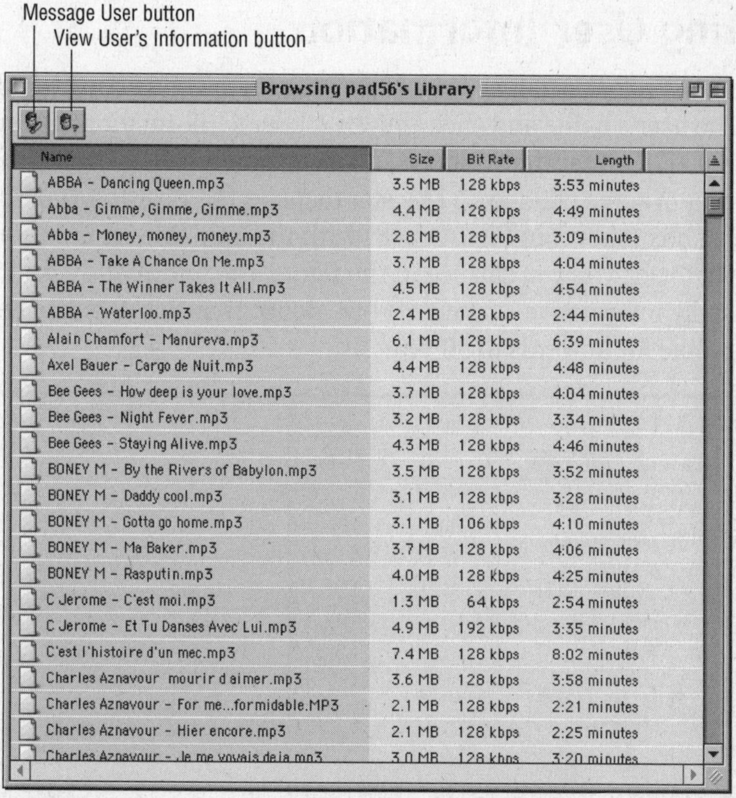

Message User button
View User's Information button

Name	Size	Bit Rate	Length
ABBA - Dancing Queen.mp3	3.5 MB	128 kbps	3:53 minutes
Abba - Gimme, Gimme, Gimme.mp3	4.4 MB	128 kbps	4:49 minutes
Abba - Money, money, money.mp3	2.8 MB	128 kbps	3:09 minutes
ABBA - Take A Chance On Me.mp3	3.7 MB	128 kbps	4:04 minutes
ABBA - The Winner Takes It All.mp3	4.5 MB	128 kbps	4:54 minutes
ABBA - Waterloo.mp3	2.4 MB	128 kbps	2:44 minutes
Alain Chamfort - Manureva.mp3	6.1 MB	128 kbps	6:39 minutes
Axel Bauer - Cargo de Nuit.mp3	4.4 MB	128 kbps	4:48 minutes
Bee Gees - How deep is your love.mp3	3.7 MB	128 kbps	4:04 minutes
Bee Gees - Night Fever.mp3	3.2 MB	128 kbps	3:34 minutes
Bee Gees - Staying Alive.mp3	4.3 MB	128 kbps	4:46 minutes
BONEY M - By the Rivers of Babylon.mp3	3.5 MB	128 kbps	3:52 minutes
BONEY M - Daddy cool.mp3	3.1 MB	128 kbps	3:28 minutes
BONEY M - Gotta go home.mp3	3.1 MB	106 kbps	4:10 minutes
BONEY M - Ma Baker.mp3	3.7 MB	128 kbps	4:06 minutes
BONEY M - Rasputin.mp3	4.0 MB	128 kbps	4:25 minutes
C Jerome - C'est moi.mp3	1.3 MB	64 kbps	2:54 minutes
C Jerome - Et Tu Danses Avec Lui.mp3	4.9 MB	192 kbps	3:35 minutes
C'est l'histoire d'un mec.mp3	7.4 MB	128 kbps	8:02 minutes
Charles Aznavour mourir d aimer.mp3	3.6 MB	128 kbps	3:58 minutes
Charles Aznavour - For me...formidable.MP3	2.1 MB	128 kbps	2:21 minutes
Charles Aznavour - Hier encore.mp3	2.1 MB	128 kbps	2:25 minutes
Charles Aznavour - Je me voyais deja.mp3	3.0 MB	128 kbps	3:20 minutes

FIGURE 5.46: Macster lets you browse another user's library.

If both your computer and the computer you're trying to access are firewalled, you'll see the error message box shown in Figure 5.47.

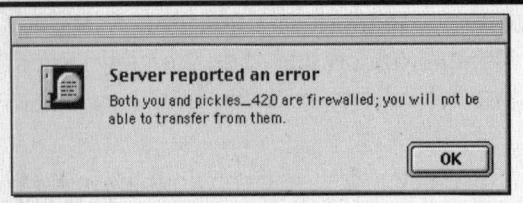

Server reported an error
Both you and pickles_420 are firewalled; you will not be able to transfer from them.

FIGURE 5.47: Macster warns you if it's not able to transfer files from the user you're interested in.

Getting User Information

To get information about a Napster user, select a listing that has the user's name and click the View User's Information button in one of the Macster windows. (This button is called User's Information in some windows.) Macster displays the User Information dialog box (shown in Figure 5.48) with the available information on that user. (As you can see in the figure, the information isn't necessarily informative or accurate—we doubt that this user has been online for upwards of 30 years.)

User Information

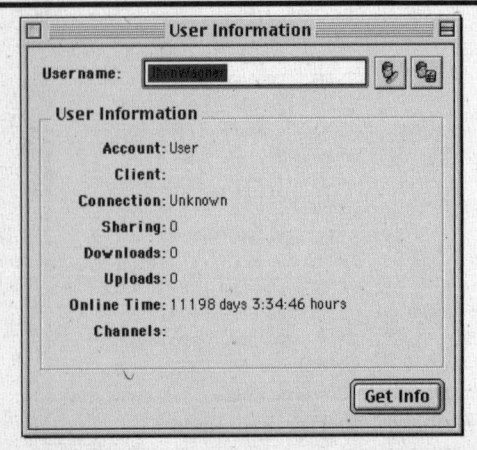

Username:

User Information
Account: User
Client:
Connection: Unknown
Sharing: 0
Downloads: 0
Uploads: 0
Online Time: 11198 days 3:34:46 hours
Channels:

Get Info

FIGURE 5.48: The User Information dialog box does its best to give you information about a selected user.

Once you have the User Information dialog box open, you can get information about another user by typing the user's name in the Username text box and clicking the Get Info button. (This technique is useful for finding out information about a user who's not currently listed in one of the Macster windows.)

Sending a Message to a User

Macster supports instant messaging between users. To send a message to a user listed in one of the Macster Windows, click the Message User button in that window. Macster displays the Private Message To dialog box (shown in Figure 5.49). Enter the message in the text box and click the Send button to send it.

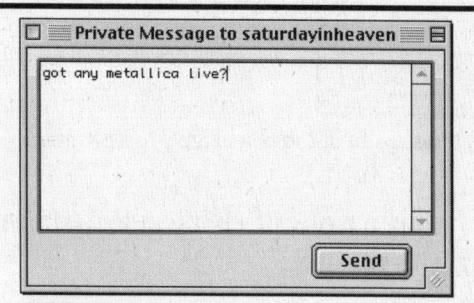

FIGURE 5.49: Use the Private Message To dialog box to send a private message to another Napster user.

When someone sends you a message (or a reply), Macster displays it in the Incoming Message From dialog box (shown in Figure 5.50).

FIGURE 5.50: When you receive a message, Macster displays the Incoming Message From dialog box.

If you don't want to reply, click the Dismiss button to dismiss the Incoming Message From window. To reply to the message, click the Reply button. Macster displays the Reply Message To dialog box (shown in Figure 5.51).

FIGURE 5.51: Use the Reply Message To dialog box to reply to a private message.

Click the Chat button to open a private chat window (shown in Figure 5.52) for chatting with the user.

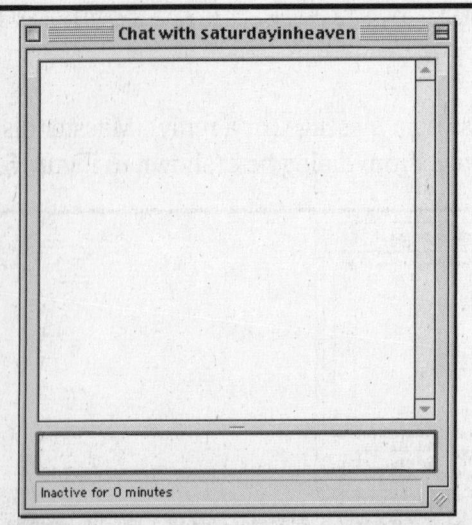

FIGURE 5.52: To take your relationship to the next stage, open a private chat window.

Chatting with Macster

Like Napster, Macster provides a full-fledged implementation of chat. Not only can you join any of the channels that already exist on the Napster server to which you're connected, but you can also create new chat channels of your own.

To join a chat channel, click the Chat button on the Macster toolbar and choose Join from the resulting drop-down menu. Macster displays the Select a Channel dialog box (shown in Figure 5.53), taking a moment to download the latest list of chat channels from the Napster server that you're currently connected to.

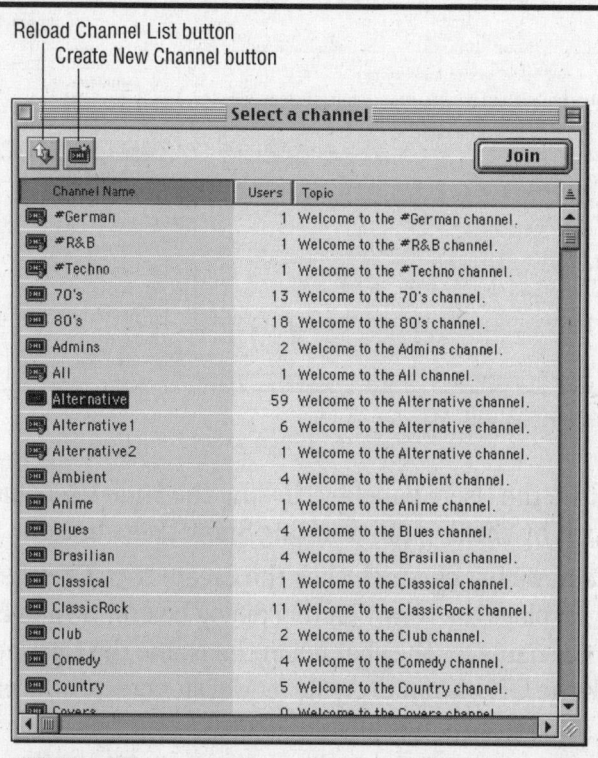

FIGURE 5.53: Use the Select a Channel dialog box to choose the chat channel that you want to join.

If you've had the chat channel open for a while, or if you want to get a listing for new channels that users have created, click the Reload Channel List button to refresh the list of channels.

To join a channel, select it in the list box and click the Join button. Macster displays the chat window for the channel you chose (shown in Figure 5.54).

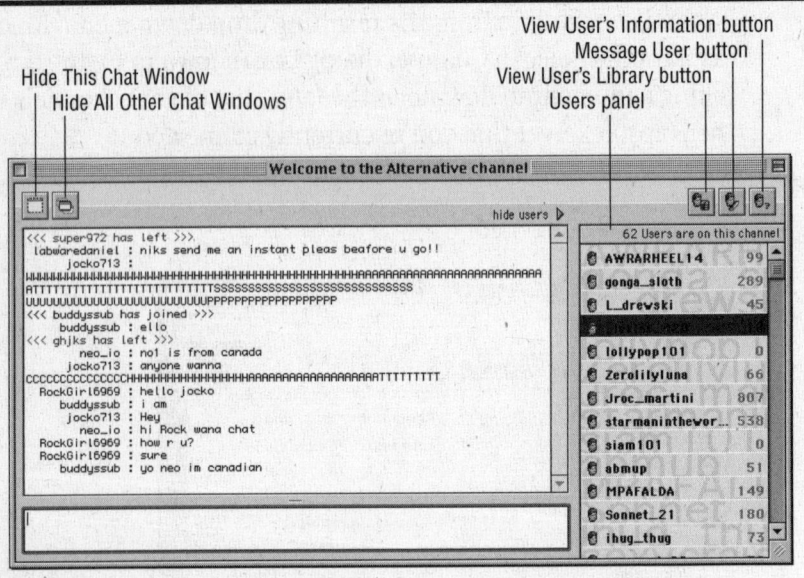

FIGURE 5.54: Chatting with Macster

You can close the Users panel by clicking the Hide Users button, and redisplay it by clicking the resulting Show Users button.

To create a new chat channel, click the Create New Channel button. Macster displays the New Channel dialog box (shown in Figure 5.55). Enter the name for the channel in the Name the Channel text box and click the OK button to create it. Macster creates the chat channel and joins it automatically.

FIGURE 5.55: You can create new chat channels by using the New Channel dialog box.

Using Napster on Linux

At this writing, there are multiple Linux versions of Napster being developed, including gnap, Gnapster, GNOME-Napster, and knapster. Gnapster, gnap, and GNOME-Napster are for the GNOME environment, and knapster is for the KDE environment.

In this section, we'll discuss Gnapster briefly. We'll expect you to have read the general sections earlier in this chapter, so that you know what Napster is and what it does.

Gnapster is a relatively full implementation of Napster for the GNOME desktop. It supports most of the "regular" Napster features, including searching for tracks, downloading and uploading them, and chatting with other users. Gnapster doesn't support a hot list as such, but it lets you easily browse another user's files—which, as you'll see, can be more useful than a hot list. What's more, you can create and use multiple accounts on Gnapster.

At this writing, Gnapster does not show you the ping time or frequency when you search. Because most people rip music from CD-quality sources—44.1kHz—the frequency isn't usually a big issue. But not seeing the ping time to hosts means that you won't be able to tell which hosts are close and which are far—so you may get slower downloads than you'd like.

gnap is currently in what the developer terms "pre-alpha private release," with the annotation "Do not use it unless you are a developer. All it does is crash!" We won't discuss it here but if you're reading this in Fall 2000 or later, you might want to look up gnap and see how it's doing. The current URL is gnap.sourceforge.net. If that link has gone south, look for a link from the Napster FAQ (currently faq.napster.com).

GNOME-Napster, on the other hand, is well under way, and bears investigation at this writing. Knapster is currently in beta, but it looks promising.

Using Gnapster

In this section, we'll run through the key points of Gnapster, one of the implementations of Napster for GNOME.

Getting, Installing, and Configuring Gnapster

Download the latest version of Gnapster from www.faradic.net/~jasta/Gnapster.html. Get either the source (if you feel like compiling the application or you need to compile it) or a suitable distribution package for the version of Linux you're using. Then install Gnapster using the standard installation procedure for the version of Linux you're running.

The first time you run Gnapster, it automatically displays the Gnapster Properties dialog box. Figure 5.56 shows the User Information page of this dialog box.

Enter your username and password in the text boxes. If this is a new account, select the New Account check box. If you're transferring an existing account to Gnapster, make sure this check box is cleared.

In the Data Port text box, leave the default setting, 6699, alone unless you know you need to use a different data port. If your computer is behind a firewall and cannot accept inbound connections, select the Firewalled Without the Ability to Accept Connections check box.

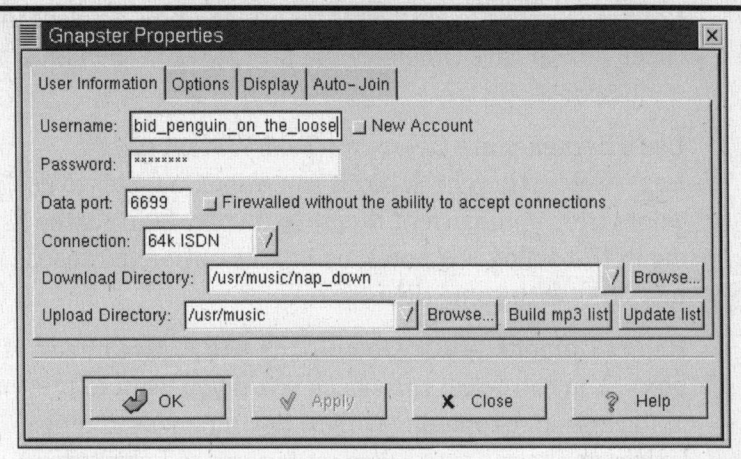

Finding MP3 files Using Napster and Its Friends

FIGURE 5.56: Enter your user information on the User Information page of the Gnapster Properties dialog box.

In the Connection drop-down list, select the connection speed you want to have listed. Remember that this setting doesn't affect the speed of your connection, just the speed that is reported to other users.

Specify your download directory in the Download Directory text box and your upload directory in the Upload Directory text box, and then click the Build MP3 List button to have Gnapster create a list of the MP3 files in your upload directory.

On the Options page of the Gnapster Properties dialog box (shown in Figure 5.57), make your choices for the following options:

Auto-Query a User Upon Incoming Message check box Select this check box to have Naptster automatically finger a user with whom you receive a message. If you find yourself checking the information for people who contact you, this option can prove useful.

Convert Spaces to Underscores? check box Select this check box to have Gnapster change spaces in filenames to underscores.

Use Themes State Colors for Text Widget check box Select this check box if you want Gnapster to use colors from your current theme to display text. As the listing in the dialog box notes, using this option may cause problems with some themes.

Reject Uploads While Downloads Are Active check box You can select this check box if you want to prevent uploads from happening while a download is running. Unless you're running a very underpowered computer with a high-bandwidth connection, uploading and downloading at the same time should not be a problem.

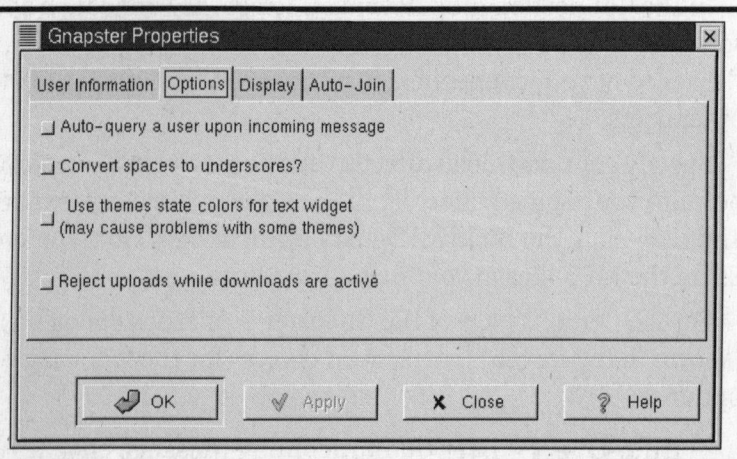

FIGURE 5.57: Choose options on the Options page of the Gnapster Properties dialog box.

On the Display page of the Gnapster Properties dialog box (shown in Figure 5.58), you can specify the font you want Gnapster to use. You will need to restart Gnapster to apply the new font.

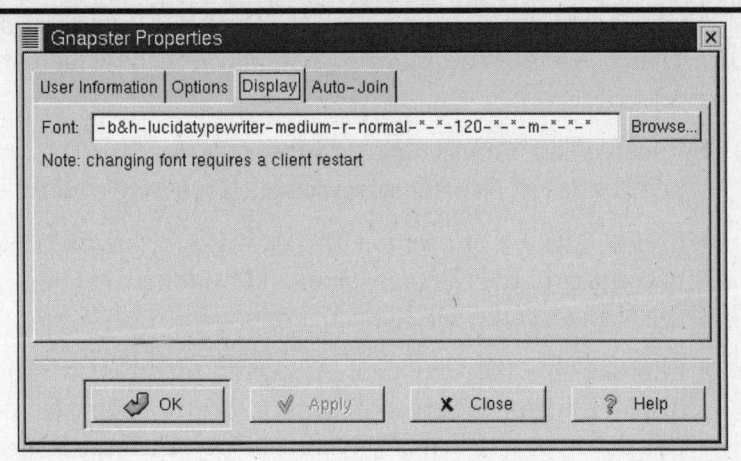

Finding MP3 files Using Napster and Its Friends   195

FIGURE 5.58: The Display page of the Gnapster Properties dialog box

On the Auto-Join page of the Gnapster Properties dialog box (shown in Figure 5.59), you can specify the channels you want to join automatically when you connect to a Napster server.

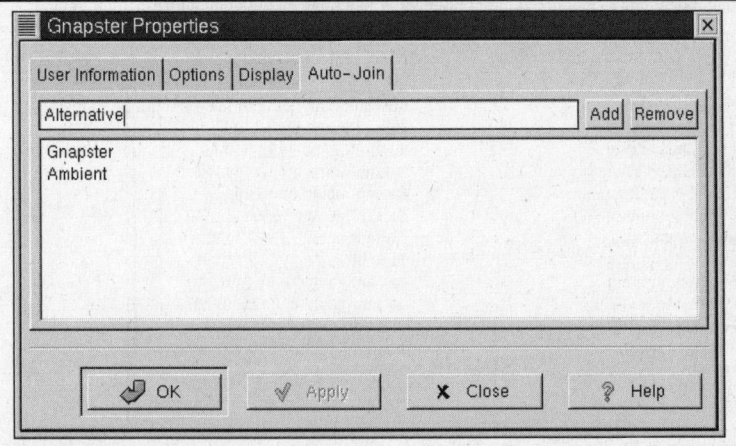

FIGURE 5.59: On the Auto-Join page of the Gnapster Properties dialog box, specify the channels you want to join automatically.

Chapter Five

Apply your preferences and close the Gnapster Properties dialog box. Then use one of the following options on the File menu to connect to a server:

- ▶ Choose File ➢ Connect to Last Server (or press Ctrl+C) to connect to the last Napster server to which you were connected.

- ▶ Choose File ➢ Connect to Official Server (or press Ctrl+O) to connect to the Napster server and be doled out to one of the Napster servers in the usual way.

- ▶ Choose File ➢ Browse OpenNAP Servers (or press Ctrl+B) to display the Browse Servers dialog box. When you first display this dialog box, its list of servers is empty. Click the Refresh List button to download an up-to-date list of the OpenNAP servers available. (Gnapster downloads this list from the Napigator Web site.) Figure 5.60 shows the Browse Servers dialog box with the latest list of servers loaded.

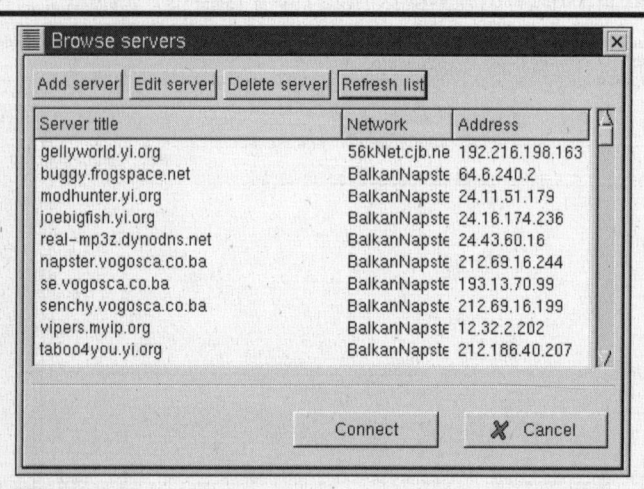

FIGURE 5.60: Use the Browse Servers dialog box to identify the server you want to connect to.

To add a server to the list manually, click the Add Server button and use the Add Server dialog box (shown in Figure 5.61) to enter the IP address, port number, and description for the server.

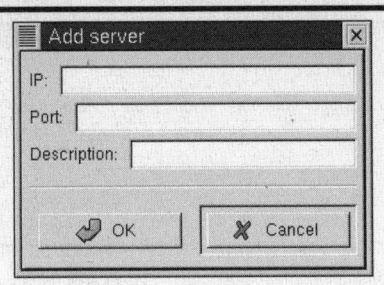

Finding MP3 files Using Napster and Its Friends 197

FIGURE 5.61: You can add a server to the Gnapster list manually by using the Add Server dialog box.

You can edit a server's entry by selecting it in the list box and clicking the Edit Server button, then working in the Edit Server dialog box (shown in Figure 5.62).

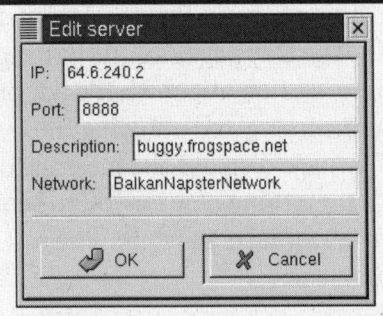

FIGURE 5.62: The Edit Server dialog box lets you edit a server entry in the Browse Servers list.

To connect to a server, select it in the list box and click the Connect button.

If you see the Error dialog box shown in Figure 5.63, you'll know that the username you created was already in use. Return to the User Information page of the Gnapster Properties dialog box and choose another. (If you already have the username registered to you, chances are you've entered your password incorrectly.)

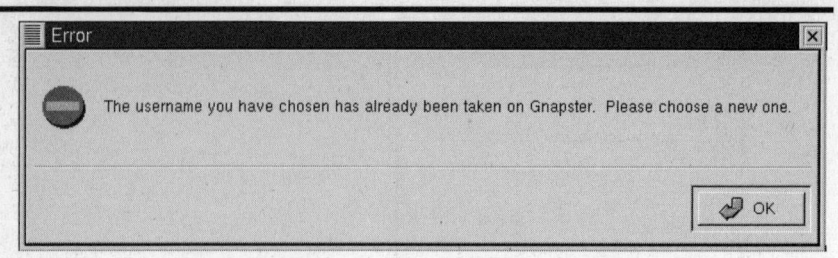

> Error
>
> The username you have chosen has already been taken on Gnapster. Please choose a new one.
>
> OK

FIGURE 5.63: If you see this Error dialog box, it means either that the new username you're trying to create has already been taken or that you entered your password incorrectly for your existing username.

Finding and Sharing Music with Gnapster

Like Napster, Gnapster uses a multipage interface that gives you quick access to its features, providing Search, Browse, Download, Upload, Console, and Message of the Day pages at this writing. The Console page displays textual information about what's happening in Gnapster, including chat and incoming and outgoing file requests. The Message of the Day page displays the message of the day from Napster. When there's something new for you to see on one of the pages, the text on its tab appears in white. The rest of the time, the tab text appears in black.

As usual, you can move from page to page by clicking the tabs on the pages. Alternatively, make sure the focus is on the tabs, then press the Tab key to highlight each tab in turn (from left to right) or Shift+Tab (from right to left), and then press the spacebar or the Enter key to display the page for the highlighted tab.

Figure 5.64 shows the Gnapster window.

> **NOTE**
>
> To disconnect from your current server, choose File ➢ Disconnect. You may want to disconnect and connect again in order to be assigned to a Napster server that has MP3 files you're looking for.

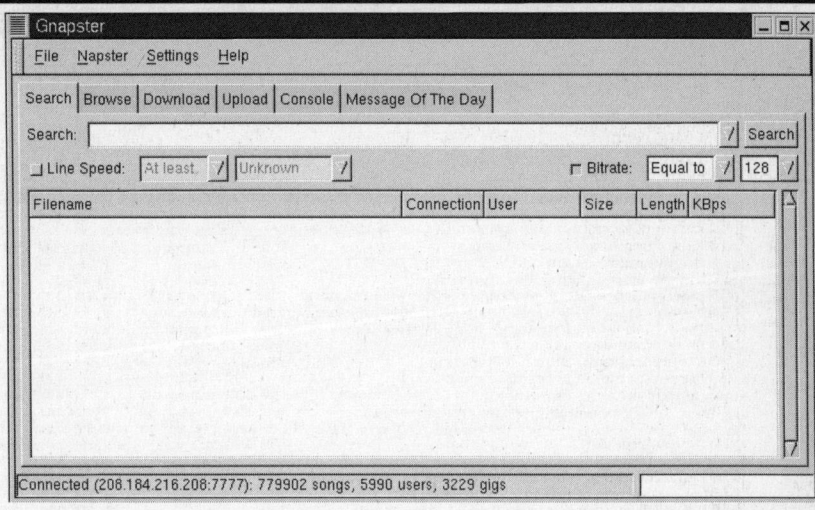

Finding MP3 files Using Napster and Its Friends 199

FIGURE 5.64: The Gnapster window uses a multipage interface much like Napster's.

Searching for MP3 Files

To search for MP3 files, you use Gnapster's Search page (shown in Figure 5.65 after a successful search). The process is very similar to the Napster process, with the following main differences:

- Instead of providing a text box for the artist's name and a text box for the track name, Gnapster provides only the Query text box. Enter the text that you want to search for—either the artist or the track name, or both, in any order you want.

- While the search is running, you'll see the indicator in the right-hand panel of the status bar moving to the left and right, and the word "Searching" appears at the left-hand end of the status bar. If the search is successful, the results are displayed.

200 **Chapter Five**

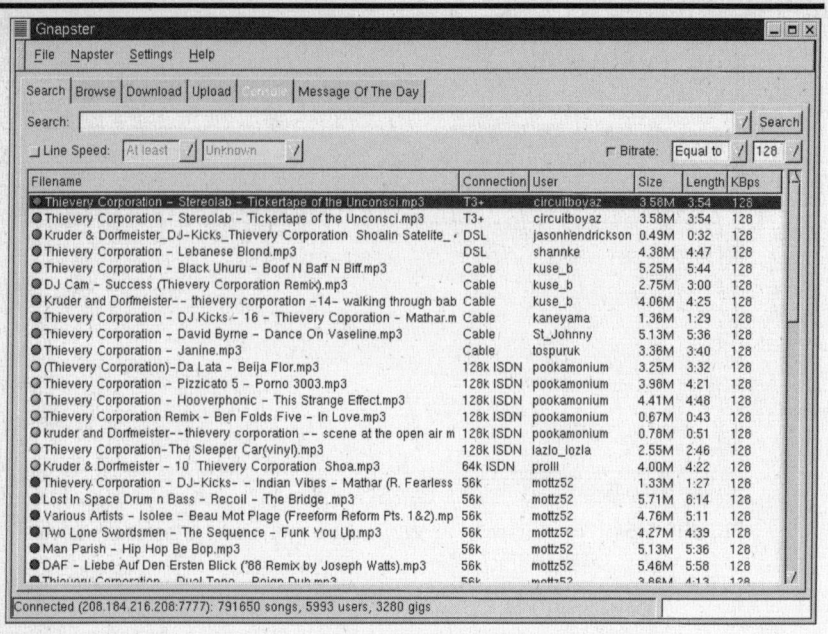

FIGURE 5.65: The Gnapster Search page after a successful search

Downloading MP3 Files

To download a track, double-click it on the Search page, or right-click it and choose Download from the context menu. Gnapster submits a download request to the host and, on getting a positive answer, begins the download. Unlike Napster, Gnapster doesn't automatically display the Download page when you submit a download request.

Once you've chosen to download one or more tracks, click the Download tab to display the Download page. Figure 5.66 shows the Download page with one track being downloaded, one being requested, one remotely queued, and several queued in the lower panel.

Finding MP3 files Using Napster and Its Friends

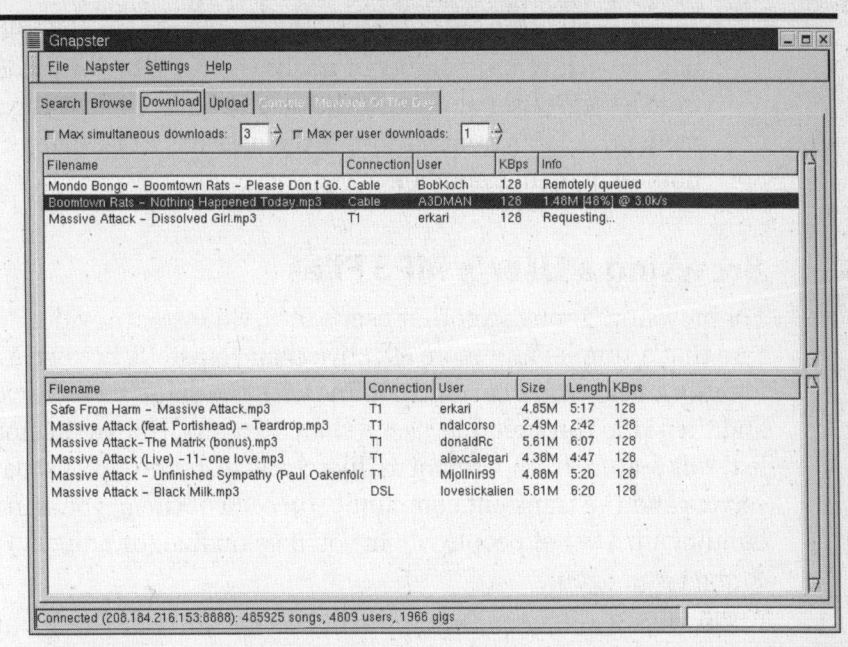

FIGURE 5.66: The Gnapster Download page with three tracks being downloaded

To cancel a download, right-click it on the Download page and choose Cancel Download from the context menu. To delete a download, right-click it and choose Cancel and Remove File from the context menu.

To keep your downloads running smoothly, choose appropriate settings for the Max Simultaneous Downloads and Max Per User Downloads features:

- ▶ Use the Max Simultaneous Downloads feature to make sure you're not trying to force too much data at once through your connection. Select the Max Simultaneous Downloads check box and enter in the text box the maximum number of tracks that you want to download at once. For a 56k modem connection, a number of 1–3 usually works best.

- ▶ Use the Max Per User Downloads feature to make sure you're not slowing your download speed by demanding too many files from a single user at the same time. Select the

Max Per User Downloads check box and enter in the text box the maximum number of tracks you want to download from a single user at once. If the user in question is using a modem, set this number to 1. If the user has a fast connection, set a higher number.

Browsing a User's MP3 Files

For browsing through another user's files, Gnapster provides a feature that's simpler and more effective than Napster's hot list. You identify a user who's currently online with the same server as you and then rifle through that user's shared folders. Unlike the hot list, this feature is impermanent, like the Napster group of separate servers and the transient community on each of them; you're not building up a list of people whom you'll be unable (or unlikely) to contact ever again.

The disadvantage to this approach is that you can check out only one user's shared folders at once—but this failing is easy to put up with.

To browse a user's shared library of MP3 files, right-click an entry for the user on the Search page or Download page and choose Browse User's MP3s from the context menu. You'll see the message "Retrieving MP3 List" in the status bar as Gnapster finds out which MP3 files the user is sharing. Click the Browse tab to display the Browse page, which displays a list of the user's shared MP3 files (shown in Figure 5.67). When something catches your fancy, you can download it or queue it as usual.

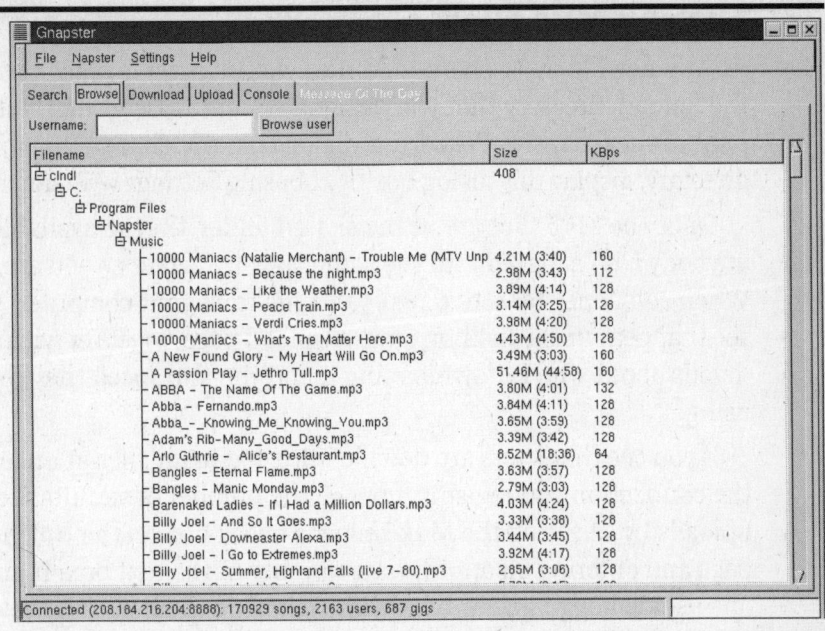

Finding MP3 files Using Napster and Its Friends

FIGURE 5.67: Gnapster lets you easily browse a list of the MP3 files that another user is sharing.

You can also browse a user's library by entering the user's name in the Username text box on the Browse page and clicking the Browse User button.

> **NOTE**
>
> If nothing happens when you try to browse a user's shared library, check the Console page. If you see the message "Error: Parameter is unparsable," it means that your request has gone off into the ether. Try someone else.

Getting Information on a User

To get information on a user, right-click a listing featuring the user on the Search page and choose Who is User from the context menu. Then switch to the Console page to view the result.

Sharing MP3 Files

All you need to do to share MP3 files via Gnapster is place them in the upload directory that you designated on the User Information page of the Gnapster Properties dialog box. (To change the upload directory, display this dialog box by choosing Settings ➢ Preferences.)

Once the MP3 files are in the shared folder, they're available to anybody who's logged into the same Napster server as you are. When someone starts to download a file from your computer, you'll see it appear in the list box on the Upload page, together with details about who is downloading it and the line speed they're using.

If you see that users are downloading too many files at once for the connection you're using, change the number of simultaneous uploads by selecting the Max Uploads check box on the Upload page and entering an appropriate number in the text box. If any one user is hogging your bandwidth, throttle them back by selecting the Max Per User Uploads check box and entering a modest figure (for example, 1) in the text box.

Chatting on Gnapster

Gnapster implements chat on its Console page via subpages.

To display a list of chat channels, choose Napster ➢ List Channels. Gnapster displays the Channel Listing dialog box (shown in Figure 5.68).

Finding MP3 files Using Napster and Its Friends

Channel	Users	Topic
70's	9	Welcome to the 70's channel.
80's	18	Welcome to the 80's channel.
Admins	2	Welcome to the Admins channel.
Alternative	73	Welcome to the Alternative channel.
Ambient	3	Welcome to the Ambient channel.
Anime	4	Welcome to the Anime channel.
Blues	3	Welcome to the Blues channel.
Brasilian	0	Welcome to the Brasilian channel.
ClassicRock	13	Welcome to the ClassicRock channel.
Classical	2	Welcome to the Classical channel.
Club	4	Welcome to the Club channel.

FIGURE 5.68: Use the Channel Listing dialog box to join chat channels.

To join a channel, select it and click the Join button. Gnapster adds a chat page for the channel, shown in Figure 5.69. You can then participate in the chat by typing into the text box at the bottom of the chat page and pressing the Enter key. To leave the chat channel, select it by clicking its tab, and then choose Napster ≻ Part Channel.

To chat with a user, choose Napster ≻ Query User. Napster inserts a query stub—/query—in the text box. Type the user's name and press the Enter key. Gnapster opens a private chat channel with the user, with its own tab for access.

To stop chatting with a user, select the tab for the private chat and choose Napster ≻ Unquery User.

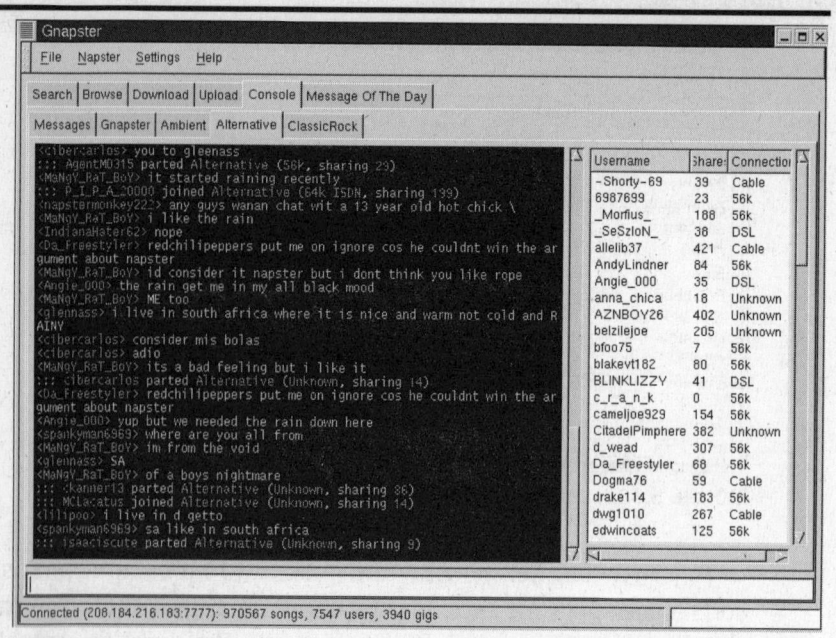

FIGURE 5.69: Chatting on Gnapster

You can also use text commands if you find them easier. Here are the basics:

- Use the /join or /j commands to join a channel. For example, the following commands join the Alternative channel:

    /join alternative
    /j alternative

- Use the /part command to leave a channel. For example, the following command leaves the Alternative channel:

    /part alternative

- Use the /msg or /m commands to send a private message to a user. For example, the following command sends the message "Are you in Houston?" to the user LiveHerald:

    /m LiveHerald Are you in Houston?

- Use the /raw command to send a message to everyone in the channel. For example, the following command sends the message "The Cleaners from Venus rule!" to everyone in the current channel:

```
/raw The Cleaners from Venus rule!
```

- Use the /whois command to display information about a user. For example, the following command displays information about the user voodoosweeney:

```
/whois voodoosweeney
```

A regular message shows up in the list box on the Console page preceded by the name of the user who sent it, enclosed in angle brackets. For example, a message from the user voodoosweeney would appear like this:

```
<voodoosweeney> Anyone got Metallica live MP3 files?
```

A private message shows up in the list box on the Console page preceded by the name of the user who sent it, a slash, and privmsg, enclosed in angle brackets. For example, a private message from voodoosweeney would appear like this:

```
<voodoosweeney/privmsg> Wanna meet?
```

Exiting Gnapster

To exit Gnapster, choose File ➤ Exit or press Ctrl+Q.

Using Wrapster

As you saw in the Napster section, Napster is built to share MP3 files—and only MP3 files. If you put other file types in the Napster folder, Napster simply ignores them.

If you want to transfer files other than MP3 files using Napster, you need to disguise the files as MP3 files. Wrapster is software that lets you do this disguising. It marks them as being encoded at a special bitrate (32kbps) and frequency (32kHz), so that you can search for them using Napster. You can put one file or multiple files in a Wrapster archive.

Download the latest version of Wrapster from the Wrapster Web site (at this writing, `notoctavian.tripod.com/`). Then double-click the Wrapster distribution file to start the setup routine. Choose the installation location and the Start menu folder as usual, and then launch Wrapster from the Start menu folder you specified.

To use Wrapster, create a new archive by choosing File ≻ New Archive or pressing Ctrl+N, specifying the name and location for the archive in the New Wrapster File dialog box, and clicking the Save button. Then, in the Wrapster window (shown in Figure 5.70 with an archive underway), you add files to the archive by choosing Actions ≻ Add Files (or pressing Ctrl+A) and using the resulting Open dialog box to specify the files. If you need to remove files, choose Actions ≻ Remove Files ≻ All (or press Ctrl+R) or Actions ≻ Remove Files ≻ Selected (Ctrl+Shift+R).

Then you put the archive in one of your shared Napster folders, and users logged in to the same Napster server as you can search for it. To find Wrapster files yourself, specify any relevant artist or song information, then set the bitrate to be equal to 32kbps and the frequency to be equal to 32kHz, and perform the search. When you find a file that interests you, download it as usual.

> **WARNING**
>
> **Wrapster files can contain *anything*, including executable files, viruses, and worms. Run a virus checker on any Wrapster files you download, both before and after you extract them.**

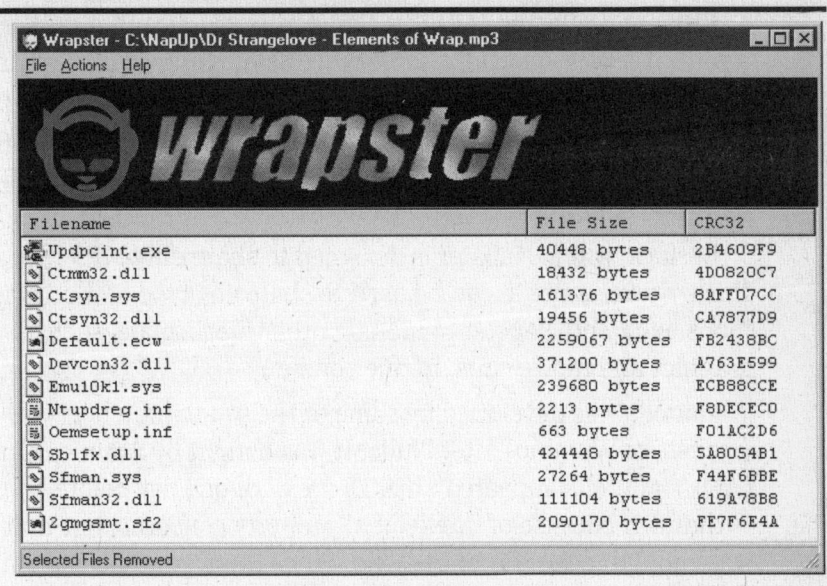

Finding MP3 files Using Napster and Its Friends 209

FIGURE 5.70: Wrapster lets you create archive files disguised as MP3 files and trade them via Napster.

To extract files from a Wrapster archive, choose Actions ➢ Extract Files ➢ All (or press Ctrl+E) or Actions ➢ Extract Files ➢ Selected (Ctrl+Shift+E). Wrapster displays the Browse for Folder dialog box. Identify the target folder and click the OK button, and Wrapster extracts the file or files.

To exit Wrapster, choose File ➢ Exit or press Ctrl+X or Alt+F4.

USING GNUTELLA

As we've mentioned, Napster is being sued by the RIAA and Metallica for encouraging copyright infringement. In the Napster setup, users log in to the individual Napster servers, which are coordinated by the master server, and can then share files directly with each other. The centralization provides an easy and effective target for the lawsuit: Close down the Napster servers, and nobody will be able to trade MP3 files (or other files disguised as MP3 files) via Napster.

Enter gnutella. gnutella is a Napster-like service that doesn't use a central server. Instead, people who install gnutella can establish their own connections to one another, setting up and tearing down virtual networks at will. This makes gnutella more resilient—more Internet-like, you might say—and as a result, harder to target and harder to shut down than Napster.

Besides, where Napster is designed to share only MP3 files at this writing, gnutella can be used to share any type of file. (Napster plans to extend Napster to include other file formats, such as graphics and movie clips, in due course.)

gnutella was developed by some of the programmers at Nullsoft (makers of Winamp) after Nullsoft was bought by America Online (AOL). gnutella appeared on AOL for all of one day before being withdrawn because of intellectual-property concerns, but that day was enough to get it into the wild. Since then, gnutella versions have been developed by a loose army of volunteers.

You can download gnutella from a number of Web sites, including `gnutella.wego.com`. Double-click the distribution file to start the Setup routine, which features Winamp-style llamas in the Installation Options dialog box (shown in Figure 5.71).

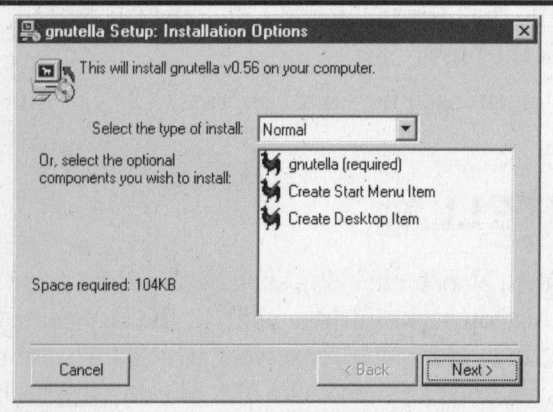

FIGURE 5.71: Choose installation options for gnutella in the gnutella Setup: Installation Options dialog box.

Finding MP3 files Using Napster and Its Friends 211

> **NOTE**
>
> At this writing, gnutella is in an early beta, so be aware that it may well have changed by the time you read this.

After the Setup routine finishes, you'll see the gnutella window, shown in Figure 5.72. The gnutella interface is a little inscrutable at first, but you'll get used to it quickly. The list box in the upper-left portion of the screen toggles you between the different pages of the gnutella interface: gnutellaNet, Uploads, Downloads, Search, Monitor, and Config (at this writing).

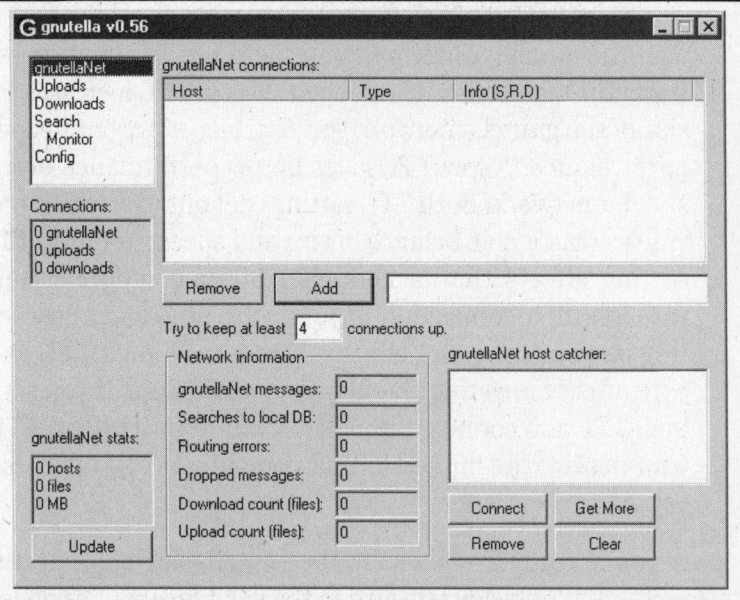

FIGURE 5.72: The gnutella window without anything happening yet

Once you've installed gnutella, display the Config page (shown in Figure 5.73) by clicking the Config entry in the upper-left list box, and adjust your configuration as necessary:

▶ Set your download directory on the Save New Files To button.

- Set your shared directories in the Path(s) to Files text box, and then click the Rescan button to force gnutella to read the files in each directory.

- If necessary, change the long default list of file extensions to be searched for in the Search Extensions text box. If you change the list, make sure you follow the proper format—no periods, and semicolons to separate the entries.

- The Listen port is the logical connection through which gnutella communicates. Don't change your Listen port from the default setting of 6346 unless you're sure of what you're doing.

- The gnutellaNet TTL Settings text boxes control the *time to live*—the number of computers a packet of information can travel through before it is stopped. A high TTL increases the size of the gnutella network you're attached to, but it slows performance. A low TTL gives better performance over a smaller network. Both TTL settings default to 7, which provides a reasonable balance of size and speed. Your My TTL setting affects the packets that other computers send through their connection to your computer, and a low setting on your computer effectively reduces a high TTL on a computer connecting through yours. Likewise, if you set a high TTL and connect through a computer with a low TTL, your packets are limited to that computer's TTL once they get to that computer.

Now you're ready to connect to the gnutellaNet by connecting to a computer that's already attached to the net. Once you're connected to that computer, you're connected to the rest of the network through it, and gnutella can search recursively through the network, starting with the network to which your computer is connected.

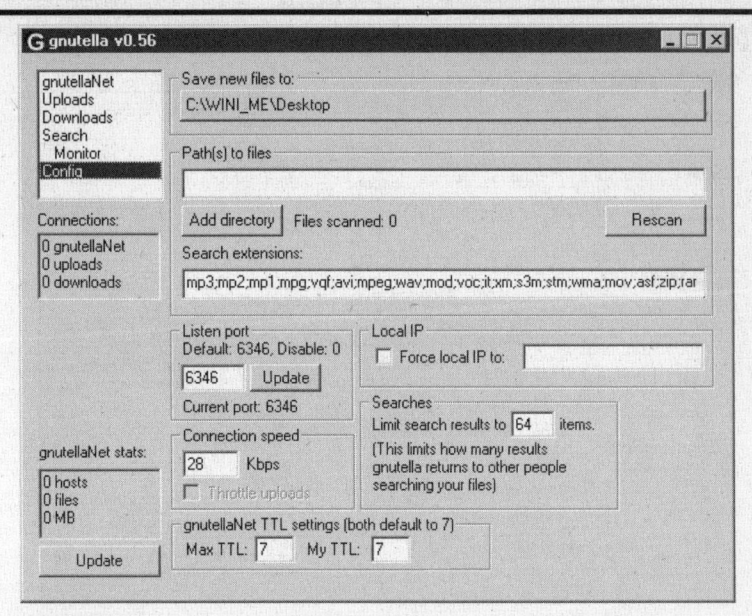

Finding MP3 files Using Napster and Its Friends   213

FIGURE 5.73: Set your configuration information on the Config page.

To connect to a computer on gnutellaNet, you need to know its IP address. If you can't hit up a friend who's currently on gnutellaNet, one of the best ways to find a current IP address is by checking the #gnutella group on the EFNet channels on IRC. (If you don't know how to do this, follow the tutorial at gnutella.wego.com. This tutorial recommends the mIRC client, which we've found works well.) This group usually shows a current IP address in its topic and often evicts people who fail to notice it and ask for an IP address.

Enter the IP address in the text box to the right of the Add button on the gnutellaNet page of the gnutella interface and click the Add button. If you're lucky, you'll get connected, as shown in Figure 5.74, in which two connections are connected and two are trying to connect. If you look in the gnutellaNet Connections text box, you can see that three of the connections use the default port for gnutella, 6346.

Chapter Five

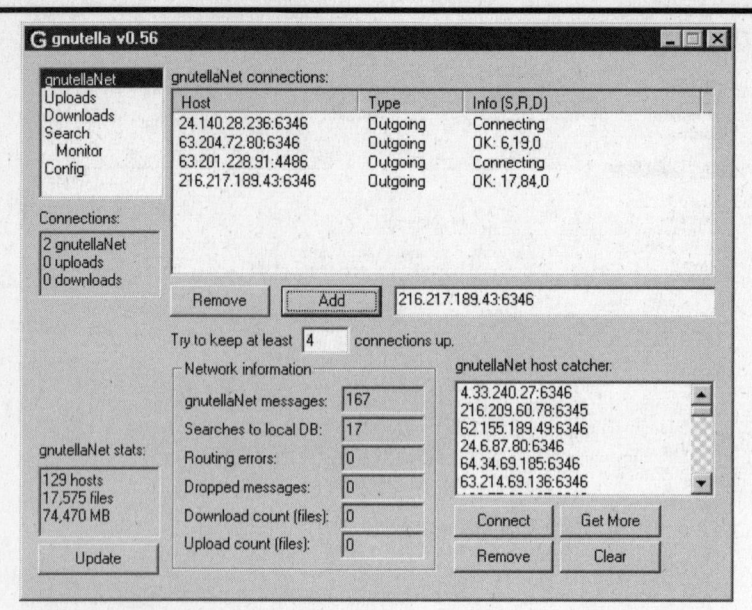

FIGURE 5.74: gnutella with two outgoing connections up and two trying to connect.

You can add further connections from the gnutellaNet Host Catcher text box—click a connection and click the Connect button. You can also add further connections as necessary by using the Add button. You can remove current connections by selecting them in the gnutellaNet Connections list box and clicking the Remove button.

Searching via gnutella is easy. Click the Search entry in the list box in the upper-left corner to display the Search page. Enter your search terms in the text box at the top, specify a minimum connection speed in the Minimum Connection Speed text box if necessary, and click the Search button. gnutella canvasses the assembled hosts it can take a while, so be patient—and return—any results. Figure 5.75 shows the result of a modestly successful search: one result.

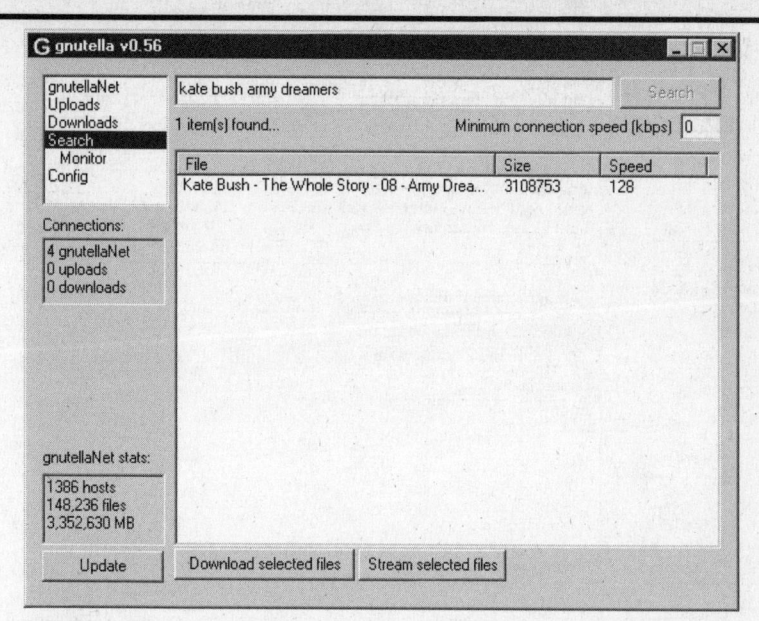

Finding MP3 files Using Napster and Its Friends 215

FIGURE 5.75: gnutella's Search page with the result of a successful search.

If gnutella has found one or more files you want to download, select them and click the Download Selected Files button. They appear on the Downloads page (shown in Figure 5.76), which shows you the progress of each download. If you have a fast connection, you may want to increase the number in the Maximum Simultaneous Downloads text box from its default of 4 until you're downloading from enough hosts to use most of your available bandwidth. Downloads beyond this number are queued in the Download Queue list box.

To stream the files (in sequence, not in parallel), click the Stream Selected Files button.

Select the Auto Clear Completed Downloads check box if you want gnutella to remove entries from the Downloads list when their files have been downloaded.

To cancel a download, select it and click the Abort Selected button.

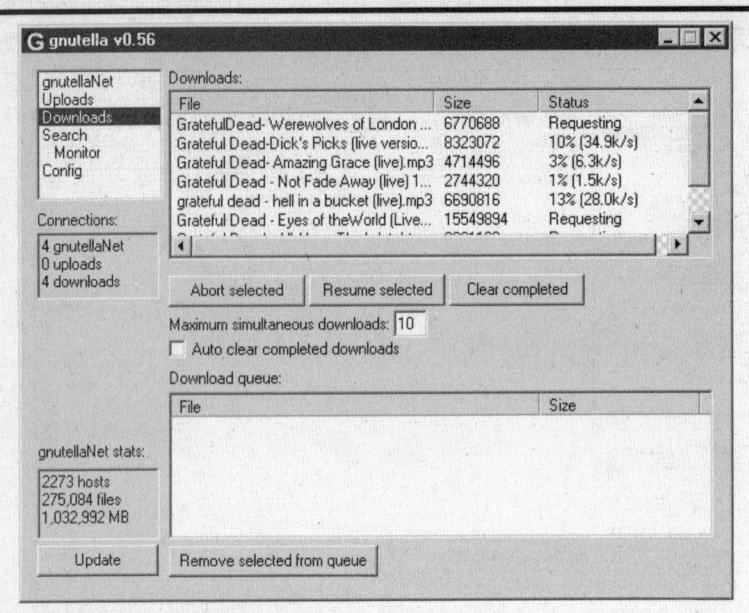

FIGURE 5.76: gnutella's Downloads page shows you the progress of your downloads.

The Uploads page shows you the files being uploaded from your computer, together with the host getting them and the status of the transfer. To prevent a transfer from occurring (or completing), select it and click the Kill Selected button. Use the Clear Completed button to clear the Uploads pane of transfers that have taken place. Select the Auto Clear Completed Uploads check box if you want gnutella to automatically remove transfers from the list once they're complete.

To close gnutella, click its Close button (the X button).

Using audioGnome

audioGnome is a post-Napster, user-to-user file-sharing technology designed at the time Napster seemed in imminent danger of being shut down. audioGnome was first released in July 2000. Should Napster be shut down, audioGnome would be unlikely to follow, because it doesn't use its own servers.

audioGnome lets you connect to multiple servers at once, which means that you can access a wide variety of files. At this writing, audioGnome is under extremely rapid development—so the version you look at is likely to be substantially different than the version described briefly in this section.

Installing audioGnome

Download the latest version of audioGnome from the Naphoria Web site (www.napster.org.uk) and install it by running the distribution executable file.

At this writing, the setup routine is unremarkable. You get to choose the destination folder and Start menu group to which you want to add audioGnome, and that's it.

The first time you run audioGnome, you have to agree to a license agreement in which you essentially agree not to do anything illegal with the software. After that, the Pick User Profile dialog box appears. Click the Add button to display the New Profile dialog box (shown in Figure 5.77).

218 Chapter Five

[New Profile dialog box image]

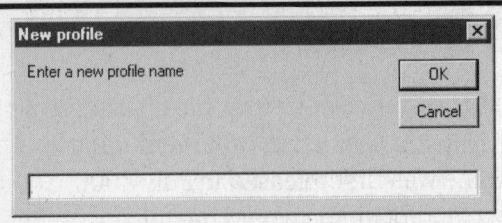

FIGURE 5.77: Use the New Profile dialog box to create a new user profile for yourself.

Enter the name for your profile in the text box and click the OK button. audioGnome creates the profile and adds it to the Pick User Profile dialog box (shown in Figure 5.78).

[Pick User Profile dialog box image]

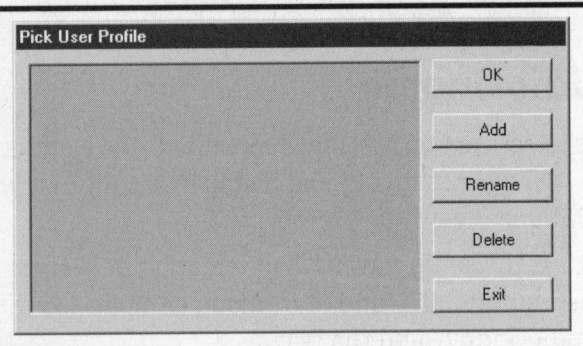

FIGURE 5.78: From the Pick User Profile dialog box, create a new user profile for yourself.

With your profile selected, click the OK button. audioGnome then walks you through the creation of a default nickname and a default password for your profile. After that, it displays the Browse for Folder dialog box once for you to specify which folder on your computer to share with other users and a second time for you to specify a download folder.

After that, you see the audioGnome window (shown in Figure 5.79), which has a multipage interface for audioGnome's various functions—search, file transfers, chat, and so on.

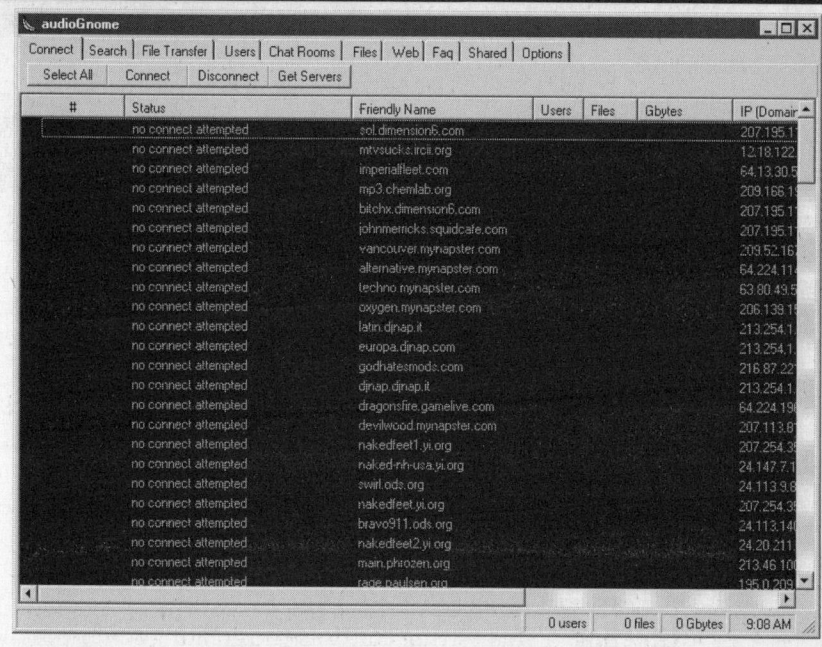

Finding MP3 files Using Napster and Its Friends 219

FIGURE 5.79: The audioGnome interface has multiple pages for audioGnome's various functions.

Configuring audioGnome

Once you've completed the setup routine, audioGnome is set up ready for use with default settings—but you should change some of these default settings immediately.

First, stop audioGnome from sharing your download folder. Click the Shared tab to display the Shared page (shown in Figure 5.80). In the left-hand list box, select the entry for your download folder and click the Delete button to remove it.

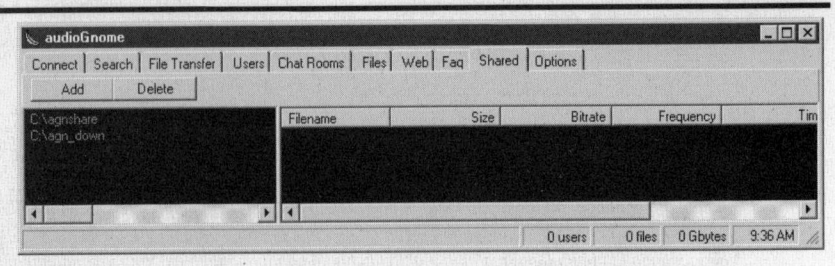

FIGURE 5.80: Before you do anything else, stop audioGnome from sharing your download folder.

Next, click the Options tab to display the Options page (shown in Figure 5.81). Then choose settings for the options as appropriate:

> **Data Listen Port** This setting controls the port on which audioGnome listens for data. Don't change this setting unless you're sure that you need to use a different port.
>
> **Greeting** This setting controls the greeting sent by audioGnome. Change this to something that amuses you—and change it frequently if you hope to amuse others.
>
> **Share MP3** This drop-down list controls whether audioGnome shares MP3 files in your shared folder. Unless you have MP3 files that you can legally distribute, choose No.
>
> **Share WMA** This drop-down list controls whether audioGnome shares WMA files in your shared folder. Unless you have WMA files that you can legally distribute, choose No.
>
> **Share WAV** This drop-down list controls whether audioGnome shares WAV files in your shared folder. Unless you have WAV files that you can legally distribute, choose No.
>
> **Shared Path** This label displays the path to the folder you're sharing. To change the folder, click the label and use the resulting Browse for Folder dialog box to choose the new folder.

Save Path This label displays the path to your download folder. To change the folder, click the label and use the resulting Browse for Folder dialog box to choose the new folder.

Max Uploads This setting controls the maximum number of files that audioGnome uploads at once from your computer. At this writing, the default setting is 5. If you have a modem connection, reduce the number to 1 or 2. (Remember that even a 56k modem delivers only 33.6k upstream—much less than a single 56k modem at the other end can suck down.)

Max Downloads This setting controls the maximum number of files that audioGnome tries to download at once. At this writing, the default setting is 5. If you have a modem connection, reduce the number to 1, 2, or 3 so that you can download MP3 files within a reasonable amount of time. (If you try to download too many files at once over a modem connection, each will take a long time.)

Max Concurrent Downloads from One User This setting controls the maximum number of files that audioGnome tries to download at once from any one user. The default setting is 1.

Max Concurrent Uploads from One User This setting controls the maximum number of upload requests from any one user that audioGnome tries to execute at one time. Unless you have a very fast connection, leave this setting set to its default value, 1.

Max Transfers This setting controls the maximum number of transfers (uploads and downloads together) that audioGnome tries to execute at one time. The default setting is 6. Increasing this number significantly may bog down the performance of all transfers.

Max Upload Rate This setting controls the maximum speed at which audioGnome uploads data from your computer. The setting allows you to prevent audioGnome from using the whole of your available bandwidth. For example, if you have a fractional T1 connection that can transfer 50 kilobytes (kBps) per second, you might want to set a Max Upload Rate of 25kBps so that audioGnome doesn't use more than half of the bandwidth at any one given time. (Note that these figures are *kilobytes*—kB—rather than *kilobits*, kb.) If you have a modem, you probably won't want to worry about this setting. You *can* use the setting to throttle down audioGnome on a modem connection—for example, by setting a Max Upload Rate of 2kBps compared to the approximately 3.5kbps that a 56k modem delivers upstream—but the resulting uploads will be painfully slow.

Transfer Timeout Interval (Seconds) This setting specifies the number of seconds that it takes for a transfer to time out (and be canceled). The default setting is 180 seconds—three minutes. Valid settings are from 20 seconds to 180 seconds.

Show Opennap Controls This drop-down list controls whether audioGnome displays Opennap controls. The default setting is No.

Auto Change to Transfer Tab This drop-down list controls whether audioGnome automatically displays the Transfer page when you set a download running. The default setting is Yes, which lets you see immediately whether audioGnome succeeds in establishing the connection and getting the transfer going.

Auto Change to Users Tab This drop-down list controls whether audioGnome automatically displays the Users tab when you perform an action such as adding a user to your list of users. The default setting is Yes.

Finding MP3 files Using Napster and Its Friends 223

Connection Speed (type) Use this drop-down list to specify the connection speed that other users see for you. This connection speed has no effect on the speed of your uploads and downloads. The default setting, Unknown, is suitably uninformative.

IRC Nickname If you want audioGnome to know your IRC nickname, enter it here.

IRC Password If you enter your IRC nickname, enter your IRC password here.

List Ignored at Connection This setting controls whether audioGnome automatically clears your Ignore list (the list of users you have chosen to ignore) when you connect. The default setting is Yes.

Auto Clear Ignored at Connection This setting controls whether audioGnome loads your Ignore list when you connect. The default setting is No.

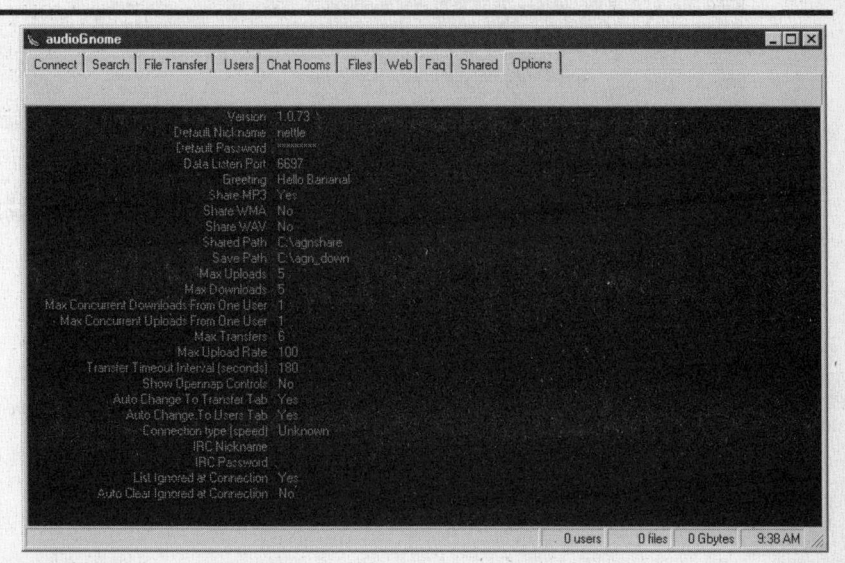

FIGURE 5.81: Use the Options page to configure audioGnome.

Connecting to a Server

To connect to a server, click the Connect tab to display the Connect page. Then either double-click a server to connect, or select one or more servers and click the Connect button.

Figure 5.82 shows audioGnome with connections established to three servers. For each active server, Active appears in the Status column, and the Users, Files, and Gbytes columns show the number of users, files, and gigabytes of data available on those servers.

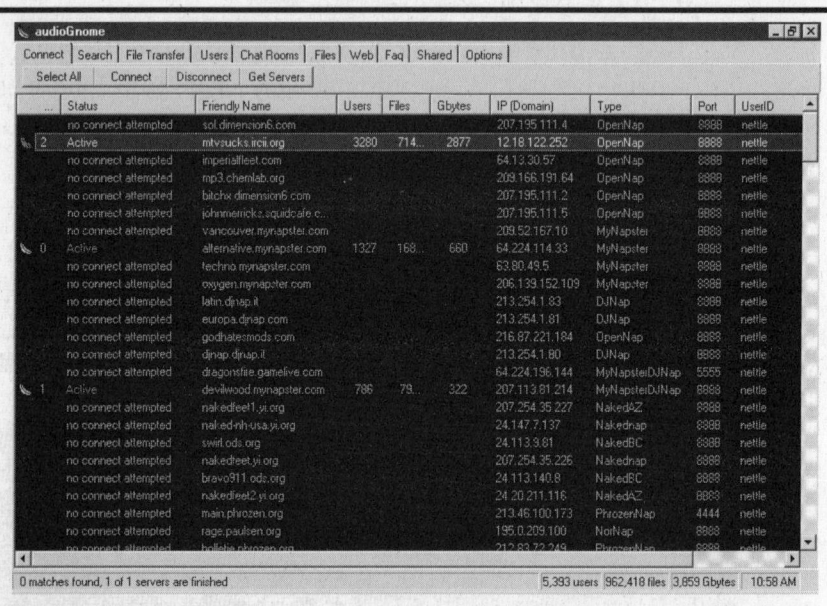

FIGURE 5.82: audioGnome with three connections established

To disconnect from a server you're connected to, select the server and click the Disconnect button, or right-click the server and choose Disconnect from Server from the context menu.

Finding MP3 files Using Napster and Its Friends

> **TIP**
>
> To connect to as many servers as possible, click the Select All button and then click the Connect button. Because there are a large number of servers, trying to connect to all of them isn't usually a good idea, but you may want to try it in desperation. You'll typically end up connected to a good number of servers, but not to anywhere near all of them.

Finding Music with audioGnome

Once you've connected to one or more servers, you're ready to start searching. Here's what to do:

1. Click the Search tab to display the Search page. Figure 5.83 shows the Search page with search criteria specified and a search executed.

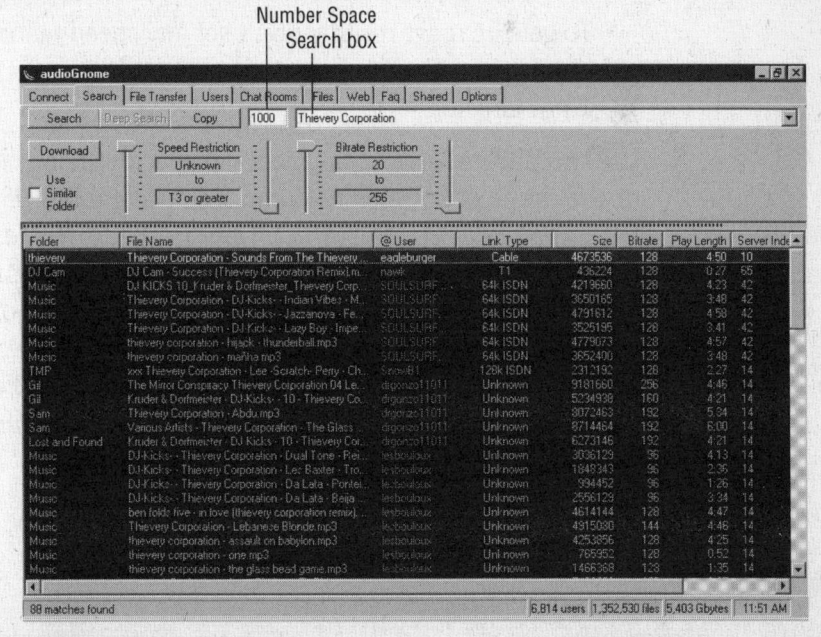

FIGURE 5.83: The audioGnome Search page after a successful search

2. Enter your search term in the Search box.

    ▶ To exclude a word from a search, put a minus sign in front of it. For example, if you want to find tracks by the Boomtown Rats other than "I Don't Like Mondays," you might use `Boomtown Rats -Mondays`.

    ▶ You can retrieve search terms that you've used earlier in the audioGnome session by using the drop-down list.

3. In the Number Space, enter the maximum number of search results you want. (The default setting is 1000.)

4. If you want, use the Speed Restriction sliders to set the range of connection speeds that you're interested in. The left-hand slider controls the speed in the upper text box, which sets the slower end of the range. The right-hand slider controls the speed in the lower text box, which sets the faster end of the range.

    ▶ To get the most results, don't set any speed restrictions: Leave the range set to its default Unknown to T3 or Greater.

5. Use the Bitrate Restriction sliders to specify the bitrate or the range of bitrates that you find acceptable. The left-hand slider controls the bitrate in the upper text box, which sets the lower end of the range. The right-hand slider controls the bitrate in the lower text box, which sets the faster end of the range. If you want, you can set the upper and lower bitrates to be the same. For example, set 128 to 128 if you want to find only files encoded at 128kbps.

Finding MP3 files Using Napster and Its Friends

6. Select the Use Similar Folder check box if you want audioGnome to put the downloaded file in a folder with the same name as the folder that contains it on the host machine. This check box is cleared by default, but you may want to experiment with this feature.

7. Click the Search button to execute the search.

   If the Deep Search button is available, you can click it to search all the servers to which you're connected 11 times. Performing a deep search takes much longer than performing a regular search, but it can turn up many more results.

Downloading Files with audioGnome

To download a file with audioGnome, double-click it on the Search page. Alternatively, select multiple files and click the Download button. audioGnome displays the File Transfer page, shown in Figure 5.84 with a number of downloads happening.

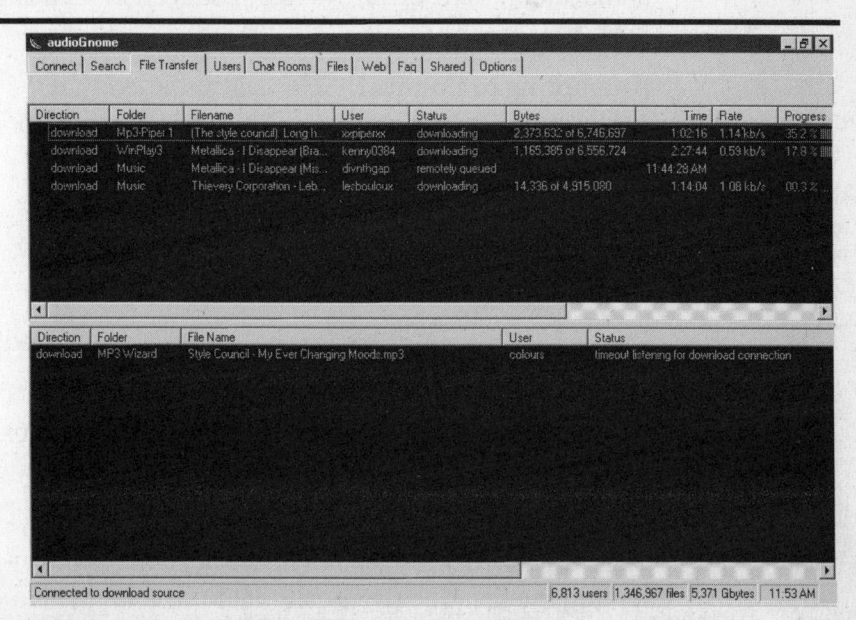

FIGURE 5.84: The File Transfer page shows the files you're uploading and downloading.

The File Transfer page contains two list boxes. The upper list box displays current transfers, and the lower list box displays transfer history—transfers that have been completed and transfers that cannot be completed. Each of the list boxes contains a number of columns, most of which are shown in Figure 5.84. Here's what the columns show:

- The Direction column shows whether you're downloading or uploading a file.

- The Folder column shows the folder in which the MP3 file is stored.

- The Filename columns shows the filename of the MP3 file.

- The User column shows the name of the user supplying the file.

- The Status column shows the status of the download, using the following terms:

    Resolving Remote Port　　This status means that audioGnome is resolving the port connection with the host.

    Attempting to Connect　　This status means that audioGnome is trying to establish a connection with the host.

    Listening for Download Connection　　This status means that audioGnome is waiting to start the download.

    Queued　　This status means that the track is queued for download on your computer.

    Remotely Queued　　This status means that the track is queued for download on the host's computer.

    Downloading　　This status means that audioGnome has established a connection to the host and is downloading the file. The Bytes column, Rate column, and Progress column show the progress of the download.

Finding MP3 files Using Napster and Its Friends 229

>**Timeout Listening for Download Connection** This status means that audioGnome has timed out.
>
>**Dormant** This status means that the download is still active, but nothing much is happening.
>
>**Canceled** This status means that you have canceled the download.
>
>**Finished Receiving Data** This status means that audioGnome has finished receiving the file.

- The Bytes column shows the number of bytes in the file and the number of bytes transferred so far. This information appears only when the download is running (or dormant).

- The Time column displays the length of time left on a running download. When a download is not running, it displays the time at which the file was queued.

- The Rate column displays the rate of a running download in kilobytes per second.

- The Progress column displays a percentage and a visual indicator showing the progress of a running download.

- The Server# column displays the number of the server to which the user supplying the file is connected.

- The Server Name column displays the name of the server to which the user supplying the file is connected.

To cancel a transfer, right-click it and select Cancel/Remove Transfer(s) from the context menu.

Browsing a User's Library

Like Napster, audioGnome lets you browse the files that other users are sharing. The easiest way to browse a user is to right-click a listing on the Search page that features them and choose Browse

User from the context menu. audioGnome displays a list of the user's shared files on the Search page, as shown in Figure 5.85. From there, you can download the files as usual.

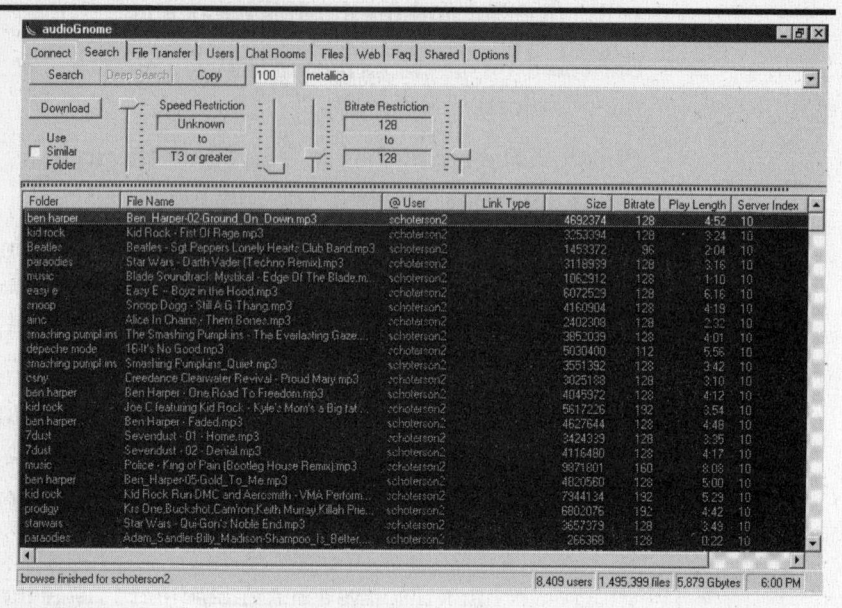

FIGURE 5.85: audioGnome lets you browse another user's library to see which files they're sharing.

Sharing Files

To share files with audioGnome, place them in your shared folder and make sure that the Share MP3 drop-down list on the Options page is set to Yes. (If you're sharing WMA files and WAV files as well, make sure that the Share WMA drop-down list and the Share WAV drop-down list are also set to Yes.) The files are then visible to other users, who will be able to download them.

Finding MP3 files Using Napster and Its Friends 231

To quickly see what's in your shared folder or folders, click the Shared tab to display the Shared page. Figure 5.86 shows the Shared page.

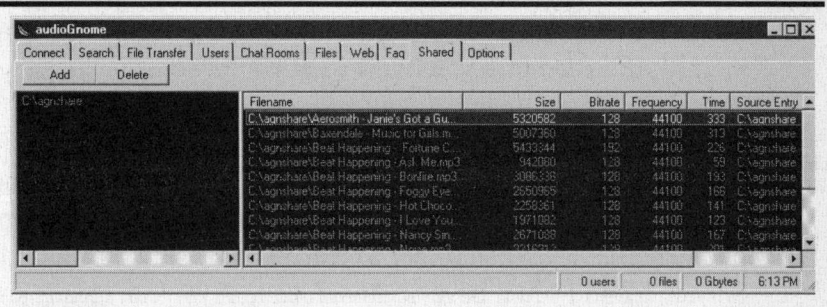

FIGURE 5.86: Use the Shared page to see which folders and files you're sharing.

CuteMX, iMesh, and SpinFrenzy

CuteMX, iMesh, and SpinFrenzy are three Napster-like technologies that (at this writing) are working to gain in popularity. In this section, we'll discuss them just briefly, leaving you to investigate them in detail if you want to.

CuteMX

CuteMX (Cute Media eXchange) is software created by GlobalScape, the makers of the popular CuteFTP FTP software. GlobalScape describes CuteMX as "your own personal file server and a powerful search engine rolled into one." Like Napster, CuteMX lets you share MP3 files, but it also lets you share other types of media files, including video and graphics files. Instead of a hot list, CuteMX lets you maintain lists of Friends and Enemies. At this writing, CuteMX runs on Windows 95, 98, ME, and 2000.

We don't much like CuteMX because it forces you to share files in order to download files from other users. We feel this is designed to encourage people to share files that they don't have the legal right to share, pushing them toward breaking the law. (As mentioned earlier, we don't have any problem with your sharing files illegally, provided that you know what you're doing is illegal, you're aware of the consequences, and you're breaking the law of your own free will.) If you want to use CuteMX but don't have any files that you can legally share, we suggest you create some by firing up Sound Recorder and recording several short WAV files of microphone noise. Save each under a creative name such as "Sound of Silence 1," and you'll have original files that you can legally share.

Download the latest version of CuteMX from www.cutemx.com, double-click the distribution file, and follow the setup routine for creating a new user account (or setting up an existing account, if you have one), specifying your connection speed (for which it claims that an accurate answer helps increase performance), selecting a shared folder and a default download folder, and specifying the file types you want to share. At this point, switch to Explorer and put your newly created WAV files there if necessary, before CuteMX can object that you're not sharing any files and therefore force you to use Browse mode.

Once you've finished setting CuteMX up, you'll find it easy to use. Figure 5.87 shows the CuteMX interface, which features a button panel on the left-hand side for navigating between the different pages. (This figure shows the Search page.)

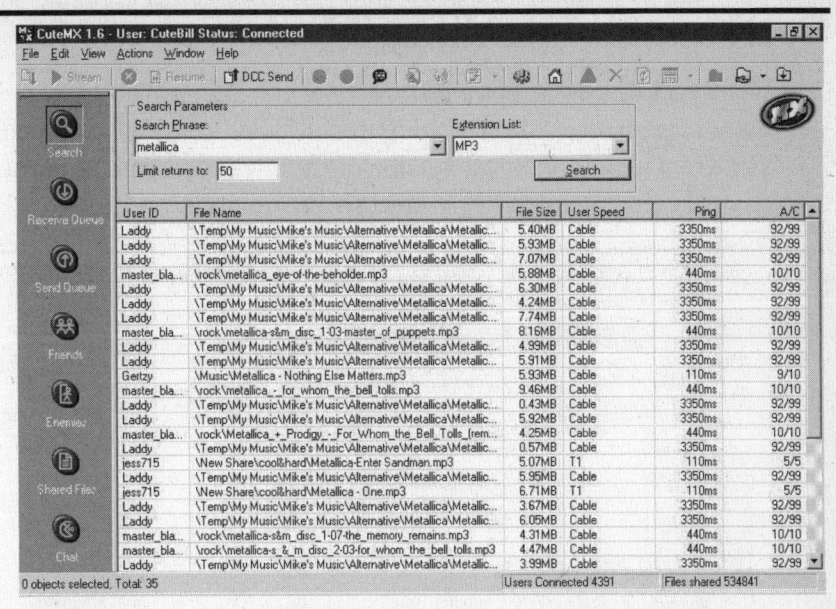

Finding MP3 files Using Napster and Its Friends 233

FIGURE 5.87: CuteMX lets you search for MP3, video, and graphics files.

iMesh

Like CuteMX, iMesh is a search tool for music, video, and graphics files. Unlike the current version of CuteMX, iMesh supports skins (of which you can download a number from www.imesh.com) and plug-ins, such as a plug-in for Winamp that lets you search for files from Winamp.

WARNING

At this writing, the iMesh software is in beta and is highly unstable. We suggest that you back up your system files before installing and running iMesh.

Getting and Installing iMesh

To get iMesh, steer your browser to the iMesh Web site, www.imesh.com (shown in Figure 5.87). Follow the Download link and download the latest version of the client software, and then run the downloaded file to start the installation routine.

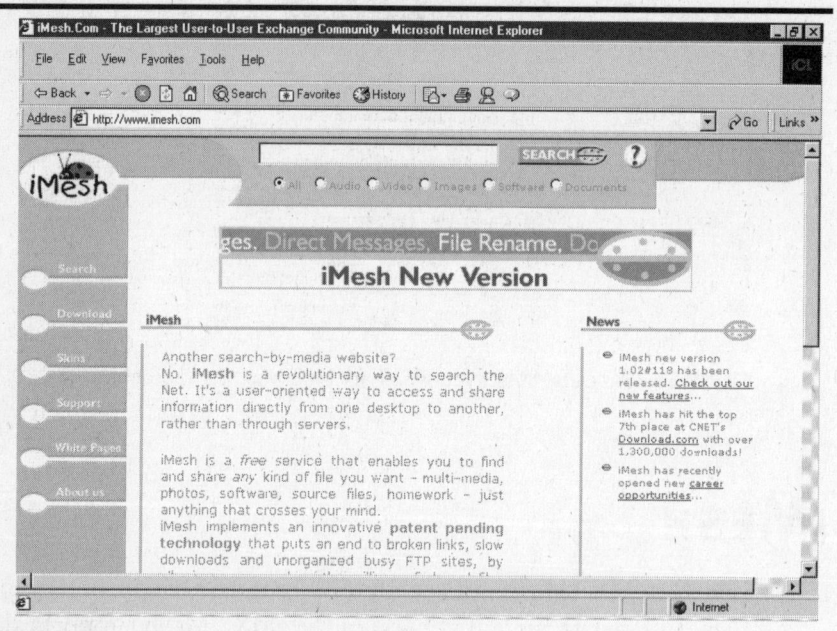

FIGURE 5.87: The iMesh home page

iMesh has a straightforward installation routine: You need to agree to a license agreement, select a program folder, specify a download folder, and choose whether to create an iMesh icon on your Desktop.

The first time you start iMesh, the Registration Wizard runs. Figure 5.88 shows the first screen of the Registration Wizard.

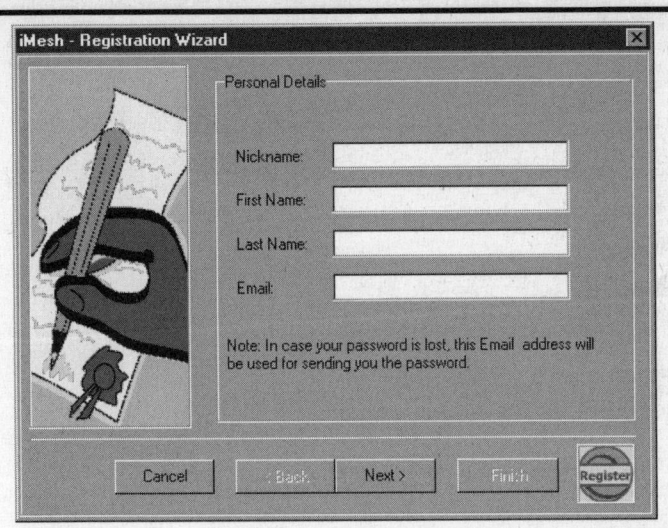

Finding MP3 files Using Napster and Its Friends 235

FIGURE 5.88: The first time you start iMesh, the Registration Wizard runs. Supply your personal information on this page.

Fill in the information in the text boxes in the Personal Details group box:

- ▶ Your iMesh nickname (which needs to be unique)
- ▶ Your first and last names (real or otherwise)
- ▶ The e-mail address to which you want iMesh to send your password should you lose it

Then click the Next button to move along to the second screen of the Registration Wizard (shown in Figure 5.89), which requests information about your location.

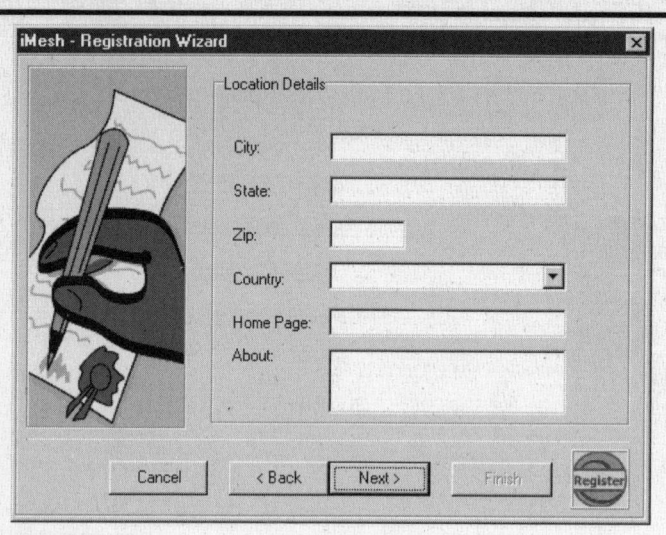

FIGURE 5.89: You don't need to supply any information on the second screen of the Registration Wizard if you don't want to.

None of the fields in the Location Details group box is required information, so you can leave these fields blank if you prefer. Click the Next button to proceed to the third screen of the Registration Wizard (shown in Figure 5.90), which contains settings that require more attention than those on the second screen do.

Use the Gender drop-down list and the Age drop-down list to specify your gender and age if you want to. You'll need to specify an age of 13 or older: If you leave the Age drop-down list set to its default setting of 0, or if you set an age younger than 13, iMesh displays the iMesh dialog box shown in Figure 5.91 telling you that, in accordance with the Children's Net Privacy Law (also known as COPPA), it will not allow ages under 13 to be registered. If iMesh displays this dialog box, click the OK button to return to the third screen of the Registration Wizard. You can specify an age as old as you like, but iMesh reduces any age over 120 to 120.

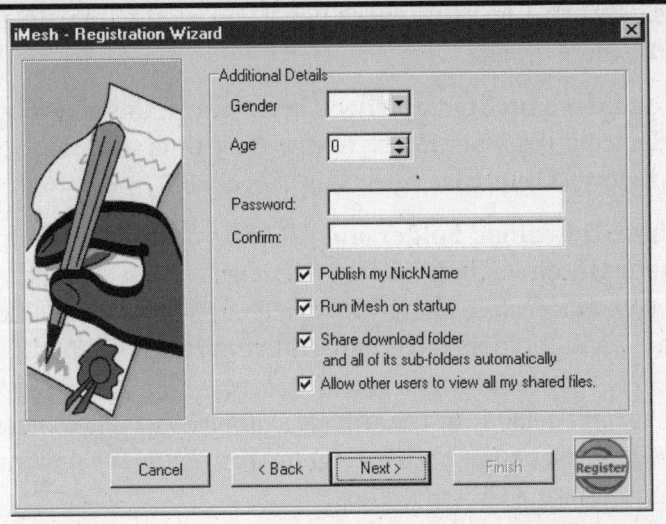

Finding MP3 files Using Napster and Its Friends 237

FIGURE 5.90: The third screen of the Registration Wizard includes some required information and other important choices.

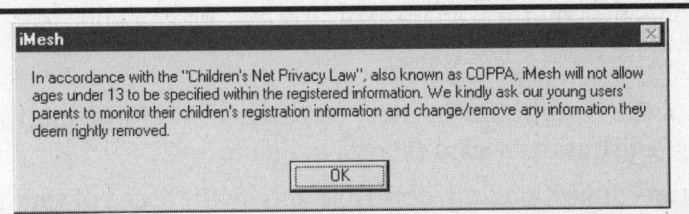

FIGURE 5.91: If you give an age under 13 (or if you leave the default setting of 0 in the Age drop-down list), iMesh displays this dialog box telling you that it will not allow ages under 13 to be registered.

Also on the third screen, enter an unguessable password in the Password text box and in the Confirm text box. Then specify settings for the following four check boxes, all of which are selected by default:

Publish My NickName check box Leave this check box selected if you want iMesh to publish your nickname on its network. Clear this check box if you want to remain a little more private.

Run iMesh on Startup check box   Leave this check box selected if you want iMesh to run every time you start Windows. Otherwise, clear this check box.

Share Download Folder and All of Its Subfolders Automatically check box   Leave this check box selected if you want iMesh to share your designated download folder and any subfolders it contains. *Sharing your download folder is almost always a bad idea, because it may cause you to commit a felony by unwittingly sharing copyrighted material that you do not have the right to distribute.* We recommend clearing this check box.

Allow Other Users to View All My Shared Files check box   Select this check box if you want other users to be able to view all the files that you're sharing as opposed to only files that you share explicitly. We recommend clearing this check box too.

Click the Next button to move on to the fourth (and final) screen of the Registration Wizard (shown in Figure 5.92).

In the Connection drop-down list, specify the speed of your Internet connection if you want to. This speed is the connection speed that other users will see listed for you. It doesn't affect the speed at which you can upload and download files. So you can leave the setting at its default, I Don't Know, if you want.

If you know that your computer connects to the Internet through a proxy server, select the I Am behind a Proxy check box and enter the proxy server's details in the Proxy Address and Proxy Port text boxes. (If you don't know the details of your network's proxy server, ask your network administrator.)

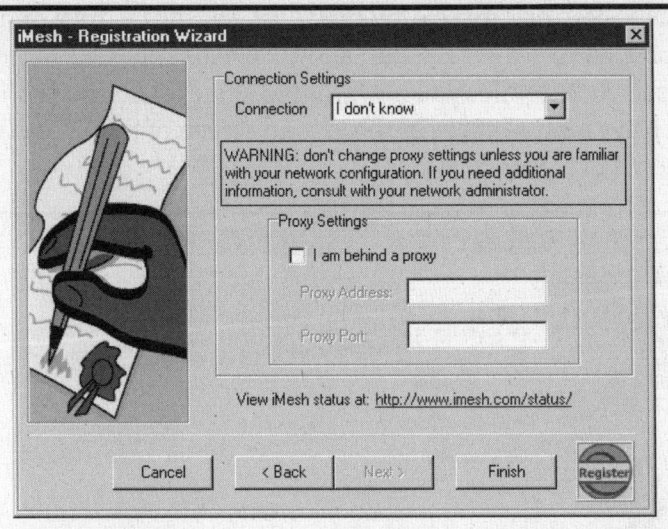

Finding MP3 files Using Napster and Its Friends 239

FIGURE 5.92: Choose connection settings on the fourth screen of the Registration Wizard.

Click the Finish button to finish the registration process and to dismiss the Registration Wizard. iMesh starts the Share Wizard. Figure 5.93 shows the first screen of the Share Wizard.

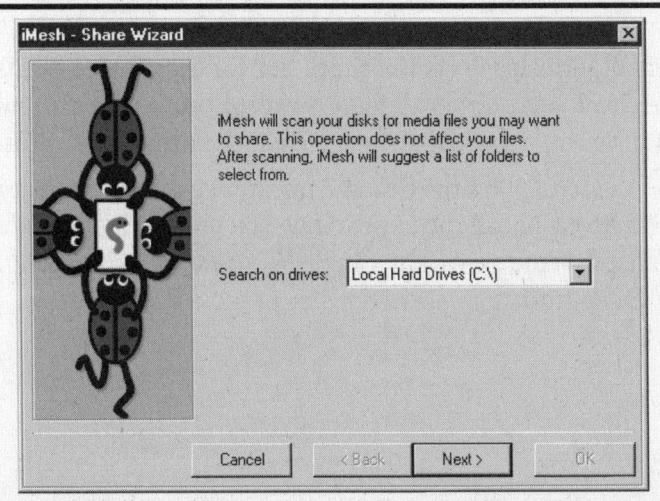

FIGURE 5.93: The first screen of the Share Wizard

Chapter Five

In the Search on Drives drop-down list, select the drive or drives that you want to search for files, and then click the Next button. iMesh searches for files you may want to share (such as MP3 files) and displays a list of them in the second screen of the Share Wizard (shown in Figure 5.94).

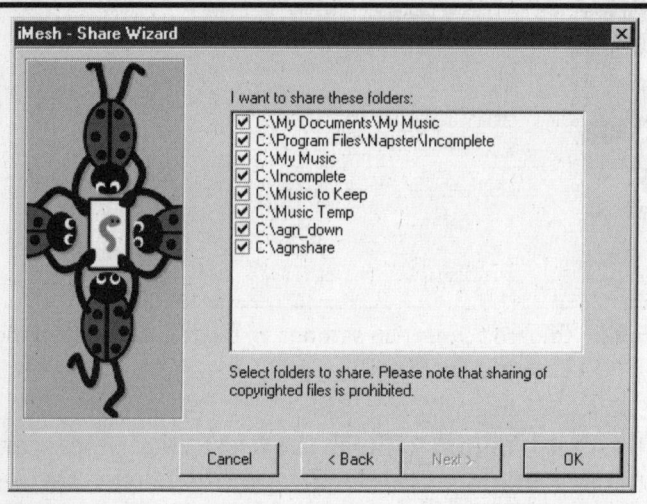

FIGURE 5.94: The second screen of the Share Wizard gives you a list of folders that you might want to share.

By default, iMesh selects the check box for each folder it lists. Clear the check boxes from all folders except those that contain files that you have the right to distribute. Then click the OK button.

Next, iMesh displays the Select Appearance dialog box (shown in Figure 5.95). Choose the appearance you want iMesh to have—Skin, Multiple Windows; Skin, Single Window; or Skinless—and click the OK button.

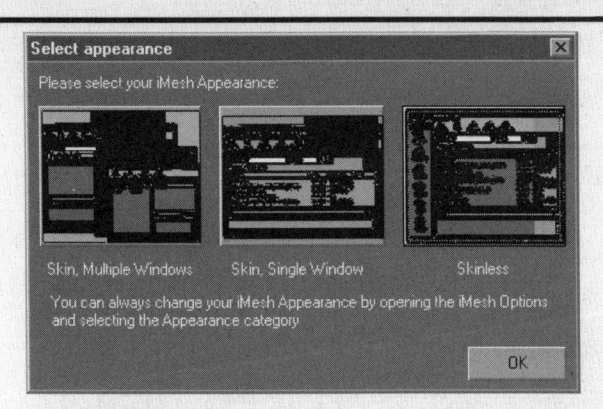

Finding MP3 files Using Napster and Its Friends

FIGURE 5.95: In the Select Appearance dialog box, choose the appearance you want iMesh to have.

Here's how the different appearances of iMesh look:

▶ Figure 5.96 shows the Skin, Multiple Windows appearance, with the Search Results window appearing on top of the Contact window. You may prefer this appearance if you have a large enough monitor to view several windows at once, because this appearance lets you keep an eye on your searches, downloads, uploads, and contacts simultaneously. At this writing, iMesh doesn't have consistently effective navigation from one window to another, which makes this appearance more difficult to use.

FIGURE 5.96: iMesh in its Skin, Multiple Windows appearance

▶ Figure 5.97 shows iMesh in its Skin, Single Window appearance. This appearance provides easy navigation via multiple pages and lets you change the look by switching from one skin to another. We'll use the Skin, Single Window appearance for the rest of this section—except to show you features that are not currently accessible from this appearance.

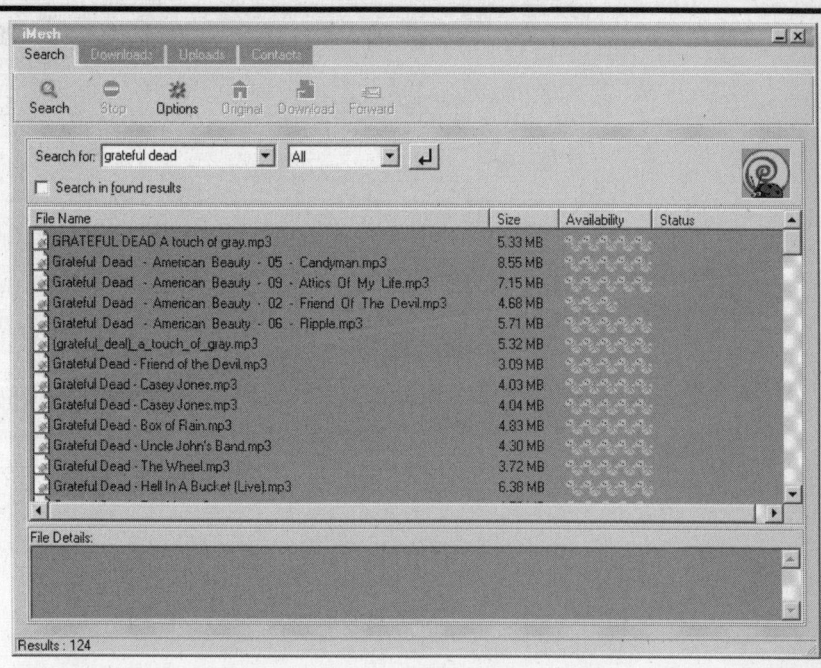

Finding MP3 files Using Napster and Its Friends 243

FIGURE 5.97: iMesh in its Skin, Single Window appearance

▶ Figure 5.98 shows iMesh in its Skinless appearance, which also uses a single window but implements navigation via a panel of buttons on the left-hand side. This appearance also has a menu bar, unlike the other appearances.

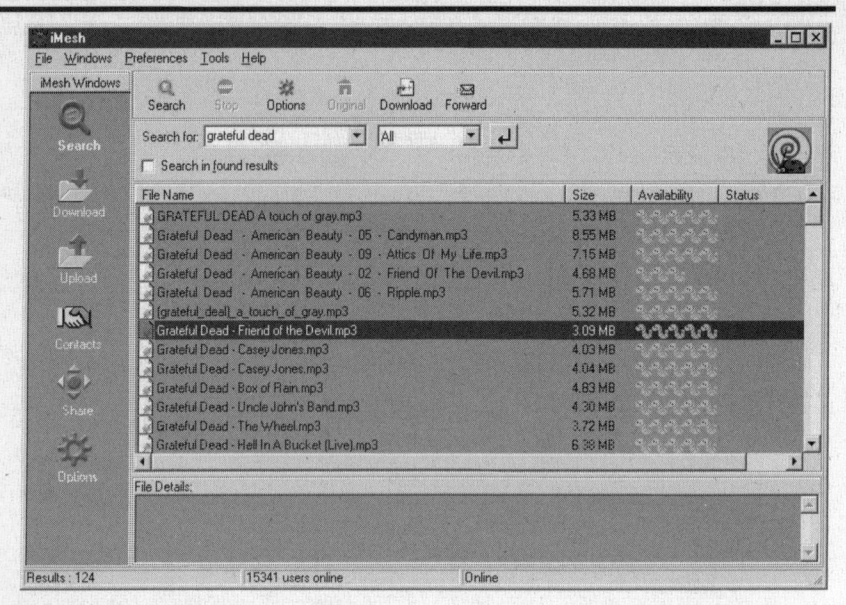

FIGURE 5.98: iMesh in its Skinless appearance

> **TIP**
>
> At this writing, iMesh's various appearances provide different commands from each other, with only the Skinless appearance providing a full set of commands. If you can't find a command you're looking for in the iMesh appearance you're using, try switching to the Skinless appearance or using the context menu from the iMesh icon in the system tray.

When you dismiss the Select Appearance dialog box, you should see the small iMesh window (shown in Figure 5.99). (Instead, you may see the Search Results window. If so, close it to reach the iMesh window.) This window displays information such as the number of users online and whether you're currently online or offline. It also provides quick access via its buttons to the main areas of iMesh, which we'll discuss in the rest of this section.

FIGURE 5.99: The iMesh window

Configuring iMesh

Click the Options button to display the Options dialog box, and choose options as discussed in the following sections.

General Page

The General page of the Options dialog box (shown in Figure 5.100) contains the following options:

Launch on Startup check box   Select this check box to make iMesh launch each time you start Windows. Clear this check box if you want to launch iMesh manually.

Always on Top check box   Select this check box if you want to run iMesh on top of any other active application. To run iMesh as a "normal" application window, clear this check box.

Show Splash check box   Select this check box if you want to see the iMesh splash screen (the opening graphical logo) each time you run iMesh. Clear this check box to skip the splash screen.

Show Desktop Icon check box   Select this check box if you want to have an iMesh icon (a shortcut) on your desktop. If you don't want a shortcut, clear this check box.

Sticky Windows (Uploads & Downloads) check box   Select this check box if you want iMesh to remember the position of the Uploads window and the Downloads window each time it displays them. Clear this check box if you prefer to position the windows manually.

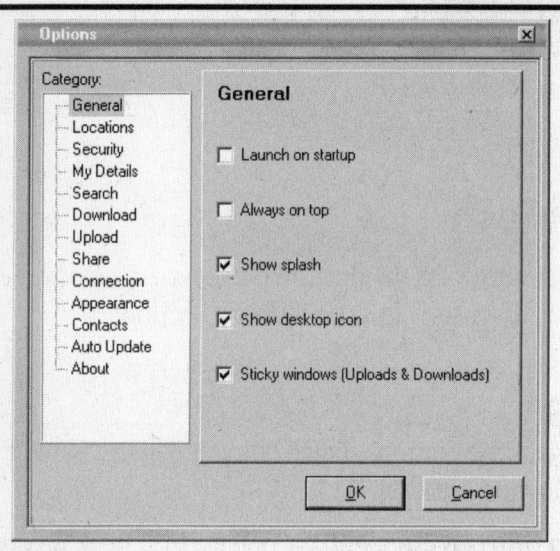

FIGURE 5.100:   The General page of the Options dialog box

Locations Page

The Locations page of the Options dialog box (shown in Figure 5.101) lets you specify the folder in which you want iMesh to save files you download via iMesh. To change the folder, either type directly into the Default Location text box or click the Change button, use the resulting Browse for Folder dialog box to navigate to and select the folder, and click the OK button.

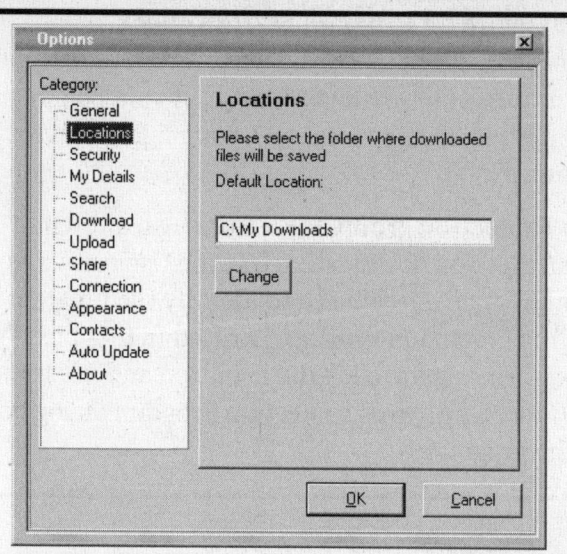

Finding MP3 files Using Napster and Its Friends

FIGURE 5.101: The Locations page of the Options dialog box

Security Page

The Security page of the Options dialog box (shown in Figure 5.102) provides the following options:

> **Set Password group box** The Password text box and the Confirm text box contain the password you entered during the setup of iMesh.
>
> **Publish My NickName check box** Select this check box if you want iMesh to publish your nickname on its network. Clear the check box to maintain somewhat greater privacy. (People from whom you download files, and people who download files from you, will of course see your nickname whatever the setting in this check box.)

Ask for Password on Program Startup check box Select this check box if you want iMesh to prompt you for your password when you start it. If your computer is shared (even in a family location), you might want to select this check box.

Antivirus Protection group box To use an anti-virus program on files you download, select the Use Antivirus Protection Program check box and identify the program in the Antivirus Protection Program Located In text box. (To navigate to the program, click the ... button and use the resulting Choose Antivirus Protection Program dialog box to select the program.)

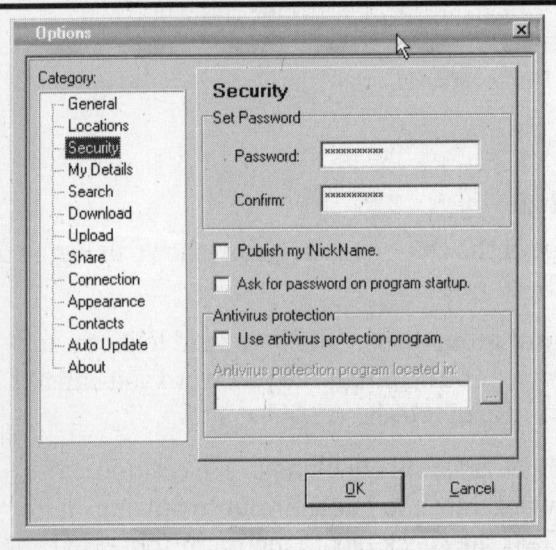

FIGURE 5.102: The Security page of the Options dialog box

Finding MP3 files Using Napster and Its Friends

My Details Page

The My Details page of the Options dialog box (shown in Figure 5.103) contains three pages that store the information you entered during the registration process. You can change this information as necessary by working on the My Details page.

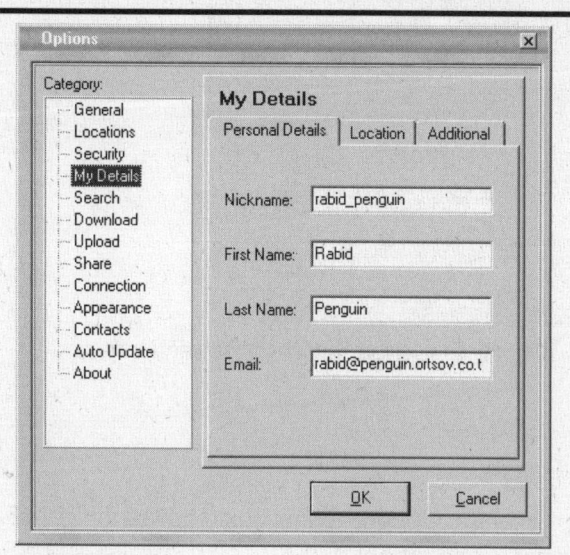

FIGURE 5.103: The My Details page of the Options dialog box

Search Page

The Search page of the Options dialog box (shown in Figure 5.104) contains only two options:

Show Only Available Results check box Leave this check box selected (as it is by default) to have iMesh show you only results that are available. Select this check box if you want iMesh to display unavailable results as well.

Clean Search History button Click this button to clear the information that iMesh has stored on the searches you have performed.

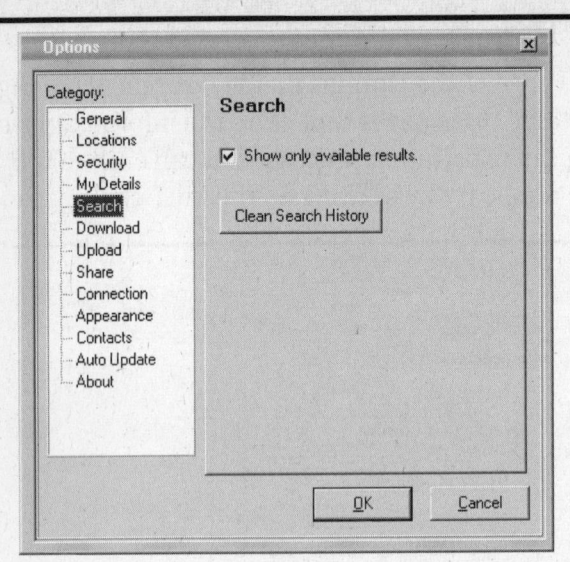

FIGURE 5.104: The Search page of the Options dialog box

Download Page

The Download page of the Options dialog box (shown in Figure 5.105) contains the following four options:

Maximum Concurrent Downloads text box In this text box, enter the maximum number of downloads that you want to have running at the same time. The default setting is 3, but if you use a modem connection, you may want to set this value to 1 or 2 instead. If you have a very fast connection, try setting this value to a higher number.

Message Alert check box Select this check box to have iMesh display a notification message when a file finishes downloading.

Tray Icon Alert check box Select this check box to have iMesh display a notification in the system tray when a file finishes downloading.

Finding MP3 files Using Napster and Its Friends

Sound Alert check box Select this check box to have iMesh play a sound to get your attention when a file finishes downloading.

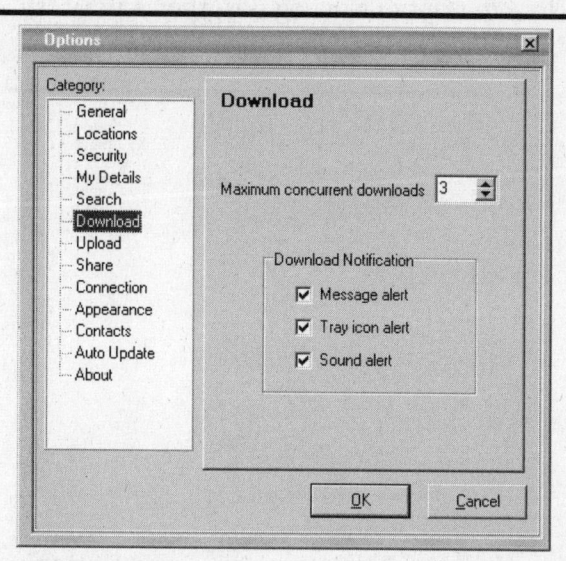

FIGURE 5.105: The Download page of the Options dialog box

Upload Page

The Upload page of the Options dialog box (shown in Figure 5.106) contains these two options:

Maximum Concurrent Uploads text box In this text box, enter the maximum number of uploads you want to have running at once. The default setting is 20, which is far too high for a modem connection; a setting of 1 or 2 is much more suitable. For a fast connection, such as an ISDN, cable, or a DSL, try a setting of between 3 and 5.

Ports Restricted for Use by iMesh text box In this text box, you can enter the numbers of ports that you want to prevent iMesh from using. For example, if you don't want iMesh to use ports 80 and 8080, enter **80, 8080** in the text box. (If you don't know what different ports do, leave this text box empty.) To apply these settings, click the OK button to close the Options dialog box, then exit iMesh and restart it.

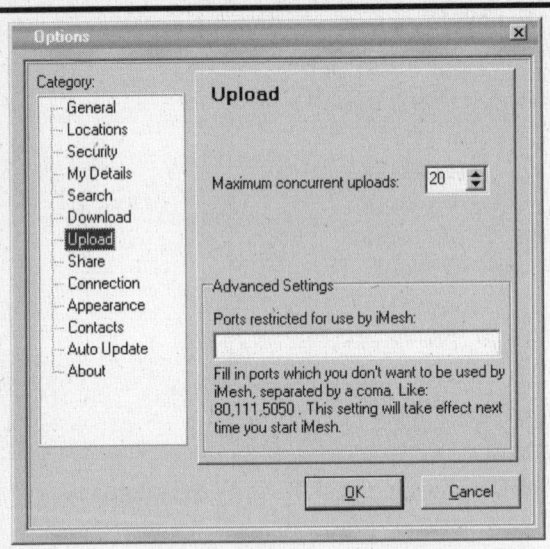

FIGURE 5.106: The Upload page of the Options dialog box

Share Page

The Share page of the Options dialog box (shown in Figure 5.107) contains these options:

Scan for Changes in Shared Directories group box Use the settings in this group box to specify how you want iMesh to scan for changes in your shared directories. (For example, when you add music files to a shared folder, or remove files from a folder, iMesh won't be aware

Finding MP3 files Using Napster and Its Friends 253

of the changes until it performs a scan of the folder.) In the Period drop-down list, choose the interval at which you want iMesh to scan the directories: 1 hour, 3 hours, 6 hours, 12 hours, 1 day, or 3 days. Select the Tray Animation While Scanning check box if you want iMesh to display an animation in your system tray to indicate that scanning is taking place. Click the Scan Now button to perform a scan immediately.

Allow Other Users to View All My Shared Files check box Select this check box if you want other users to be able to view all the files you're sharing.

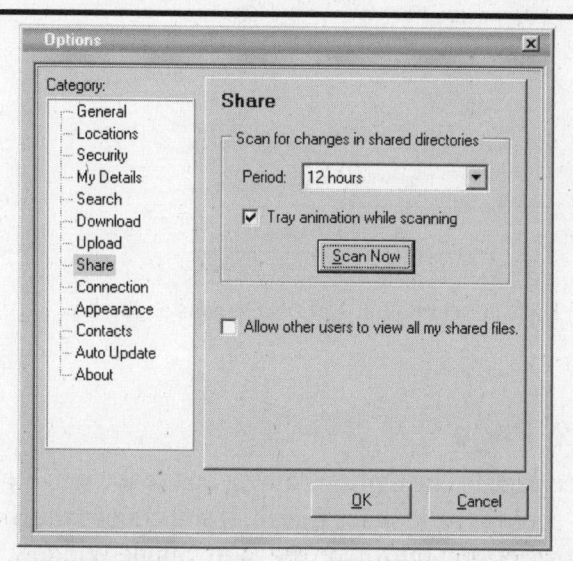

FIGURE 5.107: The Share page of the Options dialog box

Connection Page

The Connection page of the Options dialog box (shown in Figure 5.108) lets you update the connection and proxy server information that you supplied during the registration process.

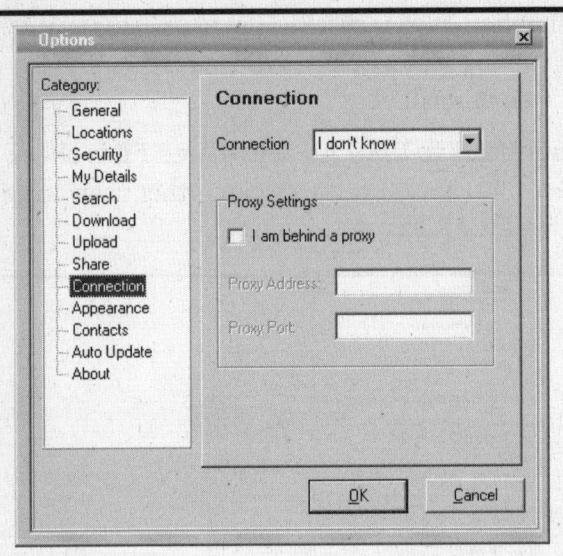

FIGURE 5.108: The Connection page of the Options dialog box

Appearance Page

The Appearance page of the Options dialog box (shown in Figure 5.109) lets you choose the look for iMesh. If you choose the Skin, Multiple Windows option button or the Skin, Single Window option button, you can choose the skin to use in the list box. Click the link at the bottom of the page to download more skins from the iMesh Web site.

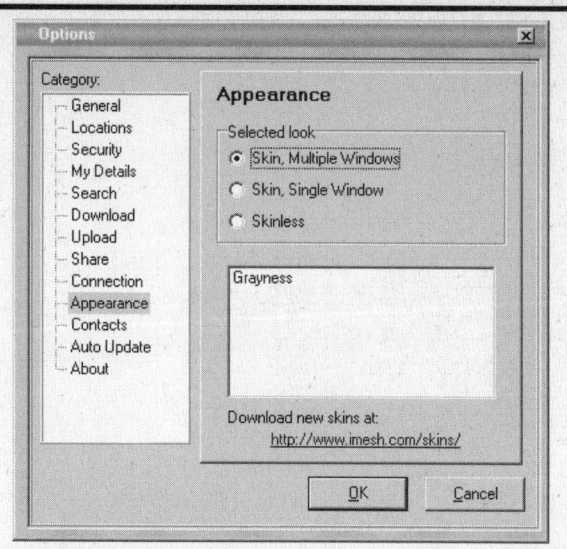

FIGURE 5.109: The Appearance page of the Options dialog box

Contacts Page

The Contacts page of the Options dialog box (shown in Figure 5.110) contains the following options:

> **Accept Instant Message from Other Users check box**   Select this check box if you want to receive instant messages from other iMesh users. Clear this check box if you want to be left alone.
>
> **Incoming Message Notification group box**   In this group box, specify the type or types of notification you want iMesh to give you when you receive an instant message. Select the Popup Message Dialog check box, the Sound Alert check box, and the Tray Icon Alert check box as appropriate.

Chapter Five

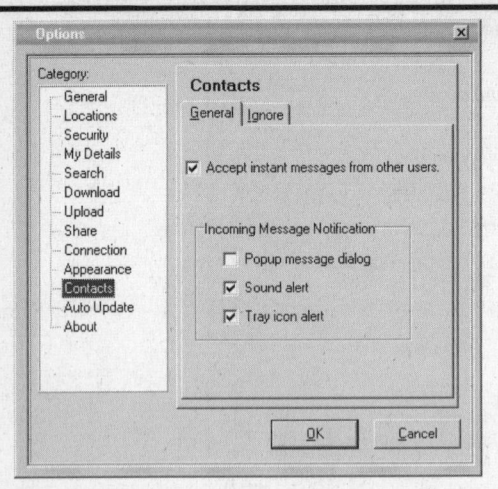

FIGURE 5.110: The Contacts page of the Options dialog box

The Ignore subpage of the Contacts page (shown in Figure 5.111) lets you maintain the list of iMesh users you're ignoring. Use the Remove button to remove a selected contact from the Ignore list. Use the Move to Contacts button to move a selected contact from the Ignore list to the Contacts list.

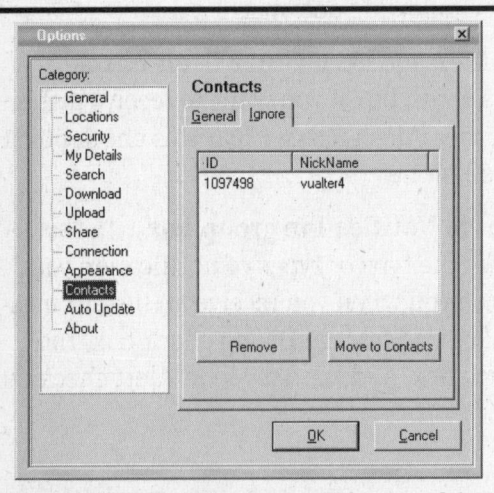

FIGURE 5.111: The Ignore Subpage of the Contacts page of the Options dialog box

Finding MP3 files Using Napster and Its Friends

Auto Update Page

The Auto Update page of the Options dialog box (shown in Figure 5.112) lets you specify whether and (if so) how frequently iMesh should try to update itself automatically. Leave the Automatically Check for a New Version check box selected (as it is by default) to have iMesh check automatically, and use the Every drop-down list to specify your chosen interval in days.

FIGURE 5.112: The Auto Update page of the Options dialog box

About Page

The About page of the Options dialog box (shown in Figure 5.113) contains information about the version and build of iMesh that you're using. It also contains your iMesh ID number. If you chose not to have iMesh update itself automatically, use the version and build information to determine whether you need to update iMesh manually.

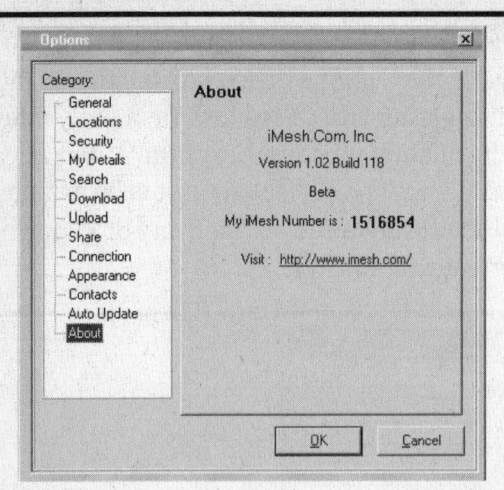

FIGURE 5.113: The About page of the Options dialog box shows you which version of iMesh you're using.

Searching with iMesh

To search with iMesh, use the Search page (shown in Figure 5.114) or the Search window, depending on which appearance you're using.

1. In the Search For text box, enter the text that you want to search for. For example, enter a band's name to search for all available tracks by that band, or enter the band's name and keywords from a track title to search just for that track.

> **TIP**
> Once you've performed some searches, you can select one of your previous searches from the Search For drop-down list.

2. In the drop-down list to the right of the Search For drop-down list, choose the category of file to search for: All,

Finding MP3 files Using Napster and Its Friends 259

Audio, Video, Images, Software, or Documents. For example, to search for music files, select Audio.

3. Click the ➢ button to execute the search.

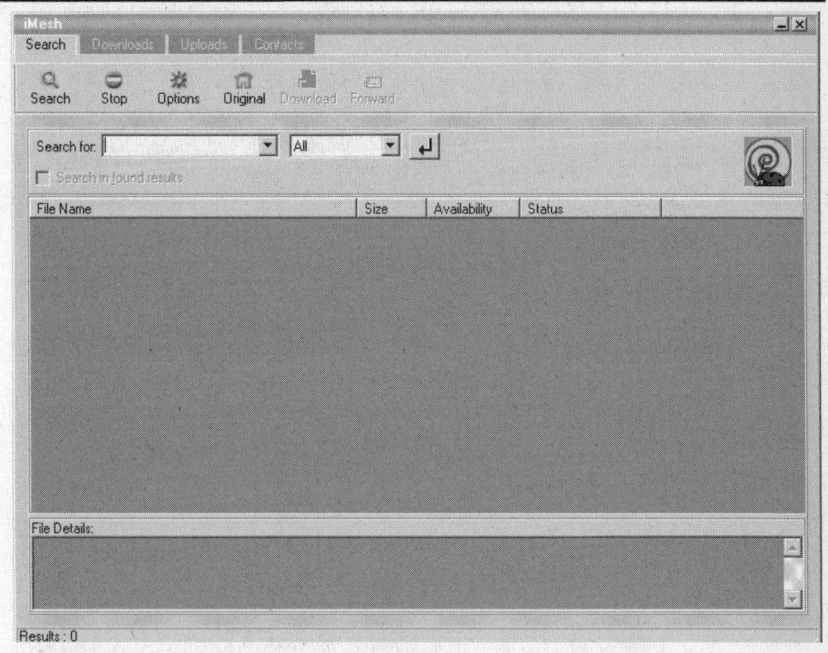

FIGURE 5.114: The iMesh Search page

Figure 5.115 shows the Search page of iMesh after a successful search for Smashing Pumpkins tracks. The green worms in the Availability column indicate the relative availability of the tracks: The more worms there are, the better the chance that you'll be able to download the track.

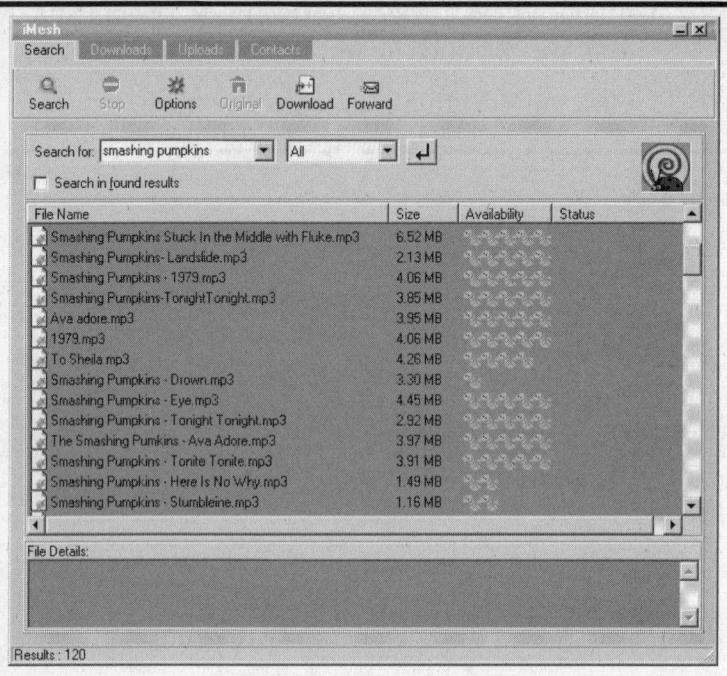

FIGURE 5.115: The Search page showing the results of a successful search

You can sort the results on the Search page by clicking the column headings. For example, you might want to sort by the File Name column so that you can see what's available, or by the Availability column so that you can assess the relative availability of the tracks.

> **TIP**
>
> If you get a lot of results, you can refine a search. Select the Search in Found Results check box, specify additional criteria in the Search For text box, and click the Search button. iMesh searches through the search results for the criteria you've specified and returns any matches.

ated) and creates a
Forwarding Information about a Track to a Friend

To forward the information about a track you've located to a friend, select the track and click the Forward button. iMesh launches your e-mail client (or activates it if it's already running) and creates a canned message with information about the track included as an attachment. Figure 5.116 shows Outlook Express with such a message underway.

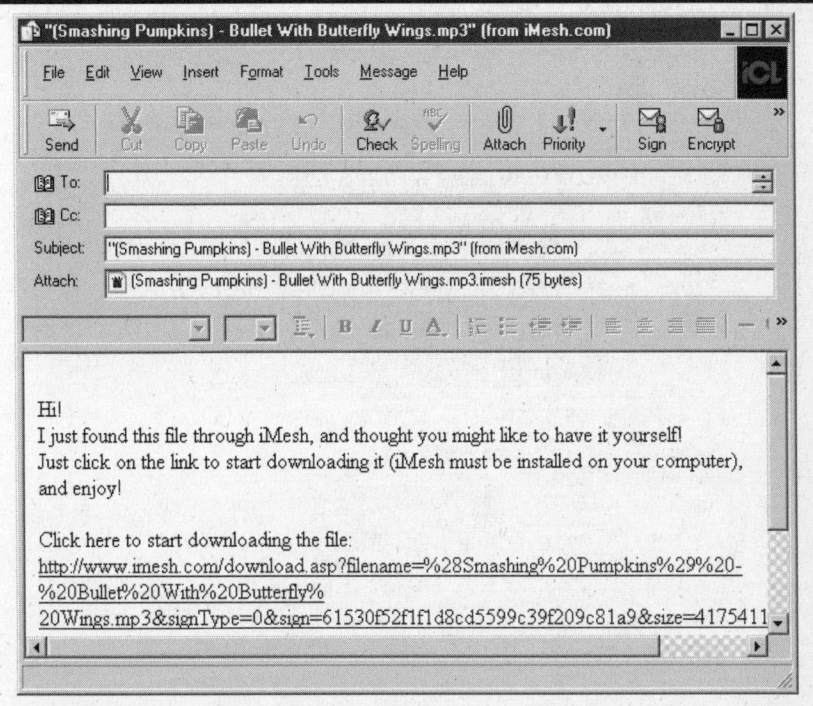

FIGURE 5.116: iMesh makes it easy to forward the information about a track to a friend.

Edit the message as you want, address it, and send it on its way.

Downloading with iMesh

To download a track, select it on the Search page and click the Download button. (To download multiple tracks, Shift+click or Ctrl+click to select them.) Alternatively, to download a single track, double-click it.

Figure 5.117 shows the Downloads page with one download in progress and a second download getting connected.

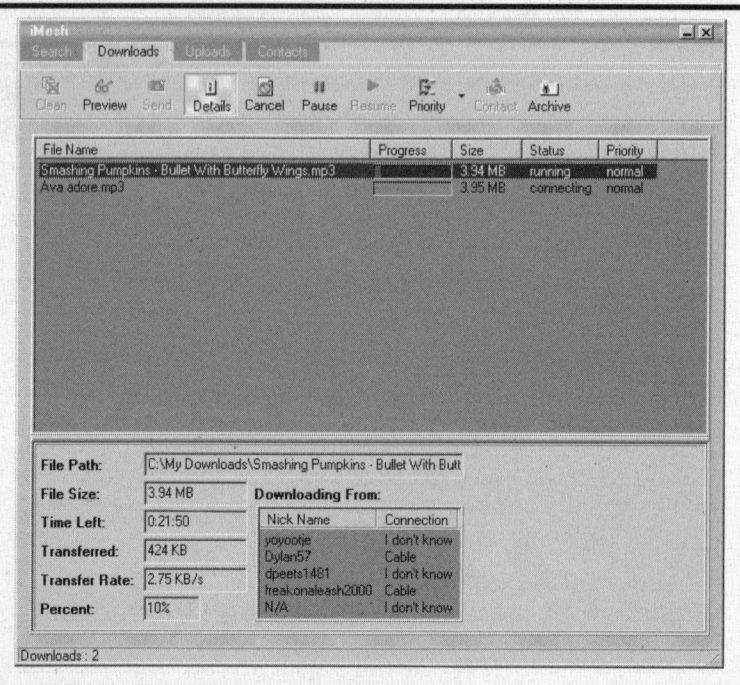

FIGURE 5.117: The Downloads page with some downloads in progress

To cancel a download, right-click it and choose Cancel from the context menu. Alternatively, select the download and click the Cancel button on the toolbar. iMesh displays a confirmation dialog box to make sure that you want to cancel the download. Choose the Yes button.

To pause a download, right-click it and choose Pause from the context menu, or select it and click the Pause button on the toolbar. iMesh displays "Paused" in the Status column. You can then resume the download by right-clicking it and choosing Resume from the context menu or by selecting it and clicking the Resume button on the toolbar.

To preview a download (for example, to make sure you're getting the track you hoped for), right-click it and choose Preview from the context menu. Alternatively, select the download and click the Preview button on the toolbar. iMesh starts as much of the track as it has downloaded playing in your default music player.

By default, iMesh assigns each download Normal priority. To raise the priority of a download, right-click it and choose Set Priority ➢ High from the context menu. (To return the priority to Normal, right-click and choose Set Priority ➢ Normal from the context menu.) Alternatively, select the download and click the Priority button on the toolbar to toggle the priority between Normal and High.

When iMesh has finished downloading files, it displays the iMesh dialog box shown in Figure 5.118.

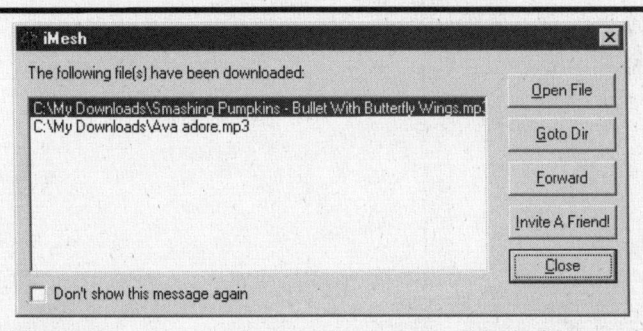

FIGURE 5.118: Until you tell it to desist, iMesh displays this iMesh dialog box after it finishes downloading files.

From this dialog box, you can take the following actions:

- To open one of the files you've downloaded, select it in the list box and click the Open File button. Opening a music file starts it playing in your default music player.

- To open an Explorer window showing the folder into which the track was downloaded, select it in the list box and click the Goto Dir button.

- To forward the information on the track to a friend, select the item and click the Forward button. iMesh creates an e-mail message in your default e-mail application, as discussed in the previous section.

- To send a recommendation for the track to a friend, click the Invite a Friend button and use the resulting Invite a Friend dialog box (shown in Figure 5.119) to specify the friend (or friends), then click the OK button.

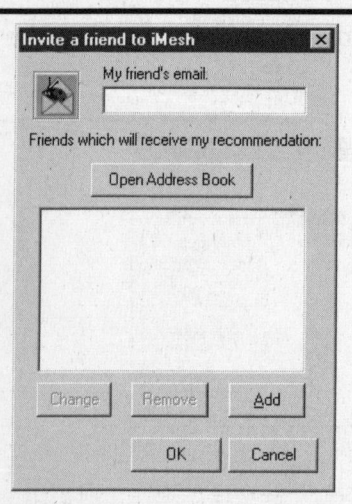

FIGURE 5.119: Use the Invite a Friend dialog box to send information about an item you downloaded to a friend.

Finding MP3 files Using Napster and Its Friends 265

▶ Click the Close button to close the iMesh dialog box. To prevent iMesh from displaying this information dialog box again, select the Don't Show This Message Again check box before closing the iMesh dialog box.

Sharing Files with iMesh

As you saw a little earlier, iMesh sets you up with shared files at the end of the setup and registration routine—but you may want to change the files and folders you're sharing later. Here's how to do so:

1. If you're not using the Skinless appearance, switch to it: Display the Options dialog box, select the Appearance category, select the Skinless option button, and click the OK button.

2. Choose Preferences ➢ Share to display the Share dialog box (shown in Figure 5.120).

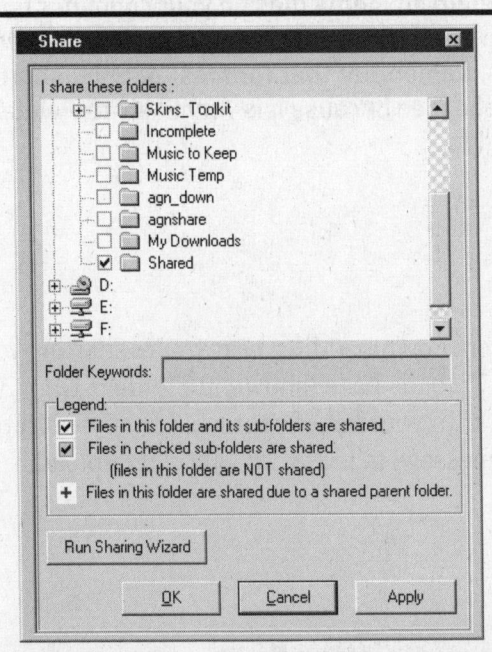

FIGURE 5.120: Use the Share dialog box to specify which files and folders to share.

3. Select the check boxes for the folders you want to share. Clear the check boxes for any previously shared folders that you no longer want to share. Read the legend carefully: A check mark on a gray background means that files in a subfolder of the selected folder are shared, but that the selected folder itself isn't shared. A red plus sign means that files in a folder are automatically shared because their parent folder is shared.

4. Click the Apply button to apply your changes.

5. Click the OK button to close the Share dialog box.

6. If you were using an appearance other than Skinless, restore it by choosing Preferences ➤ Select Appearance and selecting the appearance from the submenu.

WARNING

If you want to set up all media files on your computer for sharing, click the Run Sharing Wizard in the Share dialog box and follow its prompts. Remember that for most people, sharing all media files is a bad idea because it is very likely to violate other people's copyrights.

Uploading Files

When other iMesh users download files that you're sharing, you'll see the details on the Uploads page (shown in Figure 5.121). From here, you can add a user to your list of contacts (discussed in the next section), send a message to a user, or cancel an upload.

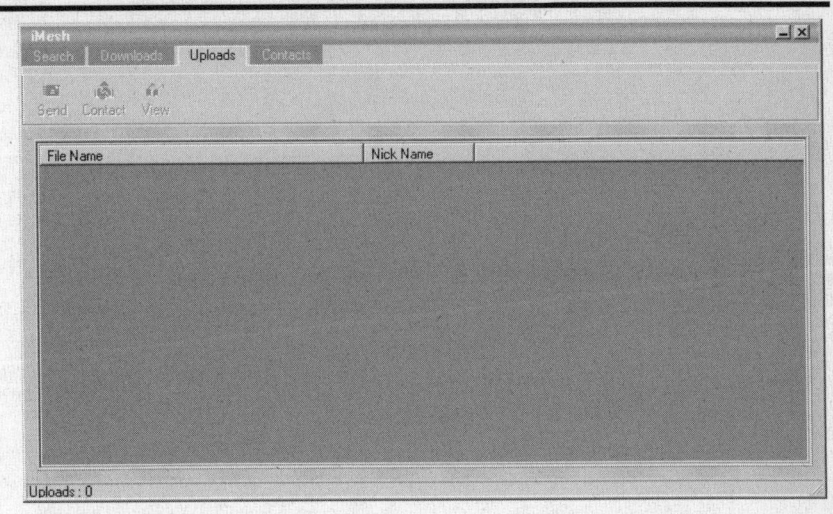

FIGURE 5.121: The Uploads page shows any uploads currently running—in this case, none.

Using Contacts

iMesh provides features for building a list of contacts with whom to exchange messages or files.

To add a user to your list of contacts, right-click an entry featuring the user on the Downloads page or the Uploads page and choose Add to Contacts from the context menu. iMesh adds the user to your list of contacts and displays the Contacts page (shown in Figure 5.122).

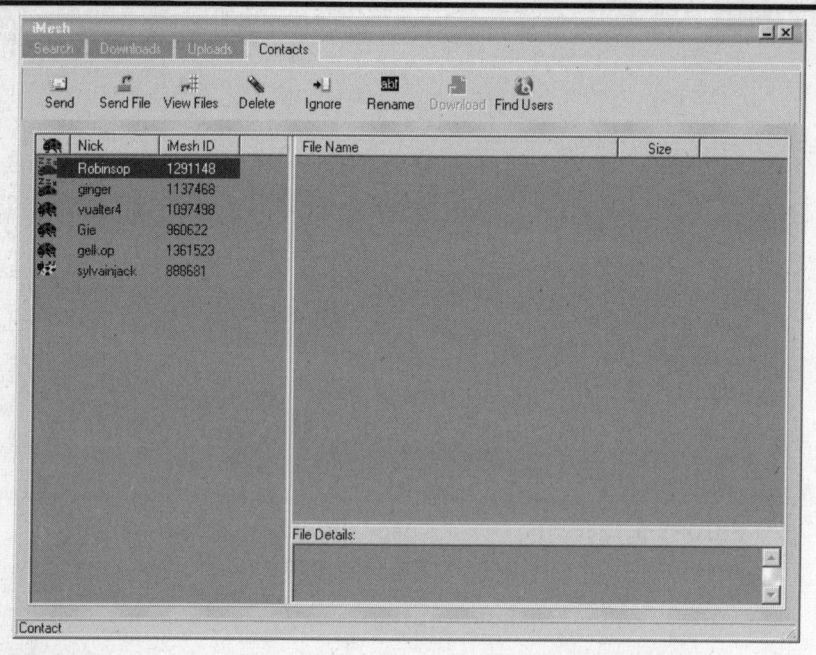

FIGURE 5.122: Use the Contacts page to manage your contacts.

You can take the following actions with contacts on the Contacts page:

- To remove a contact from your list of contacts, right-click the contact's name and choose Delete from the context menu. Alternatively, select the contact and click the Delete button on the toolbar.

- To ignore a contact, right-click their name and choose Move to Ignore List from the context menu. Alternatively, select the contact and click the Ignore button on the toolbar.

Finding MP3 files Using Napster and Its Friends 269

NOTE

To rescind your ignoring of a contact, use the Move to Contacts button on the Ignore subpage of the Contacts page in the Options dialog box.

► To view a contact's files, right-click the contact on the Contact page and choose View Files from the context menu. (Alternatively, select the contact and click the View Files button on the toolbar.) iMesh retrieves the list of files that the user is sharing and displays it on the Contacts page. Figure 5.123 shows an example of such a list. To display the file's details in the File Details pane, select one of the files. You can then download a file by right-clicking it and choosing Download from the context menu.

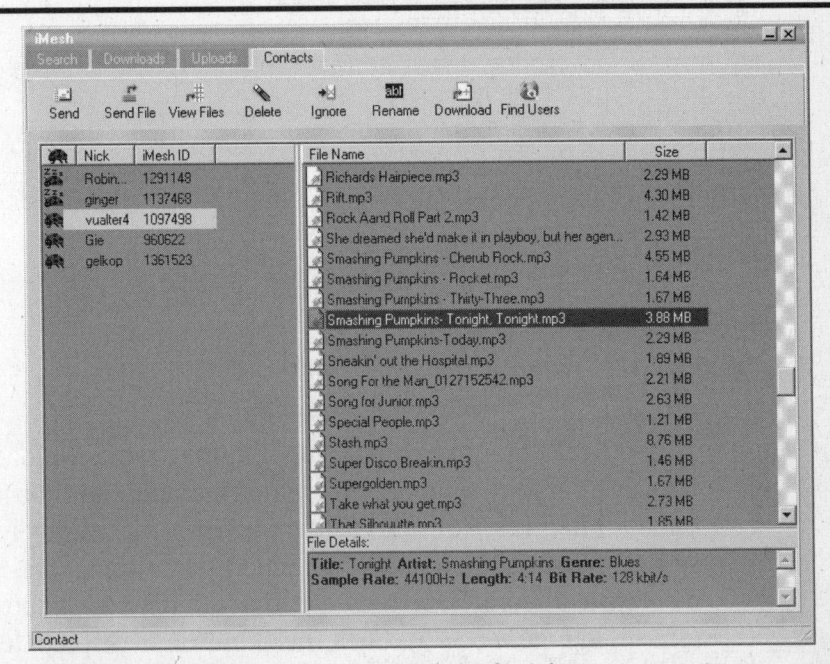

FIGURE 5.123: iMesh lets you browse the files that your contacts are sharing.

- To rename a contact (for example, to give them a name that makes it easier for you to identify them), right-click the contact and choose Rename from the context menu. (Alternatively, select the contact and click the Rename button on the toolbar.) iMesh displays an edit box around their name. Enter the new name and press the Enter key. (The renaming happens only at your end; the contact's name remains the same for everybody else.)

- To send a message to a contact, right-click the contact's name and choose Send a Message from the context menu. (Alternatively, select the contact and click the Send button on the toolbar.) iMesh displays the Send Message to iMesh User dialog box (shown in Figure 5.124). Enter the message in the text box and click the Send button.

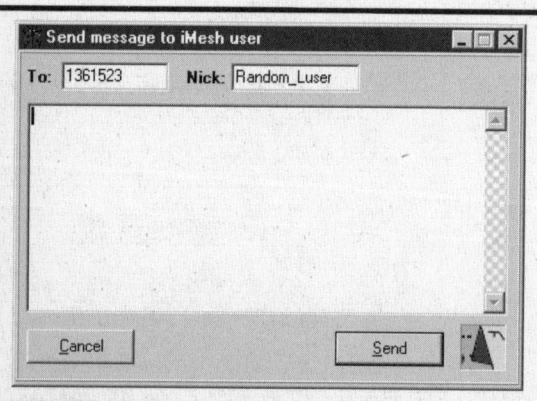

FIGURE 5.124: Sending a message to a contact

- To send a file link to a contact (so that they can download it easily from you), right-click the contact's name and choose Send a File Link from the context menu. (Alternatively, select the contact and click the Send File button.) iMesh displays a different Send Message to iMesh User dialog box (shown in Figure 5.125). Click the ... button to display the

Finding MP3 files Using Napster and Its Friends

Choose File You Want to Recommend to Your Friend dialog box, navigate to and select the file, and click the Open button to enter its details in the File Name text box. Enter a description in the File Description text box so that your contact knows what you're sending, and click the Send button to send the file link.

> **NOTE**
>
> If the folder that contains the file you recommend is not shared, iMesh prompts you to share it.

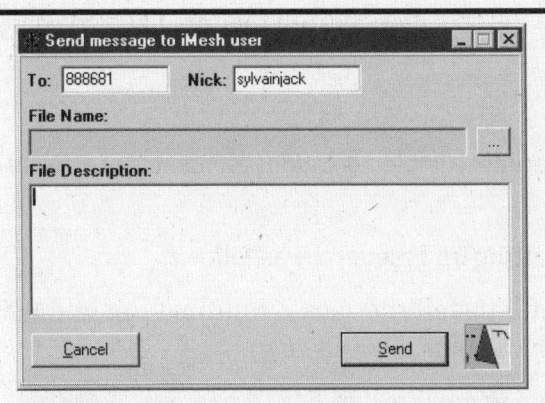

FIGURE 5.125: Sending a file link to a contact

Exiting iMesh

To exit iMesh, right-click the iMesh icon in your system tray and choose Exit from the context menu. (Clicking the Close button—the X button—on the iMesh window closes the iMesh window but does not exit iMesh.)

Freenet

Freenet is an ambitious file-sharing project that's currently under heavy development. Unlike Napster, Freenet does not use a centralized system of servers and is deliberately designed to be hard (perhaps impossible) to shut down by human intervention. Freenet also uses encryption to provide privacy for the nodes on its network, allowing users of Freenet to become anonymous.

Compared to technologies such as Napster, audioGnome, gnutella, and Freenet is more difficult to set up. This section outlines the general steps for getting Freenet up and running on Windows. Because the project is being developed at a cracking pace, this section does not give the specifics because they are likely to change.

> **NOTE**
>
> Linux and Macintosh implementations of Freenet are also available.

The steps for setting up Freenet are as follows:

- ▶ Download and install the Java 2 Runtime Environment (unless you have it installed already).
- ▶ Download and install Freenet.
- ▶ Download and install a GUI for Freenet (if you don't want to run Freenet from the command line).
- ▶ Find the files you want.

We'll look at each step in turn.

> **WARNING**
>
> Freenet is designed for sharing all kinds of files without restriction or oversight. You'll find a lot of music files on Freenet, but you'll also find politics, philosophy, software, videos, and pornography—among other things.

Downloading and Installing the Java 2 Runtime Environment

First, establish whether you have the Java 2 Runtime Environment (JRE) installed on your computer.

The easiest way to find this out is to open a command-prompt window (for example, by choosing Start ➤ Programs ➤ Accessories ➤ MS-DOS Prompt in Windows 98 or Windows Me), type **java** at the command prompt, and press the Enter key. If you get a list of command options, the JRE is installed. If you get the message "Bad command or file name", the JRE is not installed. Download the JRE from the Sun Java site, java.sun.com. Be sure to get the Java Runtime Environment, which is about 5MB, rather than the Java Software Developer's Kit (SDK), which is about 30MB.

Double-click the file that you downloaded to unpack its contents. The installation routine then runs automatically, presenting you with nothing more complex than a license agreement and the task of choosing a destination location for the files. If you're lucky, you won't need to restart Windows.

Downloading and Installing Freenet

Next, download the latest version of Freenet from `download.sourceforge.net/freenet/`. Unzip it to the folder from which you want to run it.

You can then run Freenet from the command prompt. These are the three critical batch files:

- `fserve.bat` starts the Freenet server program running on your computer.
- `frequest.bat` requests the specified file from Freenet.
- `finsert.bat` inserts a file into Freenet, thus making the file available for other users.

In this graphical day and age, however, most Windows users are much happier with a GUI. Read on.

Downloading and Installing a GUI for Freenet

If you're not comfortable putting your life on the command line, download a GUI for Freenet. At this writing, these are your best bets:

- FNC (shown in Figure 5.126), which is available from the FreenetCentre home page, `ironbark.bendigo.latrobe.edu.au/FNC/`
- FreenetGUI, which is available from the FreenetGUI Web site, `freenetgui.virtualave.net/`

Install, configure, and run the GUI according to the latest instructions on the site from which you download it.

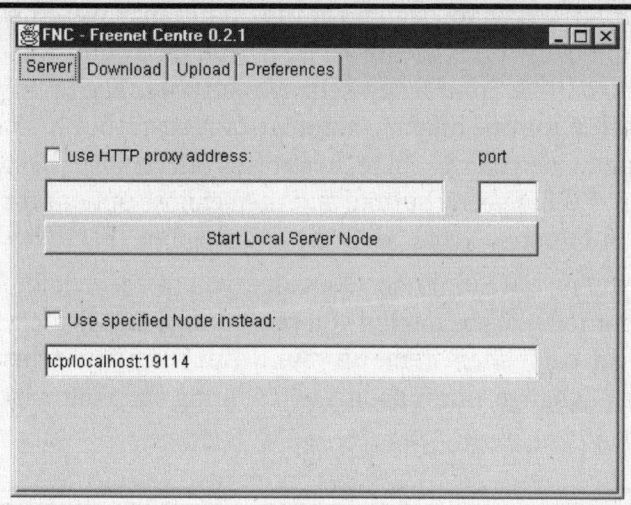

FIGURE 5.126: FNC is an effective front end for Freenet

Finding the Files You Want

At this writing, Freenet is not searchable, so you need to browse through its keys. (A *key* is a kind of description of the information posted. By using the right key, a Freenet user can retrieve a specific file.)

To get started, check freenet.sourceforge.net for information on *key servers*—servers that list available keys.

SpinFrenzy

Like CuteMX and iMesh, SpinFrenzy is a search tool for music, video, and graphics files. The SpinFrenzy search tool is implemented as a Web site, but you need to install the SpinFrenzy Xchange client component to be able to download and upload files.

Chapter Five

To use SpinFrenzy, you sign up at the SpinFrenzy Web site (www.spinfrenzy.com), create a user ID and password, and download and install the SpinFrenzy Xchange software. The SpinFrenzy Xchange setup routine offers to automatically scan your hard disk for audio and video files to share. Resist this offer by clicking the Don't Scan, I Will Specify button, and then choose options for sharing in the SpinFrenzy Xchange–Options dialog box that follows.

Before you install SpinFrenzy Xchange, you can search for items on the SpinFrenzy Web site, but you can't download the items you find, and you can't share items on your drive. Once you've installed SpinFrenzy Xchange, downloading and sharing snap into place.

Figure 5.127 shows the SpinFrenzy Web site.

FIGURE 5.127: SpinFrenzy is a search site for music, video, and graphics files. You need to install the SpinFrenzy Xchange client in order to download and upload files.

Up Next

In this chapter, we've discussed Napster and related technologies for sharing files directly between end users: Macster, Gnapster, Wrapster, gnutella, audioGnome, CuteMX, iMesh, Freenet, and SpinFrenzy. You've seen how you can easily share files located on your system and how you can search for and download files from others.

Much of the music that you'll run into when using the applications and technologies discussed in this chapter will be illegal copies. To balance the karma of the book a bit, in the next chapter, we'll show you a source of music on the Internet that's much more likely to be legal streaming audio and Internet radio stations. Turn the page.

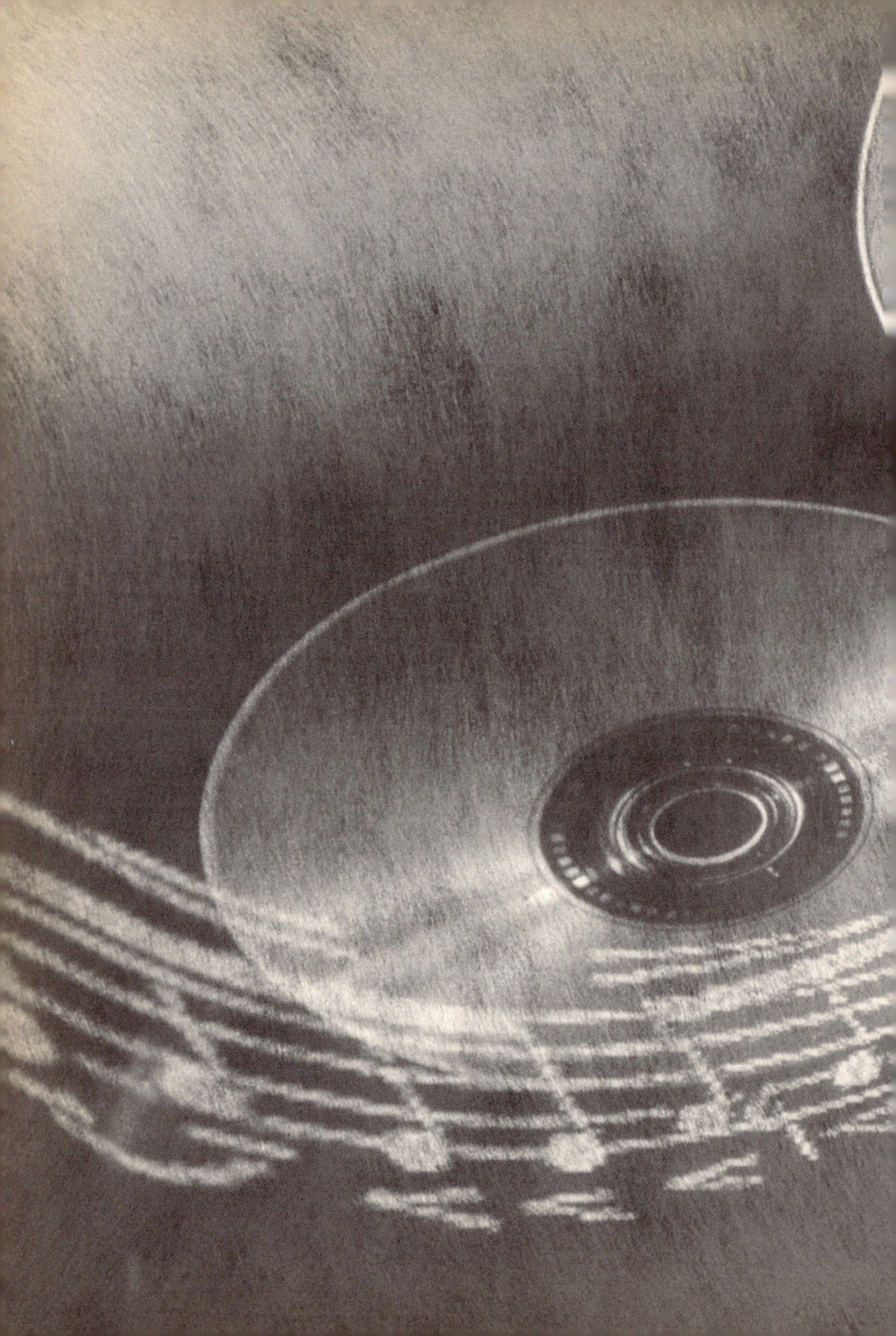

Chapter 6

Tuning In to Internet Radio

FEATURING

- Streaming audio and Internet radio
- Installing and configuring RadioSpy
- Finding and listening to Internet radio stations

In this chapter, we'll briefly discuss how to listen to streaming audio—audio delivered across the Internet that you can listen to in real time, as opposed to downloading to your hard disk for listening to later.

By using streaming audio technologies such as SHOUTcast and icecast, you can broadcast music and speech over the Internet and create your own Internet radio station. As you'll see, you can find a large number of Internet radio stations playing a wide variety of music, so you can listen to new material pretty much all day long if you want to.

If you're planning to tune into Internet radio broadcasts, your starting point should be RadioSpy from GameSpy Industries (www.radiospy.com). RadioSpy is a tool for finding SHOUTcast broadcasts of MP3 music. At the risk of oversimplifying, RadioSpy is like a smart radio tuner for the Web, searching out signals and listing them for you so that you can play them back.

Streaming Audio and Internet Radio

Briefly put, *streaming audio* is audio delivered to you in real time across your network connection or Internet connection. Instead of downloading a block of audio, such as an entire MP3 track, and then listening to it, you can listen to it as you download it. Instead of being saved to disk, the audio is played to you in real time and then discarded.

There are two forms of streaming audio:

On-demand streaming audio   As its name suggests, this is an audio stream that you, the listener, start and stop at your convenience. You usually listen to it by using your default MP3 player. For example, if you're surfing Riffage.com or MP3.com and come across a track you'd like to hear, you can click its streaming link in your browser

(Navigator, Internet Explorer, Opera, or whatever). Your browser activates your default MP3 player and sets it playing the stream back to you. When you listen to a music track on demand, it'll start playing at the beginning of the track.

Broadcast streaming audio   Also known as *Internet radio*, this is streaming audio broadcast across a network or the Internet much as it would be broadcast by a conventional radio station. The broadcast is in real time, so when you tune in, you hear what the DJ is currently playing or saying. To tune in to an Internet radio broadcast, you can use either a custom tool such as RadioSpy, which we discuss in this chapter, or an MP3 player such as Winamp. RadioSpy gives you powerful tuner capabilities, letting you jump nimbly from one station to another, maintain a list of favorite stations, and even chat with the other listeners of your current station. An MP3 player, on the other hand, lets you add Internet radio streams to your playlists and tune into them when you want, but it gives you fewer capabilities for finding Internet radio streams in the first place.

On-demand streaming audio is great for music sites and other Web sites that have content they want people to hear but of which, they do not want (or are not legally permitted) to distribute copies. Because streamed audio isn't saved to the user's hard disk (unless the user rigs a way of saving it), many tedious legalities are avoided.

On-demand streaming audio is good for users who have plenty of bandwidth, because they can listen to the audio they want to hear when they want to hear it. They don't even need to wait for a download to complete before the stream starts playing, so they get almost instant gratification. But if you don't have the bandwidth, on-demand streaming audio has little appea—it'll choke your Internet connection, and you'll get choppy, lo-fi audio.

Internet radio is likewise great for people who want to broadcast their thoughts or music for free, and for those who have enough bandwidth to listen to it. We'll show you how to broadcast with SHOUTcast and icecast in Chapter 17, "Getting Your Music Up on the Web."

Getting, Installing, and Configuring RadioSpy

Download the latest version of RadioSpy from the RadioSpy Web site (www.radiospy.com), then install RadioSpy by double-clicking the distribution file and following the setup routine. Apart from choosing the appropriate language for your needs, the only part of the installation worth noting is the Select Components dialog box, which lets you select which components you want to install. You'll probably want to install both the Winamp Skin and the RadioSpy QuickStart.

When you first launch RadioSpy (which you can do from the Installation Complete dialog box), you'll need to set a number of configuration options. We'll run you through these options in the next few paragraphs.

RadioSpy displays the Configuration dialog box with its General page displayed (see Figure 6.1). Choose options as follows:

> **WinAmp Directory text box**   Make sure RadioSpy has identified your Winamp directory. (If not, click the folder button to the right of the WinAmp Directory text box and use the Browse for Folder dialog box to identify the directory.) To use a different MP3 player, click the Other button and use the Select an Alternate MP3 Player dialog box to identify the player.
>
> **Chat Nick text box**   In this text box, enter your handle for chat rooms. Be original.

Net Connection drop-down list In this drop-down list, select the speed and type of your Internet connection. RadioSpy uses this setting to deliver the appropriate quality of music to you, so enter the correct speed.

Stream Buffer drop-down list Set the size of the buffer that you want to use for RadioSpy broadcasts—the amount of information you want to hold in memory to smooth out unevenness in the sound stream. The bigger the buffer, the smoother the sound, but the longer it will take for the sound to start.

Disable Banners check box This check box is disabled until you register your copy of RadioSpy—you can't get rid of the ad banners without paying for the privilege.

Show RadioSpy in System Tray check box Select this check box if you want RadioSpy to display an icon in the system tray on the Taskbar rather than an item in the Taskbar. This icon usually provides the most convenient access to RadioSpy.

Interface Style group box In this group box, choose Basic or Advanced. The Basic interface style provides a little less information than the Advanced interface style, but it's easier to use. Start with Basic; you can easily switch to Advanced later.

Demographic Information group box Enter information in this group box as you see appropriate. If you want to be on RadioSpy's mailing list, make sure the Notify Me When a New Version Comes Out check box is selected; if not, make sure it's cleared. The Click Here to Find Out Why We're So Darn Nosey button displays a message box with a humorous explanation of why RadioSpy wants your demographic information (or an approximation of it).

Chapter Six

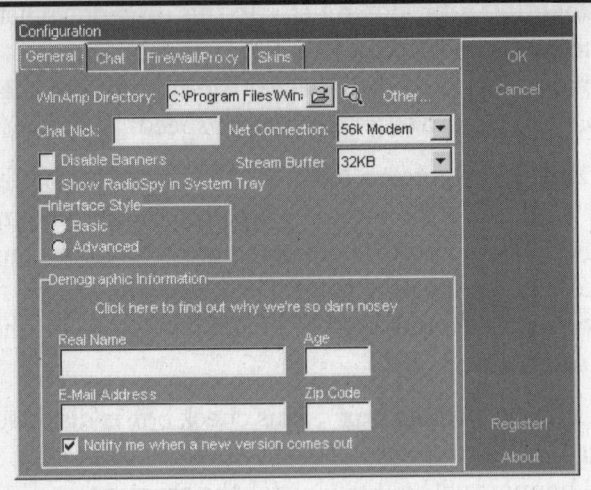

FIGURE 6.1: Setting options on the General page of the RadioSpy Configuration dialog box

Click the Chat tab to display the Chat page (the top part of which is shown in Figure 6.2), and select the following options as appropriate:

Connect to Chat on Startup check box   Select this check box if you want to connect to the chat group when you start RadioSpy.

Hide Join/Parts in Chat check box   Select this check box if you want to suppress messages about people's leaving and joining chat rooms (often a good idea).

Don't Set Auto-Away check box   Select this check box if you want to suppress messages indicating that you've left a chat room when you change to the News or Server pages in RadioSpy.

Home Channel text box   In this text box, enter the name of the channel that you want RadioSpy to use as your home channel. (This feature is only accessible in the registered version.)

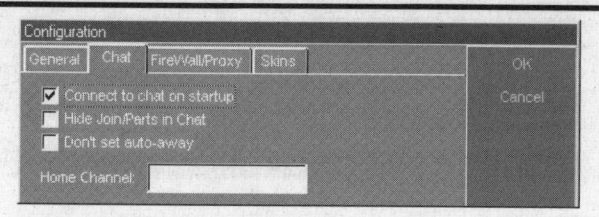

FIGURE 6.2: Choose your desired chat options on the Chat page of the Configuration dialog box.

If you use a firewall or a proxy server, click the Firewall/Proxy tab to display that page and enter your firewall or proxy server settings. (You might need to ask your system administrator for these settings; if you do, explain that you need RadioSpy to listen to business and technical broadcasts.)

To change the skin (the graphical look) that RadioSpy uses, click the Skins tab to display the Skins page. Click the Get Skins Here link to download skins for RadioSpy, then select the skin in the Skin Name drop-down list.

Finally, click the OK button to apply your configuration settings and launch RadioSpy.

Understanding the RadioSpy Interface

RadioSpy has a complex interface that takes a minute or two to grasp—and that's too complex for us to label all in one figure. So we've broken it up into three parts to show it to you more effectively. Figure 6.3 shows the entire RadioSpy interface without labels, and the next three figures show the RadioSpy interface piece by piece with labels.

Chapter Six

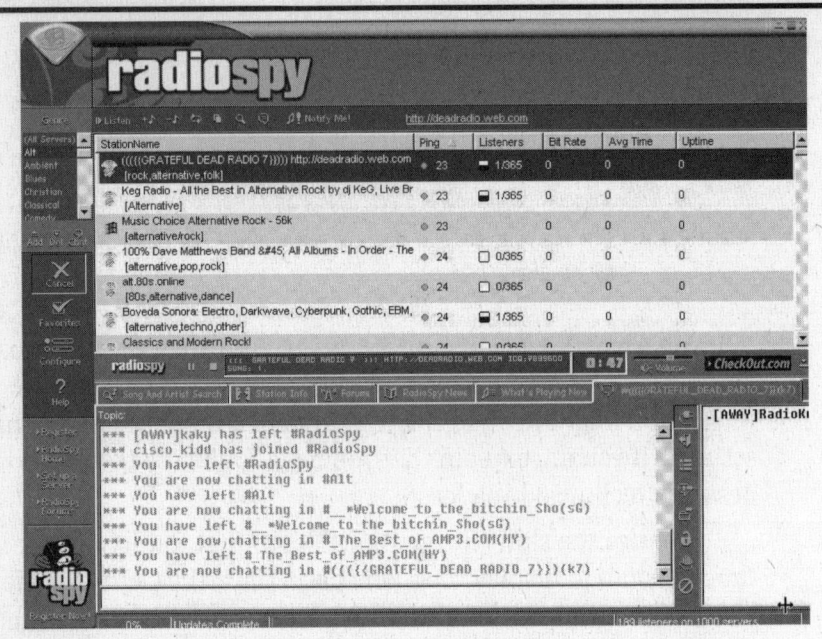

FIGURE 6.3: RadioSpy has a complex interface to give you access to all its features.

Figure 6.4 shows the top part of the RadioSpy screen.

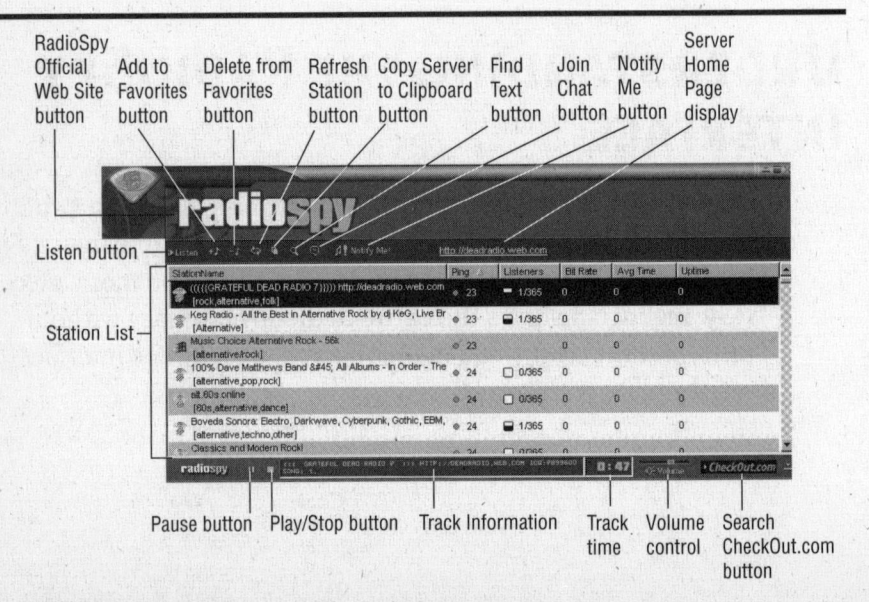

FIGURE 6.4: The top part of the RadioSpy screen

Tuning into Internet Radio 287

Figure 6.5 shows the controls on the left-hand side of the RadioSpy screen.

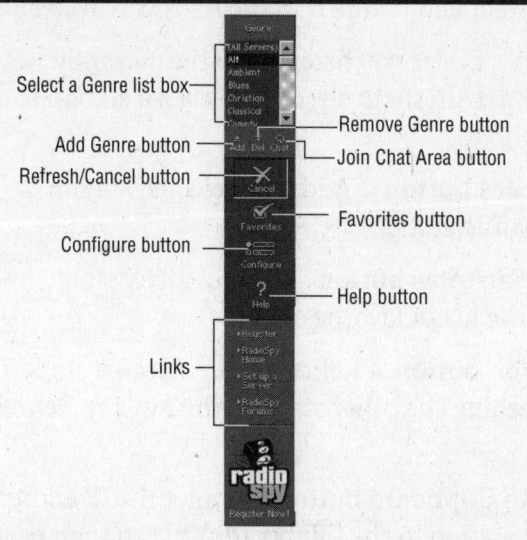

FIGURE 6.5: The left-hand side of the RadioSpy screen

Figure 6.6 shows the bottom portion of the RadioSpy screen.

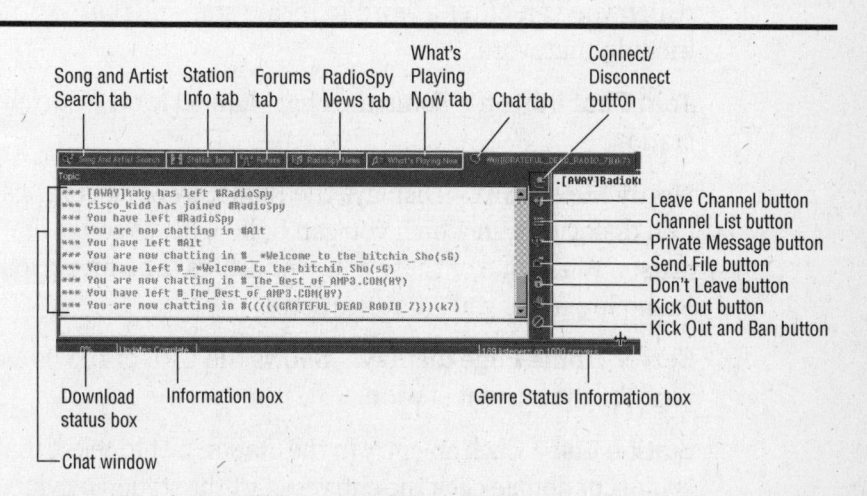

FIGURE 6.6: The bottom portion of the RadioSpy screen

Here's what the components of the RadioSpy interface do:

RadioSpy Official Web Site button   Starts or activates your Web browser and points it to the RadioSpy Web site.

Listen button   Starts you listening to the currently selected station. (Alternatively, double-click a station to start listening to it.)

Add to Favorites button   Adds the selected station to your list of favorite stations.

Delete from Favorites button   Deletes an existing favorite from the list of favorite stations.

Refresh Station button   Refreshes the selected station (without refreshing the other stations the way the Refresh button does).

Copy Server to Clipboard button   Copies the IP address of the current station to the Clipboard. You can then paste it into a player (such as Winamp) or into a playlist.

Find Text button   Displays the Find dialog box, in which you can enter a word to locate stations that include that word.

Join Chat button   Joins the chat channel for the current station.

Notify Me button   Displays the RadioSpy Song Notification dialog box, in which you can build a list of songs or artists. When one of these songs or artists is being played, RadioSpy sends you a notification.

Server Home Page display   Shows the URL of the home page for the current station.

Station List   Click an entry in the Station List to select that station, or double-click the entry to start the station playing.

Play/Stop and Pause buttons   Play, stop, and pause the current station. The Play button and Stop button replace each other as appropriate.

Search CheckOut.com button   When available, this button takes you to an online music vendor to buy the CD from which the current track is playing. It's also handy for finding out more about a CD or artist when you have no intention of buying.

Track Information   This display shows the time elapsed on the current track.

Track time   This display shows infomation about the current track.

Volume control   This control lets you adjust the volume at which RadioSpy is currently playing. You may want to use the Windows volume control or an external volume control to adjust the volume instead.

Select a Genre list box   Lets you select a genre of SHOUTcast station to display.

Add Genre button   Displays the Add a Genre dialog box, in which you can add a genre to the list of genres.

Remove Genre button   Removes the selected genre from the list.

Join Chat Area button   Joins the chat area for the current genre.

Refresh/Cancel button   Refreshes the server list displayed. While the refresh is taking place, the Cancel button is displayed in place of the Refresh button. Click the Cancel button to cancel the refresh if it's taking too long.

Favorites button   Displays in place of the station list a list of the stations that you've designated as your favorites. Click the button again to return to the station list.

Configure button   Displays the Configuration dialog box.

Help button   Displays the Tips dialog box.

Links These links provide quick access to RadioSpy registration and information.

Status Bar (containing the Download Status, Information, and Genre Status Information boxes) Provides updates on what's happening in the RadioSpy window.

Connect/Disconnect button Connects you to and disconnects you from the current chat channel.

Leave Channel button Removes you from the current chat channel.

Channel List button Displays the Channel List dialog box, which contains a list of channels that you can join.

Private Message button Starts a private message to the selected chat participant.

Send File button Starts the process of sending a file via DCC connection to the selected chat participant.

Don't Leave button Prevents RadioSpy from leaving this channel automatically when you join another channel. When this button is selected, it appears pushed in.

Kick Out button and **Kick Out and Ban button** The Kick Out button kicks the selected user out of the channel. The Kick Out and Ban button kicks the user out *and* prevents them from rejoining. In our experience, kicking out works well, but kicking out and banning tends to throw errors.

Chat window This window displays the ongoing chat in the current channel.

The six tabs on the lower part of the RadioSpy window give you quick access to the six pages of information that RadioSpy supports:

▶ **Song and Artist Search page** Use this page to search for a particular artist or a song title in the stations' playlists.

Tuning into Internet Radio 291

- **Station Info page**   This page displays information about the current station.

- **Forums page**   This page provides quick access to any forums associated with the stations you're listening to.

- **RadioSpy News page**   This page displays headlines with links to the current news on RadioSpy's Web site.

- **What's Playing Now page**   This page displays a list of the tracks currently being played by the stations.

- **Chat page**   This page provides a chat area that you can navigate by using the buttons on its right-hand side.

CONNECTING TO A STATION

To connect to a station, make sure your Internet connection is fired up. Then choose the genre of music in the Select a Genre list box to display the list of Internet radio stations available in that genre, as shown in Figure 6.7.

FIGURE 6.7:   To connect to a station, double-click it in the server list.

Here's what you see in the station list:

StationName column   Displays the name of the server and station.

Speed bar or Ping dot The Speed bar (in the Basic interface) or the Ping dot (in the Advanced interface) shows the health of the server signal. A long green bar or a green dot represents a strong signal; a shorter orange bar or an orange dot shows a server that's getting a lot of traffic; and a short red bar or a red dot indicates that the server is either down or having problems with the signal skipping.

Listeners column Shows the number of people listening to the station, from Empty to a few people to many people to Full. If a station is listed as Full, you won't be able to access that station. Click the Listeners column once to rank the stations in ascending order of number of listeners; click it again to rank the stations in descending order of number of listeners.

Quality or Bit Rate column The Quality column (in the Basic interface) or the Bit Rate column (in the Advanced interface) shows the speed of the signal, from 16kbps (which sounds horrible even for spoken audio) to 128kbps (which is near CD quality). Pick a high-quality or high-bitrate station over a low-quality or low-bitrate station any day.

Uptime column The Uptime column, which appears only in the Advanced interface, shows how long the station has been on the air this session. This information isn't usually relevant to the listening experience, although you've got to figure that any station with long airtime is more technically competent than a station that seldom breaks a couple of hours.

Once you've connected to a server and got it playing to your liking, you can minimize RadioSpy by clicking its minimize button. If you chose to display the system tray icon during configuration, RadioSpy won't appear in the Taskbar; click the RadioSpy button in the system tray to restore RadioSpy.

Using Favorites

RadioSpy makes it easy to maintain a list of your favorite stations for quick access:

- To add a station to your list of Favorites, press Ctrl+A or right-click it and choose Add to Favorites from the context menu.

- To toggle your list of favorites on and off, click the Favorites button.

- To remove a station from your Favorites list, press Ctrl+D or right-click it and choose Remove from Favorites on the context menu.

NOTE

You can also listen to Internet radio stations and streaming audio using MP3 players such as Winamp and Sonique. We'll show you how to do so in the chapter that discusses those players.

Up Next

In this short chapter, we've shown you how to use RadioSpy to find and listen to Internet radio stations. We've also mentioned another way of listening to streaming audio—by using some of the MP3 players that we'll show you a little later in this book.

That's the end of this part of the book. In the next part, we'll show you how to create and listen to MP3 files on Windows.

But in the meantime, now that you've seen how many people are on the air with their own Internet radio station, you may want to get on the (virtual) air yourself. We'll show you how to do that in Chapter 17.

PART III
MP3 on Windows

LEARN TO:

- Choose the right stand-alone MP3 player PC
- Make the most of Windows Media Player
- Play music with Winamp and Sonique
- Decide between a ripper/encoder combination and a ripper/player/jukebox
- Rip with AudioCatalyst
- Encode with MP3Enc, LAME, and LameBatch
- Rip, encode, play, and burn CDs with MusicMatch Jukebox
- Rip, encode, and play music with RealJukebox

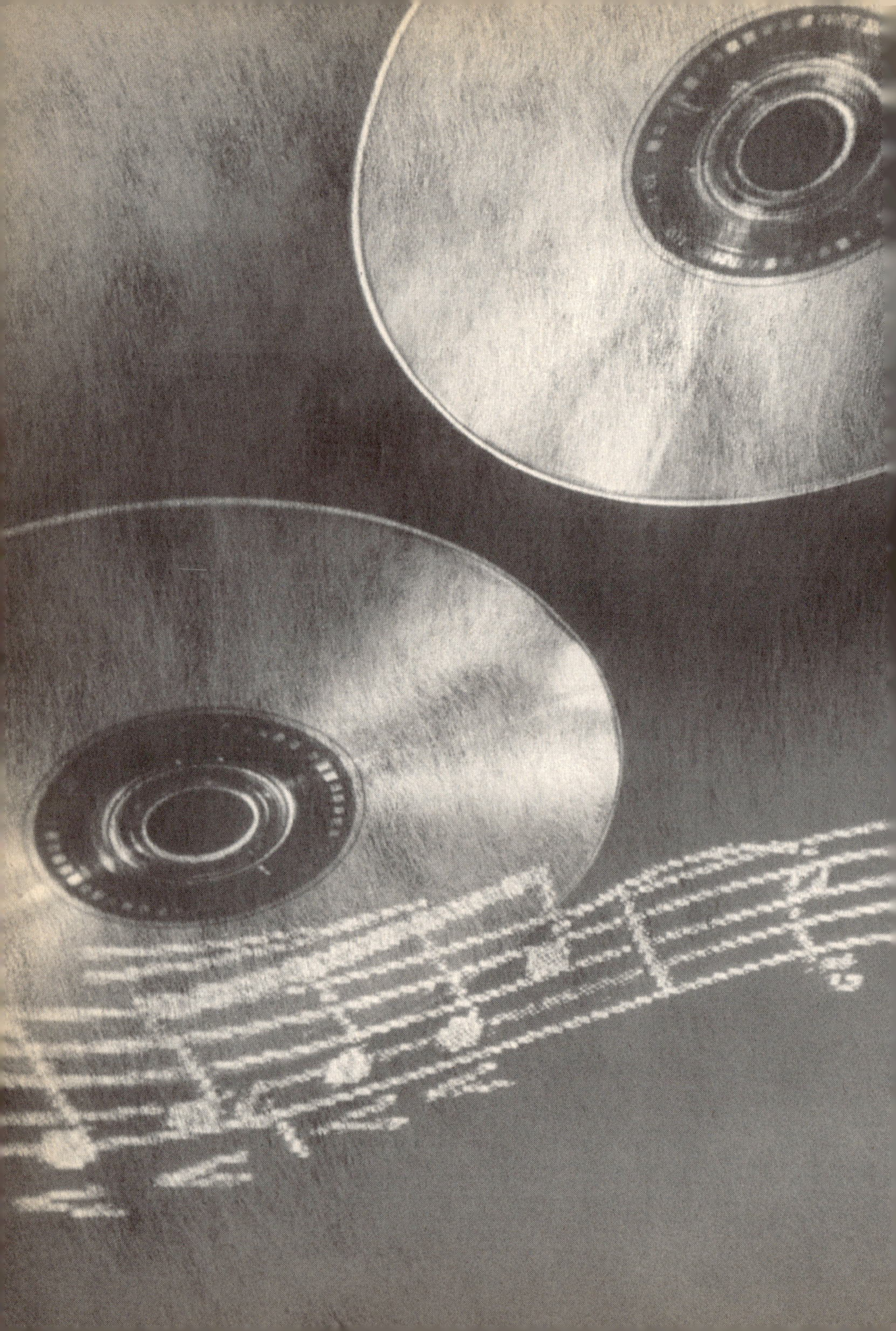

Chapter 7
Windows Players

FEATURING
- Windows Media Player
- Winamp
- Sonique
- Other players

In this chapter, we'll introduce you to the wide world of MP3 players for Windows. Because Windows is still the most widely used operating system in the world, it has the greatest variety of MP3 players available, and (as you'd imagine) these vary widely in capabilities and appeal. We'll show you the best players and the most popular players, mention some of the rest, and ignore the others.

All the players discussed in this chapter are stand-alone players in that they don't do the ripping and encoding that full-fledged ripper/player/jukeboxes do. If you want, you can dispense with a stand-alone MP3 player and just use a ripper/player/jukebox, but most people find they're better off getting a player for regular use. We'll discuss the reasons why at the beginning of this chapter, and we'll suggest some guidelines for choosing a stand-alone player that fits your needs.

Then we'll show you how to make the best use of the most ubiquitous but least powerful MP3 player—Windows Media Player for 32-bit Windows versions before Windows Millennium Edition (Windows Me). For those of you who are already using Windows Me, we'll then show you how to enjoy MP3 on the much more powerful Windows Media Player that Windows Me provides.

The various versions of Windows Media Player together form the most ubiquitous MP3 player, because they're distributed with almost all known versions of Windows. The best MP3 players are a different kettle of fish. We reckon the two best players are Winamp and Sonique, and we'll discuss them in some depth later in this chapter. Each provides an impressive set of features, including playlists for organizing your music, graphic equalizers for adjusting its sound, skins for changing the looks of the players, and visualizations for spacing your mind out while listening to the music. Winamp and Sonique are both free. Winamp is distributed as part of Netscape Communicator and AOL, but you can also get it separately on its own.

At the end of this chapter, we'll mention some of the more interesting of the less popular MP3 players for Windows, leaving you to explore these in depth if you so choose.

Choosing a Stand-Alone MP3 Player

In this chapter, we'll describe in detail several stand-alone MP3 players, and mention quite a few more. Chances are, you won't want to install all of these players on your computer. They'll take up disk space, they'll squabble with each other over file extensions, and they may even try to overwrite one another's DLLs (dynamic link libraries, repositories of shared Windows functions). In this section, we'll discuss how to evaluate stand-alone MP3 players and choose between them.

First up, you may decide that you don't need a stand-alone player. If you wish, you can do all your playing with an MP3 jukebox and not use a separate player at all. (We'll discuss MP3 jukeboxes for Windows in Chapter 9, "Windows Jukeboxes.") But while a good ripper/player/jukebox can take care of almost all your MP3 needs, most people find that they like to have a stand-alone player as well. This is because the best stand-alone MP3 players not only have more playback features and tend to be cooler looking and easier to manipulate than most ripper/player/jukeboxes, but they're also smaller in both screen space and the demands they place on your computer.

There are so many Windows MP3 players available now that it makes little sense to try each one unless you suffer from a surfeit of spare time. You'll probably do best to stick with the better known players at first—in most cases, you'll find there are good reasons for a popular player's being popular—and graduate to lesser known players if the better known ones prove unsatisfactory.

Here are our suggested criteria for evaluating MP3 players. For some, you'll need to use the player; for others, reading its specs or asking about other users' experiences should set you on the right path.

How much load does the player impose on your computer? Any player that monopolizes your processor cycles is going to cause problems if you run it regularly and expect to do anything constructive at the same time. Particularly if your computer is underpowered—say, a Pentium MMX rather than a Celeron, Pentium II, Pentium III, Athlon, or Duron—you'll want to make sure that your player is modest in its CPU requirements.

Does it have the features you need? At a minimum, you'll need a comprehensible interface that lets you control the playback easily, preferably including a volume control. For conventional use, you'll want a readout of the song and artist, plus playlist capabilities and a playlist editor (for creating the playlists).

Is it stable? There are enough good, mature players out there that you'll have little reason to use buggy, underdeveloped players, unless a certain player has a killer feature (or interface) that redeems its wickedness.

Do you like the way it looks? If you need to choose between two players that offer otherwise identical sets of features, you'll want to go with the one that looks better. If a player is ugly, does it have skins (graphical looks) that can make it look better? Chances are, you'll have the player open on your desktop much of the time you'll be using your computer, so it'll be in your face as well as in your ears.

Does the player have a system-tray icon? For quick and easy access, make sure that the player puts an icon in your system tray. This allows you to bring up the player instantly (or control it from the system tray) without having to resort to its Taskbar item or Alt+Tab through a stack of windows.

Is the price right? Many MP3 players cost only a few bucks, but others are free. Don't pay for a player unless you have a compelling reason to do so or unless your pocketbook is overflowing.

Does it automatically inform you about upgrades and add-ons? If you're frequently online looking for new versions, or if you don't always want to keep your software absolutely up-to-date, you may not be too worried about having the MP3 player manufacturer automatically inform you that a later and greater version has become available. But for most people, this feature can be useful.

With these half-dozen points in mind, you should have little difficulty finding a stand-alone MP3 player that meets your needs. In the following sections, we'll introduce you to some of the prominent contenders for your playing time.

Windows Media Player

Because it's distributed with almost all known versions of Windows, Windows Media Player is undoubtedly the most widely available MP3 player for Windows. But because the versions of Windows Media Player in Windows 95, Windows 98, Windows NT 4, and Windows 2000 are extremely limited in their capabilities, Windows Media Player has also been one of the least-used MP3 players around.

The version of Windows Media Player included in Windows, Windows Me, Windows Media Player 7, aims to change that. Windows Media Player 7 has much fuller features, including better playlist features and the ability to rip and encode to WMA format.

In the next section, we'll show you what (little) you can do with MP3 files using the earlier versions of Windows Media Player. In the section after that, we'll outline how Windows Media Player 7 improves on its predecessors.

Windows Media Player Versions up to 7

Windows Media Player versions before version 7 (in other words, the versions of Windows Media Player shipped with or available for Windows 9*x*, Windows NT 4, and Windows 2000) are so limited in their MP3 capabilities that they're primarily of interest if you want to play MP3 tracks on a work computer that you're not allowed (or able) to install software on. These versions of Windows Media Player let you open only one file at a time, but because that file can be a playlist, you can keep the music rolling without constantly having to reach for your mouse to load another track.

Start Windows Media Player as usual by choosing Start ➤ Programs ➤ Accessories ➤ Multimedia ➤ Windows Media Player or Start ➤ Programs ➤ Accessories ➤ Entertainment ➤ Windows Media Player, depending on the version of Windows you're using. Open an MP3 file by choosing File ➤ Open (or pressing Ctrl+O) to display the first Open dialog box and clicking the Browse button to display the second Open dialog box. Then open the MP3 file or playlist as you would any other file. (Depending on the version of Windows Media Player you're using, you may need to select a suitable file type in the Files of Type drop-down list.)

Windows Players 303

Figure 7.1 shows Windows Media Player version 6.4 playing a playlist. As you can see, this version of Windows Media Player provides the basic controls:

- buttons for Play, Pause, Stop, Skip Back, Rewind, Fast Forward, and Skip Forward
- a volume control
- a Mute button (the one with the speaker icon)
- a progress slider

The remaining button shown (the one with the three double-headed horizontal arrows) is the Preview button, which plays the first ten seconds of each file in a playlist—a great feature for finding the track whose name and number were on the tip of your tongue.

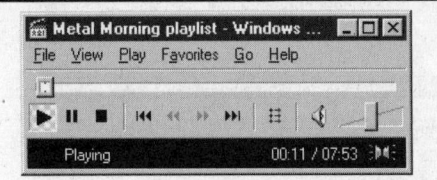

FIGURE 7.1: If you can't (or won't) install extra software on a Windows PC, you can use Windows Media Player to play MP3 files and playlists.

If you use Windows Media Player regularly, optimize the view so that it shows you what you want but doesn't waste space on screen. Choose View ➢ Compact to switch to Compact view (which saves a goodly amount of space) or View ➢ Minimal to switch to Minimal view (which saves even more space but omits features such as the progress slider). You can customize the items displayed for Compact view and Minimal view by choosing Tools ➢ Options to display the Options dialog box, selecting and clearing the check boxes as appropriate in the Compact group box and Minimal group box, and then clicking the OK button.

As mentioned a moment ago, you can use Windows Media Player to play playlists—but you can't use it to create them. If you're relying on Windows Media Player for your entertainment, you'll need to create playlists manually. To do so, fire up Notepad or another text editor and create a text document that contains the path and filename of each track in the playlist on a new line. (Copy and paste the path if you're entering multiple files from the same folder.) Figure 7.2 shows a short playlist under way in Notepad.

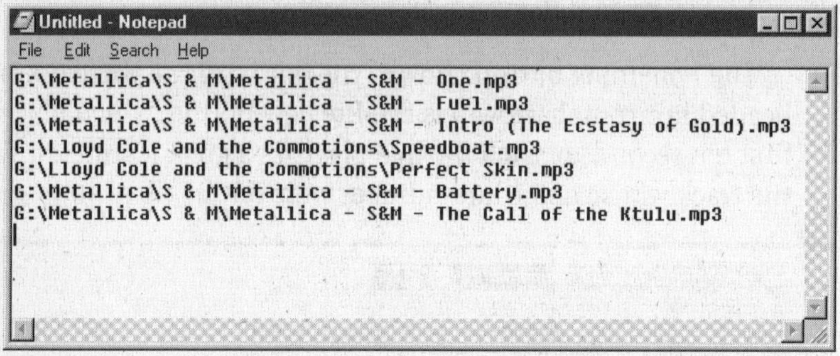
Untitled - Notepad
File Edit Search Help
G:\Metallica\S & M\Metallica - S&M - One.mp3
G:\Metallica\S & M\Metallica - S&M - Fuel.mp3
G:\Metallica\S & M\Metallica - S&M - Intro (The Ecstasy of Gold).mp3
G:\Lloyd Cole and the Commotions\Speedboat.mp3
G:\Lloyd Cole and the Commotions\Perfect Skin.mp3
G:\Metallica\S & M\Metallica - S&M - Battery.mp3
G:\Metallica\S & M\Metallica - S&M - The Call of the Ktulu.mp3

FIGURE 7.2: You can use Notepad or another text editor to create playlists for Windows Media Player.

When you save the text file, enter the name for the playlist *in double quotation marks and with the extension .M3U*. For example, to create a playlist named Slow Morning in Stockton, enter **"Slow Morning in Stockton.m3u"** (including the double quotation marks) in the File Name text box. If you don't include the quotation marks, Notepad adds a TXT extension to the filename you typed, and you won't be able to use the playlist without renaming it.

Windows Media Player 7

Windows Media Player version 7 (the version included in Windows Me) is a totally different animal from earlier versions. Among other enhancements, it can rip and encode music to the WMA format (it calls this "copying" a CD to the hard disk—peculiar terminology), it's aware of portable devices such as the Diamond Rio, and it provides full-ish jukebox capabilities. Unfortunately (and we use the word loosely, as this is clearly a very deliberate Microsoft design decision), Windows Media Player cannot rip to MP3 format, presumably in the hope of spreading the secure WMA format instead.

Start Windows Media Player by choosing Start ➢ Programs ➢ Windows Media Player. Figure 7.3 shows Windows Media Player in its Full mode, with a track playing.

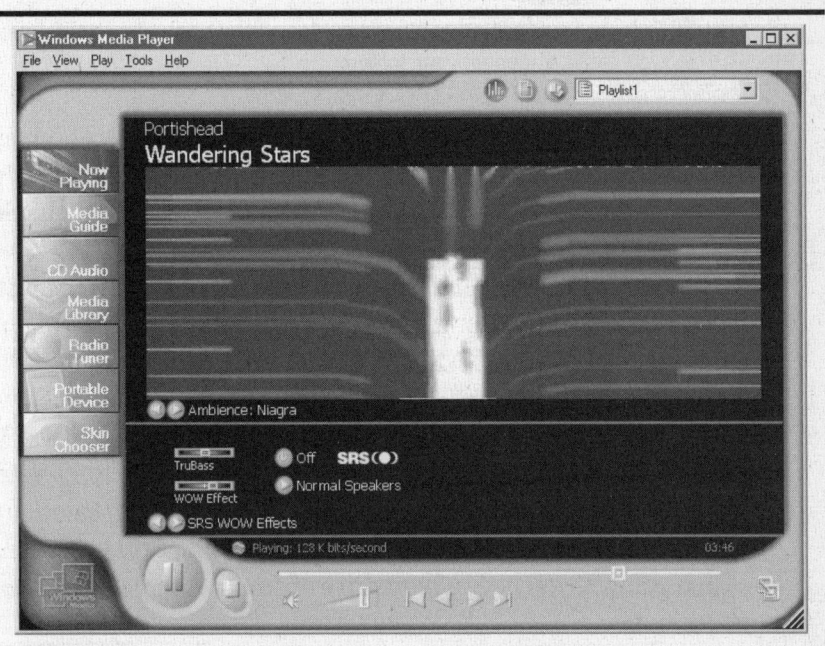

FIGURE 7.3: Windows Media Player 7, shown here in its Full mode, is a huge improvement over previous versions of Windows Media Player.

As you can see in Figure 7.3, Full mode takes up a serious chunk of a small screen. For sustained use, you'll be better off using Compact mode, shown in Figure 7.4.

FIGURE 7.4: In Compact mode, Windows Media Player occupies a more reasonable amount of your screen.

Early on, you should let Windows Media Player know about all the audio and video files on your computer. To do so, choose Tools ➢ Search Computer for Media, or press the F3 key, to display the Search Computer for Media dialog box, shown in Figure 7.5. Specify the drive in the Search for Media In drop-down list, and specify a starting folder if necessary in the Beginning In drop-down list. (If you have a typical computer setup, your best choice is Local Drives in the Search for Media In drop-down list. In this case, the Beginning In drop-down list is dimmed and unavailable.) Don't select the Include WAV and MIDI Files Found in System Folders check box unless you're longing to play Windows sounds (such as the logon and logoff sounds) through Windows Media Player. Then click the Start Search button to set the search going. If you have a hard drive of any size, the search takes a few minutes.

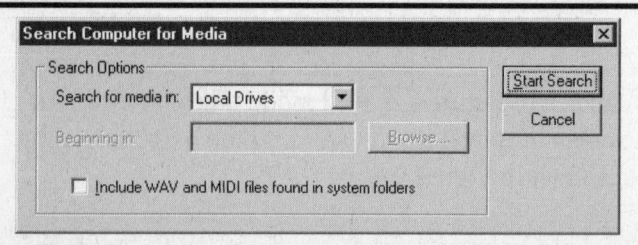

FIGURE 7.5: Use the Search Computer for Media dialog box to search your computer for audio and video files.

Once Windows Media Player has assembled the list of files, you'll be able to access them via the Media Library page in Full mode. Figure 7.6 shows the Media Library page with a modest assortment of audio tracks.

To create a new playlist, click the New Playlist button on the Media Library page, enter the name for the playlist in the New Playlist dialog box, and click the OK button. Windows Media Player creates a new playlist in the My Playlists list. You can then populate it by dragging tracks to it.

FIGURE 7.6: Windows Media Player marshals the files and lists them on the Media Library page.

To switch from one playlist to another, use the drop-down list in the upper-right corner of Windows Media Player.

Windows Media Player has a raft of configuration options on the eight pages of its Options dialog box (Tools ≻ Options). The following paragraphs and list describe the most important options, but you'll probably want to scan the other options as well.

Chapter Seven

On the Player page (see Figure 7.7), choose these options:

- In the Auto Upgrade group box, select the Once a Month option button, unless you want Windows Media Player to prompt you to upgrade more frequently. In addition, make sure that the Prompt for Codec Download check box is selected. This check box makes Windows Media Player prompt you before it installs any new codecs. If you select the Enable Automatic Codec Download check box, it goes ahead and installs the codecs on its own authority.

- In the Player Settings group box, you can choose whether to start the player on the Media Guide page, whether to display the player always on top in Compact mode, and whether to display the anchor window (a small reference window) when the player is in Compact mode. We don't find much use for the anchor window, but having the player always on top can be handy.

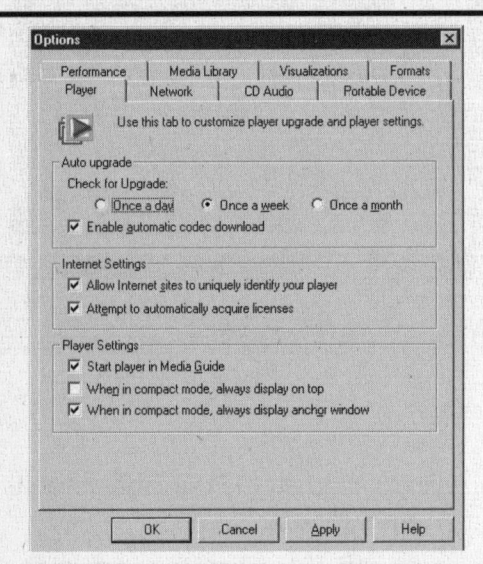

FIGURE 7.7: The Player page of the Options dialog box

On the Network page (see Figure 7.8), you can choose which protocols to use for receiving audio and video streams over a network. Unless you know your protocols, you probably shouldn't mess with the default selections.

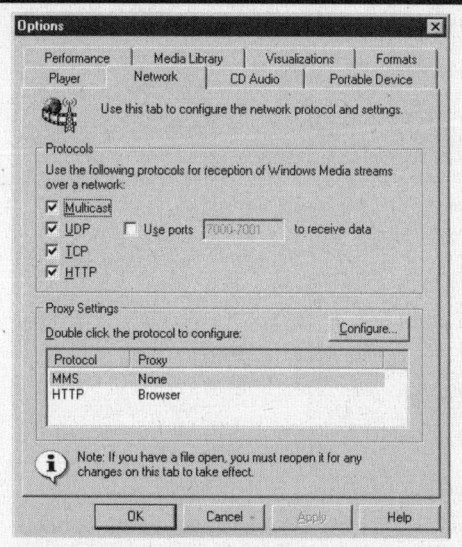

FIGURE 7.8: If you're familiar with network protocols, you can adjust them on the Network page of the Options dialog box.

On the CD Audio page (see Figure 7.9), choose the following options:

- Make sure the Digital Playback check box is selected.

- In the Copying Settings group box, select the Best Quality setting (which encodes at 160kbps) or the setting below it (which encodes at 128kbps), unless you find that either of the lower quality settings (Smallest Size, which encodes at 64kpbs, or the second setting, which encodes at 96kbps) sounds good enough to you.

Chapter Seven

- In the Archive group box, specify the folder in which you want Windows Media Player to put the copies of audio it rips and encodes.

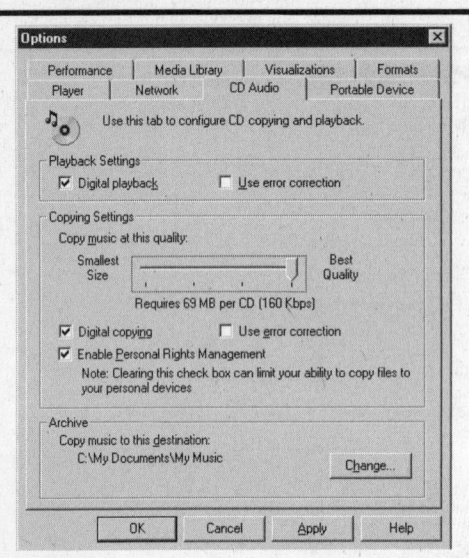

FIGURE 7.9: Choose quality settings on the CD Audio page of the Options dialog box.

On the Portable Device page (see Figure 7.10), click the Select Quality Level option button and specify Best Quality or the middle setting on the Copy Music at This Quality slider if you'll be using Windows Media Player with a portable device. Click the Details button to make your Web browser display the latest information using portable devices with Windows Media Player.

On the Performance page (see Figure 7.11), you can specify a connection speed if you want, but usually it's best to let Windows Media Player detect the connection speed.

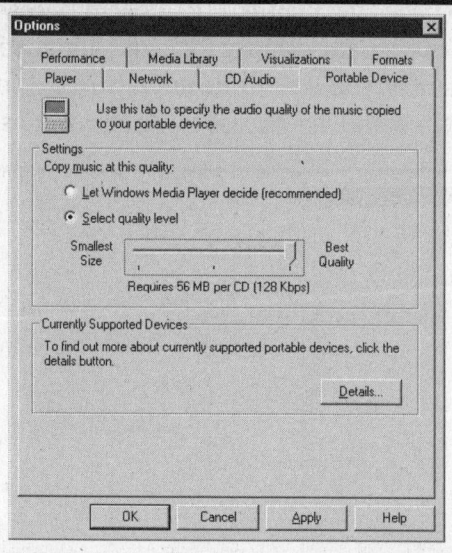

FIGURE 7.10: If you'll be using a portable MP3 player with Windows Media Player, choose the appropriate settings on the Portable Device page of the Options dialog box.

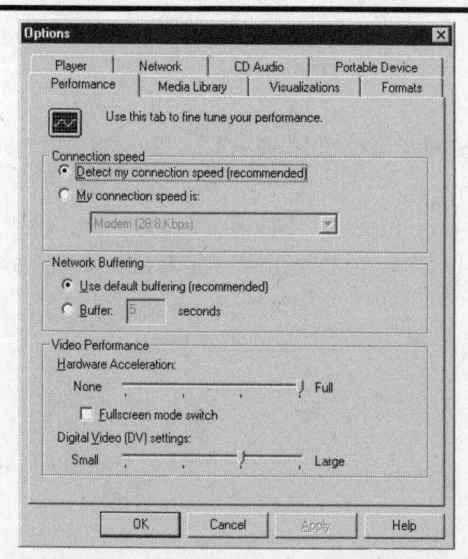

FIGURE 7.11: If necessary, specify a connection speed on the Performance page of the Options dialog box.

On the Media Library page (see Figure 7.12), specify access rights to the contents of your media library for other applications and for Internet sites. Usually, you'll want Read-Only Access or Full Access for other applications and No Access for Internet sites.

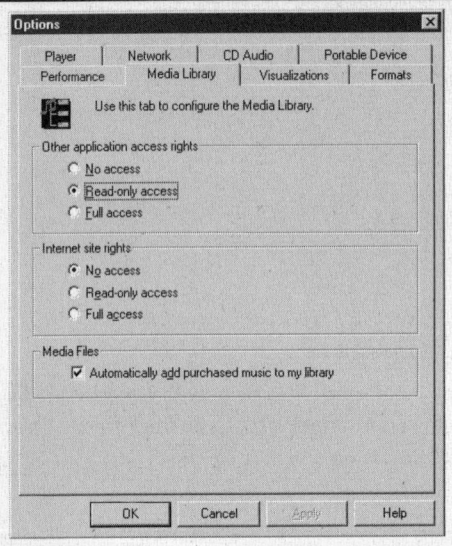

FIGURE 7.12: You can specify access rights to your media library on the Media Library page of the Options dialog box.

On the Visualizations page (see Figure 7.13), choose the visualization collection to use.

On the Formats page (see Figure 7.14), select and clear check boxes to specify which file formats Windows Media Player is associated with.

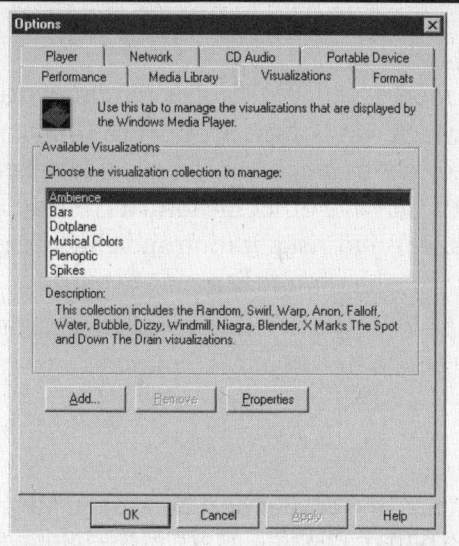

FIGURE 7.13: Choose a visualization collection on the Visualizations page of the Options dialog box.

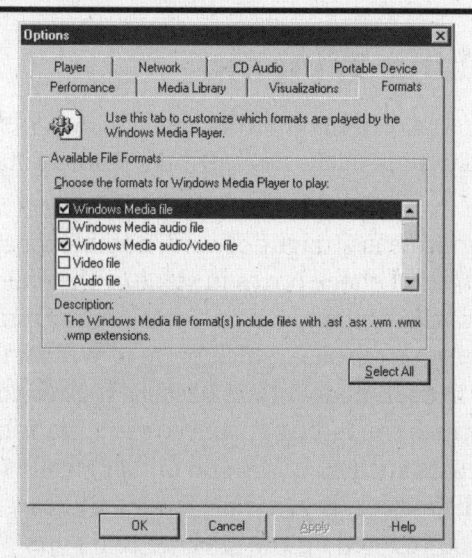

FIGURE 7.14: Use the Formats page of the Options dialog box to specify the file formats to associate with Windows Media Player.

Winamp

Winamp is perhaps the most popular MP3 player at this writing. Developed by Nullsoft, which was bought by America Online (AOL) in late 1999, Winamp provides a comprehensive set of features for playing and enjoying MP3 files and other file formats (including Windows Media and Mjuice), and visualization and plug-in capabilities to keep you entertained while you're listening to music.

Because Winamp is the leading MP3 player, we'll devote more space to it in this book than to the other MP3 players.

> **NOTE**
> If you're running Linux, one of your best bets for an MP3 player is xmms, which is a port of Winamp. Much of the information in this section applies to xmms as well as Winamp.

Getting and Installing Winamp

Download the latest version of Winamp from the Winamp Web site (www.winamp.com) and double-click the distribution file to start installing it.

The Winamp Setup routine is straightforward, notable mostly for its use of llamas instead of check boxes in some of the dialog boxes. Figure 7.15 shows the Winamp Setup: Installation Options dialog box, in which you get to choose which parts of Winamp to install. We recommend the full installation, because it gives you most flexibility and features (including advanced visualizations and support for file formats such as WMA and Mjuice) while taking up only about 4MB of disk space. If you want fewer features, select and clear llamas until you've lined up the package that suits you.

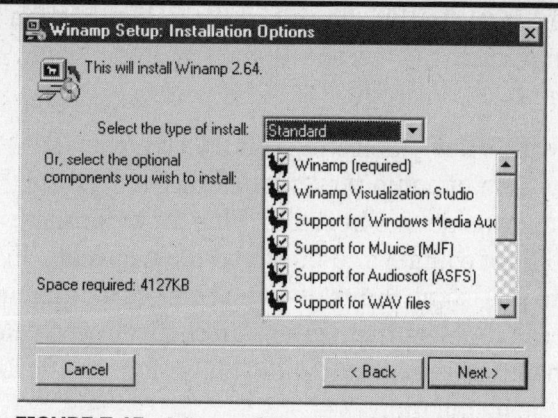

FIGURE 7.15: Winamp Setup is simple, provided you can get used to selecting and clearing the llamas for the options.

Once you've specified an installation directory and Winamp has installed itself in it, you'll see the Winamp Setup: Settings dialog box (shown in Figure 7.16).

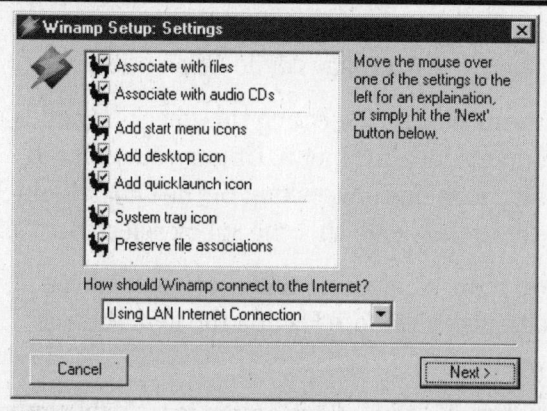

FIGURE 7.16: Choose your settings carefully in the Winamp Setup: Settings dialog box.

Here's what the items in this dialog box do. (If you've got a later version of Winamp, there may be additional features.) Again, select and clear the llamas as you see fit.

Associate with Files   Selecting this check box makes Winamp the default audio player for all files in formats that Winamp considers to be audio. This list of formats includes MP3 (of course) and most audio file formats. If you prefer to play some forms of audio through a different player, you can deselect them later. Alternatively, you can specify Winamp as the default audio player for specific formats after the installation.

Associate with Audio CDs   Selecting this check box causes Winamp to spring to life when you insert an audio CD into your computer's CD drive. If you don't like autoplay, clear this check box. Note that this setting does not change the Auto Insert Notification setting on your PC. If Auto Insert Notification is off in the CD drive's Properties dialog box, Winamp does not automatically play CDs, even if you select the Autoplay Audio CDs option.

Add Start Menu Icons   Selecting this check box adds a Winamp group to the Start menu. Unless you prefer to have a Winamp icon on the Desktop or the Quick Launch bar and nowhere else, keep this check box selected.

Add Desktop Icon   Selecting this check box adds a Winamp icon to the desktop. Having the icon there is often handy.

Add Quick Launch Icon   This option is available only if your computer is running Windows 98, Windows 2000, Windows Me, or Internet Explorer 4 or 5. Because the Quick Launch bar is always accessible, this is usually the second quickest way to get to Winamp.

System Tray Icon   This option adds a Winamp icon to the system tray so that you can quickly start Winamp, access it, and use its bookmarks. We find the system tray icon the easiest way to manipulate Winamp, although of course, your mileage may vary.

Preserve File Associations This option instructs Winamp to defend its file associations when another application tries to steal them. Leave this llama selected unless you're sure you want to let other applications grab Winamp's file associations.

How Should Winamp Connect to the Internet drop-down list This drop-down list lets you choose the way that Winamp uses the Internet. If the computer you're using doesn't have an Internet connection, or you don't want to use Winamp's Internet features, choose No Internet Connection Available. If your computer has a modem connection, choose Using Dial-Up Modem Internet Connection. If your computer connects to the Internet through a network (for example, a company's local area network or a home network, or a cable modem or DSL), choose Using LAN Internet Connection.

After you've made your choices and dismissed the Winamp Setup: Settings dialog box, you'll see the Winamp Setup: User Information dialog box. Enter information here if you want to—there's no obligation. If you don't want to be invited to register again, select the Stop Bugging Me check box. If you want to have Winamp announcements mailed to you, select the Please Send Me Winamp Announcements check box. You may find it easier to visit the Winamp Web site periodically at your convenience to scan for new information rather than having it mailed to you. If you don't want Winamp to send back to Winamp.com anonymous statistics on how much you're using Winamp, clear the Allow Winamp to Report Simple, Anonymous Usage Statistics check box.

If you fill in the user information, click the Next button to send it. Winamp connects to the Internet using the connection that you specified in the previous dialog box and sends the information to

Winamp.com. If you don't fill in the user information, click the Later button.

You'll then see the Winamp Setup: Winamp Successfully Installed dialog box. Click the Run Winamp button to run Winamp.

Using Winamp

This section explains how to use Winamp. If you've used a CD player or cassette player designed after 1980, you shouldn't have any problems coming to terms with Winamp's basic controls (such as the Play, Pause, Stop, Previous Track, and Next Track buttons). We'll steer clear of the obvious and concentrate on the less intuitive features.

Arranging the Winamp Windows

Figure 7.17 shows Winamp's basic look. As you can see, it consists of four windows: the Main window, the Playlist Editor window, the Graphical Equalizer window (as Winamp calls the graphic equalizer), and the Browser window. Here's the brief version of what each window does:

> **Main window** This window displays information about the track that's currently playing and provides CD-player–style controls. The Main window also provides quick access to the Playlist Editor window and the Graphical Equalizer window. We tend to keep the Main window open all the time that we're using Winamp.
>
> **Playlist Editor window** This window contains the current playlist, buttons for creating and manipulating playlists, and a minimal set of play controls (so that you can dispense with the Main window if you want). We tend to keep this window open all the time, too.

Graphical Equalizer window   This window provides a software graphic equalizer that you can use to tweak the sound that Winamp produces. Once you've found an equalization that works for most of your music, you'll probably want to close this window except when you're tweaking the sound.

Browser window   This window provides a quick way to enter information into your main Browser window for searching Amazon.com for music by the current artist. Whether you find the Browser window useful depends on your interests and whether you have a constant connection to the Internet. We tend to find the Browser window annoying and recommend turning it off straightaway, particularly if you find it's constantly trying to establish a dial-up connection to the Internet.

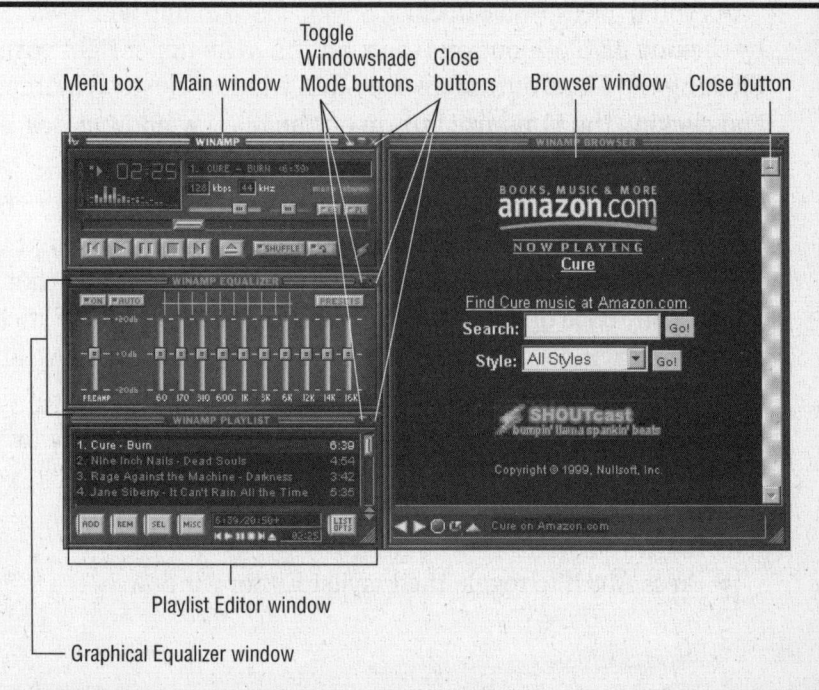

FIGURE 7.17:   Winamp uses four windows: the Main window, the Playlist Editor window, the Graphical Equalizer window, and the Browser window.

Chapter Seven

We mentioned keeping some of the windows open and closing others—but there's a third option for the Main window, Playlist Editor window, and the Graphical Equalizer window: *windowshade mode*. Windowshade mode reduces the window in question to a narrow strip that you can park comfortably in the title bar of another running application. To toggle a window to and from windowshade mode, click its Toggle Windowshade Mode button or double-click its title bar. Figure 7.18 shows the three windows in windowshade mode.

FIGURE 7.18: To save space on screen, you can switch the Main window, the Playlist Editor window, and the Graphical Equalizer window to windowshade mode, in which each window displays only the essential controls.

As you'd guess, you can close any of the Winamp windows by clicking its Close button (the x button in its upper-right corner). Clicking the Close button on the Main window closes Winamp, and clicking the Minimize button on the Main window closes Winamp.

You can arrange the Winamp windows any way you want to by dragging them about as you would any other windows—except that when you move the edge of one of the satellite windows so that it touches any edge of the Main window, the satellite window sticks to the Main window. When you then move the Main window, any windows stuck to it move along with it.

You can toggle the display of the Winamp windows easily by using the following shortcuts:

▶ Press Alt+W to toggle the main Winamp window.

▶ Press Alt+E to toggle the Playlist Editor window.

- Press Alt+G to toggle the Graphical Equalizer window.
- Press Alt+T to toggle the Browser window.

You can also toggle the display of these windows by selecting their entries from the menu that appears when you click the menu box in the upper-left corner of the Main window. And you can move the focus from one window to another by pressing Ctrl+Tab.

If you use Winamp regularly, you may want to keep Winamp on top of all other running applications so that you can access it easily. To do this, use one of the following shortcuts:

- Press Ctrl+A to toggle the Always on Top feature for all Winamp windows except the Playlist Editor window.
- Press Ctrl+Alt+A to toggle the Always on Top feature for the Playlist Editor window.

Press Ctrl+D to toggle Winamp's double-size mode on and off.

The easiest way to exit Winamp is to right-click the system tray icon and choose Exit from the menu. Alternatively, click the control menu on the Main window (or press Alt+F) and choose Exit from the menu, press Alt+F4 with Winamp active, or click the Close button (the x button) on the Main window. You can also close any of the Winamp windows by pressing Ctrl+F4 with the window active.

Playing Music with Winamp

Winamp is well designed, and you'll find it easy to use with the mouse. There are also a number of keyboard shortcuts that we'll point out for those of you who like to keep your fingers locked to the keys.

Figure 7.19 shows the components of the Main window.

Chapter Seven

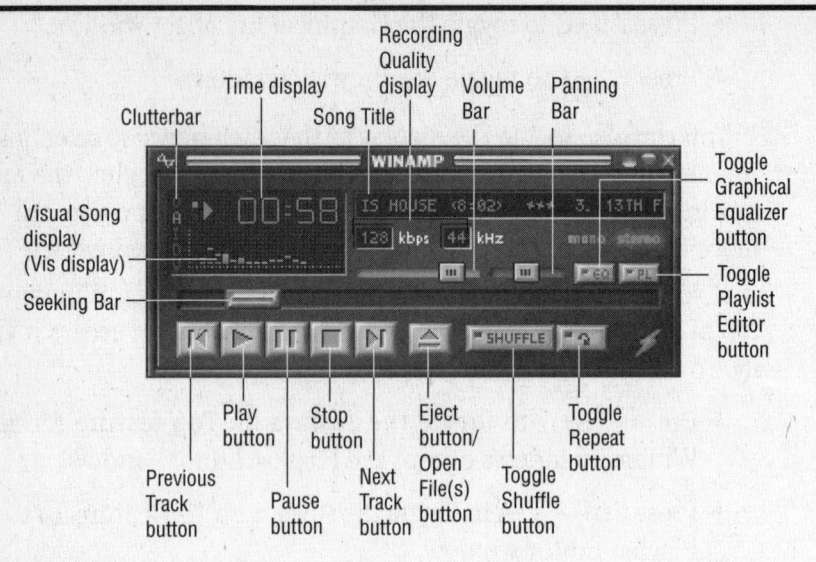

FIGURE 7.19: Winamp's Main window

Use the Open File(s) button (or press Ctrl+O) and the resulting Open File(s) dialog box to select the tracks you want to play. As usual, you can Shift+click to select a contiguous list of tracks or Ctrl+ click to add individual tracks to or remove individual tracks from your selection. When you click the Open button, Winamp adds the tracks to the current playlist and starts playing the first track. Usually Winamp decides that the last track you selected is the first track, so you may want to try selecting the tracks in reverse order.

Apart from the CD-player–like buttons, you can click most parts of the Main window to do different things in Winamp:

- ▶ Click the time in the Time display to toggle it between time elapsed and time remaining on the track.

- ▶ Click the Visual Song display (the Vis display) to switch between visualization modes.

- ▶ Click the letters in the Clutterbar at the left-hand side of the Time display window to perform the following common maneuvers:

- O displays the Options menu.
- I displays the File Info dialog box.
- A toggles the Always on Top feature.
- D toggles the double-size feature.
- V displays the Visualization menu, which contains options for the visualization feature below the Time display.
- Right-click the Song Title display to pop up a context menu for moving around the current track and current playlist. (More on these in a moment.)
- Click the lightning-flash logo in the lower-right corner to display the About Winamp dialog box.

To listen to an audio stream off the Web, press Ctrl+L or choose Play Location from the Main Winamp menu to display the Open Location dialog box. Enter the URL of a SHOUTcast stream, and click the Open button; Winamp starts playing the stream.

You can also open or play files in Winamp by pressing L to display the Open File(s) dialog box, selecting one or more files, and then clicking the Open button. Winamp adds the selected files to the playlist and starts playing the first of them. Alternatively, you can right-click one or more items in the Open File(s) dialog box and choose Play in Winamp to play the track or tracks immediately, Enqueue in Winamp to add the track or tracks to the playlist without interrupting what's currently playing, or Add to Winamp's Bookmark List.

> **NOTE**
> Many Web sites use streams that automatically start your MP3 player or browser plug-in playing the track.

TIP

You can also play CDs using Winamp—and you can use standard Winamp commands to manipulate the CD's playlist, removing and rearranging tracks to improve the artist's choice of order. If you chose the Autoplay Audio CDs option during setup, you'll be ready to roll; if not, select the Associate with Audio CDs check box on the File Types page of the Winamp Preferences dialog box (Ctrl+P). If you're using Winamp's Internet features and are connected to the Internet, Winamp contacts CDDB and downloads the track titles.

Using Playlists

Opening a few tracks one by one is all very well for brief entertainment, but for sustained listening, you'll want to build playlists. As you might guess, you use Winamp's Playlist Editor to create, manage, and manipulate playlists.

If the Playlist Editor isn't displayed, toggle it on by pressing Alt+E or by clicking the Toggle Playlist Editor button in the Main window. Figure 7.20 shows the Playlist Editor with a playlist loaded in it.

FIGURE 7.20: Use Winamp's Playlist Editor window to create, manage, and manipulate playlists.

To create a new playlist, click the List Opts button and click the New List button from the button menu that appears. Winamp clears any tracks currently in the Playlist Editor window, but continues playing any track that's currently playing.

There are three main ways to add tracks to a playlist:

- **From Explorer** Drag tracks from an Explorer window to the Playlist Editor.

- **Use the Add File(s) to Playlist dialog box** Double-click the Add button in the Playlist Editor to display the Add File(s) to Playlist dialog box, select the tracks, and click the Open button. (The first click of the Add button displays the menu of buttons, and the second click selects the Add File button, which appears in place of the Add button, but you can perform the action as a double-click.)

- **Use the Open Directory dialog box to add an entire directory of tracks** To add an entire directory to the playlist, click the Add button to display the menu of buttons, then choose the Add Dir button. Winamp displays the Open Directory dialog box. Navigate to and select the directory you want to add. If you want to add all the subdirectories under the directory you're selecting, make sure that the Recurse Subdirectories check box is selected; if you don't want to add all the subdirectories, make sure it's cleared. Then click the OK button.

NOTE

To play a track more than once in a playlist, add two or more instances of it to the playlist.

You can also add Web tracks or SHOUTcast streams to the Playlist Editor by clicking the Add button to display the menu of buttons, then choosing the Add URL button to display the Open Location dialog box, specifying the URL of the file or stream, and clicking the Open button.

Once you've added the tracks to your playlist, drag tracks up and down the playlist until you've shuffled them into the order you want. If you need to remove a track, select it and either press the Delete key or double-click the Rem button. (The first click displays the button menu, and the second click selects the Rem Sel button—Remove Selection—that replaces the Rem button.) Use the Sel button menu to select all the tracks (Sel All, or a double-click on the Sel button itself) or deselect tracks (Sel Zero).

For a bit of variety, make Winamp sort the playlist. Click the Misc button and choose Sort List from the menu of buttons to display a submenu. You can sort a list by title, by filename, or by path and filename. You can also reverse the current order of the playlist—which can be good for variety—or randomize the playlist to produce something unexpected. Even alphabetical sorting can produce entertaining results if you include a variety of music in your playlist—Winamp will put Vivaldi concertos right between the Victims of Circumstance and the Vixens from Venus.

To sort from the keyboard, press Ctrl+Shift+1 to sort by title, Ctrl+Shift+2 to sort by filename, Ctrl+Shift+3 to sort by path and filename, Ctrl+R to reverse the playlist, or Ctrl+Shift+R to randomize the playlist.

If you want to change a playlist entry so that it appears as something catchier or easier to understand, select it and press Ctrl+E to display the Edit Playlist Entry dialog box. Enter the new name in the New text box and click the OK button. Winamp then updates the playlist.

Once you've created a playlist to your satisfaction, save it by clicking the List Opts button and choosing Save List from the menu of buttons to display the Save Playlist dialog box. Specify a name and location as usual, then click the Save button. The default file format is M3U Playlist, but you can choose PLS Playlist in the Save As Type drop-down list if you want to save your playlists in the PLS format.

To open a saved playlist, double-click the List Opts button to display the Load Playlist dialog box. (The first click displays the menu of buttons, and the second click selects the Load List button that replaces the List Opts button.) Navigate to the playlist, select it, and click the Open button.

Once you've created a playlist and set it running, you can get around it quickly as follows:

- To jump to a specific time in the track that is currently playing, press Ctrl+J, or right-click the Song Title display and choose Jump to Time from the context menu to display the Jump to Time dialog box. Enter the time to which to jump in the Jump to text box in *Minutes:Seconds* format (for example, **2:15**) and click the Jump button.

- To move less precisely through a track, drag the Seeking bar to the left or right.

- To jump to another track in the current playlist, press J, or right-click the Song Title display and choose Jump to File from the context menu to display the Jump to File dialog box (shown in Figure 7.21). The Jump to File dialog box lists the tracks in alphabetical order. Double-click the track to which you want to jump. To search for text in a track's name, enter the letters in the Search for Text text box. As you type, Winamp reduces the playlist to tracks that have that sequence of letters in the title.

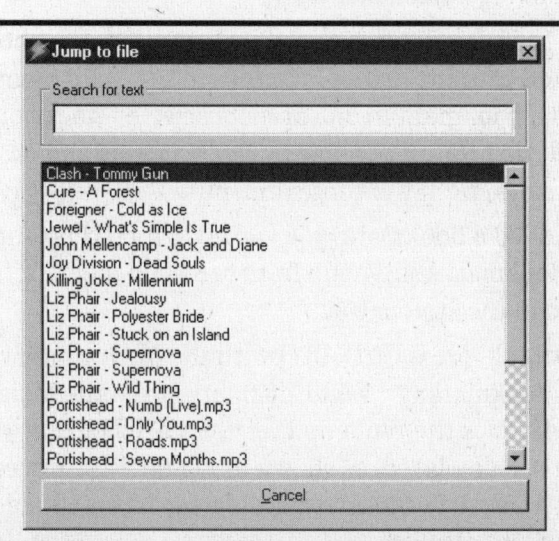

FIGURE 7.21: Use the Jump to File dialog box to move quickly to a track in a long playlist.

- You can also navigate around the playlist using the Playback submenu on the main Winamp menu. This submenu offers navigation items, including Stop w/Fadeout, Back 5 Seconds, Fwd 5 Seconds, Start of List, 10 Tracks Back, and 10 Tracks Fwd.

- Winamp uses the keys on the left-hand bottom row of the QWERTY keyboard for controlling play, as follows:
    - Press Z to move to the previous track.
    - Press X to activate play.
    - Press C to pause play.
    - Press V to stop play.
    - Press B to move to the next track.

Using Bookmarks to Access Tracks Quickly

To quickly access a track or a SHOUTcast stream in your current playlist, use Winamp's bookmarks. A *bookmark* is a virtual marker that you can use to tag a track or stream.

To bookmark the current track or stream, press Alt+I or choose Bookmarks ➤ Add Current As Bookmark from the Main menu. You can also add a bookmark to one or more selected tracks or streams in the Playlist Editor window by right-clicking and choosing Bookmark Item(s) from the context menu.

Once you've added a bookmark, you can go to it by choosing its name from the Bookmarks submenu from the Main menu or from the Winamp icon in the system tray.

To edit a bookmark, press Ctrl+Alt+I with the Main window active or choose Bookmarks ➤ Edit Bookmarks from the Main menu. Winamp displays the Winamp Preferences dialog box with the Bookmarks page displayed, as shown in Figure 7.22. You can edit a bookmark, remove it, open it (start playing it), or enqueue it (add it to your current playlist).

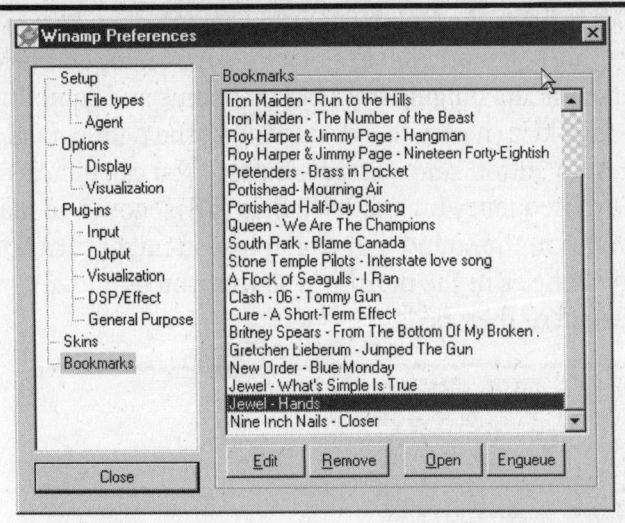

FIGURE 7.22: Edit your bookmarks on the Bookmarks page of the Winamp Preferences dialog box.

Using the Graphic Equalizer to Tweak the Sound

Winamp provides a full-featured graphic equalizer (which it calls the "graphical equalizer") for adjusting the balance of the music and compensating for any inadequacies of your sound system. For example, if you have tinny speakers in your dorm or office, you can turn down the treble frequencies to make the sound less shrill. If you like bass-heavy music, you can boost the bass frequencies to bring them out better. Better yet, Winamp's auto-load feature for presets lets you associate preset equalizations with particular tracks, then have Winamp automatically load the preset whenever you play the track.

The graphic equalizer appears in its own window and lets you increase or decrease ten different frequencies (measured in hertz—cycles per second—and kilohertz—thousands of cycles per second) in the sound spectrum to boost the parts of the music you want to hear more of and reduce those you don't.

Figure 7.23 shows the Graphical Equalizer window. As you can see, the graphic equalizer consists of a PreAmp slider on the left, ten frequency sliders ranging from 60Hz (booms and rumblings) on the left up to 16kHz (high-pitched sounds) on the right, an On/Off button, an Auto button, and a Presets button. You can increase or decrease each frequency up to 20 decibels (dB), enough to make a huge difference in the sound. For example, you might turn down the bass frequencies in the mornings so that you don't blow your housemates out of their beds.

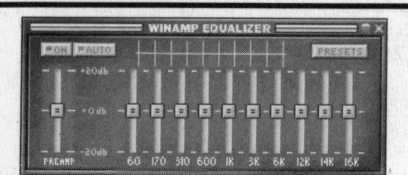

FIGURE 7.23: Use Winamp's graphic equalizer to adjust the sound.

The graphic equalizer is easy to use:

- If the Graphical Equalizer window isn't displayed, click the Toggle Graphical Equalizer button on the Main window, or press Alt+G, to display it.

- The graphic equalizer is off by default. Turn it on by clicking its On button so that it shows a light-green square instead of a dark square (in the default skin).

- If necessary, adjust the PreAmp slider to raise or lower the preamplification of the graphical equalizer all at once. Don't adjust the PreAmp slider unless you need to. For most purposes, you can control the volume better using the Volume slider on the Main window, the Windows Volume Control (usually in the Taskbar's tray), or the volume control on your amplifier or speakers. Increase the preamp setting only if you're not getting enough volume from your system otherwise. Don't set the preamp too high because that distorts the sound.

- Drag the sliders up and down to adjust the sound. Winamp takes a second or two to implement the changes, so wait until you hear the change. You'll notice that the equalizer display at the top of the Graphical Equalizer window changes shape to match the slider settings so that you can see the overall shape of the equalization you're applying.

- To create an auto-load preset equalization for a track, play the track and set the graphic equalizer sliders appropriately. Then click the Presets button to display its menu, select the Save menu to display its submenu, and choose Auto-Load Preset to display the Save Auto-Load Preset dialog box. Adjust the suggested name for the equalization (Winamp suggests the track title) as you like and click the Save button to save the preset. Then enable the auto-load presets by clicking the Auto button in the Graphical Equalizer window so that it displays a light-green light. From here on, Winamp uses your customized equalization whenever you play the song.

NOTE

When auto-load preset equalizations are enabled and Winamp finishes playing a track with a preset equalization, it continues to use that equalization for the following track if that track does not have its own equalization.

- To apply one of Winamp's built-in preset equalizations, click the Presets button, select Load to display its submenu, and choose Preset to display the Load EQ Preset dialog box (see Figure 7.24). Drag the dialog box so that you can see the Graphical Equalizer window while you work. Select the equalization you want from the list box. Wait a couple of seconds and see how it sounds. To apply it, click the Load button.

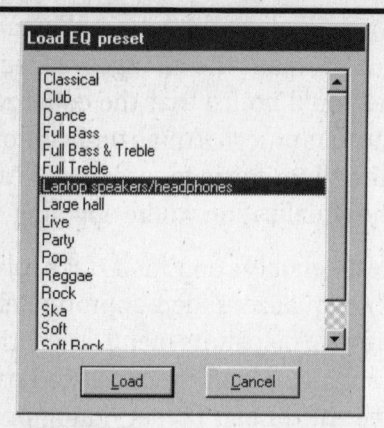

FIGURE 7.24: Winamp provides a good selection of built-in preset equalizations.

- To add to the list of preset equalizations, set the sliders for the equalization, click the Presets button, and choose Save ➢ Preset to display the Save EQ Preset dialog box. Enter the name for the new preset and click the Save button.

- To delete a preset, click the Presets button and choose Delete ➢ Preset or Delete ➢ Auto-Load Preset to display the Delete Preset dialog box or Delete Auto-Load Preset dialog box. Select the preset and click the Delete button to delete it.

- To export an equalization to an equalization setting file (EQ setting file, EQF format), click the Presets button and choose Save ➢ To EQF to display the Select File to Write dialog box. Specify the filename and location and click the Save button.

- To load an equalization from an EQ setting file, click the Presets button and choose Load ➢ From EQF to display the Select File to Read dialog box. Specify the file and click the Open button. Winamp then applies the equalization to the current track.

Editing Tag Information

Winamp provides a competent tag editor for changing the information included in the tag built into each MP3 file.

To change tag information, display the MPEG File Info Box + ID3 Tag Editor dialog box, shown in Figure 7.25, in either of the following ways:

- For the current track, double-click the track title in the Main window, or press Alt+3 from either the Main window or the Playlist Editor window.

- For a track in the current playlist, take one of the following actions in the Playlist Editor window:

    - Select the track in the Playlist Editor window and press Alt+3.

    - Right-click the track and choose File Info from the context menu.

    - Select the track and choose View ➢ File Info from the Main menu.

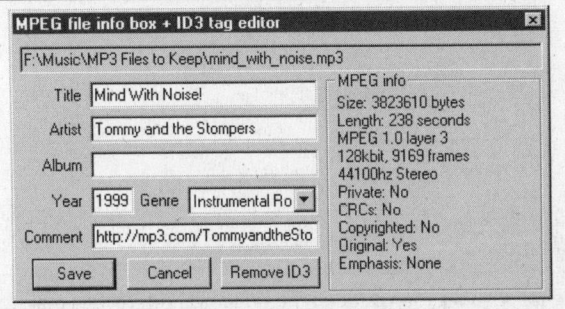

FIGURE 7.25: Use the MP3 File Info Box + ID3 Tag Editor dialog box to check and change the tag information on MP3 files.

Change the information as appropriate and then click the Save button to save it to the MP3 file. You can also click the Remove ID3 button to remove the tag information from the MP3 file.

Enjoying Visualizations

Winamp's Vis display provides *visualizations*—constantly changing graphics keyed to the frequencies of the music you're playing. In this section, we'll look quickly at the main options the Vis display provides.

You control most of the options for the Vis display from the Visualization page of the Winamp Preferences dialog box, shown in Figure 7.26. To display this page of the dialog box, right-click the Vis display and choose Visualization Options from the context menu, or choose Visualization ➢ Visualization Options from the Main menu, or press Alt+O. With the dialog box open, move it off the Winamp window so that you can see the effects of the changes you're making—Winamp applies them as you make them.

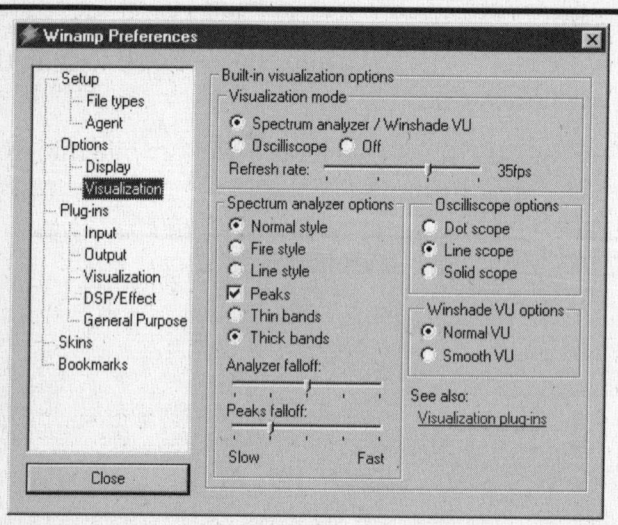

FIGURE 7.26: Use the Visualization page of the Winamp Preferences dialog box to control visualizations.

- In the Visualization Mode group box, choose the visualization mode you want: Spectrum Analyzer/Winshade VU (rising and falling columns in regular mode, a rising and falling bar in Windowshade mode), Oscilliscope (an oscilloscope waveform), or Off (nada).

> **NOTE**
> You can toggle visualization mode between Analyzer, Scope, and Off by clicking the Vis display.

- In the Spectrum Analyzer Options group box, select the options to use when you're running the spectrum analyzer. Select the Normal Style option button, the Fire Style option button, or Line Style option button to determine the style. Select the Peaks check box if you want the spectrum analyzer to mark the peaks momentarily. Select the Thin Bands option button or the Thick Bands option button to specify the width of the bands. Finally, adjust the Analyzer Falloff slider and the Peaks Falloff slider to give you the effect you want.

- In the Oscilliscope Options group box, select the option button for the oscilloscope effect you want: Dot Scope, Line Scope, or Solid Scope.

- In the Winshade VU Options group box, select the Normal VU option button for "normal," jerky movement on the windowshade meter or the Smooth VU option button for a smoother effect.

Winamp Keyboard Commands

So far in this section, we've mentioned many of the keyboard commands that Winamp supports—but there are many more. Table 7.1 lists the key presses and keyboard shortcuts for Winamp, grouped by category.

TABLE 7.1: Winamp Key Presses and Keyboard Shortcuts

Action	Key Press/Shortcut
Manipulating the Winamp Windows and Appearance	
Toggle the Main window	Alt+W
Toggle the Playlist Editor window	Alt+E
Toggle the Graphical Equalizer window	Alt+G
Toggle the Browser window	Alt+T
Toggle Always on Top for all Winamp windows except the Playlist Editor window	Ctrl+A
Toggle Always on Top for the Playlist Editor window	Ctrl+Alt+A
Exit Winamp	Alt+F4
Toggle double-size mode	Ctrl+D
Toggle easy-move mode	Ctrl+E
Display the Skins page of the Winamp Preferences dialog box	Alt+S
Display the Preferences dialog box	Ctrl+P
Toggle the time display	Ctrl+T
Display the Visualization options page of the Preferences dialog box	Alt+O
Display the Visualization plug-ins page of the Preferences dialog box	Ctrl+K
Display the Main menu	Alt+F
Configure the current visualization	Alt+K
Toggle the current visualization on or off	Ctrl+Shift+K
Start a new instance of Winamp	Ctrl+Alt+N
Playing Music	
Previous track	Z or 6 on numeric keypad
Play	X or 5 on numeric keypad
Pause/End Pause	C
Stop	V
Next	B or 4 on numeric keypad

CONTINUED →

TABLE 7.1 continued: Winamp Key Presses and Keyboard Shortcuts

ACTION	KEY PRESS/SHORTCUT
PLAYING MUSIC	
Stop with fadeout	Shift+V
Stop at the end of the current track	Ctrl+V
Jump 10 songs back	1 on numeric keypad
Jump 10 songs forward	3 on numeric keypad
Rewind five seconds	← or 7 on numeric keypad
Fast-forward five seconds	→ or 9 on numeric keypad
Display the Open File(s) dialog box	L or 0 on numeric keypad
Display the Open Location dialog box	Ctrl+L or Ctrl+0 on numeric keypad
Display the Open Directory dialog box	Shift+L or Insert
Increase the volume	↑ or 8 on numeric keypad
Decrease the volume	↓ or 2 on numeric keypad
Toggle repeat mode	R
Toggle shuffle mode	S
Display the Jump to Time dialog box	Ctrl+J
Display the Jump to File dialog box	J
MANIPULATING PLAYLISTS	
Display the Edit Playlist Entry dialog box	Ctrl+E
Create a new playlist	Ctrl+N
Display the Load Playlist dialog box	Ctrl+O
Display the Save Playlist dialog box	Ctrl+S
Select All	Ctrl+A
Invert Selection	Ctrl+I
Remove selected files from the playlist	Delete
Crop the playlist (remove all entries except those selected)	Shift+Delete
Clear the playlist	Ctrl+Shift+Delete
Move the selected files up	Alt+↑

CONTINUED →

TABLE 7.1 continued: Winamp Key Presses and Keyboard Shortcuts

Action	Key Press/Shortcut
Manipulating Playlists	
Move the selected files down	Alt+↓
Move the cursor up and down	↑ and ↓
Play the selected file or stream	Enter
Move to the end of the playlist	End
Move to the start of the playlist	Home
Move up by a fifth of the number of tracks displayed in the Playlist Editor window	Page Up
Move down by a fifth of the number of tracks displayed in the Playlist Editor window	Page Down
Remove any dead files	Alt+Delete
Manipulating the Graphic Equalizer	
Increase the equalization band	1 through 0 (left to right)
Decrease the equalization band	Q through P (left to right)
Increase the preamp	
Decrease the preamp	Tab
Toggle the graphic equalizer on and off	N
Display the Presets menu	S
Display the Load EQ Preset dialog box	Ctrl+S
Toggle equalization autoloading	A
Manipulating the Browser	
Go back	Alt+←
Go forward	Alt+→
Display the Go menu	Ctrl+L
Display the Open Location dialog box	Ctrl+O
Reload the current page	Ctrl+R
Update the link list	Ctrl+Alt+R

Applying Skins

Winamp supports different *skins*—graphical looks that you can apply with the click of a couple of buttons. By applying different skins to Winamp, you can change its look completely, while the functionality of each control remains the same. Figure 7.27 shows the Sketchamp skin, one of our favorites for its apparent simplicity.

FIGURE 7.27: Sketchamp gives Winamp the appearance of a rough sketch.

You can get skins from the skin archives online, or you can create your own skins. At this writing, the best sites for skins include the Winamp site (www.winamp.com/winamp/skins/index.phtml), the Winamp Skins Warehouse (start.at/skins), and the 1001 Winamp Skins site (www.1001winampskins.com/).

Some skin archives provides skins in a Winamp zipped format (with a WSZ extension) that installs automatically into your Skins directory and does not need unzipping. Others provide conventional zip files (with the usual ZIP extension) that you need to place in your Skins directory yourself. Once a skin is in your Skins directory, it appears in Winamp's listings of skins.

Once you've downloaded a skin, you can apply it by choosing it from the Skins submenu off the Main menu or off the context menu from the Winamp icon in the system tray. To browse the skins that you have available, you may want to use the Skin Browser instead. Press Alt+S to display the Winamp Preferences dialog box with the Skin Browser page displayed, move the dialog box off Winamp so that you can see the effect of each skin you apply, browse through the skins until you find the one you want, and then click the Close button to close the dialog box.

If you need to change your skins directory, click the Set Skins Directory button and use the Select Winamp Skin Directory dialog box to specify the directory. To have Winamp choose a random skin for you for each track you play, check the Select Random Skin on Play check box in the Skin Browser.

With a little time and creativity, you can easily create your own skins for Winamp. We'll show you how to do this in Chapter 21, "Creating Skins for Winamp and RealJukebox."

Adding Functionality with Plug-Ins

Winamp supports a variety of *plug-ins*—add-in components that enhance Winamp's capabilities and functionality. Here are a few examples of what plug-ins can do:

- Let you play RealAudio and RealMedia files so you can use Winamp instead of RealPlayer.
- Enable you to broadcast audio to a SHOUTcast server.
- Provide dreamy or intense visualizations to enhance the music you're playing.
- Let you control Winamp from an infrared remote control unit such as the IRMan.
- Display the lyrics associated with an MP3 file.
- Add reverb and other effects to the audio you're playing.
- Start Winamp playing at a given time so that you can use it as an alarm.

Winamp divides plug-ins into five categories: Input, Output, Visualization, DSP/Effect, and General Purpose. (DSP is the abbreviation for *digital signal processor*, a category of chip for manipulating and altering sound.) At this writing, most plug-ins are free, but some of the fancier ones you have to pay for.

You can get plug-ins from a number of Web sites. Unless you have a hot lead elsewhere, start at the main Winamp site, www.winamp.com, which includes a large collection of plug-ins sorted into categories. Download the plug-ins that interest you. For most plug-ins, you'll need to unzip the archive into your \Winamp\Plugins\ folder.

You can use different folders for plug-ins by setting the Visualization Plug-In Directory and DSP/Effect Plug-In Directory options in the Plug-In Settings group box in the Winamp Preferences dialog box (Ctrl+P).

These are the general steps for selecting, configuring, and running a plug-in. Depending on the capabilities and complexity of the plug-in, you may have to take extra steps.

1. Press Ctrl+K, or choose Visualization ➢ Select Plug-In from the Main menu, to display the Winamp Preferences dialog box with the Visualization page under Plug-Ins selected. (To choose a different sort of plug-in than visualization, choose Input, Output, DSP/Effect, or General Purpose in the Plug-Ins area.)

2. In the list box, select the plug-in you want to run.

3. If this is the first time you've run the plug-in, click the Configure button to display a dialog box containing any configuration options that the plug-in supports. (Some plug-ins do not support any configuration options.) Choose options as appropriate and close the dialog box.

4. Click the Start button to start the plug-in.

5. Click the Close button to close the Winamp Preferences dialog box. The plug-in should now be running.

The next sections give examples of installing and configuring some Winamp plug-ins.

Adding RealAudio Functionality to Winamp

The RealAudio plug-in from innover lets you play RealAudio files and streams—both audio and video—from within Winamp. By using this plug-in, you can avoid using the RealPlayer almost entirely.

Here's how to get, install, and configure the RealAudio plug-in:

1. Download the RealAudio plug-in from a plug-ins site and save it to your hard disk. (At this writing, Real-Networks has forced the Winamp site to remove this plug-in from their download area.)

2. Run the EXE file to install the plug-in. The plug-in locates your Winamp directory and offers to install itself there, as shown in Figure 7.28.

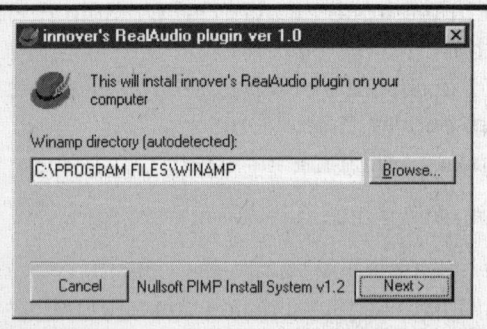

FIGURE 7.28: Installing the RealAudio plug-in for Winamp

3. Usually, it's best to install the plug-in in the suggested directory, but if you want to choose another directory, click the Browse button and use the resulting Select Your Winamp Directory dialog box to select a different directory.

4. Click the Next button when you're ready to proceed. You'll see an installation dialog box flash by, and then a message box telling you that the installation was successful. The plug-in also displays an information page in your default Web browser.

This plug-in needs no configuration, so you're all done. (If you're in any doubt that it's installed correctly, fire up Winamp and press Ctrl+K to display the Winamp Preferences dialog box with the Plug-Ins page displayed. Check the Input page for an entry called innover's RealAudio Plugin for Winamp.)

You can now use Winamp to play RealAudio audio and video files and streams. If you already have RealPlayer installed on your computer, you may need to reassign the RealAudio file associations from RealPlayer to Winamp.

Ensuring a Supply of Eye Candy

Many of the plug-ins available for Winamp provide visual effects to accompany the music you're listening to. One of our current favorites is Climax by Sergej Müller, which provides amazing graphics.

Here's how to get, install, and configure Climax:

1. Download the latest version of Climax from www.winamp.com.

2. Run the EXE file to start the installation routine. You'll see the Climax for Winamp dialog box (see Figure 7.29).

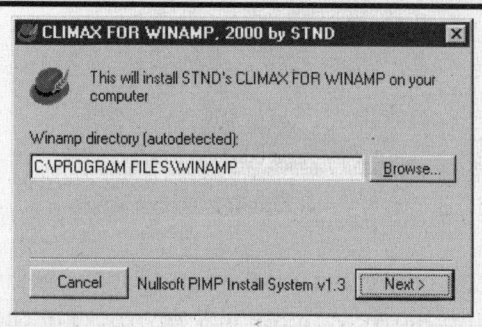

FIGURE 7.29: Installing the Climax plug-in for Winamp

3. Either accept the auto-detected Winamp directory or use the Browse button and the Select Your Winamp Directory dialog box to designate a different directory.

344 Chapter Seven

4. Click the Next button to install Climax. Once the installation has finished, Climax displays its Readme file of information.

5. Press Ctrl+K to display the Winamp Preferences dialog box with the Visualization page displayed.

6. In the Visualization Plug-Ins list box, select the entry for Climax for Winamp.

7. Click the Start button. Climax displays the Climax window with visualizations running in time to the music. Figure 7.30 shows Climax running in a window.

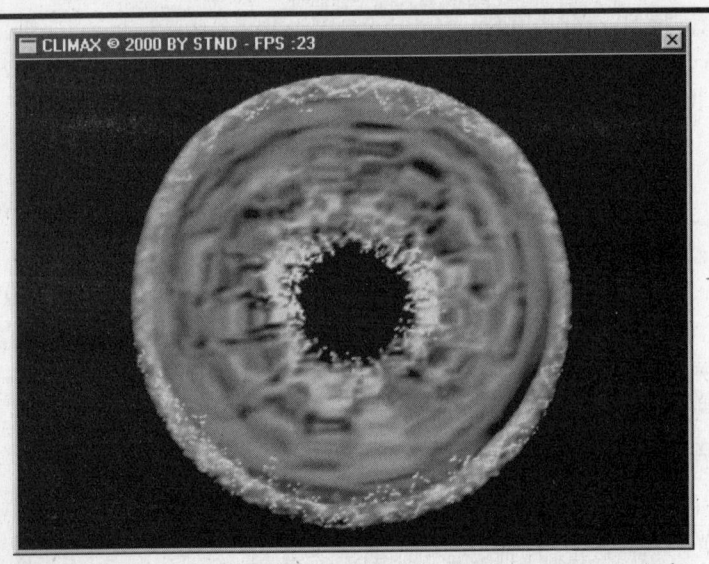

FIGURE 7.30: Climax produces intense visualizations even in a window.

You can toggle Climax between a window and full screen by pressing the F4 key. Alternatively, right-click anywhere in the Climax window or the full Climax screen, and choose Full Screen from the context menu. Figure 7.31 shows Climax running full screen.

FIGURE 7.31: Climax is even more intense when run full screen.

To configure Climax, press the F2 key. The Climax dialog box (see Figure 7.33) appears, offering a variety of information and configuration options that you can fiddle with by clicking the category on the left-hand side of the dialog box:

- On the Display page, you can set the resolution to use for running Climax full screen. This resolution doesn't have to be the same resolution at which you're running Windows. For example, you could be running Windows at 800×600 resolution and run Climax at 1024×768 if you wanted. But make sure that you don't choose a resolution higher than your monitor and graphics card support. The higher the resolution, the more processing power is needed. Unless you have a fierce graphics card, Climax may run slowly and jerkily at the higher resolutions. On the Display page, you can also choose a frame rate (in frames per second—FPS), whether you want to always start Climax in full-screen mode, and whether you want to minimize Winamp when Climax is in full-screen mode.

▶ Figure 7.32 shows the Keys page of the dialog box, which lists the keystrokes that you can use for configuring and running Climax. For example, you can press the B key to move to the next song in Winamp or press the Z key to move to the previous song so you can control Winamp easily even when you're running Climax full screen.

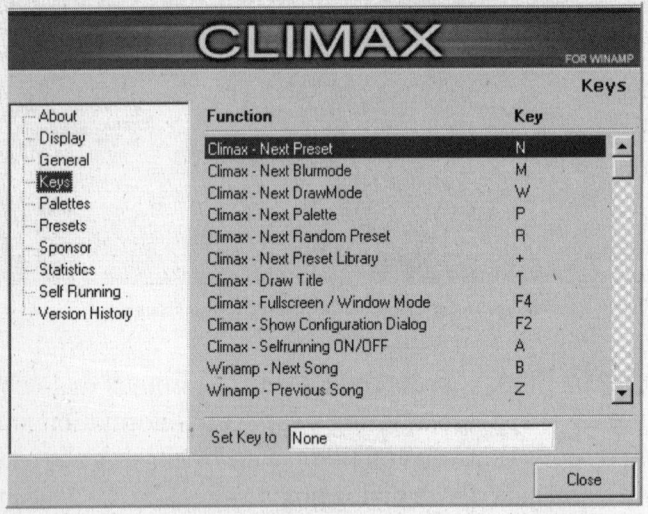

FIGURE 7.32: Configure the keystrokes for running Climax on the Keys page of the Climax dialog box.

When you've set the options to your satisfaction, click the Close button to close the Climax dialog box.

To stop Climax running, press the Esc key with the Climax window or the full-screen view active.

Adding Reverberation and Effects with DeFX

DeFX is a plug-in that lets you add effects such as reverberation, voice removal, and pitch modulation to MP3 playback.

Here's how to get, install, and configure DeFX:

1. Download the latest version of DeFX from www.winamp.com or from another Winamp plug-in site.

2. Run the DeFX file to start the installation procedure. You'll see the DeFX DSP/Effects Plug-In for Winamp dialog box, shown in Figure 7.33. Change the directory if necessary; if not, click the Next button. When the installation ends, an Installation Successful message box appears; dismiss it.

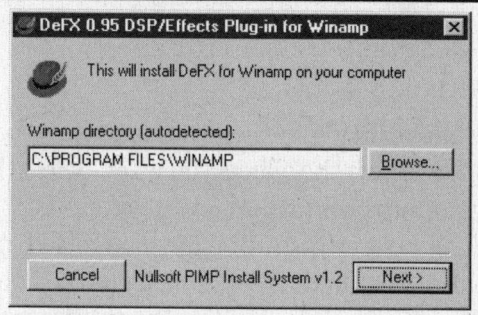

FIGURE 7.33: Installing the DeFX plug-in for Winamp

3. Press Ctrl+K to display the Winamp Preferences dialog box.

4. Click the DSP/Effect item in the left-hand list box to display the DSP/Effect Plug-In page.

5. Select the entry for DeFX in the right-hand list box. DeFX automatically displays its Console dialog box, as shown in Figure 7.34.

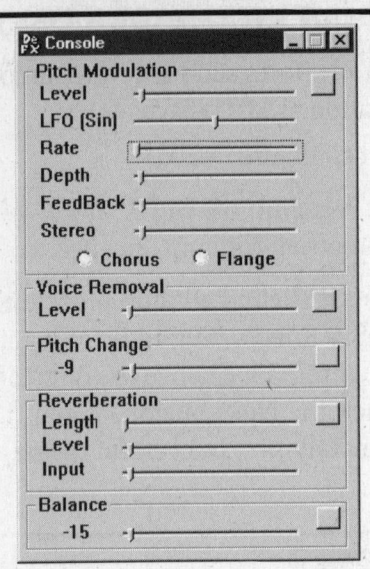

FIGURE 7.34: Use the Console dialog box to configure DeFX.

6. In the Pitch Modulation, Voice Removal, and Reverberation group boxes, select the effects you want. Select the unnamed toggle button in the relevant group box to turn the effect on (when the button appears raised, it's deselected; when pushed in, it's selected). Voice Removal is good for karaoke or Bob Dylan CDs, and Reverberation can be entertaining if you like boiler-factory sound effects.

> **WARNING**
>
> The DeFX effects take a significant amount of processing power. In particular, heavy reverberation can swamp a less-powerful processor and interrupt audio playback.

7. Click the Close button (the x button) to close the Console dialog box. (Alternatively, you can keep it open as you play music so that you can continue to make adjustments.)

8. Click the Close button to close the Winamp Preferences dialog box.

Sonique

This section discusses Sonique, which is probably the second most widely used MP3 player for Windows. Sonique owes its popularity both to being free and to being a cool-looking and highly functional MP3 player that you can customize freely with skins. Sonique started off as an independent project but was bought by Lycos in late 1999.

Sonique is one of the more idiosyncratic players that's available and it tends to receive more polarized reactions—some people love it, and others hate it—than other MP3 players. See how it suits you.

Getting and Installing Sonique

Download the latest version of Sonique from `sonique.lycos.com`. To install Sonique, double-click the distribution EXE file that you downloaded. The installation program walks you through a standard installation routine that includes choosing a language, accepting a license agreement, specifying where you want Sonique shortcuts (in your Start menu, on your Desktop, and/or on your Quick Launch toolbar), and specifying an installation directory and program folder.

The first dialog box worth noting is the page of the Sonique Installer dialog box shown in Figure 7.35, on which you specify the file types for which you want Sonique to be the default player. Unless you're using another MP3 player as your primary player, you'll want to select most of the check boxes. If you want to use Sonique as your default CD player, select the CD Audio check box. If you want Sonique to start playing the CDs automatically, also select the Auto-Play CDs When I Insert Them check box.

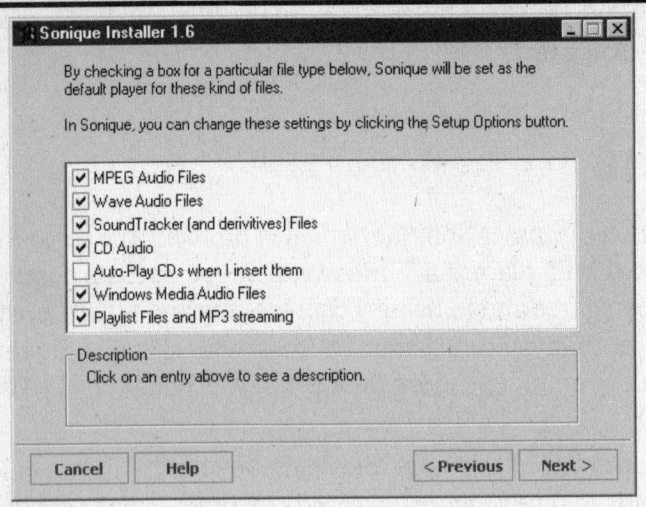

FIGURE 7.35: Choose the appropriate file types on this page of the Sonique Installer dialog box.

> **NOTE**
>
> Two quick notes here: First, at this writing, Sonique's Auto-Play feature works only with the primary CD drive on a computer—the CD drive with the lowest drive letter—not with any subsequent CD drives. Second, if you choose to use this feature, you may have to reboot a Windows 9x machine after installing Sonique—a "safe and normal operation," to use the jargon, but tedious nonetheless.

Next, the installation routine displays the page of the Sonique Installer dialog box on which you specify the type of Internet connection you're using (see Figure 7.36). In the Internet Connection Type group box, select the option button corresponding to the type of Internet connection your computer uses—a modem, a LAN, or none. If you don't want to use Sonique's Internet features, select the I Do Not Have an Internet Connection option button. (These Internet features include online updates to Sonique, including some great visualizations, and you'll probably want to use them. But if you're online infrequently, you may prefer to check for these updates manually.)

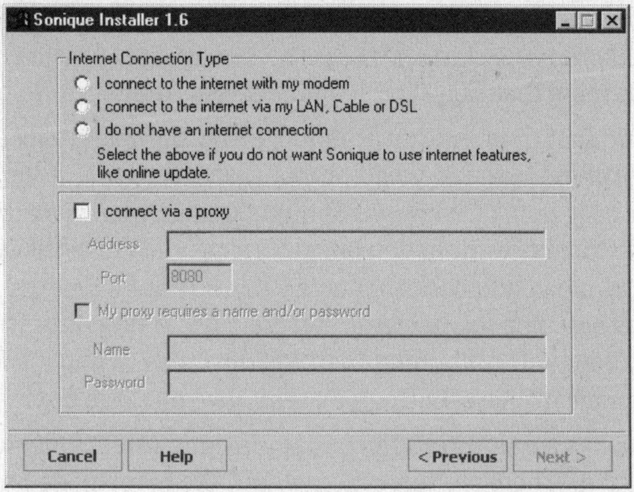

FIGURE 7.36: Specify your Internet connection (or none) and any proxy details needed on the Internet connection page of the Sonique Installer dialog box.

If your computer connects to the Internet via a proxy server, select the I Connect Via a Proxy check box. Then enter the address of the proxy server in the Address text box and enter the port number in the Port text box. The proxy server's address will probably be an IP address, something like 192.168.1.2. The port will be a number, such as 80. (Get these numbers from your network administrator if you don't know them—you won't be able to guess them unless you're psychic, and the examples in this paragraph are unlikely to be right for you.) If you need to log in to your proxy server, select the My Proxy Requires a Name and/or Password check box, and enter the name in the Name text box and the password in the Password text box.

Navigating the Interface

Launch Sonique from its Start menu item, from its Desktop item, or by clicking the Sonique QuickStart item it adds to your system tray and choosing Open Sonique from the context menu.

The first time you run Sonique, it asks you to register. Enter such information as you see fit. (Because registration is apparently inescapable, we suspect that Lycos gets a lot of people registered who claim to be more than 50 years old and living in Antarctica. So be it.)

Also, the first time you run Sonique, if you showed interest in Sonique's online updates, you'll probably see the Sonique Online Updates dialog box, offering you Sonique updates and visualizations that you may want to download. Choose the items that you want to download and click the Install Items button. Sonique downloads and installs the items and displays a text-editor window (typically Notepad) containing their Readme files. When it's finished, Sonique displays an Upgrade Complete message box.

Sonique has a unique interface that provides a short but steep learning curve. There are three modes, and the main mode has multiple screens. We'll start with the Navigation Console, the default mode Sonique initially runs in, with the Navigation screen displayed, as shown in Figure 7.37.

> **NOTE**
>
> At first, Sonique may seem unnecessarily complicated. But once you've played with it for a few minutes, you'll identify the features most useful to you and concentrate on them.

Windows Players 353

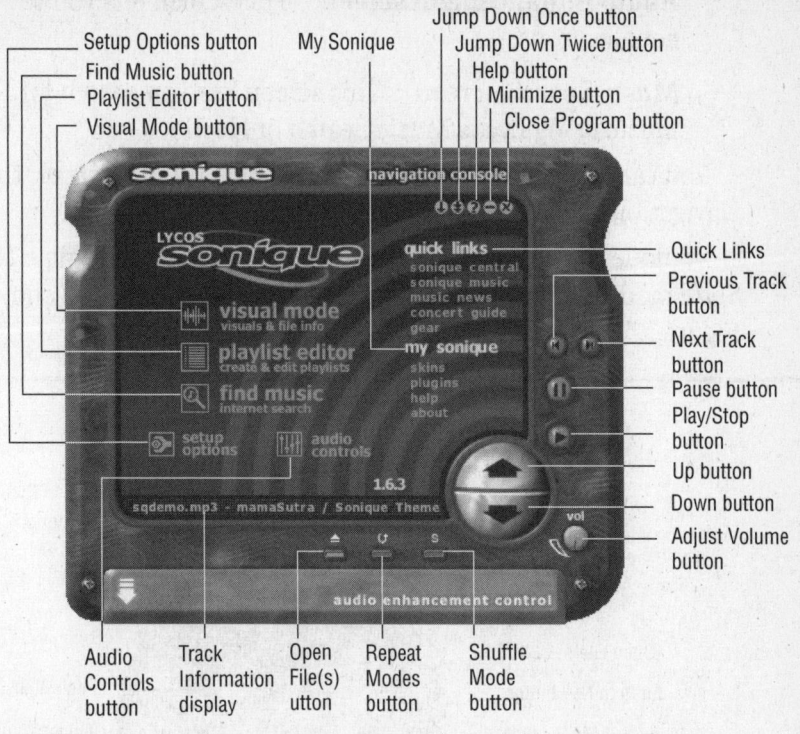

FIGURE 7.37: The Navigation Console gives you quick access to Sonique's assorted features.

Labels around the figure:
- Setup Options button
- Find Music button
- Playlist Editor button
- Visual Mode button
- My Sonique
- Jump Down Once button
- Jump Down Twice button
- Help button
- Minimize button
- Close Program button
- Quick Links
- Previous Track button
- Next Track button
- Pause button
- Play/Stop button
- Up button
- Down button
- Adjust Volume button
- Audio Controls button
- Track Information display
- Open File(s) button
- Repeat Modes button
- Shuffle Mode button

The Navigation Console offers five main screens, which we'll visit in the following sections:

Navigation screen This screen (shown in Figure 7.37) gets you around Sonique.

Playlist Editor screen This screen is used to create, save, and load playlists.

Visual Mode screen This screen provides visual accompaniment to the music that's playing.

Setup Options screen This screen lets you configure Sonique's system, audio, and visual options.

Audio Enhancement screen This screen lets you set equalizations.

Music Search screen This screen lets you search for music using Lycos Music Search or HotBot.

You can open and play tracks from any of the screens on the Navigation Console.

Sonique has two more compact modes designed for play: Mid-State mode displays Sonique as a shell-shaped player, as shown in Figure 7.38.

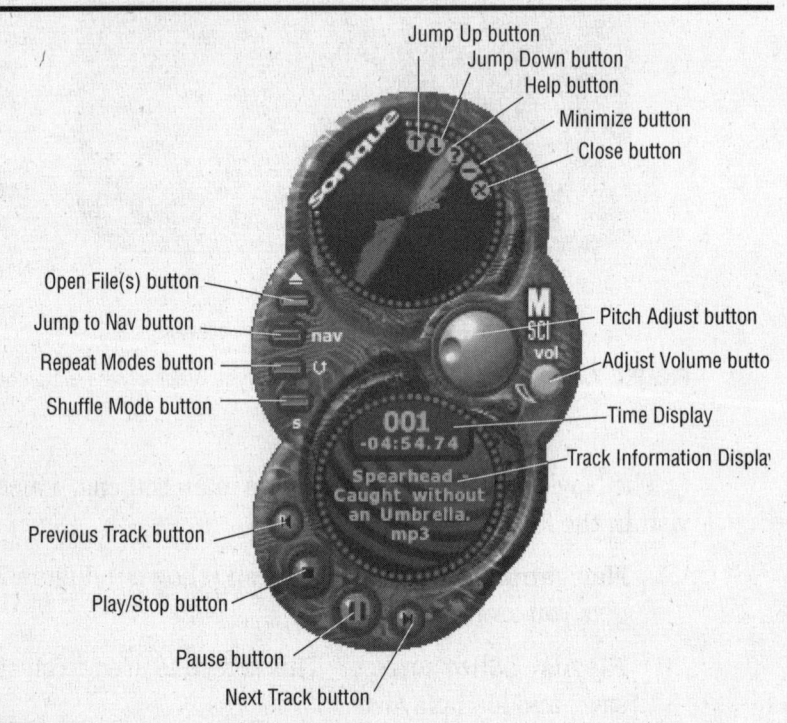

FIGURE 7.38: Sonique in Mid-State mode

Small-State mode, shown in Figure 7.39, takes up very little screen real estate. Small-State mode displays Sonique as a bar showing the track number and playing time, as you see at the top of the figure. When you move the mouse pointer over the Small-

State Mode bar, it displays the drop-down panel of controls that you see on the right.

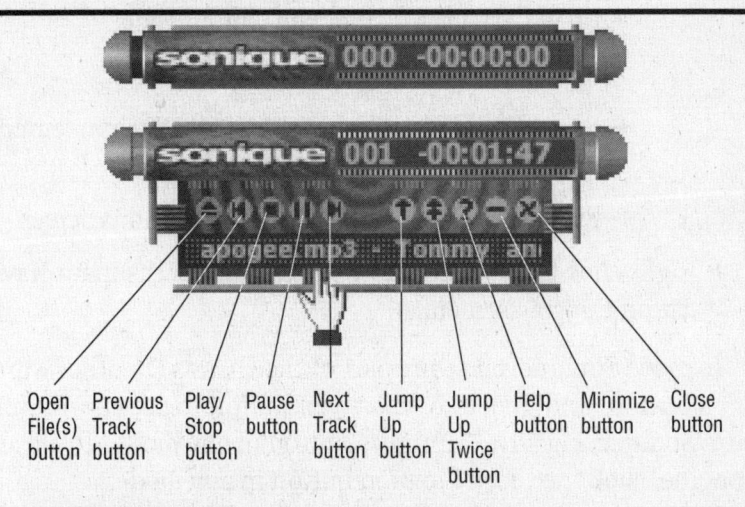

FIGURE 7.39: In Small-State mode, Sonique takes up minimal space, but displays a control panel when you move the mouse pointer over it.

You can navigate Sonique's modes with the keyboard or the mouse as follows:

- Use the navigation buttons (such as the Jump Up button) on the Sonique windows.

- Double-click any part of Sonique's chassis (the gray frame), or press Ctrl+Tab, to move between modes in the following sequence: Small-State mode, Mid-State mode, and Navigation Console. Double-click the right mouse button to move through the modes in the reverse order.

- To quickly change modes with the keyboard, use the following key presses:
    - Press Ctrl+N for the Navigation Console.
    - Press Ctrl+E for Visual mode.
    - Press Ctrl+M for Mid-State mode.
    - Press Ctrl+, (Ctrl+comma) for Small-State mode.

- To display different screens on the Navigation Console, use the following key presses:
    - Press Ctrl+O to display the Online Tools.
    - Press Ctrl+P to display the Playlist Editor.
    - Press Ctrl+R to display the Audio Enhancement screen and Audio Enhancement Control.
    - Press Ctrl+S to display the Setup Options screen.
- Right-click to move from any screen back to the main Navigation Console screen.

To move Sonique, click any part of the chassis (in other words, not a button) and drag it to where you want it to appear. To minimize Sonique, click the Minimize button in any mode. To close Sonique, click the Close Program button in any mode.

To put Sonique into always-on-top mode, so that it appears on top no matter which application is active, press Ctrl+T, or display the Setup Options screen by clicking the Setup Options button in the Navigation Console and select the Always on Top check box in the System Options area.

Playing MP3 Files and SHOUTcast Streams

Compared to getting used to the Sonique interface, playing music is a no-brainer. You can use either the button controls (which are mostly self-explanatory) or the keyboard, as follows:

- Press L to display the Add & Play Sonique Media dialog box to open MP3 files or URLs.
- Press X to start or stop the track playing.
- Press C to pause the track.
- Press B or → to move to the next track.
- Press Z or ← to move to the previous track.
- Press D to clear the current playlist.

You can control the volume by using either the Volume button (drag up or right to increase the volume, down or left to decrease it) or the keyboard, as follows:

- Press ↑ to increase volume.
- Press ↓ to decrease volume.
- Press the ` key (the accent key, not the apostrophe) to mute the volume.
- Press the numbers 1 through 0 for 10 percent through 100 percent volume.

Creating a Playlist

To create a playlist, start the Playlist Editor (shown in Figure 7.40 with a number of songs added) by pressing P or by clicking the Playlist Editor button in the Navigation Console.

The Playlist Editor is straightforward to use:

- Use the Add button (or press A) and the resulting Add & Play Sonique Media dialog box to add tracks, playlists, or streams to the playlist. Use the Remove button to remove selected tracks or streams from the playlist.
- Use the Sort button to sort the tracks in the playlist into alphabetical order, the Shuffle button (as often as you like) to shuffle them, and the Reverse button to reverse the current order.
- Use the Up and Down buttons to move to a different track in the playlist.

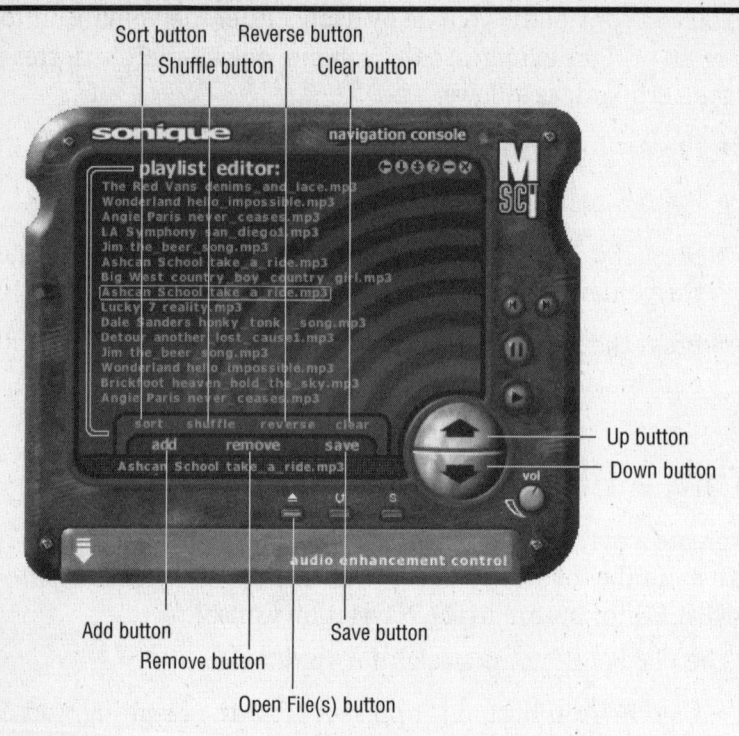

FIGURE 7.40: Creating a playlist in Sonique's Playlist Editor

- When you've got the playlist to your satisfaction, save it by clicking the Save button and using the Save Sonique Media Playlist dialog box. Sonique uses the PLS extension for playlist filenames.

- Use the Open File(s) button and the resulting Open & Play Sonique Media dialog box to open a saved playlist.

- Use the Clear button to clear the current playlist in order to start a new playlist.

- To edit the ID3 tag for the currently playing MP3 file, click the File Info button on the Navigation Console in Visual mode to display the audioEnlightenment File Information dialog box (see Figure 7.41). This dialog box shows "Edit Me!" for missing entries in the artist name, song title, album title, and comment slots of the tag. Click the Wipe Tag button if you need to remove the current tag information.

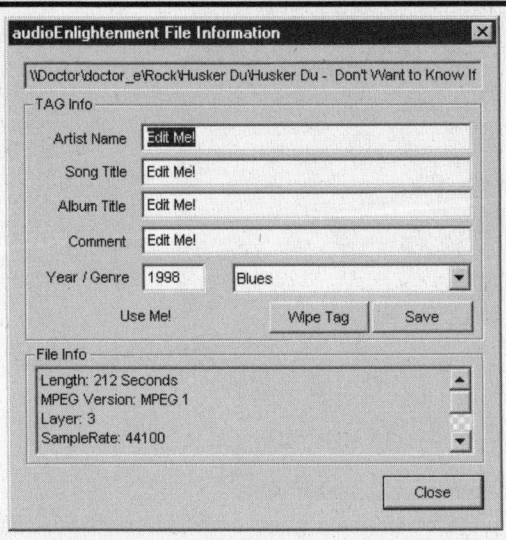

FIGURE 7.41: Use the audioEnlightenment File Information dialog box to edit ID3 tags.

Using the Audio Enhancement Control

Like Winamp, Sonique provides an effective graphic equalizer. It lacks some of the features that Winamp's graphic equalizer provides but it gives you 20 equalizer bands to Winamp's 10.

Press Ctrl+R or click the Audio Controls button on the main screen of the Navigation Console to display the Audio Enhancement screen and slide out the Audio Enhancement Control (see Figure 7.42). You can also click the Audio Enhancement Control button on the Navigation Console to display the Audio Enhancement Control at any time; click it again to slide the Audio Enhancement Control shut.

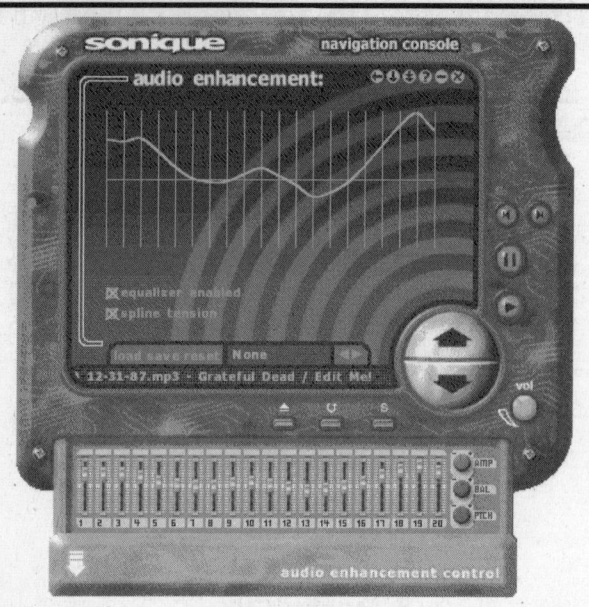

FIGURE 7.42: Sonique provides a 20-band graphic equalizer to give you fine control over the sound it produces.

By default, the graphic equalizer is turned off, so start by turning it on. Press Q or select the Equalizer Enabled check box on the Audio Enhancement screen. (To turn the equalizer off again, press Q again or clear the Equalizer Enabled check box.) You can then create an equalization by dragging the sliders for the different frequencies up and down until you get the sound balance you want.

The Spline Tension check box on the Audio Enhancement screen controls whether the pitch sliders move independently or affect nearby sliders. When this check box is selected, moving a slider moves the adjacent sliders in the same direction to a lesser degree, producing a gradual change in the wave form. If you want to set large differences between one band and the next, clear the Spline Tension check box.

To change the preamplification, click the Amp button and drag up (or left) or down (or right). Similarly, use the Balance button to adjust the left-right balance and the control to change the pitch (the speed) at which the track is playing. Use the readout in the song-title area to check the current setting.

To save an equalization, click the Save button, then select the preset save location you want to use on the Select a Preset Save Location panel of the Audio Enhancement screen (see Figure 7.43).

FIGURE 7.43: Use the Select a Preset Save Location panel of the Audio Enhancement screen to save your graphic equalizations.

To load an equalization you've created and saved, click the Load button and choose the equalization from the Select a Preset Load Location panel. To reset the graphic equalizer, click the Reset button on the Audio Enhancement screen.

Enjoying Visualizations

Sonique comes complete with built-in visualizations that provide an intense light-show accompaniment to what you're playing.

Mid-State mode displays a small-scale visualization whenever you're playing music. You can change from one visualization to the

Chapter Seven

next by pressing the comma (,) key and the period (.) key or by moving the mouse pointer over the Vis Display window so that the Vis buttons pop up (as shown in Figure 7.44), then clicking one of the buttons.

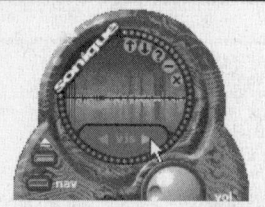

FIGURE 7.44: To move from one visualization to another in Mid-State mode, move the mouse pointer over the Vis Display window so that the Vis buttons pop up, then use the buttons.

Sonique's best effects are accessible only from the Navigation Console. From any mode, press Ctrl+E to display Visual mode. (Sonique switches to the Navigation Console if it's in another mode.) If you're already in the Navigation Console, you can also click the Visual Mode button on the Navigation screen to enter Visual mode. Figure 7.45 shows Sonique in Visual mode.

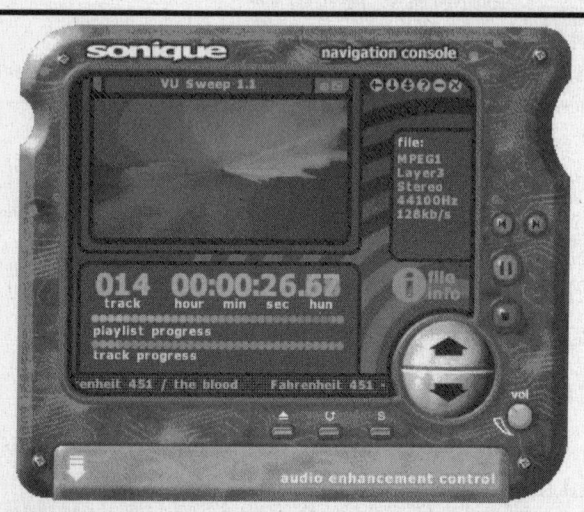

FIGURE 7.45: To enjoy Sonique's best effects, switch to Visual mode.

Click the Up and Down buttons, or press the comma (,) and period (.) keys, to change from one visualization to the next.

Click the Full Window Vis Mode button at the upper-right corner of the Vis display to enlarge the visualization to fill the Sonique screen area. You then have another choice at the upper-left corner of the Vis area—the No Extras Full Window Mode button, which removes all the information overlaid on the screen area. Click the button again to restore Full Window Vis mode with the overlaid information.

Full Window Vis mode is great for keeping your mind engaged when you're setting up monster custom playlists with Sonique. But when you've gotten a playlist rolling and you're ready to kick back and enjoy a playlist, switch to Sonique's full-bore visualizations by clicking the Full Screen Vis button. As before, press the comma (,) and period (.) keys to switch backward and forward through the available visualizations. Press Esc or Enter to exit Full Screen Vis mode.

Full Screen Vis mode makes heavy use of the processor and can overwhelm an underpowered computer. If you hear interruptions in the sound when you're trying to run Full Screen Vis mode, your computer is probably unable to handle the strain. Desist.

> **TIP**
>
> To get more impressive visualizations out of a song at the same volume, turn up the preamplification and turn down the volume to balance things out.

Changing Sonique's Skin

Sonique supports both different skins and different shapes, so you can completely change the player's appearance by applying a different skin to it. Figure 7.46 shows the Bubble Blues skin applied to Sonique.

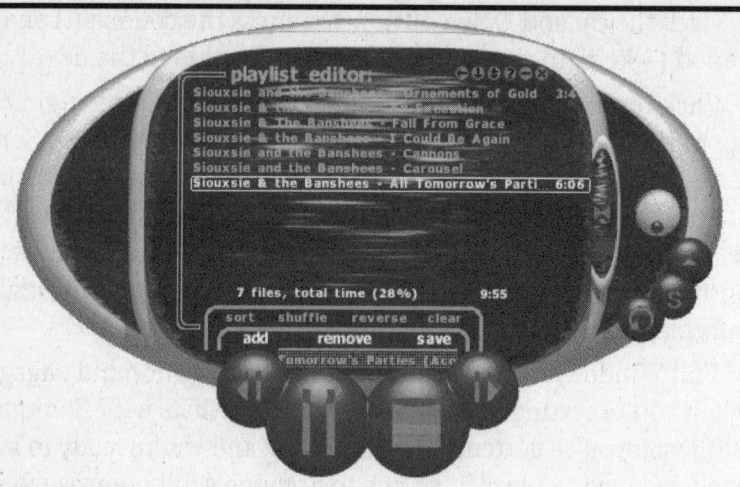

FIGURE 7.46: Sonique's skins can change both its look and its shape.

If you're looking for skins, your first stop should probably be the Sonique skins archive (skins.sonique.com). There are also plenty of other Web sites and newsgroups that carry Sonique skins. Most skin files are relatively small in size (say, from 50K to 600K), so you can download them in a minute or two even over a modem connection. The skins have the filename extension SGF.

The easiest way to install a skin is to download it directly into the \Sonique\skins\ folder. You can also copy or move a skin manually into this folder. Alternatively, right-click the skin file (which will have a SGF extension) in Explorer and choose Install into Sonique from the context menu.

To apply a skin from the Navigation Console, click the Setup Options button to display the Setup Options screen. Click the Skins button on the right-hand side to display the setup options for skins with a thumbnail of the current skin. Then use the Up and Down buttons to browse through the skins that are available in your \Sonique\skins\ folder. To apply the skin, click the back arrow button or right mouse button. Sonique applies the skin and returns you to the Navigation Console.

To apply a skin immediately, double-click it in Explorer.

Using Plug-Ins

Sonique also supports visualization and audio plug-ins that extend its functionality. For example, if you're using Sonique to play CDs, you'll probably want to get the Copah CD-Reader plug-in (from www.url.ru/~copah/CDReader.htm), which enables Sonique to access CDDB and display the names of CD tracks, an ability Sonique itself doesn't have at this writing.

If you're using Sonique's auto-update feature, Sonique automatically alerts you when new plug-ins are posted on the Sonique Web site. If not, or if you're in a tearing hurry, visit the Sonique plug-in archive (plugins.sonique.com) and download anything that catches your imagination.

Many plug-ins come in EXE files that you run to install the plug-in. Be sure to run a virus checker on EXE files to make sure they're not harboring anything unpleasant.

Some plug-ins just produce visual effects, and are configured via configuration files; read the Readme file that accompanies the plug-in for details. Other plug-ins provide options that are configurable through the Sonique interface. To configure such a plug-in, press Ctrl+S, or click the Setup Options button on the Navigation screen in the Navigation Console, to display the Setup Options screen. Then click the Plug-Ins button to display the Plug-Ins screen, and on the right-hand side of the screen, click the tab for the plug-in you want to configure. Select options for the plug-in, then click the Navigation Menu button to return to the Navigation screen.

Sonique Keyboard Commands

Because of Sonique's multiple modes, the key to using it effectively is to learn some of the many keyboard shortcuts that it supports. Table 7.2 lists the key presses and key combinations for controlling Sonique.

TABLE 7.2: Sonique Key Presses and Keyboard Shortcuts

Action	Key Press/Combination
Playing Tracks	
Next track	B or →
Pause	C
Delete the currently playing track	D
Load track	L
Playlist Editor	P
EQ enable toggle	Q
Stop	V
Play/Stop	X
Previous track	Z or ←
Scan backward	Ctrl+←
Scan forward	Ctrl+→
Visualizations	
Previous visualization	,
Next visualization	.
Changing Video Resolutions and Colors (Full-Screen Visualizations)	
Next higher resolution mode	+ (on numeric keypad)
Next lower resolution made	- (on numeric keypad)
Next higher color depth	] or Page Up
Next lower color depth	[or Page Down
Exit full-screen Vis mode	Enter or Esc
Display the current track in full-screen Vis mode	Space
Toggles between the Playlist Editor and Visual mode	Tab
Windows and Modes	
Always on top	Ctrl+A
Clear playlist	Ctrl+D
Visual mode	Ctrl+E

CONTINUED ➔

TABLE 7.2 continued: Sonique Key Presses and Keyboard Shortcuts

Action	Key Press/Combination
Windows and Modes	
Announce to IRC toggle	Ctrl+I
Mid-State mode	Ctrl+M
Nav Console	Ctrl+N
Online Tools	Ctrl+O
Playlist	Ctrl+P
Audio Controls	Ctrl+R
Setup Options	Ctrl+S
Always on top toggle	Ctrl+T
Small-State mode	Ctrl+,
Change state	Ctrl+Tab
Switch to the default skin	Ctrl+Z
Volume Controls	
Set the volume to 10 through 90 percent	1 through 9
Full volume	0
Mute volume	` (on the ~ key, not ')
Increase the volume	↑
Decrease the volume	↓

Other Windows MP3 Players

So far in this chapter, we've described the two most widely used MP3 players for Windows—Winamp and Sonique—in some depth. In this section, we'll discuss some of the other leading MP3 players available for Windows in far less depth: FreeAmp, XingMP3 Player, Audioactive, UltraPlayer, and Unreal Player MAX.

FreeAmp

FreeAmp is a competent but only modestly exciting player that has a relatively small but devoted following. As its name suggests, FreeAmp is free, developed by a dedicated group funded by EMusic.com. You can get versions of FreeAmp for Linux and various versions of Unix at this writing, and a Macintosh version of FreeAmp is in the pipeline.

Go to the FreeAmp Web site, `www.freeamp.org`, and download the latest version you find.

FreeAmp has a number of nice features, including the following:

- The ability to search your drives for music files and manage them into a database, which lets you manipulate them without knowing exactly where they're located.

- Three modes (Normal, Medium, and Mini) that let you balance your need for information about what's playing against your need for screen real estate.

- *Themes* that let you apply different color schemes to the player.

- The option to save SHOUTcast and icecast streams to your hard disk.

- The ability to download music from Web sites that support the RMP or RealJukebox download format. (You'll find plenty of such music at EMusic.com.)

- Its support of the M3U and PLS playlists formats.

At this writing, the biggest disadvantage of FreeAmp is that is doesn't have a graphic equalizer. If you're running the output through a receiver that includes graphic equalization, or if you like your music straight and your food unsalted, this may not be a problem. Otherwise, you'll lack the fine control over the sound of music that equalization-equipped players such as Winamp, Sonique, and UltraPlayer give you.

FreeAmp's installation routine is easy but it gives you more options than many other MP3 players. Here's what you should know:

- FreeAmp is provided under the GNU General Public License, which means you can redistribute and modify the software if you see fit, and you don't need to agree to a license agreement if you just want to install FreeAmp. Because this is cool, FreeAmp uses a Cool! button instead of a Next button on the license agreement.

- You get to choose between Typical, Compact, and Custom installation options. Given that the full installation takes up little less than 4MB at this writing, and that you can save only a few hundred KB by leaving out certain components, we suggest you choose the Custom option and leave all the options selected in the Select Components dialog box.

- You get to choose whether FreeAmp can reclaim stolen file types (a good idea if you want to use FreeAmp as your main player, but not a good idea if you want to use another MP3 player most of the time).

- You get to specify a download directory for music that FreeAmp downloads from within the player.

Once you've installed it, you'll find that FreeAmp (shown in Normal view in Figure 7.47) provides a straightforward and uncluttered interface that's easy to manipulate.

FIGURE 7.47: FreeAmp has a pleasant and uncluttered interface that's easy to work with.

When you start FreeAmp, it volunteers to search your disks for music and playlists to add to your music database, which is called My Music. (If you have an MP3 CD in one of your CD drives, make sure you don't let FreeAmp search that, or it will expect the CD always to be there.) You can then build playlists easily in the My Music window (shown in Figure 7.48).

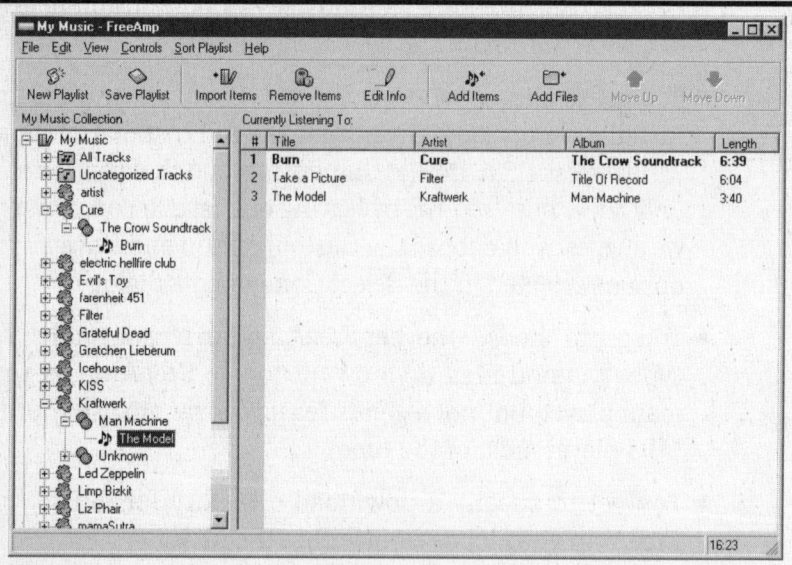

FIGURE 7.48: The My Music window provides your interface to FreeAmp's database of MP3 tracks and playlists.

XingMP3 Player

Xing Technologies, long famous for compelling audio software, makes XingMP3 Player, a solid MP3 player for Windows. (This player isn't available for other platforms such as the Macintosh or Linux.) XingMP3 Player doesn't offer as many features as Winamp or Sonique, but it has a number of strong features, including a good playlist editor and the ability to play video files such as MPEG video. And the price is right—it's free. But because Xing Technologies has been acquired by RealNetworks, and RealNetworks's primary interest on the MP3 front is promoting its ripper/player/

jukebox, RealJukebox, XingMP3 Player seems to be being neglected and it may go nowhere fast in the future.

For the moment, though, it's worth using if you're interested. Download the latest version of XingMP3 Player from the Xing Technologies Web site, www.xingtech.com, and then double-click the distribution file to start the setup routine. Be sure to select the appropriate file associations in the Select File Associations dialog box so that XingMP3 Player will play MP3 files and playlists. XingMP3 Player uses the M3U playlist format as well as its own XPL format. You'll most likely need to restart your computer before you can use XingMP3 Player.

Once Windows has restarted, start XingMP3 Player by choosing Start ➤ Programs ➤ XingMP3 Player ➤ XingMP3 Player. If XingMP3 Player isn't your default MPEG player when you start it, it warns you about the problem. If you don't want XingMP3 Player to harass you about not being the default player, select the Do Not Prompt in the Future check box before dismissing the Warning dialog box.

By default, XingMP3 Player automatically opens the Play List Editor, but you can hide it if you're not using it. You can also stop it from appearing. Clear the Auto Load Play List Editor check box on the Play List Editor page of the Properties/Settings dialog box.

Figure 7.49 shows XingMP3 Player and the Play List Editor with a number of songs added to a playlist. (When you first open XingMP3 Player, you probably won't be seeing a playlist, just the sample track that XingMP3 Player includes so that you can make sure the player is working.)

XingMP3 Player's interface is mostly intuitive to use. Here are four things about it that are perhaps less intuitive:

- ▶ Click the Launch AudioCatalyst button to launch AudioCatalyst for ripping tracks. (We'll talk about AudioCatalyst a little in the next chapter.)

- ▶ Click the Properties/Settings button to display the Properties/Settings dialog box for choosing configuration settings.

372 Chapter Seven

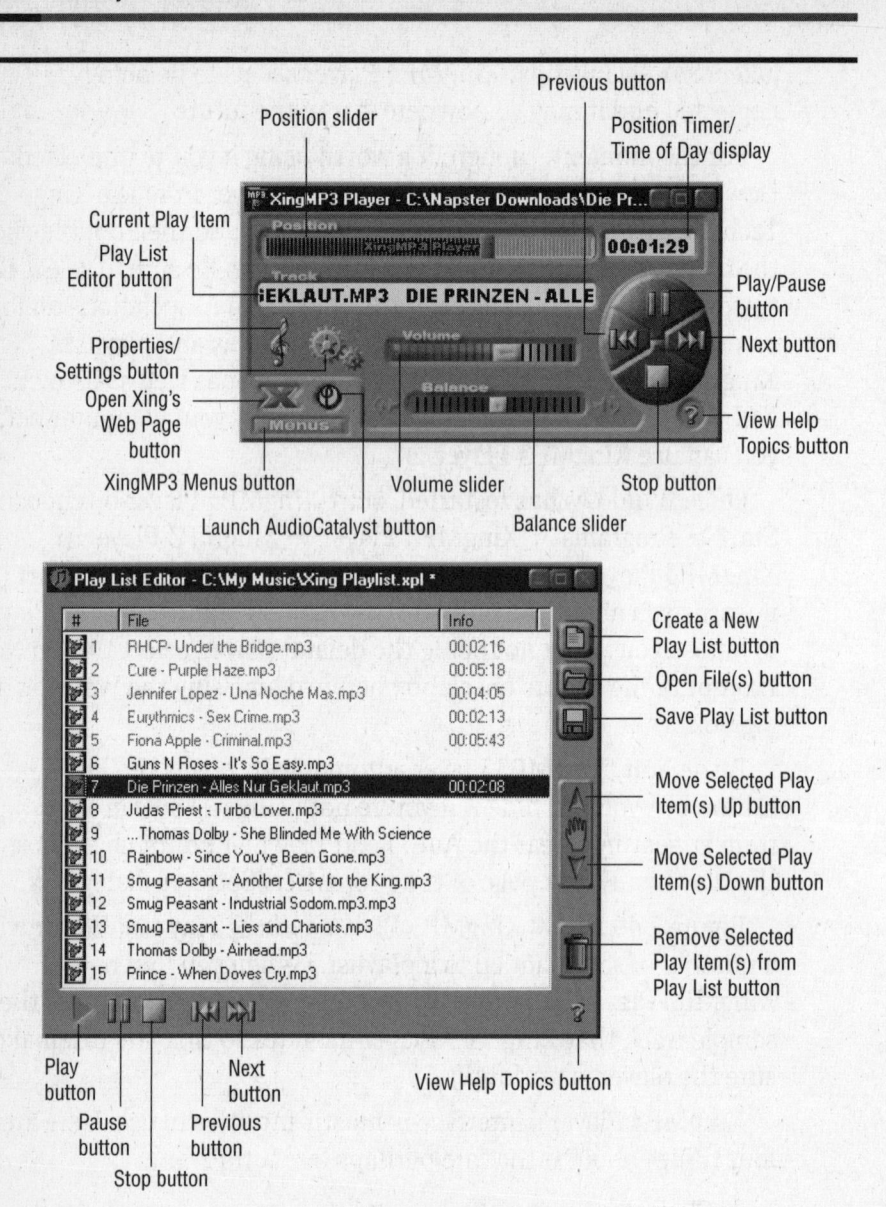

FIGURE 7.49: XingMP3 Player and the Play List Editor

▶ Click the XingMP3 Menus button to display a drop-down menu of menus: File, View, Volume, and Help. You can access most of the XingMP3 Player commands from these menus, but usually it's easier to use the graphic controls (the buttons, sliders, and so on) and the keyboard shortcuts.

▶ If XingMP3 Player displays a Warning dialog box, such as the one shown in Figure 7.50, when you try to add a file from a network drive to a playlist, you've run into an annoying bug. If you look at the dialog box shown in the figure, you'll see that the path is listed as starting with `Classical\Rock\`. In fact, it should be `h:\Rock\`, but XingMP3 Player has bollixed the path for some reason. If this happens to you, look for a newer version of XingMP3 Player with the bug fixed. Failing that, try copying the file or files to a local drive and loading them from there. For whatever reason, XingMP3 Player seems to handle local drives without a problem but seems to screw up royally on network drives.

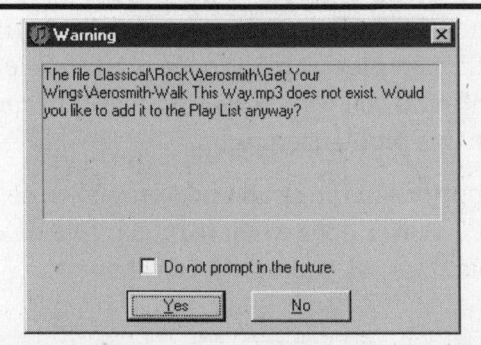

FIGURE 7.50: At this writing, XingMP3 Player has a bug that messes up when adding a file located on a network drive to a playlist.

There are a few settings in the Properties/Settings dialog box worth mentioning:

▶ In the Filters group box, leave the Always Try to Use XingMP3 Audio Decoder check box selected unless you have a good reason not to.

▶ The Auto Load Play List Editor check box controls whether XingMP3 Player opens the Play List Editor when you start XingMP3 Player. Usually, opening the Play List Editor is useful.

- The Auto Randomize on Open check box controls whether XingMP3 Player automatically randomizes each playlist as you open it. We hate this feature, but you may love it.

- The Allow Unregistered Filetypes check box governs whether XingMP3 Player lets you add to a playlist files of types that are not explicitly registered to XingMP3 Player. Don't bother adding anything that XingMP3 Player can't play.

- The Crop Saved Path Names check box controls whether XingMP3 Player stores path names at their full length or whether it crops them down to a more friendly size.

- The Opening Playlists group box lets you specify what you want XingMP3 Player to do when you open a playlist when another is already open. Select the Replace option button if you want the new playlist to get rid of the current playlist. Select the Append option button if you want XingMP3 Player to append the new playlist to the open playlist. Select the Ask option button if you want XingMP3 Player to consult you each time this problem crops up.

- The three option buttons in the Dead Links group box control what XingMP3 Player does when it runs into a dead link: allow it, forbid it, or ask you what to do about it.

Audioactive Player

Audioactive Player is a straightforward player from Telos Systems. Audioactive Player lacks a graphic equalizer, but makes up somewhat for this sad omission by providing an easy-to-use playlist editor (which bears more than a passing resemblance to XingMP3 Player's playlist editor) and an ID3 tag editor. In our experience, Audioactive Player produces good sounds. You can download the latest version of Audioactive Player from the Audioactive Web site, www.audioactive.com.

Telos Systems is a commercial concern, so they point you first toward the products they sell, which include Audioactive Productions Studio, one of the MP3-ripping and encoding solutions that we'll discuss in the next chapter. Steer your way past everything that costs money to the freebies and download the latest version of Audioactive Player. If you have time to spare, grab the latest version of Audioactive Production Studio while you're at their site. (If not, get it when you read the next chapter.)

Audioactive Player's installation routine is remarkable only for making you quit your Web browser for the installation. After you say you've done so, the installation runs without any options (except for giving you the chance to refuse the license agreement and end the installation) and starts Audioactive Player without consulting you.

Figure 7.51 shows Audioactive Player and the Audioactive Playlist Editor.

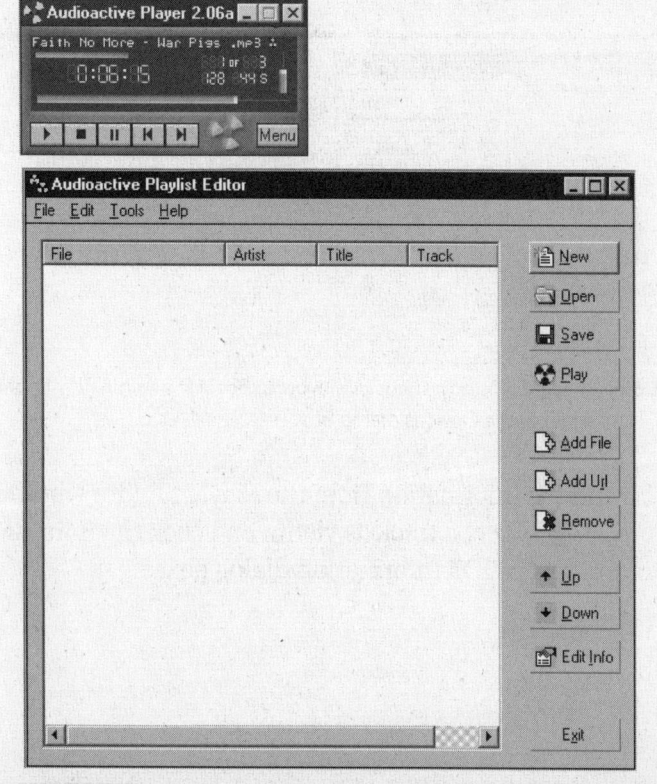

FIGURE 7.51: Audioactive Player is a straightforward player that produced good sound quality in our informal testing.

Audioactive Player's Options dialog box (shown in Figure 7.52, and which you summon by clicking the Menu button and choosing Options) has relatively few options, but two of them are worth mentioning:

- The Check File Types check box controls whether Audioactive Player tries to reclaim file associations that other applications have stolen when you run it.

- The Audio Play Priority slider lets you assign a priority to audio play. If you find you get interruptions in play, move the slider to the fourth or fifth notch. If audio quality is fine but other applications are responding like inebriated slugs, move the slider down towards the low end until audio quality starts to degrade. Otherwise, leave the slider at the midway position.

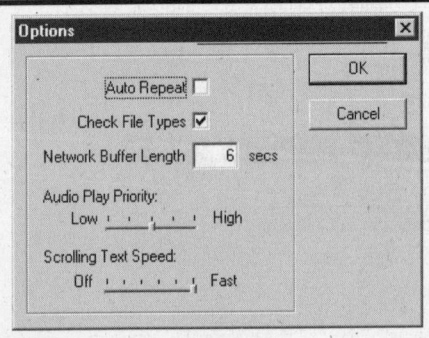

FIGURE 7.52: If you get interruptions in playback, boost the Audio Play Priority slider in the Options dialog box.

You can edit tag information from the Playlist Editor window (see Figure 7.53). Select a track as victim and click the Edit Info button to display the ID3 Information dialog box.

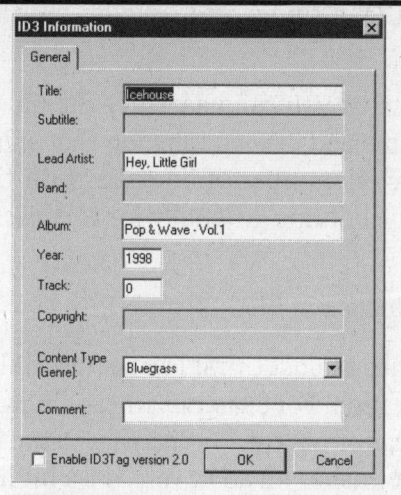

FIGURE 7.53: Audioactive Player provides tag-editing capabilities.

UltraPlayer

UltraPlayer is a relatively new MP3 player that claims to be hot on the heels of Winamp for the Windows MP3 player crown. There's some merit in this claim, as UltraPlayer has the following features:

- Plays files in a wide variety of formats, including MP3, WMA, WAV files, both the M3U and the PLS playlist formats, and of course CDA, audio CD files.
- Has a ten-band graphic equalizer.
- Uses the much-vaunted Neutrino decoder, which seems to produce high-quality sound even on modest sound cards.
- Supports skins.

- Integrates with EasyMP3, a ripper and encoder built by Proteron.
- Has an alarm function that you can use to set the music playing at a specified time and a sleep function that shuts the music off after a given number of minutes, with the option of decreasing the volume gradually for the last of those minutes.
- Saves streaming audio to disk in MP3 files.

In our eyes, the biggest strike against UltraPlayer is that it flashes ads at you between each operation. For example, when you switch from one of its pages to another (from the Playlist page to the Equalization page, for example), it flashes an ad at you. It's a bit like watching TV, but much more annoying, because it makes the transition from page to page seem glacially slow.

Download the latest version of UltraPlayer from the UltraPlayer Web site (www.ultraplayer.com) and run the EXE file to install it. UltraPlayer's installation routine is easy. On the File-Types page of the UltraPlayer Setup dialog box, make sure the file types that you want to play in UltraPlayer are selected. More to the point, perhaps, make sure that the check boxes for any file types you want other applications to play are cleared, and check whether you want to set UltraPlayer as your default player for audio CDs.

Figure 7.54 shows UltraPlayer. In this figure, it's hard to see, but UltraPlayer consists of two parts that join just above the track display. You can run the lower, smaller part on its own, but to access most of the features (the graphic equalizer, the playlist editor, the tuner for accessing streams, and so on), you need to display the upper, larger part.

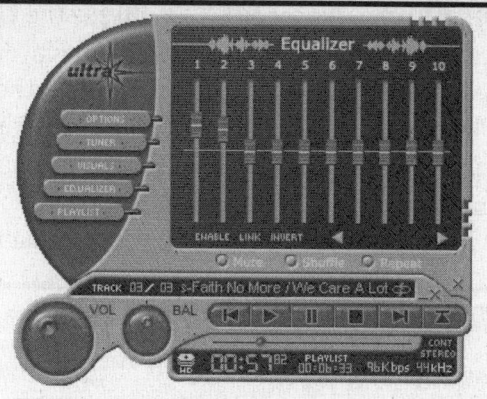

FIGURE 7.54: UltraPlayer has an innovative interface but irritates by flashing ads at you.

Unreal Player MAX

Unreal Player MAX is a capable young player that suffers at this writing from a confusing and buggy interface. Unreal Player MAX has a huge number of features, but at the moment, it's best treated with caution.

If you're the adventurous type, download the latest version of Unreal Player MAX from the Internal Corporation Web site (www.internal.co.jp), cross your fingers (or back up your system files), and run the executable.

Unreal Player MAX uses a straightforward installation routine marred (again, at this writing) by a license agreement dialog box that shows the license text in unintelligible symbols rather than readable text, so that you can't know what you're agreeing with, and by a Select Destination Directory dialog box in which some of the information is hidden by a bad choice of font.

More relevant is the Select Your Processor dialog box, shown in Figure 7.55, in which you get to specify the type of processor that your computer has. In our experience, the installation routine seems effective at detecting the type of processor, but you may need to override its selection.

Chapter Seven

The first time you start Unreal Player MAX, you'll see the Online Update dialog box, which offers to connect to the Unreal Player server to check for a new version. If you've just downloaded the latest version of Unreal Player MAX, you might be tempted to skip this check. But be aware that Unreal Player MAX offers you the chance to download extra components such as panels and plug-ins, so it might be worth your while to go ahead and check what's available.

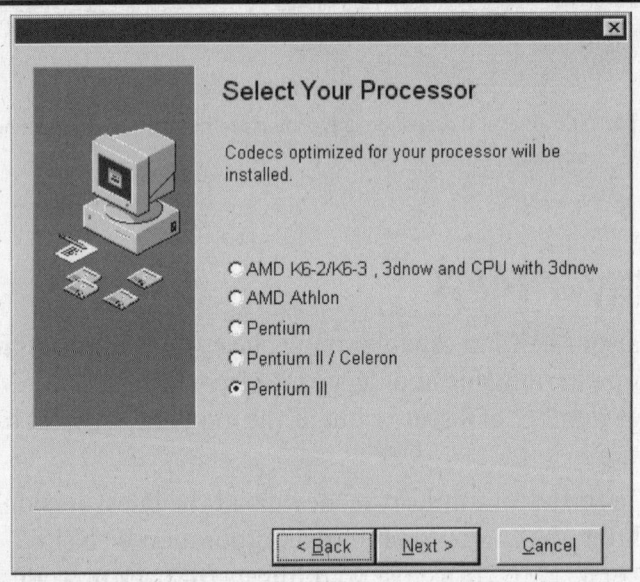

FIGURE 7.55: Unlike most other players, Unreal Player MAX makes you choose the type of processor your computer has, so that it can install the appropriate codecs.

Unreal Player MAX then grabs the details of whatever's available, like an enthusiastic Labrador finding unpleasant objects in a farmyard, and presents them to you in the Download Component dialog box, shown in Figure 7.56. Use the Install button to install each component you want, then click the OK button to close the Download Component dialog box.

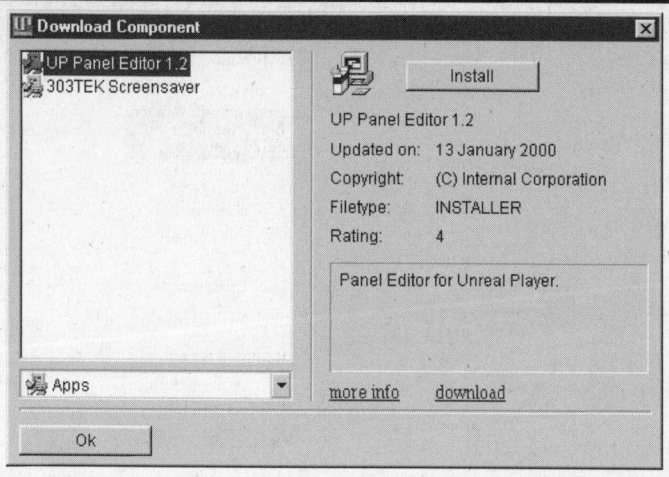

FIGURE 7.56: If you let it, Unreal Player MAX automatically checks for new components and offers to download them for you.

Once you've installed the components that interest you, you're ready to start playing music with Unreal Player MAX. Figure 7.57 shows Unreal Player MAX getting to grips with some ancient metal.

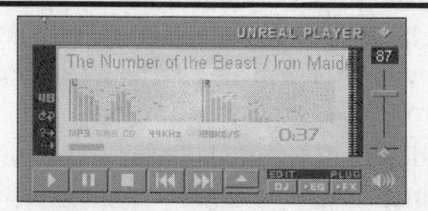

FIGURE 7.57: Unreal Player MAX in action

The features available from Unreal Player MAX's interface are easy enough to guess. In the default skin, the buttons for accessing the playlist editor (the Edit button), visualization plug-ins (the Plug button), the DJ Console feature (the DJ and FX buttons), and the graphic equalizer (the EQ button) appear to the right of the main play controls. Clicking the speaker icon at the lower-right corner of the player displays the Config dialog box (see Figure 7.58), which offers seven pages of options: Soundcard, Preferences, Appearance, Animation, Tips, Panel/Coolbar, and Playlist Editor.

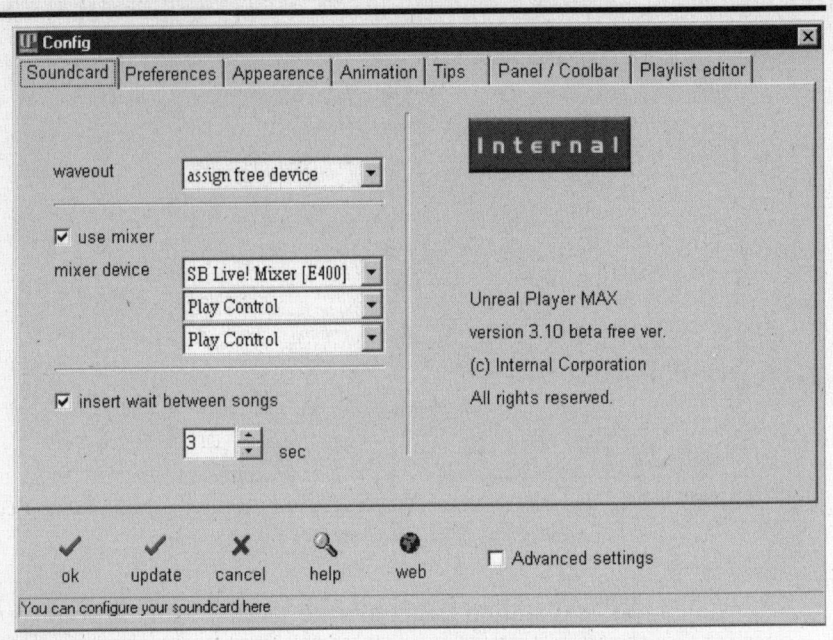

FIGURE 7.58: Unreal Player MAX comes well equipped with options.

You can access Unreal Player MAX's other features by right-clicking the player window and choosing from the resulting huge context menu and its many submenus. There are also many keyboard shortcuts that you can use to quickly access features.

Unreal Player MAX provides a full-featured playlist editor with a graphic button bar for building, manipulating, and saving playlists. By contrast, Unreal Player MAX's graphic equalizer is underpowered, offering only four bands (compared to the 10 of Winamp and the 20 of Sonique).

To display the graphic equalizer, click the EQ button on the main Unreal Player MAX window. Drag the four sliders in the resulting window to create the equalization you want. To turn the graphic equalizer off, click the EQ button again.

More interesting is the DJ Console feature (shown in Figure 7.59), which lets you add effects such as reverb and delay to the music you're playing. To display the DJ Console, click the FX button or the DJ button on the main window. Choose settings that please you, then click the close button (the x button) on the DJ Console window to close it. To turn off the DJ Console effects, click the FX button on the main Unreal Player MAX window again.

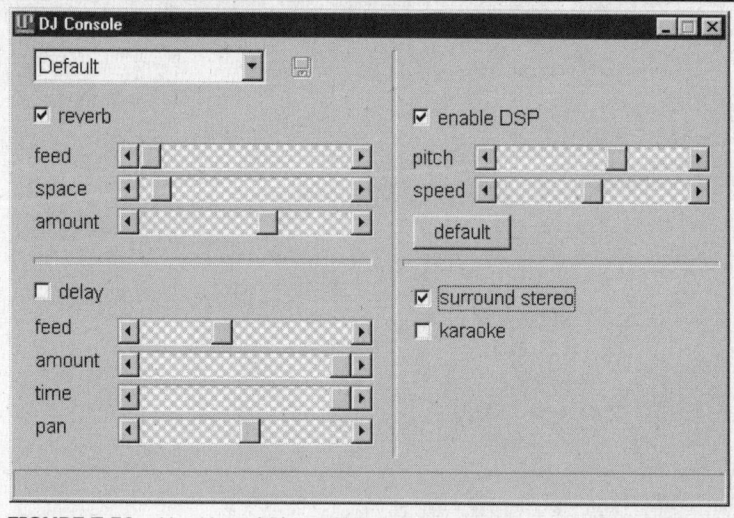

FIGURE 7.59: Use Unreal Player MAX's DJ Console to add effects to audio.

Up Next

In this chapter, we've given you a grounding in the leading MP3 players for Windows at this time: Winamp and Sonique. We've also shown you how to make the most of the ubiquitous-on-Windows-platforms Windows Media Player in versions up to 7, and how to start getting to grips with the much-improved version 7 that debuted in Windows Me. And we've drawn your attention to some of the up-and-coming MP3 players and some of those that have been moderately popular but whose stars seem to be fading.

At this point, you should be well equipped to play MP3 files on Windows. Next, we'll turn our attention to creating MP3 files of your own under Windows. The next chapter will discuss Windows rippers and encoders. We'll leave jukeboxes (almost all of which rip and encode as well) until the chapter after that.

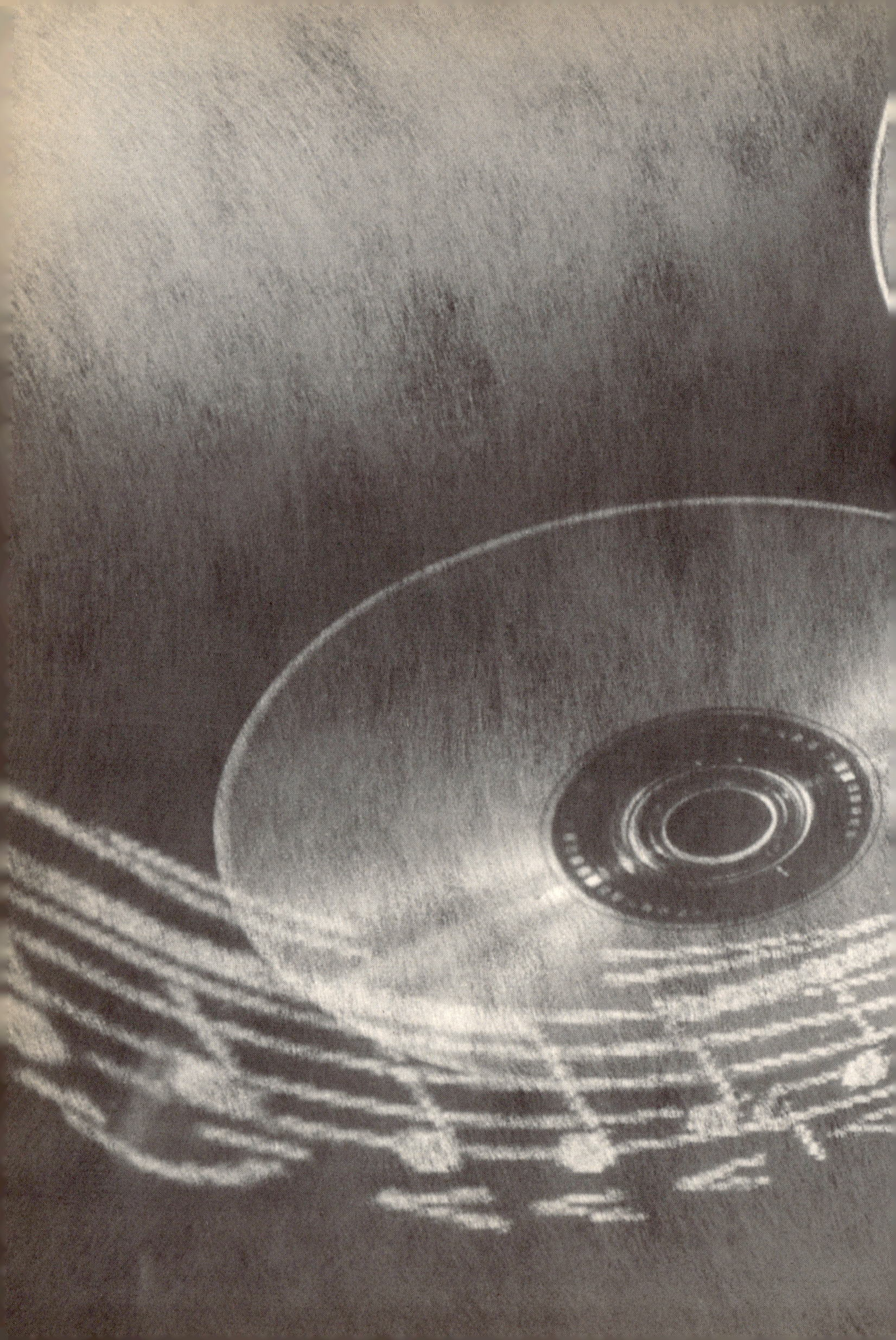

Chapter 8
Windows Rippers and Encoders

FEATURING

- AudioCatalyst
- MP3Enc
- MP3 Producer
- LAME
- BladeEnc
- Audioactive Production Studio

In this chapter, we'll discuss six of the leading MP3 rippers and encoders for Windows. These rippers and encoders are effective and powerful, and they're not very difficult to use. There's a slew of rippers and encoders that are integrated into ripper/player/jukeboxes; we'll discuss those in depth in the next chapter.

The rippers and encoders discussed in this chapter are a mixed bag:

- AudioCatalyst is a straightforward ripper and encoder from Xing Technologies.
- MP3Enc is a very expensive command-line encoder from the Fraunhofer Institute, under whose auspices the MP3 compression format was created.
- MP3 Production Studio is likewise expensive and likewise from Fraunhofer, but it has a graphical interface.
- LAME and BladeEnc are free, Open Source encoders.
- Audioactive Production Studio is a semi-professional suite of tools for creating MP3 files.

So there's a bit of something in this chapter to suit just about everyone. But you may not even need a stand-alone ripper and/or encoder. We'll deal with that question first.

Do You Need a Separate Ripper and Encoder?

Before you read the rest of this chapter, think about whether you want to get (and use) a separate ripper and encoder, or whether you'd prefer to use an all-in-one solution, a ripper/player/jukebox. (Ripper/player/jukeboxes also encode, but "encoder" isn't included in the term.) If you decide on the all-in-one solution, you probably don't need to spend time reading the rest of this chapter.

As you saw in the previous chapter, most of the MP3 players for Windows are currently free, so time is all it will cost you to try a variety of them. But because most Windows rippers, encoders, and jukeboxes cost from a fistful to a bucketful of dollars (some are free, but most cost between $30 and $199), you'll have a financial motivation to make the right decision quickly as to which ripper, encoder, or jukebox you want to buy. If your budget is limited, you'll want to get a suitable ripper and encoder or a ripper/player/jukebox with no false shots.

Quick and perhaps unnecessary recap: To create an MP3 file from a CD track, you *rip* (extract) the track from the CD and *encode* the result to MP3. CD tracks are stored as uncompressed audio marked by *handles* (pointers) and manifest themselves as 1K files in the CDA format. Because of the handles, you can't just copy an audio file off a CD the way you would copy a data file; instead, you need to rip it.

A *ripper* is a program that understands the handles and extracts the uncompressed audio from the CD. An *encoder* is a program that encodes the uncompressed audio to an MP3 file. Some ripper/encoders automatically store the ripped track as a WAV file on your hard disk before encoding it. Others perform the ripping and encoding in one apparently seamless step, without writing the extracted audio to disk. Others still let you choose whether to encode it directly, use a temporary WAV file before encoding (because this sometimes produces better results), store it as a WAV file *and* encode it, or just store it as a WAV file and leave it at that. So if you choose the right ripper/encoder, you have a good deal of flexibility. You can also get rippers that don't encode and encoders that don't rip, and treat the creation of each MP3 file as a separate step.

How you decide between a ripper and an encoder, a ripper/encoder, and a ripper/player/jukebox is of course entirely up to you, but given that you seem to be paying attention, we'll throw out a couple of observations.

As a gross generalization, stand-alone rippers, stand-alone encoders, and to a lesser extent ripper/encoders offer you more control than ripper/player/jukeboxes, which provide fewer options in order to give a more user-friendly experience. (Don't bombard us with exceptions to this—we already know that there are some.) So you'll mostly likely find there's a trade-off between convenience, quality, and control.

If your main priority is to get your CD collection ripped as soon as possible so that everybody in your house can listen to any of the tracks across your network, you'll probably want to opt for convenience. But if your aim is to make the highest-possible quality MP3 recordings that you'll be able to enjoy for decades (or until your musical tastes change), you'll need to opt for quality.

We know how the initial MP3 frenzy feels, but we've now passed over to the quality side. There's no reason that you couldn't do both—start by ripping everything quickly, and then rip each CD more slowly to get a higher quality version of each track except that most people don't have the time or persistence to carry through with doing so. Unless you're a true maniac, you'll do better to get a good setup for ripping and encoding, and then rip and encode each track just once.

Obviously, we can't tell you how to establish how high a quality you need, or whether your MP3 files sound good. As with just about everything in the computer world, many people are fiercely partisan about the rippers, encoders, and jukeboxes they use. You'll get people who swear that you'll get the best results by recording with, for example, MusicMatch Jukebox at 160kbps and playing back with FreeAmp through a Sound Blaster Live! MP3 soundcard and Altec Lansing speakers. And of course they're absolutely right, but only for the music they listen to, for their idiosyncratic speaker setup, and for how they think the music ought to sound. If you tried to duplicate their system, there's a good chance that you'll run screaming from the room within five minutes, or at least beat your speakers into silence with a baseball bat.

In other words, the MP3 solution you choose needs to be right for you, and the hell with the rest of the world. If you think you get the best results using GoatKicker 0.34a (based on the free SuperRat encoder), and playing back through a command-line program and $20 speakers, you're probably right. (At least, we won't bother to argue with you.)

All right—enough of that. We'll let you make your own decision. Let's get into the rippers and encoders.

AudioCatalyst

AudioCatalyst is a competent ripper/encoder produced by Xing Technologies. If you read the previous chapter, you'll remember that Xing Technologies also makes XingMP3 Player (an MP3 player), and that they were acquired by RealNetworks, which puts the future of their software products that overlap RealNetworks's software products in jeopardy. AudioCatalyst and XingMP3 Player together form an alternative to RealJukebox Plus, RealNetworks' premier audio product, so their days may be numbered.

In the meantime, though, both are viable products, if not best of breed. XingMP3 Player is free, and a trial version of AudioCatalyst is available. The full version of AudioCatalyst gives you excellent control over recording.

Download the trial version of AudioCatalyst 2.1 from the Xing Technologies Web site, www.xingtech.com. This trial version has some severe limitations (such as not letting you specify which tracks from a CD to record or the bitrate at which you want to record), so we recommend it only for making sure that AudioCatalyst is compatible with your CD-ROM and sound card and to see if you find the interface tolerable. If you want to use AudioCatalyst to enjoy MP3, you'll need to fork over 30 bucks for the full version.

Installing and Configuring AudioCatalyst

At this writing, you can buy the full version of AudioCatalyst for $29.99 from either the RealNetworks Web site or from e-tailers such as Beyond.com (www.beyond.com). Download the distribution file and double-click it to start the installation routine.

With AudioCatalyst, you get to choose between a Typical Installation and a Custom Installation. We suggest choosing the Custom Installation because this choice gives you the option not to install XingMP3 Player if you don't want to. However, because AudioCatalyst and XingMP3 Player are designed to integrate with each other, you may want to try them together.

As usual, you can specify the folder into which to install Audio-Catalyst. If you install XingMP3 Player, you need to choose not only the folder for it but also the file types that get associated with it. These details aside, the installation routine is, well, routine.

When you start the full version of AudioCatalyst for the first time, you are asked to agree to its license agreement before you can use the application. After that, you'll see the AudioCatalyst window.

Before you start ripping, configure AudioCatalyst. Start by choosing Settings ➤ General to display the Settings dialog box, shown in Figure 8.1.

These are the important settings to check and change in the Settings dialog box:

- ▶ Change the directory shown in the Directory to Store Files In text box by using the Browse button and the resulting Select Directory dialog box.

- ▶ In the second group box, make sure that the correct CD-ROM drive is selected in the CD-ROM Unit drop-down list.

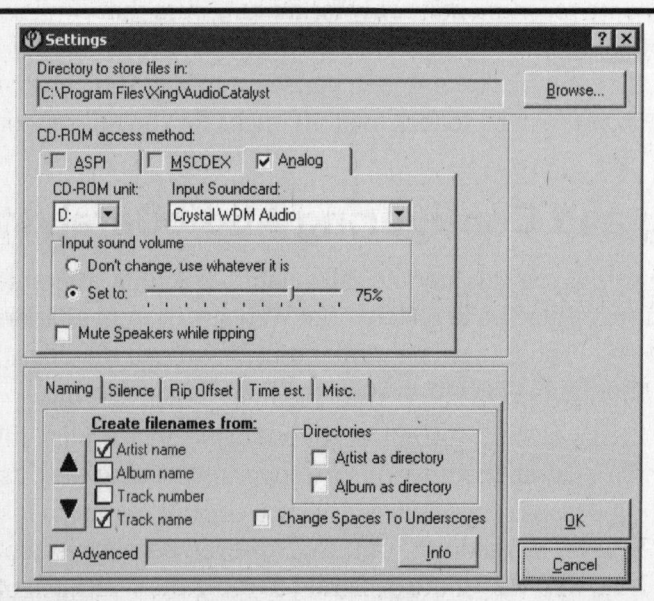

FIGURE 8.1: Choose general settings in the Settings dialog box.

- On the three tabs for the top set of pages, make sure the correct check box among ASPI, MSCDEX, and Analog is selected. Each page will be available to you only if it's an option on your computer.

    - ASPI generally gives the best performance, but isn't available for some CD-ROM drives. To have ASPI working, you need to have an ASPI-compatible CD-ROM drive and an ASPI driver loaded.

    - MSCDEX should be your second choice if ASPI isn't available or doesn't rip and encode right. However, MSCDEX isn't available if you're running Windows NT or Windows 2000.

    - Analog should be your last choice, for use only if neither ASPI nor MSCDEX is available. To use analog access to your CD, your CD needs to be connected to your sound card with a cable—not a problem on most computers.

- If you're ripping via analog access, make sure that the correct sound card is selected in the Input Soundcard drop-down list.

- If you don't want to play the music as you're ripping, select the Mute Speakers While Ripping check box.

- On the Naming page of the multi-page control in the third group box, choose how you want AudioCatalyst to name the MP3 files it creates. In the Advanced text box, you can specify a custom string for the filename instead of using the artist, album, track number, and track name options. Select the Advanced check box, then enter the string in the text box. Use the code %1 to add the artist's name, %2 for the album name, %3 for the track number, %4 for the track name, and %5 for the CDDB disc ID. For example, you can enter **%1-%2-%4** to produce a track name such as Metallica-Load-The House That Jack Built.mp3. AudioCatalyst adds the file extension automatically, so you don't need to specify it.

- On the Silence page of the multi-page control, you can specify how to delete leading and trailing silences from tracks.

- On the Rip Offset page of the multi-page control, you can specify a start offset or an end offset to help your CD-ROM drive find the beginning and end of tracks. If your CD-ROM drive seems to have problems with enhanced CDs, make sure that the Shorten Last Track by 10 Frames check box is selected (as it is by default), because enhanced CDs store some data after the last track.

- On the Time Est. (estimate) page of the multi-page control, you can specify speeds at which to normalize audio, read CD audio, and encode audio to MP3. You probably won't need to change these values unless you find that you're not getting good results in your ripping.

- On the Misc. page of the multi-page control, you can choose miscellaneous options for AudioCatalyst. The most interesting option here is the Shut Down the Computer When Finished check box, which you might want to use if you're ripping when you leave your computer for the night. More often useful is the Autosave CDDB Queries check box, which you should make sure is selected so that AudioCatalyst will already have the track information from CDDB for any CD you've previously looked up.

Close the Settings dialog box and choose Settings ➤ XingMP3 Encoder to display the XingMP3 Encoder Settings dialog box (see Figure 8.2).

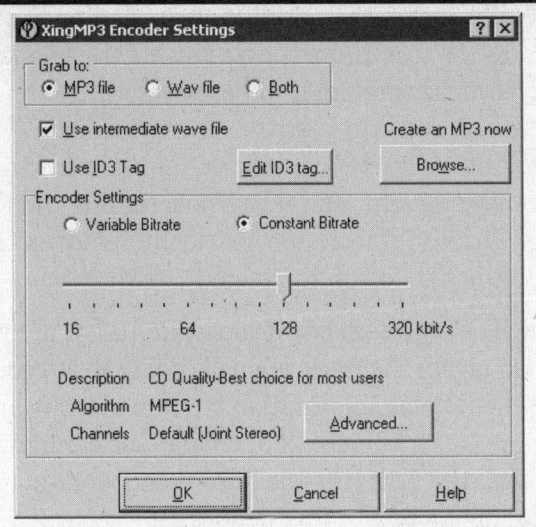

FIGURE 8.2: The XingMP3 Encoder Settings dialog box has mercifully fewer settings than the Settings dialog box—but they're important ones.

Choose settings for the following:

- In the Grab To group box, select the MP3 File option button, the Wav File option button, or the Both option button. Typically, you'll want to choose the MP3 File option button here, but you may want to try ripping to a WAV file, and then encoding that file to MP3 (perhaps with a different encoder), if you're not getting satisfactory results from ripping and encoding in a single operation. Selecting the Both option button records to a WAV file and then encodes that file to MP3, but does not remove the WAV file from disk. This option is useful primarily for troubleshooting MP3 ripping: By listening to the WAV file, you can determine whether any problems in the MP3 file come at the ripping stage or at the encoding stage. (We'll describe how to create an MP3 file from a WAV file with AudioCatalyst a little later in this section.)

- You can also select the Use Intermediate Wave File check box to force AudioCatalyst to rip to a WAV file, then encode from the WAV file, rather than ripping and encoding in one step. Use this option to improve the quality of MP3 files you get, especially if your computer is underpowered or your CD drive is slow or old. You also need to use intermediate WAV files if you use AudioCatalyst's normalization feature, which we'll discuss in a moment, and if you're accessing the CD via MSCDEX. AudioCatalyst automatically removes the WAV file after it has successfully created the MP3 file.

- ▶ Select the Use ID3 Tag check box if you want AudioCatalyst to create an ID3 tag for the track. (Usually doing so is a good idea because the ID3 tag information lets you identify and sort tracks more easily.) To check or change the content of the ID3 tag, click the Edit ID3 Tag button and work in the ID3 Tag Editor dialog box.

- ▶ In the Encoder Settings group box, choose the Variable Bitrate option button or the Constant Bitrate option button. For most music, you'll do better with a constant bitrate (CBR). Although variable-bitrate (VBR) technology is improving, some hardware MP3 players cannot play VBR files. For constant bitrate files, choose the bitrate you want to use. As mentioned earlier in the book, we recommend a bitrate of at least 128kbps for music. For variable bitrate files, you get to choose a quality: Low, Normal/Low, Normal, Normal/High, or High. You can also click the Advanced button and set advanced options in the Advanced Options dialog box. Of these, the important settings are High Frequency Mode (which makes AudioCatalyst encode frequencies up to 20kHz for constant bitrates of 112kbps and above, preventing the thin-sounding treble sounds that bedevil low-quality MP3 files) and Set Original Bit, which sets the original bit in the MP3 file. The original bit is a flag that's supposed to indicate that the MP3 file is original material. (In practice, the original bit means very little.)

Dismiss the XingMP3 Encoder Settings dialog box and choose Settings ➤ CDDB to display the CDDB Settings dialog box (see

Figure 8.3). In this dialog box, you can update the CDDB list by clicking the Get List button. But the main points of interest in the CDDB Settings dialog box are the Your E-mail Address text box (enter a different address than the default AC_user@xingtech.com if you want) and the Auto-Query CDDB If a New Disc Is Not Found in `cdplayer.ini` check box. (`cdplayer.ini` is the initialization file for the CD player. It contains information for CDs whose details you've looked up using your default CD player.)

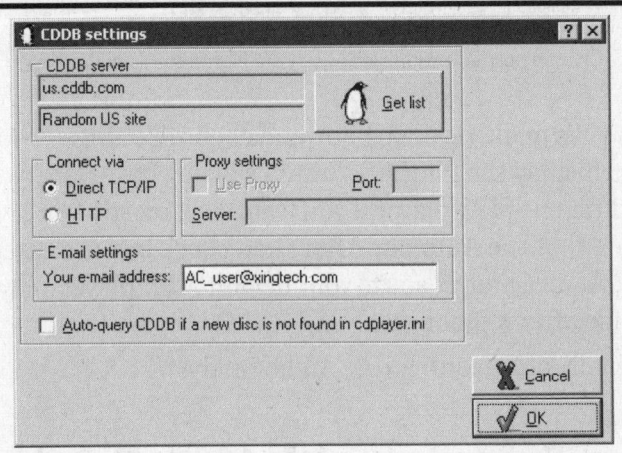

FIGURE 8.3: Check your CDDB settings in the CDDB Settings dialog box.

Close the CDDB Settings dialog box and choose Settings ➤ Normalize to display the Normalizing dialog box, shown in Figure 8.4. (*Normalization* is the process of maximizing the volume of the digital audio data without adding any distortion. Usually when ripping and encoding from CD, normalization isn't needed, but it can be valuable when the source material is too quiet. If you normalize everything you encode, it all plays back in the same relative volume range.) Then choose settings for normalization if you want to use it. Select the Use Normalizing check box, then enter the percentage in the Normalize To text box (the default setting is 98%). In the group box, you can specify normalization thresholds by selecting the But Only If the Track Is check box and specifying percentages in the Lower Than and Higher Than text boxes. You can also normalize a

WAV file on the spot by clicking the Browse button and choosing the file (or files) in the Select File(s) to Normalize dialog box.

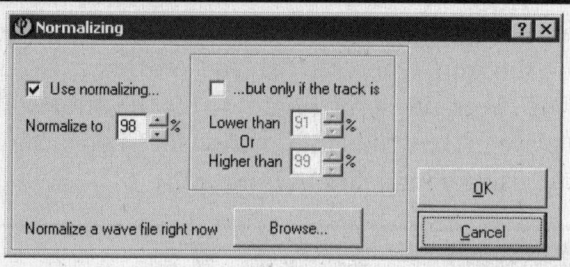

FIGURE 8.4: Choose normalization settings in the Normalizing dialog box.

Close the Normalizing dialog box and choose Settings ≻ MP3 Playback to display the Playback Settings dialog box. Here, you can identify a different MP3 player if you want. But mostly you'll want to make sure that the Autoplay After Grab check box is cleared. Otherwise, AudioCatalyst starts your default MP3 player, playing each MP3 file after it grabs one.

You're finally done configuring AudioCatalyst.

Ripping and Encoding with AudioCatalyst

Compared with configuring AudioCatalyst, ripping and encoding with it is extremely straightforward. Figure 8.5 shows AudioCatalyst with a CD loaded.

As you can see, the interface is easy to use:

- ▶ The Grab button starts the ripping or encoding process.
- ▶ The Norm and MP3 buttons display the Normalizing dialog box and the XingMP3 Encoder Settings dialog box, respectively.
- ▶ The check boxes on the Norm button and the MP3 button show when these features are switched on. The MP3 check

box appears cleared when AudioCatalyst is capturing to a WAV file.

▶ The CDDB button retrieves information about the current CD from CDDB.

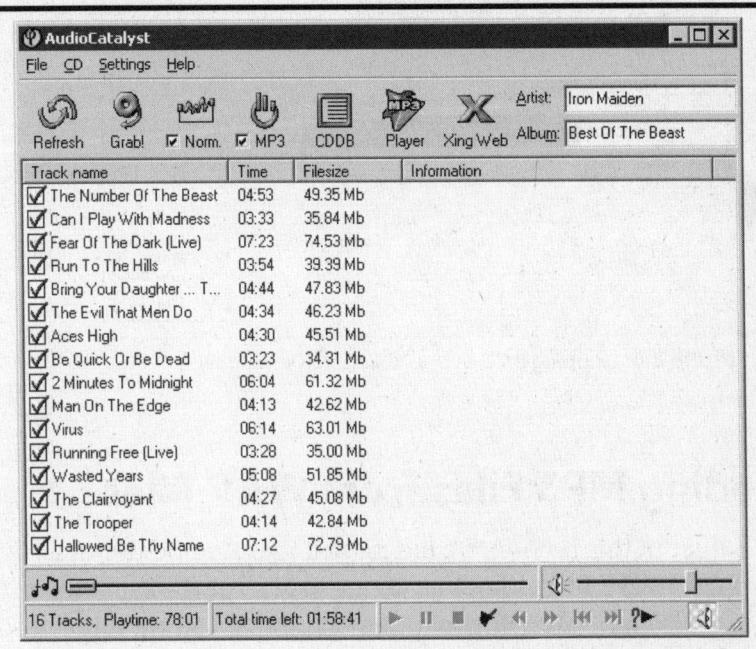

FIGURE 8.5: AudioCatalyst with a CD loaded for ripping and encoding

To get ripping, insert a CD, select the tracks you want to rip (AudioCatalyst automatically selects them all by default), and verify the settings of the Norm and MP3 check boxes. Then click the CDDB button to get the CDDB information for the CD, and the Grab button to start ripping.

Figure 8.6 shows AudioCatalyst ripping a track from a CD.

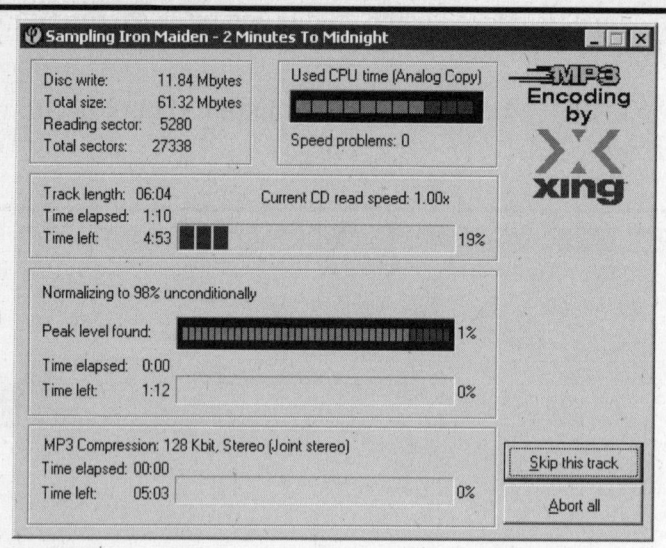

FIGURE 8.6: Ripping a CD in the AudioCatalyst window

Encoding MP3 Files from WAV Files

Earlier in this section, we mentioned that AudioCatalyst lets you rip to a WAV file without encoding to MP3 at the same time. You may also have WAV files of other audio that you want to encode to MP3—for example, your teenage ax heroics that you feel will resonate with Riffage.com's users.

AudioCatalyst lets you easily encode an MP3 file from a WAV file. Display the XingMP3 Encoder Settings dialog box by choosing Settings ➤ XingMP3 Encoder. Then click the Browse button to display the Select File(s) to Create MP3s From dialog box. Choose the WAV file or files you want to encode from, and click the Open button.

> **TIP**
>
> AudioCatalyst includes a CDDB Disk Submit Wizard that walks you through the process of submitting CD data to the CDDB database. Choose CD ➤ Submit to CDDB to start the Wizard.

MP3Enc

MP3Enc (for MPEG Layer-3 Commandline Encoder) is a very high-end encoder made by the Fraunhofer Institute, the masterminds behind the MP3 compression format.

MP3Enc is expensive ($199) and minimalist. Fraunhofer doesn't even give you a graphical interface—it's a command-line–only product. But many of those who have paid for MP3Enc swear by it, and you can use batch files to convert tracks, lessening the amount of typing required. But if you want Fraunhofer quality with a graphical interface, try MP3 Producer Professional, which we will discuss in the next section.

Fortunately—because of the price—Fraunhofer realizes that you probably won't want to take the quality of MP3Enc on trust, so it provides a free demo version limited to recording 30 seconds of a track. You can download this demo version from the Fraunhofer Web site's downloads section, www.iis.fhg.de/amm/download/index.html#2.

The demo needs no installation beyond unzipping to a convenient folder. You can then run it from a command prompt the way you would run any command-line program.

MP3Enc comes with good explanations of its commands. To test the demo version, these are the important parameters you'll want:

Parameter	Meaning	Example
br	Bitrate	br=128000
if	Input file	if = "c:\My Music\Travis\Travis-Luv.wav
of	Output file	of = "c:\My Music\Travis\Travis-Luv.mp3
q	Quality	q = 3

The following command-line example encodes a WAV file to a 128kbps MP3 file at quality 3:

```
mp3enc -br = 128000 -if = "c:\My
➥Music\Travis\Travis-Luv.wav" -of = "c:\My
➥Music\Travis\Travis-Luv.mp3" -q = 3
```

> **NOTE**
>
> Recently (as of this writing), Fraunhofer released a new MP3 encoder named FastEnc. FastEnc is included in other products, including MusicMatch Jukebox 5.

MP3 Producer and MP3 Producer Professional

MP3 Producer and MP3 Producer Professional are high-end encoders that both use a graphical interface from Fraunhofer IIS. MP3 Producer Professional costs $199; MP3 Producer, the regular edition, costs $49 and is the same as MP3 Producer Professional, except that you cannot record at bitrates of more than 128kbps. Because of this limitation of MP3 Producer, the painful price of MP3 Producer Professional, and their minimalist features and slightly awkward interface, we find them hard to recommend unless you believe that Fraunhofer, having invented MP3, has a lock on the highest-quality encoding.

We find MP3 Producer and MP3 Producer Professional good but not *that* good. They're also not the fastest encoders on the street, but to make up for this, they include a batch processor that lets you encode any number of files in a single operation.

Price aside, the other key disadvantages of MP3 Producer and MP3 Producer Professional are as follows:

▶ You'll need to use (and probably pay for) a separate ripper.

- You'll need to add ID3 tag information to the tracks manually—a great waste of time.

Getting and Installing MP3 Producer

You can find details about MP3 Producer and MP3 Producer Professional on the Fraunhofer Web site (www.iis.fhg.de/amm/), and you can buy them online from Opticom (www.opticom.de/). The transaction is actually handled by Digital River, a big name in online sales that you may well be familiar with already.

MP3 Producer uses a straightforward setup routine. The only unusual element is the Fraunhofer IIS MPEG Layer-3 Audio Decoder ACM Component dialog box (see Figure 8.7), which checks to see if you want to install the ACM component, an MP3 decoder and player plug-in for the Windows audio codec manager. Click the Yes button. You'll then be asked to agree to a license agreement for this component, which tells you that you can install it on as many computers as you like, copy it, and distribute it freely. Don't get too excited—that's just the ACM component, not MP3 Producer itself, whose license agreement is the first one that you have to deal with and which has the usual heavily restrictive terms.

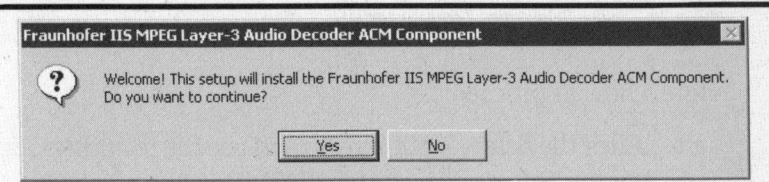

FIGURE 8.7: When you see the Fraunhofer IIS MPEG Layer-3 Audio Decoder ACM Component dialog box, agree to install the ACM component.

The first time you run MP3 Producer, you'll need to enter your name and license key in the License Registration dialog box. Opticom sends you an e-mail containing your license key when you buy the product, and because the license key is long, alphanumeric, and mixed case, you'll usually do best to paste it in from the e-mail message. Make sure that you use the same version of your name in the License Registration dialog box as Opticom used in the license message. The license key is linked to your name, and if you get it even a character wrong, the License Registration dialog box will beep at you when you click the OK button but give you no other indication of what's amiss.

Encoding with MP3 Producer

MP3 Producer has so few features that it's easy to use. Figure 8.8 shows MP3 Producer Professional loaded and ready to go.

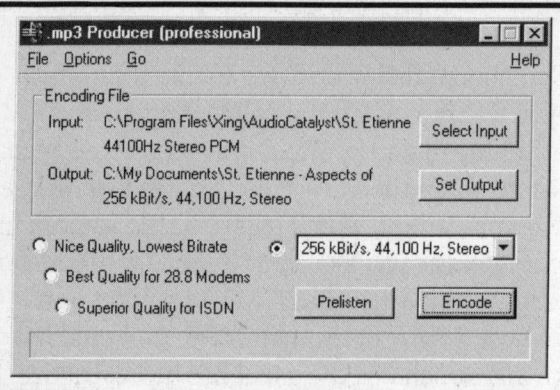

FIGURE 8.8: MP3 Producer Professional is a very expensive and very simple encoder from Fraunhofer IIS.

Here's how to proceed:

1. Click the Select Input button and use the resulting Open dialog box to select the WAV file that you want to encode from.

2. On the Options menu, make sure that the Write RIFF/WAV-Format Files item is not selected and that the High Quality Encoding item is selected. Set the Beep When Done item on that menu as you wish.

3. To specify the directory in which the converted MP3 files are to be saved, choose File ➢ Set Conversion Directory and use the resulting Open dialog box to specify

Windows Rippers and Encoders

the directory. Click the Choose button to select the directory.

4. By default, MP3 Producer saves the MP3 file under the same filename as the WAV file but with the MP3 file type and extension. To specify a different filename, click the Set Output button and enter the name in the Save As dialog box.

5. In the lower half of the dialog box, choose the option button for the quality you want: Nice Quality, Lowest Bitrate (8kbps, 11,025Hz, mono), Best Quality for 28.8 Modems (24kbps, 11,025Hz, stereo), Superior Quality for ISDN (112kbps, 44,100Hz, stereo), or the option button with the drop-down list from which you can select a rate. Given that even 112kbps makes for poor listening for music for most people, you'll probably want to choose one of the higher values from the drop-down list.

6. You can then click the Prelisten button to get a preview of how the first five seconds of the WAV file will sound when encoded as an MP3 file. When you're satisfied with your choice, click the Encode button to encode the track. MP3 Producer replaces the Encode button with a Cancel button while the encoding is proceeding.

Batch-Processing Files

To protect itself from accusations of being incredibly overpriced, MP3 Producer includes a batch processor that lets you line up a slew of files and encode them all in one process. Given that encoding takes a fair amount of both computational horsepower and time, this feature is great for encoding a huge number of MP3 files while you sleep.

Choose File ➢ Batch Processor to display the Batch Processor, shown in Figure 8.9 with a batch of tracks added.

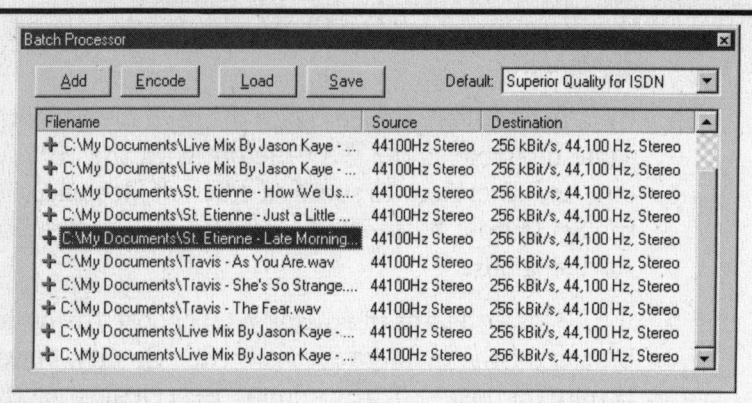

FIGURE 8.9: Use MP3 Producer's Batch Processor to encode a batch of tracks in one operation.

Use the Add button and the resulting Open dialog box to add tracks to the Batch Processor. The Batch Processor automatically includes for conversion each track that you add to the batch, putting a plus sign to the left of its listing. To exclude a file from the batch, right-click its entry and choose Exclude from Batch from the context menu. The Batch Processor places a minus sign next to the track to indicate that it won't be encoded.

You can set the default rate for all the tracks in the batch by using the Default drop-down list, but this offers only the Nice Quality, Best Quality, and Superior Quality Options, none of which is (we think) high enough for music. Select all the tracks, right-click in the selection, and choose the bitrate you want from the context menu. You can also set a different bitrate for any track by choosing the bitrate from the context menu.

When you're all set for encoding, click the Encode button. You'll see the Batch Progress dialog box, shown in Figure 8.10, while MP3 Producer encodes the files.

FIGURE 8.10: The Batch Progress dialog box lets you know how MP3 Producer is progressing on encoding the batch of files.

Should you need to, you can save a batch file list by using the Save button, and load a saved batch file list by using the Load button.

LAME

At this point in the chapter, we hop nimbly from one extreme to another. Where MP3Enc is perhaps the most expensive encoder that you might consider using, LAME is as free as the polluted air we breathe.

LAME is a Unix-style recursive acronym that stands for "LAME Ain't an MP3 Encoder" (compare GNU, which stands for "GNU's Not Unix"). The name was originally true, but LAME has now been updated so that it does indeed encode.

You can download the source code of LAME from the official LAME Web site, www.sulaco.org/mp3/. But unless you have a compiler and know how to use it, you'll be better off downloading a compiled binary file for the platform you're using. LAME binaries are available from a number of sites, including MP3`Tech (www.mp3-tech.org). Expand the distribution file to a suitable folder (most distribution files for Windows are zip files rather than executables).

Running LAME from the Command Line

If you get just LAME itself, you'll need to run it from the command line. Open a command-prompt window and enter the lame command. Running LAME from the command line is a little forbidding, because there are several dozen switches you can set to specify what kind of file you're inputting, which filters to apply, the bitrate at which to encode, the information for the ID3 tag, and so on.

To find out the details of the switches, use the --help command from a command prompt (note the two hyphens) as follows:

    lame--help

Instead, you may prefer to use one of the front ends that puts a graphical interface on LAME in much the same way Windows puts a graphical interface on DOS. If so, read on.

Using a Front End with LAME

With a little patience, you can run LAME from the command line effectively enough. But if you prefer the comfort and convenience of a graphical interface, you needn't do things the hard way. Several Windows front ends are available for LAME. Of those we've used, our favorite is LameBatch, which is described briefly in this section.

Download the latest version of LameBatch from its home page (www.uic.nnov.ru/~loea/index-en.html) or wherever fine freeware MP3 tools are found and extract it to a convenient folder. (Because the program comes as a single executable with no ancillary files, you may want simply to put it in the same folder as your installation of LAME.) Then double-click the file to start it running; for regular use, you'll probably want to create a shortcut to the file on your Desktop, Start menu, or Quick Launch toolbar.

The first time you start LameBatch, check its settings before you start encoding anything. Figure 8.11 shows the Settings page for LameBatch.

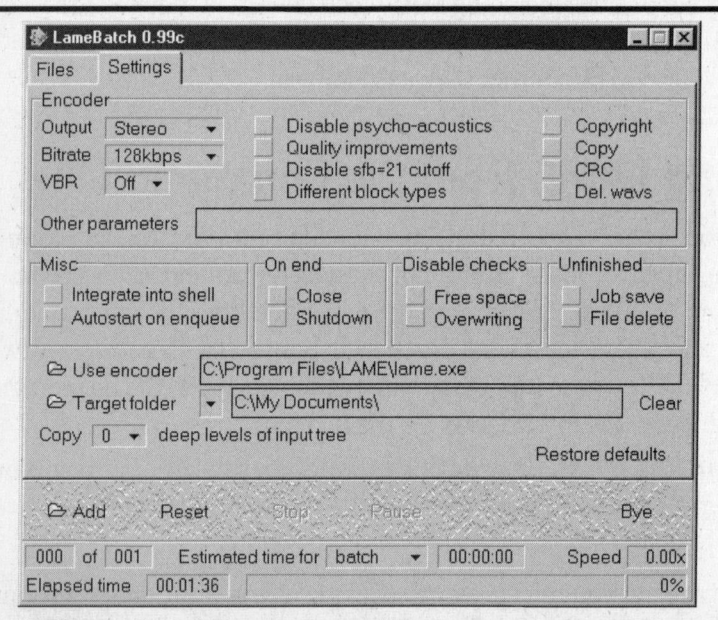

FIGURE 8.11: Before you start encoding, choose appropriate settings on the Settings page of LameBatch.

Windows Rippers and Encoders

As you can see in this figure, the options are broken up into several different categories. These are the important settings you'll need to choose:

- In the Encoder group box, make sure that Stereo is selected in the Output drop-down list, that an appropriate bitrate (for example, 160kbps) is selected in the Bitrate drop-down list, and that Off is selected in the VBR drop-down list (unless you're sure you want to do variable bitrate encoding rather than constant bitrate encoding). Of the eight options on the right-hand side of the Encoder group box, you probably won't want to select any right off the bat. The Copyright check box and the Copy check box toggle the copyright bit and copy bit (respectively) on the MP3 file that is created. Selecting the CRC check box causes LAME to perform a CRC check, and selecting the Del. Wavs check box makes it delete each WAV file after it has successfully created an MP3 file from it. You may want to select the Del. Wavs check box once you've established that LAME is making MP3 files that you like the sound of.

- In the Misc. group box, select the Autostart on Enqueue check box if you want LAME to start encoding as soon as you drop a file on it rather than wait for you to start it manually.

- In the On End group box, select the Close check box if you want LameBatch to close itself when it has finished the current encoding session, and select the Shutdown check box if you want LameBatch to try to shut down Windows.

- In the Disable Checks group box, select the Free Space check box to prevent LAME from checking that there's enough free space on your drive for the files it's creating, and select the Overwriting check box to avoid having LAME question you before it overwrites an existing file.

- In the Unfinished group box, you can choose whether LAME should save an unfinished file (select the Job Save check box) or delete it (select the File Delete check box).

- Click the Use Encoder button and use the resulting dialog box to identify the folder in which you installed LAME.

- Click the Target Folder button and use the resulting dialog box to identify the folder in which you want to save the MP3 files.

To start encoding files, you can either drag files to LameBatch from Explorer or another file-management application, or you can use the Add button and the resulting Open dialog box to identify the tracks. Once you've lined up the tracks you want to encode, you can set different options for each track by selecting the track and choosing options from the drop-down lists. You can also set ID3 tag information for a track by selecting the track, clicking the ID3 button, and working in the ID3 Tag dialog box.

Once you've set all the parameters and ID3 tag information you want, click the Encode button to start encoding the MP3 files. Figure 8.12 shows LameBatch encoding a file.

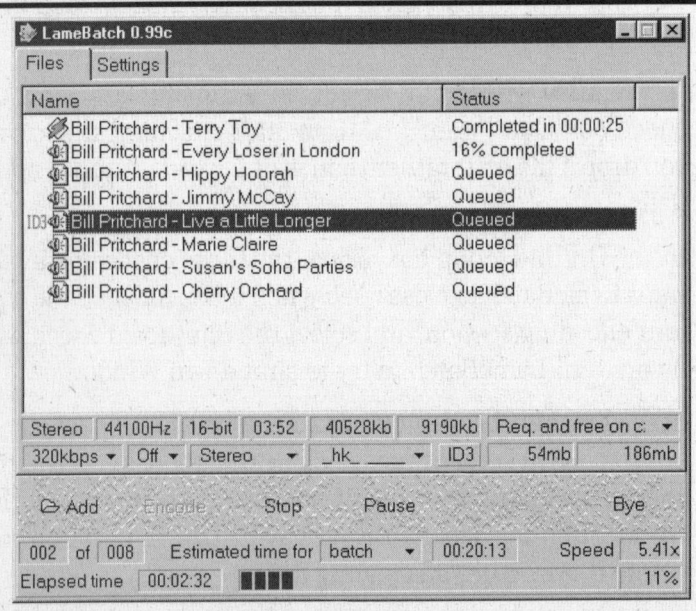

FIGURE 8.12: LameBatch provides an easy-to-use graphical front end for the freeware LAME encoder.

To remove the completed tracks from the LameBatch window, right-click the tracks and choose Remove Completed from the context menu.

BladeEnc

Another freeware MP3 encoder that you may want to try is BladeEnc—but right now it's difficult to try. BladeEnc comes highly recommended, because its creator, Tord Jansson, concentrated on high music quality to the exclusion of almost everything else. (For example, speed: BladeEnc usually takes much longer than LAME to encode a track). Unfortunately, at this writing, Jansson has removed the binaries of BladeEnc from the BladeEnc Web site, bladeenc.mp3.no, because of receiving "threats from large companies" that hold MP3 patents. Jansson is still providing the source code for BladeEnc, but you'll have to compile it yourself—no terrible task if you have a compiler, but a severe pain in the seat if you don't.

Given that BladeEnc isn't easy to get (or at least, to get working) at the moment, we won't discuss it here. But should Jansson repost the binaries of BladeEnc, we think you'll find it well worth a try. BladeEnc itself is a command-line program, but you can get various graphical front ends for it, including BladeBatch, a straightforward front end coded by the creator of LameBatch.

Audioactive Production Studio

If you read the previous chapter, you'll probably remember Telos Systems, which makes the Audioactive Player that we described toward the end of the chapter. Telos System also makes Audioactive Production Studio, an MP3 ripper and encoder, which comes in both Lite and Professional versions. Audioactive Production Studio Lite costs $34.95 and encodes at bitrates up to 128kbps. Audioactive Production Studio Professional costs $149.95, records at up to 256kbps, and includes options such as high-quality encoding, scripting support, and batch encoding of an unlimited number of files.

We're less than convinced of the merits of Audioactive Production Studio. Unless you feel that you can live with a maximum bitrate of 128kbps, we suggest you avoid the Lite edition. And unless you have money to burn, you probably won't want to commit to the Professional edition.

To help you make up your mind that it's worth spending the money, Telos provides a 30-day trial of Audioactive Production Studio. You can download this trial version from the Audioactive Web site, www.audioactive.com.

Audioactive Production Studio uses a mostly standard installation routine, with these two exceptions:

- ▶ It offers to install a version of CDFS (the CD file system) that can digitally read audio data directly from audio CDs. To use this version of CDFS, you need to have a CD-ROM drive that supports digital audio extraction. If you've been performing digital-audio extraction with another ripper already, you should be safe here, but check the specifications of your CD-ROM drive to be sure that the drive supports digital-audio extraction. (Most modern drives do.) Then, when you see the Install CDFS dialog box, choose appropriately.

- ▶ Audioactive Production Studio also installs the Fraunhofer IIS MPEG Layer-3 Audio Decoder ACM Component—the same one that MP3 Producer installs. You'll need to accept a separate license agreement for this component.

> **WARNING**
>
> Don't install this version of CDFS if your drive doesn't support digital-audio extraction, because it has been known to cause Windows 95 and 98 to spontaneously reboot when trying to access the CD-ROM drive or to identify the CD-ROM drive as a removable disk. If you do install it and start having problems, you may be able to uninstall the version of CDFS by choosing the Uninstall CDFS item from the Audioactive Production Studio submenu on the Start menu. But if the uninstall feature doesn't work for you (it didn't work for us), you may need to manually remove the CDFS drivers by removing entries from the System control panel applet and also deleting the appropriate DLLs. This is as ugly as it sounds, and if you're not up to speed on this sort of under-the-hood Windows tweaking, you may end up having to reinstall Windows to fix the problem.

The first time you run Audioactive Production Studio, you'll need to enter your license number and key, then restart the application. (For the trial version, specify that you're using the trial version.)

Once you've got Audioactive Production Studio running, you'll find it easy enough to use. As you can see in Figure 8.13, Audioactive Production Studio uses a four-page interface, with pages for Encode, Decode, MP3 Convert, and CD Copy.

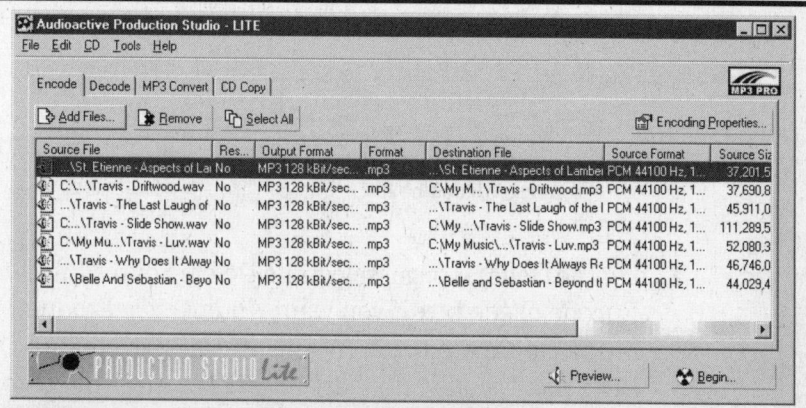

FIGURE 8.13: Audioactive Production Studio lets you convert audio files to and from the MP3 format, as well as rip audio files from a CD.

To encode WAV files to MP3 files, work on the Encode page (shown in Figure 8.13) as follows:

1. Use the Add Files button and the resulting Select File(s) to Encode dialog box to add WAV files to the list box.

2. Select the files you want to encode.

3. Click the Encoding Properties button to display the Encoding Properties dialog box (see Figure 8.14). In this figure, the dialog box has three pages; when you're ripping from CD, it displays a fourth page, for selecting PCM options.

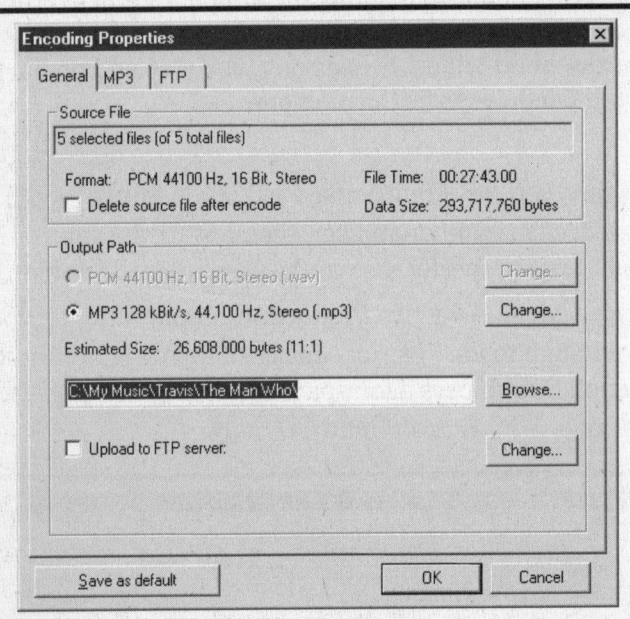

FIGURE 8.14: Before encoding, choose the appropriate settings in the Encoding Properties dialog box.

4. On the General page, select the Delete Source File after Encode check box if you want Audioactive Production Studio to delete the WAV file after it has created the MP3 file. Usually, it's best to test the MP3 file before

deleting the WAV file, but you may want to delete the WAV file if you're running out of disk space.

5. Still on the General page, change the output path if necessary.

6. On the MP3 page (see Figure 8.15), change the bitrate in the Compression drop-down list if necessary. If you're using Audioactive Production Studio Professional, make sure the Higher Quality Encode option button is selected.

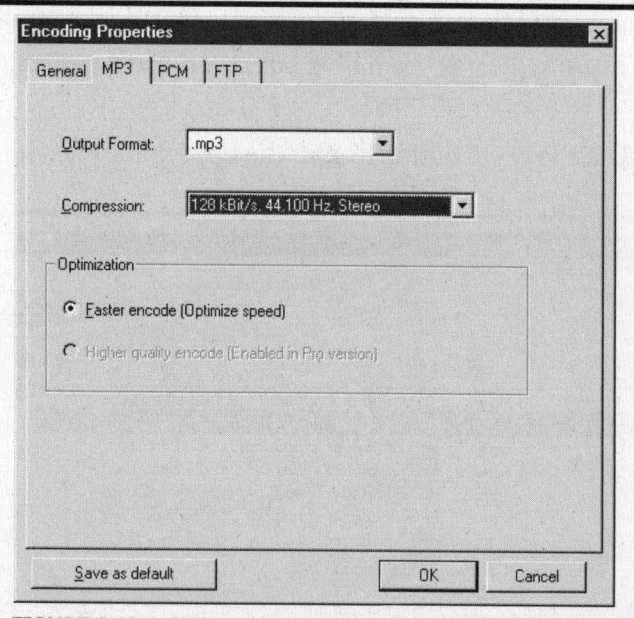

FIGURE 8.15: Choose the output format and bitrate on the MP3 page of the Encoding Properties dialog box.

7. Click the OK button to close the Encoding Properties dialog box.

8. Click the Begin button to start encoding the files.

Chapter Eight

To rip from CD, use the CD Copy page (see Figure 8.16). These are the general steps:

1. Click the Scan CD button to force Audioactive Production Studio to read the CD, if it hasn't already done so.
2. Click the CDDB button if you want to get the CD information and track names from CDDB.
3. Select the tracks you want to encode. (Use the Select All button if appropriate.)
4. If you need to change the encoding properties for MP3 files, click the Encoding Properties button to display the Encoding Properties dialog box, then choose settings on the MP3 page.
5. Click the Begin button to start the ripping and encoding.

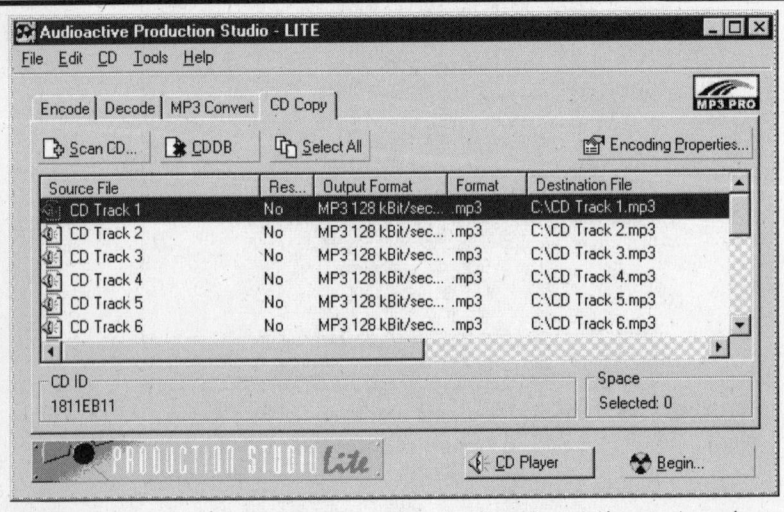

FIGURE 8.16: Use the CD Copy page of the Audioactive window to rip and encode from CD.

> **TIP**
>
> To submit information to CDDB for a CD that's not yet listed there, choose CD ➤ CDDB Submit, enter the information in the Edit CD Related Information dialog box, and send it off.

Up Next

In this chapter, you've met six of the leading stand-alone rippers and encoders for Windows. You've seen how to rip and encode in a single operation, and how to rip and encode separately and how you can pay anything from nothing to nearly 200 dollars for the privilege of encoding.

In the next chapter, we'll show you the alternative to these stand-alone rippers and encoders: the ripper/player/jukeboxes for Windows. We'll examine MusicMatch Jukebox and RealJukebox Plus in some detail, and then look at some lesser-known but promising jukeboxes. Turn the page.

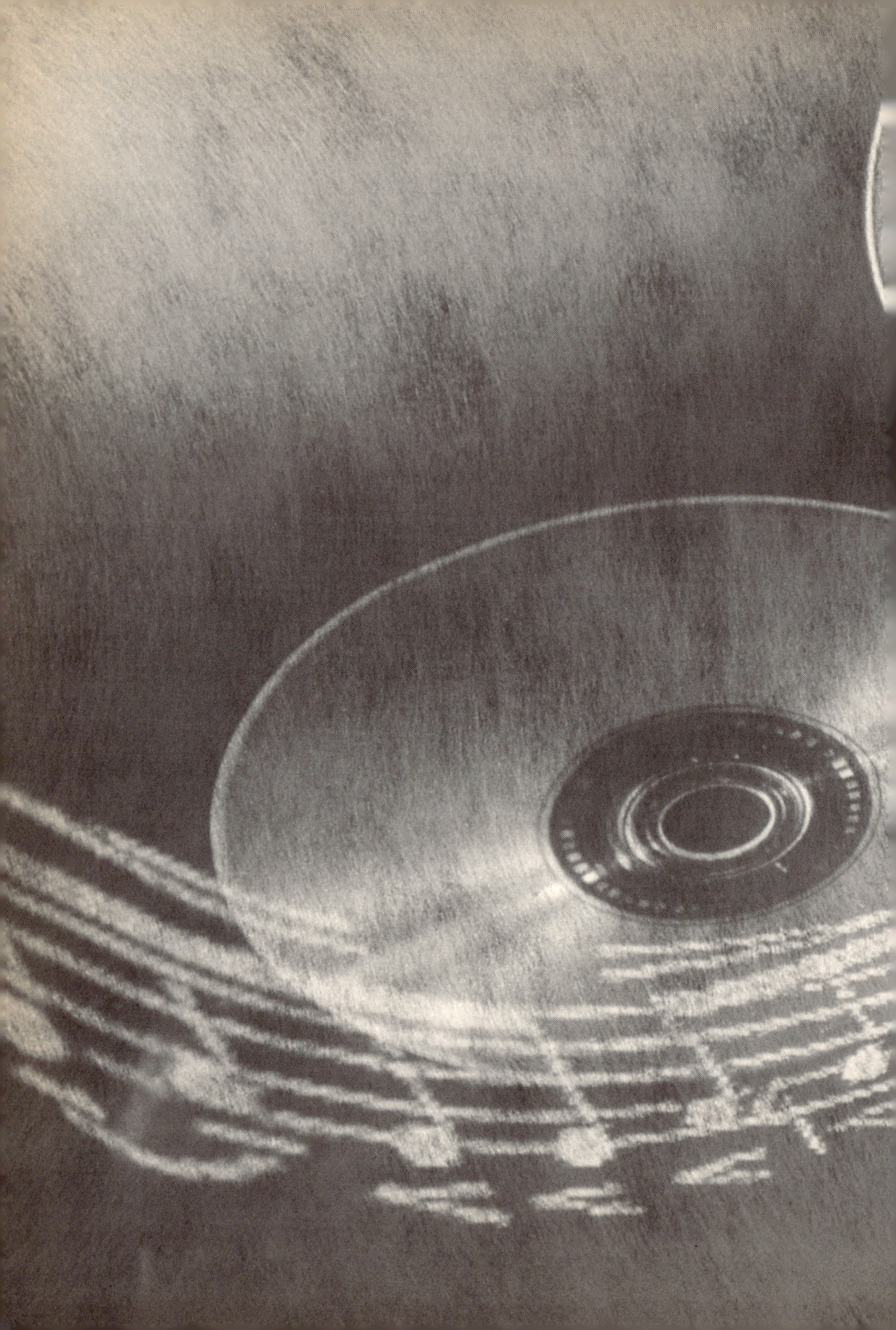

Chapter 9
Windows Jukeboxes

FEATURING
- MusicMatch Jukebox
- RealJukebox
- Siren Jukebox and Visiosonic PCDJ

In this chapter, we'll discuss ripper/player/jukeboxes for Windows. As you'll see, a ripper/player/jukebox can provide a complete MP3 solution, covering all the functions from ripping and encoding to maintaining a database of all the tracks and playlists on your system *and* playing them back for you.

We'll look at the two leading MP3 ripper/player/jukeboxes for Windows—MusicMatch Jukebox and RealJukebox—and then briefly visit two other ripper/player/jukeboxes, Siren Jukebox and Visiosonic PCDJ.

MusicMatch Jukebox is one of the most popular ripper/player/jukeboxes currently available. MusicMatch Jukebox offers a standard version that you can download for free and that rips at all bitrates up to 320kbps, providing enough flexibility for most people. There's also a registered version that costs $29.99, uses the Fraunhofer FastEnc encoder, and seems (to us, at least) to deliver higher quality sound at the same bitrates as well as marginally faster performance than the standard edition.

RealJukebox is a ripper/player/jukebox from RealNetworks. RealJukebox is available in a Basic edition that's free but is limited to recording at 96kbps—too low a rate for music, unless you have tin ears—and a Plus edition that costs $29.99 but lets you rip at decent quality. Because we figure you want decent quality, this chapter concentrates on RealJukebox Plus, but we'll show you a screen or two from RealJukebox just so that you don't feel left out if you're stuck with the freebie.

MusicMatch Jukebox

In this section, we'll discuss how to use MusicMatch Jukebox, our favorite Windows jukebox software.

Getting, Installing, and Configuring MusicMatch Jukebox

Download the latest version of MusicMatch Jukebox from the MusicMatch web site, www.musicmatch.com. At this writing, MusicMatch Jukebox is around 7MB—a hefty download if you're using a modem, an inconsequential one if you have cable or a DSL. MusicMatch Jukebox requires a processor with a minimum clock speed of 166 MHz (preferably with MMX support), but you'll find a faster processor helps greatly.

MusicMatch Jukebox has a fairly standardized installation routine, in which only the following merit mention:

- You need to enter information in the User Registration Info dialog box in order to proceed with the installation. You have to enter at least one character each in the Name text box, the Email text box, and the Postal/Zip Code text box in order to enable the Next button. We feel that you shouldn't have to give this information, but you can't install MusicMatch Jukebox without appearing to give it. (If you have qualms about supplying this information, you might want to be less than honest.) Either way, think twice before you leave the Notify Me When Software Upgrades Are Available check box and the Send Me Music-Related News and Special Offers check box selected, as they are by default.

- The Personalize Net Music dialog box, shown in Figure 9.1, invites you to let MusicMatch Jukebox upload information on the music you listen to, save, and download to a MusicMatch server. MusicMatch uses this information to deliver personalized recommendations to you, and assures you that "your personal music preferences...will never be sold or shared." But the idea of MusicMatch Jukebox automatically uploading information about our listening habits creeps us out too much for us to recommend using this feature. Choose the Yes (Recommended) option button rather than the No option button if you're less paranoid than we are.

The option buttons are implemented a little strangely, and to access the No button via the keyboard, you'll need to press one of the arrow keys (for example, →) rather than the Tab key.

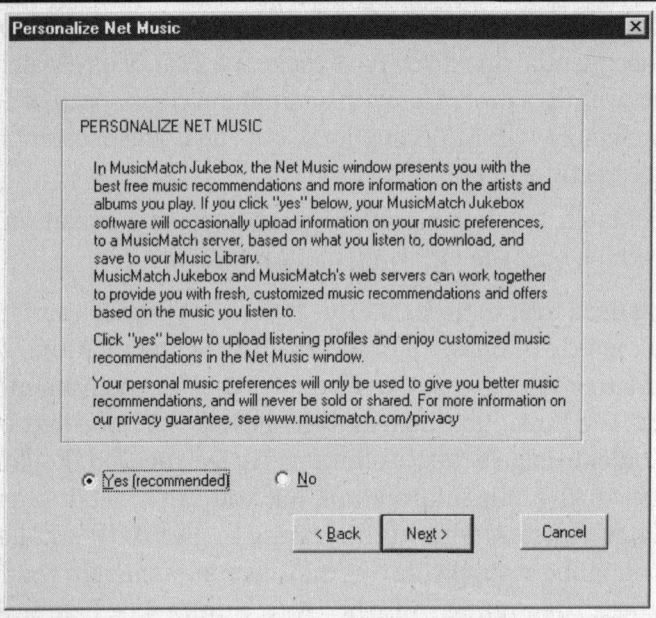

FIGURE 9.1: In the Personalize Net Music dialog box, choose whether you want MusicMatch Jukebox to upload your listening habits to the MusicMatch server so that it can offer you personalized music.

- Be sure to select an appropriate destination folder for your music in the Choose Music Folder Destination dialog box.
- The Filetype Registration dialog box (see Figure 9.2) lets you choose the file types for which you want to use MusicMatch Jukebox. If you're using another MP3 player (for example, a stand-alone one), you'll probably want to clear some or all of these check boxes. If you'll be using MusicMatch Jukebox primarily or exclusively, leave them selected.

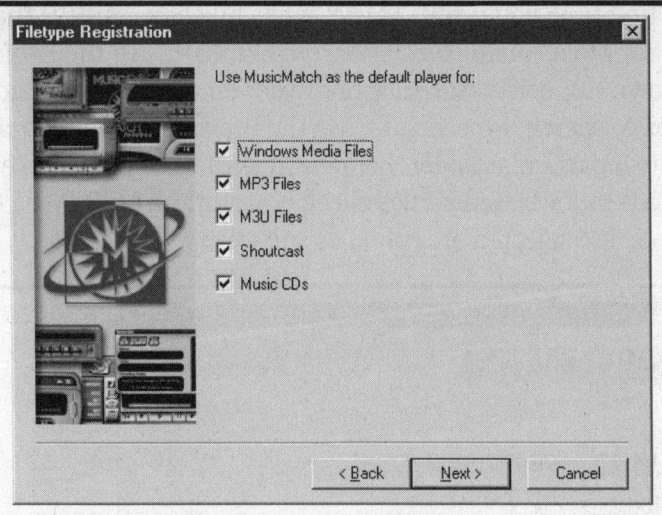

FIGURE 9.2: Choose carefully which file types you want MusicMatch Jukebox to handle in the Filetype Registration dialog box.

> **NOTE**
>
> If you do choose to make MusicMatch Jukebox your default MP3 player, it monitors your file associations aggressively to see if any have been stolen by another application. Typically, this happens when you install another MP3 player or jukebox after installing MusicMatch Jukebox, but it may also happen when you run another player or jukebox that reclaims file associations it finds that MusicMatch Jukebox has stolen from it. If MusicMatch Jukebox detects that it no longer has its associations, it displays the MusicMatch Jukebox File Associations dialog box, inviting you to reclaim them. To restore the associations, leave the Reclaim File Associations option button selected (it's selected by default), and click the OK button. To leave the file associations with whichever application has stolen them, select the Do Not Reclaim File Associations option button, and click the OK button. You can prevent MusicMatch Jukebox from bugging you about this by selecting the Don't Ask Me Again check box before closing the MusicMatch Jukebox File Associations dialog box.

Chapter Nine

The first time you run it, MusicMatch Jukebox displays the Search for Music dialog box, shown in Figure 9.3. In the Look In drop-down list, select the drive or drives you want MusicMatch Jukebox to search. If necessary, use the Browse button to limit the search to a particular folder. Before you start searching, make sure that the Windows Media Files check box and the MP2/MP3 Files check box are selected or cleared as suits you.

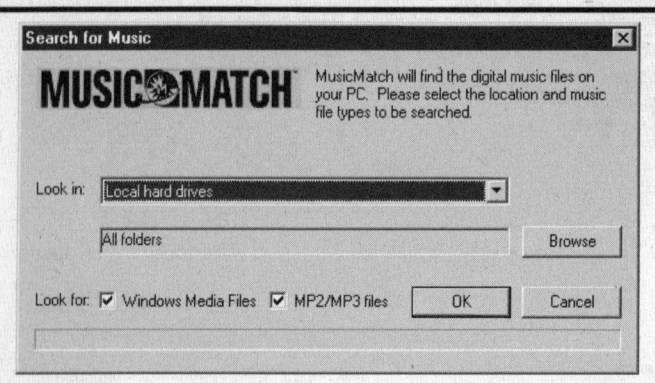

FIGURE 9.3: The first time you run it, MusicMatch Jukebox offers to search your hard drive for music.

You may also see the Confirm Association dialog box, which tells you that MusicMatch Jukebox is trying to grab some unspecified file associations from another application. If you're planning to use MusicMatch Jukebox as your primary MP3 tool, you'll probably want to choose the Yes button in this dialog box.

After that, you're ready to start using MusicMatch Jukebox. Figure 9.4 shows the Main window, and Figure 9.5 shows the Music Library window. You'll probably see them joined together, but we've pulled them apart so that we could label them better. You'll also see the Recorder window, which we'll show you how to use in a few pages' time, and a Welcome Tips window, which we'll let you explore on your own.

Windows Jukeboxes 423

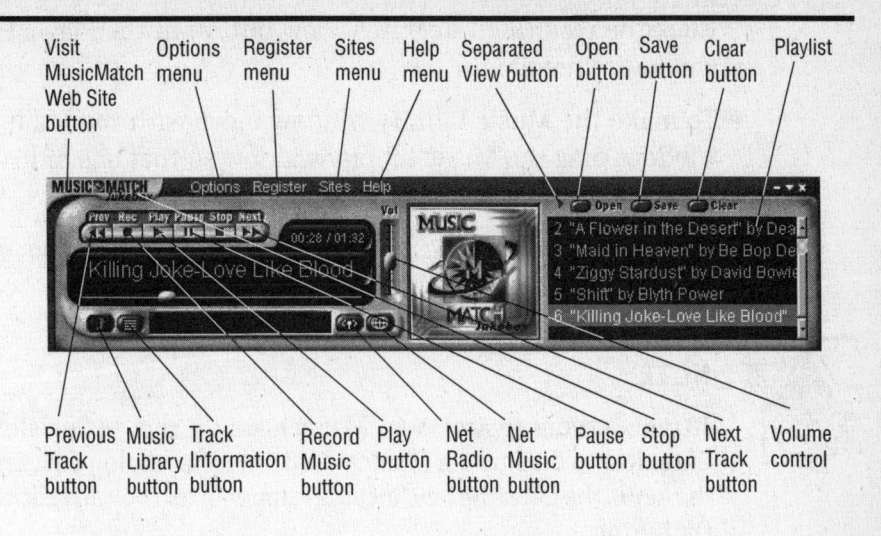

FIGURE 9.4: The MusicMatch Jukebox Main window

FIGURE 9.5: The MusicMatch Jukebox Music Library

The MusicMatch Jukebox windows are mostly straightforward and intuitive to handle:

- You can drag the windows around as you want.
- You can click the Separated View button on the Main window to separate the Playlist window (on the right-hand side of the Main window in Figure 9.4) from the Main window.

Click the resulting Integrated View button in the Playlist window to reunite the two.

- ▶ To make the Music Library window move with the Main window, drag the Music Library window so that one of its sides sticks to a side of the Main window.

- ▶ You can resize the Music Library window by clicking its border and dragging.

> **NOTE**
>
> To register your copy of MusicMatch Jukebox, choose Register ➤ Enter Key to display the MusicMatch Enter Key dialog box. Enter the key in the Enter the Key (Include Hyphens) text box and click the OK button.

Configuring CDDB

If your computer has an Internet connection, make sure that MusicMatch Jukebox is configured correctly to use CDDB, the online database of CD information. You only need to do this once, and it'll save you plenty of time in your ripping and playing of CDs.

To configure CDDB, choose Options ➤ Settings to display the Settings dialog box, then click the CDDB Preferences tab to display the CDDB/Connectivity page, shown in Figure 9.6.

To use CDDB, make sure the Enable CDDB CD Lookup Service check box is selected. Then, with your Internet connection up and running, click the Refresh Site List button to get the latest CDDB sites available.

In the Double Click a CDDB Site as Your Default list box, double-click the CDDB site that you want to use. Start with one that's geographically close to you if possible, but switch to another if that one is flaky. Your selection appears in the Current Default Site text box. Then click the Set as Default button to set the site as your default.

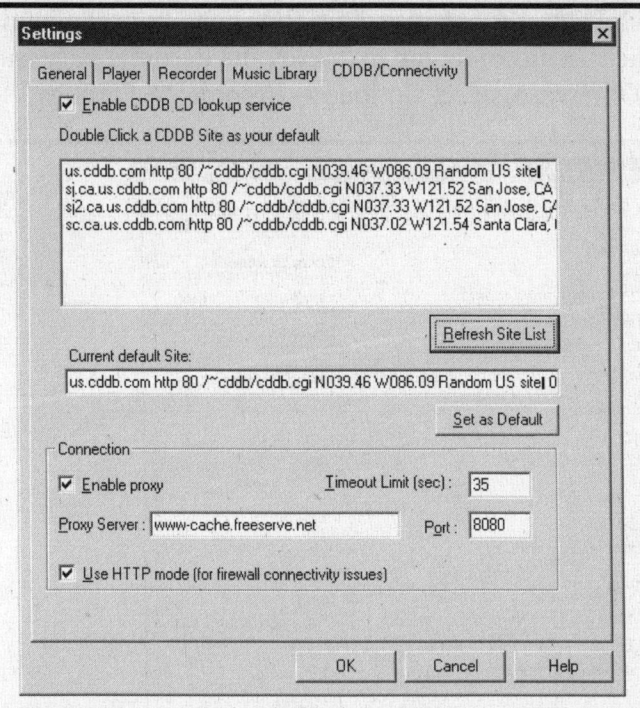

FIGURE 9.6: Configure CDDB on the CDDB/Connectivity page of the Settings dialog box.

If you need to use a proxy server, select the Enable Proxy check box in the Connection group box and enter the server's details in the Proxy Server text box and the Port text box. (Consult your network administrator for this information if you don't know it.) You can also change the timeout limit from its default setting in the Timeout Limit (Sec) text box.

Choosing Recorder Options

Next, choose the sampling rate and other details to use for your encoding. Like CDDB, these are details you'll typically want to set and forget so that all your MP3 files are encoded at the same bitrate and quality.

If you still have the Settings dialog box open from configuring CDDB, click the Recorder tab to display the Recorder page (see Figure 9.7). Otherwise, select Options ➢ Recorder ➢ Settings.

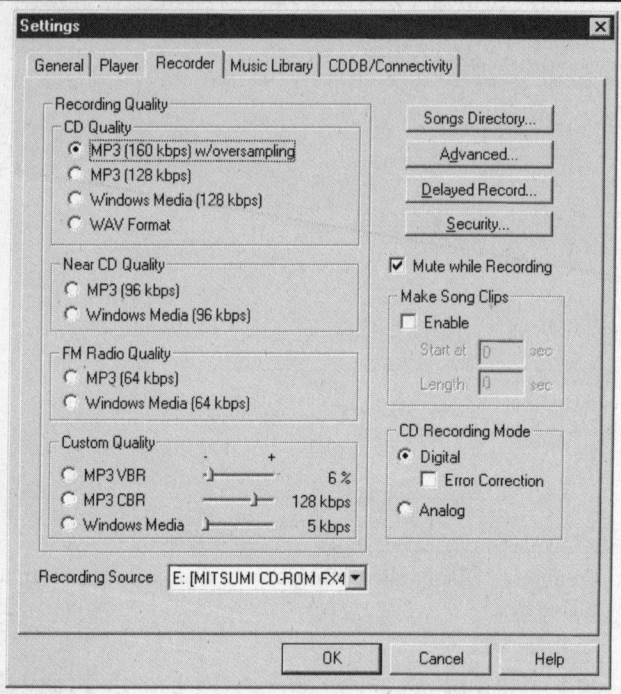

FIGURE 9.7: Choose a sampling rate on the Recorder page of the Settings dialog box.

In the Recording Quality group box, select the sampling rate at which to record. For most music, we suggest starting with the MP3 (128kbps) setting. If you find the quality not high enough, try the MP3 (160kbps) w/Oversampling setting. For spoken audio, experiment with the MP3 (96kbps) and MP3 (64kbps) settings found in the Near CD Quality and FM Radio Quality group boxes, respectively. For special purposes, you can use the MP3 VBR and MP3 CBR options found in the Custom Quality group box.

▶ VBR stands for *variable bitrate* and lets you emphasize the quality of the audio. The amount of information recorded (the *bitrate*) varies according to the complexity of the music.

Windows Jukeboxes

Be warned that VBR can produce large files, and some MP3 players cannot play back VBR files successfully.

- To squeeze even more audio into each megabyte of storage, select the MP3 CBR option button and drag its slider to the left to reduce the bitrate. CBR stands for *constant bitrate*. This option lets you reduce the size of the MP3 files you're encoding, but you can also use it to set a high bitrate (for example, 192kbps or 320kbps).

In the Recording Source drop-down list, select the CD or DVD drive from which you want to record. If you have an audio CD in the drive, the Recording Source drop-down list displays its title; if the drive is empty, the drop-down list displays a generic description, such as Toshiba CD-ROM.

Click the Songs Directory button to display the New Songs Directory Options dialog box, shown in Figure 9.8. Check the directory identified in the Directory for New Songs text box, and change it if necessary by typing in a new directory or by using the ... button and the resulting Browse for Folder dialog box.

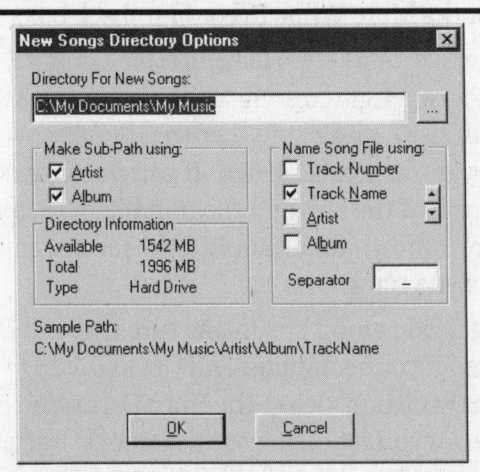

FIGURE 9.8: Choose a location and naming for MP3 files in the New Songs Directory Options dialog box.

In the Make Sub-Path Using group box, select the Artist check box and Album check box as appropriate to include them in the name of the subfolders that'll be created. For example, if you're ripping the album *Sound of Water* by St. Etienne, having the Artist and Album check boxes selected creates the subfolder `\St. Etienne\Sound of Water\`. The Sample Path label at the bottom of the New Songs Directory Options dialog box displays a generic path reflecting your choices.

In the Name Song File Using group box, select the information to include in the track file by selecting the check boxes for Track Number, Track Name, Artist, and Album as appropriate. You can change the order of these items by selecting one of them and using the up and down arrow buttons to move it to where you want it. In the Separator text box, enter the separator character to use between these components. The default is an underscore, but you can use a different character (or several characters) if you prefer. For example, you might prefer to use two or three hyphens, or a space, a hyphen, and a space (for readability).

Close the New Songs Directory Options dialog box to return to the Recorder page of the Settings dialog box (shown in Figure 9.7).

If you want MusicMatch Jukebox to rip without playing the music at the same time, select the Mute While Recording check box.

Unless you want to make short clips of songs (for example, for sharing a small part of a copyrighted song while remaining within shouting distance of fair use), make sure that the Enable check box in the Make Song Clips group box is cleared. If you do make clips, you can specify the length of the clip and the number of seconds into the track to start recording—for example, a 29-second clip starting at second 30 of the track.

In the CD Recording Mode group box, make sure that the Digital option button is selected if your computer and CD-ROM drive are capable of digital-audio extraction. Select the Error Correction check box if you want to use error correction in your recordings. It'll slow down the recording (on our test system, from 5.1× to 1.8×), so if you're in a hurry, you may want to use it only if you get clicks and pops on a recording. (If you're not in a hurry, error correction can't hurt.)

> **TIP**
>
> You can also quickly change the sampling rate by choosing Options Recorder Quality and choosing the appropriate setting on the Quality submenu.

Ripping

By this point, you should be all set to record. Slip a CD into your drive. MusicMatch Jukebox reads the CD and—if you're using CDDB and connected to the Internet, or if it's a CD your CD-ROM drive has looked up before—displays the album's name, the artist's name, and the track titles. If CDDB can't decide between a couple of possible listings for the CD, it displays a dialog box to let you decide.

If the Recorder window isn't displayed, click the Record Music CDs into Digital Tracks button to display it. Figure 9.9 shows the Recorder window, in action ripping and with labels.

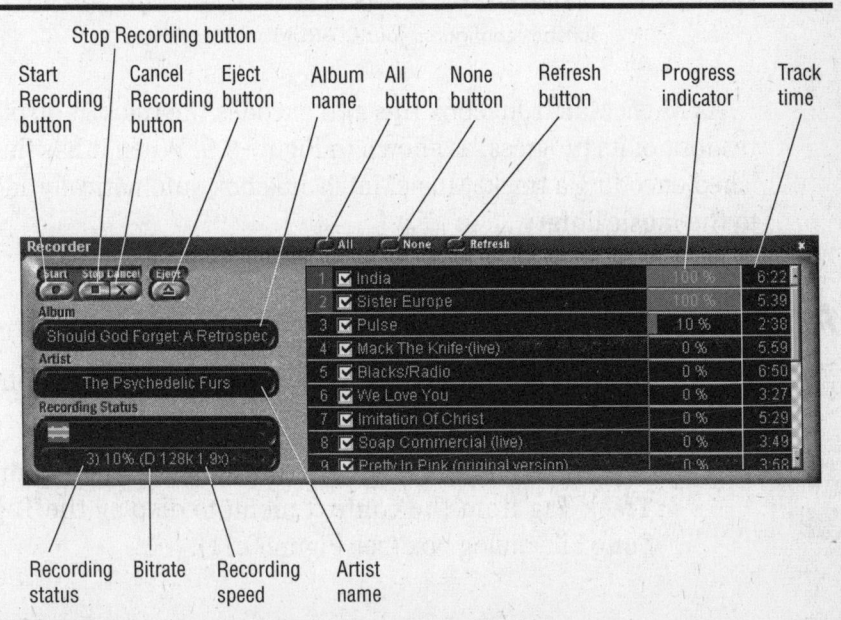

FIGURE 9.9: The MusicMatch Jukebox Recorder window

Specify the tracks that you want to record by selecting their check boxes. Use the All button to select all tracks and the None button to deselect all tracks. Click the Refresh button to force MusicMatch Jukebox to reread the CD's contents.

Click the Start Recording button to start ripping and encoding. The first time you go to rip tracks from a CD and encode them to MP3 files, MusicMatch Jukebox configures your CD drive or drives. The CD-ROM Preparation dialog box, shown in Figure 9.10, appears. Make sure that each of your CD drives and DVD drives that you'll ever want to use for recording contains an audio CD and then click the OK button. MusicMatch Jukebox configures the drive or drives for you and then starts ripping and encoding.

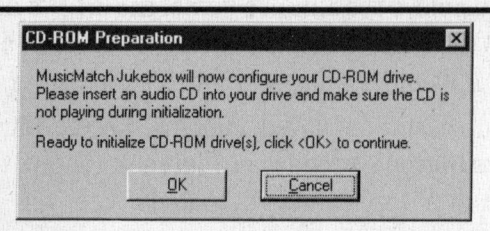

FIGURE 9.10: The first time you rip with MusicMatch Jukebox, MusicMatch Jukebox configures your CD-ROM drive or drives.

As MusicMatch Jukebox rips and encodes the track, it displays a readout of its progress, as shown in Figure 9.9. When it has finished encoding a track, MusicMatch Jukebox automatically adds it to the music library.

Adding and Editing Tags

MusicMatch Jukebox makes it easy to add ID3 tag information to all the tracks from the same album:

1. Right-click a track in the Music Library and choose Edit Track Tag from the context menu to display the Tag Song File dialog box (see Figure 9.11).

Windows Jukeboxes 431

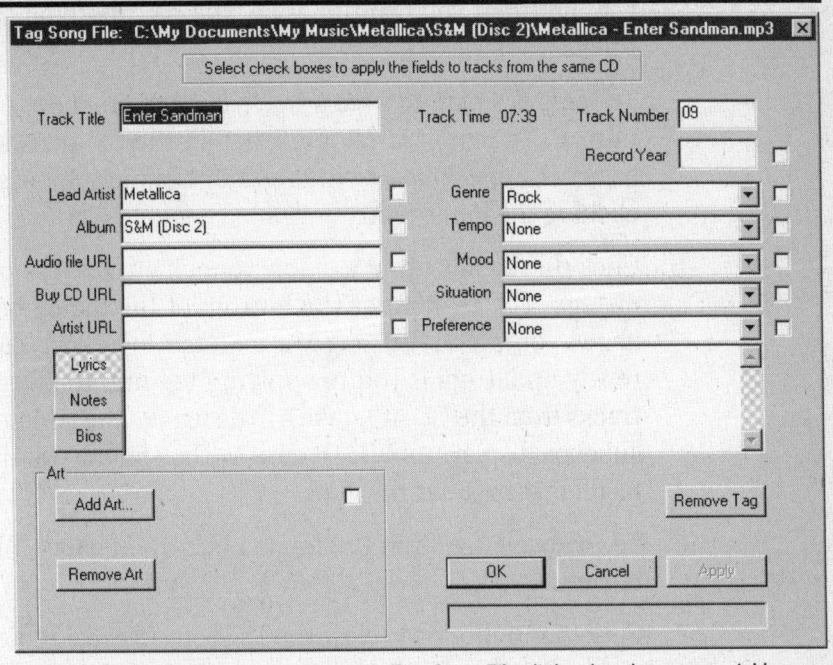

FIGURE 9.11: MusicMatch Jukebox's Tag Song File dialog box lets you quickly add and edit ID3 tags.

2. Enter information for the track by typing the information in the text boxes and by choosing items in the drop-down list boxes. If you want to apply the same information to all the tracks from the same CD, select the check box to the right of the text box or drop-down list box.

3. To add lyrics, notes, or bios to the track, click the Lyrics, Notes, or Bios button and enter the information in the text box.

4. To add a bitmap or JPEG picture to the track, click the Add Art button to display the Open dialog box. Navigate to and select the picture file, then click the Open button. The selected picture appears to the right of the Remove Art button. Select the check box to the right of

the picture if you want to apply the picture to all the tracks from the CD.

To remove a picture from a track, click the Remove Art button. To remove a picture from all the CD's tracks, select the check box to the right of the picture before clicking the Remove Art button.

5. Click the Apply button to apply your changes to the tag or tags. The readout at the bottom of the dialog box shows you which file's tag MusicMatch Jukebox is currently updating. If you're applying tag info to all the tracks from the CD, it'll take a little while. MusicMatch Jukebox displays an MMJB message box telling you the results when it has finished.

6. To remove a tag from the track, click the Remove Tag button.

7. Click the OK button to close the Tag Song File dialog box.

Building Your Music Library or Libraries

Like most jukeboxes, MusicMatch Jukebox lets you keep a database of your music files, enabling you to manage and find them easily.

You can create as many music libraries as you want. If you prefer to have all your music in one music library, that's fine, but be warned that it may become unmanageably large. We suggest segmenting your music into the different themes, moods, or occasions by which you'll want to play it. MusicMatch Jukebox lets you put any individual track into multiple music libraries.

If you don't have the Music Library window displayed, click the Music Library button on the Main window to display it.

Planning Your Music Libraries

Before you create a music library, choose options for the music libraries that you're planning to create. (You can choose options for a music library after creating it, but you'll save time by setting things up right before creating any libraries.) Here's what to do:

1. Choose Options ➤ Music Library ➤ Music Library Settings to display the Music Library page of the Settings dialog box, shown in Figure 9.12.

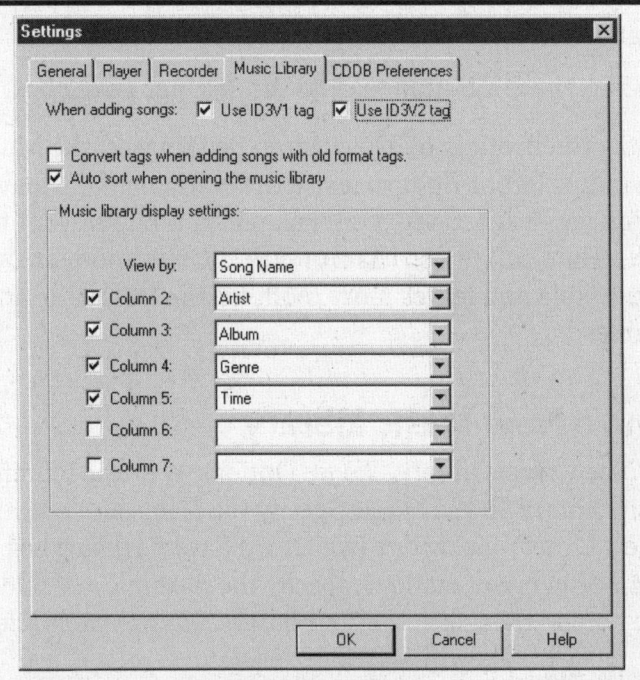

FIGURE 9.12: Choose options for your music library on the Music Library page of the Settings dialog box.

2. Make sure that both the Use ID3V1 Tag check box and the Use ID3V2 Tag check box are selected so that MusicMatch Jukebox adds all the available tag information to the music library. (ID3V1 tags can contain title, artist, album, year, comment, and genre data. ID3V2 tags include more information, such as lyrics, and a picture.)

3. Select the Convert Tags When Adding Songs with Old Format Tags check box if you want to convert tags from older tag formats to new ones when you add them.

4. Select the Auto Sort When Opening the Music Library check box to have MusicMatch Jukebox automatically sort the tracks in the library each time you open it.

5. In the Music Library Display Settings group box, select the columns that you want to have appear in the Music Library window. For each column, select the appropriate contents in the list box.

6. Click the OK button to close the Settings dialog box.

Now drag the dividers on the column headings in the Music Library window left or right to resize the columns to display the information you want to see. For example, you might want to narrow the Time column so that it takes the minimum amount of space possible and leaves more room for the track title and album names.

Creating a New Music Library

To create a new music library, choose Options ➤ Music Library ➤ New Music Library. In the Please Specify the Name and Location of Your New Library dialog box (which is a Save As dialog box after a quick name-change operation), specify the filename and folder for the music library, then click the Save button. MusicMatch Jukebox saves the music library with a DDF extension.

Adding Tracks to a Music Library

MusicMatch Jukebox automatically adds to the current music library any new MP3 files that you rip with it. But you'll need to add any existing MP3 files that you have to the database so that you can work with them through MusicMatch Jukebox. The same goes for any MP3 files that you download.

To add files to the current music library, click the Add button in the Music Library window to display the Add Songs to Music Library dialog box, shown in Figure 9.13. Then select the directory and files you want, and click the OK button. If the directory contains subdirectories that you want to add, select the Include Subdirectories check box.

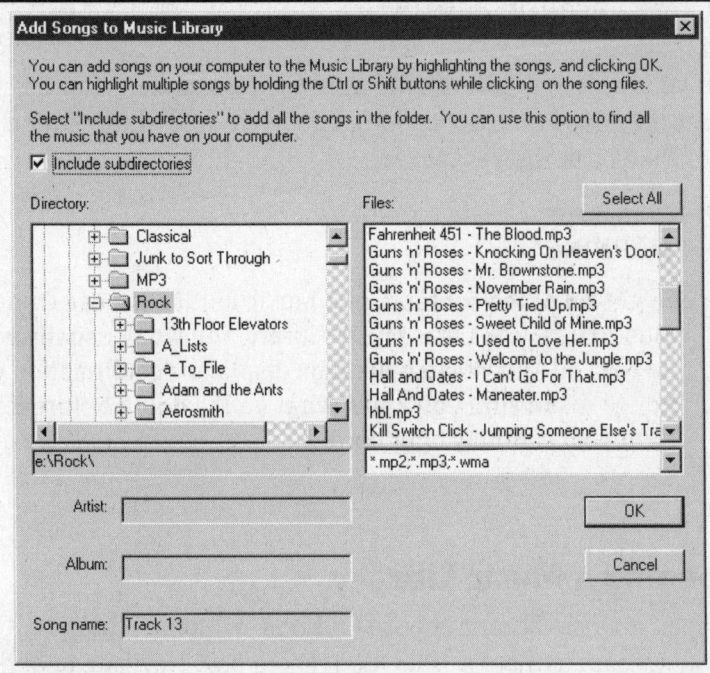

FIGURE 9.13: Use the Add Songs To Music Library dialog box to add tracks to your current music library.

Deleting Tracks from a Music Library

To delete a track from a music library, select the track and click the Delete button (or press the Delete key). MusicMatch Jukebox displays the MusicMatch Jukebox dialog box shown in Figure 9.14.

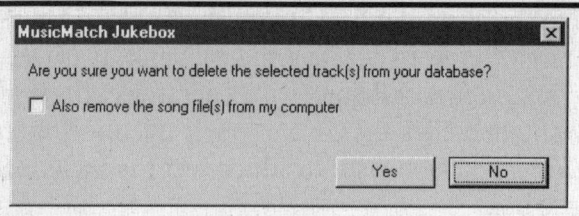

FIGURE 9.14: When deleting a track from a music library, you can choose also to delete it from your drive.

If you want to delete the file from your computer's hard disk, select the Also Remove the Song File(s) from My Computer check box. Then click the Yes button.

> **WARNING**
>
> **To get rid of the contents of a music library, choose Options ➢ Music Library ➢ Clear Music Library. You won't usually want to do this, so MusicMatch Jukebox displays a confirmation dialog box to make sure you know what you're doing before it wipes clear your carefully built library.**

Opening a Music Library

To open a music library, choose Options ➢ Music Library ➢ Open Music Library to display the Open dialog box. Navigate to and select the music library, then click the Open button. MusicMatch Jukebox opens the music library, and closes any music library that is currently open.

Sharing a Music Library with a Friend

To share a music library with a friend, take the following steps:

1. Export it to a text file by choosing Options ➢ Music Library ➢ Export Music Library.
2. Enter a filename in the Save As dialog box.
3. Click the Save button.

You can then e-mail the text file to your friend, and they can import it by choosing Options ➢ Music Library ➢ Import Music Library.

Sharing a music library like this gives your friends only the list of tracks in the library. They need to have the MP3 files that the music library references in order to play them back—but you knew that already.

Finding Tracks in Your Music Library

To find tracks in a music library, press Ctrl+F (or choose Options ➢ Music Library ➢ Find Music in Music Library) to display the Find in Music Library dialog box (see Figure 9.15). Take the following steps:

1. Enter your search term in the Find What text box.
2. Select or clear the Match Complete Name Only check box and the Match Case check box as appropriate.
3. Choose a direction.
4. Click the Find First button.

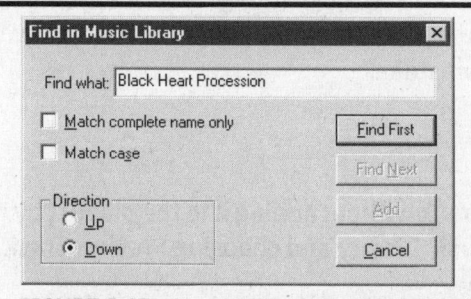

FIGURE 9.15: Use the Find in Music Library dialog box to track down lost music in the far reaches of your music libraries.

If it finds an instance of your search term, MusicMatch Jukebox scrolls the Music Library to display it. You can then click the Add button to add that track to your current playlist or click the Find Next button to find the next instance of the search term.

Playing Music with MusicMatch Jukebox

Once you've got your music organized into music libraries, you can create playlists, save them, and play them back. You can also use the AutoDJ feature to create automatic playlists for you.

Creating, Saving, and Opening Playlists

The Playlist window initially appears docked to the Main window. When you're working with it, you'll usually want to display it separately so that you can expand it to see more of its contents. Click the Separated View button to display the Playlist window as a separate window. Click the Integrated View button to attach the Playlist window to the Main window again.

To create a playlist, clear the current playlist of any superfluous tracks by clicking the Clear button. Then add tracks to the Playlist window by dragging them from the Music Library window or by selecting them in the Music Library window, right-clicking, and choosing Add Track(s) to Playlist from the context menu. Then drag the tracks up and down the playlist to get them into the order you want. Use the Delete button to delete any track that you've added to the playlist by mistake.

> **TIP**
>
> You can preview a track without adding it to the playlist by right-clicking it in the Music Library and choosing Preview Track from the context menu.

When you've assembled your playlist, save it by clicking the Save button to display the Save Playlist dialog box, entering a name, and clicking the Save button. MusicMatch Jukebox supports really long names for playlists, but anything over about 40 characters tends to be hard to work with, so you'll probably want to keep them concise but descriptive.

To open a playlist, click the Open button on the Playlist window and use the resulting Open Music dialog box to identify the playlist.

Using the AutoDJ Feature

MusicMatch Jukebox's AutoDJ feature lets you specify vague guidelines by which MusicMatch Jukebox should put together automatic playlists for you. This feature is worth trying, if only for amusement. You may have thought that nobody could put together a worse playlist than your beloved sibling, but MusicMatch Jukebox stands ready to prove you wrong time and again.

To use the AutoDJ feature, press Ctrl+D or click the AutoDJ button in the Main window to display the AutoDJ dialog box (see Figure 9.16). Specify the number of hours in the Enter Play Time text box (we suggest keeping this number low when you're testing the AutoDJ feature). Then use the First Criteria, Second Criteria, and Third Criteria group boxes to specify the type of music you want. Use the Preview button to get a readout of how many matching tracks AutoDJ has found and the combined playing time. Then click the Get Tracks button to add the tracks to your current playlist, from which you can rearrange them as you want and play them as usual.

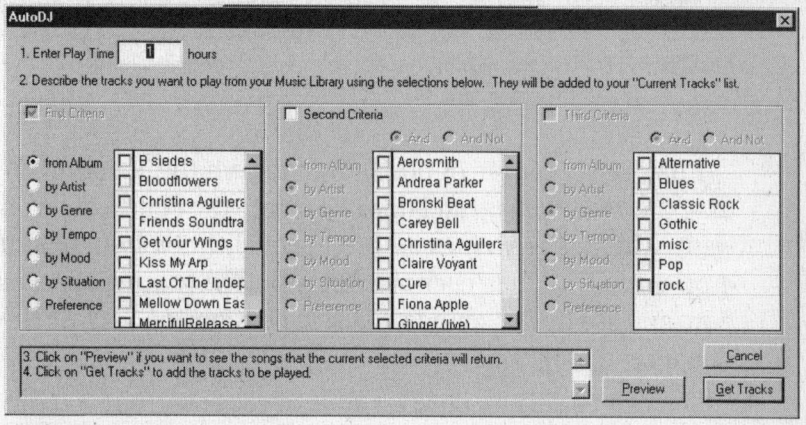

FIGURE 9.16: If you're feeling adventurous, try MusicMatch Jukebox's AutoDJ feature.

Using the Graphic Equalizer

Like the better MP3 players, MusicMatch Jukebox provides a graphic equalizer that you can use to tweak the music to your liking. Unfortunately, the graphic equalizer is much less useful than it might be, and it's implemented as a dialog box rather than as a window, so you can't keep it open while you manipulate the rest of MusicMatch Jukebox.

To use the equalizer, display the Equalizer dialog box (see Figure 9.17) by choosing Options ➢ Player ➢ MP3 Equalizer.

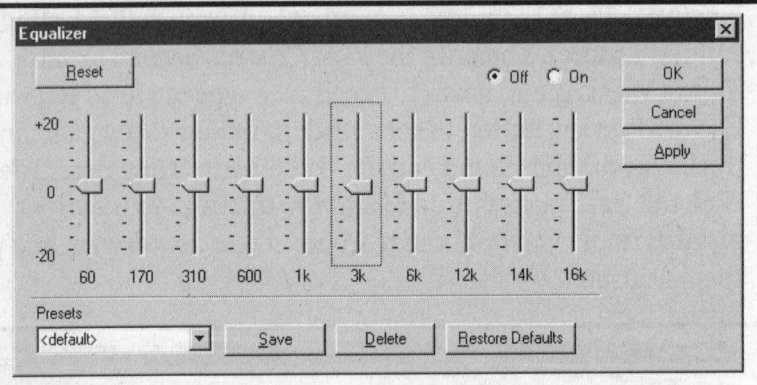

FIGURE 9.17: Use the graphic equalizer to remedy deficiencies of your music or your speakers.

First, select the On option button to turn the equalizer on. Next, drag the 10 sliders up and down to create the equalization you want. Alternatively, choose a preset equalization from the Presets drop-down list. Then click the Apply button to apply the equalization, and see how it sounds. Click the OK button to close the Equalizer dialog box.

You can't save new equalizations of your own, but you can change the preset equalizations that MusicMatch Jukebox provides using the following steps:

1. Choose the preset equalization from the Presets drop-down list.

2. Change the slider positions as necessary.
3. Click the Save button.

If you goof up, you can restore the default settings for all preset equalizations—not just the currently selected one—by clicking the Restore Defaults button.

Use the Net Music Feature to Access Music on the Internet

To keep you up to date with what's happening in music on the Internet, and to deliver that customized music it promised you during the installation, MusicMatch Jukebox provides its Net Music feature. To use Net Music, click the Net Music button in the Main window to display the Net Music window. As you can see in Figure 9.18, the Net Music window contains six pages: Home (shown in the figure), Best Matches, Charts, New, Find Music, and More Music. You access each page by clicking its tab below the ever-changing and relentless ads that barrage you from the upper reaches of the window.

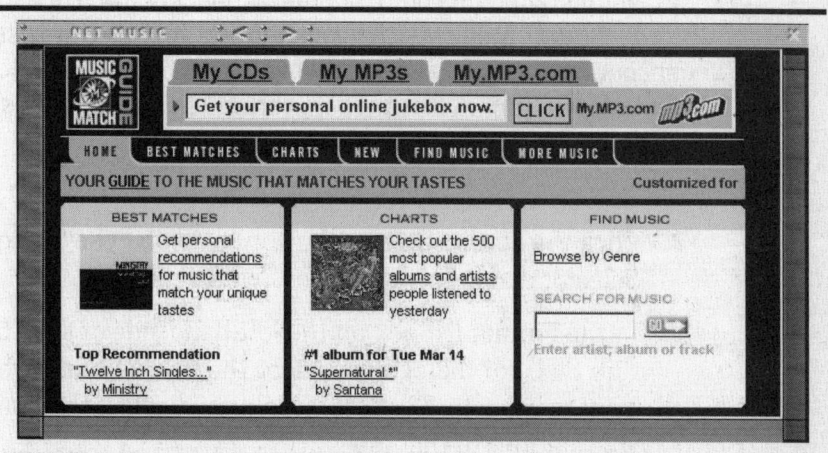

FIGURE 9.18: Use MusicMatch Jukebox's Net Music feature to access music on the Internet.

Playing Net Radio

MusicMatch Jukebox provides a feature called Net Radio that lets you play Internet radio streams. Here's how to use the Net Radio feature:

1. Click the Net Radio button in the Main window to display the Net Radio window, shown in Figure 9.19 with a station playing.

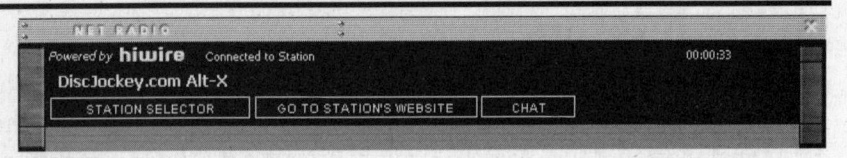

FIGURE 9.19: Use the Net Radio feature to listen to radio broadcasts across the Internet.

> **NOTE**
>
> If you don't have the latest version of Microsoft Windows Media Player installed on your computer when you first click the Net Radio button, MusicMatch Jukebox starts your Web browser and encourages you to download that version. Comply and follow the installation procedure, then restart MusicMatch Jukebox and click the Net Radio button again.

2. Click the Station Selector button to display the Station Selector dialog box, shown in Figure 9.20.

3. In the Format list box on the left-hand side of the Station Selector dialog box, select the type of music you want to listen to. The second column displays the available stations of that type.

   Alternatively, enter a search term in the text box at the bottom of the Station Selector dialog box and click the Search button. Again, the second column displays the available stations that match the text you specified.

Windows Jukeboxes

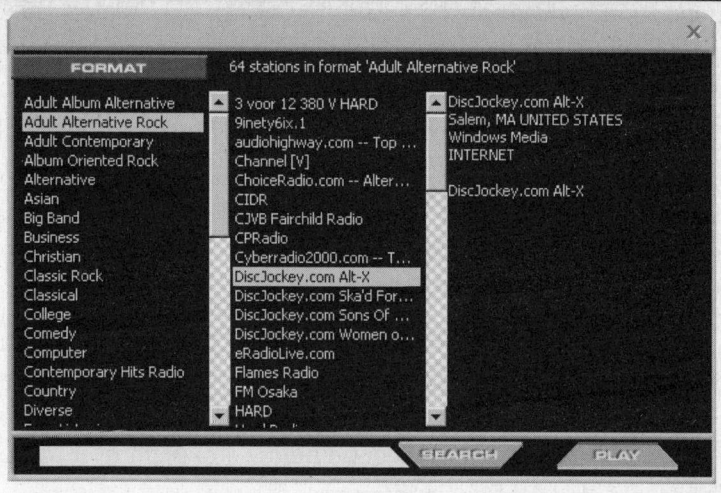

FIGURE 9.20: The Station Selector dialog box lets you access the wide variety of stations that are available.

4. In the second column, select the station that interests you. The third column displays the details of the station, as shown in Figure 9.20.

5. Click the Play button to start playing the station. Depending on the speed of your Internet connection and the strength of the signal, MusicMatch Jukebox needs a few seconds to buffer the signal before it starts playing. You'll see a Buffering label and a growing percentage readout on the right-hand side of the Net Radio window while MusicMatch Jukebox is filling the buffer.

You can control the Net Radio station's play using the controls in the Main window. For example, click the Stop button to stop the current station playing.

Burning CDs

If you have a CD-R or CD-RW drive, MusicMatch Jukebox's most compelling feature over most of the other ripper/player/jukeboxes available is its ability to burn CDs. Compared to a semi-professional

CD-creation package such as Adaptec's Easy CD Creator, this feature is limited, but you'll probably find that it's good enough to get the job done.

Before you start trying to burn CDs with MusicMatch Jukebox, check the MusicMatch Web site for a list of supported CD recorders. At this writing, the URL is www.musicmatch.com/jukebox/player/cdr.cgi.

Here's how to create a CD:

1. Assemble a playlist containing the tracks that you want to put on the CD, preferably in the order in which you want them to appear on the CD. Try the playlist and make sure it sounds good before you commit it to CD.

2. Save the playlist. (That way you won't have to suffer the tedium of having to recreate it if things go disastrously wrong and your PC crashes.)

3. Click the Create CD button in the Main window (or in the Playlist window, if you're using Separated view), or right-click in the playlist and choose Create CD from Playlist from the context menu. Either way, MusicMatch Jukebox displays the Create CD from Playlist dialog box in its more compact format. Figure 9.21 shows the Create CD from Playlist dialog box in its expanded format, which it displays when you click the Options button.

4. In the CD Format area at the top of the dialog box, make sure that the Audio (Default) option button is selected if you want to create an audio CD—one that you can play in a CD player. The Data (MP3, WMA, WAV) format lets you pack far more music onto a CD, but you'll need to play it in a computer (or in a special CD player that can handle the MP3 format, such as the D'music MP3 CD player from Pine Technology).

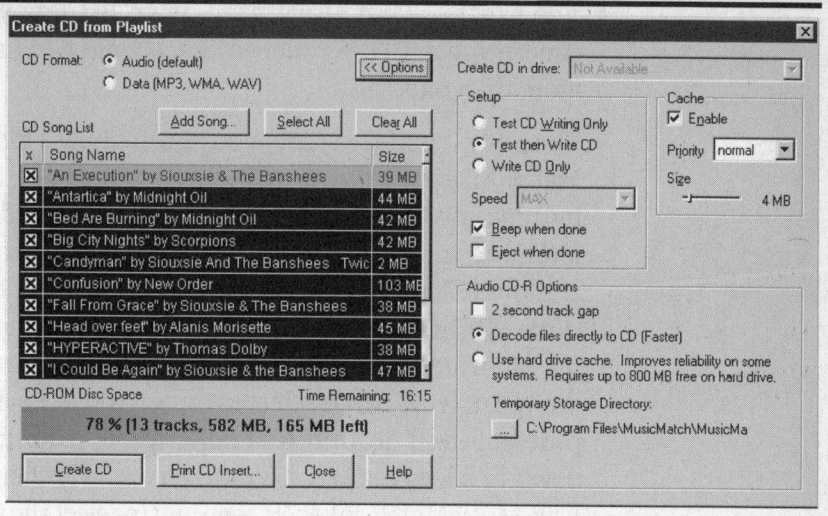

FIGURE 9.21: MusicMatch Jukebox's killer feature is its ability to burn audio CDs.

5. Scan through the tracks in the CD Song List and see how things look:

    ▶ Use the CD-ROM Disc Space readout to see if there's extra space on the CD.

    ▶ To add a track to the CD, click the Add Song button, use the resulting Open dialog box to specify the track, and click the Open button. MusicMatch Jukebox adds the track to the end of the CD, so you may well want to move it to a better position.

    ▶ To change the order of tracks, select a track and drag it up or down the list to where you want it to appear.

    ▶ To remove a track from the CD, clear its check box in the list.

6. To choose further options for creating the CD, click the Options button. The Create CD from Playlist dialog box displays its previously hidden right-hand half, which contains the following options:

- The Create CD in Drive drop-down list lets you choose which CD recorder to use, should you have more than one.

- The Setup group box lets you specify how Music-Match Jukebox writes the CD. In the group of option buttons, use the Test Then Write CD option the first few times you burn a CD with MusicMatch Jukebox and this CD recorder. After that, if all is well, use the Write CD Only option, which dispenses with the testing phase and hence is quicker. In the Speed drop-down list, leave MAX selected unless you're having problems and need to try cranking the recording down to a lower speed. You can choose whether to have MusicMatch Jukebox beep and/or eject the CD when it has finished creating it; either option can be a useful cue that it's time to start the next CD.

- The Cache group box controls whether and how MusicMatch Jukebox creates a cache space for buffering data that it's feeding to the CD recorder. Leave the Enable check box selected unless you have a very good reason for clearing it. Leave the Priority drop-down list set to Normal unless you're having problems burning CDs, in which case you may want to try setting it to High. And leave the Size slider at its default setting of 4MB unless you're having problems burning CDs; if you have problems, try increasing the size in gradual increments.

- The Audio CD-R Options group box offers three more options that you need to know about. First, select the 2 Second Track Gap check box if you want MusicMatch Jukebox to add a gap of two seconds between tracks on the CD. Second, choose one of the two option buttons to specify whether to decode the MP3 files directly to the CD or to use a cache on your hard drive. Writing directly is faster, but if

Windows Jukeboxes 447

you're not getting satisfactory results from it, try the cache; be aware that you need 800MB of free space on the hard drive in question. Third, the Temporary Storage Directory button controls where Music-Match Jukebox places the disk cache. You need to change this setting only if the default drive is short of that 800MB of space.

7. Make sure your CD recorder is loaded with a blank disk, then click the Create CD button to start creating the CD. MusicMatch Jukebox displays the CD Creation Progress dialog box, shown in Figure 9.22, to show you how things are going.

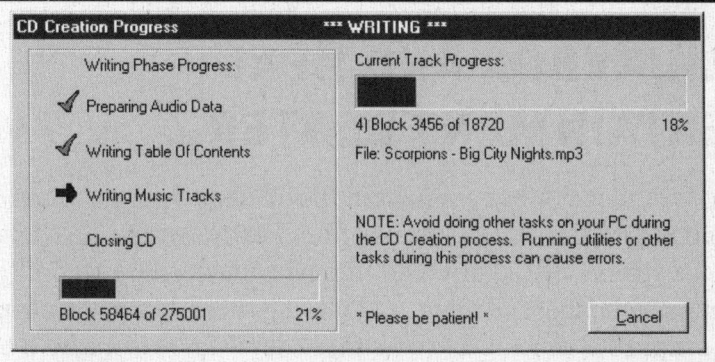

FIGURE 9.22: You'll see the CD Creation Progress dialog box as MusicMatch Jukebox creates the CD.

NOTE

The CD Creation Progress dialog box enjoins you from doing other tasks on your PC while the CD is being created. If you have a reasonably powerful PC and you're using Windows NT Workstation or Windows 2000 rather than Windows 95, Windows 98, or Windows Me, you may be able to get away with multitasking. But if your CD recorder is reasonably quick or has a small on-board RAM buffer, you'd do better to take a break until the recording is finished.

8. When the recording is finished, MusicMatch Jukebox displays a dialog box that tells you the CD was created successfully, beeps (depending on the setting in the Create CD from Playlist dialog box), and ejects the CD (likewise). Dismiss the dialog box and remove the CD.

9. If you want to create an insert card for the CD, click the Print CD Insert button, specify the details in the Print CD Insert dialog box, and click the OK button.

10. Click the Close button to close the Create CD from Playlist dialog box.

Now label your CD and test it.

RealJukebox and Real Entertainment Center

The second major heavyweight in the all-in-one ripper/player/jukebox category is RealJukebox from RealNetworks. RealJukebox can be an effective solution for ripping and encoding MP3 files, keeping a database of them, and playing them, but many people are suspicious of RealNetworks these days—for reasons we'll mention in due course.

RealJukebox comes in a Basic edition that's free but it's too limited for most people—it's maximum bitrate is 96kbps, which isn't enough for quality music—and a Plus edition that costs $29.99. At this writing, RealNetworks has started pushing its Real Entertainment Center package, which includes RealJukebox, RealPlayer, and RealDownload. There's a standard version of Real Entertainment Center that you can download for free (which contains RealPlayer Basic and RealJukebox Basic) and a Plus version that costs $49.99 and contains the Plus versions of the products.

RealNetworks is one of the most aggressive companies that we've ever bought software from. Not only does it sell beta versions of its software for the full price (you can get the upgrades in due course), but it constantly tries to upsell you on other products. So when you're buying—or simply downloading—from RealNetworks, be on the lookout. Check every page carefully for already-selected check boxes by which you agree to receive mailings, get trial versions of products that you'll later be charged for, buy eternal upgrades, or get add-on packages called things like Power Pack.

$49.99 for Real Entertainment Center Plus doesn't seem too bad, but when you add $29.99 of upgrades and another $29.99 of Power Pack, your credit card may start to buckle under the heat. At this writing, the Real Entertainment Center Power Pack contains iQfx, an audio-enhancement product, and FreeMem Professional for freeing RAM. iQfx is an interesting product that you may want to give a spin, but we don't think much of FreeMem. You're better off investing in more physical RAM or simply practicing the self-restraint to run fewer applications at the same time rather than kludging about with software-based solutions. Feel free to disagree about the value of FreeMem and prove us right.

Why Some People Don't Like RealNetworks

Before discussing RealJukebox, we should mention that it and RealNetworks have some history that you need to be aware of, because it may affect your decision to pay for and try RealJukebox Plus or Real Entertainment Center Plus. (In fact, it may put you off the free Basic versions as well.)

In 1999, RealNetworks made front-page headlines across the U.S. by being caught perpetrating some truly disgusting marketing practices. Unknown to users, RealJukebox would send information on the user's listening and ripping habits to RealNetworks, together with a unique player ID number that identified the computer in use. This information included the number of songs the user had recorded onto their hard drive, the music CDs they were listening to, and even the type of portable MP3 player they had (if they were connecting it to the computer on which RealJukebox was installed)—exactly the sort of information that's most valuable to marketers. If you had registered RealJukebox with your real e-mail address, RealNetworks was in a perfect position to market suitable music directly to you—or to sell your information to someone else for them to market to you.

When this spying on users was revealed, a minor furor broke out. RealNetworks issued an apology for collecting this information and made available a patch that prevented RealJukebox from sending further information. However, by that time, more than 12 million people were using RealJukebox—and you can bet that a sizable percentage of them either never learned of the patch or were too lazy to apply it.

At this writing, RealNetworks has a Privacy Guarantee prominently displayed on their Web site that reads as follows:

```
We will not sell, rent, or give away your e-mail
address or personal information. RealJukebox does not
contain a unique identifier that could theoretically
be used to track the actions or listening habits of
individuals.
```

Does this clear everything up? The wording could certainly be plainer. The "unique identifier" wouldn't need to be in RealJukebox. Instead, it would typically be generated by using a hardware ID in your computer, such as the MAC address of your network card (if you have one) or the serial number of your Pentium-III computer (likewise). Similarly, a unique number generated by some algorithm could be stored in the Windows Registry, where it wouldn't be "contained" by RealJukebox. If you're thinking along these lines, visit the RealNetworks Consumer Software Privacy Statement (currently at `www.realnetworks.com/company/privacy/software.html`) and see if it sets your mind at rest.

If you already have RealJukebox installed, be sure to update to the latest version available, or at least to download and install any patches that are released.

Installing and Configuring RealJukebox

The best place to get RealJukebox is, needless to say, the RealNetworks Web site, `www.real.com`. Download the package that you feel most comfortable with. Real Entertainment Center Basic is a much heftier download than RealJukebox Basic, but you may want to take the extra time if you want the added features it provides.

RealJukebox requires Windows, a minimum of a modest-powered processor—a Pentium 200, a Cyrix 233, or an AMD K5 PR-200—32MB RAM, 15MB of free space for software and 200MB of free space for music, plus the obvious: a full-duplex sound card, speakers, and an Internet connection.

> **WARNING**
>
> If you're downloading RealJukebox (rather than RealJukebox Plus), be sure not to install it over an earlier version of RealJukebox Plus. Doing so disables the RealJukebox Plus features, such as being able to record at an acceptable bitrate.

RealJukebox has a straightforward but extremely long installation routine. These are the points of interest:

- You need to supply an e-mail address (or text that looks like one).

- As mentioned earlier, watch out for already-selected check boxes and options by which you automatically sign up for updates, events, and so on.

- If you're installing RealJukebox Plus or Real Entertainment Center Plus, you'll need to enter your serial number. You should have received this number in your browser when you placed your order, and RealNetworks should have sent you an e-mail containing it.

- RealJukebox asks if you have a portable music player or storage device—a portable player, a CD-R or CD-RW, or a portable drive such as a Zip, a Jaz, or an Orb. If you do, select the Yes option button in the first Portable Players/Storage dialog box, click the Update List button in the second Portable Players/Storage dialog box to download the latest list of portable players and storage devices from RealNetworks, then select the player or device you have. Depending on which player or device you choose, you may see the Missing Plugin dialog box, telling you that RealJukebox Plus needs to download a component to support the device. Let it do so.

▶ If another application currently holds the file associations that RealJukebox wants, RealJukebox asks your permission to grab the file associations so that it can be your default player. If you want to know which file associations RealJukebox is after, or you want to modify them, click the Detail button to display the Reclaim – Advanced dialog box.

▶ When RealJukebox displays the Configuration Options dialog box (see Figure 9.23), you can click the Finish button to finish the installation with default settings. However, we recommend that instead you click the Change button to go step-by-step through the configuration options, which are discussed in the next few paragraphs.

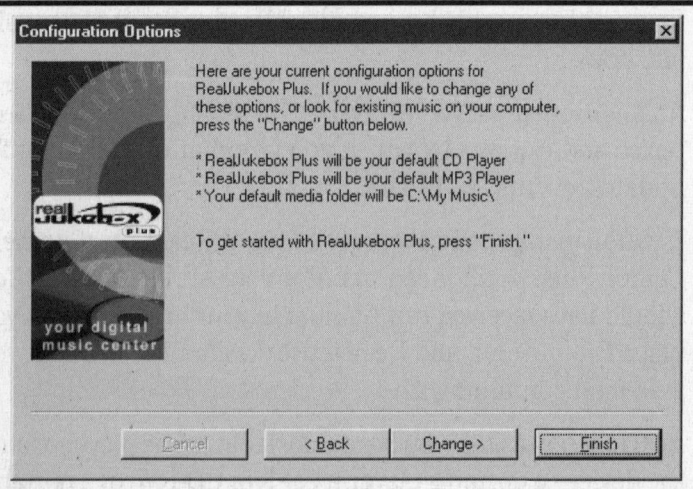

FIGURE 9.23: When you reach the Configuration Options dialog box, you can choose either to finish the installation with the default settings or plod through each of the configuration options manually.

▶ The Configuration – Audio Playback dialog box lets you choose which file types RealJukebox is the default player for, and whether to reclaim these file types without prompting. If you plan to use RealJukebox exclusively, select both these options. If you'll be using other players or jukeboxes, assign to RealJukebox only those music file types that you want it to play, and clear the Reclaim RealNetworks Music Types without Asking check box.

- The Configuration – Find Music dialog box offers to search your hard disk and other local drives for music files. Select the Yes option button to perform the search now; otherwise, leave the No, Don't Look for Music at This Time option button selected, as it is by default. (You can make RealJukebox Plus search for music later if you want.) If you choose to search, you get to specify which drives and folders to search.

- The Configuration – Music File Location dialog box lets you tell RealJukebox where to store your music files.

- The Configuration – AutoStart dialog box lets you specify whether RealJukebox should automatically start recording each new CD you put in your CD-ROM drive. Clear this check box because you won't want to record every CD, and you can start the recording process easily enough manually when appropriate.

- The Security Feature dialog box offers to enable the "security feature which protects your recordings from unauthorized use." This feature creates music files that you will be able to play only in RealJukebox, not with any other MP3 player, and only on the computer on which you recorded it (unless you install the same security key on another computer). From the recording industry's point of view, this security feature (which is enabled by default) is probably welcome; for the consumer, it's limiting. For example, if you have two computers and you want to share music between them (which you can do legally even if you don't hold the copyright to the music), you'll need to disable the security feature.

454 Chapter Nine

> **NOTE**
>
> When you clear the Secure My Music Files When Encoding check box, RealJukebox displays the Confirm Security Choice dialog box, warning you about copyright law and informing you that "by unchecking 'Security,' you are assuming the obligation to comply with all legal restrictions regarding extracted material." Read the information, select the I Accept the Above Terms option button, and click the OK button to close the dialog box. (If you think about it, these "terms" are very peculiar. You're explicitly assuming obligations that you have already to comply with the copyright laws of wherever you are. Essentially, RealNetworks is trying to make you agree you've been read the riot act.)

- The Configuration–CD Recording Options dialog box (see Figure 9.24) is even more important because it lets you choose whether to record in MP3 format, RealAudio format, or WAV format, and lets you choose which bitrate to use for MP3 or RealAudio. We recommend the MP3 Audio format and a bitrate of at least 128kbps (if you're using RealJukebox Plus rather than RealJukebox, which is limited to 96kbps).

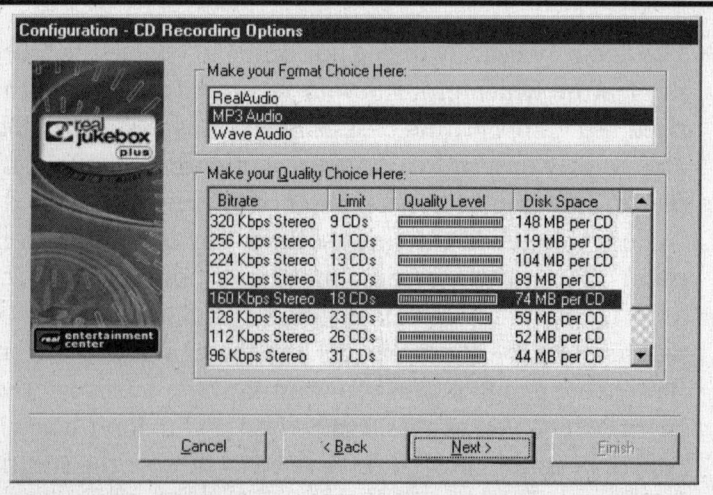

FIGURE 9.24: In the Configuration – CD Recording Options dialog box, you'll probably want to choose the MP3 Audio format.

- The Configuration – Internet dialog box lets you change five settings: Automatic Update Notification, Automatic CD Lookup Information, Faster Access to Technical Support, Automatic "Net Music" Updates, and Enable Track Info Presentations. You can turn off the automatic update notification for 30 days if you want—perhaps a sensible maneuver if you've just downloaded RealJukebox. The Faster Access to Technical Support feature, when selected, enables RealJukebox to automatically transmit information about your computer configuration so that RealNetworks's tech support can help you troubleshoot problems. Depending on your views, this may be a great idea or an invasion of privacy. Enable Track Info Presentations allows RealJukebox to present extra track information (such as lyrics, or where to buy the track) as well as CDDB information.

- The Recording Options dialog box invites you to optimize your system for recording. This is a good idea, so leave the Yes option button selected, load an audio CD in the CD-ROM drive, and click the Start Test button. Leave your keyboard and mouse alone while running the test—using either input device can screw up the test. After a bit, RealJukebox displays a Test Complete message telling whether the drive's up to ripping digitally or whether you'll have to slum it with analog. (If running the test makes your computer hang, skip the test next time and complete the configuration, then run the test from the Recording page of the Preferences dialog box.)

NOTE

If RealJukebox doesn't like your CD-ROM, you may see the Use of Generic CD-ROM Driver dialog box, warning you that you may need to upgrade the generic driver you're using in order to record successfully. If your CD-ROM has been behaving to date, we suggest you stick with it and choose the Yes button in this dialog box to see if it will work for you, but leave the Don't Ask Me Again check box cleared until you've found out whether the driver is up to snuff. Then select the Don't Ask Me Again check box the next time RealJukebox Plus displays it.

> **TIP**
>
> If necessary, you can rerun the Configuration Wizard by choosing Options ➤ Configuration Wizard.

RealJukebox is now all set up, but there's some more configuration you need to do. Choose Tools ➤ Preferences to display the Preferences dialog box, then take the following steps:

- On the General page, make sure that the Enable AutoPlay While Recording check box setting is suitable. When this check box is selected, you get to listen to the CD as RealJukebox rips it, even if RealJukebox is able to rip faster than real time. Check the status of the CD AutoPlay check box and the CD AutoRecord check box as well; many people find autoplay a boon, but it drives us up the wall.

- On the Recording page, shown in Figure 9.25, make sure that the Digital option button is selected if your CD drive can handle digital extraction. Otherwise, make sure that the Analog option button is selected, and set an appropriate recording volume by using the Record Volume slider. If you're using digital recording, you may want to select the Use Error Correction check box to implement error correction on the recording. (Because using error correction slows down the recording, most people turn error correction on only if they're not getting good results from recording without it.) You can also click the Advanced CPU Options button to display the Advanced CPU Options dialog box, in which you can adjust RealJukebox's CPU usage. Crudely put, the higher CPU usage you set, the faster encoding will be, but the worse the performance of other applications will be when you're encoding.

Windows Jukeboxes

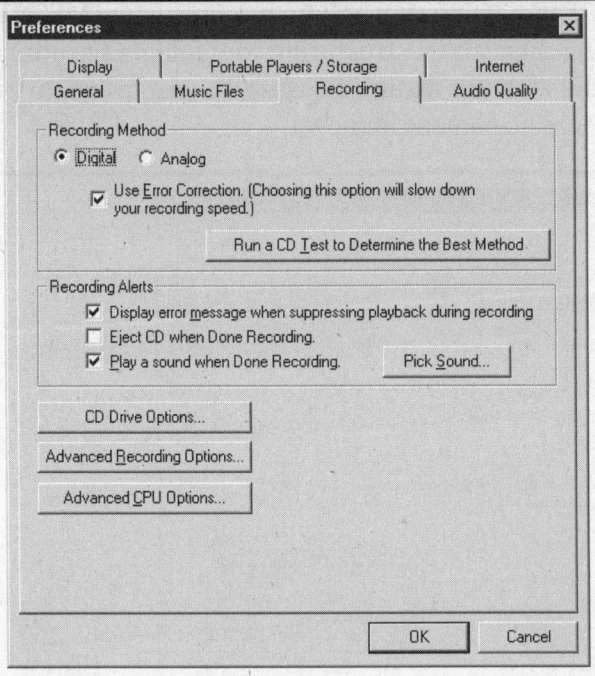

FIGURE 9.25: Choose the desired recording options on the Recording page of the Preferences dialog box.

- On the Audio Quality page, you can change the format and bitrate at which RealJukebox encodes—but you probably just set those during the installation routine. You can also enable and disable the security feature by selecting or clearing the Secure My Music Files When Encoding check box.

- On the Music Files page of the Preferences dialog box, shown in Figure 9.26, specify how RealJukebox should name the files for the tracks that you rip and encode. For example, click the Change Filenames button to display the Change File Naming Convention dialog box (see Figure 9.27), which gives you four drop-down lists to specify how to name each track—such as by the artist's name, the album name, and the track name. The most interesting feature here is the Apply to Existing Music button, which displays the Apply Convention to Existing Music dialog box. This feature applies your naming convention to your existing MP3 files, renaming them and restructuring your folders accordingly. Be careful with this feature, because it's easy to end up with a lot of folders named Unknown.

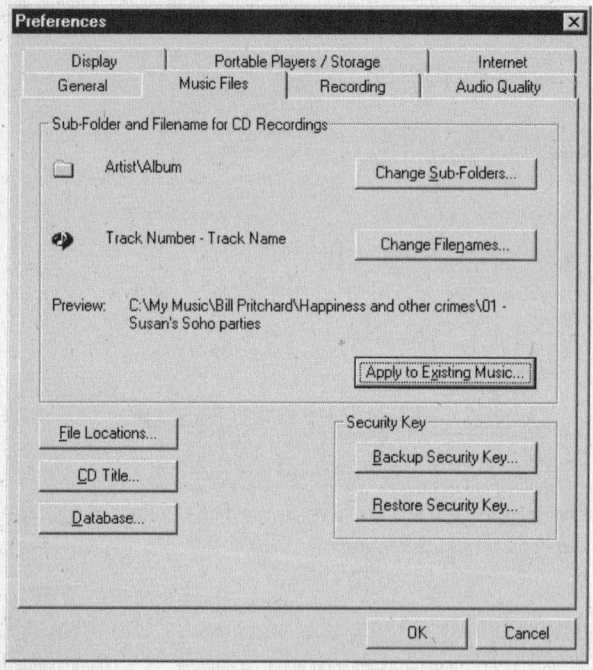

FIGURE 9.26: On the Music Files page of the Preferences dialog box, specify how RealJukebox should name the files it creates for you.

FIGURE 9.27: Use the Change File Naming Convention dialog box to tell RealJukebox how to name the MP3 files you encode from CD.

Close the Preferences dialog box. You're ready to use RealJukebox.

… Windows Jukeboxes 459

Getting around RealJukebox

Start RealJukebox by clicking the RealJukebox icon on your Quick Launch toolbar, by double-clicking the RealJukebox icon in the system tray, by double-clicking the RealJukebox icon on your Desktop, or by choosing Start ➤ Programs ➤ Real ➤ RealJukebox.

RealJukebox has two very different visual modes: Full mode and Skin mode. Full mode is the one you're most likely to see at first—a conventional-looking application window, like the one shown in Figure 9.28.

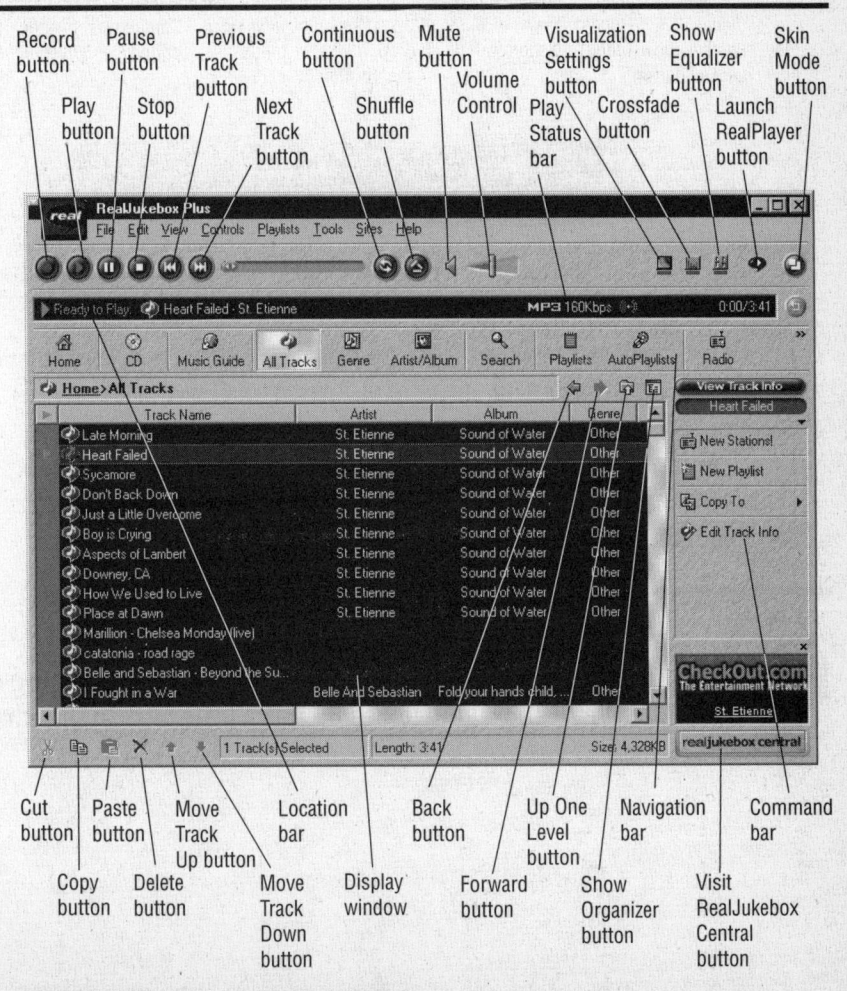

FIGURE 9.28: RealJukebox in Full Mode

Chapter Nine

Most of the buttons and other interface items are easy enough to understand, with the possible exception of the following features:

- Clicking the Visit RealJukebox Central button launches (or activates) your default Web browser and takes you to the RealJukebox Central Web site.

- Clicking the Skin Mode button displays RealJukebox in Skin mode, a mode that applies a custom skin (a look) to RealJukebox. Figure 9.29 shows RealJukebox in Skin mode in its Stainless Steel skin.

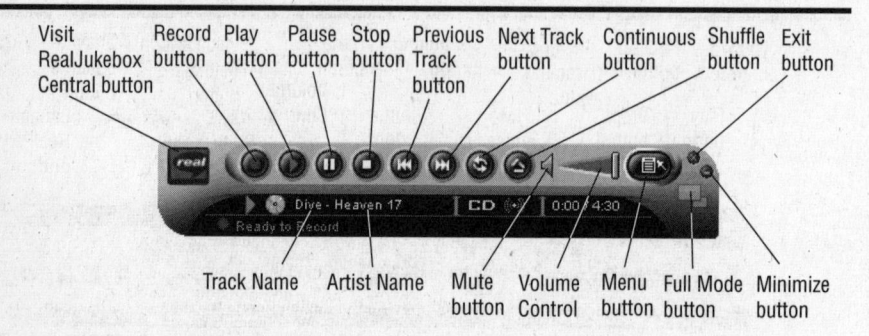

FIGURE 9.29: In Skin Mode, RealJukebox takes up less space and looks far more interesting. This is the built-in Stainless Steel skin.

Again, these buttons and controls are easy enough to understand. As you'd expect, clicking the Full Mode button returns RealJukebox to Full Mode.

> **NOTE**
> You can change RealJukebox's look further by applying other skins. We'll show you how to do this a little later in this chapter.

Ripping

To rip with RealJukebox, put a CD in your CD-ROM drive and close the tray.

If you're connected to the Internet, RealJukebox automatically contacts the CDDB database and returns the CD info—artist name, album name, and track names—if they're available. If RealJukebox isn't able to make a definitive match with an entry in CDDB, it may ask you to choose between two or more entries competing for your attention. Figure 9.30 shows RealJukebox with a CD loaded and CDDB information already looked up.

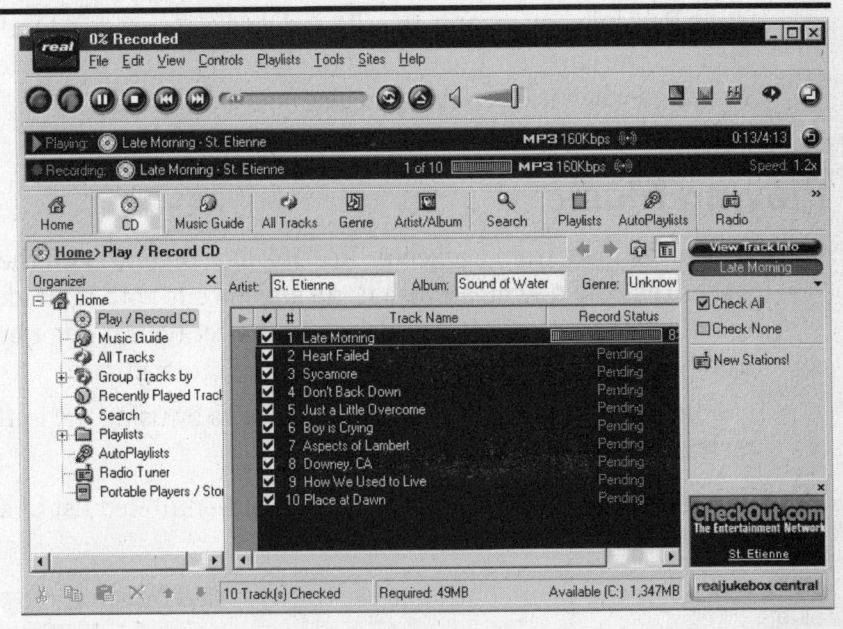

FIGURE 9.30: RealJukebox automatically downloads CD information from CDDB if you're connected to the Internet.

Read through the information that CDDB produces, and edit the titles as necessary. To edit a title, use Windows Explorer techniques:

1. Click a title twice *slowly* (in other words, with a pause between the clicks) to select it and place the insertion point, or select the title and press the F2 key.

2. Press Enter when you've finished modifying the name of the track.

Select the check boxes for the tracks you want to record. (RealJukebox selects them all by default.) Then click the Record button to start ripping and encoding.

As RealJukebox records the CD, it displays its progress and changes the entry for the track in the Record Status column to Recorded when it has finished recording.

Playing Music

As you'd expect from a jukebox, RealJukebox organizes all the tracks that you download with it, rip and encode with it, or identify to it (by letting it search your drives during configuration or by using the Import Wizard on the File menu) into a library.

You can view this library in different views by using the buttons on the Navigation bar:

- Click the All Tracks button to view an unfiltered list of all tracks.

- Click the Genre button to see tracks sorted by genre.

- Click the Artist/Album button to see tracks sorted by artist and album.

Within any view, you can click a column heading to sort in ascending order by that column; click again to sort in descending order.

The Location bar shows you which category you're currently in. If you want a more Explorer-like view of the categories, display the

Windows Jukeboxes 463

Organizer panel by choosing View ➤ Organizer. When you display the Organizer panel, the Navigation bar is largely redundant, and you may want to hide it by choosing View ➤ Navigation Bar.

The easiest way to create a playlist is to select tracks in the current view, then press Ctrl+W or choose Playlists ➤ New Playlist to display the New Playlist dialog box (shown in Figure 9.31 with choices entered). Enter the name for your playlist in step 1, select an option in step 2 if more than one is available, choose a location in step 3 (create a new folder if necessary), and click the OK button.

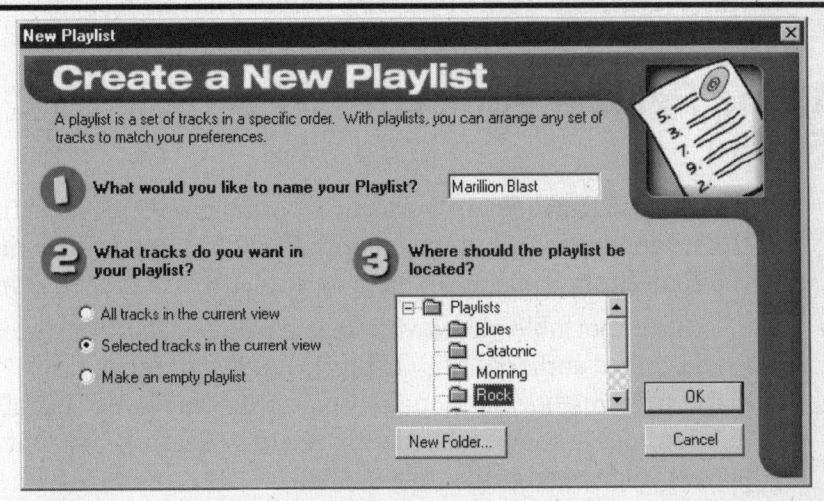

FIGURE 9.31: Use the New Playlist dialog box to start creating a new playlist. You can create a playlist from selected tracks in the current view, from all tracks in the current view, or by adding individual tracks afterwards.

If you chose to create an empty playlist, or if you need to bulk up a playlist, click the Add Tracks button in the Command bar from the Playlists panel and use the Add Tracks dialog box to select and add the tracks.

Then sort your playlist as desired by either dragging the tracks up and down in the playlist or by selecting a track and using the Move Track Up button or Move Track Down button.

RealJukebox automatically saves any changes you make to a playlist, so you don't need to save it explicitly.

Once you've created a playlist, you can play it by selecting it in the Playlists list and clicking the Play button. If you don't have the Playlists panel displayed, display it by clicking the Playlists button on the Navigation bar or the Playlists entry in the Organizer panel.

RealJukebox includes an AutoPlaylist feature that, like Music-Match Jukebox's AutoDJ, attempts to mix a playlist to your specifications. To use the AutoPlaylist feature, choose Playlists for New AutoPlaylist and work in the New AutoPlaylist dialog box.

Using RealJukebox with a Portable MP3 Player

You can use RealJukebox to gas up a portable MP3 player with tracks, and in fact, a number of portable MP3 players, including the Yepp (from Samsung), ship with RealJukebox as their software.

To use a portable player with RealJukebox, install RealJukebox (as described earlier in this chapter), and install the portable player following its instructions. Some portable players' installation routines automatically identify them to RealJukebox, but most players you'll need to identify manually.

Identifying Your Portable MP3 Player to RealJukebox

To identify a portable MP3 player to RealJukebox, connect the player and turn it on. Then choose Tools ➢ Preferences to display the Preferences dialog box and click the Portable Players/Storage tab to display the Portable Players/Storage page. Click the Add button to display the Add Portable Players/Storage dialog box.

Connect to the Internet (if you're not already connected), and click the Update List button to update the list of supported devices. In the list box, select the entry for the portable player you have, and click the OK button. RealJukebox will probably display the Missing Plugin dialog box, telling you that it needs to download a component to add support for the device. Click the OK button and let it proceed.

If downloading the plug-in takes a while, or if your portable player has ADD, the player may switch itself off before RealJukebox identifies it. If so, you'll see a dialog box such as the Driver Problem Detected dialog box (see Figure 9.32). Click the Done button.

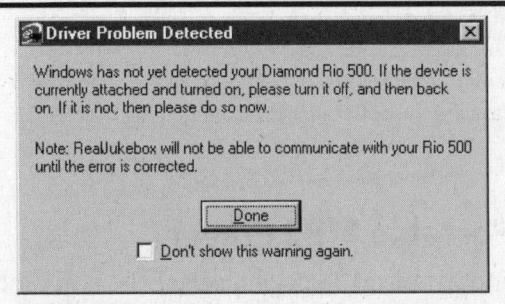

FIGURE 9.32: The Driver Problem Detected dialog box may mean that your portable MP3 player has gone to sleep before RealJukebox could identify it.

Once you've successfully identified a portable player to RealJukebox, you may need to configure it by clicking the Configure button on the Portable Players/Storage page of the Preferences dialog box (Tools ➢ Preferences) and working in the resulting Configure dialog box. Figure 9.33 shows the Configure dialog box with the options for the Diamond Rio 500 player; you'll see different options for other players.

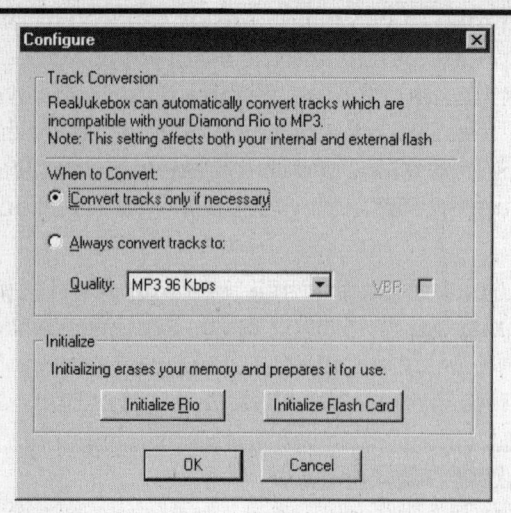

FIGURE 9.33: Use the Configure dialog box to configure your portable MP3 player. These are the options for the Diamond Rio 500 player.

Loading Your Portable MP3 Player

To see what's on your portable MP3 player, select the entry for the portable player (or its external memory) in the Portable Players/Storage tree.

You can add tracks to your portable player by selecting them in the Display window, right-clicking, choosing Copy to Device from the context menu, and specifying the player or component (for example, its internal or external memory) in the Copy to Device dialog box. Alternatively, you can select the player (or its component) in the Portable Players/Storage tree, choosing Tools ≻ Add Tracks to Device, and specifying the tracks in the Add Tracks dialog box.

Removing a Portable MP3 Player from RealJukebox

To remove a portable player from RealJukebox's awareness, select it in the Installed Devices list box on the Portable Players/Storage page of the Preferences dialog box and click the Remove button. You'll need to confirm your decision in the Remove Device dialog box.

Changing RealJukebox's Skin

As you'd guess from its Skin mode, RealJukebox is thoroughly skinnable—you can change its look by applying skins. It comes with several skins, which you can apply at will, and you can download a variety of other skins, both from RealNetworks and from other locations on the Internet.

To change skin, choose View ➤ Skins to display the Skins submenu, then choose the skin you want to apply. Figure 9.34 shows the Wood and Water skin.

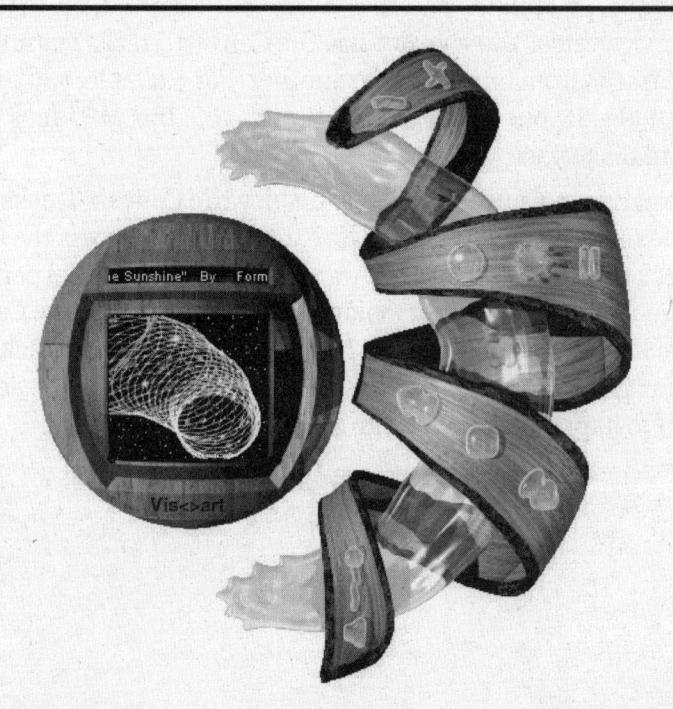

FIGURE 9.34: You can download a wide variety of skins from RealJukebox Central and other Web sites.

If you're looking for skins to download, start at the RealJukebox Central site. To get there, choose View ➤ Skins ➤ Get Skins. RealJukebox fires up your default Web browser and connects to the site. Select a skin, and RealJukebox automatically downloads it.

By default, RealJukebox switches the view to a new skin as soon as you download it. To prevent RealJukebox from doing so, clear the Switch to New Skin after Download check box on the General page of the Preferences dialog box (Tools ➤ Preferences).

Converting Tracks from One Format or Bitrate to Another

RealJukebox lets you convert tracks from one format to another. For example, you might want to convert your RealAudio files to MP3, or vice versa. You can also use the Convert Tracks feature to convert tracks from one bitrate to another. For example, you could downsample all your 320kbps MP3 files to 160kbps MP3 files to save hard disk space.

Choose File ➤ Convert Tracks to display the Convert Tracks dialog box (see Figure 9.35). The first time that you access the Convert Tracks feature, RealJukebox warns you of the potential perils of using the feature. We suggest making sure that the Erase the Current Track from My Hard Drive When Done with Convert Tracks check box is cleared until you've tested Convert Tracks and made sure you're happy with the results it's giving you.

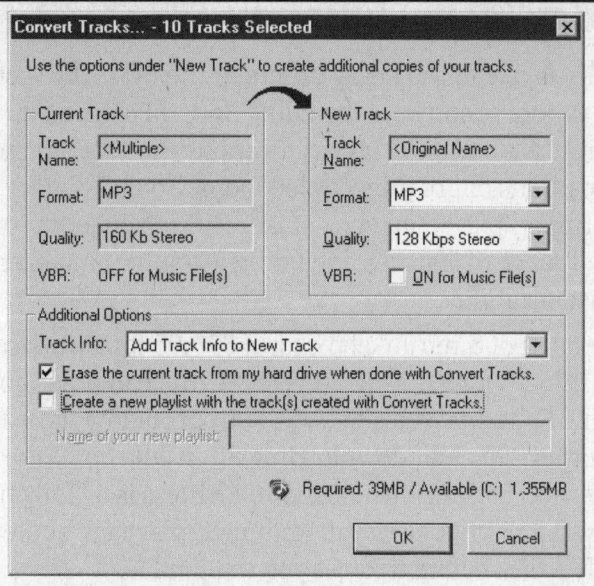

FIGURE 9.35: Use the Convert Tracks dialog box to convert a track from one format to another (for example, from RealAudio to MP3) or from one bitrate to another.

SIREN JUKEBOX AND VISIOSONIC PCDJ

This section describes two other ripper/player/jukeboxes for Windows that you may want to try: Siren Jukebox and Visiosonic PCDJ. Each offers strong features, but we feel that at this point neither stands up to the free version of MusicMatch Jukebox.

Sonic Foundry Siren Jukebox

Sonic Foundry is one of the heavy hitters in the PC-audio scene, producing a variety of software including Sound Forge, an audio-editing application, and Acid Music, its application for assembling music compositions out of prerecorded loops. Sonic Foundry's entry in the ripper/player/jukebox stakes is Siren Jukebox, which provides a full range of features, including a graphic equalizer, skins, and visualizations.

The full version of Siren Jukebox costs $39.95 for a physical package and $35.95 for a download version. You can order both from the Sonic Foundry Web site, www.sonicfoundry.com. Before you pay for either, consider downloading Siren Jukebox XPress, an evaluation version of Siren Jukebox. Siren XPress is a "fully functioning free version" that gives you unlimited playback but lets you encode 20 MP3 files before it forces you to upgrade.

Siren Jukebox and Siren Jukebox XPress use a standard installation routine that should cause you no problems. The first time you start Siren Jukebox, you need to enter your serial number (if you purchased a full copy) or specify that you want to use XPress (with the limitations outlined above). The Configuration Wizard then walks you through configuring Siren Jukebox.

> **WARNING**
>
> By default, Siren Jukebox records to the Windows Media Audio format. To record to MP3 instead, change the setting in the Record to Library Format drop-down list on the Recording page of the Preferences dialog box (Options ≻ Preferences).

Figure 9.36 shows Siren Jukebox XPress in action.

Windows Jukeboxes 471

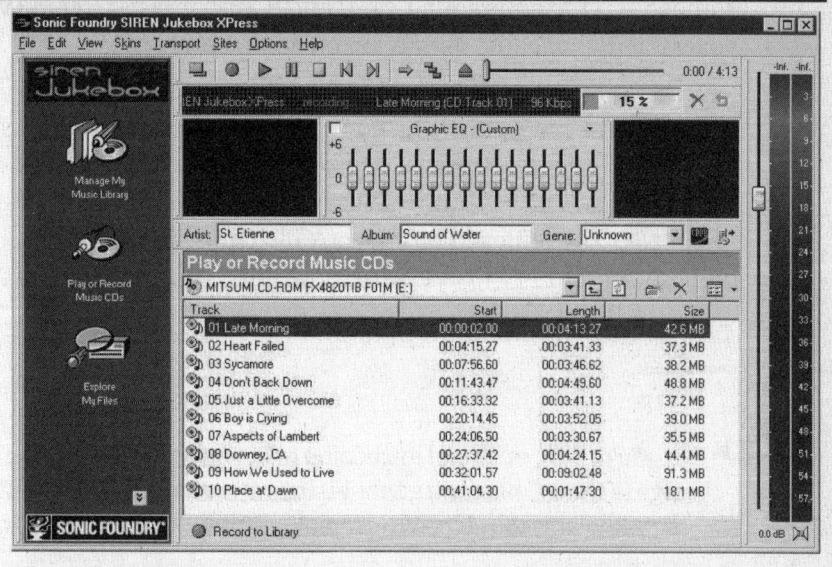

FIGURE 9.36: Siren Jukebox is a competent ripper/player/jukebox from Sonic Foundry. This illustration shows the free XPress version, which we suggest you try before you buy the full version.

Visiosonic PCDJ

Visiosonic PCDJ is something of an anomaly among ripper/player/jukeboxes—it comes in more versions, and at more widely varying price-points, than just about any other ripper/player/jukebox, and most of the versions are specialized tools designed for DJs. All the versions are available from the Visiosonic Web site, www.visiosonic.com.

PCDJ PHAT is a free version that can encode only Windows Media Audio (WMA) files—it can't encode MP3 files. This version is aimed at the average consumer, but it's too limited for most people—especially as it barrages you with ads.

PCDJ Mixmaster is a $49.99 product that supports full MP3 encoding, but at this writing, it has no trial version. PCDJ Mixmaster requires Windows 95 or 98, a Sound Blaster Live! or Turtle Beach

Montego A3D Xtreme sound card, and a 20× or faster CD-ROM capable of digital audio extraction on a hardware level.

PCDJ 1200sl is a $499 product (currently available for $199) that supports encrypted MP3 encoding and is aimed at professional DJs. PCDJ 1200sl has the same hardware requirements as PCDJ Mixmaster but requires either a Sound Blaster Live! sound card or *two* Turtle Beach Montego A3D Xtreme sound cards. If you're interested in PCDJ 1200sl, download the 30-day evaluation version of PCDJ 1200sl.

> **TIP**
>
> If you're a DJ, or intend to become one, you may also want to investigate the PC hardware that Visiosonic makes for DJs. You'll find details of this too at the Visiosonic Web site, www.visiosonic.com.

Up Next

In this chapter, we've examined the two major ripper/player/jukeboxes for Windows—MusicMatch Jukebox and RealPlayer—in some depth. We've also looked briefly at a couple of other ripper/player/jukeboxes for Windows: Siren Jukebox, which is suitable for conventional use, and Visiosonic PCDJ, whose multiple versions are primarily aimed at the DJ market.

In the next part of the book, Part 4, we'll show you how to enjoy MP3 music on the Macintosh. If you're not interested in the Mac, you might skip ahead to Part 5, which discusses MP3 on Linux. If you're not interested in Linux either, pick up the trail in Part 7, which shows you how to publish your own music via MP3; Part 8, which discusses other digital-music formats; or Part 9, which shows you a number of more advanced maneuvers for MP3.

PART IV

MP3 ON THE MACINTOSH

LEARN TO:

- Play MP3 files with QuickTime and RealPlayer Basic
- Make the most of SoundApp and QuickAmp
- Enjoy music with MACAST
- Use GrayAMP and MACAST Lite
- Rip and encode with AudioCatalyst and MPegger
- Use the jukeboxes SoundJam and MusicMatch Jukebox for the Macintosh

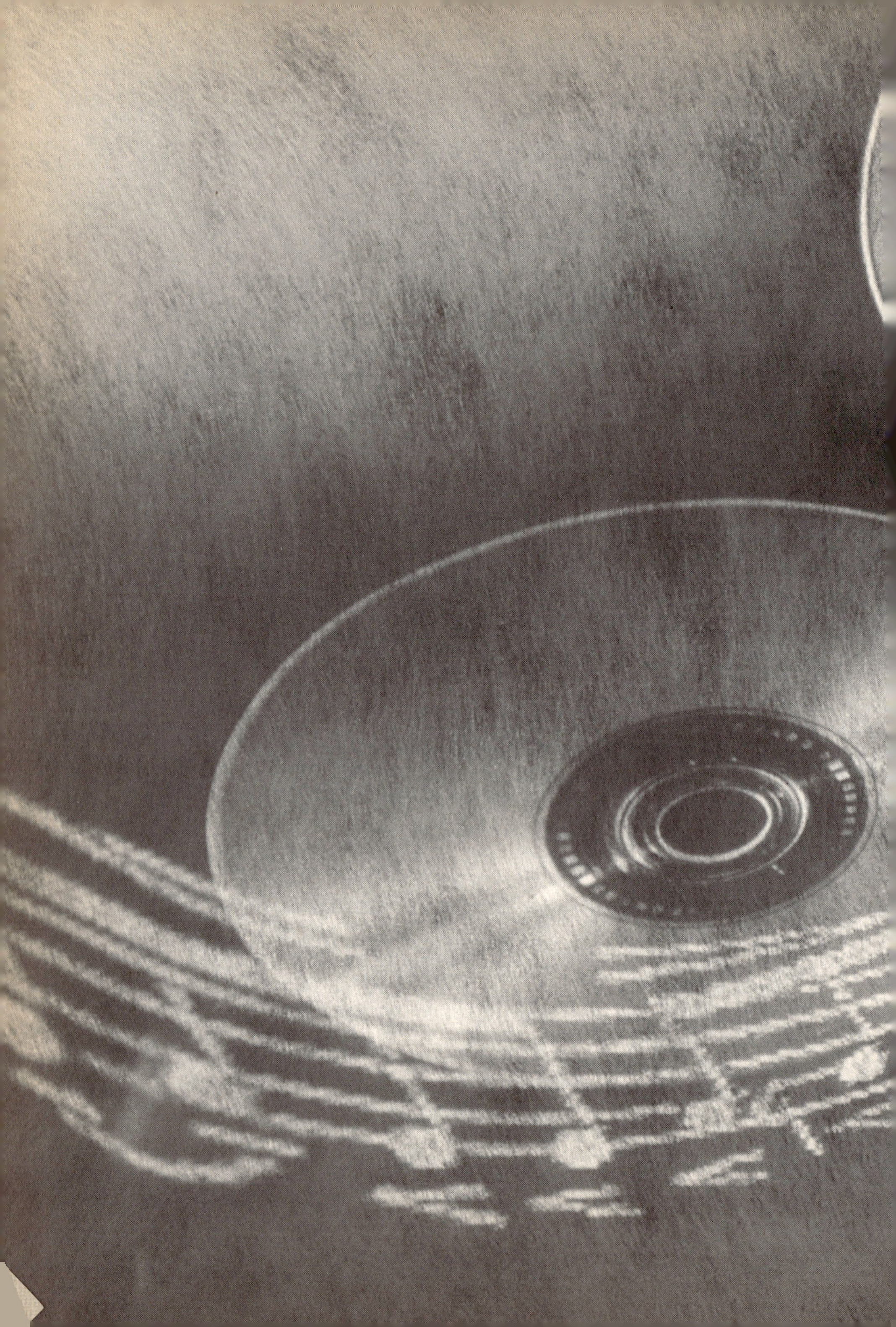

Chapter 10
Macintosh MP3 Players

FEATURING

- Playing MP3 files with QuickTime
- Playing MP3 files with RealPlayer Basic
- SoundApp
- QuickAmp
- MACAST
- GrayAMP
- MACAST Lite

In this chapter, we'll discuss the best MP3 players for the Macintosh: SoundApp (which is free), QuickAmp (which is free), MACAST (which costs $24.95), and GrayAMP (which is free). We'll also briefly discuss MACAST Lite (which costs $15), and two applications that you may already have that you can use to play MP3 files in a pinch: RealPlayer Basic and QuickTime.

As with many other kinds of software, your choices of MP3 software for the Mac are much more limited than those for Windows, mostly because the Mac market is much smaller than the Windows market, so fewer developers can make a decent living developing applications for the Mac. But although there's not the overabundance of choices that you'll find for Windows, some of the software written for the Mac is as good as (if not better than) its Windows counterparts, and you'll have no problem creating and enjoying MP3 files on the Mac.

Playing MP3 Files with QuickTime and RealPlayer Basic

If you're unwilling or unable to install any software on your Macintosh (for example, in a school or business environment), you may already have on your Mac one or both of two widespread applications that you can use to play MP3 files: QuickTime from Apple and RealPlayer Basic from RealNetworks. Neither is a dedicated MP3 player, but each can handle the MP3 file format well enough. Neither has the sophisticated features of dedicated MP3 players such as those you'll meet later in the chapter, though, so we doubt you'll want to use them for playing MP3 files if you have a choice.

If you have neither QuickTime nor RealPlayer Basic, you can get them easily enough. They're so necessary for watching and listening to multimedia on your Mac that you should be able to persuade your system administrator to install them for you without even needing to mention the dreaded term "MP3."

Playing MP3 Files with QuickTime

If you don't have QuickTime, go to www.apple.com, click the QuickTime tab, and you'll be up and running in no time.

To play an MP3 file with QuickTime, choose File ➢ Open Movie (life's a movie to QuickTime). Select the MP3 file in the resulting dialog box and click the Convert button. QuickTime opens the file and along the way, converts it to a format that QuickTime can handle. (The MP3 file on the disk remains intact.)

You can then play the file using the QuickTime controls as usual. QuickTime doesn't provide a full equalizer, but you can tweak the sound a little. From QuickTime's default compressed manifestation (shown in the upper part of Figure 10.1), click the Expand button (the one with the four dots on it) to display the expanded window (shown in the lower part of Figure 10.1) with the full set of controls. Now you have access to the balance, bass, and treble controls, which can help you remedy major equalization disasters but don't give you the fine-tuning capabilities of a graphic equalizer.

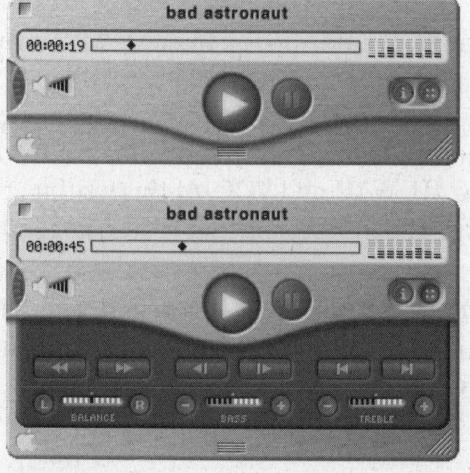

FIGURE 10.1: You can use QuickTime to play MP3 files in a pinch.

Playing MP3 Files with RealPlayer Basic

If you don't have RealPlayer Basic, you can download it from www.real.com. RealPlayer Basic is free, but if you want, you can go for RealPlayer Plus, which will set you back $29.99.

To play an MP3 file with RealPlayer Basic, drag the MP3 file and drop it on RealPlayer, which starts playing it. Alternatively, use the File ≻ Open File command to open a file or the File ≻ Open Location command to open a stream. You can then use the RealPlayer controls as usual. Figure 10.2 shows RealPlayer Basic in Compact view (View ≻ Compact) playing an MP3 file.

FIGURE 10.2: RealPlayer Basic can also play MP3 files.

SoundApp

Created by Norman Franke, SoundApp is a freeware MP3 player that supports playlists and can perform batch conversions of files. The price is right, and SoundApp is an effective player. SoundApp 2.7 supports MP3 and a multitude of digital-audio formats including AIFF, QuickTime MOV, AU, WAV, and VOC. At this writing, the one serious disadvantage of SoundApp is that it does not support streaming audio.

SoundApp requires MacOS System 7 or better and Sound Manager 3.1 or greater; if you have System 7.5.3 or higher, you'll have Sound Manager already.

Macintosh MP3 Players 479

Download the latest version of SoundApp from the SoundApp Web site, www-cs-students.stanford.edu/~franke/SoundApp/, and unstuff the distribution file if it doesn't unstuff itself.

You can then run SoundApp by double-clicking the SoundApp icon. Alternatively, you can drag an MP3 or other file in a supported audio file over the SoundApp icon and drop it there. SoundApp takes over the menu bar and displays the SoundApp Status window and Controls window, shown in Figure 10.3. (If you don't see the Controls window, press Apple+H or choose Options ≻ Show Controls.) If you drag and drop an MP3 file, SoundApp just starts playing it.

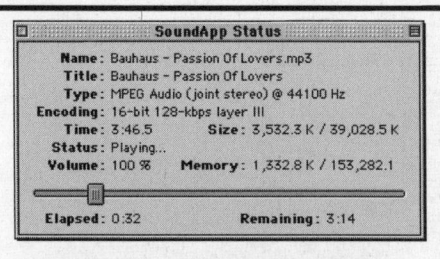

FIGURE 10.3: SoundApp is a freeware MP3 player with impressive capabilities for everything but playing streaming audio.

To open one or more files, click the Play button in the Controls window when SoundApp isn't playing. Use the resulting Play: SoundApp PPC dialog box to navigate to and select the file or files and then click the Play button.

The SoundApp playback and volume controls are easy to manipulate with the mouse. You can also adjust the volume from the keyboard by pressing Apple+= to increase the volume and Apple+- to decrease it.

Creating and Using Playlists

When you add MP3 files as described in the previous section, SoundApp doesn't automatically create a playlist that you can save, but you can create a playlist as follows:

1. Choose File ➤ New Play List, or press Apple+N, to open an untitled playlist window.

2. Add MP3 files to the playlist by using the Add SoundApp dialog box (File ➤ Add, or Apple+D) or by dragging files to the playlist window and dropping them there. Figure 10.4 shows a playlist under construction.

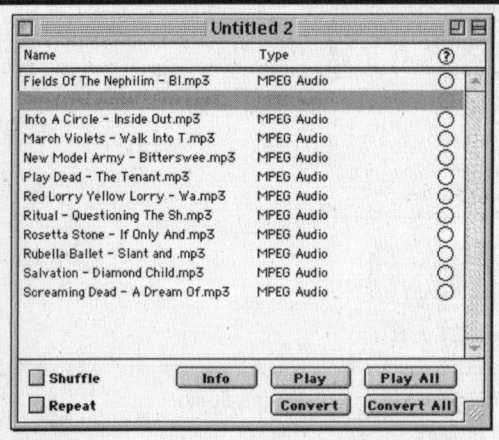

FIGURE 10.4: Creating a playlist in SoundApp

3. Drag the tracks up and down in the playlist window to get them into the order you want. To remove any track you don't want, select it and press the Delete key.

4. Choose File ➤ Save to display the Save: SoundApp dialog box, specify the location and name for the playlist, and click the Save button.

To play the playlist, click the Play All button in the playlist window. To shuffle or repeat tracks, select the Shuffle check box and Repeat check box first.

To close a playlist, choose File ➢ Close. To open a playlist, choose File ➢ Open, or press Apple+O, to display the Open: SoundApp dialog box. Navigate to and select the playlist, and click the Open button.

Viewing the Information for a File

To view the information for a file, select it in the playlist and click the Info button. SoundApp displays the Info dialog box (see Figure 10.5) with the information for the track, including the path to its location, its encoding information, and its bitrate. Click the Show Original button in the Info dialog box to open the folder containing the file.

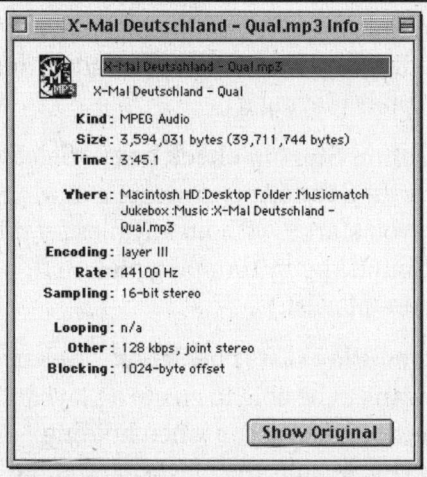

FIGURE 10.5: Use the Info dialog box to view the information on a file.

Choosing Preferences in SoundApp

To make SoundApp behave as you want it to, and to make it produce the best sound, you probably need to change some settings. Choose Options ➢ Preferences to display the Preferences dialog box and set the appropriate options for your needs.

The following sections discuss the options on the five pages of the Preferences dialog box that are relevant to playing MP3 files and audio CDs. (We don't discuss the options on the MIDI page and the MOD page because these apply only to MIDI files and MOD files, respectively.)

Each page contains a Use Defaults button and a Revert button. Each Use Defaults button reapplies the default settings for that page. Each Revert button reapplies the previously saved settings.

General Page Preferences

The General page of the Preferences dialog box (see Figure 10.6) offers the following options:

Auto Quit When Done check box   Select this check box to cause SoundApp to quit when it has finished playing its current playlist (including any tracks that you add to the playlist while SoundApp is playing it).

New Untitled Play List on Startup check box   Select this check box if you want SoundApp to create a new, untitled playlist when you start it without any files for it to process. (If you start SoundApp by dropping files on it, SoundApp won't create a playlist.)

Auto Play Drag-Created Play Lists check box   Select this check box if you want to be able to create a playlist by dragging files onto the SoundApp icon when holding down the playlist key. (By default, the playlist key is the Option key, but you can change this setting on the Keys page of the Preferences dialog box.)

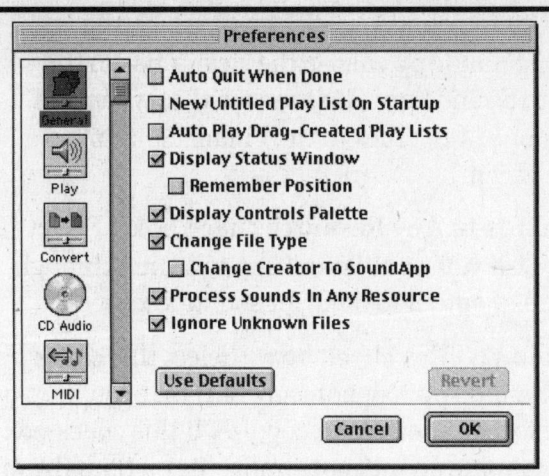

FIGURE 10.6: Choose SoundApp-wide options on the General page of the Preferences dialog box.

Display Status Window check box and Remember Position check box   Select the Display Status Window check box to make SoundApp display the Status window by default. Select the Remember Position check box if you want SoundApp to remember the position of the Status window (and put it in the same place each time you start SoundApp).

Display Controls Palette check box   Select this check box to make SoundApp display the Controls palette by default.

Change File Type check box and Change Creator to SoundApp check box   Select the Change File Type check box if you want SoundApp to change the file types of sound files you play that have the file type set incorrectly. Selecting the Change File Type check box enables the

Change Creator to SoundApp check box, which you can select to have SoundApp change the creator flag of the sound files to SoundApp. (This means that when you double-click one of the files in the Finder, SoundApp launches to play it.)

Process Sounds In Any Resource check box Select this check box if you want SoundApp to search through all files dropped onto it looking for sound resources.

Ignore Unknown Files check box Select this check box if you want SoundApp to ignore any files that you drop on it whose file format it cannot recognize. If this check box is cleared, dropping an unrecognizable file on SoundApp results in an error dialog box.

Play Page Preferences

The Play page of the Preferences dialog box (see Figure 10.7) contains the following options:

Play a/µ-Law As 8-Bit check box and Smart a/µ-Law Playback check box If you have a Mac that isn't capable of 16-bit playback, select the Play a/µ-Law As 8-Bit check box to have SoundApp perform linear interpolation and play back µ-law and a-law files at 8-bit resolution. Selecting the Play a/µ-Law As 8-Bit check box enables the Smart a/µ-Law Playback check box, which you can select to make SoundApp prescan µ-law and a-law files to find the best scaling factor for 8-bit playback.

Default Sampling Rate drop-down list Use this drop-down list to set the sampling rate at which you want SoundApp to play sound files that do not have headers.

Macintosh MP3 Players 485

(Usually, uncompressed SoundCap files are the only files in this category. With MP3 files, you don't need to worry about this setting.)

Double Buffer (K) drop-down list Use this drop-down list to control the size of the buffer SoundApp uses for playing files. The choices are Don't, 64, 96 (the default), 128, 192, 256, 384, or 512. If you have plenty of memory, you may want to try the Don't setting, which forces SoundApp to load the entire sound file into memory before starting to play it.

Volume drop-down list Use this drop-down list to set the SoundApp playback volume relative to the system volume. The default setting is 100%, which typically gives good results. You can boost the setting above 100% (the range is 10% to 150%) to get more volume (but that may distort the audio) or lower it to reduce the overall volume.

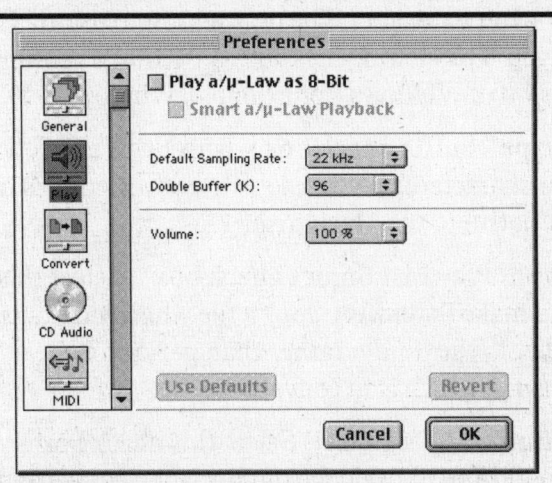

FIGURE 10.7: Choose playback options on the Play page of the Preferences dialog box.

Convert Page Preferences

The Convert page of the Preferences dialog box (see Figure 10.8) offers the following options for converting sound files into output files:

Convert a/µ-Law As 8-Bit check box and Smart a/µ-Law Conversion check box If you have a Mac that isn't capable of 16-bit playback, select the Convert a/µ-Law As 8-Bit check box to have SoundApp perform linear interpolation and convert µ-law and a-law files at 8-bit resolution. Selecting the Convert a/µ-Law As 8-Bit check box enables the Smart a/µ-Law Conversion check box, which you can select to make SoundApp pre-scan µ-law and a-law files to find the best scaling factor for 8-bit conversion.

DOSify Output Filenames check box Select this check box only if you want SoundApp to save the converted files with filenames in the 8.3 format—an 8-character filename and a 3-character extension. The only reason to use this option is if you'll be sharing files with a PC that's running a 16-bit version of Windows (for example, Windows 3.1).

Append ".type" Suffix check box Select this check box to add three-character file extensions to converted files in formats not native to the Macintosh.

Dragging from Play List Copies check box Select this check box to make SoundApp copy a file when you drag it from a playlist to the Finder rather than perform its default behavior, which is to convert the file.

Use Large Buffers check box Select this check box if you want SoundApp to use large buffers when converting files.

Macintosh MP3 Players

Output Location drop-down list Use this drop-down list to specify how SoundApp creates output files. Your choices are as follows:

- The Auto-Create Folder item automatically creates a folder in the folder where the first file is located. SoundApp then places all the converted files in the new folder.

- The Prompt for New Folder item makes SoundApp display a dialog box asking where you want to place all the converted files.

- The Prompt for Each File item makes SoundApp display a dialog box asking where you want to place each converted file.

- The Prompt for Existing Folder item makes Sound-App display a dialog box asking you to select an existing folder in which to place the converted files.

- The Use "Convert To" Folder item places all files in the folder that you specify by using the Set button.

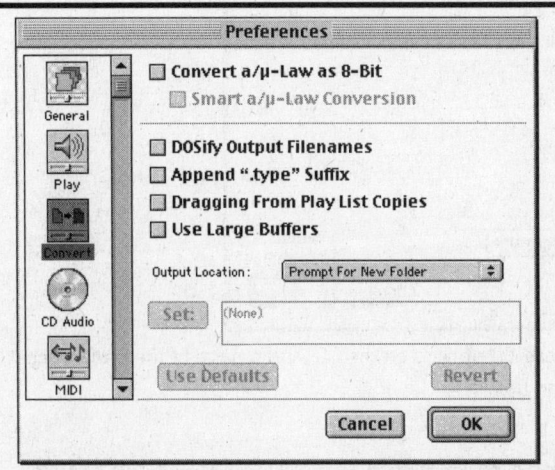

FIGURE 10.8: Choose file-conversion options on the Convert page of the Preferences dialog box.

CD Audio Page Preferences

The CD Audio page of the Preferences dialog box (see Figure 10.9) contains these options:

Monopolize CPU While Importing check box   Select this check box to make SoundApp not yield precedence to background tasks that your Mac is running when SoundApp is converting a CD audio track. Because selecting this check box can interrupt other tasks by hogging the processor, it's best to use this option only if you have problems when converting audio from CDs.

High-Speed Import check box   Select this option (which is selected by default) to have SoundApp use the capabilities of a multi-speed CD-ROM drive to read data faster. Clear this option if you're having trouble converting audio from CDs.

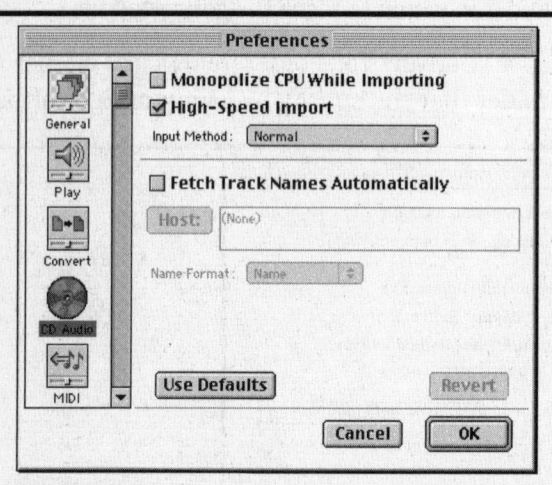

FIGURE 10.9:   Choose CD options on the CD Audio page of the Preferences dialog box.

Input Method drop-down list   Use this check box to specify how SoundApp should read the blocks of audio data on a CD. Use the default setting, Normal, unless you're having problems with clicks and pops. In that case, use the slower Overlap on Sync Loss setting, which causes SoundApp to reread some data to ensure that it gets a continuous data stream.

Fetch Track Names Automatically check box Select this check box to make SoundApp automatically connect to a CDDB server to download CD and track information. Selecting the Fetch Track Names Automatically check box enables the Host button and the Name Format drop-down list. Click the Host button and use the resulting CDDB Host Selection dialog box (see Figure 10.10) to select the CDDB host you want to use, and then click the OK button. Use the Name Format drop-down list to specify the track name format for SoundApp to use.

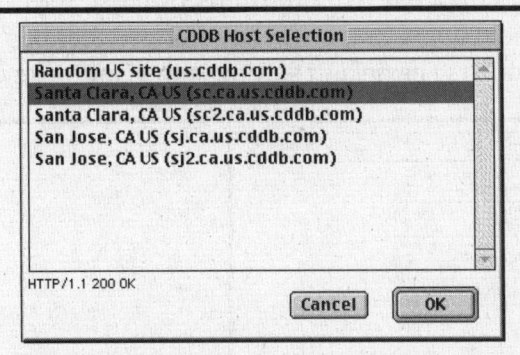

FIGURE 10.10: If you choose to have SoundApp download CD information automatically, select the CDDB host you want to use in the CDDB Host Selection dialog box.

Keys Page Preferences

The Keys page of the Preferences dialog box (see Figure 10.11) provides four drop-down lists for specifying what happens when you hold down a modifier key (for example, the Ctrl key or the Option key) when dragging files onto SoundApp:

Play drop-down list   In this drop-down list, select the key to be held down to specify that dropped files be played. The default setting is None, so that when you drop files on SoundApp without holding down a key, SoundApp starts to play them.

Convert drop-down list   In this drop-down list, select the key to be held down to specify that the dropped files be converted. The default setting is the Shift key.

Dialog drop-down list   In this drop-down list, select the key to be held down (at the same time as the Convert key) to cause SoundApp to display the Conversion Parameters dialog box when you drop files on SoundApp. The default setting is the Ctrl key.

Play List drop-down list   In this drop-down list, select the key to be hold down to specify that dropped files be placed in a play list. The default setting is the Option key.

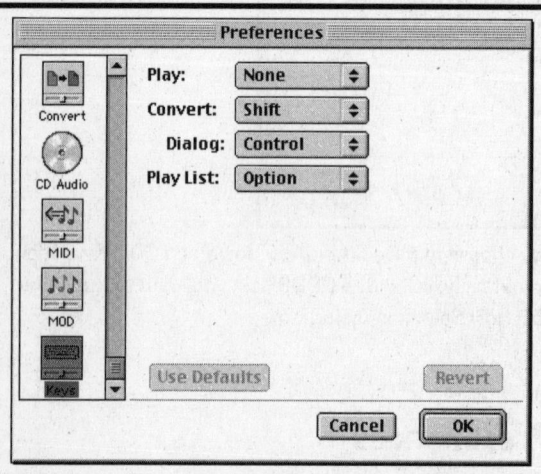

FIGURE 10.11: Choose keyboard assignments for SoundApp on the Keys page of the Preferences dialog box.

QuickAmp

QuickAmp is a free player with several attractive features, including support for playlists and skins. It also has a Timer feature that lets you shut down QuickAmp—and, if you choose, your Mac as well—after a specified time, so you can use QuickAmp to lull yourself to sleep. Against this, it lacks a graphic equalizer.

Download the latest version of QuickAmp from the QuickAmp site, `homepage.mac.com/gtijerino/index.html`, and unstuff it if it doesn't automatically unstuff itself. Then run QuickAmp by double-clicking the QuickAmp icon in the QuickAmp folder created by the installation.

At first, QuickAmp appears in its minimized format (see Figure 10.12). As you can see in this figure, the play controls are more or less conventional—Stop, Play, Pause, Rewind, and Fast Forward buttons, plus a Select button—but the Play, Rewind, and Select buttons also have downward-pointing arrows that produce drop-down menus:

- The Play button's drop-down menu offers a Play Selected item (for playing the currently selected tracks) and a Play Random item for playing random tracks.

- The Rewind button's drop-down menu offers the choices Rewind Current (rewind to the start of the current track) and Play Previous.

- The Select button's drop-down menu lists the tracks in the playlist, letting you easily start any track playing.

FIGURE 10.12: QuickAmp in its minimized format offers quick access to tracks through its Select button's drop-down menu.

To create a playlist, you'll need to display QuickAmp in its enlarged format, which includes the playlist editor. To display QuickAmp in the enlarged format, click the short, thin, darker line below the Rewind button. (You can barely see this line in Figure 10.12.) Figure 10.13 shows QuickAmp in its enlarged format.

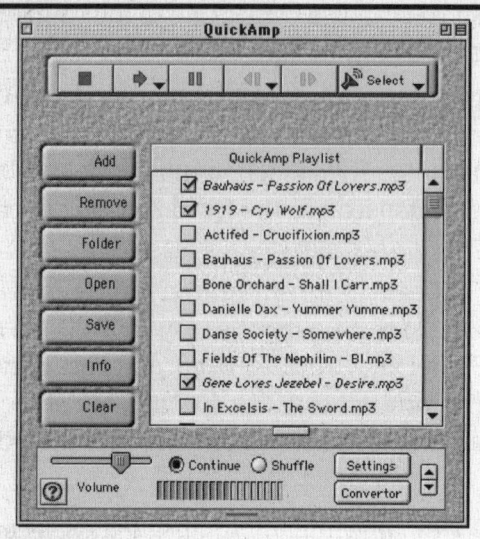

FIGURE 10.13: QuickAmp's enlarged format includes the playlist editor.

To return QuickAmp to its minimized state, click the short dark line again.

Creating and Using Playlists in QuickAmp

To get music playing in QuickAmp, you need to create a playlist. To do so, display QuickAmp in its enlarged format (as described in the previous section) and add tracks or a folder as follows:

▶ To add a track, click the Add button, use the resulting Open dialog box to navigate to and select the track, and click the Open button.

- To add all the tracks in a folder, click the Folder button, use the resulting dialog box to navigate to and select the folder, and click the Choose button. QuickAmp adds all the tracks in the folder to the playlist in alphabetical order of their filenames.

To remove a track from the playlist, select it and click the Remove button. (It's much quicker to add a folder's worth of tracks and then remove some that you don't want than to add individual tracks one by one.)

To move a track up or down the playlist, select it and click the up-arrow button or down-arrow button in the lower-right corner of the QuickAmp window as appropriate.

To save the playlist, click the Save button. QuickAmp displays the Save Options dialog box shown in Figure 10.14 to let you specify whether to save all the tracks in the playlist or to save only the tracks that you've marked (by checking their check boxes). Choose the Marked button or the Save All button as appropriate; then use the Save dialog box to save the playlist.

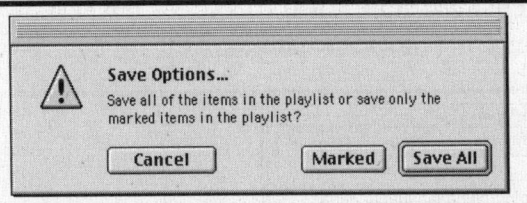

FIGURE 10.14: When you're saving a playlist, QuickAmp lets you specify whether you want to save all the tracks in the playlist or only the marked (selected) items.

To open a playlist you've saved, click the Open button. Use the resulting Open dialog box to navigate to and select the playlist, and then click the Open button.

> **WARNING**
>
> If you value the changes you've made to your current playlist, save it before opening a new playlist. Otherwise, QuickAmp discards the changes.

Choosing Settings for QuickAmp

To get the performance and the aspect you want from QuickAmp, you'll need to choose settings to suit your needs. To choose settings for QuickAmp, click the Preferences button in the QuickAmp window, or choose Edit ➤ Preferences, to display the Settings dialog box.

The General page of the Settings dialog box (see Figure 10.15) offers the following options:

Gradual Window Growth check box Select this check box (which is selected by default) if you want QuickAmp to use a scrolling effect when switching between its small state and its enlarged state. Clear this check box if you want the change to take place more rapidly.

FIGURE 10.15: The General page of the Settings dialog box

Live Window Dragging check box Select this check box to improve how QuickAmp looks when you drag the window about. (This check box didn't have much effect on our Mac.)

Reverse Controls check box Select this check box to switch positions of the play controls (the buttons that appear in QuickAmp's small mode and at the top of the window in enlarged mode) and the set of controls that appear at the bottom of the window in enlarged mode (the volume control and so on). Figure 10.16 shows Quick-Amp with the controls "reversed."

FIGURE 10.16: QuickAmp lets you switch the position of its upper and lower controls.

Sound Monitoring check box Select this check box to enable sound-in monitoring.

Allow Songs to Repeat check box   Select this check box if you want to songs to be allowed to repeat during random play.

Enable Keyboard Support check box   Select this check box to enable keyboard control of play. Press the spacebar to start and stop play; press ↑ and ↓ to select a track in the playlist, and then press Return to play it.

The Playlist page of the Settings dialog box (see Figure 10.17) contains the following settings:

Remember Playlist check box   Select this check box if you want QuickAmp to remember changes to your playlists and to save track information with the playlists.

Play on Startup check box   Select this check box (if it is available) to make QuickAmp play on startup.

Enable Drag & Drop check box   Select this check box (if it is available) to enable you to use drag-and-drop in QuickAmp.

FIGURE 10.17: Choose playlist settings on the Playlist page of the Settings dialog box.

Text Font drop-down list   In this list, select the font you want to use for text in the QuickAmp window.

Text Size drop-down list In this list, select the font size you want in the QuickAmp window.

Playlist Item Playing icon To change the icon for the currently playing track in the playlist, click the icon and use the resulting Open dialog box to select the icon you want.

Playlist Item Not Playing icon To change the icon for non-playing tracks in the playlist, click the icon and use the resulting Open dialog box to select the icon you want.

The Appearance page of the Settings dialog box (see Figure 10.18) lets you change the appearance of QuickAmp, including the color for the three levels of volume LEDs, the panel color, and the rollover color (the color that the text in a clickable box changes to when you move the mouse pointer over the box).

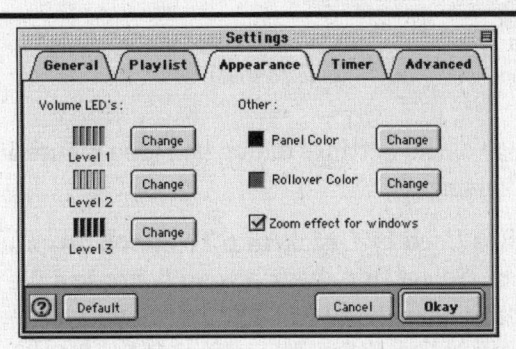

FIGURE 10.18: You can change the color scheme for QuickAmp on the Appearance page of the Settings dialog box.

The Timer page of the Settings dialog box (see Figure 10.19) contains three settings for QuickAmp's Timer feature:

Timer Settings slider Use this slider to specify the length of time for which the timer is to run. QuickAmp supports settings in 10-minute increments from 10 minutes up to 90 minutes.

Quit QuickAmp check box Select this check box if you want QuickAmp to quit after the specified time.

Quit and Shut Down System check box Select this check box if you want QuickAmp to shut down not only itself but also your system.

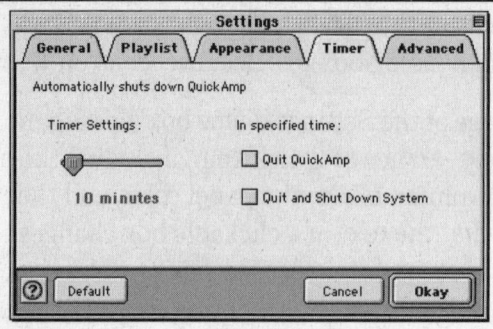

FIGURE 10.19: Use the Timer page of the Settings dialog box to specify when and how QuickAmp should shut down.

The Advanced page of the Settings dialog box (see Figure 10.20) contains these four settings:

Convert All Files Used by QuickAmp To check box and drop-down list Select this check box and choose a file format in the drop-down list if you want to convert all the files that you play in QuickAmp to a different file format. (For example, you could convert the files to the Quick-Time format.)

Enable Visual Plugins check box and drop-down list Select this check box and choose a plug-in in the drop-down list if you want to use visual plug-ins with QuickAmp. (This check box is disabled if the functionality is not available.)

Macintosh MP3 Players

Enabled Folder Scanning check box Select this check box if you want QuickAmp to be able to scan your folders for music files. (This check box is disabled if the functionality is not available.)

Simple Controls (Less Functions) check box Select this check box if you want QuickAmp to display a smaller set of controls for simplicity. (This check box is disabled if the functionality is not available.)

FIGURE 10.20: You can choose four extra options on the Advanced page of the Settings dialog box.

Adding Information to Tracks

QuickAmp doesn't support ID3 tag editing as such, but it lets you add information to tracks. To do so, select the track in the playlist and click the Info button to display the Info dialog box (see Figure 10.21). Enter the information as appropriate—including a volume setting if you want to specify one—and click the Okay button. To save the information, you need either to save the playlist or you need to have the Remember Playlist check box on the Playlist page of the Settings dialog box selected.

Chapter Ten

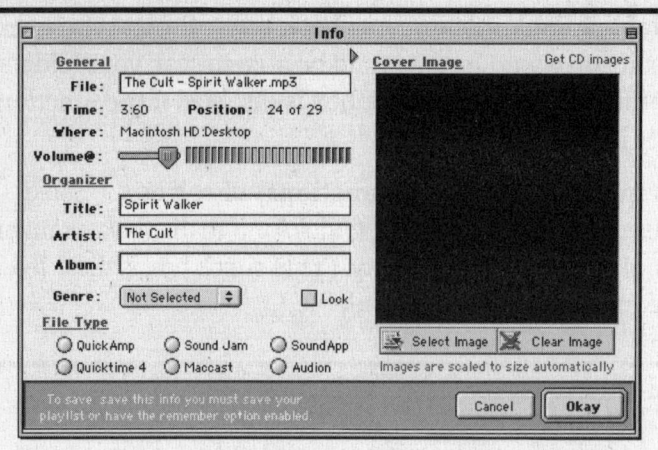

FIGURE 10.21: QuickAmp lets you add information to tracks, including the volume at which you want them to play.

Applying Skins to QuickAmp

QuickAmp supports skins, which let you apply a different look to the player in seconds. You can download a variety of skins from the QuickAmp home page.

To change a skin:

1. Choose Appearance ➢ Custom/Other. QuickAmp displays the Custom Skin Info dialog box (see Figure 10.22).

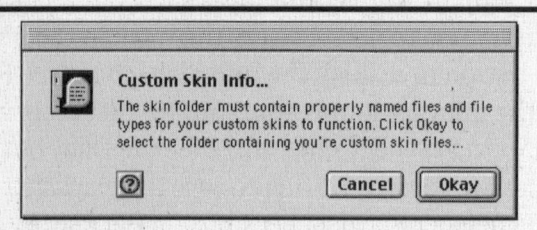

FIGURE 10.22: The Custom Skin Info dialog box

2. Click the Okay button. QuickAmp displays an untitled dialog box.

3. Navigate to and select the folder that contains the skin you want to apply.
4. Click the Choose button. QuickAmp applies the skin.

Figure 10.23 shows QuickAmp using the Thunderstorm skin.

FIGURE 10.23: QuickAmp wearing the Thunderstorm skin

To restore the default theme, press Apple+O, or choose Appearance ➢ Default Theme.

MACAST

From @soft, MACAST (formerly MacAMP) is a slick and friendly player whose features include support for SHOUTcast and icecast streaming audio, full graphic equalization, visualizations, skin support, and a sleep timer that can even shut down your computer (if you tell it to). MACAST is shareware that costs $24.95. It requires a PowerPC processor, MacOS System 7 or (preferably) System 8 or System 9, and 4MB of available RAM. @soft offers a demo version of MACAST that can play only the first two minutes of each track. As far as we can judge, this limitation is enough to force most people to pay for the registered version—or head for a free player such as SoundApp or GrayAMP.

To get the latest version of MACAST, visit www.macamp.net. Double-click the distribution file to unstuff MACAST—if it doesn't unstuff itself automatically. MACAST automatically configures some Web browsers, such as Internet Explorer, to play MP3 files directly from your browser. If you're using Netscape, you're probably out of luck; you'll need to configure the MPEG Audio Stream item manually in the Preferences dialog box.

Installing MACAST presents no problems. Unstuff the distribution file if necessary, then run the installer. You get to choose between the default Easy Install option, which gives you a full installation of MACAST, and a Custom Install option, which lets you choose the elements of MACAST. Figure 10.24 shows the MACAST Installer dialog box for the Custom Install.

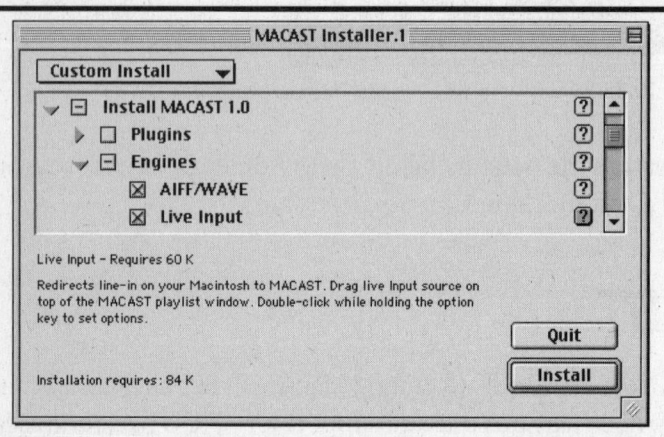

FIGURE 10.24: If you want to specify which elements of MACAST are installed, choose the Custom Install option.

Macintosh MP3 Players

After that, choose which disk to install MACAST onto, and the installation is on its way. To launch MACAST, double-click the MACAST icon in the folder created by the installation routine.

The first time you run MACAST, it displays the Welcome dialog box, which sings the virtues of registration (it'll make MACAST work properly) and offers you information on how to get it. Click the OK button to proceed with your evaluation of MACAST.

Playing Music

In its default skin, MACAST offers a straightforward interface, as you can see in Figure 10.25.

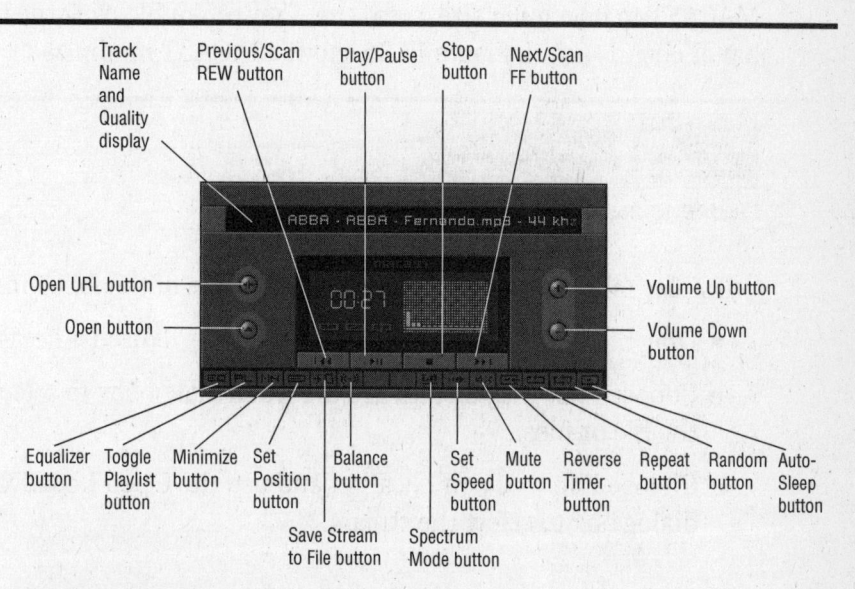

FIGURE 10.25: MACAST in its default skin

MACAST is easy to use with the mouse, but you'll probably want to use the following keyboard controls as well:

Action	Key
Play	Spacebar
Pause	Spacebar

Action	Key
Next track	Tab
Previous track	Shift+Tab
Decrease volume	←
Increase volume	→
Minimize MACAST	` (the accent key, not the single quote key)

At its regular size, MACAST doesn't take up much space, but you can minimize it by clicking the Minimize button, pressing the ` key (the accent key), or double-clicking its title bar or chassis. To restore MACAST to its regular size, press the ` key or double-click the title bar or chassis again. Figure 10.26 shows MACAST minimized.

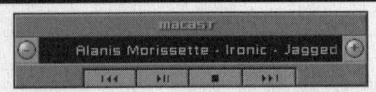

FIGURE 10.26: You can also minimize MACAST.

To play music with MACAST, you can do one of the following:

- Drag files to the Playlist window (which we'll discuss next).
- Choose File ➤ Open and use the Open dialog box to select the file or files.
- Choose File ➤ Open Location and use the Open Location dialog box to select the stream.

Creating and Using Playlists

Here's how to use playlists with MACAST:

- Click the Toggle Playlist button to display the Playlist window, shown in Figure 10.27 with a playlist created and playing. Tracks that haven't yet been played appear in white; tracks that have been played appear in dull green; and the active track is highlighted. The Elapsed Time readout at the bottom of the Playlist window shows how much of the playlist has been played so far, together with the total playlist time.

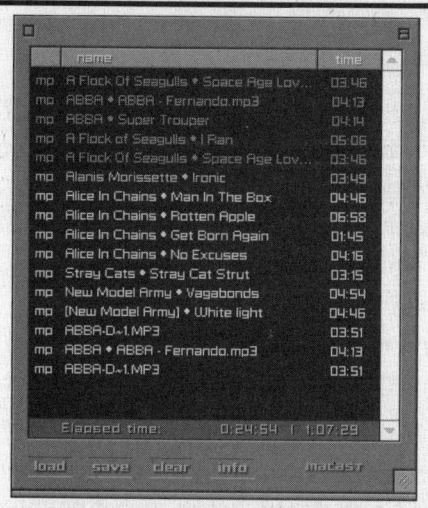

FIGURE 10.27: Use the Playlist window to create and play playlists.

- To add tracks to the playlist, drag tracks to the Playlist window and drop them there. You can drag tracks from a CD to a playlist by opening a window for the CD.

- To arrange the playlist, drag tracks up and down.

- To save a playlist, click the Save button. In the Save dialog box, specify the name and location for the playlist, and then click the Save button to save it.

- To load a playlist, click the Load button. In the Open dialog box, select the playlist you want to load, and click the Open button to open it.

- To clear a playlist, click the Clear button.

- To make MACAST remember your current playlist between sessions, select the Remember Playlist check box on the Playlist page of the Preferences dialog box.

> To make MACAST pick up playing your playlist from where you ended your last session, select the Resume Playlist check box on the Playlist page of the Preferences dialog box.

Using the Equalizer

Like Windows players such as Winamp and Sonique, MACAST includes a graphic equalizer that gives you fine control over how the music you're playing emerges from your computer. MACAST's graphic equalizer provides a number of preset equalizations (from Live, Classical, and Jazz to Uphill and PowerBook) and it also lets you create your own equalizations.

Click the Equalizer button to display the equalizer in the main MACAST window (see Figure 10.28). Then work with the equalizer as follows:

> Click the up and down arrow buttons on the left-hand side of the display to move through the list of preset equalizations.

> To create a preset equalization of your own, click in the frequency bars to set equalization for the different frequencies. When everything sounds right, click the + button at the right-hand side of the equalizer display to save the preset.

> To delete the current preset equalization, click the – button at the right-hand side of the equalizer display.

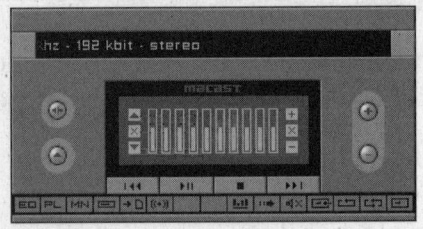

FIGURE 10.28: Use the Equalizer to hone the sound MACAST is producing.

MACAST automatically removes the equalizer display when you leave it alone for a few seconds after using it.

Applying Skins and Using Visualizations

To keep your Mac's desktop looking good, MACAST not only supports skins but it also provides visualizations. Figure 10.29 shows MACAST in its built-in subrad skin.

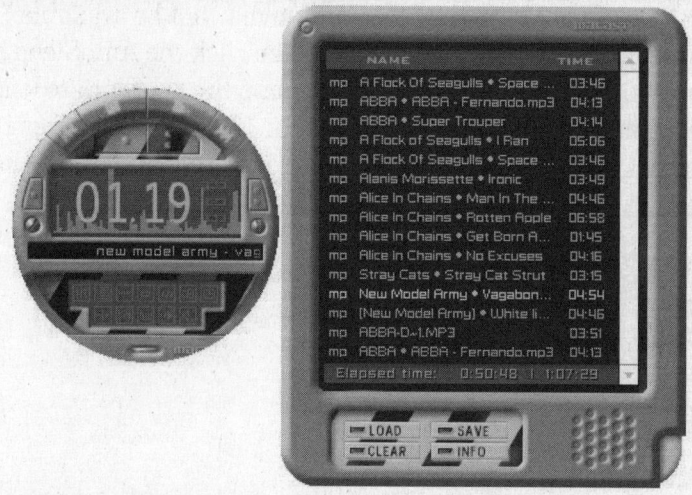

FIGURE 10.29: MACAST in its built-in subrad skin

To apply one of MACAST's built-in skins, pull down the Skins menu and choose the skin from it. To apply a skin that you've downloaded from the Internet, choose Skins ➢ Other and specify the skin in the resulting Open dialog box.

MACAST provides both tiny visualizations within its main window and larger scale visualizations in separate windows. To run through the main window visualizations, click in the track name display area in the main window. To turn on the external visualizations, pull down the Plugins menu and select the G-Force, Reflections, RGB Spectrum, Star Lyrics, or WhiteCap item. Each opens in a separate window. You can run two or more visualizations at once if your processor can stand the strain.

Using the AutoSleep Feature

MACAST's AutoSleep feature lets you use your Mac as a high-tech clock radio. AutoSleep can even turn your Mac off for you if you choose.

To use AutoSleep, choose Edit ➤ Preferences to display the Preferences dialog box (see Figure 10.30) and select the Misc. page by clicking its tab. In the AutoSleep Action drop-down list, choose the action you want MACAST to take: Quit MACAST, Sleep, or Shutdown. (On some Macs, the Sleep option may not be available.) Click the Save button to save your choice. Then click the AutoSleep button until the Sleep Timer message displays the appropriate length of time you want: 5, 10, 15, 30, 60, 90, or 180 minutes. (After 180, it loops back to Off.) Then load a playlist, let it roll, and hit the hay.

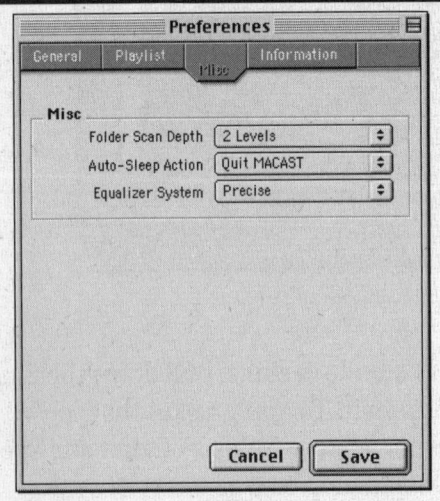

FIGURE 10.30: Use MACAST's AutoSleep feature to lull you off to the Land of Nod.

GrayAMP

GrayAMP is a straightforward, lightweight player that plays MP3 files without any fuss. When we say that GrayAMP is lightweight, we mean that in a good way. Because it doesn't support visualization plug-ins, it's light on processor demands, which means that you can run it without difficulty on older and less powerful Macs. It also doesn't support skins, which (although off-putting to some people) at least makes sure that you won't waste bandwidth downloading them or time worrying about which skin to apply for the perfect listening experience. More limiting are some of the other features GrayAMP doesn't have: fast-forward and rewind functionality (moving through a track), graphic equalization, and ID3 tag editing.

To offset these lacks, GrayAMP has a couple of really nice features:

- GrayAMP can keep track of files when you move them about on your system, whereas many other players simply lose them.
- You can set custom key bindings for the Play, Pause, Stop, Previous, Next, Shuffle, and Loop functions, enabling you to create a custom way of controlling GrayAMP from the keyboard.

GrayAMP is freeware but if you care to support it, the authors invite you to send them a three-pound lobster (or, if you find it more manageable, a check for the amount such a lobster would cost). They note that they also "happily accept jars of pickles," although most people find pickles almost as finicky to ship as lobsters—less sensitive to temperature, for sure, but eminently more breakable (assuming that the lobster is dead).

Download the latest version of GrayAMP from the Digital Thoughts Web site, digithought.net/software/grayamp/ If the distribution file doesn't unstuff itself, unstuff it manually. Then run GrayAMP by clicking the GrayAMP icon in the GrayAMP folder that the distribution file installed.

GrayAMP could hardly be easier to use. As you can see in Figure 10.31, its interface is self-explanatory. There are two things that we should mention, however. First, you can toggle the display of the playlist window (the lower part of the window shown) by clicking the arrow labeled Playlist. Second, to remove a selected track from the playlist, you press the Delete key.

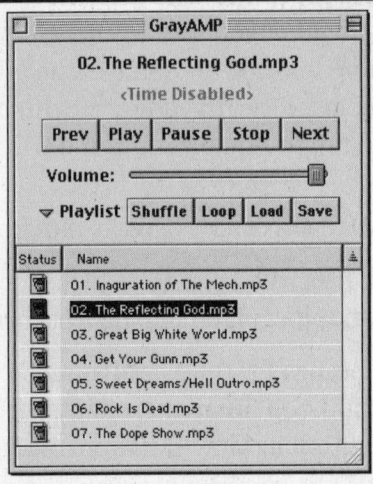

FIGURE 10.31: GrayAMP is a straightforward and free MP3 player that produces good sound and runs well on less powerful Macs.

GrayAMP offers a number of options that you can set on the three pages of the Preferences dialog box (Edit ➢ Preferences). Of these, a couple are worth trying:

- ▶ The Fade Out on Quit option on the Interface page of the Preferences dialog box (see Figure 10.32) gradually fades the volume as you quit GrayAMP.

- ▶ The Strict File Adding option on the General page of the Preferences dialog box (see Figure 10.33) lets you add only files with the correct file type to your playlists.

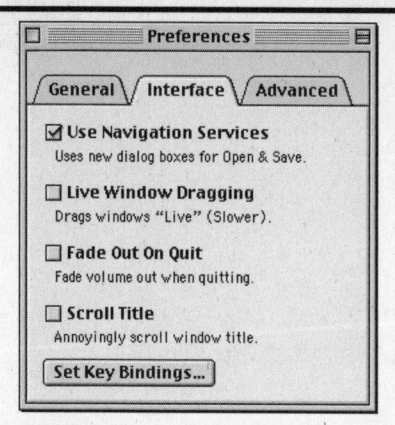

FIGURE 10.32: The Fade Out on Quit option on the Interface page of the Preferences dialog box produces interesting effects.

FIGURE 10.33: Use the Strict File Adding option on the General page of the Preferences dialog box to prevent yourself from adding files with incorrect file types to your playlists.

On the Advanced page of the Preferences dialog box (see Figure 10.34), you can adjust the depth to which GrayAMP scans into folders to find files, and the foreground and background sleep times for GrayAMP.

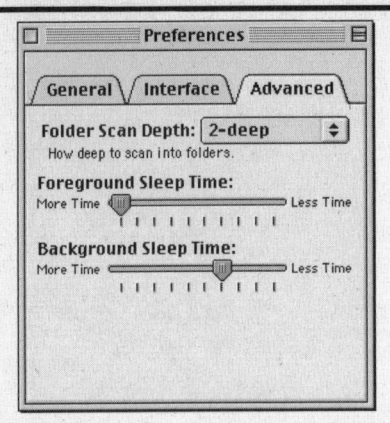

FIGURE 10.34: The options on the Advanced page of the Preferences dialog box let you adjust the folder scan depth and the foreground and background sleep times.

To set custom key bindings for running GrayAMP, click the Set Key Bindings button on the Interface page of the Preferences dialog box and work in the resulting Set Key Bindings dialog box (see Figure 10.35).

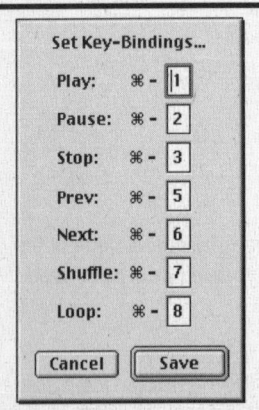

FIGURE 10.35: GrayAMP also lets you set custom key bindings so that you can run the player more easily.

MACAST LITE

MACAST Lite, MACAST's smaller sibling, is made (you've guessed it) by @soft and can also be found at www.macamp.net. MACAST Lite provides fewer features than MACAST, but they're enough to be useful. It has a simple, unobtrusive interface and takes less memory than MACAST, but it supports playlists (via a pop-up menu) and skins. If you like MACAST Lite, pay $10 (or more, if you choose) to register it. If you then choose to upgrade to MACAST, you save $5 off the $24.95 registration price.

UP NEXT

In this chapter, we've looked at several of the most popular MP3 players for the Mac, from the free SoundApp, QuickAmp, and GrayAMP to the much more expensive but also more powerful MACAST. We've also shown you how to play MP3 files with QuickTime and RealJukebox Basic for the times when you must have the music but can't install MP3-specific software on your computer.

In the next chapter, we'll discuss rippers and jukeboxes for the Mac.

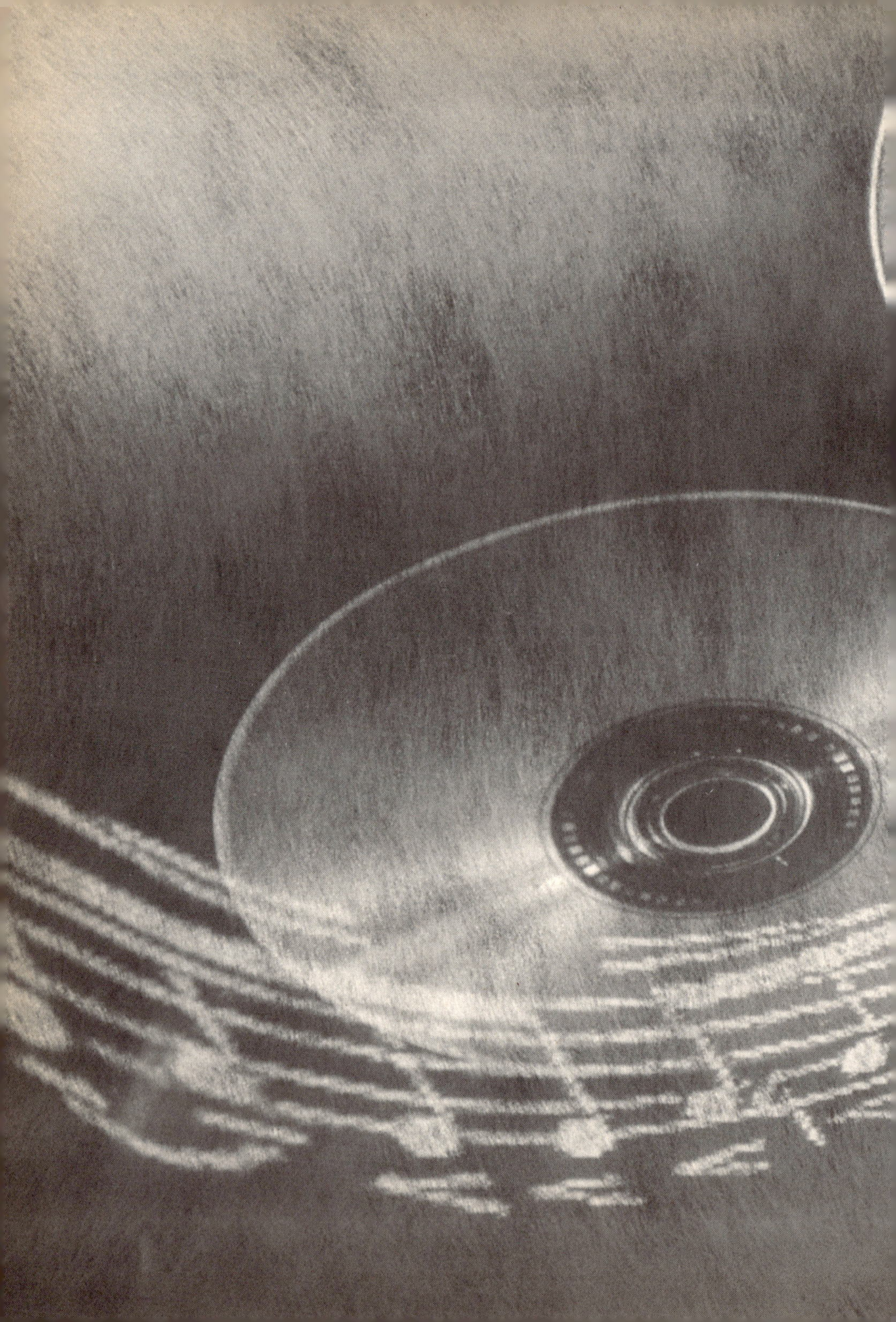

Chapter 11
Macintosh Rippers and Jukeboxes

FEATURING
- AudioCatalyst
- MPegger
- SoundJam MP
- MusicMatch Jukebox for the Macintosh

In this chapter, we'll show you two of the leading ripper/encoders and the two leading ripper/player/jukeboxes for the Macintosh. AudioCatalyst and MPegger are the ripper/encoders, and SoundJam MP and MusicMatch Jukebox are the ripper/player/jukeboxes. As you might guess by seeing these names, the range of MP3 software available for the Mac is much narrower than for Windows—but the quality of what's available is high.

AudioCatalyst

AudioCatalyst is one of the relatively few ripper/encoders for the Mac—and in our estimation, it's the best. However, it has two things going against it:

- First, although it's a commercial product, and although there's an evaluation copy available of its PC version, there's no evaluation copy for the Mac version. So you can't try it before you buy it.

- Second, AudioCatalyst is built by Xing Technologies, a company acquired by RealNetworks, which seems more enthusiastic about its main line of audio and video products (such as RealPlayer and RealJukebox) than about the Xing line. That said, AudioCatalyst is available and functional at this writing. If you can't find where to buy it on RealNetworks's Web site (`www.real.com`), try an electronic software retailer such as Beyond.com (`www.beyond.com`).

AudioCatalyst for the Mac requires a PowerPC processor, MacOS System 8 or higher, and a compatible CD drive. It costs $29.95.

Installing and Configuring AudioCatalyst

Once you've downloaded AudioCatalyst, unstuff it to a convenient location (if it doesn't unstuff itself) and launch it. Then configure AudioCatalyst as described in the following steps:

1. Choose Preferences ≻ General, or press Apple+G, to display the General Preferences dialog box (see Figure 11.1).

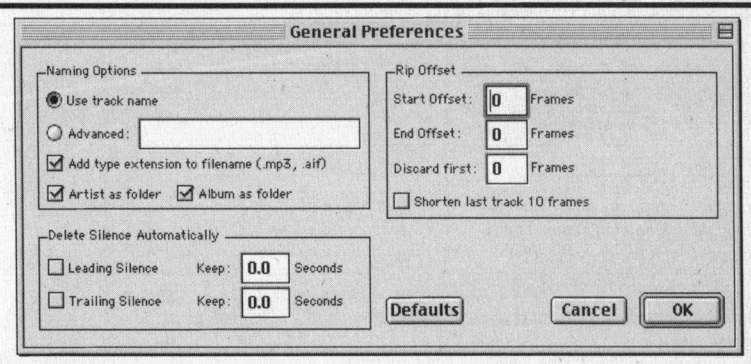

FIGURE 11.1: Start configuring AudioCatalyst in the General Preferences dialog box.

2. In the Naming Options group box, choose between the Use Track Name option button and the Advanced option button. If you're using CDDB, the Use Track Name option is usually a better bet because it saves you time and effort. Make sure the Add Type Extension to Filename check box is selected. If you want to create folders named after the artist and album, select the Artist As Folder check box and the Album As Folder check box. (We recommend these options, but they may not suit you.)

3. Leave the check boxes in the Delete Silence Automatically group box cleared, and leave the text boxes in the Rip Offset group box set to 0 frames.

4. Click the OK button to close the General Preferences dialog box.

5. Choose Preferences ➢ Encoder, or press Apple+P, to display the Encoder Preferences dialog box (see Figure 11.2).

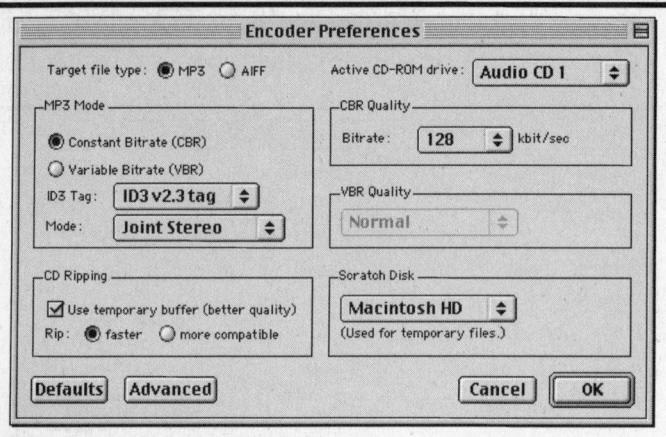

FIGURE 11.2: Continue setting preferences in the Encoder Preferences dialog box.

6. At the top of the Encoder Preferences dialog box, make sure that the MP3 option button is selected and that AudioCatalyst has identified the right CD drive.

7. In the MP3 Mode group box, select the Constant Bitrate option button, choose ID3 v2.3 Tag in the ID3 Tag drop-down list, and choose Joint Stereo in the Mode drop-down list.

8. In the CD Ripping group box, select the Use Temporary Buffer check box and the Faster option button.

9. In the CBR Quality group box, select the bitrate you want to use. We recommend 128kbps as the right place to start.

10. Click the OK button to close the Encoder Preferences dialog box.

11. Choose Preferences ➤ Normalization, or press Apple+N, to display the Normalization dialog box (see Figure 11.3).

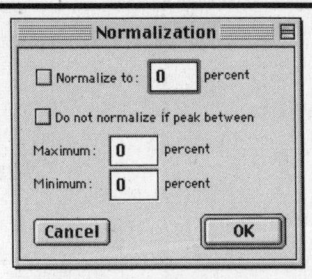

FIGURE 11.3: Continue setting preferences in the Normalization dialog box.

12. If you want to apply normalization to record MP3 files from all your CDs at the same volume, select the Normalize To check box and enter an appropriate value in the Percent text box. What's appropriate depends on the variation in the volume among the CDs that you listen to, and you'll probably need to experiment to determine it. You can tweak the normalization by selecting the Do Not Normalize If Peak Between check box and specifying Maximum and Minimum percentages in the text boxes. (Again, you'll need to experiment with this.)

13. Click the OK button to close the Normalization dialog box.

14. Choose Preferences ➤ Setup CDDB/ID3, or press Apple+S, to display the CDDB/ID3 Preferences dialog box (see Figure 11.4).

15. In the CDDB group box, enter the name of a CDDB server in the CDDB Server text box and a port in the Port text box. (You can try accepting the default settings on these and see what happens.) Enter your e-mail address in the Your E-Mail Address text box, and make choices for the four check boxes below. (We recommend leaving all four selected.)

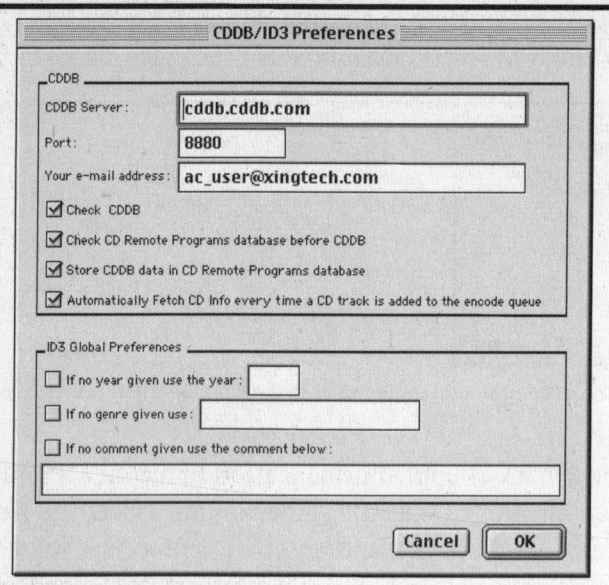

FIGURE 11.4: Finish by setting preferences in the CDDB/ID3 Preferences dialog box.

16. If you want to enter default text for tracks that otherwise won't have any, select one or more of the check boxes in the ID3 Global Preferences group box as appropriate and enter the corresponding text. Unless you're very confused by minimally tagged tracks, entering default text doesn't seem to be a good idea.

17. Click the OK button to close the CDDB/ID3 Preferences dialog box. You're nearly done.

18. Choose Player ➢ Set Player. In the resulting dialog box, navigate to the player that you'd like to launch from AudioCatalyst for playing MP3 files, and click the Open button.

Ripping and Encoding with AudioCatalyst

As you just saw, AudioCatalyst takes a while to configure—but once it's configured, you'll find that ripping and encoding (which Audio-Catalyst does in a single step) are easy.

With a CD inserted in your CD-ROM drive, click the Add from CD button in AudioCatalyst to display the CD Tracks dialog box (see Figure 11.5). Use the Add All button or the Add Selected button to identify the tracks you want to rip. AudioCatalyst accesses CDDB, downloads track information, and then displays the track names in the AudioCatalyst window. It also closes the CD Tracks dialog box, returning the focus to the AudioCatalyst window.

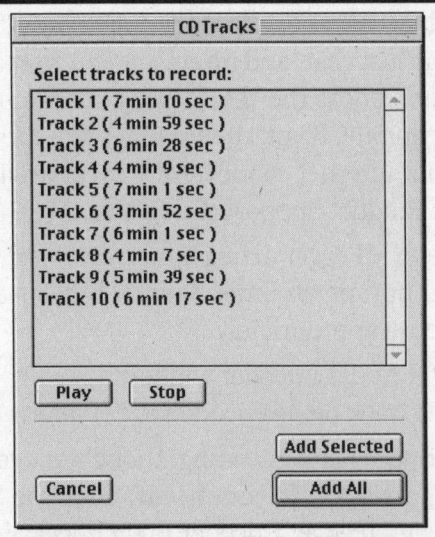

FIGURE 11.5: In the CD Tracks dialog box, select the tracks that you want to rip and encode.

Click the Encode button. When AudioCatalyst displays the Select Destination Folder dialog box, choose the destination folder for the MP3 files and click the Select button. AudioCatalyst starts the ripping and encoding.

MPegger

MPegger, from Proteron, is a ripper and encoder for the Macintosh. MPegger requires a PowerPC chip and MacOS System 7 or better, supports CDDB, and provides normalization. The full version of MPegger costs $24.95, but you can get an evaluation version that lets you encode 20 full-length MP3 files but then cuts off any further files at a minute apiece.

Download the latest version of MPegger from the Proteron Web site (`www.proteron.com`) and let the distribution file unstuff itself. Then run it by double-clicking the MPegger icon in the MPegger folder created by the unstuffing.

The first time you run it, MPegger displays the Free Product Support dialog box, offering you just that, and promising not to spam or abuse the address you enter. Choose the Yes, Please button or the No, Thanks button as appropriate. If you choose to receive the free support, make sure that your Internet connection is up or available when you dismiss the Free Product Support dialog box.

After that, the Welcome to MPegger dialog box appears, which offers you a Demo MPegger button, an Enter Serial # button, and a Purchase Now button. Choose appropriately.

Then the MPegger Digital Audio Encoder window appears, shown in Figure 11.6 with a track being encoded to MP3 format.

Before you get down to ripping and encoding, though, make sure that MPegger's preferences are set to fit your needs. Click the Preferences button to display the MPegger Encoder Preferences dialog box, whose Encoding Options page is shown in Figure 11.7. Then check the settings in the Layer drop-down list (you'll probably want Layer III Constant Bitrate for your music recordings), the Stereo Bitrate drop-down list (128kbps or higher for quality music), and the Stereo Mode drop-down list (probably Stereo rather than Joint Stereo). If you want to normalize the volume levels of the tracks that you're encoding, select the Normalize Audio Source

Macintosh Rippers and Jukeboxes

check box. If you're recording at a low bitrate (say, 32kbps or 64kbps), select the Low Bitrate Frequency Clamp check box, which helps prevent the encoder from producing a "washy" effect.

FIGURE 11.6: MPegger encoding a track to MP3

FIGURE 11.7: Before you start encoding, choose suitable settings in the MPegger Encoder Preferences dialog box. The Encoding Options page contains several important settings.

Chapter Eleven

> **NOTE**
>
> You may also want to try selecting the Asynchronous IO check box on the Encoding Options page of the MPegger Encoder Preferences dialog box. Asynchronous I/O lets the computer work on the encoding even when it's busy writing to disk. This speeds up the encoding a little bit. Be warned, though, that asynchronous I/O disagrees with some device drivers—so if this setting seems to cause trouble on your computer, clear this check box again.

On the I/O & System Options page of the MPegger Encoder Preferences dialog box (see Figure 11.8), use the Change Destination button to specify the output destination folder for the MP3 files that you encode. In the System Options group box, you may also want to select the Delete Source Files after Encoding check box (to have MPegger delete any WAV files that you encode to MP3 files) and the Monopolize the CPU check box (if you want to sacrifice the performance of any other applications you're running in order to get the encoding finished faster).

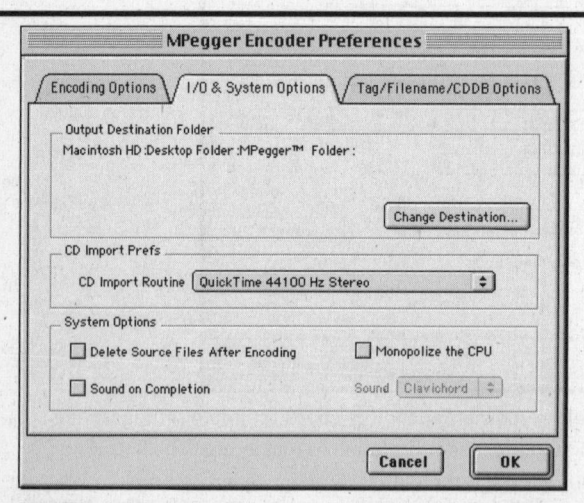

FIGURE 11.8: Specify the output destination folder for MP3 files on the I/O & System Options page of the MPegger Encoding Preferences dialog box.

On the Tag/Filename/CDDB Options page of the MPegger Encoding Preferences dialog box (see Figure 11.9), choose options for naming and tagging the MP3 files you create:

- Select the Add mpN to Name check box to add the appropriate extension (for example, MP3) to the filename.

- Select the Separate CDs into Subfolders check box to put each CD's tracks into a separate folder.

- Select both the Name Using CD Remote Database check box and the Tag Using CD Remote Database check box if you want to use information stored in your CD Remote Database (your local information store for CDs you've played on your Mac) for naming and tagging the files. Select the Query CDDB If Necessary check box to have MPegger query CDDB for song data that's not stored in your CD Remote Database.

- Select either the Add ID3 V2 Tags check box (more likely) or the Add ID3 V1 Tags check box (less likely, but preferable if the MP3 player or jukebox you're using has compatibility problems with ID3 V2 tags).

- In the File Type drop-down list, select the default player for your MP3 files.

- You can also specify a default genre for tracks that do not have genre information attached.

Once you've set the preferences, load a CD in your CD drive and click the Open CD button. If you chose to use CDDB, MPegger queries it. Then the Select Tracks for Encoding dialog box, shown in Figure 11.10, appears. Select the tracks you want to encode, and click the Encode button.

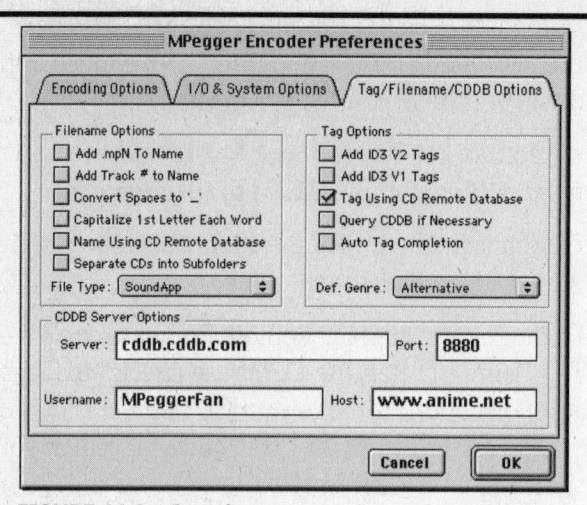

FIGURE 11.9: Specify naming and tag information for your music files on the Tag/Filename/CDDB Options page of the MPegger Encoder Preferences dialog box.

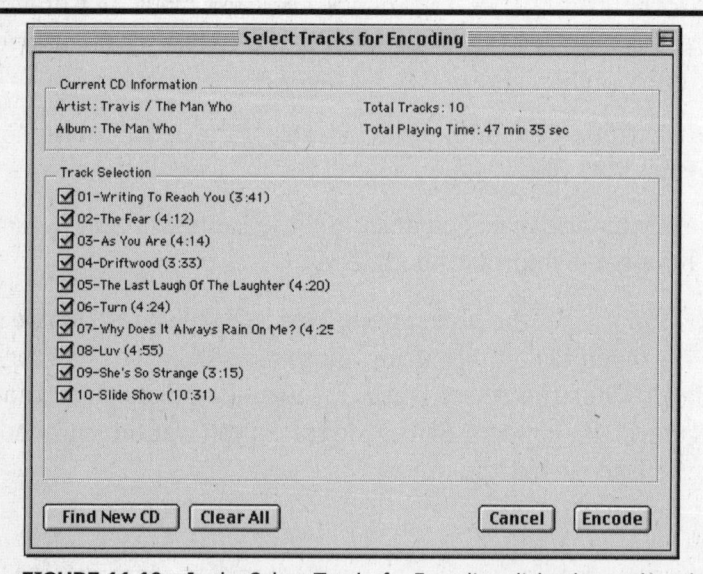

FIGURE 11.10: In the Select Tracks for Encoding dialog box, select the tracks from which you want to create MP3 files.

To encode WAV files to MP3 files, click the Open File button and use the Open: Select Files for Encoding dialog box to identify the source files.

SoundJam MP

SoundJam was the first full-fledged ripper/player/jukebox for the Macintosh, and as such, has proved to be a big hit. SoundJam offers a strong set of features, including the following:

- High-quality ripping and encoding (of course)
- The ability to create an effective jukebox database of your music
- A ten-band graphic equalizer
- Visualizations
- Skins
- Built-in Web connectivity that lets you download MP3 files directly from the Web

SoundJam costs $39.99–$10 more than AudioCatalyst and $15 more than MPegger—and comes either as a download or as a retail package that you can find in many physical stores and at online retailers. There's also a seven-day demo that you can download from the SoundJam Web site, www.soundjam.com, if you want to check the product out before buying—a good idea for most people.

Installing and Configuring SoundJam

Both the downloaded version of SoundJam and the retail version are easy to install:

- To install the downloaded version of SoundJam, unstuff the self-extracting archive and run the SoundJam MP Installer in the resulting SoundJam MP Demo folder.

- To install SoundJam from the retail package, insert the CD-ROM into your CD drive. Your Mac automatically opens a window displaying the contents of the CD. Drag its folder from the distribution CD onto a convenient location on your Mac, so that your Mac copies it there.

Configuring SoundJam is straightforward. The first time you run SoundJam, the SoundJam MP Software License Agreement dialog box appears. Once you agree to that, SoundJam displays the Personalize SoundJam MP dialog box, in which you enter (or correct) your name, add a company name if you want, and type the serial number from the CD sleeve or the manual into the Serial Number text box.

If you're using virtual memory, SoundJam displays the dialog box shown in Figure 11.11 to alert you to that fact and to tell you that as a result of using virtual memory, you may experience slowdowns in playback. This won't necessarily happen. Using virtual memory isn't a bad thing in itself—it just may indicate that your computer is light on physical memory (RAM), and this shortage of memory may cause problems with playback. If you have a lot of RAM but have configured your Macintosh to use virtual memory as well so that you can have a number of large applications or huge files open at once, you can probably safely ignore this warning.

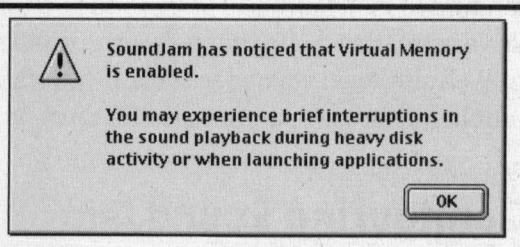

> ⚠ **SoundJam has noticed that Virtual Memory is enabled.**
>
> You may experience brief interruptions in the sound playback during heavy disk activity or when launching applications.
>
> [OK]

FIGURE 11.11: Don't worry if SoundJam displays this dialog box warning you that you're using virtual memory—it isn't necessarily a problem.

Next, SoundJam displays the dialog box shown in Figure 11.12, asking if you want to set SoundJam as the handler for MP3 files and MP3 audio streams. If you want to use a different MP3 player

Macintosh Rippers and Jukeboxes 529

most of the time, click the No button. But for most installations, it makes sense to accept the default Yes button.

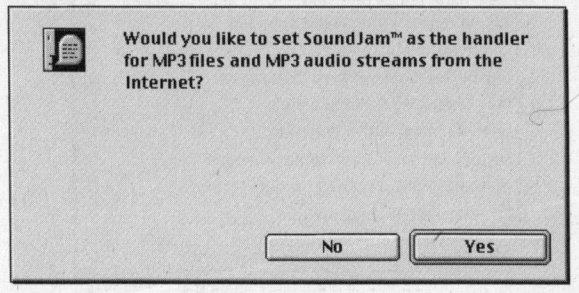

FIGURE 11.12: SoundJam asks if you want to use it as the default handler for MP3 files and audio streams.

After this preliminary skirmishing, SoundJam displays its Player window. Before you start playing or recording music with SoundJam, make sure that your preferences are set suitably, as discussed in the following sections.

Choose Edit ➢ Preferences to display the Preferences dialog box. This dialog box has seven pages of options. You access the different pages via the list of items on the left-hand side of the dialog box.

General Page Preferences

These are the options on the General page of the Preferences dialog box (see Figure 11.13):

Display Track Number in Name check box Controls whether SoundJam includes the track numbers in the titles of tracks.

Chapter Eleven

[Preferences dialog box screenshot]

- ☐ Display Track Number in Name
- ☑ Display Skins Using Transparency
- ☐ Live Window Dragging
- ☑ Ask Before Saving Playlist Changes
- ☑ Play Tracks While Converting
- ☑ Use CD Digital Audio Playback
- ☐ Reduce CPU Use When in Background
- ☑ Quit Application When Closing Player
- ☐ Reverse Left/Right Speakers

Use SoundJam™ for Internet Playback

On CD Insert: Do Nothing

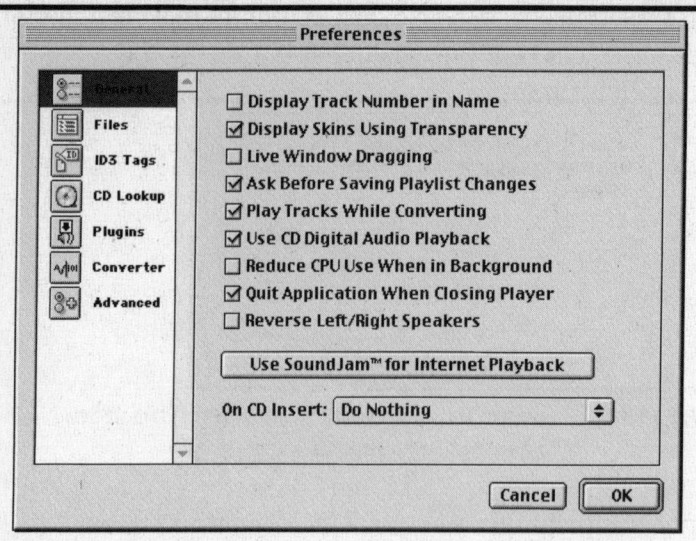

FIGURE 11.13: The General page of the Preferences dialog box

Display Skins Using Transparency check box Controls whether SoundJam lets you see through lightly shaded parts of SoundJam skins to another application below.

Live Window Dragging check box Controls whether SoundJam displays the contents of a window when you drag it or just the outline.

Ask Before Saving Playlist Changes check box This check box controls whether SoundJam prompts you to save any unsaved changes to a playlist when you close the Playlist window. If you clear this check box, SoundJam saves the changes automatically without prompting you.

Play Tracks While Converting check box Controls whether SoundJam plays CD tracks as it converts them. Doing so doesn't slow down the recording speed unless your processor and/or CD drive are very slow. (If so, you may need to turn this option off in order to rip effectively.)

Use CD Digital Audio Playback check box Controls whether SoundJam routes CD audio through your Mac's sound circuitry or directly to the sound output. Keep this check box selected; if you clear it, you won't be able to use SoundJam's visualizations or graphic equalizer.

Reduce CPU Use When in Background check box Controls whether SoundJam throttles back its demands on the processor (the CPU) when you have another application in the foreground. If you're experiencing a slow response in other applications when playing or ripping with SoundJam in the background, try selecting this check box to see if it improves matters.

Quit Application When Closing Player check box Controls whether closing the SoundJam Player window quits the application as well. This check box is selected by default.

Reverse Left/Right Speakers check box Controls whether SoundJam reverses left and right channels in output. Useful only if you've crossed your speaker wires under the floor or in the paneling.

On CD Insert drop-down list Lets you specify what SoundJam should do when you insert a CD in your CD drive: Do Nothing, Begin Playing, Convert All Tracks, or Convert All Tracks & Eject.

Files Page Preferences

These are the options on the Files page of the Preferences dialog box (see Figure 11.14).

Ask Before Removing Tracks check box Controls whether SoundJam prompts you for confirmation when you press the Delete key to remove a file from a playlist.

Change File Creator to SoundJam check box Controls whether SoundJam changes the creator code on MP3, MP2, AIFF, or WAV files to associate the file with SoundJam. (The creator code is a kind of tag on the file.) If you use SoundJam exclusively for your MP3 needs, make sure this check box is selected.

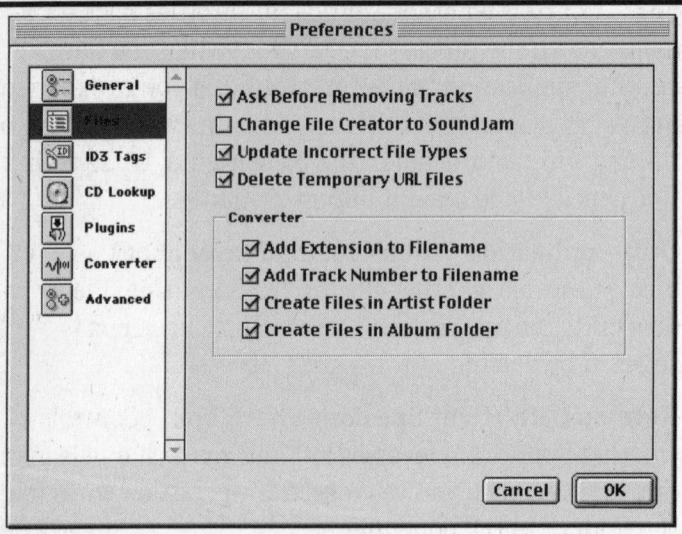

FIGURE 11.14: The Files page of the Preferences dialog box

Update Incorrect File Types check box Controls whether SoundJam adds a creator code to a sound file that seems to be lacking one. Typically, the reason for a sound file lacking a creator code is that it comes from a non-Mac machine (for example, from a Windows machine). Leave this check box selected.

Delete Temporary URL Files check box Controls whether SoundJam automatically deletes temporary files created by playing streaming audio from the Web. Deleting these files automatically is usually a good idea.

Converter group box The four check boxes in this group box control how SoundJam names the MP3 files it creates, and where it stores them.

ID3 Tags Page Preferences

These are the options on the ID3 Tags page of the Preferences dialog box (see Figure 11.15):

Add Missing ID3 Tags check box and **Update Existing ID3 Tags check box** These two options tell SoundJam to add missing tags and update tags using information that you enter in the Track Information dialog box. Typically, you'll want to leave these two check boxes selected.

Create ID3 Tags as drop-down list Select the ID3 tag version that you want to use. At this writing, v2.2 is selected by default, since it seems to be becoming the most widely used tag standard. If you're using SoundJam almost exclusively, you might want to choose v2.3, which can store more information.

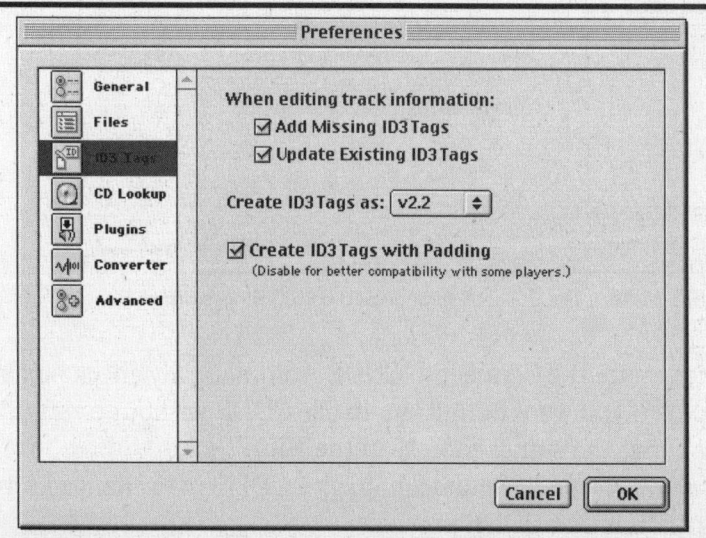

FIGURE 11.15: The ID3 Tags page of the Preferences dialog box

Create ID3 Tags with Padding check box This check box controls whether SoundJam uses padding (extra space) in tags. If you're having problems using SoundJam-created files with padded tags in other MP3 players, try clearing this check box.

CD Lookup Page Preferences

On the CD Lookup page of the Preferences dialog box (see Figure 11.16), you can select the CDDB server to use (in the CDDB Database Server text box) and the port (in the Port text box). We see little reason to mess with the default settings, cddb.cddb.com and port 80, unless you find they're not working.

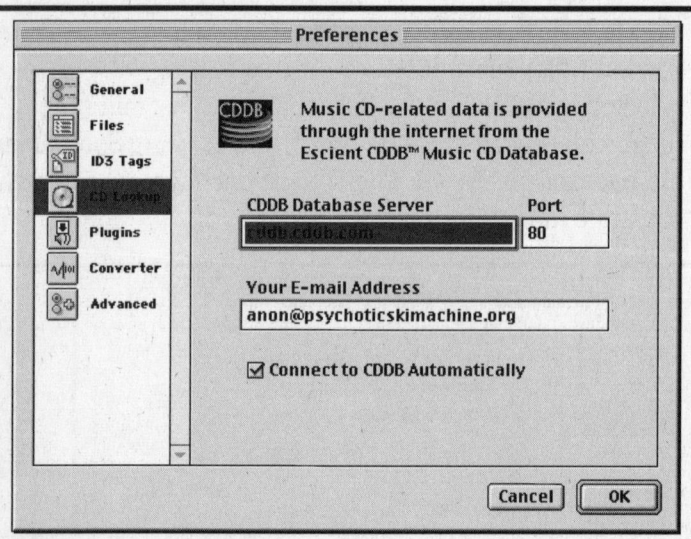

FIGURE 11.16: The CD Lookup page of the Preferences dialog box

Make sure the Connect to CDDB Automatically check box is selected if you want SoundJam to use CDDB without prompting. Check that the e-mail address in the Your E-mail Address text box is the one you want SoundJam to give CDDB in exchange for the information that CDDB provides.

Plugins Page Preferences

The Plugins page of the Preferences dialog box (see Figure 11.17) offers options for the plug-ins that you're using with SoundJam. At this writing, SoundJam comes with the Eclipse, Melt-O-Rama, and Thumper plug-ins, but you can add other plug-ins to customize your copy of SoundJam as you feel necessary.

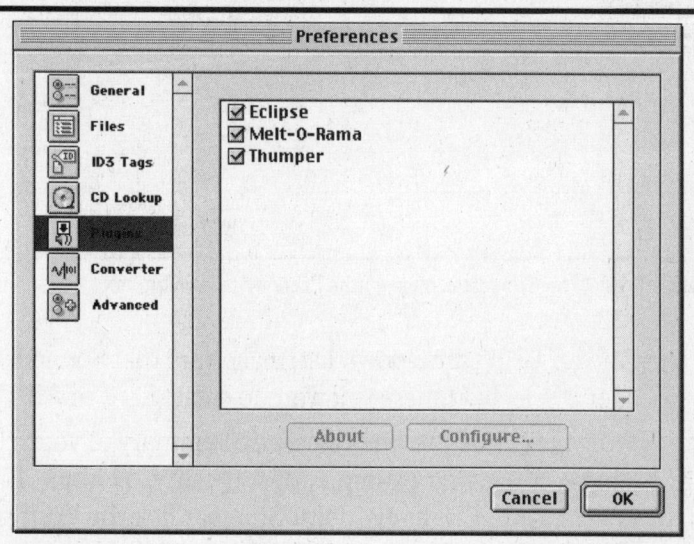

FIGURE 11.17: The Plugins page of the Preferences dialog box

Some plug-ins provide configuration options. To access these options, select the desired plug-in in the list box and click the Configure button. Make the appropriate choices and click the OK button to close the configuration dialog box.

Converter Page

The Converter page of the Preferences dialog box (see Figure 11.18) lets you specify what kinds of files to create and where SoundJam stores them.

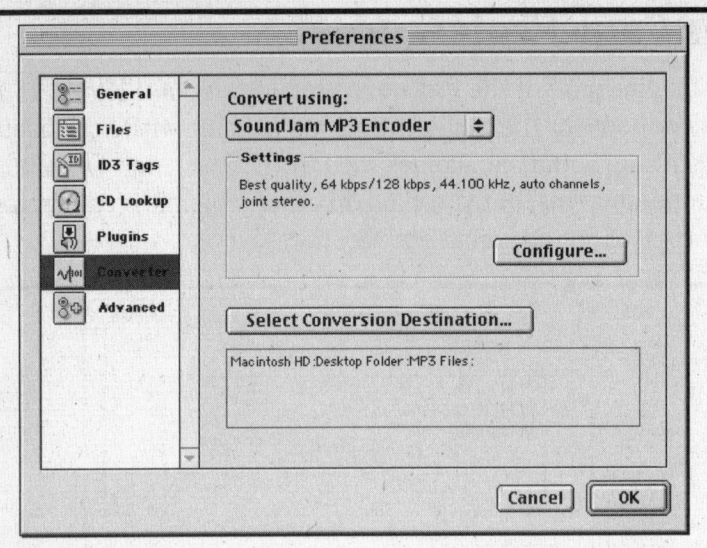

FIGURE 11.18: The Converter page of the Preferences dialog box

In the Convert Using drop-down list, make sure that SoundJam MP3 Encoder is selected unless you want to create MP2 or AIFF files.

The Settings text box provides a cryptic summary of your current encoding settings—for example, Best Quality, 64 kbps/128 kbps, Auto kHz, Auto Channels, Joint Stereo. Click the Configure button to display the SoundJam MP3 Encoder dialog box (see Figure 11.19).

FIGURE 11.19: The SoundJam MP Encoder dialog box contains some of the most important settings for producing high-quality MP3 files.

Then make your choices for the following settings:

Bit Rate group box Select suitable bitrates for the MP3 files that you're creating. For example, select 128 kbps in the Stereo drop-down list.

Performance group box Make sure that the Best Quality option button is selected. (In our opinion, the Faster option button isn't worth using.)

Channels group box Make sure that the Auto option button is selected.

Stereo Mode group box Make sure that the Joint Stereo option button is selected.

Advanced button To choose advanced encoding options, click this button and make choices in the second SoundJam MP3 Encoder dialog box.

Select Conversion Destination text box Check the folder shown in this text box; this is where SoundJam stores the MP3 files you create. To change the destination folder, click the Select Conversion Destination button and use the resulting dialog box to specify the folder.

Advanced Page Preferences

These are the options you can choose on the Advanced page of the Preferences dialog box (see Figure 11.20):

Add Encoded Files to drop-down list Select the playlist to which you want the ripped and encoded files to be added: Master Playlist, New Playlist, or None. The default setting is Master Playlist, which tends to be the most useful for conventional purposes.

Add Opened Files to drop-down list Choose the playlist in which you want the files you open to be added. Again, your choices are Master Playlist, New Playlist, or None, and Master Playlist is the default setting.

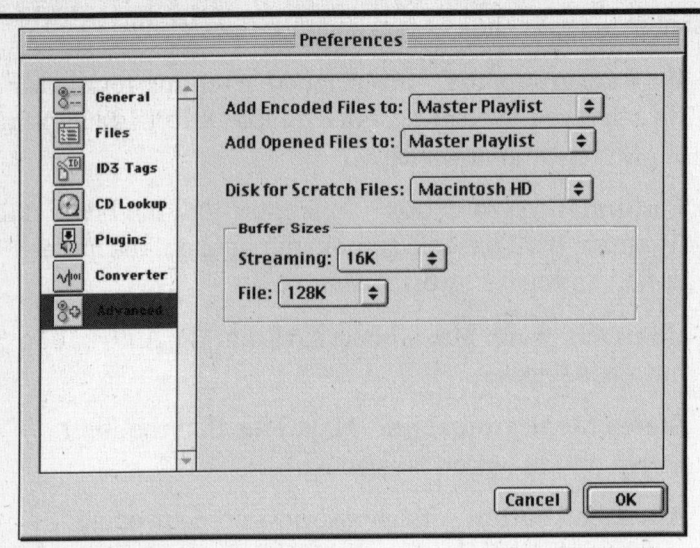

FIGURE 11.20: The Advanced page of the Preferences dialog box

Disk for Scratch Files drop-down list   Choose the location in which SoundJam should store temporary (scratch) files while processing audio. Unless you find yourself running out of disk space, you'll probably want to use your hard drive for temporary storage.

Buffer Sizes group box   Specify a buffer size for streaming and for writing to files. The Streaming buffer defaults to 16K, while the File buffer defaults to 128K. If playback seems choppy, try increasing the buffer sizes.

Navigating the SoundJam Interface

SoundJam's interface is friendly and easy to navigate, at least in its default skin. Figure 11.21 shows the Player window, all of whose controls are self-explanatory and straightforward to use.

Macintosh Rippers and Jukeboxes 539

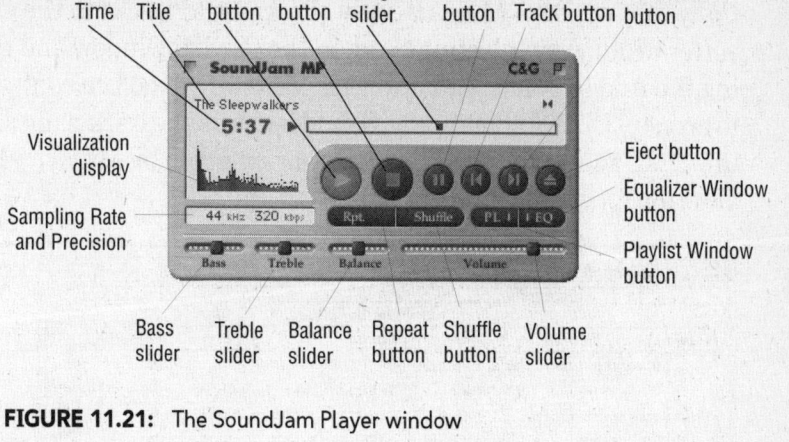

FIGURE 11.21: The SoundJam Player window

In addition to the Player window, SoundJam has an Equalizer window, a Master Playlist window, and a Converter window. You'll meet each of these in due course in the following sections.

Ripping and Encoding with SoundJam

Probably the first thing you'll want to do with SoundJam is rip and encode some MP3 files. SoundJam uses the Fraunhofer MP3 compression technology, and in our experience, it delivers consistently good results.

To get ripping, display the Converter window by choosing Window ➢ Converter or by pressing Apple+3. If you skipped the section on configuring SoundJam earlier in this chapter, check the Settings text box in the Converter window to make sure that all is in order. If anything looks wrong, click the Configure button to display the SoundJam MP3 Encoder dialog box, and check the settings there.

Load a CD in your CD drive, and then drag the CD's icon to the Converter window. (Alternatively, you can add tracks to the Converter window by selecting them in the Playlist window and clicking the Add to Converter button.) If you have SoundJam configured to access CDDB automatically, SoundJam lists the track names. Figure 11.22 shows the CD *The Last Tour on Earth* by Marilyn Manson all ready for ripping and encoding.

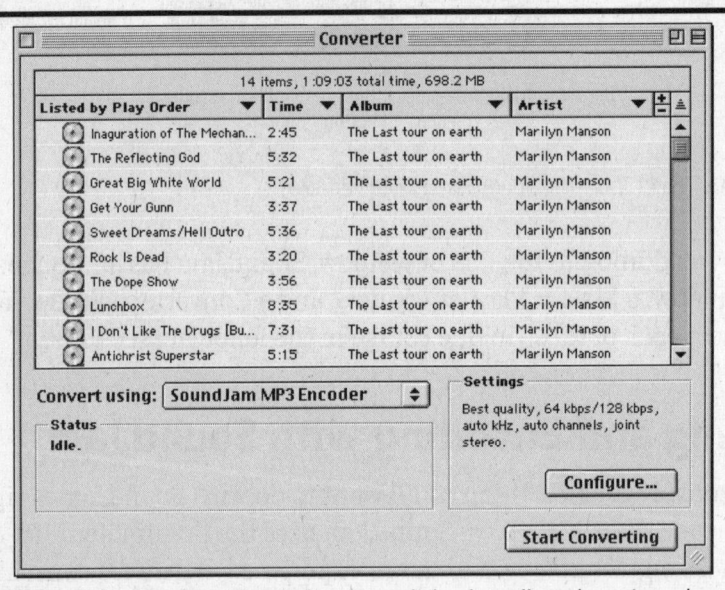

FIGURE 11.22: SoundJam's Converter dialog box all ready to rip and encode Marilyn Manson

In the Convert Using drop-down list, make sure that SoundJam MP3 Encoder is selected. (At this writing, the alternatives are SoundJam MP2 Encoder and SoundJam AIFF Encoder; we're betting you'll never need to use either of these.)

Click the Start Converting button to start ripping the CD tracks to MP3 files. SoundJam springs into action, and as the ripping takes place, SoundJam keeps you updated in the Status group box.

By default, SoundJam plays the tracks from the CD as it rips the files, which helps keep you entertained. You can prevent SoundJam from playing the files by clearing the Play Tracks While Converting check box on the General page of the Preferences dialog box. If you need to interrupt the ripping, click the Stop Converting button, into which the Start Converting button will have changed itself.

> **NOTE**
>
> You can convert files from other formats such as AIFF, QuickTime, or WAV into the MP3 format by dragging them to the Converter window and clicking the Start Converting button.

Adding and Updating Track Information

To change the tag information for a track, choose File ➤ Get Info, or press Apple+I, to display the Track Information dialog box, shown in Figure 11.23. Change the information as appropriate, and then click the OK button to close the Track Information dialog box.

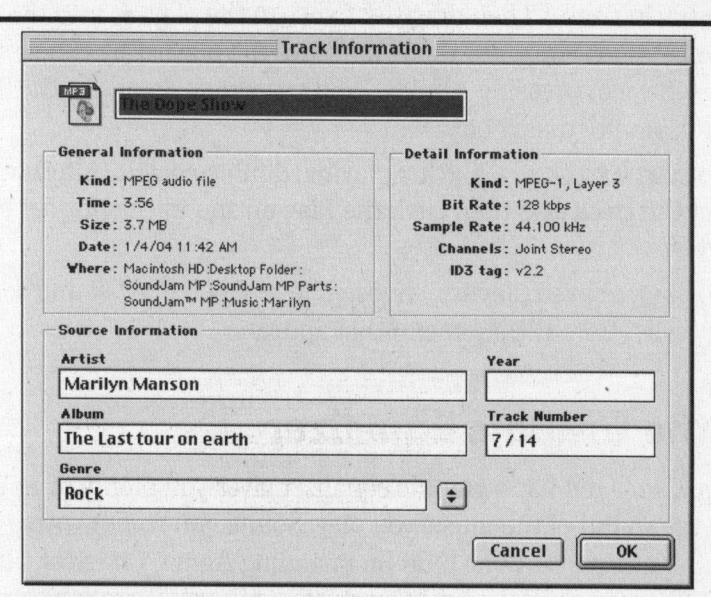

FIGURE 11.23: Use the Track Information dialog box to change the tag information for a track.

> **TIP**
>
> To make SoundJam update the tag information for the track, make sure the Update Existing ID3 Tags check box on the ID3 Tags page of the Preferences dialog box (Edit ➢ Preferences) is selected. Select the Add Missing ID3 Tags check box as well if you want SoundJam to add ID3 tags to tracks that are missing them.

Creating and Using Playlists

You can (of course) play individual tracks with SoundJam with no problem, but usually you'll want to create playlists. To do so, choose File ➢ New Playlist, or press Apple+N. SoundJam opens a new window named Untitled Playlist, into which you can drag tracks from anywhere convenient. (If you're keeping most of your tracks in your Master Playlist, that's probably the easiest place to drag tracks from.) Then drag the tracks in the playlist into the order in which you want them, and save the playlist by choosing File ➢ Save or pressing Apple+S and specifying details in the Save: SoundJam MP dialog box.

To start a track in a playlist playing, double-click it. Alternatively, select the track and then click the Play button in the playlist's window.

To open a saved playlist, choose File ➢ Open Playlist and select the playlist from the submenu that appears.

Using the Graphic Equalizer

SoundJam's ten-band graphic equalizer gives you plenty of control over the sound of the music you play. SoundJam comes with a number of equalizations built in, including Arena, Classical, Hall, Jazz, Rock, and Vocal, to get you started, but you'll probably want to create your own custom equalizations to supplement them.

To display the equalizer (see Figure 11.24), choose Window ➢ Equalizer, or press Apple+2. Then make sure the equalizer is switched on; if the Off button is showing, click it to change it into the On button.

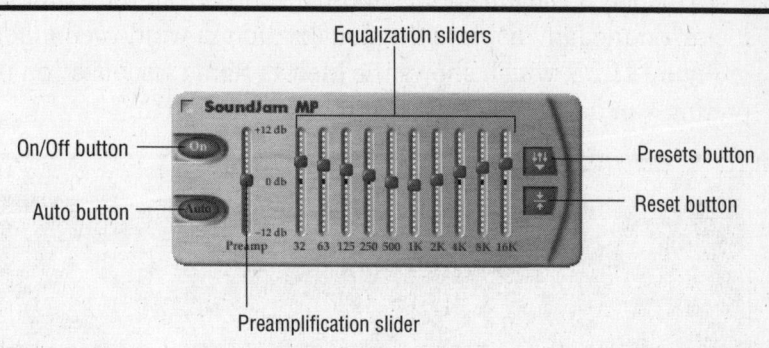

FIGURE 11.24: Use SoundJam's graphic equalizer to fine-tune the sound.

To adjust the current equalization, drag the Equalization sliders up and down. To apply a preset equalization, click the Presets button and make your choice from the context menu.

Most of the time, you won't need to move the Preamplification slider from its default midline position. But if you do increase the preamplification, click the Auto button so that it's turned on. This feature monitors SoundJam's output and prevents you from pumping a higher level of sound through your Mac's audio circuitry than it can comfortably support. (If you manage to do this, you'll get a form of distortion that's called *clipping*.)

To save a preset, move the sliders to create the sound you want. Click the Presets button and choose Save Settings from the pop-up menu, then use the Save: SoundJam MP dialog box to give the preset a name. You'll then be able to choose it from the pop-up menu like the built-in equalizations.

Visualizations

SoundJam comes with a number of built-in visualizations, and you can add further visualizations as you find them on the Web.

To display a visualization, choose its entry from the Window menu. SoundJam displays the visualization in windowed mode, as in Figure 11.25, which shows the Melt-O-Rama visualization interpreting Van der Graaf Generator's "Scorched Earth."

FIGURE 11.25: You can watch SoundJam's visualizations either in windows (as shown here) or in full screen.

To display the visualization in full-screen mode, choose Window ➢ Use Full Screen, or press Apple+F. To return from the full-screen visualization to the windowed visualization, click the mouse, press the Esc key, or press Apple+F again.

Applying Skins

SoundJam's default, brushed-aluminum–style skin is easy to understand and to use but if you want a little variety, you can apply any of SoundJam's other 17 built-in skins directly from the Skin menu. Figure 11.26 shows the WonderJelly skin.

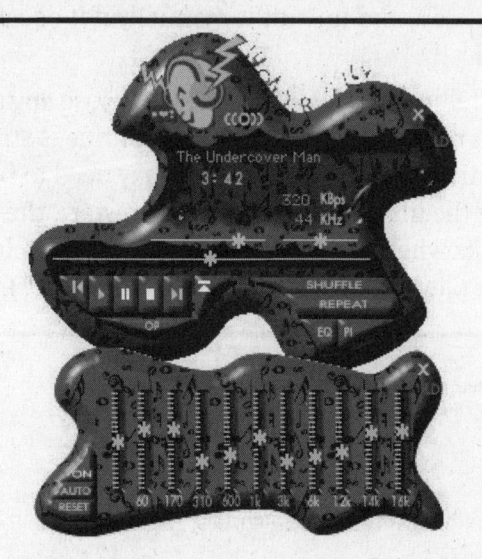

FIGURE 11.26: SoundJam includes 18 skins, including WonderJelly (shown here).

MusicMatch Jukebox for the Mac

As you'd guess, MusicMatch Jukebox for the Mac is the Mac version of MusicMatch Jukebox, one of the most popular ripper/player/jukeboxes for Windows.

As does the Windows version, MusicMatch Jukebox for the Mac comes in a free version that records at all bitrates and a paid version that records somewhat faster and claims to deliver better quality. We recommend starting with the free version and making sure it agrees with your Mac and yourself before paying for the premium version. Download the latest version from the MusicMatch Web site, `www.musicmatch.com`, and unstuff it manually if it doesn't unstuff itself automatically.

Before you start installing MusicMatch Jukebox, close any applications that you've got running. The installation routine is straightforward, apart from warning you that your Mac may need to be restarted at the end of the installation. Before the restart, the installation routine asks whether you want to set MusicMatch Jukebox as the default player for MP3 files (see Figure 11.27).

FIGURE 11.27: Choose whether to use MusicMatch Jukebox as your default MP3 player.

When you start MusicMatch Jukebox the first time, it displays the MusicMatch Jukebox – Find Songs dialog box, shown in Figure 11.28. Letting MusicMatch Jukebox find the music files is usually easier than adding them manually on your own (although you can do this later if you prefer). So we suggest clicking the Find Songs Now button. The only down side is that finding the files takes a few minutes, depending on the size of your hard drive and the speed of your Mac.

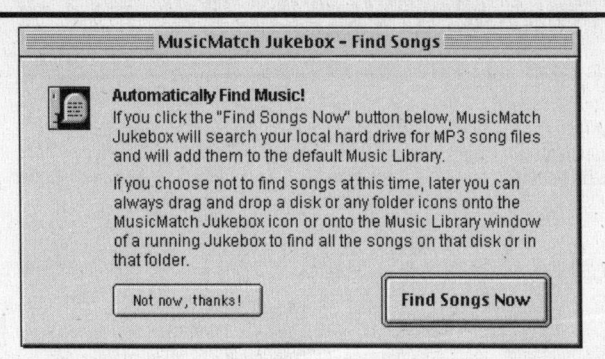

FIGURE 11.28: The first time you run it, MusicMatch Jukebox offers to search your hard drive for MP3 files.

You'll see the MusicMatch Jukebox – Add Songs dialog box (see Figure 11.29) as it works.

FIGURE 11.29: MusicMatch Jukebox takes a few minutes to search your hard drive for MP3 files.

Next, the MusicMatch Jukebox Welcome Tips dialog box appears. Browse these tips as you wish. You'll probably want to clear the Always Show These Welcome Tips at Startup check box before you dismiss the dialog box so that you'll be able to open MusicMatch Jukebox in the future without it bugging you.

After that, MusicMatch Jukebox appears. By default, MusicMatch Jukebox displays the Main window, the Music Library window, and the Recorder window, placing the windows in a vertical stack. You can return the MusicMatch Jukebox windows to this stack by choosing Window ➢ Auto Arrange Components.

548 Chapter Eleven

Figure 11.30 shows the Main window.

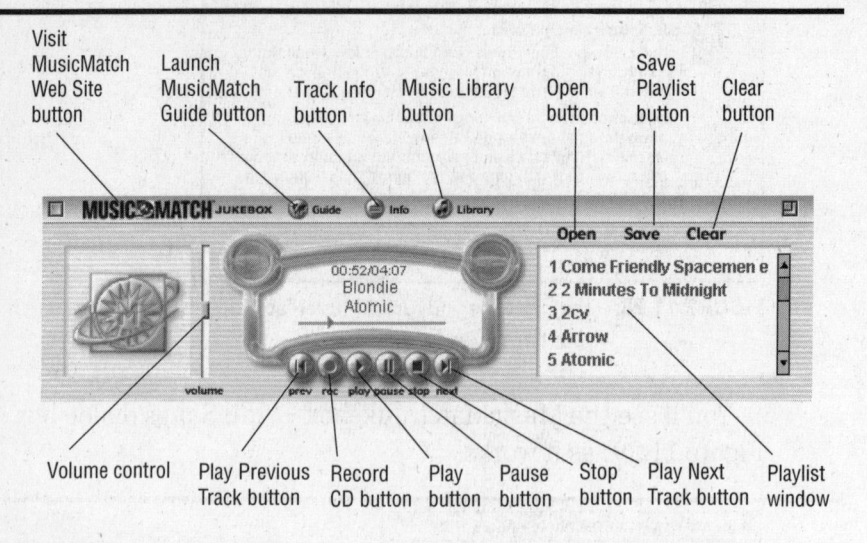

Visit MusicMatch Web Site button — Launch MusicMatch Guide button — Track Info button — Music Library button — Open button — Save Playlist button — Clear button

Volume control — Play Previous Track button — Record CD button — Play button — Pause button — Stop button — Play Next Track button — Playlist window

FIGURE 11.30: MusicMatch Jukebox for the Mac is a new contender in the ripper/player/jukebox stakes.

Figure 11.31 shows the Music Library window.

Add button — Delete button — Tag button — Find button — AutoDJ button

Title	Artist	Album	Genre	Time
Be Quick Or Be Dead	Iron Maiden	Best Of The Beast	rock	03:23
Maria	Blondie			00:00
Atomic	Blondie			04:07
Bone Orchard - Shall I Carry	Various Artist	Gothic Rock 3 (Disc 2)	Rock	02:39

FIGURE 11.31: The Music Library window

The MusicMatch Jukebox windows are mostly straightforward and intuitive to handle:

- You can drag the windows around as you want.
- To make the Music Library window move with the Main window, drag the Music Library window so that one of its sides sticks to a side of the Main window.
- You can resize the Music Library window vertically by clicking its bottom border and dragging it up or down.
- You can display MusicMatch Jukebox in Small view (see Figure 11.32) by choosing Window ➢ Small View. To restore MusicMatch Jukebox to Full view, choose Window ➢ Full View.

FIGURE 11.32: MusicMatch Jukebox for the Mac in Small view

NOTE

To register your copy of MusicMatch Jukebox, choose Register ➢ Enter Key to display the MusicMatch: Enter Key dialog box. Enter your key in the Enter the Key (Include Hyphens) text box and click the OK button.

Configuring MusicMatch Jukebox

Before you start working with MusicMatch Jukebox, configure it by choosing settings suitable for you in the Preferences dialog box. Choose Edit ➢ Preferences to display the Preferences dialog box.

General Page Preferences

The General page of the Preferences dialog box (see Figure 11.33) contains only three options:

Add Song to Music Library check box Leave this check box selected (as it is by default) if you want MusicMatch Jukebox to add new tracks to the music library when you open them.

Add Song to Play List check box Leave this check box selected (as it is by default) if you want MusicMatch Jukebox to add new tracks to the playlist when you open them.

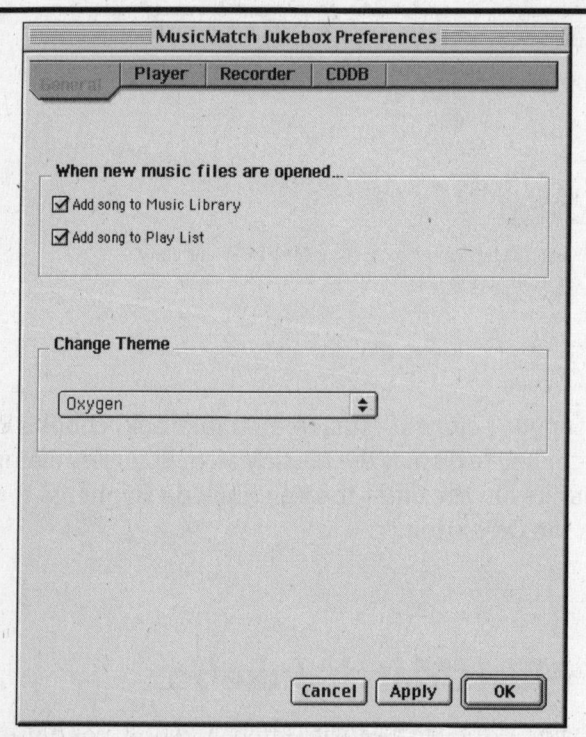

FIGURE 11.33: The General page of the Preferences dialog box has options for specifying what happens when you open new music files and for changing MusicMatch Jukebox's theme.

Change Theme drop-down list Use this drop-down list to specify the theme (the visual look) for MusicMatch Jukebox.

Player Page Preferences

The Player page of the Preferences dialog box (the business part of which is shown in Figure 11.34) contains these two options:

Seek Increment text box Use this text box to specify the number of seconds that MusicMatch Jukebox moves forward or back when you issue a seek command (Controls ➤ Player ➤ Play Control ➤ Seek Backward or Controls ➤ Player ➤ Play Control ➤ Seek Forward). The default setting is 5 seconds.

Song Skip Increment text box Use this text box to specify how many tracks MusicMatch Jukebox skips when you issue a skip command (Controls ➤ Player ➤ Play Control ➤ Skip Back Songs or Controls ➤ Player ➤ Play Control ➤ Skip Forward Songs). The default setting is 5 songs.

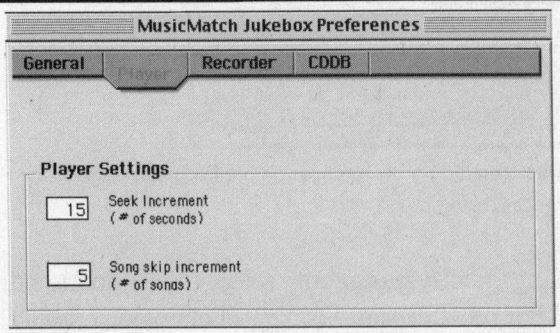

FIGURE 11.34: The business part of the Player page of the Preferences dialog box

Recorder Preferences

The Recorder page of the Preferences dialog box (see Figure 11.35) contains options that control the encoding rate and location for the MP3 files that you encode.

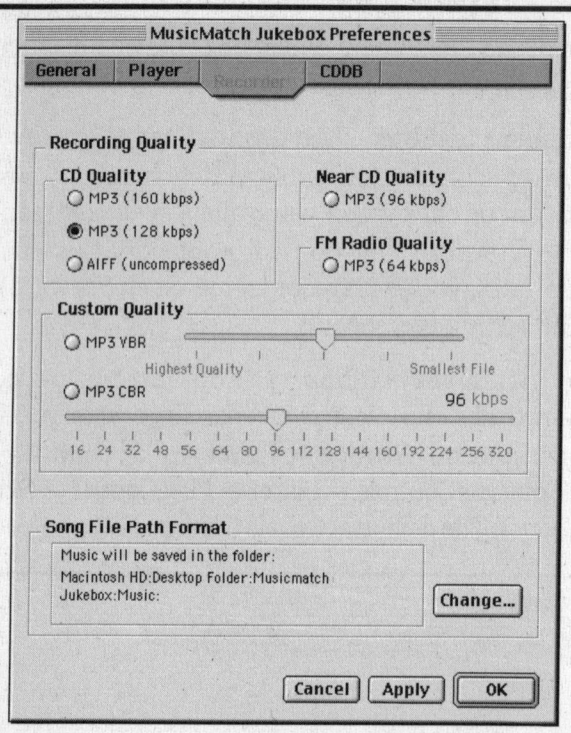

FIGURE 11.35: Choose encoding preferences on the Recorder page of the Preferences dialog box.

In the Recording Quality group box, select the sampling rate at which to record. For most music, we suggest choosing one of the CD Quality options—either the MP3 (128kbps) option button or the MP3 (160kbps) option button. (The AIFF setting creates uncompressed audio files.) For spoken audio, try the Near CD Quality setting by choosing the MP3 (96kbps) option button, or the FM Radio Quality setting by choosing the MP3 (64kbps) option button.

For special purposes, you can use the MP3 VBR (variable bit rate) and MP3 CBR (constant bitrate) options found in the Custom Quality group box. The VBR option lets you specify the quality you want, and the CBR option lets you specify the bitrate.

The Song File Path Format text box displays the folder in which MusicMatch Jukebox saves the MP3 files that you encode. To change the folder, click the Change button and use the resulting Choose a Folder dialog box to navigate to and identify the appropriate folder.

> **TIP**
> You can also quickly change the sampling rate by choosing Controls ≻ Recorder ≻ Quality and choosing the appropriate setting on the Quality submenu.

CDDB Page Preferences

The CDDB page of the Preferences dialog box (see Figure 11.36) contains settings that let you control whether and how MusicMatch Jukebox accesses CDDB, the online database of CD information.

To use CDDB, make sure the Enable CDDB Service check box is selected. (This check box is selected by default.) Then, make sure that the address of an appropriate CDDB server is entered in the CDDB Server text box, and an appropriate port is entered in the Port text box. (The default settings are cddb.cddb.com and 80, respectively.)

Change the e-mail address in the Your Email Address text box if you want. By default, MusicMatch Jukebox enters your real e-mail address (if it can learn it), and you may not want to broadcast this address.

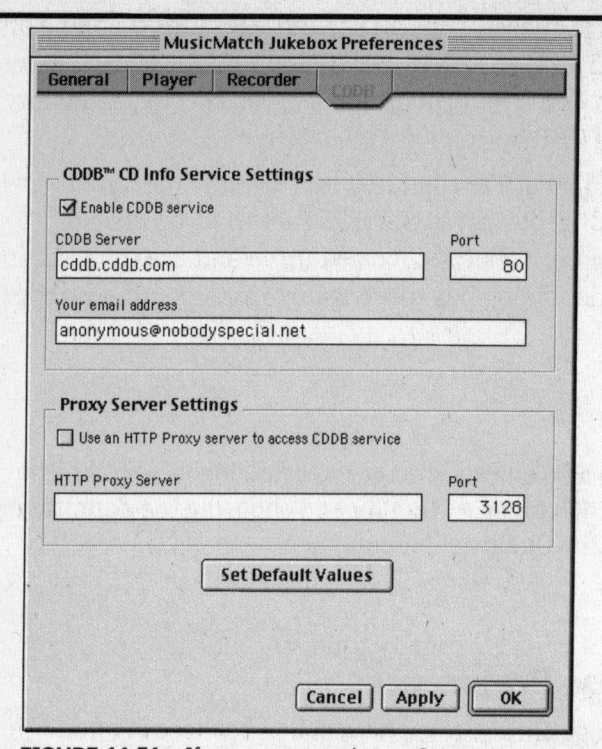

FIGURE 11.36: If your computer has an Internet connection, make sure that MusicMatch Jukebox is configured correctly to use CDDB.

> **NOTE**
>
> At this writing, MusicMatch Jukebox doesn't provide a way to retrieve a list of CDDB servers, so if you want to use a different CDDB server, you'll need to find out its address from another source.

If you need to use a proxy server, select the Use an HTTP Proxy Server to Access CDDB Service check box in the Proxy Server Settings group box. Enter the server's details in the HTTP Proxy

Ripping and Encoding with MusicMatch Jukebox

You're now ready to start ripping and encoding with MusicMatch Jukebox.

Put a CD in your CD drive and close the drive. MusicMatch Jukebox reads the CD and—if you're using CDDB and connected to the Internet, or if it's a CD that your CD-ROM drive has looked up before—displays the album's name, the artist's name, and the track titles. If CDDB can't decide between a couple of possible listings for the CD, it displays a dialog box to let you decide.

If the Recorder window isn't displayed, click the Record Music button to display it. Figure 11.37 shows the Recorder window ripping and encoding a CD.

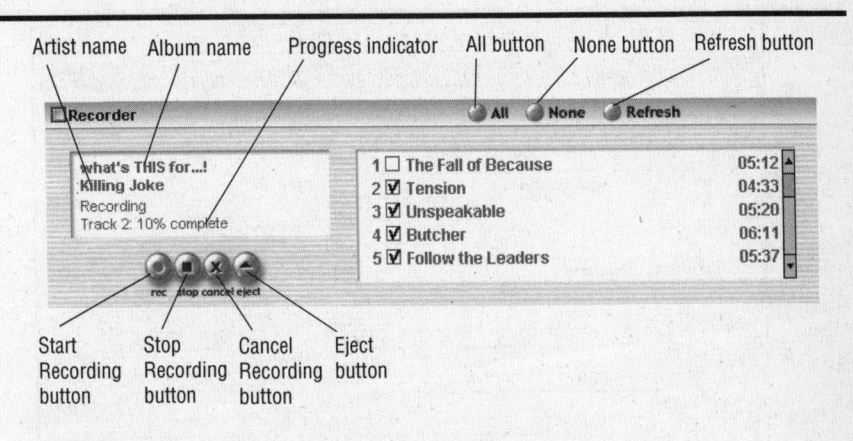

FIGURE 11.37: The MusicMatch Jukebox Recorder window

Specify the tracks that you want to record by selecting their check boxes. Use the All button to select all tracks and the None button to deselect all tracks. Click the Refresh button to force MusicMatch Jukebox to reread the CD's contents (or to read them if you've set MusicMatch Jukebox not to look up CDs automatically).

Click the Start Recording button to start ripping. As MusicMatch Jukebox rips and encodes the track, it displays a readout of its progress. When it has finished encoding a track, MusicMatch Jukebox automatically adds it to the music library.

Adding and Editing Tags

MusicMatch Jukebox makes it easy to add ID3 tag information to all the tracks from the same album:

1. Select a track in the Music Library window and click the Tag button to display the MusicMatch Jukebox – MP3 Tag Editor dialog box (see Figure 11.38).

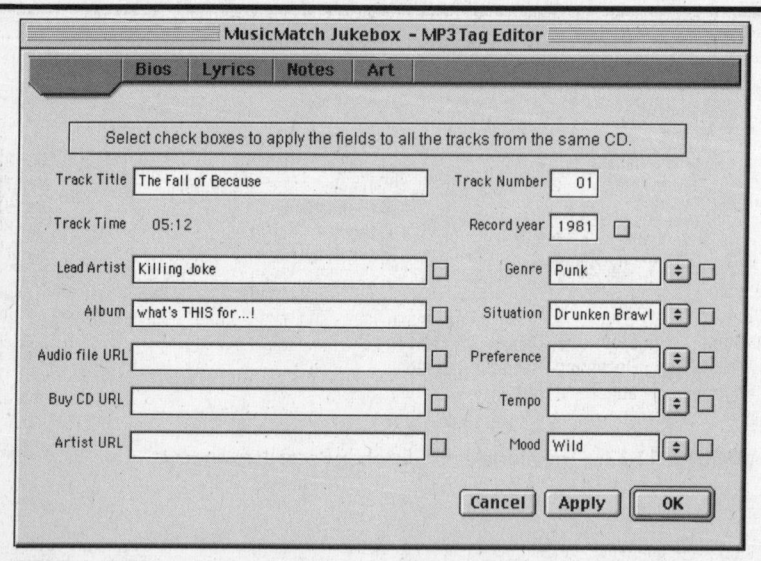

FIGURE 11.38: Use the MusicMatch Jukebox – MP3 Tag Editor dialog box to add and edit ID3 tags.

2. Enter information for the track by typing the information in the text boxes and by choosing items in the drop-down list boxes. If you want to apply the same information to all the tracks from the same CD, select the check box to the right of the text box or drop-down list box.

3. To add lyrics, notes, or bios to the track, click the Lyrics, Notes, or Bios tab and enter the information in the text box on that page.

4. To add a JPEG picture to the track, click the Art tab to display the Art page. Click the Load New Artwork button and use the resulting MusicMatch Jukebox: Choose Art File dialog box to navigate to and select the art file. Then click the Open button. (To remove the art from a tag, click the Remove Art from Tag button.)

5. Click the Apply button to apply your changes to the tag or tags.

6. Click the OK button to close the MusicMatch Jukebox – MP3 Tag Editor dialog box.

Building Your Music Library or Libraries

Like most jukeboxes, MusicMatch Jukebox lets you keep a database of your music files, enabling you to manage and find them easily.

You can create as many music libraries as you want. If you prefer to have all your music in one music library, that's fine, but be warned that the library may become unmanageably large. We suggest segmenting your music into the different themes, moods, or occasions by which you'll want to play it. MusicMatch Jukebox lets you put any individual track into multiple music libraries.

If you don't have the Music Library window displayed, click the Music Library button on the Main window to display it.

Creating a New Music Library

To create a new music library, choose Controls ➤ Music Library ➤ New Music Library. In the MusicMatch Jukebox: Music Library dialog box, specify the filename and folder for the music library, then click the Save button.

Adding Tracks to a Music Library

MusicMatch Jukebox automatically adds to the current music library any new MP3 files that you rip with it. But you'll need to add any existing MP3 files to the database so that you can work with them through MusicMatch Jukebox. The same goes for any MP3 files that you download.

To add files to the current music library, click the Add button in the Music Library window to display the MusicMatch Jukebox: Add Tracks dialog box. Then select the directory and files you want, and click the Open button.

Removing Tracks from a Music Library

To remove a file from your music library, select it in the Music Library window and click the Delete button. MusicMatch Jukebox displays the Jukebox – Confirm Removal dialog box (see Figure 11.39). Proceed as follows:

- To remove the track from your music library but leave the file for the track on your computer, click the OK button.
- To remove the track from your music library and delete the file for the track from your computer, select the Also Remove

the Song Files from My Computer check box and click the OK button.

- If you want to commit yourself one way or the other on deleting files from your computer when removing them from your music library, select the Never Ask Me This Again check box before dismissing the Jukebox – Confirm Removal dialog box.

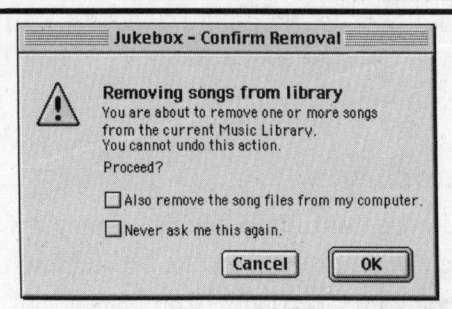

FIGURE 11.39: In the Jukebox – Confirm Removal dialog box, confirm that you want to remove the track or tracks from your music library. You can also choose to delete the file for the track from your computer.

Clearing a Music Library

To get rid of the contents of a music library, choose Controls ➢ Music Library ➢ Clear Music Library. You won't usually want to do this, so MusicMatch Jukebox displays the Confirm Clear dialog box (see Figure 11.40) to make sure that you're aware of the significance of the action. Click the OK button to clear the music library. If you want to be able to blow away the contents of a music library without MusicMatch Jukebox questioning your actions, select the Never Ask Me This Again check box before clicking the OK button.

FIGURE 11.40: MusicMatch Jukebox displays the Confirm Clear dialog box before clearing the contents of a music library.

Opening a Music Library

To open a music library, choose Controls ➤ Music Library ➤ Open Music Library. MusicMatch Jukebox displays the MusicMatch Jukebox: Music Library dialog box. Navigate to and select the music library, then click the Open button. MusicMatch Jukebox opens the music library, and closes any music library that is currently open.

Finding Tracks in Your Music Library

To find tracks in a music library, choose Controls ➤ Music Library ➤ Find Track in Music Library to display the Find in Music Library dialog box (see Figure 11.41). Take the following steps:

1. Enter your search term in the Find What text box.

2. Select or clear the Match Complete Name Only check box and the Match Case check box as appropriate.

3. Choose a direction by selecting the Up option button or the Down option button. (The Down option button is selected by default.)

4. Click the Find First button.

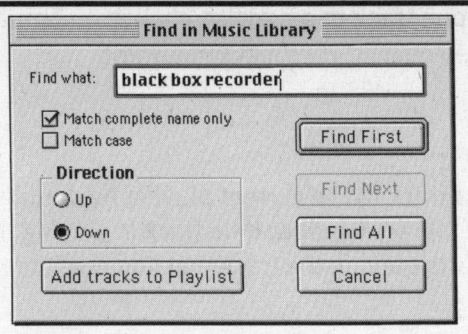

FIGURE 11.41: Use the Find in Music Library dialog box to find tracks in your music library.

If it finds an instance of your search term, MusicMatch Jukebox scrolls the Music Library to display it. You can then click the Add Tracks to Playlist button to add that track to your current playlist or click the Find Next button to find the next instance of the search term. Click the Find All button to find all instances of the search term. (The Find All feature is useful for adding all the tracks matching a certain description to a playlist.)

Playing Music with MusicMatch Jukebox

Once you've got your music organized into music libraries, you can create playlists, save them, and play them back. You can also use the AutoDJ feature to create automatic playlists for you.

Creating, Saving, and Opening Playlists

To create a playlist, clear the current playlist of any superfluous tracks by clicking the Clear button. Add tracks to the Playlist window by dragging them from the Music Library window. Drag the tracks up and down the playlist to get them into the order you want.

To select more than one track in a playlist, click in an empty area and drag until you've selected all the tracks you want.

> **TIP**
>
> You can also add a track to the current playlist by double-clicking it in the Music Library window. If no track is playing, MusicMatch Jukebox starts playing the track that you just added.

When you've assembled your playlist, save it by clicking the Save button to display the Save dialog box, entering a name, and clicking the Save button.

To open a playlist, click the Open button on the Playlist window. Use the resulting MusicMatch Jukebox: Open Playlist Files dialog box to navigate to and select the playlist, and then click the Open button.

> **TIP**
>
> To play tracks, you can drag them from the Finder and drop them in the Playlist window.

Using the AutoDJ Feature

MusicMatch Jukebox's AutoDJ feature lets you specify vague guidelines by which MusicMatch Jukebox should put together automatic playlists for you. This feature is usually irritating, but you may find it amusing on occasion.

To use the AutoDJ feature, click the AutoDJ button in the Music Library window to display the AutoDJ dialog box (see Figure 11.42). Specify the number of hours in the Enter Play Time text box, then use the First Criteria, Second Criteria, and Third Criteria group boxes to specify the type of music you want. Use the Preview button to get a readout of how many matching tracks AutoDJ has found and the combined playing time. Then click the Get Tracks button to add the tracks to your current playlist, from which you can rearrange them as you want and play them as usual.

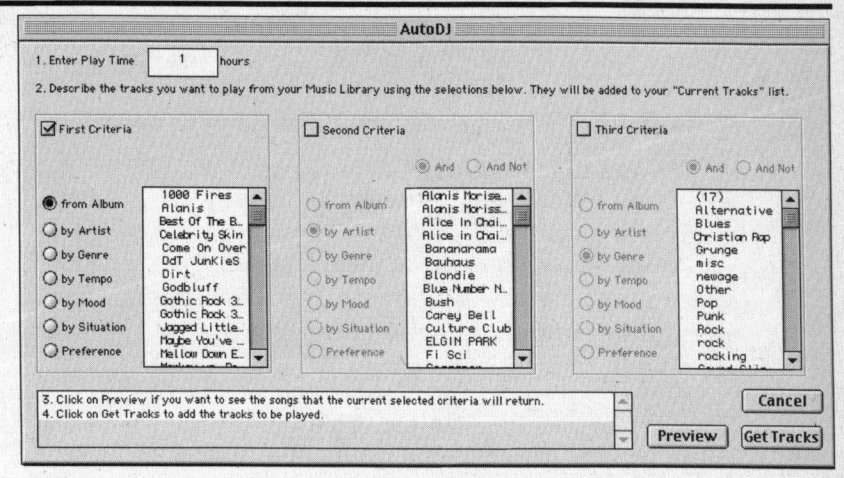

FIGURE 11.42: MusicMatch Jukebox's AutoDJ feature creates playlists based on criteria you specify.

Applying Themes to MusicMatch Jukebox

MusicMatch Jukebox for the Macintosh supports different looks called *themes*. It comes with two themes built in—Oxygen (shown in the screens so far) and Digital Age—and you can add more themes that you download from sites such as the MusicMatch Web site.

To apply a different theme, choose Window ➢ Change Theme. MusicMatch Jukebox displays the General page of the Preferences dialog box. In the Change Theme drop-down list, select the theme, then click the Apply button to apply it. Click the OK button to close the Preferences dialog box.

Figure 11.43 shows MusicMatch Jukebox in its Digital Age theme.

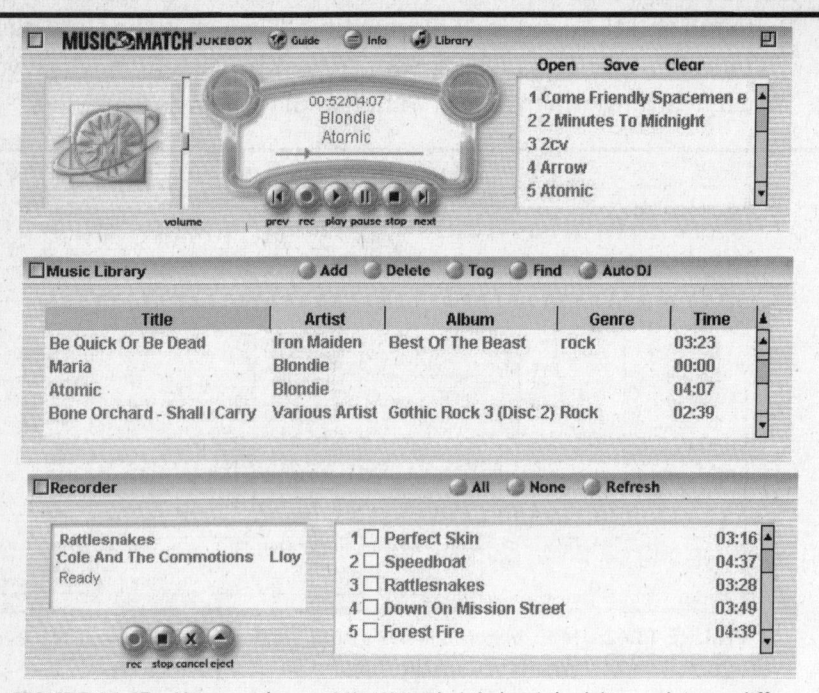

FIGURE 11.43: You can change MusicMatch Jukebox's look by applying a different theme.

Up Next

In this chapter, we've looked at two of the leading rippers for the Macintosh—AudioCatalyst and MPegger—and at the two leading ripper/player/jukeboxes, SoundJam MP and MusicMatch Jukebox for the Mac. As we mentioned at the start of the chapter, the amount of MP3 software available for the Mac is much more limited than for Windows, but the quality of what is available is plenty high enough to get you ripping and encoding comfortably.

That's the end of the Macintosh part of this book. In Part 6, we'll discuss how to play, rip, and encode MP3 files on Linux.

PART V
MP3 ON LINUX

LEARN TO:

- **USE MP3 PLAYERS ON LINUX**
- **USE RIPPERS AND JUKEBOXES ON LINUX**

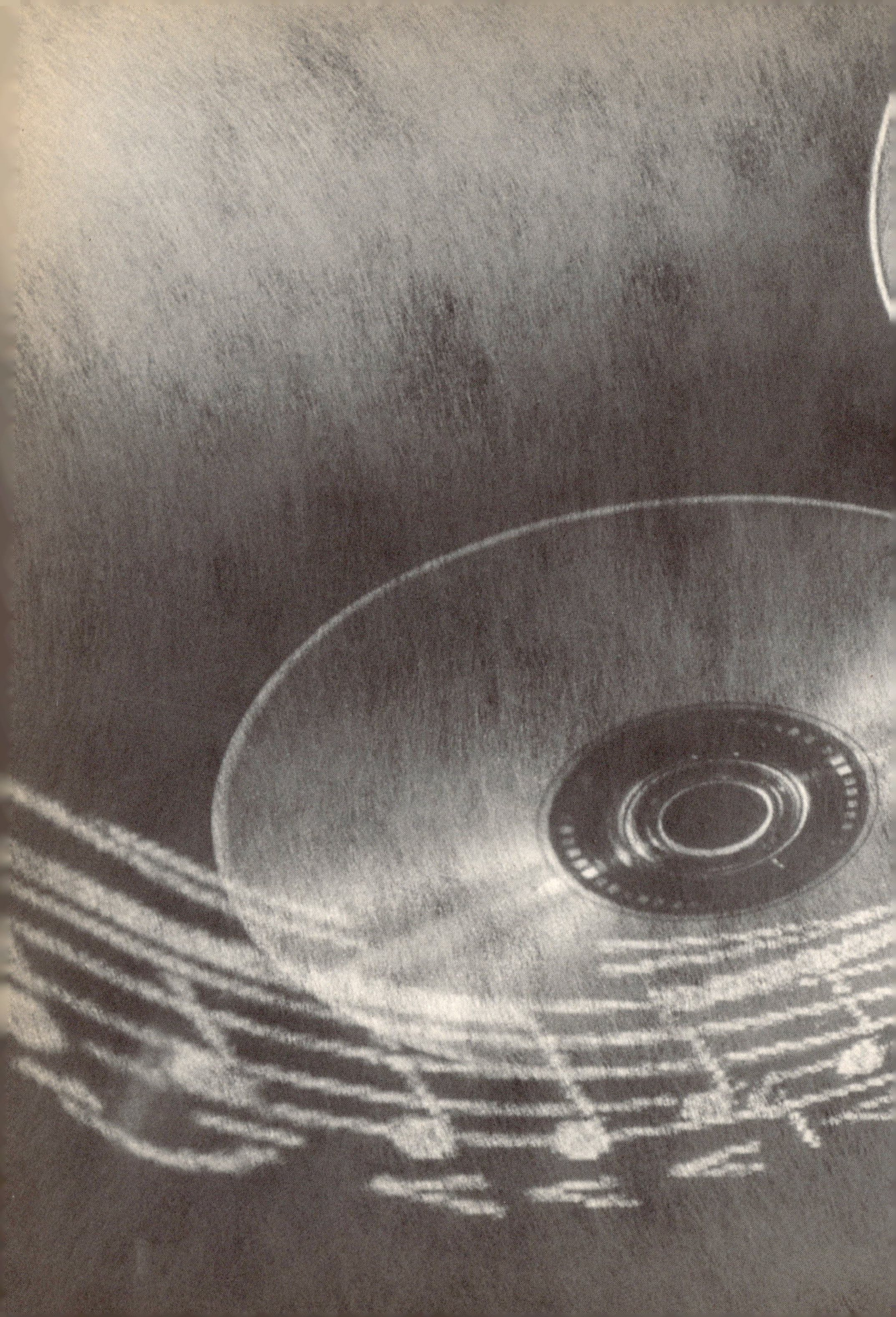

Chapter 12
Linux Players

FEATURING

- XMMS
- FreeAmp
- MPG123

In this chapter, we'll introduce you to three MP3 players for Linux: xmms, FreeAmp, and mpg123. If you're familiar with the Linux operating system, it won't be any surprise to find that these three MP3 players only scratch the surface of the huge number of MP3 players written for Linux—but they should be enough to get you started.

xmms (X Multimedia System) is essentially a Linux incarnation of Winamp, the Windows MP3 player discussed in Chapter 7, "Windows Players." xmms is a terrific player, but we'll cover it lightly here, referring you back to the Winamp section for most of the information on it so as not to repeat ourselves. FreeAmp, which we also visited (albeit more briefly) in Chapter 7, is a cross-platform player with a straightforward and functional graphical user interface (GUI). And mpg123 is a command-line player that we decided to include for a bit of variety.

As you'll know from your experience using Linux, you can get many distributions of the operating system, and you can install your chosen distribution with different degrees of completeness. We can't see what you're looking at, so you'll need to be able to navigate the intricacies of Linux libraries, packages, and the utilities tar and make on your own.

The examples in this chapter use Red Hat Linux 6, perhaps the most widespread distribution of Linux among Linux enthusiasts in North America at this writing. We're not putting down other distributions such as Caldera's OpenLinux, Mandrake Linux, Corel Linux, or S.U.S.E. Linux—they can rip and rock right along with Red Hat. However, we did have to choose one distribution to focus on in the wide-open world of Linux.

XMMS

The Player Formerly Known as x11amp, xmms (X Multimedia System) is included in a number of Linux distributions, including Red Hat Linux 6.

If your distribution of Linux doesn't include xmms, get the latest version of it from the xmms Web site, www.xmms.org. Compile it if necessary, and install it using the usual methods.

> **NOTE**
>
> Before you can install xmms, you need to have gtk+/glib 1.2.2 or better. If you don't have these libraries, you can download them from various sources on the Web.

Once you've got xmms started, you should be seeing something like Figure 12.1. (We've added in a number of MP3 tracks for visual excitement.)

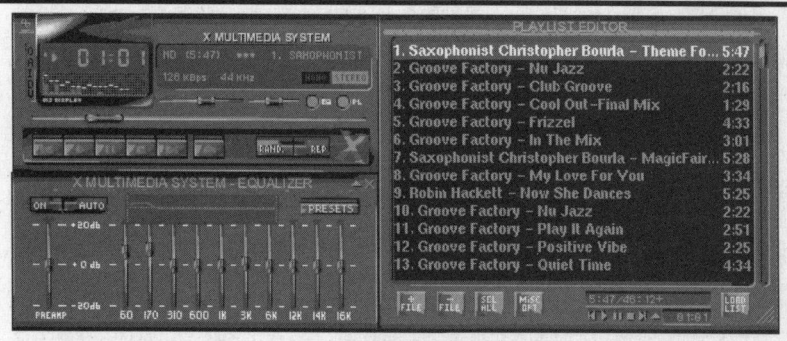

FIGURE 12.1: xmms is a Linux version of Winamp.

As you'll see, just about everything works the same as in Winamp—the Main window, the Playlist Editor, the Graphical Equalizer window, and so on. (For full coverage of Winamp, see Chapter 7.) The most notable differences between xmms and Winamp are relatively minor:

Different default skin xmms comes with its own slick-looking skin, rather than the Winamp-clone skin that x11amp sported. xmms can use Winamp's skins. Download a skin, install it in the /skins/ directory, and then press Alt+S to display the Skin Selector dialog box to select and apply it.

No preset equalizations At this writing, xmms doesn't have one of Winamp's strongest features—preset equalizations. You'll probably want to create some EQ presets of your own right away, perhaps taking a look at some of Winamp's preset equalizations for inspiration if you have Windows.

Different preference options You'll find that the Preferences dialog box is the area that appears to be the most different from Winamp, although many of the preference options themselves are the same. Figure 12.2 shows the Options page of the Preferences dialog box.

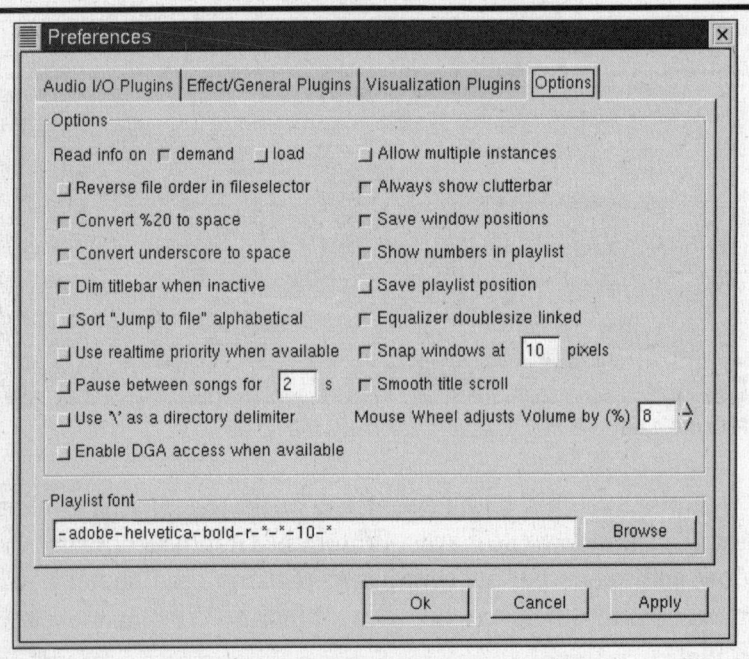

FIGURE 12.2: The Preferences dialog box is where you'll find most of the differences between xmms and Winamp.

> **TIP**
>
> Like Winamp, xmms supports a variety of plug-ins for providing additional features. If you're into MPEG video, you'll probably want to try the smpeg-xmms plug-in from 4Front Technologies (www.opensound.com), which enables xmms to play back MPEG video files.

FreeAmp

FreeAmp—Free Audio Music Player—is a free MP3 player that's currently available for Linux, Windows 9x and NT on Intel hardware, and Windows NT on Alpha hardware. Macintosh, BeOS, and Solaris versions are underway. As you'd expect, FreeAmp plays MP3 files; it also supports both SHOUTcast and icecast streams.

Download the latest version of FreeAmp from the FreeAmp Web site (www.freeamp.org) and install it as is appropriate for your distribution of Linux. For example, if your distribution uses the Red Hat Package Manager, you'll probably want to download an RPM file rather than getting the source code and compiling it yourself although there's nothing to stop you from compiling FreeAmp if you wish.

Once you've installed FreeAmp, start it. Figure 12.3 shows FreeAmp playing a minor classic.

FIGURE 12.3: FreeAmp is an effective MP3 player with a straightforward graphical interface.

Chapter Twelve

To open MP3 files in FreeAmp, click the Files button on the FreeAmp window and use the resulting Select a File to Play dialog box to select the file. But you'll want to do most of your file management from the FreeAmp – My Music window, which provides useful features for organizing your music and creating and manipulating playlists. Figure 12.4 shows the FreeAmp – My Music window with a short playlist underway.

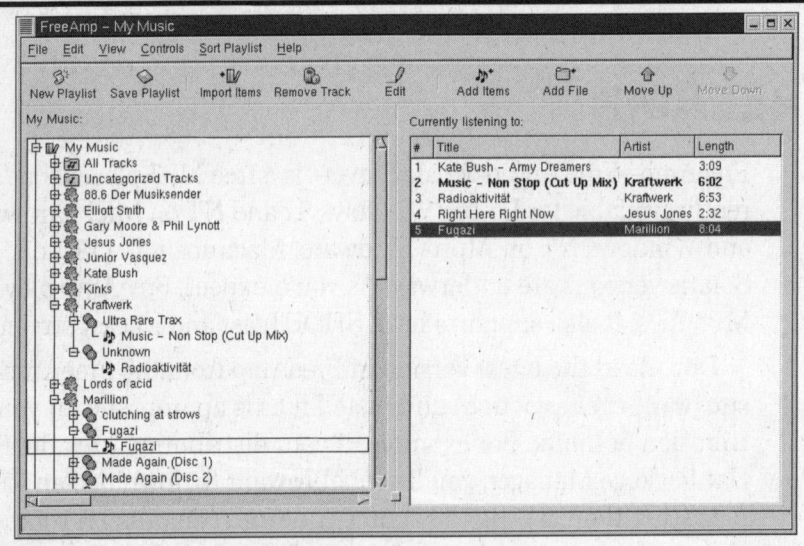

FIGURE 12.4: The FreeAmp – My Music window gives you access to your music collection and lets you build playlists.

To make the music on your computer known to FreeAmp, choose File ➢ Search Computer for Music from the FreeAmp – My Music window. In the FreeAmp – Search for Music dialog box, shown in Figure 12.5, specify the areas of your computer to search for files and click the Start Search button. Give the feature a few minutes, and it will marshal your files into a neat list in the FreeAmp – My Music window.

FIGURE 12.5: Use FreeAmp's Search for Music feature to have FreeAmp identify the music files on your computer.

FreeAmp includes a Download Manager feature that enables you to download music from Web sites that support the RMP or Real-Jukebox download format. (EMusic.com is one of the sites that supports this format.) To access the Download Manager, click the Download button on the FreeAmp window.

FreeAmp lets you save SHOUTcast or icecast streams to your hard disk. To do so, select the Save SHOUTcast/icecast Streams Locally check box on the Streaming page of the FreeAmp Preferences dialog box (displayed by clicking the Options button on the FreeAmp window) and specify the location to which to save them in the Save Location text box.

Other options you may want to set in the FreeAmp Preferences dialog box include the following:

General page Set your default music folder in the Save Music Folder Text box. In the Miscellaneous group box, you can select the By Default Queue Tracks Rather Than Play Them Immediately check box if you want to be able to add tracks to your playlist by double-clicking them in the My Music pane of the FreeAmp – My Music dialog box. (Double-clicking a track here starts it playing if this check box is not selected.) In the File Associations group box, specify whether FreeAmp should reclaim file associations, and whether it should ask you before doing so.

Streaming page Specify a different buffer length in the Buffer Streams For NN Seconds text box if you want to try to smooth out buffering problems for streaming audio. On this page, you can also specify proxy information and an alternate IP address.

Advanced page On this page, you can adjust the sizes of the input buffer, output buffer, and prebuffer.

MPG123

mpg123 is a free command-line player for Linux that produces good-quality sound.

mpg123 is included in a number of distributions of Linux, including Red Hat Linux 6.x. Check to see if your distribution of Linux includes it; if not, download the latest version of mpg123 from the mpg123 Web site, `www.mpg123.de`. Compile mpg123 if necessary, and install it as usual.

Once you've installed mpg123, you can start a track playing by issuing the `mpg123` command followed by the filename for the track. For example, the following command plays the track `Kate Bush - Sat in Your Lap.mp3` in the `/usr/music/` directory:

```
mpg123 "/usr/music/Kate Bush - Sat in Your Lap.mp3"
```

If you're playing a single track, press Ctrl+C to stop play. If you're playing multiple tracks, press Ctrl+C twice to stop play, because the first press of Ctrl+C stops the current track but automatically starts the next track.

One way to start multiple tracks playing is to specify them in sequence after the `mpg123` command, as follows:

```
mpg123 "Metallica - Unforgiven.mp3" "Junior Vasquez - Do It Again.mp3"
```

But usually you'll find it easier to create a playlist and feed it to mpg123 using the `@` flag:

```
mpg123 -@ /playlists/green_skies.pls
```

As a command-line program, mpg123 doesn't offer much visual entertainment. If you want to know a bit about what's going on, you can run it in verbose mode by using the -v switch:

mpg123 -v "/usr/music/Joan Jett - Bad Reputation"

Figure 12.6 shows mpg123 playing in verbose mode, with frame information running at the bottom of the window.

```
Joan Jett - Bad Reputation.mp3                              _ □ x
 File  Edit  Settings  Help
[root@performance /root]# mpg123 -v "/usr/music/Joan Jett - Bad Reputation.mp3"
High Performance MPEG 1.0/2.0/2.5 Audio Player for Layer 1, 2 and 3.
Version 0.59r (1999/Jun/15). Written and copyrights by Michael Hipp.
Uses code from various people. See 'README' for more!
THIS SOFTWARE COMES WITH ABSOLUTELY NO WARRANTY! USE AT YOUR OWN RISK!

Directory: /usr/music/
Playing MPEG stream from Joan Jett - Bad Reputation.mp3 ...
MPEG 1.0, Layer: III, Freq: 44100, mode: Joint-Stereo, modext: 0, BPF : 417
Channels: 2, copyright: No, original: Yes, CRC: No, emphasis: 0.
Bitrate: 128 Kbits/s, Extension value: 0
Audio: 1:1 conversion, rate: 44100, encoding: signed 16 bit, channels: 2
Frame#  1509 [ 4899], Time: 00:39.41 [02:07.97],
```

FIGURE 12.6: mpg123 is an effective command-line MP3 player for Linux and various Unix distributions.

Up Next

This brief chapter outlined three MP3 players for Linux: the Winamp look-alike xmms, the straightforward FreeAmp, and the command-line mpg123. As mentioned at the start of the chapter, Linux boasts many other MP3 players but we'll leave you to investigate them on your own.

In the next chapter, we'll discuss Linux rippers and encoders.

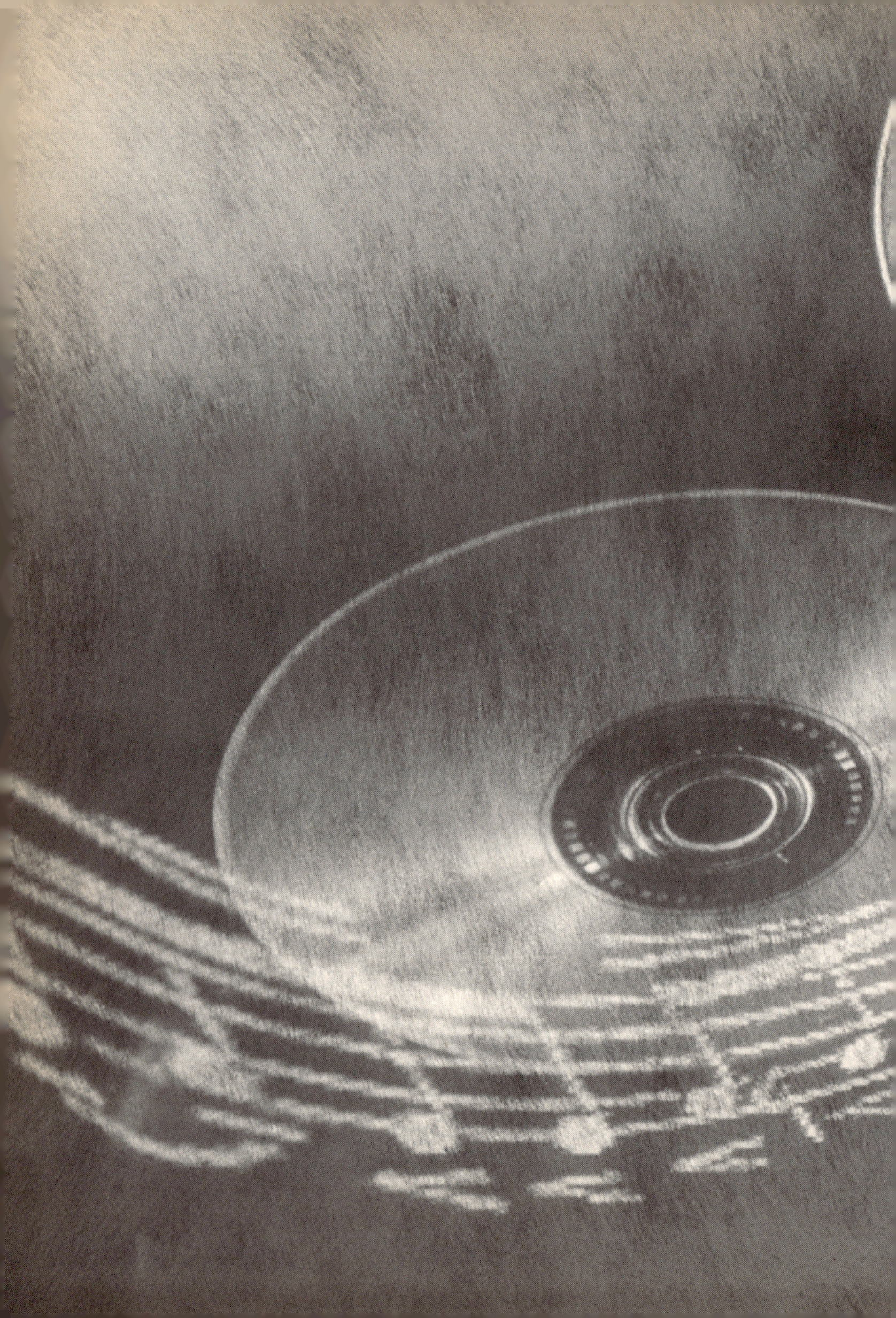

Chapter 13
Linux Rippers and Encoders

FEATURING
- Grip
- cdparanoia
- ripperX
- NotLame
- GOGO-no-coda
- BladeEnc
- MP3Enc

In this chapter, we'll show you some of the ripping and encoding solutions for Linux. Because of Linux's status as the hacker's operating system, there's a vast amount of Linux audio software available, much of it freeware or shareware.

Some of the Linux audio software solutions produce great results, some produce good results, and some produce indifferent to disappointing results. Much of the ripping and encoding software for Linux is easy to install, configure, and use. However, with other applications, you may struggle through a bear of a configuration process only to find that for some reason, that application won't work on your system. So be prepared to put in some trial and error—and to dedicate some time to finding the right solution for you.

While much of the software is freeware or shareware, there are commercial packages as well, such as the MP3 Encoder for Linux from Xing Technologies and the $199 MP3Enc from Fraunhofer IIS. While you can get combined rippers and encoders for Linux, you may want to use a separate ripper and encoder to give yourself more flexibility and control over the processes.

In this chapter, we'll start off with the one-stop solutions: Grip, a GUI freeware ripper and encoder that we've found to be fast and effective, and ripperX, which matches Grip for results and outdoes it with its user interface. We'll then move behind the scenes and discuss cdparanoia, the ripper used by various front ends (including Grip and ripperX) and a couple of command-line encoders, NotLame and GOGO. We'll also mention a couple of other encoders that you may want to try: BladeEnc and MP3Enc.

Grip

If you want to do your ripping and encoding in a single step, the freeware ripper and encoder Grip by Mike Oliphant is a great place to start. You can find Grip at a variety of sites including www.freshmeat.net. Download Grip and install it to an appropriate directory. (Consult the documentation for where to install Grip if you're root and if you're not root. If you don't know what "root" means, break open the Linux documentation or reach for your nearest guru.)

Grip comes with the ripper cdparanoia built in and works with MP3 encoders such as LAME, GOGO, BladeEnc, l3enc, MP3Enc, and others. If you have one of these encoders, you should be all set. If you have several of these encoders, you can use whichever one you feel gives you the best results. If you don't have any of these encoders, see the sections on NotLame, GOGO, BladeEnc, and MP3Enc near the end of this chapter for information on where to find them.

Launch Grip as usual. Figure 13.1 shows Grip with a fresh CD in the CD drive.

As you can see, the main Grip window has five pages:

- The Tracks page lists the tracks on the current CD.
- The Rip page contains options for ripping.
- The Config page contains the configuration information.
- The Help page tells you to read the Readme file and provides a button for submitting bug reports to the author.
- The About page displays information about the version of Grip and its author.

580 Chapter Thirteen

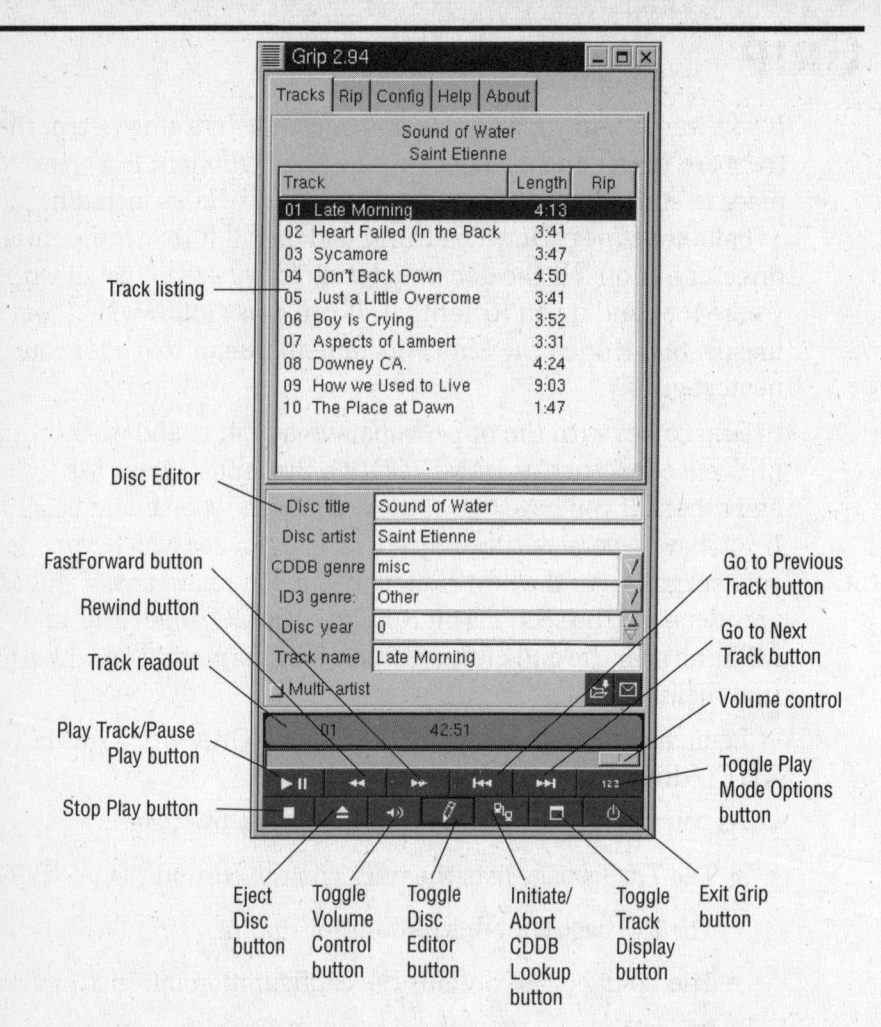

FIGURE 13.1: Grip is a freeware ripper and front end that works with a number of encoders.

Grip has a ton of configuration options, some of which are less obvious than others. We'll walk you through the main ones here:

1. Start by clicking the Config tab to display the Config page, which has six subpages. The four options on the CD page affect CD playback only and need no explanation.

2. Click the Rip tab on the Config page to display the Rip subpage (shown in Figure 13.2).

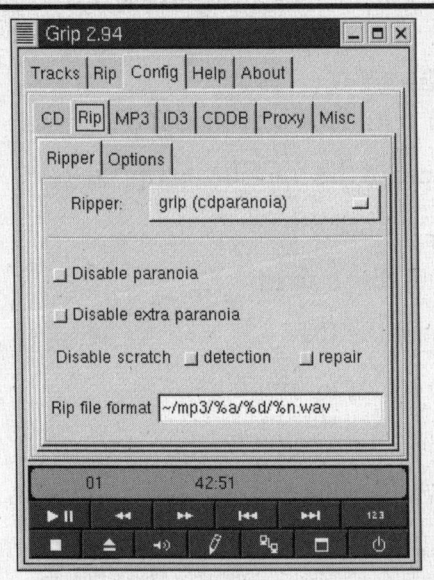

FIGURE 13.2: The Ripper subpage of the Rip subpage of Grip window

3. Make sure the Ripper subpage of the Rip subpage is showing, and then choose ripper options as follows:

   Ripper drop-down list   Usually you'll want to choose grip (cdparanoia) in this drop-down list, but you can also use cdparanoia itself, cdda2wav, or another ripper if you have it installed.

   Disable Paranoia, Disable Extra Paranoia, Detection, and Repair check boxes   Leave these check boxes unselected. (The Disable Paranoia check box and the Disable Extra Paranoia check box are available only if you use the built-in cdparanoia ripper.)

Rip File Format text box   Enter **%n.mp3** in this text box to make Grip record the tracks as MP3 files that use the track's name. The switches for rip file format are as follows:

Switch	Designation
%n	Name of the track being ripped
%t	Number of the track being ripped
%a	Current track's artist
%A	Current disc's artist
%d	Name of the CD
%b	Begin sector for ripping
%e	End sector for ripping
%c	CD drive involved
%I	CDDB ID of the CD in hexadecimal format
%g	Number for the ID3 genre tag
%G	Word for the ID3 genre tag

4. Now click the Options tab to display the Options subpage of the Rip subpage, shown in Figure 13.3, and choose options as follows:

Rip 'nice' Value text box   To change the priority given to Grip, enter a value in this text box.

Auto-Rip on Insert, Beep after Rip, and Auto-Eject after Rip check boxes   Select these check boxes as you see fit. If you select the Auto-Eject after Rip check box, you can specify a delay (in seconds) in the Auto-Eject Delay text box.

Linux Rippers and Encoders

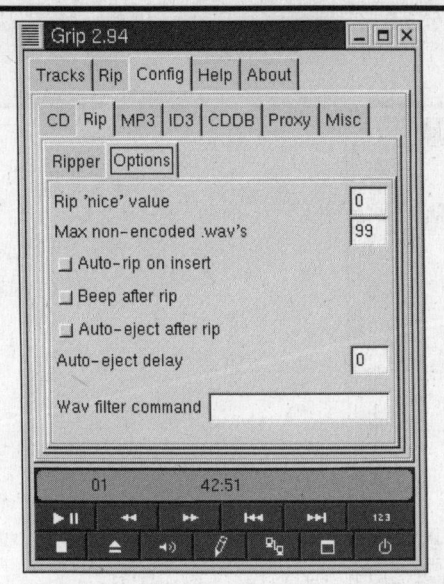

FIGURE 13.3: Choosing options on the Options subpage of the Rip subpage

5. Click the MP3 tab to display the MP3 subpage (shown in Figure 13.4). If the Encoder subpage isn't displayed, click the Encoder tab. Then choose options as follows:

   Encoder drop-down list   Select the encoder you want to use: BladeEnc, LAME, l3enc, xingmp3enc, mp3encode, GOGO, or Other.

   MP3 Executable and MP3 Command-Line text boxes   Grip enters the expected path to the encoder in the MP3 Executable text box and the command parameters in the MP3 Command-Line text box. Adjust these as necessary for your system: %b specifies the bitrate in kbps, %f specifies the WAV filename, and %o specifies the MP3 filename.

   MP3 File Format text box   Change the default setting of ~mp3/%a/%d/%n.mp3 if you want to name the MP3 file differently than by its name in a directory named after the CD in a directory named after the artist.

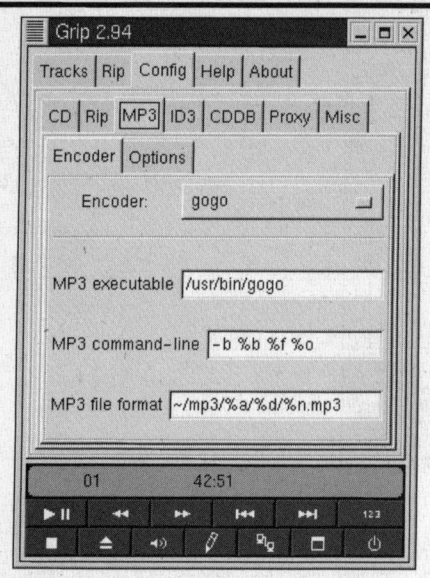

FIGURE 13.4: Choosing options on the Encoder subpage of the MP3 subpage

6. Click the Options tab to display the Options subpage (shown in Figure 13.5) and choose options as follows:

Delete .WAV after Encoding check box Clear this check box if you want to keep the WAV file for whatever reason.

Insert Info into SQL Database check box Select this check box if you're running a program such as DigitalDJ that logs audio tracks in a SQL database.

Create .m3u Files check box This check box controls whether Grip automatically creates a playlist of the CD's tracks in the M3U format.

Use Relative Paths in .m3u Files This check box controls whether Grip uses relative paths (relative to the location of the playlist file) or absolute (full) paths in the playlist files.

M3U File Format text box Use this text box to specify the file format of the M3U playlist file (if you're creating one). The switches are the same as for the rip file format (discussed earlier in this section).

Encoding Bitrate text box Make sure that this text box shows a suitable bitrate, such as 128 or 160.

Number of CPUs to Use and MP3 'Nice' Value text boxes Change the numbers in these text boxes if appropriate for your system.

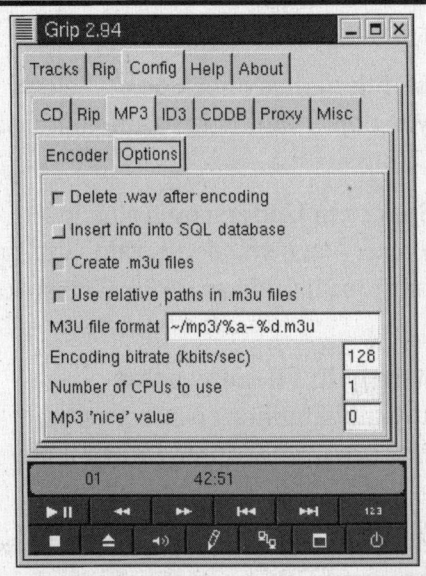

FIGURE 13.5: Choose a bitrate and other encoding options on the Options subpage of the MP3 subpage.

7. Click the ID3 tab to display the ID3 subpage, and make sure that the Add ID3 Tags to MP3 Files check box is selected (unless for some reason you do not want to add tags to your tracks).

8. Click the CDDB tab to display the CDDB subpage and choose CDDB settings. On the Primary server subpage and Secondary Server subpage, enter settings for the CDDB servers you want to use. Unless you don't want to use CDDB, leave the Perform CDDB Lookup Automatically check box selected.

9. If you use a proxy server to connect to the Internet, click the Proxy tab and enter appropriate settings on the Proxy subpage.

10. Click the Misc tab to display the Misc subpage and choose options as follows:

    Email Address text box   Adjust the address in this text box as necessary.

    Do Not Lowercase Filenames check box   Select this check box if you don't want Grip to automatically lowercase filenames.

    Do Not Change Spaces to Underscores check box   Select this check box if you don't want Grip to automatically substitute an underscore for each space in a track name.

    Characters to Not Strip in Filenames text box   Enter any non-alphanumeric characters that you want to prevent Grip from stripping when it creates filenames.

    Keep Application Minimum Size check box   Select this check box if you want Grip to minimize its demands on your screen real estate.

Ripping and Encoding

Finally, you're ready to rip. Insert a CD, and you're off. On the Tracks page, right-click the tracks you want to rip. (Click the Rip column header to toggle selection of all tracks at once.) Then click the Rip+Encode button to start the ripping and encoding of the tracks you selected. As Grip rips the tracks, the Rip meter and the MP3 meter displays its progress, as shown in Figure 13.6.

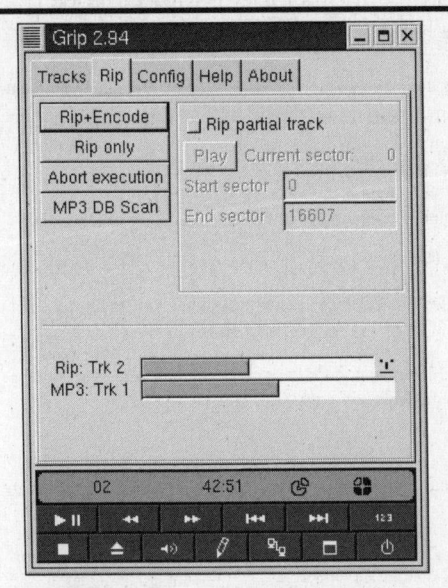

FIGURE 13.6: Grip at work ripping and encoding

CDPARANOIA

One of the primary rippers for Linux, cdparanoia gets its name from its creator's obsession with high-quality audio. cdparanoia is renowned for its extremely thorough error-checking, including the paranoia and extra paranoia features. To deliver perfectly ripped copies of CD tracks, cdparanoia extracts audio directly from the CD drive, bypassing the sound card, thus removing the chance that a low-quality sound card might degrade the sound.

cdparanoia is freeware. You can download it from the Xiphophorus company (www.xiph.org/paranoia). You'll also find copies and packages of it in many of the Linux archives on the Internet.

cdparanoia is a command-line program, but various front ends—including Grip and ripperX—work with it, making it easy to use cdparanoia with a graphical user interface (GUI). Table 13.1 lists the important command-line options for cdparanoia. (See the cdparanoia man pages for other options.)

TABLE 13.1: Important Command-Line Options for cdparanoia

Option	Meaning
-v	Verbose: Prints lots of information about auto-sensing and reading.
-q	Quiet: Does not print progress or error information.
-Q	Query: Auto-senses the CD-ROM drive, queries it, prints the table of contents for the CD-ROM to the screen, and quits.
-s	Search for drive: Makes cdparanoia perform a complete search for a CD-ROM drive even there's a /dev/cdrom link already.
-B	Batch mode.
-S	Force read speed: Sets the read speed of the CD-ROM (on supported CD-ROMs).
-Z	Disable paranoia: Disables the data-verification and error-correction features.
-Y	Disable extra paranoia: Disables the intra-read data-verification feature.
-X	Disable scratch detection: Disables the scratch-detection feature. When scratch detection is disabled, cdparanoia aborts reading the disc when it encounters a scratch.
-W	Disable scratch repair: Disables the scratch-repair feature, which attempts to repair damaged data.

Install cdparanoia as appropriate for the version that you download and the distribution of Linux you're using.

To make sure that cdparanoia is running correctly, load a CD and issue the `cdparanoia -vQ` command from a terminal window. If all is well, you'll see a table of contents for the CD, as in Figure 13.7.

Once that's happening, you're ready to start ripping. You can rip a specific track to a file with the default name of `cdda.wav` in the current directory by issuing the `cdparanoia` command with the

Linux Rippers and Encoders

track number. For example, the following command rips track 10 from the CD:

```
cdparanoia 10
```

This is fine for a single track, but usually you'll want to specify a filename and directory name. To do so, specify them after a tilde (~), as in the following command, which creates the file beatles_let_it_be.wav in the /music/ directory:

```
cdparanoia 1 ~/music/beatles_let_it_be.wav
```

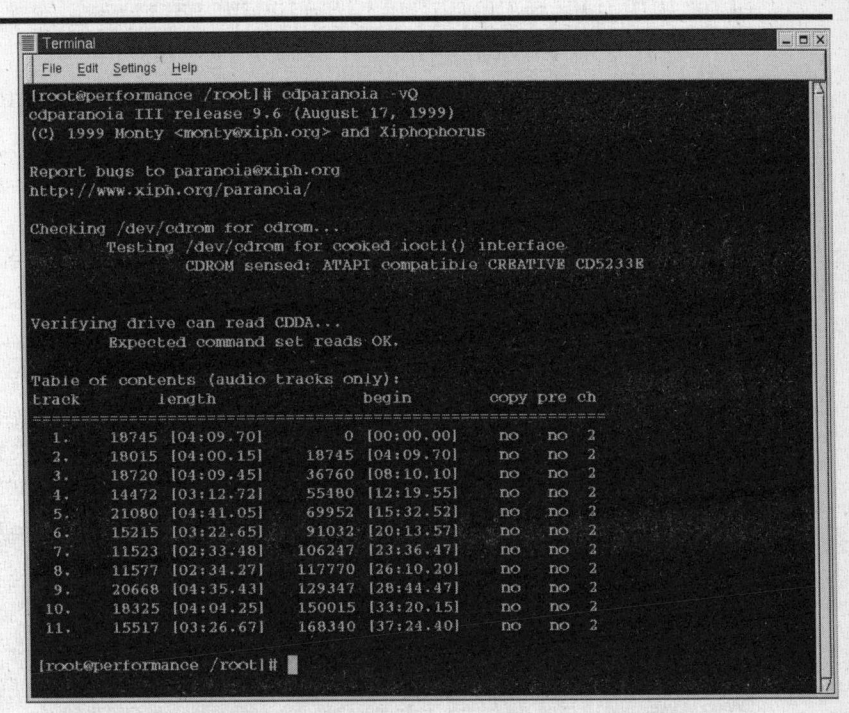

FIGURE 13.7: Issue the cdparanoia -vQ command to make sure cdparanoia is working correctly.

You can perform batch rips by using the -B flag with arguments to specify the tracks, and specifying the output directory for the

the files. In a batch encode, cdparanoia splits the tracks at their track boundaries and names them `trackn`, where *n* is the appropriate number. For example, the following command rips all the tracks on the CD (from track 1 to the last track) to the `/music/` directory, naming the tracks automatically:

```
cdparanoia -B 1- ~/music/
```

You can rip only part of certain tracks by specifying the start and end times in brackets and the track numbers in double quotation marks. For example, the following command rips the second minute of the fifth track of the current CD to the file `part.wav`:

```
cdparanoia "5[1:00]-5[1:59]" part.wav
```

You can also use this capability to rip two or more tracks into the same WAV file. For example, the following command rips the first three tracks of the current CD to the file `medley.wav`:

```
cdparanoia "1[0:00]-3[4:42]" medley.wav
```

While cdparanoia is ripping, it displays its progress in glyphs, as shown in Figure 13.8.

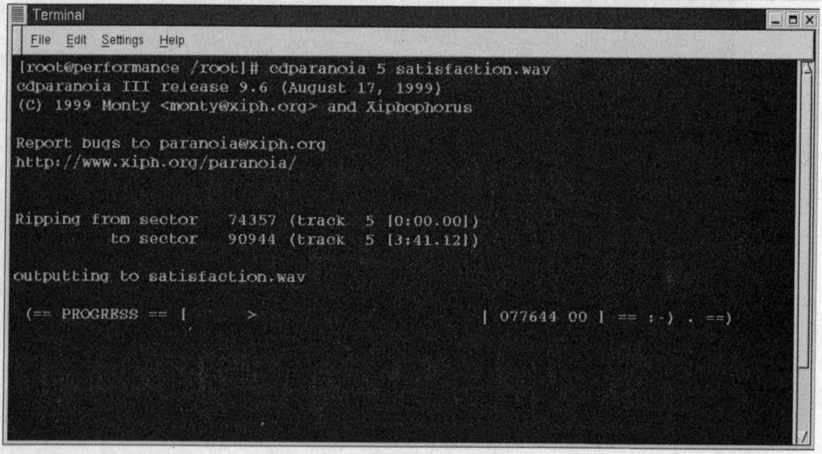

FIGURE 13.8: cdparanoia displays glyphs to show its progress as it rips.

Once you've ripped the tracks with cdparanoia, you're ready to encode them using an encoder such as MP3Enc or BladeEnc.

RIPPERX

ripperX is a freeware ripper and encoder with an attractive graphical user interface. ripperX requires cdparanoia to extract audio from CDs, and can use a variety of encoders, including BladeEnc, LAME, Xingmp3enc, and Fraunhofer's MP3Enc.

Download the latest version of ripperX from the ripperX Home Page, www.digitallabyrinth.com/linux/ripperX/. Before installing ripperX, download and install cdparanoia. (If you don't, ripperX will complain.) Before running ripperX, put an audio CD in your CD drive. (If you don't, cdparanoia will complain.) Either make cdparanoia setuid root or run ripperX as root. (If you don't, cdparanoia will give you an Error Code 14.)

The first time you run ripperX, it displays the Wanna Create Config File dialog box (shown in Figure 13.9). Agree to do so.

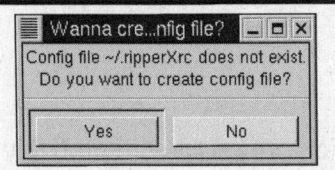

FIGURE 13.9: The first time you run ripperX, it invites you to create the ripperXrc config file.

Figure 13.10 shows ripperX running, with a CD loaded.

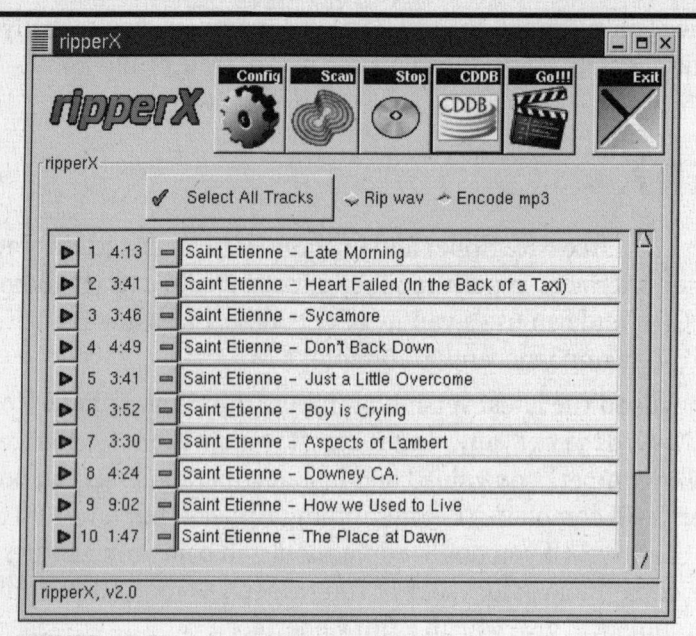

FIGURE 13.10: ripperX is a graphical ripper and encoder that works with cdparanoia and a variety of encoders, including LAME, BladeEnc, and MP3Enc.

Configuring ripperX

ripperX offers plenty of configuration options. You'll probably want to check through these and change some of them before you start ripping and encoding. The following sections discuss each page in the Configuration dialog box in turn.

General Page

On the General page (shown in Figure 13.11), specify the target directories for the WAV files and the MP3 files.

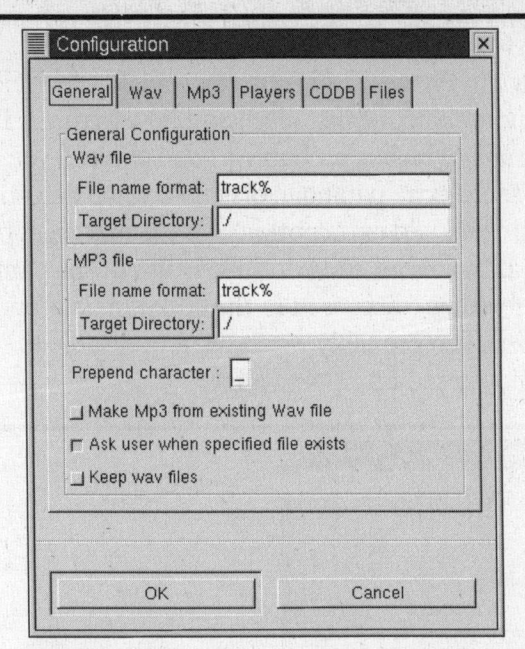

FIGURE 13.11: Choosing options on the General page of ripperX's Configuration dialog box

The Make MP3 from Existing WAV file check box lets you encode a group of WAV files you've previously ripped from a CD in a separate step. For this to work, you need to keep the filenames in the text boxes exactly the same as when the WAV files were ripped.

Select the Keep WAV Files check box if you want to keep the WAV files after encoding them to MP3 files. This option is useful when you're testing MP3 encoding quality.

Wav Page

The Wav page (shown in Figure 13.12) lets you specify which ripper to use (if you have more than one installed) and how to run it. If you're using cdparanoia (which is probably a good choice), you can disable paranoia, disable extra paranoia, disable scratch detection, disable scratch repair, and add extra options. Given that most people who choose cdparanoia over cdda do so because of the paranoia and extra paranoia features (discussed in the cdparanoia section earlier in this chapter), you probably won't want to disable them although doing so may speed up ripping a bit.

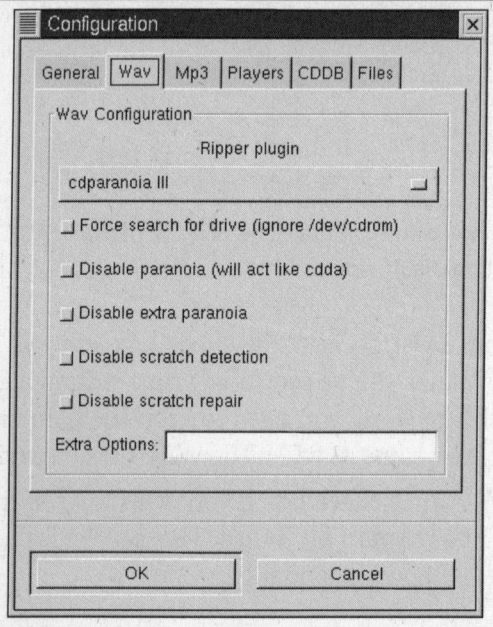

FIGURE 13.12: Configure your ripper on the Wav page of the Configuration dialog box.

MP3 Page

The MP3 page (shown in Figure 13.13) lets you specify which encoder to use, which bitrate to use, and options such as high-quality mode and CRC error protection.

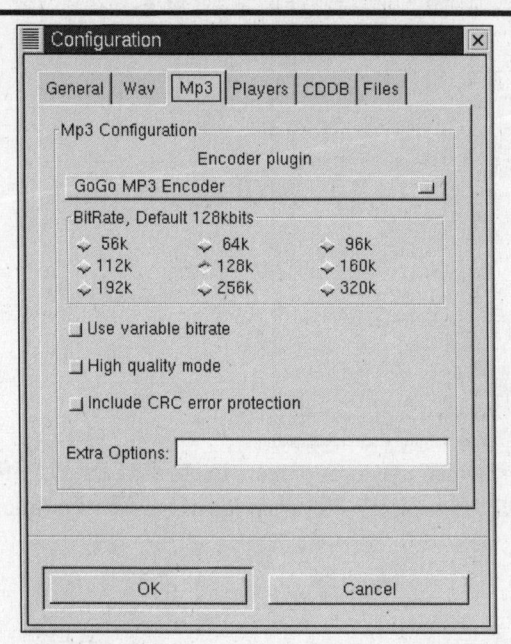

FIGURE 13.13: Choose MP3 encoding options on the MP3 page of the Configuration dialog box.

Players Page

The Players page (shown in Figure 13.14) lets you specify which player or players to use for CDs, WAV files, and MP3 files.

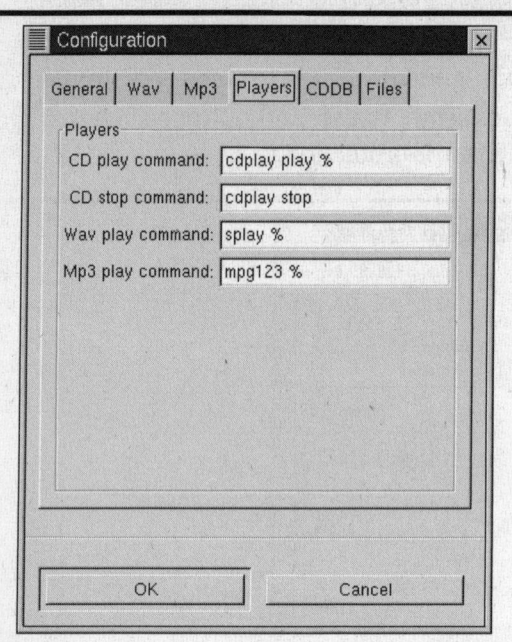

FIGURE 13.14: Specify which player or players to use for CDs, WAV files, and MP3 files on the Players page of the Configuration dialog box.

CDDB Page

The CDDB page (see Figure 13.15) lets you specify which CDDB server to use. ripperX uses freedb.org as its default CDDB server rather than cddb.com. freedb.org is perhaps ideologically sounder than cddb.com, but its listings may not be as up to date as those at cddb.com.

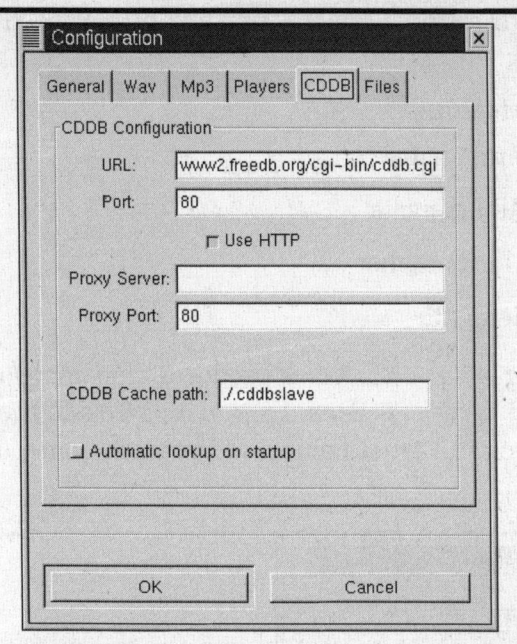

FIGURE 13.15: Specify CDDB settings on the CDDB page of the Configuration dialog box.

If you want to use cddb.com rather than freedb.org, change the URL in the URL text box on the CDDB page to **us.cddb.com** and the port to **888**. (For HTTP access, change the URL to **us.cddb.com/~cddb/cddb.cgi** and the port to **80**.) Select the Automatic Lookup on Startup check box if you want ripperX to check for the CD listing each time you start ripperX.

Files Page

On the Files page of the Configuration dialog box (shown in Figure 13.16), specify the file-naming format and directory-naming format that you want by entering codes in the Filename Format

String text box and Directory Format String text box, respectively. These are the codes:

Code	Meaning
%a	Artist name
%v	Album name
%#	Track number
%s	Song title

The default string is %a - %s, which produces filenames such as `Christina Aguilera - I Turn to You.mp3` To add the album name between the artist name and the track name, use %a - %v - %s.

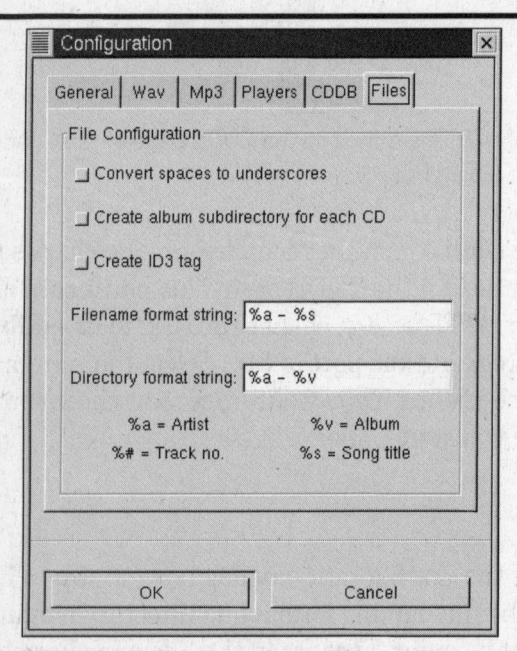

FIGURE 13.16: Specify your file-naming and directory-naming formats on the Files page of the Configuration dialog box.

You'll probably want to select the Create ID3 Tag check box so that ripperX creates ID3 tags in the MP3 files.

If you want to put each album into a separate subdirectory, select the Create Album Subdirectory for Each CD check box and specify the naming format in the Directory Format String text box. For example, you can use %a/%v to create a subdirectory containing the name under the artist's subdirectory. This produces folders such as `Richard Ashcroft/Alone with Everybody`.

Ripping and Encoding with ripperX

Once you've configured ripperX to your satisfaction, you should be ready to rip and encode. Select the tracks that you want to rip and encode. You can click the Select All Tracks button to select all tracks or, when all tracks are selected, to deselect them. Alternatively, click the button to the left of the track name so that its minus sign (–) changes to a check mark.

If you want to rip to WAV file but not encode, select the Rip WAV option button. Otherwise, make sure that the Encode MP3 option button is selected.

If you don't have ripperX configured to contact CDDB automatically, click the CDDB button to get the CD information. Then click the Go button to start ripping and encoding. Figure 13.17 shows ripperX at work ripping and encoding.

> **NOTE**
>
> With some encoders, ripperX is able neither to gauge the time remaining accurately (see the 186:48 reading for time remaining in Figure 13.17) nor to update the bar graph for the encoding progress. Chances are, though, that behind the scenes, all is going well—as in this example.

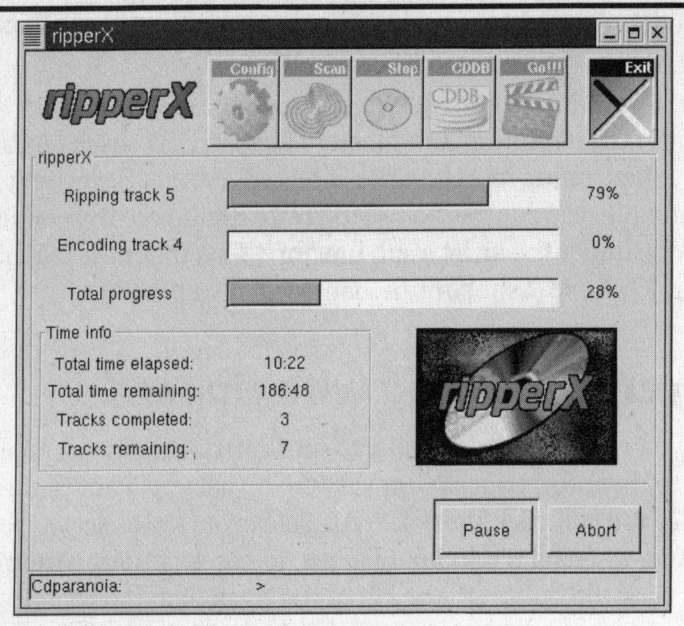

FIGURE 13.17: ripperX ripping and encoding

Once ripperX has finished ripping and encoding, it displays the Status dialog box (shown in Figure 13.18).

FIGURE 13.18: The Status dialog box lists the results of the ripping and encoding operations.

NotLame

The NotLame MP3 encoder is based on the LAME encoding engine. LAME has a reputation for high quality, and in May 2000, the r3mix.net site claimed that LAME produced better results than Fraunhofer's MP3Enc because MP3Enc sometimes "deforms" the range of 16kHz to 22kHz tones. (At this writing, you can find the analysis at `users.belgacom.net/gc247244/analysis.htm#MP3ENC31`.) Not everyone agrees, of course, but there are strong arguments for giving LAME a spin, perhaps in the shape of NotLame, and seeing how the results sound to you.

To do so, download the latest version of NotLame from the Not-Lame Web site, `hive.me.gu.edu.au/not_lame/`. Compile it if necessary, and install it as usual. (In most cases, you'll need to `su` to root for the installation.) Run NotLame from a terminal window.

Table 13.2 lists the important command-line options for NotLame.

TABLE 13.2: Important Command-Line Options for NotLame

Option	Meaning
-m	Specifies the mode: m for mono, s for stereo, j for joint stereo, f for forced mid/side stereo.
-k	Disables all filtering, causing NotLame to keep all frequencies.
--athonly	Causes NotLame to ignore the psychoacoustic model.
-b *n*	Specifies the bitrate. Can be 32, 40, 48, 56, 64, 80, 96, 112, 128, 160, 192, 224, 256, or 320.
-h	Specifies higher quality recording (this takes longer).
-f	Specifies fast encoding, which loses some audio quality.
-v	Specifies variable bitrate recording.
-V *n*	Specifies the variable bitrate quality, where *n* is a number between 0 (highest quality) and 9 (lowest quality).
-b *n*	Specifies the minimum bitrate for variable bitrate recording.
-B *n*	Specifies the maximum bitrate for variable bitrate recording.
-F	Strictly enforces the minimum bitrate.

CONTINUED →

TABLE 13.2 continued: Important Command-Line Options for NotLame

Option	Meaning
--tt "*text*"	Adds the text as the track title (30-character maximum) in the ID3 tag.
--ta "*text*"	Adds the text as the artist name (30-character maximum) in the ID3 tag.
--tl "*text*"	Adds the text as the album name (30-character maximum) in the ID3 tag.
--ty "*text*"	Adds the text as the year (4-character maximum) in the ID3 tag.
--tc "*text*"	Adds the text as the comment (30-character maximum) in the ID3 tag.
--tg "*text*"	Adds the text or number as the genre in the ID3 tag.
-c	Marks the MP3 file as copyrighted.
-o	Marks the MP3 file as a copy (non-original).
-p	Turns on CRC error protection. (Adds 16 bits per frame.)

Here are some examples:

- The following command encodes the WAV file heart_failed.wav at 320kpbs to the MP3 file heart_failed.mp3:

    ```
    notlame -b 320 heart_failed.wav
    heart_failed.mp3
    ```

- The following command encodes the WAV file heart_failed.wav at the default 128kpbs (which you don't need to specify) to the MP3 file heart_failed.mp3, with all filtering disabled:

    ```
    notlame -k heart_failed.wav heart_failed.mp3
    ```

- The following command encodes the same WAV file to the same MP3 file at a bitrate of 160kpbs, in joint stereo, with CRC error protection, and with the track title "Heart Failed," the artist name Saint Etienne, and the album name *Sound of Water*:

    ```
    notlame -b 160 -m j tt "Heart Failed" ta
    "Saint Etienne" tl "Sound of Water" -p
    heart_failed.wav heart_failed.mp3
    ```

Figure 13.19 shows NotLame encoding a file at 320kpbs.

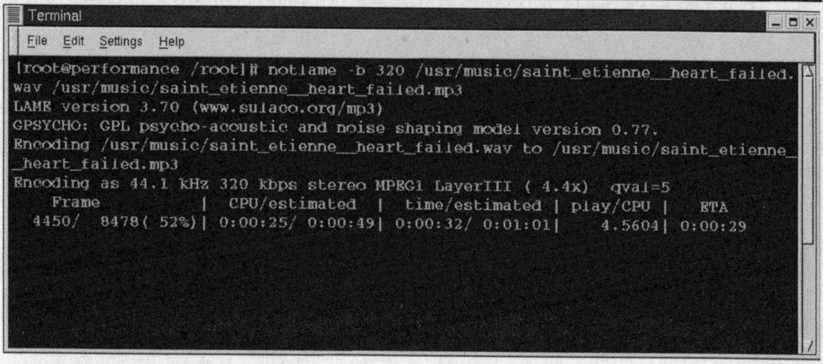

FIGURE 13.19: NotLame at work encoding

GOGO-NO-CODA

The strangely named GOGO-no-coda, or GOGO for short, is a Japanese reworking of LAME that provides great performance and high sound quality. (The name, a deliberate misspelling of "GOGO-no-coder," is a pun on "gogo no kōcha," Japanese for "afternoon tea.") Not only is GOGO faster than LAME, but (unlike LAME and most other encoders), it's designed to make use of multiple processors—so if you have a multiprocessor machine, it's doubly worth a try. GOGO works with a number of ripper/encoders, including Grip and ripperX.

Download the latest version of GOGO from homepage1.nifty.com/herumi/gogo_e.html. Compile it if necessary, and install it. Then run GOGO from a terminal window.

Table 13.3 lists the important command-line options for GOGO.

TABLE 13.3: Important Command-Line Options for GOGO

Option	Meaning
-b n	Specifies the bitrate. Can be 32, 40, 48, 56, 64, 80, 96, 112, 128, 160, 192, 224, 256, or 320.
-m	Specifies the mode: m for mono, s for stereo, or j for joint stereo.
-nopsy	Disables the psychoacoustic model, giving faster encoding but lower quality.
-cpu n	Allows you to specify the number of CPUs to use. Usually, it's best to let GOGO automatically detect the number of CPUs available.
-f	Specifies fast encoding, which loses some audio quality.
-V n	Specifies the variable bitrate quality, where n is a number between 0 (highest quality) and 9 (lowest quality).
-lpf on/off	Turns the 16kHz filter on and off. By default, this filter is used at bitrates of 128kbps and below and not used at bitrates of 160kpbs and above.

Here are a couple of examples using GOGO:

- The following command encodes the WAV file `fuel_live.wav` at a bitrate of 192kpbs to an MP3 file of the same name. (If you don't specify a name for the output file, GOGO creates a file with the same name as the input file but with the MP3 extension.)

    ```
    gogo -b 160 fuel_live.wav
    ```

- The following command encodes the WAV file `fuel_live.wav` in stereo at a bitrate of 128kbps to the MP3 file `fuel_live.mp3` in the /mp3/ directory, disabling the psychoacoustic model:

    ```
    gogo -m s -b 128 -nopsy fuel_live.wav /mp3/fuel_live.mp3
    ```

BladeEnc

The BladeEnc encoder has been widely used for several years now. But as mentioned in Chapter 8, "Windows Rippers and Encoders," BladeEnc's creator, Tord Jansson, has removed the binaries of BladeEnc from his Web site (bladeenc.mp3.no) at this writing because some big MP3-related companies with patents have been breathing down his neck. Jansson is still providing the source code, so if you're happy to compile BladeEnc yourself, go ahead and download it. But you'll probably be able to find binaries on the Web with a little searching.

You can run BladeEnc from the command line, add a graphical front end such as Krabber or KBlade, or use it as the encoder for a ripper/encoder such as Grip or ripperX.

MP3Enc

At $199, MP3Enc is absurdly expensive compared to most other Linux encoders—but it's made by the Fraunhofer Institute, it has a great reputation, and many people swear by the results it gives.

If you're interested in trying MP3Enc, download the demo version from the Fraunhofer IIS-A AMM Download Area (www.iis.fhg.de/amm/download/index.html). The demo creates files 30 seconds long, which may be enough to give you an idea of the quality it produces.

You can run MP3Enc from the command line for the authentic Fraunhofer "hardways" experience, or use it as the encoder for a ripper/encoder such as Grip or ripperX.

Up Next

In this chapter, we've looked at a cross-section of the ripping and encoding solutions available for Linux—from free to expensive, from command-line to graphical, and from slow to speedy.

This concludes our coverage of MP3 software for the time being. In Part 8 of the book, "Advanced Digital-Audio Maneuvers," we'll show you a variety of advanced maneuvers for digital audio, from burning CDs to editing your music files. But in the meantime, we'll take a short detour. In the next part, we'll show you how to take MP3 beyond your computer with portable MP3 hardware and with car and home stereo players.

PART VI
Taking MP3 Beyond the Computer

LEARN TO:

- **Select and use a portable MP3 player**
- **Play MP3 files on a pocket PC or Palm-size PC**
- **Play MP3 files on a hand-held PC**
- **Play MP3 files on a Handspring Visor**
- **Play MP3 files through your stereo system**
- **Play MP3 files in your car**

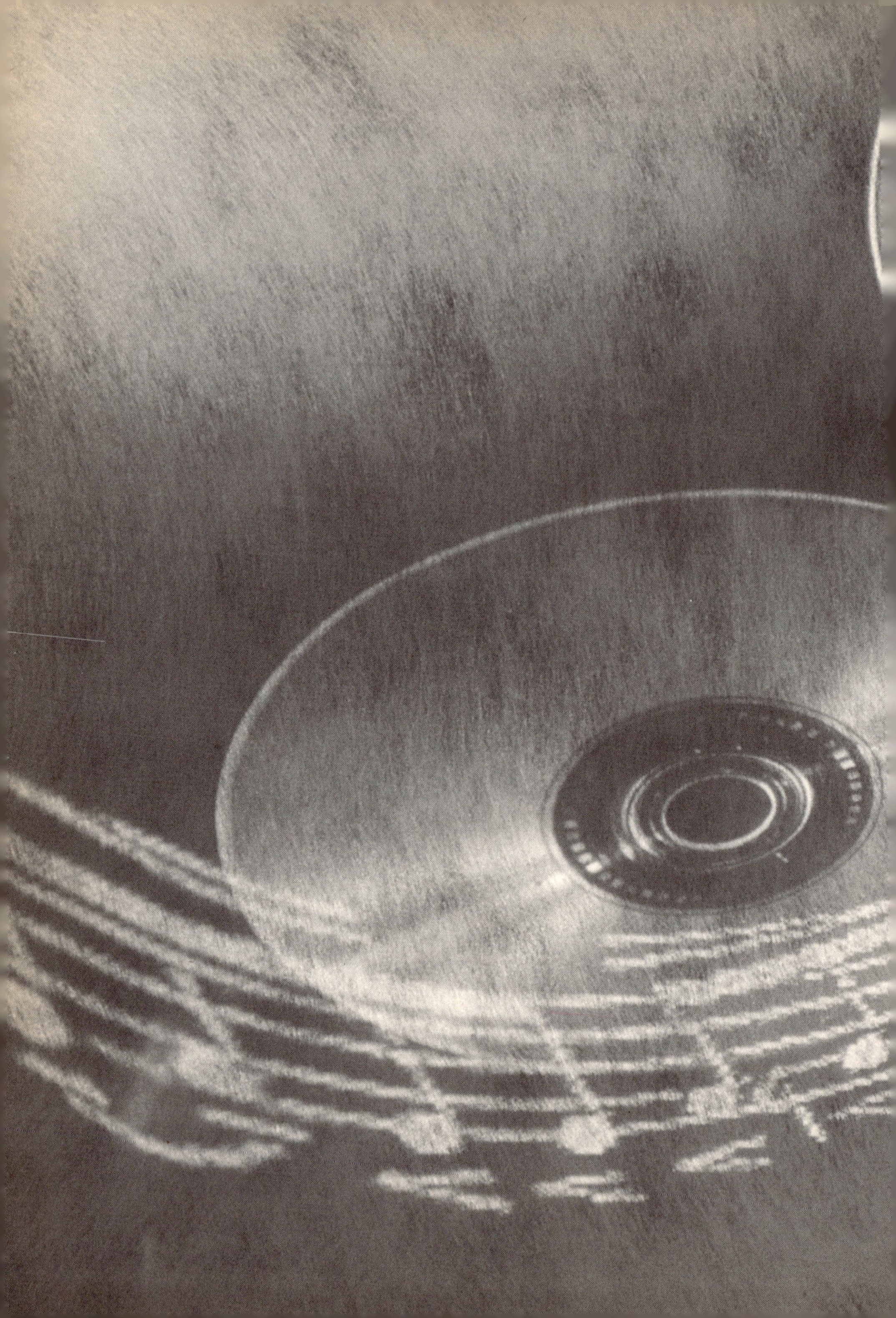

Chapter 14

Choosing a Portable MP3 Player

FEATURING

- The five categories of products that take MP3 beyond the computer
- Why there's no category-killer portable player yet
- Choosing the right portable player

In this chapter, we'll discuss how to go about choosing a portable MP3 player that meets your needs. At this writing, the range of portable players available is not only impressive but growing week by week, so you'll need to do a little research to find exactly the right player for you. We'll suggest the considerations you should keep in mind while looking for a player and the features you should look for. Along the way, we'll give you specifics on a few of the current players—but given how many of them are now available, and how quickly new models are being released, we won't even attempt anything like full coverage.

We'll start by casting our net a little wider: At the beginning of this chapter, we'll outline not only the various types of portable players that you'll be able to find, but also the other alternatives for enjoying MP3 music wherever you are, away from your computer. We'll then discuss the portable (and ultraportable) players in this chapter, and the other categories of MP3 hardware in the next chapter.

MP3s Beyond the PC: Five Categories

Depending on how you count, there are about five categories of products that let you enjoy MP3 music without directly using a personal computer. These categories are somewhat fluid, because new products are being introduced at a frantic clip (thus changing the categories) and because some devices slop over from one category into another. But these categories are usable enough for roughly describing the different types of players you'll be considering for taking MP3 beyond your PC.

The categories are as follows:

> **Ultraportable players** An ultraportable player is typically smaller than a packet of cigarettes and uses flash memory for storage. Ultraportables' main appeal is their

extremely compact size. Their main problem is their lack of storage space.

Portable players A portable player is bigger and heavier than an ultraportable—up to the size of a medium-thick novel. Portables are (needless to say) bigger than ultraportables and typically contain much more storage than do ultraportables.

Car players Car players come in a variety of sizes and shapes, ranging from portable players that do double duty as in-car players to players specifically designed to fit into the car-dash sleeve or into the trunk.

Stereo components Stereo components are MP3 players designed to fit into a home stereo system.

Computers that aren't PCs Various portable computer-like devices can also play MP3 files. These devices include hand-held PCs, Palm-size PCs, Pocket PCs, and PDAs such as the Handspring Visor (which takes MP3 player Springboard modules).

We'll discuss the first two categories in the rest of this chapter, and the other three categories in the next chapter.

DO YOU HAVE A DEVICE THAT CAN ACT AS A HARDWARE MP3 PLAYER?

Before you decide to buy a hardware MP3 player, make sure that you *need* one. If you already have a device you can use for MP3 playback for the time being, you may be able to wait until the market matures a little before opening your wallet again.

If you have a Palm-size PC that supports stereo audio, such as the Cassiopeia E-100 or E-105, or a hand-held computer such as the HP Jornada 680, you can turn it into an MP3 player in just a few minutes. Many of the later Palm-size computers

CONTINUED ➡

and a number of the hand-held computers have audio hardware built in, so you need only install software to make them into MP3 players. The new Pocket PCs (for example, the Cassiopeia E-115) already have the software built in, so all you need to do is load some music.

If you have a Palm-size PC, check to make sure that its output jack supports stereo. Some of them can manage only mono and make any music sound terrible. (By contrast, all Pocket PCs support stereo, as it's part of the specification.)

With most Palm-size PCs and Pocket PCs, you'll need to add a CompactFlash card to supplement the computer's built-in memory and give you enough space to carry a decent amount of music.

The disadvantage of playing music on a Palm-size PC or Pocket PC is that you'll usually be dealing with software-based controls rather than hardware-based controls. For example, to start the music playing, you'll tap on a Play icon rather than pressing a Play button. That means you'll need to look at the screen rather than working by touch, which (for most people) means pulling out the device each time you need to manipulate it, rather than keeping it in a belt case or a pocket the way you might do with a dedicated MP3 player.

If you have a Handspring Visor, you can get a Springboard module containing an MP3 player. (Actually, strike that "can get" and make it "will soon be able to get." Although Innogear announced its MiniJam Springboard module in September 1999, and Diamond Multimedia's RioPort announced a Digital Audio Player Springboard the same month, neither is available at this writing—and Visor owners are beginning to champ through the bit.) These players have hardware buttons, so they're easy to use.

We'll look at how to play MP3 files on Palm-size PCs, Pocket PCs, and Handspring Visors in the next chapter. For the rest of this chapter, we'll assume you've established that you do need a hardware MP3 player.

Portable MP3 Players: A Burgeoning Market

The market for portable MP3 players was born in November 1998 when Diamond Multimedia released the first Diamond Rio. The product's launch was delayed when the RIAA sued to prevent Diamond from releasing it. But when the RIAA lost the lawsuit, the Rio quickly became a hit. The Rio wasn't the first hardware MP3 player to be released; the Eiger MPMan was released before it. But the MPMan didn't get wide distribution in North America until after the Rio was released.

After the Rio proved a hit, other portable MP3 players were quickly released, some by major players, such as Creative Labs (makers of the Sound Blaster sound cards and other audio hardware) and RCA, and others by startup companies. At this writing, more than 50 portable MP3 players of various descriptions are available, and new ones are being announced or introduced most every week. They vary widely in size, style, looks, capacity, and capabilities, not to mention price. And so far, none of them is a category killer—a product that blows away all the other products in its category.

There are several reasons for the lack of a category killer to date:

- First, the market is fragmented. Because portable MP3 players can come in a variety of sizes and capacities, there's no one compelling size for manufacturers to concentrate on. For example, the Walkman's size was dictated by the audio cassette that would go inside it and by portability. The player needed to be bigger than a cassette but small enough to be portable. The resulting size fits into a good-sized pocket but is big enough to easily accommodate all the controls needed. By contrast, an MP3 player need contain only memory chips about the size of a big toenail, a small amount of circuitry, and a headphone jack, so it can be made any size from matchbox upward.

- Second, the players are still too expensive to go mainstream. For a portable player to go *really* mainstream, it needs to sell for less than $100 and have decent features—say, 64MB memory minimum (although 128MB would be much better), a USB connection, and good headphones. At this writing, memory prices are about as good as they've ever been, at around $1 per MB. But even that low price means that a 64MB player is going to cost more like $200 at retail, which is too much for the product to go mainstream. We'd say there's an opportunity here for an enterprising company that's prepared to lose a lot of money in the short term to lock up the market for the long term.

- Third, the MP3 players are not good enough to go mainstream. Many of them are well designed and well made, and they execute well enough the functions that they're designed to perform, but none is so compelling in and of itself to make people pay above the odds for it. As it stands, most portable MP3 players don't expand significantly on the basic functionality of the Walkman—they simply provide a similar set of functions using a different technology. So right now, the players are competing with each other on price, features, advertising, and distribution. And the more different players that are on the market, the more confusing it gets.

- Fourth, for all but a few MP3 players, you need to have a computer to get MP3 files and load them into the portable unit. Computer ownership in United States and Canada households is approaching 50 percent—but even that means that half the people in the continent have no interest in portable MP3 players.

Choosing the Right Portable Player

This section discusses the main considerations you should keep in mind when deciding which MP3 player to buy.

You'll probably find that some of the considerations are crashingly obvious, while others are less so. That's fine. We've listed them all in the hope that you will avoid the mistakes that we've made when buying portable players.

How Much Storage Do You Need?

The amount of audio storage available is perhaps the most important feature when choosing a hardware MP3 player. As you know, a minute of near–CD-quality audio (encoded at 128kbps) takes up about a megabyte of storage, so if you want to be able to tote an hour of music around with you, you'll need at least 64MB of memory. Few people are satisfied with an hour of music—they want at least two or three.

> **NOTE**
>
> As mentioned earlier in this book, if you're interested in spoken audio, you'll be able to get away with a lower quality (and a lower compression rate) than for music. 64MB of memory on a hardware MP3 player can contain a good two to three hours' worth of spoken audio—enough for even severe commutes or tedious lectures.

At this writing, many ultraportable players come with 64MB of memory on board. Most have an expansion slot that can hold another 16MB or 32MB, resulting in a total of 80MB or 96MB. That's enough to keep most people entertained for a while, but not enough for that category killer we're eager to see. We'd like to see an ultraportable with 128MB on board and an expansion slot that can hold another 64MB or 128MB—maybe even 256MB for audiophiles with fat wallets.

To bring prices down on ultraportables, some manufacturers are sadly skimping on primary memory. Where the Rio PMP5000 had 64MB base memory, the Rio 600 has only 32MB—although you can add snap-on backpacks of 32MB, 64MB, or 340MB each.

The upgrade cards, which are typically in MultiMediaCard format, are expensive—about $50 for 16MB and $90 for 32MB at this writing. They're tiny—smaller than a quarter. And they're delicate. So they're really portable, but you won't want to handle them any more than you have to. Even if you can afford a clutch of them, you usually won't want to carry them around with you and swap them back and forth. Even if you manage not to damage them, you'll find them too small to label, so it'll be hard to keep track of what each card contains. Instead, you'll want to get the biggest upgrade card your player supports, slide it in, and leave it there permanently. If you arrange your music libraries effectively, you can group tracks in hour-long clumps (for a 64MB machine) and quickly upload a new mood, CD, or artist's greatest hits.

Because each MP3 track is an integrated unit, the entire track needs to fit in the available memory—you can't wedge 4MB of a 5MB track into the last 4MB free on a player the way you could cram four minutes of a five-minute track onto the end of a cassette. Either you have enough space to fit the whole track on the player or none of it goes on. This means that you'll usually have up to a couple of megabytes free when you've loaded a player "full." And if the player's memory is split into internal and external, those usually act as two separate areas—you can't break an MP3 file across them. So you'll almost always end up with some empty space in each area.

Bottom line: When buying an ultraportable MP3 player, get as much on-board memory as you can. You won't regret paying more for the memory-heavy models—at least, not until a model with more memory comes out at a lower price.

Portable players are a better bet than ultraportables when it comes to storage—but you'll still be paying top dollar for the space. The eGo has one or two CompactFlash slots, which can hold either CompactFlash cards or IBM Microdrives, giving you up to 680MB of storage for a cost somewhere north of $1000 (that's including the Microdrives). A loaded eGo will keep you in music for a day or two, but you'll usually want to change the tracks after that.

By contrast, the HanGo Personal Jukebox contains a 4.8GB hard drive and costs $799. The Personal Jukebox provides enough storage for you to carry a decent chunk of your music collection around with you.

An alternative type of portable player that offers inexpensive storage is the MiniDisc recorder/player. These players are made by a number of manufacturers and store about an hour of audio on discs that cost a couple of dollars each. The drawback is that when you transfer music to a MiniDisc unit, you've got to play it back on the source device while recording it to MiniDisc. So, to record an hour's worth of music, it takes an hour of recording time.

Another disadvantage of a MiniDisc player is if you are transferring MP3 files to a MiniDisc, each MP3 file must be decoded to full digital, then to analog, piped into the MiniDisc unit, then sampled back to digital, then re-encoded to MiniDisc's ATRAC compression scheme, which is comparable but not compatible with MP3. Some MiniDisc units have digital inputs that let you skip a couple of these steps, and some (such as the Sharp MiniDisc player MiniDisc-MT15) come with hardware and software packages designed to simplify the process of getting MP3 files onto them.

Does It Support Your Operating System?

Which operating system will you be using with your portable MP3 player? If it's Windows 9*x* or Windows Millennium Edition (Windows Me), it won't be a limitation. Most MP3 players come with software for Windows 9*x*/Windows Me and nothing else. If you want to use another PC operating system, you'll have to download some third-party software and expend a little more effort configuring it.

If you want to use the Macintosh, you'll need to make sure that your portable comes with a USB connection and with Mac software, because a parallel port won't be an option with the Mac. Now that more USB devices are being released, using them with the Mac is less of a problem. But make sure that the player comes with Mac software (or that you can download Mac software that will work with it).

Does It Have the Basic Controls You Need?

Make sure that the portable MP3 player you choose provides the basic playing functionality you need, especially pause, fast forward, and rewind. Here, MP3 players differ from most CD players and cassette players.

First, the pause functionality on many portable MP3 players is somewhat impaired, at least compared to what people typically expect in a Pause button. When you press the Pause button, you want the audio to stop, and you want to be able to resume from that point. However, on some portable MP3 players, pressing the Pause button pauses play for about 15 seconds, but after that the player registers a Stop instruction and turns itself off. This saves battery power but usually loses your place in the track. When you restart play, some players start from the beginning of that track, while others start again from the beginning of your playlist.

Second, most players totally lack fast-forward and rewind capabilities within a track, so you can't move quickly through a track to find the section you want to hear. All the players we've used have Previous Track and Next Track buttons, so you can jump to the previous track or to the next track with no problem. In some players, pressing the Previous Track button while playing a track takes you to the beginning of that track rather than to the beginning of the previous track.

How Does It Sound?

If the suggestions in the preceding sections haven't helped you decide which MP3 player to get, the final test should be your ears. Listen to the players you're evaluating for as long as possible. Play with those equalization and volume controls. Jog around the store with the player if you can do so without attracting any undue attention from the store detectives.

If you can, listen to the same types of music that you're planning to listen to in the long term. For example, if your musical tastes encompass everything from Bach to Britney Spears to Metallica, listen to examples of each extreme of the range of music when evaluating the player. Don't listen to evaluation tracks that contain different types of music: A Julio Iglesias evaluation track will tell you little about how Korn will sound on a player.

If you're evaluating a player that uses removable media—CompactFlash cards, say—you might even be able to take in some music of your own to listen to, although in doing so you might run the risk of being suspected of shoplifting.

Do You Need to Play Music Files Other Than MP3 on It?

Not surprisingly, most portable MP3 players are designed primarily for playing MP3 files. But some players can play other music formats as well. If you've committed yourself to an audio format other than MP3, you'll certainly want to get a portable player that can handle that format.

At this writing, coverage is scanty. Some of the later portable models, such as the Rio 600 and the latest models of the Creative Labs Nomad, can play WMA files as well as MP3 files. Sony hardware, such as Sony VAIO Music Clip and the Sony Memory Stick Walkman, can play audio in both the Sony OpenMP3 format (which is anything but open) and the ATRAC3 format. However, you're not likely to go looking for a portable player that plays files in these formats. Rather, you'll use these formats because they're the only ones with which the Sony hardware will deign to work.

Do You Need to Be Able to Record?

Some MP3 hardware players include microphones and the ability to record audio (either as MP3 files or in other audio file formats), usually for making voice notes or practicing dictation. Others don't. If you need to record, this feature may be a deal-breaker when you're choosing a player. Most of these microphones are designed for recording voice rather than music, so if you try to bootleg a concert with one of them, you'll wish you hadn't bothered.

For good results when recording music via a microphone, make sure that the MP3 device supports stereo recording and provides a microphone input, not just a low-quality built-in microphone.

Do You Need a Tuner?

If you need a tuner in your MP3 player, you'll be able to narrow down your choices still further. Relatively few of the MP3 players have built-in tuners. Those that do, such as most of the Creative Labs Nomad models, advertise them prominently.

How Are the Size and Ease of Use?

Next, consider size and ease of use. All the ultraportables are much smaller than Walkmans and Discmans, while some of the portables are a little bigger than a Walkman, though a little differently proportioned.

Because many MP3 players are so small, those of you with larger hands may actually prefer the larger players or those that offer larger buttons for controlling play. For example, most people find the pinkie-nail–sized buttons on the Rio easier to use than the tiny buttons on the top of the MPMan or the match-head–sized buttons on the side of the Yepp. However, when you're working by touch, even the larger buttons are easy enough to get wrong.

Most players have a Hold button or a Lock button that disables the controls. Use the Hold button or Lock button with the player switched off to make sure it doesn't get turned on accidentally in your pocket. Use it with the unit running to make sure you don't bump the player when jogging, working out, or packing yourself into a crowded subway train.

Do You Need a Line-Out Jack?

If you're seriously into MP3, you may want to be able to plug your MP3 player directly into your stereo system or into an input jack on your car. If so, look for a line-out jack in addition to the headphone jack. The line-out jack provides what is known as a *line-level output signal*. This signal is compatible with standard line-level inputs such as those you might find on your home stereo amplifier or cassette deck.

In many cases this isn't a big deal, but the output on some headphone jacks can be high enough to damage the inputs on a receiver that's geared to the more moderate output of a line-out jack. If you end up using the headphone jack, turn the volume down completely before making the connection. Then increase the volume very cautiously until it reaches the level you want.

What Battery Type, What Battery Life?

Next, what kind of batteries does the player use—removable batteries or a built-in rechargeable battery? Will it make a difference to you? And what kind of battery life will you get from the player?

As long as a built-in rechargeable battery is powerful enough to provide decent battery life, it's typically a good solution. What constitutes decent battery life will depend on your needs, but it'll probably be on the order of 6 to 12 hours a day. You can then recharge the battery while you're asleep—but bear in mind that recharging typically involves a hefty AC adapter that you'll need to schlep around with you.

If you need to be able to use the player for extended periods away from a battery charger, you may prefer removable batteries. Once you've burned through one set of batteries, you can pop in the next set and keep rocking. And of course, these removable batteries can be rechargeable batteries—for example, rechargeable AA or AAA batteries—although there's a downside to rechargeables. The main disadvantage of rechargeable batteries is that they never deliver their full voltage. Even when they're in theory fully charged, they deliver much less than a disposable battery does at the start of its life. For example, a disposable AA battery gives its rated 1.5 volts at the start of its life, whereas a rechargeable AA battery typically starts with more like 1.2 volts. A secondary disadvantage is that their battery life is usually much shorter than that of quality disposable alkaline batteries.

Battery life on the ultraportables and portables we've used has ranged from magnificent to miserable. For example, the Rio 500 delivers 8 to 12 hours on a single AA battery, and the Yepp gives us around 8 hours on two AAA batteries. But the eGo, with its monster capacity (two CompactFlash cards, either or both of which can be IBM Microdrives, which hold 340MB apiece), finishes off a pair of Duracell Ultra AA batteries in less than an hour and a half. (To be fair, we should mention that the eGo is designed primarily for use in the car with an adapter cable.) The HanGo Personal Jukebox comes with a rechargeable lithium-ion battery that provides 8 to 10 hours—and which you can replace with another battery if necessary, giving you great flexibility.

For a player that you'll use in the car or attached to your stereo system, make sure that you can get a lighter-socket cable or an AC cable so that you can plug it in and forget about the batteries.

How Will You Carry It?

If you'll want to wear the player on a belt, make sure that it comes with a belt clip or a case that offers a belt clip. A surprising number of players don't come with a belt clip or a belt-friendly case. The MPMan F10 and the D'music come with drawstring pouches that are decorative but essentially useless. The pouches keep the player and its headphones together in your pocket, but you have to take the player out to access its controls. The I-JAM comes with a cute case with a strong belt clip, and the case provides easy access to the controls.

While the Rio PMP300 (the original Rio) has a sturdy and removable belt clip, the Rio PMP500 comes with a case that clips firmly to your belt but that prevents you from easily accessing any of the controls other than the On/Off/Hold switch. This severely diminishes the appeal of the player for anyone who wants to use it as part of an active lifestyle. The Yepp, on the other hand, doesn't look nearly as good as the Rio, and the Nex looks decidedly clunky, but each comes with a good belt clip that's far more effective than the Rio PMP500's case.

The Sony VAIO Music Clip comes with a neck strap and a shirt-pocket clip. This clip is feeble and barely holds the VAIO Music Clip in place even when you're stationary.

The eGo (which is primarily designed for the car) also comes with a belt clip, but the clip is so poorly located that you have to loosen and swivel the belt clip in order to change the batteries on the player. (And, as mentioned in the previous section, you'll be needing to change the batteries frequently if you're using the eGo as a portable player.)

At this writing, about the coolest MP3 player to have is the Wrist Audio Player from Casio, which is basically a watch on steroids, with the capacity to hold less MP3 music than you probably want. (The current model maxes out at 30 minutes of music.) The Wrist Audio Player looks satisfyingly unique, but we wonder how you'll avoid snarling the headphone cord on things as you boogie down the street playing windmill air guitar *à la* Pete Townshend.

On the horizon—actually, make that "appearing soon at a boutique near you"—are MP3 players integrated into pieces of clothing. The Levi ICD+ collection is a collaboration between Philips (the notorious Dutch electronics company), Levi Strauss (which should need no introduction), and the designer Massimo Osti (who's perhaps best known for the Equipment for Legs project for Dockers). The Levi ICD+ collection includes a range of jackets made by Levi's that incorporate mobile phones and MP3 players, together with some intelligence. For example, when the phone rings, the MP3 player pauses the audio so that you can hear the phone.

The jackets are apparently fully washable and flexible—but we wonder who will want electronics that are available only when they're wearing a particular piece of clothing. For most people, portable players work best as independent units—integrated with a PDA, mobile phone, and GPS, perhaps, but a small unit that you can clip on or pocket as you need—until wetware is commercially available and we can patch the electronics directly into our nervous systems.

How Are the Headphones?

Next, consider the headphones included with the player. Because you can easily replace the headphones with better or more comfortable ones, the ones included with the player shouldn't be a deciding factor in your choice. But headphones can certainly be a tiebreaker if two players around the same level of price and features are deadlocked for your affections and your dollars.

Most ultraportable and portable players come with ear-bud headphones—either the kind that wedge into your ears or the headband-mounted ones that poke into your ears. Some of these ear buds are higher quality than others; some are more comfortable than others. But in most cases, you won't know until you try them on, which you may be unable to do in the store.

Other players are more ambitious in their choice of headphones. For example, the Rio PMP500 includes Koss sport-clip headphones, which are an interesting choice. People tend to find them comfortable provided they're not wearing glasses (or shades) at the same time. Because the headphone clip goes over the ear, it's right where the earpiece of your glasses wants to go. The clips hold the ear buds steady under modest movement, but if you jog with them, you'll find the buds flapping away from your ears, and the music flapping with them. The HanGo Personal Jukebox comes with a pair of folding supra-aural headphones that we found quite comfortable.

Whichever headphones you end up with, try not to use them regularly at high volumes. You can cause permanent, irreversible ear damage that way. Sermon over.

Does the Software Want to Manage Your Life?

The software that comes with the MP3 players that we've used varies widely in its scope, capabilities, and ambitions. If possible, find out approximately what the software attempts to do and make sure that this meshes with your needs.

The most basic software lets you download MP3 files—to the player, rearrange them, and delete them to make space for further tracks. For copyright reasons, the software that comes with most players does not let you upload MP3 files from the player to your computer, although some software and players let you upload other files, such as audio files that you've recorded on the player. You can fool some such software by changing the file extension on the MP3 files—but then the player probably won't play them.

The software doesn't care where you keep your MP3 files—it lets you deal with such questions—and doesn't try to start ripping any audio CD that gets within kissing distance of your computer. We like this approach because the software is easy to use and isn't constantly imposing itself on you.

One example of this kind of software is the MPDJ software included with the Audiovox MP1000 (shown in Figure 14.1). The MPDJ software provides a simple four-pane interface with an Explorer-style tree on the upper-left, an information pane on the lower-left, a file-selection pane on the upper-right, and a player pane on the lower-right. This makes for easy file management.

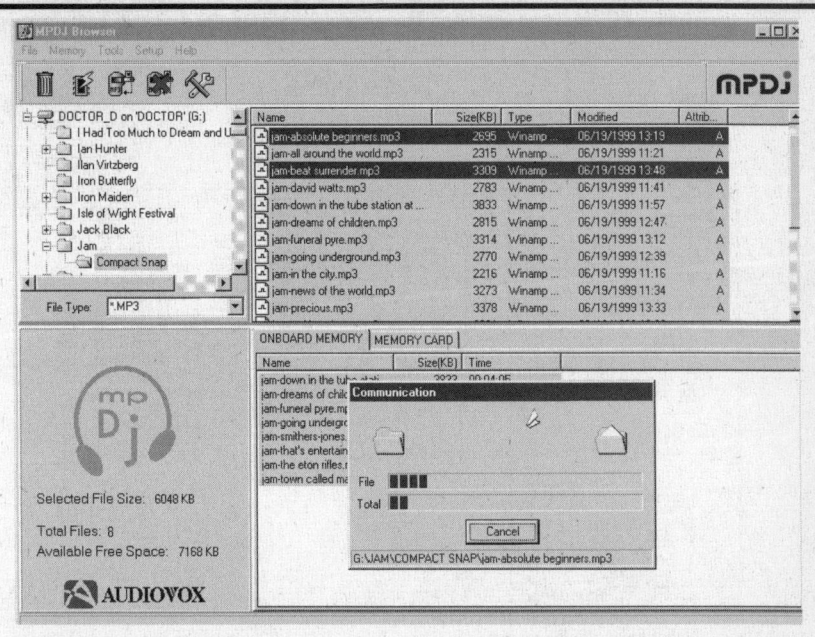

FIGURE 14.1: The MPDJ software included with the Audiovox MP1000 has a straightforward interface that lets you transfer files easily.

Another example of straightforward software is mp3Agent, the software included with the i2Go eGo. As shown in Figure 14.2, mp3Agent provides a two-pane interface:

- The left-hand pane contains trees for the Browser, Programs and Content, Portable Players (here, just the i2Go eGo), and My Computer.

- The right-hand pane displays the contents of the current selection.

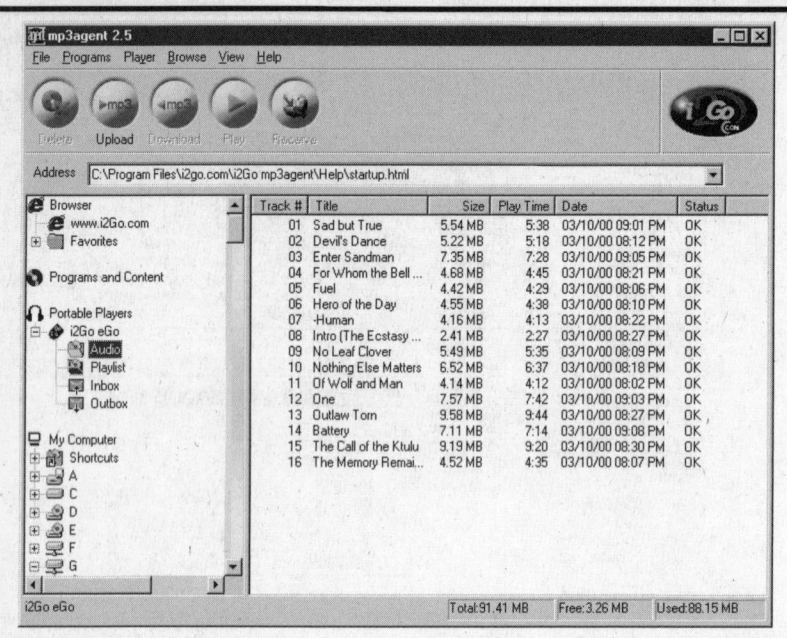

FIGURE 14.2: mp3Agent, included with the i2Go eGo, is also straightforward to use.

The more "advanced" software wants to manage your life for you. Before you can put any tracks on the player, you need to tell the software about them so that it can manage them into a library. Then (depending on the software) you may have to build a playlist before exporting the tracks to the PC. And if you put an audio CD in your computer, the software starts trying to rip it, probably without consulting you.

We don't like this approach much. We can see the advantages, but unless the software is exceptionally well designed, it tends to be harder to use.

For example, the RioPort Audio Manager software included with the Diamond Rio PMP500 tries to keep a very close rein on what you do with digital audio on the computer. When you install the software, it displays the File Monitor dialog box (shown in Figure 14.3), asking for your agreement for it to monitor the music files that you create.

Choosing a Portable MP3 Player

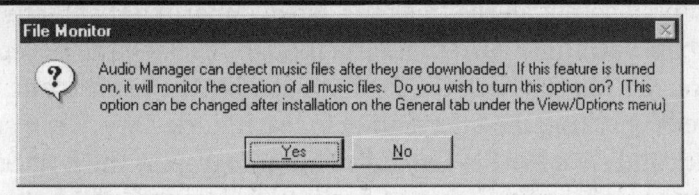

FIGURE 14.3: Controlling software: The File Monitor dialog box of the Rio's RioPort Audio Manager software wants to keep track of every music file you create and download.

Audio Monitor makes it easy to keep track of your MP3 files. However, you may dislike the Big Brother implications of its peering over your virtual shoulder the whole time and choose to turn it off.

But even if you turn off the Audio Monitor, you need to let the RioPort Audio Manager know about every track that you want to be able to use on the Rio. Typically, you'll need to search your hard disk for music, then review the results in the Review New Songs dialog box (shown in Figure 14.4).

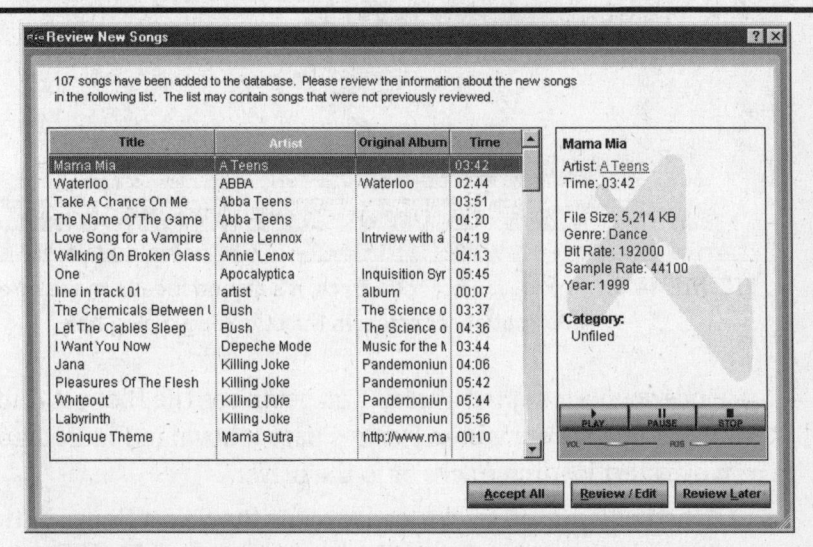

FIGURE 14.4: Before you can put a track on your Rio, you need to "review" it.

You can accept all the tracks as listed, importing them into the database with their current information, by clicking the Accept All button. Or you can click the Review Later button to postpone the chore of checking the information for each track. Or you can select a track and click the Review/Edit button to display the Edit Song dialog box, shown in Figure 14.5, check and fix the information, and then click the Save/Close button.

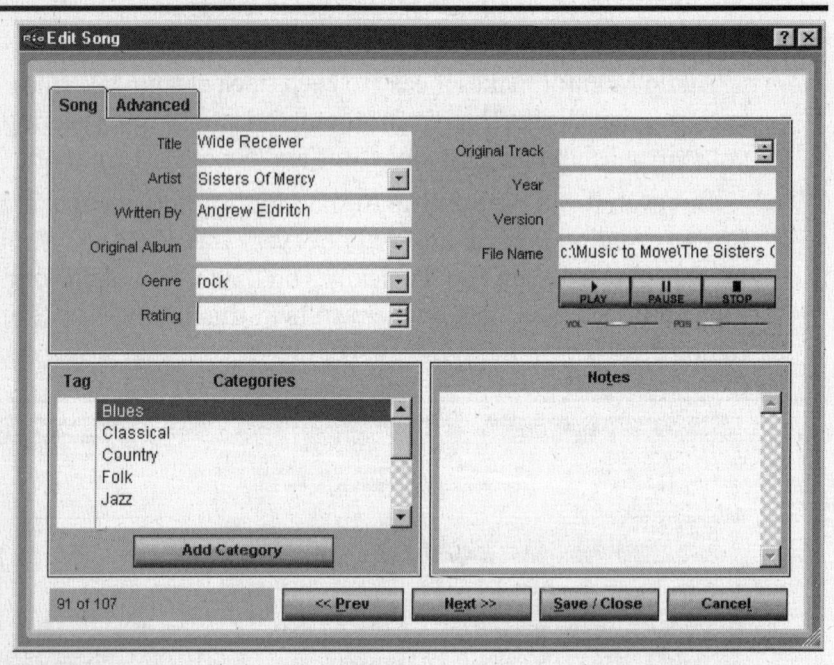

FIGURE 14.5: Before you accept a track, it's a good idea to make sure its information is correct in the Edit Song dialog box.

Once you've accepted a track, you get to see the RioPort Audio Manager itself, from whose Devices page (shown in Figure 14.6) you can start loading tracks onto the player.

To actually get the tracks loaded, click the Select Songs button and work in the Select Songs dialog box (shown in Figure 14.7). To load entire albums, click the Select Albums button and work in the Select Albums dialog box.

Choosing a Portable MP3 Player 631

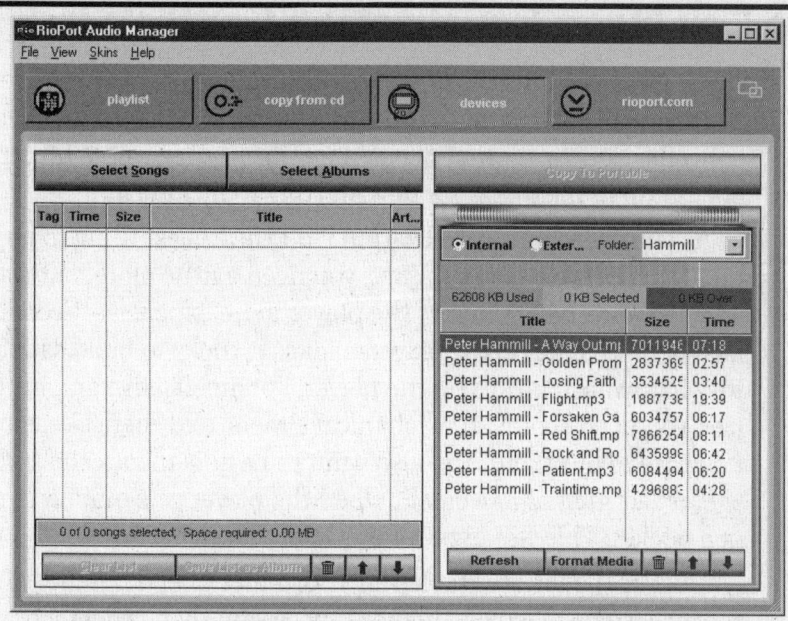

FIGURE 14.6: The Devices page of the RioPort Audio Manager software is where you start the process of loading tracks onto your player.

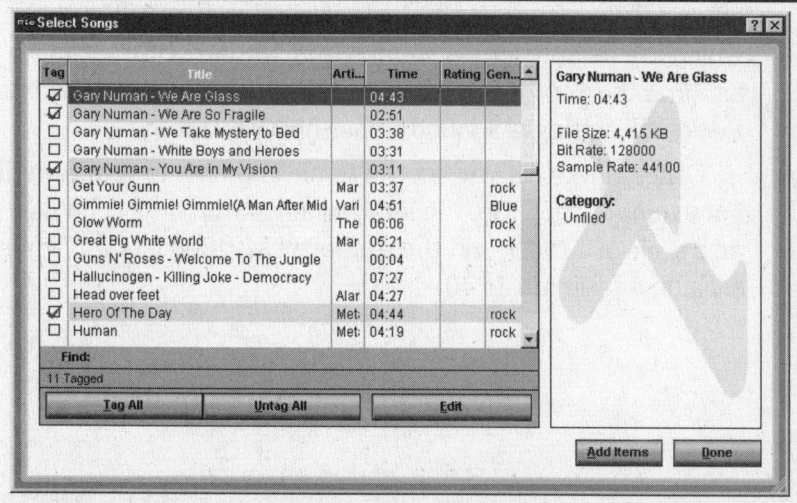

FIGURE 14.7: You use the Select Songs dialog box to select tracks to load onto your player.

Do You Need Equalization Controls?

If you want the music that you play on your portable player to sound good, make sure that the player has adequate equalization controls. Equalization has been a weakness of portable MP3 players, but manufacturers are now starting to include it.

As you'd imagine, equalization isn't the easiest thing to implement on portable players. First, you need a little more hardware and software, which makes the player more expensive. Second, the lack of real estate on the players makes it tricky to build satisfactory hardware controls on the player. For an effective graphic equalizer, you need six to ten mechanical sliders, and there's essentially nowhere to put them. You also want to be able to lock the sliders against accidental movement when the player gets bumped or put in a pocket. This would be a miracle of design.

Most of the ultraportables and portables offer a number of DSP settings, some of which are more successful than others. For example, the Pine D'music has a five-position DSP that offers Flat, Pop, Classic, Jazz, and Ex-Bass (extra-bass) settings. The Samsung Yepp has a seven-position DSP, three of the settings being 3D options that didn't do much for us (although the non-3D settings were effective). The Sony VAIO Music Clip offers four DSP settings, of which the default setting sounds fine, the Jazz DSP setting is pleasant, and the Pop DSP setting is crisp and just about right, but the Rock DSP setting is a muddy, bass-heavy disaster.

Other players let you set the treble and bass to your own liking. For example, the i2Go eGo lets you adjust the treble and bass each on a scale of 1 to 10, and the Audiovox MP1000 lets you adjust each on a scale of 1 to 20.

Are Looks Important?

We put the question of looks right down at the bottom of the list because with many of the players, you get little if any choice of looks. Either you like the player the way it's designed, or you're straight out of luck. Given this lack of choice, you'll probably be buying on the basis of features rather than looks.

Some players, including some Diamond Rio models and the i2Go eGo, come in a choice of colors; other players offer no choice. Some have visual gimmicks. For example, the Frontier Nex claims to be the first player with changeable skins. These "skins" are small, colored cutouts that you slide into a transparent pocket on the front of the players. They do give the Nex a different look, and you can make your own skins easily enough—but they're incredibly cheesy.

Up Next

In this chapter, we've suggested how you might approach choosing between the several dozen different portable and ultraportable MP3 players now available. We've discussed the important features that you'll want to look for, and we've given examples of some of the current and recent players that have or lack these features.

In the next chapter, we'll discuss how to enjoy MP3 on your PDA, on your home stereo, and in your car.

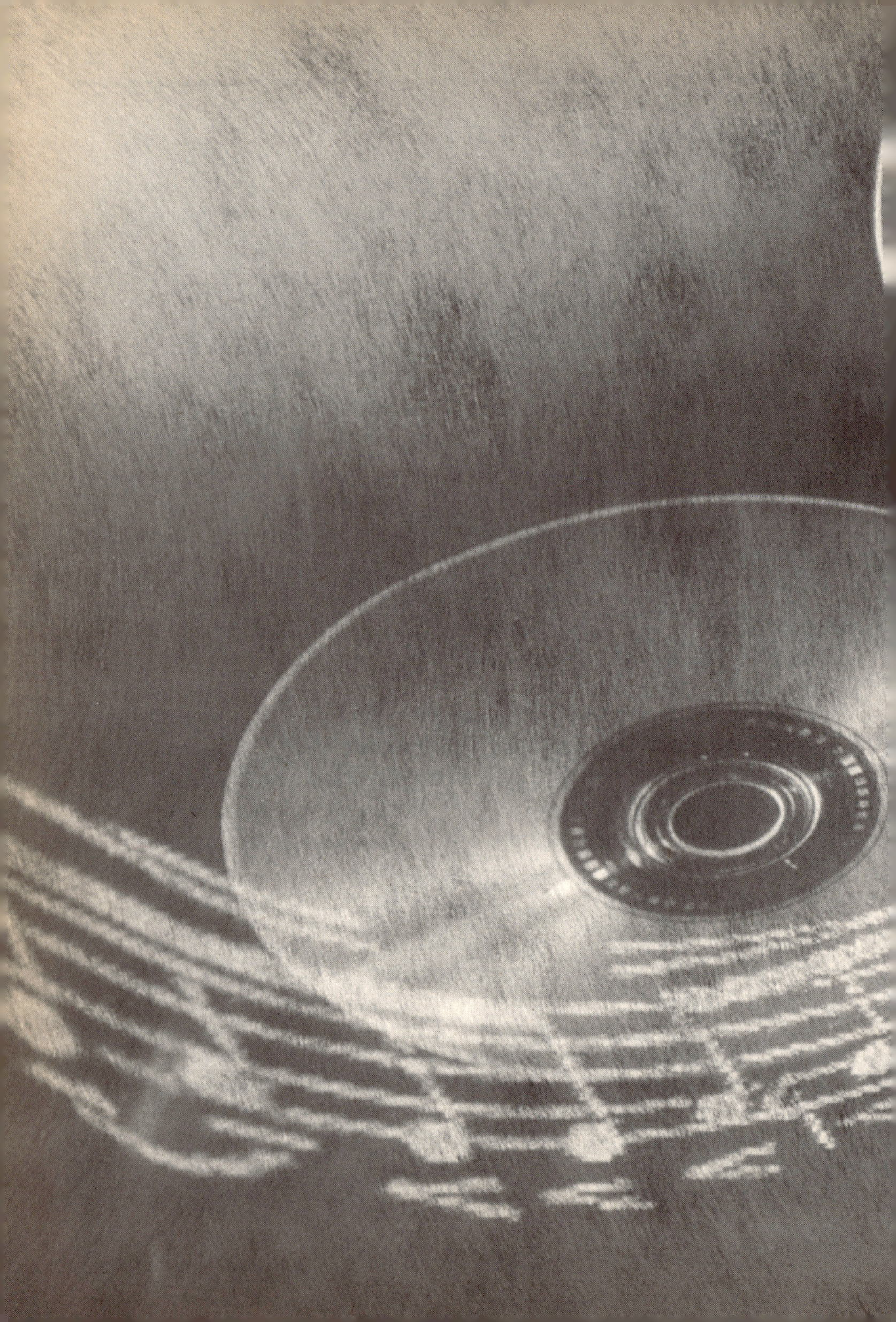

Chapter 15

MP3 on Your PDA, on Your Home Stereo, and in Your Car

FEATURING

- Playing MP3 files on a Pocket PC or Palm-size PC
- Playing MP3 files on a hand-held PC
- Playing MP3 files on a Handspring Visor
- Playing MP3 files through your home stereo
- Playing MP3 files in your car

The previous chapter looked at the various ultraportable, portable, and semi-portable MP3 players that let you take MP3 music with you wherever you go, and suggested how to go about choosing among them. In this chapter, we'll continue our exploration of how you can take MP3 beyond the computer.

We'll start by discussing briefly how to play MP3 files on portable computers that you may already have—Pocket PCs, Palm-size PCs, hand-held PCs, and the Handspring Visor. Then we'll turn our attention to how you can play MP3 audio through your home stereo; it's not difficult, but there are a couple of mistakes you should avoid. Lastly, we'll go over the possibilities for adding MP3 to your car's repertoire of tricks—and how to do so both with and without breaking your budget.

Playing MP3 Files on a Pocket PC or Palm-Size PC

If you've shelled out the money for a Pocket PC, you should definitely play music on it, because you have all the necessary software built in. If you have a Palm-size PC (one of the predecessors of the Pocket PC), you should definitely consider trying to play music on it. (If your company or school has provided you with a Palm-size PC, you should probably try as well. Should your systems people object, tell them you're, uh, leveraging their investment in technology.)

Multimedia is a strong selling point of the Pocket PCs in their battle against the Palm platform, so any Pocket PC should be capable of delivering quality stereo sound, should have a CompactFlash slot, and should come with the Windows Media Player built in. If you don't have a CompactFlash card, you'll probably want to get one so that you can carry a decent amount of music around with you.

Most of the Palm-size PC available at this writing are multimedia-capable to a greater or lesser degree. If you're considering a

Palm-size PC (as opposed to a Pocket PC) and want to play MP3 files on it, keep these two key criteria in mind:

- First, make sure that it has full audio capabilities, including stereo playback. (Some Palm-size PCs do not support stereo.)
- Second, make sure it has plenty of storage space. Because MP3 files are typically a few megabytes each and Palm-size PCs are typically light on memory (8, 16, or 32MB for both applications and storage), you'll usually want a Palm-size PC with a CompactFlash slot.

Apart from capacity, the critical advantage of a CompactFlash card is speed. You can quickly transfer information (read: a boatload of MP3 files) to it from your PC by using a CompactFlash reader or a PC Card adapter, then slot it into the Palm-size PC and play them from there. This beats transferring MP3 files via the docking cable, which can take half an hour or more to transfer a single track.

Using the Windows Media Player for Palm-Size PCs

Your best bet for playing MP3 files on a Palm-size PC is to use the Windows Media Player for Palm-size PCs.

Download the Windows Media Player for Palm-size PCs from www.microsoft.com/windows/mediaplayer/en/download/WinPortPlay.asp. If you're not already registered with Microsoft, you'll need to do so, but after that, the download is free. At this writing, there are three different versions of the Windows Media Player for Palm-size PCs available:

- One for the Cassiopeia E100 and E105
- One for the Compaq Aero 1500 and 2100
- One for the Hewlett Packard Jornada 430se

Make sure you get the right one.

> **NOTE**
>
> You can also download skins for the Windows Media Player for Palm-size PCs from the same Web site.

After downloading Windows Media Player for Palm-size PCs, run the executable file. It takes you through a CE installation routine that involves making sure your player is connected, accepting an end-user license agreement, and agreeing to the default application installation directory (or choosing a different directory). After devoting a small chunk of your life to watching the progress indicator crawl along the Installing Applications dialog box as Windows forces the application down the serial cable, you'll see the Application Downloading Complete dialog box, instructing you to see if your Palm-size PC needs any further attention. Do so, and you should be ready to rock.

Other Options for Playing Music on Palm-Size PCs

If for some reason you choose not to use the Windows Media Player for Palm-size PCs, this section describes two other possibilities for playing music on a Palm-size PC.

Hum for CE

Hum for CE from UtopiaSoft (www.utopiasoft.com) lets you play actual MP3 files on a Palm-size PC. Hum provides an easy-to-use interface and supports skins. In May 2000, UtopiaSoft started giving Hum away free—good news for everyone except those who paid $19.95 for it earlier.

Mobile Audio Player

Some Palm-size PCs, including the Cassiopeia E-100 and E-105, come with Mobile Audio Player, a Windows CE application for playing music in the WMA (Windows Media Audio) format. Mobile Audio Player isn't wonderful, because you have to convert your MP3 files to WMA format in order to play them, but it does work. Here's the short version:

1. Dock your Palm-size PC so that it establishes a connection to the computer. (If you need to establish a connection manually, do so.)

2. On your PC, launch the Mobile Audio Player Manager application. (By default, it's installed to the Windows Media group on the Start menu.)

3. In the left-hand list box, navigate to and select the file you want to transfer.

4. In the right-hand list box, select the folder on the Palm-size PC to receive the track. Mobile Audio Player suggests using the My Documents folder.

5. Click the ➤ button to convert the file to WMA format and transfer it. This typically takes several times as long as the playing time of the file.

6. On the Palm-size PC, you can then play the tracks by launching the Mobile Audio Player (Start ➤ Programs ➤ Mobile Audio Player) and using its play controls.

Playing MP3 Files on a Hand-Held PC

Another possibility for playing MP3 files is a hand-held PC.

A hand-held PC isn't a Palm-size PC or Pocket PC (as its name suggests), but rather, it's a small computer with a keyboard but no hard drive. Some of the more successful hand-held PCs have been the IBM WorkPad Z50 and some of the HP Jornada hand-held PCs. (Before you ask, IBM and HP make things confusing by using the WorkPad and Jornada names for their Palm-size PCs as well as for their hand-held PCs.)

Hand-held PCs have been going out of fashion in the last few months as of this writing, which is both bad news and good news for their fans. The bad news is that hand-held PCs aren't going to be very important in the future of computing. The good news is that right now you can pick one up for a song. If you do, make sure that it has either a good amount of on-board memory or a CompactFlash socket that you can use for MP3 files. You'll usually do better with CompactFlash, because you can load it with music far more quickly than you can get the music to the hand-held's on-board memory using the serial cable.

Your best bet for playing MP3 files on a hand-held PC is to get Hum from UtopiaSoft. (As mentioned in the previous section, Hum is now free.) Read the Hardware Compatibility List at UtopiaSoft's Web site first to make sure that your hand-held PC is up to the job, and be warned that some hand-helds can manage only mono rather than stereo.

Download the latest version of Hum from UtopiaSoft's Web site (www.utopiasoft.com) and unzip the distribution file to a temporary directory of your choice. Then double-click the Setup.exe file to run the Setup routine and follow through a, well, routine routine: an end-user license agreement, your choice of installation directory for the application, and time to enjoy a couple of medium-length tracks while your computer forces Hum down the serial cable onto the hand-held.

When the Application Downloading Complete dialog box instructs you to check your mobile device screen to see if additional steps are necessary to complete this installation, do so. Chances are, you'll find your hand-held ready to go, and you'll be able to launch Hum by choosing Start ➤ Programs ➤ UtopiaSoft Hum, whereupon Hum starts walking you through the creation of a new playlist.

Playing MP3 Files on a Handspring Visor

If you have a Handspring Visor, you can play MP3 files through it by adding an MP3 player Springboard module to it.

The MiniJam MP3 Player from Innogear (www.innogear.com) is due to be released in summer 2000—but given that it was originally announced in September 1999, we and other Visor owners will believe it only when we see it. Diamond Multimedia, makers of the Rio portable players, announced a Digital Audio Player Springboard at around the same time, but it seems to have vanished off the face of the earth.

Playing MP3 Files through Your Stereo System

Once you get into MP3, you'll probably amass a number of tracks that you have only in MP3 format, and you won't want to be confined to playing them through your PC speakers. You may well also find that MP3 provides a far more convenient way of managing your vast music collection than does a wall-full of CDs or a basement full of LPs and bootleg cassettes.

In short, sooner or later you'll want to play MP3 files through your stereo system. There are three ways in which you can do this:

- First, connect your PC to your stereo system.
- Second, connect a portable MP3 player (or a car player) to your stereo system.
- Third, get a home-stereo component designed for MP3.

In the following sections, we'll consider each of these three possibilities in turn.

Connecting Your PC to Your Stereo System

If you have a good component stereo system, you'll probably want to connect your PC to it so that you can play MP3 tracks through the stereo and record MP3 files from your cassettes and LPs. If your hi-fi system has a receiver (or separate amplifier) with a graphic equalizer, you can make good any shortcomings—real or perceived—in the equalization your MP3 player delivers.

Connecting your PC to your stereo system is almost as easy as getting the right cable and plugging it into the right sockets at either end—but there's one nasty mistake you'll want to avoid.

Typically, you need a quality cable with a ⅛-inch stereo mini-plug for your computer's end and two RCA plugs on the receiver's end. Check your equipment before you go to buy the cable, because some high-end sound cards offer different outputs, and some receivers boast a ⅛-inch stereo input jack for connecting personal electronics such as portable CD players.

Make sure the ⅛-inch mini-plug is stereo—it's easy to get a mono one by mistake, and it'll sound horrible. If this discussion sends you rooting through the back of your closet for old cables, a stereo mini-plug has two black plastic rings around its prong, while a mono mini-plug has only one. If you want to use your PC to record MP3 files from your cassette deck or record player, you'll need a second cable of the same sort. Again, check the input connector or connectors on your sound card and the output on your receiver or cassette deck before you buy.

Plug the mini-plug into the line-out jack on your sound card—*not* the speaker jack—because its signal is amplified and is not a line-level signal. Then plug the RCA plugs into a free pair of input jacks on the amplifier. If your receiver has auxiliary jacks (typically labeled AUX or AUX1 and AUX2), those are a good bet. These days, the input most likely to be free on your amplifier is the one that you mustn't connect your PC to—the Phono input. The Phono input is intended to interface with the feeble output of a record player. It includes built-in equalization intended to shape the signals coming off vinyl into ones that sound correct to our ears. Applying this power and equalization to an already correct MP3 signal results in a mangled signal if it doesn't destroy the Phono input at first blast.

Check the connections and make sure that the input selection button on the receiver is set to the input jacks to which you connected the cable from the PC. Then, set the volume on both your MP3 player and your receiver right down near the bottom of their ranges and start an MP3 track playing on the PC. Turn the volume up a little bit on both the MP3 player and the receiver until you can hear the music quietly. Increase the volume on the player until it is halfway up or so, if you can, and then adjust the receiver volume accordingly. The connection between the two devices will have an inherent amount of hiss and noise present. You want to feed the receiver a fairly strong audio signal so that when the receiver amplifies the mixture, you are amplifying a lot more signal than you are noise. (This is an example of the much touted "signal-to-noise ratio" that you may have heard about. Some people also think this applies to user ramblings on Usenet...but we digress.)

Once that's working, you can set up a connection to carry sound from your stereo to your sound card. You'll want to do this if you need to make MP3 files from your band's old cassettes. Grab another cable with the same specs as the first, and slide the RCA plugs onto a set of output jacks on the receiver. Plug the mini-plug into the line-in jack on your computer's sound card (*not* the microphone jack). Choose the right output channel on the receiver, and test the connection to make sure that the stereo is delivering sound to the PC and that the sound is clean and undistorted.

Choosing an MP3 Home Stereo Component

If—for whatever reason—you don't want to rely on your PC as the source for MP3 audio to your home stereo, you have an alternative: You can get a dedicated MP3 stereo component. If you were into marketing, you'd see MP3 stereo components as a new and exciting product category. But if you're a seasoned computer user, you'll probably regard them as special-purpose computers that are deliberately limited in what they do—and you'd be right.

Right now, the field of home-stereo components is just starting to develop. Several companies are now bringing products to the market. At this writing, the top contenders are the AudioReQuest from ReQuest, Inc. (www.request.com) and the SongBank from Lydstrom (www.lydstrom.com—not www.songbank.com, which is a music site). Each has an Ethernet jack for connectivity; each has a small built-in screen on which it can display information and visualizations, but can also output to your television; and each accepts input from a keyboard.

AudioReQuest

The AudioReQuest is a stereo component–like CD player with a built-in 17GB hard drive. At 128K, that'll hold 320 hours of music—enough to keep you running for a solid month or so. You can rip from CDs directly to the hard drive, or you can copy existing files to the AudioReQuest.

The AudioReQuest has a built-in LCD display but also can interface with your television if you want to get a bigger picture of what's on it, if you want to use its custom graphical user interface (GUI), or if you want visualizations to enhance your appreciation of the music.

The AudioReQuest comes with a remote control, but you can also add a keyboard, either through the AT keyboard port or through one of the USB ports. The AudioReQuest can connect to your PC via its parallel port, via USB, or via its built-in Ethernet port, so you shouldn't have any problem getting music onto it.

The AudioReQuest costs $799, making it a serious investment.

SongBank

Like the AudioReQuest, the SongBank is a stereo component-like CD player with a built-in hard drive capable of holding a large number of songs. At this writing, the SongBank has been announced in three different models, of which only one is available at this writing. The SongBank SL ($799) stores up to 350 hours of music, the SongBank SZ stores up to 450, and the SongBank MZ stores up to 900 hours of music. To each SongBank you can attach additional storage units, which are due to be released in fall 2000.

The SongBank SL and the SongBank SZ each have a single stereo output, whereas the SongBank MZ has four stereo outputs and can output a different audio stream to each simultaneously.

WARNING

Lydstrom has one of the more annoying Web sites that we've seen within living memory—a Flash monstrosity that loads at sub-glacial speed over a modem connection but insists on playing sub-Wolfenstein music at you until you stop it. To keep your sanity, locate and click the Sound Off button at the first chance.

Playing MP3 Files in Your Car

Once you're heavily into MP3, you'll want to be able to play MP3 files wherever you go. The good news is that there are already many ways to play MP3 audio in your car. The bad news is that most of them will set you back some serious bucks.

This section examines two main ways of playing MP3 audio in your car, discussing their advantages and disadvantages.

Connecting Your Portable Player to Your Car Stereo

The first way to add MP3 to your car, and the least expensive, is to connect your portable player to your existing car stereo. The advantages of doing this are that the cost can be minimal, the sound quality high, and the task trivial. The disadvantages are that the task can be Herculean, the sound quality horrible, and the amount of music you can take disappointing.

In other words, it all depends.

The first thing it depends on is your car stereo. Some car stereos have an auxiliary input into which you can slap a signal from a portable player. This input might be a mini-plug socket on the front face of the car stereo, but it's more likely to be a pair of wires with RCA jacks protruding from the back of the player (or a socket into which such wires would go). So you'll have to go hunting for it, and if professionals installed the stereo for you, they probably bundled up and hid the extra wire, so you may have to dig it out. If you find this wire, you'll probably need an adapter for it, which means a trip to your local car stereo outlet (or Radio Shack) for some high-quality connectors. You'll then most likely need to enable the auxiliary input on the stereo and switch to it, and you'll be in business.

If your stereo doesn't have an auxiliary input, but it has a cassette player, your best bet is to use a cassette adapter. Some portable players, such as the i2Go eGo and some RCA Lyra packages, come with cassette adapters included in the package. If yours doesn't, you should be able to buy one easily enough either at a retail outlet or online. Once you've got that, plug the adapter into the player and the stereo, flip any switches necessary, set the volume low at both ends, and see if it works.

If your stereo doesn't have a cassette player either, you may be able to patch your portable player into your existing wiring by using an RF modulator (*RF* stands for *radio frequency*). Unless you're experienced at handling electronics, you probably should let your car stereo dealership handle this task.

The second thing it depends on is (obviously enough) your portable player. If you're planning to use the player in the car, make sure that

- It has enough memory for your needs.
- It can use a car adapter for power if it's at all heavy on the batteries.
- It produces a sound signal of a quality high enough for your car stereo.

Depending on your vehicle and the player, you may be able to bundle the player into the glove compartment rather than having it flapping loose the whole time. Some players, such as the i2Go eGo, come with custom car mounts.

Whatever your mounting arrangement, the player is almost certainly going to be much more vulnerable to theft than your car stereo, so you'll probably want to unplug it and take it with you when you leave the vehicle.

Getting an In-Dash Player or In-Car Jukebox

The other way to add MP3 to your car is to get a custom in-dash player or in-car jukebox. An in-dash player fits into the car-stereo slot in the dashboard of the car, while an in-car jukebox usually lives in the trunk and feeds into a dashboard unit that acts as a controller, in an arrangement similar to that used by in-car CD jukeboxes (also known as *CD changers*). The jukebox may connect to the dashboard unit either via a wire or via an RF modulator.

Both in-dash players and in-car jukeboxes are for the serious MP3 fan because they involve a serious chunk of dough (think several hundred to much more than a thousand dollars). An in-dash player also means getting rid of your car's current CD player or cassette deck (or having one of the two dangling loosely or strapped to the dash with duct tape).

The advantage of the in-dash player is clear—it doesn't take up extra space. The advantage of the jukebox is that the amount of space available for the main unit is limited by the size of the trunk rather than by the size of the dash slot, so (in most cars) you can include a much larger player.

Most of the jukeboxes that are currently available or in development range in size from the size of a shoebox to the size of a VCR and have one or more hard drives inside. Most of the in-dash players use a hard drive, although some in-dash players are CD drives that can read both regular audio CDs and data CDs containing MP3 or other audio files. (If you remember that a CD can hold about 11 hours of MP3 files at 128K, these CD drives should sound pretty good to you.)

At this writing, there are about two dozen competing products in this category, most of them from small companies who, although selling energetically over the Web and developing their products fast enough to give larger companies indigestion, have yet to make a major impact. Given that the picture will certainly have changed by the time you read this, we won't attempt to round up the current players. Instead, we'll point you to a good source of information on car MP3 players: www.mp3car.com. And in the next section we'll examine one in-car player that has more or less broken free of the pack—the empeg car.

If you're in the market for an in-dash or in-car player, these should be your main considerations:

Price Basically, whichever in-car player you're looking at, it's a serious purchase—around the cost of a modest-to-good new computer. We can't help you much with this consideration except to advise you to shop around as much as possible.

Size An in-dash player is going to look much more attractive than a jukebox if you've got a small trunk and aren't prepared to sacrifice your luggage space for your listening. Given that some in-dash players can hold as much as 36GB—600 hours of MP3 files encoded at 128kbps—you may not need a jukebox.

Medium   You can choose a CD or hard drive—or another medium such as Zip drive. Decide what's going to work best for you.

Data Transfer   How will you get the files onto the player? If the player has a non-removable hard drive and is permanently installed in your car, you're probably looking at running an Ethernet network connection out to the street, testing the length limitations of USB cables, or hauling your computer out to the garage. An Ethernet cable can be up to 328 feet long, so running one from your home to the car is workable if absurd, but most likely you'll be better off with a removable player or jukebox.

empeg car

The empeg car, from the U.K. company Empeg Ltd. (www.empeg.com), is one of the longest-lived and leading in-dash MP3 players for the car. The empeg car Mark 1 player, released in 1999, helped define the car MP3 player market, but was rough around the edges. In particular, the controls and interface needed refinement. The empeg car Mark 2, released in June 2000, delivers significant improvements, including fully revamped controls and a much clearer interface.

In a nutshell, the empeg car is a player built around one or two hard drives and an optional FM tuner crammed into a car stereo that fits into the car-stereo slot in your dashboard. The empeg car plays MP2, MP3, and WAV files, and will soon play WMA files as well.

The empeg car comes in a variety of capacities offering up to 36GB of storage. As you'd expect, the larger the capacity, the higher the cost, but (as usual) we recommend getting the most storage you can reasonably afford. As you'll see in a minute, it's easy enough to add music to the empeg car and remove music from it. But if you're anything like us, you'll want to gradually build on your empeg car a library of all the music you might ever possibly want to listen to in your car, and just keep it there. That way, you'll never be without the tracks you need.

> **TIP**
>
> At this writing, the empeg car Mark 2 is available in 6GB, 12GB, 18GB, and 36GB configurations. Each of the first three configurations uses a single hard drive, and the fourth configuration uses two 18GB drives. For most people, the 12GB model is the best entry-level configuration, because (at this writing) it costs only a little more than the 6GB version and substantially less than the 18GB version. You can then add a second drive when you have more money available. By that time, drives even larger than 18GB may be available and affordable.

The empeg car Mark 2 runs Linux on a 220MHz StrongARM processor, has 12MB RAM and 1MB of flash ROM, uses a custom in-car DSP, and has a five-band equalizer for each of the four output channels.

The empeg car is designed to play a dual role. It comes with a removable chassis so that you can yank it quickly from the dashboard of your car and carry it inside to connect it to your PC or your stereo. For non-car use, the empeg car uses a standard power cable and an AC adapter, so you can plug it in just about anywhere. If you have multiple vehicles, you can get an extra car mounting bay and simply plug the empeg car into whichever vehicle you're using.

By connecting it to your PC, you can load and unload music from the empeg car. By connecting it to your stereo, you can use the empeg car as a stereo component. Chances are, the empeg car won't match your stereo components for size or look, but with the quantity of music it can hold, you probably won't care too much.

MP3 on Your PDA, on Your Home Stereo, and in Your Car

The empeg car connects to your PC via either a serial cable or a USB cable. If you have any choice in the matter, go with the USB cable, because file transfers will be an order of magnitude faster with the USB cable than with the serial cable. Note that you'll need to keep the serial cable in case you want to upgrade the software on the empeg car unit with a later release—for this task, the USB cable is no use.

The empeg car uses custom software punningly named emplode that installs easily on Windows 9x or Windows 2000. emplode installs using a standard InstallShield installation routine involving nothing more challenging than entering the player's serial number (which you should find on the unit). As usual with USB-connected hardware, you should install the software before connecting the unit via USB. If you connect the hardware first, Windows starts demanding a driver information file for the unknown device it has just encountered.

Once you've installed emplode and plugged in the empeg car, you're ready to start transferring files. emplode, shown in Figure 15.1, provides a simple interface that lets you easily manage the contents of the empeg car.

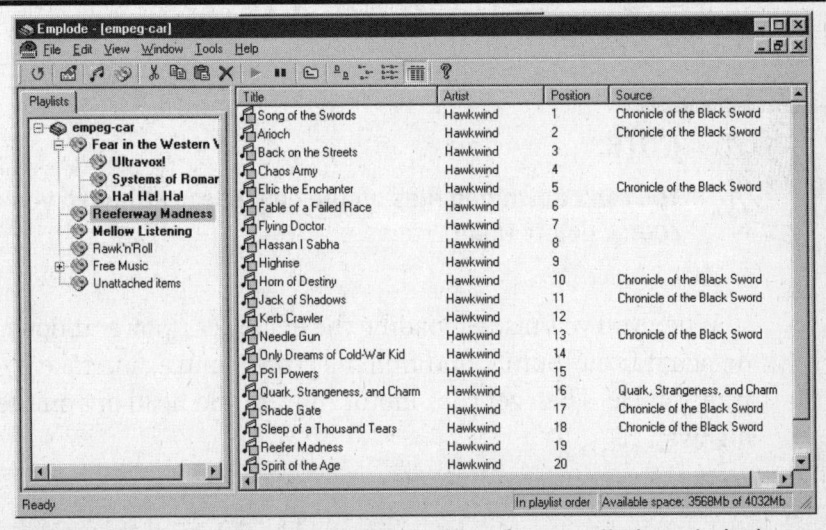

FIGURE 15.1: The empeg car comes with software called emplode that provides full management functions.

You can add tunes and playlists to the empeg car. (A *tune* is essentially the same thing as a track or a song.) You can nest one playlist within another or keep all your playlists at the empeg-car root of the tree.

Once you've arranged tunes and playlists to your heart's content in emplode, you synchronize the changes to the empeg car unit by issuing a `Synchronize` command. Depending on how much music you're transferring to the empeg car, synchronization can take anything from a few minutes to a few hours. During synchronization, emplode displays the Synchronising dialog box, shown in Figure 15.2, to tell you what's happening. In the Operation group box, you can see the operation that's being performed (Uploading to Unit) and the track (item) being processed (Dateline).

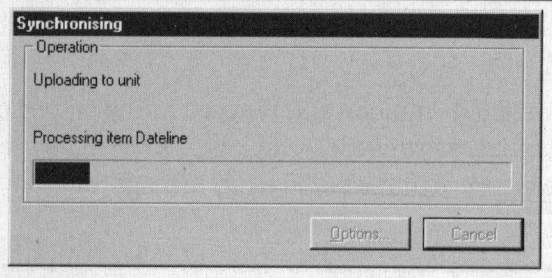

FIGURE 15.2: Loading the empeg car

> **NOTE**
> You can't download files off the empeg car, although you can of course delete them.

When you've finished loading the empeg car, power it down, detach it from your PC and from its power source, and take it out to your vehicle. Then get your motor runnin' and head out on the highway...

> **NOTE**
>
> If you don't fancy spending upwards of $1000 on a custom-built MP3 player for your car, and if you have some old hardware lying around that you'd like to reuse, you can always build your own in-car player yourself. One project for building such a player is Route 66, which you'll find detailed on the Maximum PC Web site (www.maximumpc.com/route66/index.html).

Up Next

In this chapter, you've seen the possibilities for playing MP3 music on your PDA or hand-held computer, in your home, and in your car.

That's the end of the MP3-beyond-the-computer part of the book. In the next part, we'll show how to publish, promote, and broadcast your audio on the Web. Turn the page.

Part VII
Publishing, Promoting, and Broadcasting Your Music on the Web

LEARN TO:

- Understand the opportunities the Web offers artists
- Be realistic about piracy—and use it to your advantage
- Develop a promotional strategy for your band
- Make your tracks available on major music Web sites
- Build your own Web site to promote your music
- Start an electronic newsletter to keep your fans up to date
- Use SHOUTcast and icecast to broadcast audio across the Internet

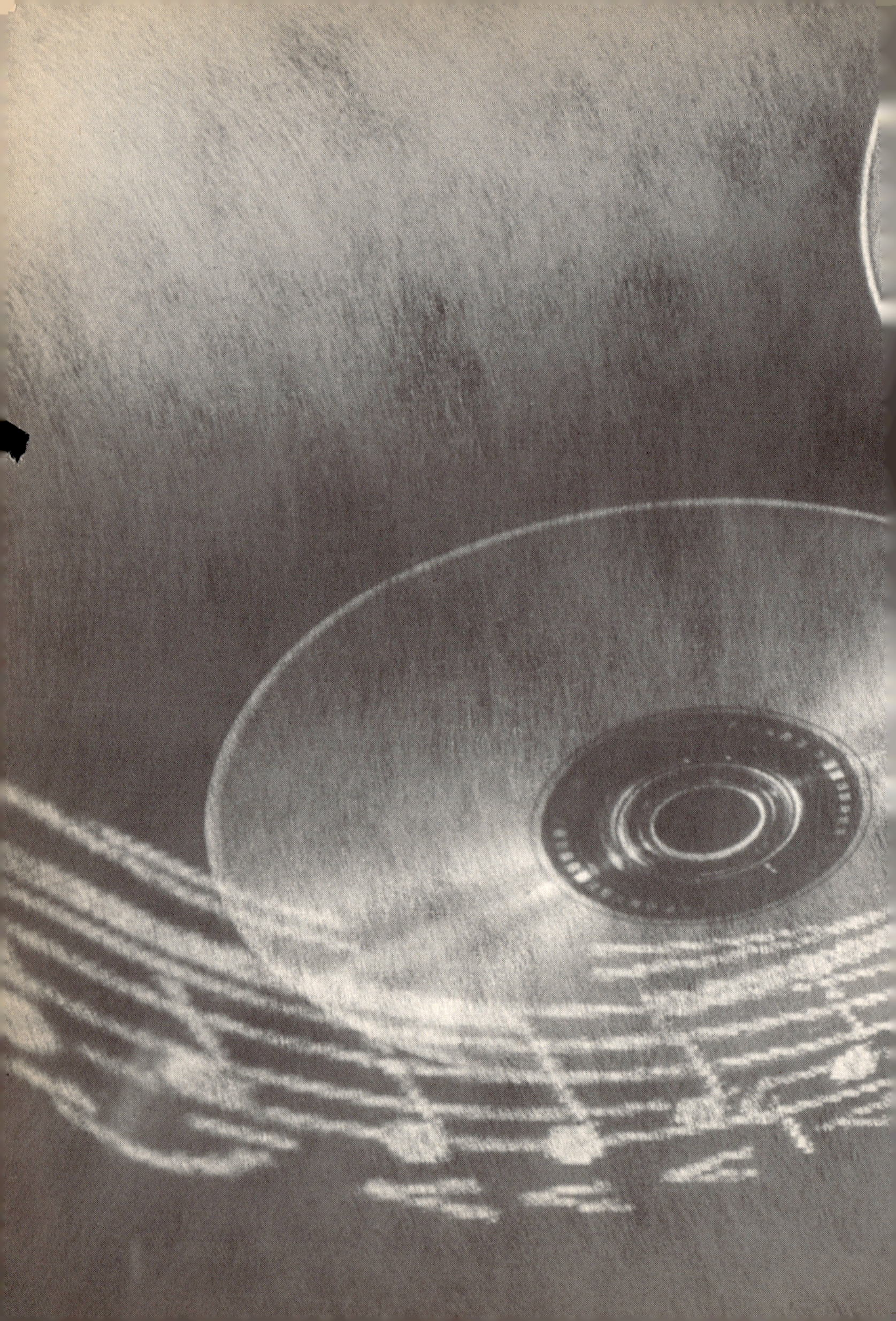

Chapter 16

Grasping the Opportunities the Web Offers

FEATURING
- Advantages and disadvantages of digital audio for the artist
- Being realistic about piracy
- Establishing your goals
- Developing a promotional strategy
- Choosing the best music format for your needs

As you saw earlier in this book, the Internet, the Web, and the new digital-audio formats present a fantastic opportunity for musicians to publish, distribute, and promote their own work—and an equally fantastic opportunity for music lovers to hear a wider variety and greater quantity of music than ever before.

If you're an artist, the digital-music formats offer you unprecedented new opportunities for promoting your music on the Web and the Internet. Freed from the constraints of the record companies that used to effectively filter all the music that was widely released, the artist can now release and promote their music as they wish. The artist can connect directly with their audience and have a chance at gaining new listeners, without needing to have a huge marketing machine behind them.

This chapter will discuss the opportunities that the Web offers, the threats that to some extent counterbalance them, and how to decide the best way to proceed. The next chapter then outlines the best ways to promote your music on the Web.

Along the way, we'll try to resist the temptation to give you the history of recorded music. We're sure you know enough of that already, from wax cylinders through vinyl records through cassettes, CDs, DATs, and MiniDiscs. We'll also try to avoid advising you on how to develop yourself as a musician, as an artist, or both. If you've decided that you're going to dedicate any substantial chunk of your time to playing, creating, and publishing music, you probably have a better idea of what you're up to than we do.

That said, one of the things that seems clear when you look at the contemporary scene is that it's the distinctive artists and bands who gain the most from being on the Web, while the more-of-the-same artists and bands fail to stand out in the crowd. While it's great that you no longer have to deal with a record company or have some heavy-handed producer messing with your artistic vision, make sure that you do *have* an artistic vision, that it's accessible enough to your fans, and that your production values are at least adequate. There's little profit in releasing music that sounds terrible because nobody bothered to mix it correctly. And if you're constantly "challenging" your existing audience to keep up with you, you may not stand much chance of breaking through to new listeners.

Okay, lecture over. Let's get into it.

Promises and Threats of Digital Audio

As discussed in Chapter 1, "MP3 and Digital Audio," digital audio provides great opportunities for you as an artist, but it also threatens your livelihood by simplifying piracy and magnifying its effects. In this section, we'll quickly recap what digital audio promises and threatens. You'll want to keep these threats and promises at the front of your mind when developing a Web-savvy promotional strategy for your music.

Advantages and Disadvantages of MP3

Because the MP3 format is not secure, it offers the clearest illustration of the advantages and disadvantages of digital audio for the artist.

The first advantage is that with digital audio, you have the freedom to publish and distribute your own music over the Internet as you want and when you want. If you wish, you no longer have to have anything to do with a record company or a producer, or with all the delays, restrictions, and hassles that they bring. Instead, you can retain complete creative control over your work. You can record your music yourself, either on conventional (analog) media or (better) on digital media, mix it yourself, create MP3 files, and distribute them via the Web and the Internet. You can sell tracks and CDs, either from your own Web site or via an existing music site, or you can give tracks away for promotional or altruistic purposes.

The second advantage is that you can promote your work online, in the various ways that we'll discuss in this chapter and in the next chapter. Instead of needing the record company (or, more likely, its PR agency) and a ton of money to promote your music via conventional media, you can achieve fair publicity and distribution online.

The third advantage, which ties closely into the first, is that you're no longer constrained by the limitations of conventional media. You no longer need to produce several singles' (and B sides') worth of material in order to get a track released. As soon as you've created anything that you'd like other people to listen to, you can make it available on the Web. If you want, you can release multiple mixes or versions of a track and ask your audience for feedback, which you can get instantly. That's the fourth main advantage: much closer contact with your audience.

Put these four advantages together, and you'll see much of the reason for the recent explosion of music available online. With the artificial restrictions of the record companies and the fiscal restrictions imposed by the distribution of music on physical media (LPs, cassettes, CDs) removed, a large number of new artists have been able to release their material. In addition, many existing artists have been able to release material in digital formats that they would not have been able to release commercially on physical media.

But while it frees the artist from the shackles of the record company, MP3 also has the massive disadvantage of enabling piracy. Using (by today's standards) a modest computer and a poky dial-up connection or ubiquitous CD-R drive, consumers can create and distribute illegal copies of the artist's work, costing the artist money that they would have earned on sales or as royalties on sales. Any CDs that an artist has released can be ripped (extracted) from the CD, encoded to MP3 files, and distributed either on physical media or electronically. Each additional copy made of an MP3 file is perfect—it does not lose audio quality in the way that audiotape copies do from generation to generation—and it costs virtually nothing.

As you've seen already in the book, many people are using technologies such as Napster and gnutella to share illegal copies of music. All it takes is for one person to encode and share an MP3 file of an artist's music, and it quickly becomes available to just about anybody on the Internet.

Advantages and Disadvantages of Other Digital-Audio Formats

The various secure digital-audio formats—such as a2b, Liquid Audio, Mjuice, and ATRAC3—promise far more to the artist than does MP3. In theory, they offer features such as the following:

- The ability to lock a track to a particular computer
- The ability to prevent piracy
- The ability to create a track that expires after a number of plays or at a certain date
- The ability to create a track that the user can purchase if they like it

Chapter 23, "Other Digital-Audio Formats," discusses the assorted secure digital-audio formats.

But despite the best intentions of their creators, the other digital-audio formats pose essentially the same threat to the artist as MP3 does. The artist's music can be distributed in an insecure digital-audio format, leading to full-scale piracy. The only difference is that with the secure digital-audio formats, the user needs to perform an extra step. Instead of ripping directly from the CD to an MP3 file, the user needs to use software that can circumvent the built-in protection of the digital-audio format and output it to an MP3 file. (Typically, this circumvention involves hijacking the sound stream at the sound card. In some cases, the sound stream is converted to analog and then back to digital, losing some fidelity, but not enough to worry most listeners.) After that, they can play and distribute the MP3 file as usual.

If the original track is in a format that includes an audio watermark, it may be possible to trace the derivation of the insecure file back to the original purchaser. In theory, someone could be prosecuted for illegally copying and sharing a track—but by that time, the cat would be thoroughly out of the bag, and illegal copies of the track would probably have reached every wired corner of the earth.

Being Realistic about Piracy

As we see it, the first thing you need to do as a recording artist is come to terms with piracy. For any creator of audio content, piracy is a major issue, but it's not one you can do a great deal about. Realistically, you should expect that any music you release on CD will be ripped to MP3 files within hours of its becoming available, and that illegal copies will begin to circulate. And supposedly secure digital-audio formats are only a tiny bit more secure than CDs.

The following sections discuss some measures you might consider taking against piracy, and how effective or ineffective each is. We should warn you ahead of time that none of these measures is effective in the long term.

Release Lo-Fi Versions of Tracks

Releasing low-fidelity versions of tracks for free public consumption is an effective but limited anti-piracy measure. For example, you might choose to release free versions of files recorded at something approaching FM-radio quality. (For MP3 files, this would probably mean using a bitrate of 64kbps.) People would be able to download the music freely and quickly, listen to it, and share it with whomever they wished, and the music would sound borderline acceptable—probably just bad enough that anybody who wanted to listen to the music often would feel the need to get a better version. You could then sell a higher fidelity version of the tracks to them, preferably via the Web.

The limits of releasing lo-fi versions are clear. First, your music will sound much worse than it should, and that may cost you the listeners you're coveting. (It won't necessarily be apparent to many listeners that the defects in the sound quality are the result of your deliberate choice—they may just think your music sounds that way.) And—if people like your music—as soon as you release a higher fidelity version of a track, no matter what format you use, it will be encoded to an MP3 file and distributed freely.

Release Tracks in a Secure Format

Were any digital-audio format totally secure, releasing tracks in that format would of course be the perfect solution to piracy problems. Needless to say, in the real world, no format is secure, despite the best efforts of a number of heavy hitters in the field.

As things stand at this writing, some formats (such as Liquid Audio and Sony's ATRAC3) provide solid security against the user's being able to copy a file against the wishes of its creator; the user can copy the file, but the copy won't play for them. But even the most secure, SDMI-fortified track can be piped out of one sound card, into another, and captured there. With the right software, you can hijack the audio stream from the sound card and write it to a file. The result loses a little of the fidelity of the digital original, but not enough to worry people who are eager to hear the track.

By using a (supposedly) secure format, you can increase the amount of effort and ingenuity that someone has to employ in order to make an MP3 file from your original, but that's about it. You might as well not bother.

Release No Music at All

The ultimate deterrent against piracy, and (as far as we can tell) the only effective one, is to release no music at all. Sadly, this has also proven to blight an artist's career.

If Piracy Is Inevitable, What Can You Do?

If you accept that piracy of your music is more or less inevitable whatever you do, the question becomes how you can best turn it to your advantage.

Because the music scene is changing rapidly at this writing because of MP3, the answer isn't entirely clear yet. But it seems to us that the most successful artists will be those who use MP3 (and other digital-audio formats) to help spread their music and increase the popularity of their works, thus driving sales of music on physical media and of ancillary products. Although some (perhaps many) people will adopt MP3 to the exclusion of all physical media, others will still want to have the music on a physical medium for convenience, for the perception of conferred status, or to have the ultimate in sound quality. Others are more concerned with remaining on the right side of the law. Others yet actively want to support the artist, and do so by buying CDs, concert tickets, t-shirts, and so on.

We suggest that you work to spread your music so widely that, despite a high level of piracy, you still achieve strong sales of CDs and cassettes. At the very least, you will probably increase the audience for your concerts. But to maximize your revenues, create and sell ancillary products, such as posters, t-shirts, baseball caps, pens, and whatever other items your audience chooses to demonstrate its musical allegiances by purchasing. If you follow this trend to its extreme, you may find that more of your revenue comes from selling clothing (for example) than selling music. It may be disconcerting (pun not really intended) to be earning your money from the t-shirt rather than from the Telecaster, but if you're building your audience and making enough money, who's to care?

Encourage Bootlegs of Live Performances

To fuel the spread of your music, aggressively encourage bootlegs of your live performances. As you no doubt know, this tactic has a long and honorable history, and has worked for artists spanning the full music range from the Grateful Dead to Metallica. If your live performances are worth experiencing, you can bet that some of the fans who were at any given performance will want to relive it, and that fans who weren't there will want to know what happened.

We doubt we need tell you this, but the more unique or compelling your live performances, the more likely fans will want recordings of them. Play your cult-appeal tracks more often, play covers, or even develop the art of telling stories in between tracks—anything to avoid giving the cookie-cutter performances that make gigs a grind for audience and artist alike.

In the old days of analog recordings, the ultimate gift an artist could give their fans (short of dying onstage in dramatic fashion) was to let them plug in to the mixing desk during a show and get a high-quality copy of the sound rather than an open-mike copy full of the audience stamping on each other's feet, cheering drunkenly, and breaking beer glasses. With MP3, you can go one step further: Record each performance at the mixing desk the way you would normally do, then release those tracks as MP3 files. Don't remix them unless you have a huge amount of time on your hands. If the performance was worthwhile, your fans will want them as they are; if the tracks are worthless, they'll be relegated to digital oblivion before too long.

ESTABLISHING YOUR GOALS

At this point, you need to decide what goals you have in developing an online presence. Your list of goals will vary, but the chances are it will include at least some of the following:

- ▶ Get exposure by distributing promotional tracks or live tracks. If you're a new artist who's trying to build a following, you'll probably want to distribute music files that people can pass along to their friends without running into usage restrictions. If you're an established artist, you may also want to consider releasing time-out versions or limited-play versions of tracks by using a format other than MP3.

> **WARNING**
>
> If you're signed to or working with a record company already, make sure that you have the rights to distribute the tracks in question.

- Develop the interest and loyalty of your existing audience by keeping your fans informed about your music releases and your concert schedule, by letting them contact you easily, and by providing them with more information about you (or your band) and your music.

- Expand your audience by getting your music to new listeners.

- Sell electronic copies of your music.

- Increase sales of your work on physical media.

- Increase sales of your ancillary products (t-shirts, baseball caps, posters, pens, bumper stickers, etc.). As discussed earlier in this chapter, these products can represent a significant chunk of the income that you will derive from your musical career.

- Provide booking agents with your contact information. If you arrange your own bookings, supply your booking information so that prospective contact people can reach you easily. Maintain a calendar of confirmed bookings on your Web site so that agents can see when you're free and your fans can see when you'll be playing.

Developing a Promotional Strategy

Once you've identified your goals, develop a promotional strategy for the Web that encompasses them. Your strategy will depend largely on the amount of time and money you can afford to put into promoting yourself and your music—but at a minimum, your options should include the following:

- Developing a presence on some of the major digital-music sites, such as Riffage.com, MP3.com, and EMusic.com. Doing so takes a little time and effort, but costs next to nothing.

- Building a simple Web site of your own to communicate with your fans. Unless you have a friend willing to host the site for free, this will cost you some money each month, and you'll need to put in a fair amount of time keeping the site up to date and interesting.

- Building a more complex Web site of your own with a Web host that provides e-commerce capabilities so that you can sell your merchandise online. This will be more expensive than a simple Web site, and you'll need to fulfill (or arrange fulfillment for) the orders you receive—preferably promptly.

TIP

If you decide to build a Web site, try to get a snappy domain name that is or evokes the name of your band. You can search for and register domain names at a number of sites, of which Network Solutions, Inc. (www.networksolutions.com) is perhaps the most authoritative (having held a monopoly on domain names for several years) and the Germany-based Joker.com (www.joker.com) one of the least expensive. Once you've registered the name, resist any record company contracts that try to appropriate it for their own use.

- Creating an e-mail newsletter to keep your fans in touch with you. This will cost you more time than money.

We'll discuss how to put these four options into effect in the next chapter.

If you have money to spare and are looking to make a splash, consider the following:

- ▶ Hire a company that specializes in Web-based publicity to promote your music on the Web.
- ▶ Buy banner ads on music sites or other related sites. If you have your own Web site, you might also be able to trade ads with artists you know or artists whose music is similar.
- ▶ Arrange giveaways of your CDs and ancillary products.

Choosing the Best Digital-Audio Format for Distribution

Next, you need to choose the best digital-audio format for distributing your tracks. Given the small number of formats available, the number of tracks that each currently has in circulation, and the relative popularity of the different formats with the consumer, this shouldn't be too tough a decision.

For most artists, the deciding factor is usually the level of security that they want the files to have. In theory, a digital-audio format that offers security features, such as a2b or Liquid Audio, will protect your tracks from piracy. But as we've discussed in this chapter, the security in all the currently available file formats can be bypassed either directly (using software) or by outputting the sound signal from the sound card and back into the computer (or into another computer). Some sound quality will be lost if the signal needs to be converted from digital to analog and back again, but the resulting track will be plenty high enough quality to listen to. So if somebody wants to create an MP3 file of a secure track, they can do so without undue effort.

If you've decided to circulate files of either your live performances or some of your recordings in the hope of getting viral marketing to work for you, MP3 is by far the best format. By using MP3 (and perhaps adding a "please distribute freely" message and your URL in the tag information), you can encourage people to circulate your music and give yourself global exposure within a very short time.

> **NOTE**
>
> If you feel limited in your choice of viable digital-audio formats, consider how much more limited your choice of physical media for distribution is. These days, pretty much every artist must distribute their work on CD and cassette, with vinyl tailing off as a specialty option for aging audiophiles. Now, as you saw earlier in this book, the CD is the most eminently rippable medium. It delivers high-quality audio, and almost every current computer has a drive that can provide digital audio from a CD. So you might choose to take the view that just about any digital-audio format is better than the CD—except that the CD has the advantage inherent to all physical media, that someone has to buy (or steal) a physical unit in order to get access to its contents.

Up Next

In this chapter, we've looked at the opportunities that MP3 offers you as an artist, and the threats to your livelihood that counterbalance those opportunities. We've discussed how it is inevitable that any appealing music you release will be pirated, no matter which digital format (secure or otherwise) you use for distribution. We've also looked at what we consider to be the best way of dealing with piracy: Turn it to your advantage by leveraging the exposure that it will give your music.

Beyond that, we've outlined how to establish your goals in developing an online presence, how to plan a promotional strategy for your music, and how to choose the best audio format to meet your needs.

In the next chapter, we'll discuss how to put these goals into practice by getting your music up on the Web and by developing an e-mail newsletter to communicate with your audience.

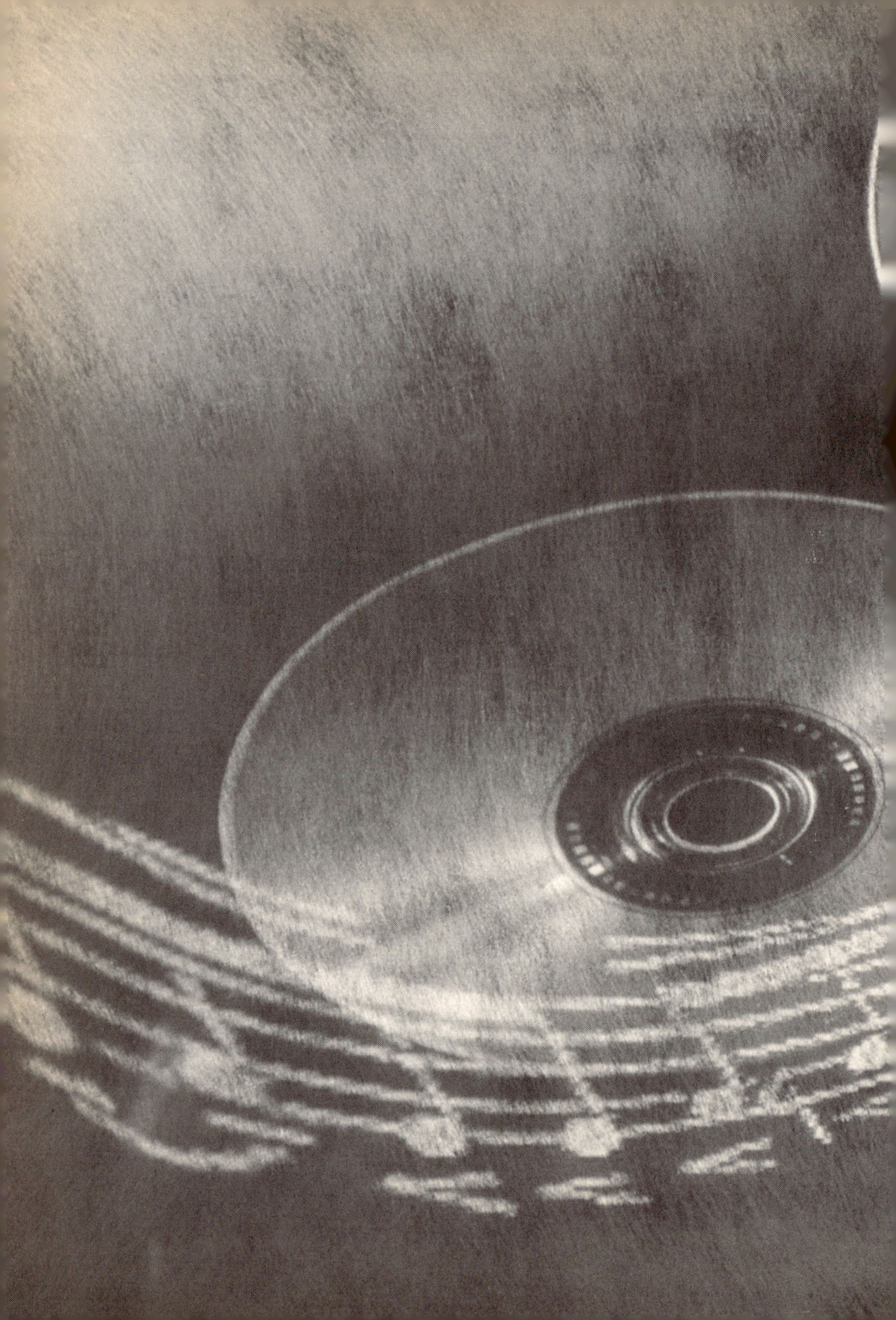

Chapter 17
Getting Your Music Up on the Web

FEATURING
- Getting your tracks onto online music sites
- Planning your Web site
- Starting an e-mail newsletter

In this chapter, we'll discuss how to put into practice some of the decisions you made in the previous chapter for promoting your music on the Web.

First, we'll show you how to get your MP3 files up onto a couple of the major MP3 sites: Riffage.com and MP3.com. This is usually the easiest way for an artist or a band to start getting worldwide exposure for their music. It's fast, and it costs you only a little time and effort.

After that, we'll discuss how to go about planning and building your own Web site. Because of the many different Web site–hosting possibilities these days, and because we have no idea what kind of software you're using, we won't go into the details of constructing the Web site. (For that, you'll probably want to get a book that discusses in depth how to construct a Web site.) But we'll point out the major considerations, from establishing which capabilities your ISP will need to deciding what types of content you'll put up on your site.

Last, we'll talk about how to develop an e-mail newsletter for keeping your audience up-to-date with your music and your movements.

Getting Your Music onto Online Music Sites

If you have rights to music and want to distribute that music in MP3 format, your first move toward developing an online presence should be to get some of your tracks up on major music sites such as Riffage.com and MP3.com. This involves little time, less effort, and zero expense, so you've got no excuse for not doing it.

Both these sites, and many of their competitors, let you both provide free tracks and sell tracks via their built-in mechanisms. The disadvantage to selling tracks via these sites is that, naturally enough, they take a hefty cut of the selling price. As a result, you'll notice that many artists prefer to give away a bunch of tracks on

Getting Your Music Up on the Web   673

the major sites to help build their audience but sell tracks through a Web site of their own where they get a better percentage of the price.

The process for each music site is simple but relatively volatile—the pages involved change frequently—so in this section we'll merely point out how to get started, leaving you to handle the details.

Before you start, arm yourself with the following:

- An image of your band. For Riffage.com, make the image 150×200 pixels (150 pixels wide by 200 pixels high). For MP3.com, make it 270×180 pixels, and save it in JPEG or GIF format. For MP3.com, you'll also need the album or track picture that you want to use. Trim this to 70×70 pixels. Use an image-editing program such as Microsoft Paint (which ships with Windows) to trim the pictures to the right size.

- Your band name or artist name (the hardest decision, but one you should have taken a while ago).

- A description of your band, a list of members, any press reviews you want to post, a list of instruments played, and so on. Create this information ahead of time and have your other band members review it before you post it. If you flip through a number of the pages that other bands have posted, you'll soon see the inadvisability of putting this information together on the fly.

- A short passage on the background and history of the band, a list of its top musical influences, a list of similar artists, and the URLs of any online reviews of your band. All these are optional, but you'll probably want to enter them if you have them.

- The band's main contact, together with the address and the name to which checks should be made out.

- The e-mail address that you want to use for the band. Consider setting up a custom e-mail address for the band if you haven't already done so. You won't want thousands of new fans barraging your personal e-mail address.

- ▶ A custom URL of 20 characters or fewer derived from the band name and consisting of only letters (uppercase and lowercase) and numbers.
- ▶ The MP3 files that you want to post. Don't forget these—neither site will be much interested in you if you don't provide any music. (MP3.com will let you sign up, but nobody's going to pay any attention to you.) Have a description and credits for each MP3 file you plan to post.

Signing Up As an Artist on Riffage.com

To sign up as an artist on Riffage.com, click the Artist Sign In button on the navigation bar on the left-hand side of the Riffage.com home page. This takes you to the Artist Zone on Riffage.com, where you can click the Sign Up Now link to start the registration process.

Once you're safely registered, you can click the Login Here link on the Artist Zone page to log in as your artist persona (as opposed to your user persona) and manipulate your account. For example, you might need to update your contact information or add further tracks to your offerings.

Signing Up As an Artist on MP3.com

To sign up as an artist on MP3.com, follow the New Artist Sign Up link, which currently resides near the bottom of the MP3.com home page. Wade through the page of propaganda ("Earn CA$H – through our Payback for Playback promotion!") and click the Sign Me Up button at the bottom.

You then get to log in with your e-mail address but without a password, which gets you to the Creating New Master Admin Logon page, in which you create a password. MP3.com then sends you an e-mail for confirmation with a special URL to unlock your MP3.com Master Page. Click or double-click the URL's link (depending on the e-mail package you're using) to unlock the page, then click the Sign Up New Artist link in the Artist Management section of the resulting page to begin the signup procedure.

> **NOTE**
>
> MP3.com automatically creates an instant-play version of any tracks you upload.

> **TIP**
>
> Given Napster's current extreme popularity (assuming that it survives the legal attacks it's battling at this writing), you may also want to sign up as an artist on Napster so that prospective listeners can track you down by your music style or name. Go to `artist.napster.com` and create an artist profile.

Building Your Own Web Site

Given how easy and inexpensive it is to build a Web site, you should certainly build a site of your own to promote your music. But unless you're overburdened with time or resources, we suggest using your personal Web site as a supplement to the online presence you establish on large sites such as Riffage.com or MP3.com rather than using it instead of them. These professional sites will get far greater traffic than your site, so by making your music available on them, you have the potential to reach a much wider audience. You can use one or more of these major sites as a gateway, introducing people to your music and directing them to your personal site for more information. Include in your artist biography the URL of your Web site and brief details of what people will find there; make it sound as tempting as possible to draw people in.

The advantage of running your own Web site is, obviously enough, that you get to control what goes on it. The disadvantage is that you have to create and maintain the site.

If you want, you can also control access to your site (for example, by using passwords), but this tends to be an extreme measure that may lose you fans. Because a username and password can be distributed easily and instantly across the Internet (for example, by a participant in a chat room or by a member of a mailing list), having password-protected areas of a Web site offers little effective defense against unauthorized visitors.

The first role of your personal Web site should be to provide information to your listeners. Consider putting the following on it:

Lyrics to tracks Unless your songs plumb new depths of banality, lyrics tend to be a strong draw for fans. Some fans will just want to know what those indecipherable phrases in the middle of the third verse actually are, just for the sake of knowing. Other fans will want to be able to sing along. If you're lucky, still other fans will want to perform your songs. It's hard to see any downside to people singing along or performing your songs, although you may need to chase down royalties if anybody starts performing them in public or recording them.

Commented lyrics or explanations of lyrics Anybody can publish the lyrics to your songs on the Web. You may be able to take a leaf out of the Harry Fox Agency's book (the agency that shut down the International Lyrics Server in 1999 on copyright grounds) and prevent them from doing so. But only you can give people authentic commented lyrics or explanations of the lyrics. Your fans will love these.

Background information on you, your band, and your music If people like your music, they'll probably want to know how and why you started playing, what your musical influences are, and so on. Your Web site is a great place to provide this information.

Music you recommend to your fans   Point your fans toward the artists that you find interesting. (If those artists have Web sites, consider doing cross-promotions with them.)

Demo versions of tracks   If you feel confident enough in your work, you may want to release some demo versions (or alternative mixes) of tracks. Some of these versions will be music for the hardcore fan rather than for the casual fan—but that's what your Web site should be about.

Works in progress   You may even choose to let your fans listen to the music you're working on. You can conduct surveys or polls to see which version of a track your audience prefers—and find out why they prefer it.

Your concert schedule   Post your concert schedule as far in advance as you can. If possible, include details on the venues, directions to them, and maps, or link to information on the venue's own Web site.

MP3 files of live recordings that you want to distribute
As discussed in the previous chapter, providing MP3 files of tracks recorded at your concerts is a great way to maintain your audience's interest. The more regularly you provide live MP3 files, the more selective you can afford to be, and the less unauthorized recording will happen at your concerts.

Forms, surveys, questionnaires, and contests   Interactive features such as these can help retain visitors' interest in your site, but they can also greatly increase the amount of time you need to spend maintaining it. We'll discuss such features in the next section.

> **TIP**
>
> Include the URL of your Web site in all your MP3 files and other promotional tracks, and on all your correspondence.

Choosing an ISP

Unless you have a wholly satisfactory ISP already, choosing an ISP will be one of the major decisions you need to make for your Web site.

Entire books have been written on finding a suitable ISP—and if you're in any doubt as to what you need from your ISP, you might want to read one of the books. Briefly, though, here are the important points to keep in mind:

- Make sure that the ISP offers all the features you need, from plenty of e-mail addresses and plenty of Web space to advanced features (such as a shopping cart, a list server, or message boards) if you need them. If you're planning to use Microsoft FrontPage to create and edit your Web pages, check that the ISP supports FrontPage server extensions. (FrontPage is so widespread these days that this isn't a problem with most ISPs.) And if you want to include forms on your Web site, make sure that the ISP supports them.

- If you'll be offering MP3 files for download, check not only that the ISP offers enough space to host the files but that you won't incur extra fees when a huge number of people download them. Some ISPs allow you a number of gigabytes of data transfer before they start charging extra, while others let you shove any amount of data across the wires for a flat fee.

- Make sure that the ISP offers the connection speeds you need. For example, if you have a cable modem or a DSL, an ISP that offers only 56k dial-up access is likely to be of little interest. That said, if you have a cable modem or a DSL, you may be locked into using a particular ISP for your basic connection. In this case, consider a dedicated Web-hosting service for your Web site.

▶ Check the ISP's reliability and the percentage of uptime they promise. These days, they should probably be promising "four nines" (99.99 percent) or "five nines" (99.999 percent) uptime, which translates to between 20 minutes (five nines) and several hours (four nines) of unplanned downtime a year. However, many ISPs miss these marks by the proverbial mile.

▶ Check that you'll be able to access the ISP via dial-up access at local rates from everywhere you expect to be. For example, if you careen around the country on tour, you'll probably do better with an ISP that has points of presence (POPs) nationwide rather than with a local provider whose POPs are concentrated in one geographical area.

▶ Check the ISP's Web site to see if it's organized well enough that you can find all the information you need. Try calling technical support a couple of times and see how long it takes to get an answer.

▶ Unless cents are at a premium, avoid like the plague the free ISPs that barrage visitors to your site with banner ads and advertising windows. We've yet to meet anyone who likes these ads, and they give your site—however well it's designed and constructed—all the glamour of yet another cheapo fan site for Liz Hurley, Denise Richards, or Russell Crowe.

▶ If you're registering a domain name for yourself or your band, find out how much the ISP will charge to host it.

INTERACTIVITY AND FEEDBACK

If you have the time and the inclination to develop your Web site beyond providing information and music to your visitors, consider whether you should add interactive feedback features to it. Depending on who your listeners are and why they come to the site, they may be willing to interface with forms, surveys, questionnaires, and contests—and even provide you with some useful information.

Before we get into this subject, a quick warning: Don't add interactivity and feedback mechanisms to your site for their own sake, because it will be a dreadful waste of time. Add them only if you have a solid reason to do so, and if they will deliver—or (if you're feeling cynical) will appear to deliver—a concrete benefit to your visitors. A modest site that provides solid information is much more useful to your typical fan that an overambitious site that wastes their time.

How you create forms will vary depending on your computer, your operating system, your ISP, and your patience—but you shouldn't find it hard. Even a limited application such as FrontPage Express, which comes free with Windows 98 and Windows Me, can create basic forms. FrontPage itself can do complex forms. You can also use a scripting language such as JavaScript or VBScript, or you can create a script either using CGI directly or by using a tool that generates CGI.

Proceed with Caution

When planning feedback features for your Web site, proceed with caution. Think hard to design features that will benefit both you and your visitors.

Above all, don't bite off more than you can chew. If your site becomes successful, you may draw hundreds or thousands of individual visitors a day. Be careful not to put yourself in a position where you're obliged to spend an ever-increasing percentage of your precious time responding to individual e-mails, feedback forms, or questionnaires.

What Are the Interactive Features For?

Start by establishing what you're trying to do with your feedback features. For example, do you have a strong relationship with live audiences, and are you trying to recreate that relationship online? If so, you'll probably have hard time doing so, because the medium is so different. On the other hand, if you have a widely dispersed audience that's shown an interest (or a determination) in communicating with you, interactive features may well be worthwhile.

One driving reason for implementing interactive features is to collect information about your audience. Read on.

Collecting Information about Your Audience

The reason you're most likely to have for collecting information from visitors to your Web site is so that you can give them information related to you and your music. For example, if you're going to send people a hardcopy newsletter about your music and concert schedule, you'll need the name and full postal address of each recipient. If you're going to send an e-mail newsletter, you'll need a valid e-mail address and perhaps a name.

Some people will tell you that you should try to collect personal information about your visitors—their ages, hobbies, pets, and so on—so that you can customize your messages to them. We feel that this isn't a good idea. Unless your audience is so small that you can actually try to know something about each member individually, or if you have a team of highly enthusiastic people running your fan club, you won't be able to sustain this illusion for long, and your efforts will seem increasingly peculiar to your audience.

If you do feel the need to collect information beyond the basics, a better idea is music-related information. For example, you might ask which other artists they like. If you find you have a large overlap in audience with one or more other artists, you could consider linking to their Web sites, promoting your music together, or even playing gigs together.

There's a right way and many wrong ways to go about collecting information about your listeners. Generally speaking, many people consider it an intrusion of privacy for a Web site to require any piece of information from them that it doesn't actually need for the transaction they're expecting of the site. For example, if you buy a book from Amazon.com, you expect to give them your name, address, telephone number, e-mail address, and payment information, because they need that information to conduct the transaction and get the book to you by mail or delivery. But if they asked for your Social Security number or your best friend's name, you wouldn't see any reason to give it to them—and you'd be right.

If you require information that people feel you shouldn't, you'll typically get one of three reactions:

▶ Some people will shrug (perhaps just mentally) and give you true information.

▶ Some people will abandon the form. (Some will also flame you.)

▶ Some people will give you false information.

One of the easiest ways to get more information from people is to give them a good reason to give it to you. For example, on a form for signing up for an e-mail newsletter, the one piece of information you absolutely need is a valid e-mail address for the person. Most people would think it legitimate for the form to request a name as well, because that will help you administer the e-mail—list for example, deleting an old e-mail address in favor of a new one. (A few people will see the name request as unreasonable and will give a false name. This is fine.) But if you were to request the city or zip code people lived in, they might well think that unreasonable.

However, if you give an apparently valid reason for requesting the information, most people will give it. For example, if you preface the request for the city or zip code by saying that it will enable you to mail people about shows in their area, most people will find that reasonable and provide that information. Some people will still not want to give the information, so you may do better to make it optional.

If you're hell-bent on squeezing information out of people, or if you really want feedback, run a contest. If the prize is a physical object, you will of course need the full mailing address of each person who signs up. If you send the object via a delivery service, you can probably squeeze a home phone number out of people as well. And if there's the prospect of winning something worth having, many people will gladly part with extra information. If you're feeling truly inquisitive, or just curious about which information people will give, look at a few of the warranty cards you considered too intrusive to send in, and derive some survey questions of your own along those lines. (More sensibly, you might ask which of your CDs—or which tracks—they own, and which their favorite tracks are.)

DEVELOPING A PRIVACY POLICY

If you're collecting information from the visitors to your Web site, develop and publish a privacy policy so that visitors know what you'll be doing with the information you request from them.

Developing a privacy policy sounds like a major pain in the seat, but it doesn't need to be. You probably just need to tell visitors to your site that the information you're collecting is to enable you to understand your audience better; inform them of your music, releases, concerts, and promotions; and (if appropriate) send them the information they've requested or any prizes they've won.

Tell them that you will not sell the information to other people. (If you will sell it, have a prominent opt-out option on the sign-up page telling people.) And then back up your privacy policy by doing what you say.

> **WARNING**
>
> Be triply careful about collecting information from children, because much child-protection legislation is belatedly hitting the Web following some vile exploitative marketing toward children by some major companies. Consider including a mechanism (such as a check box or command button) by which the user attests that they're an adult or a mechanism for getting parental consent.

Designing Your Web Site

In designing your Web site, keep the following points in mind.

Focus, Jack! Focus!

First, your site needs to present your message clearly. That means identifying that it's a music site, giving your name (or your artist name) or your band's name, your logo, and the type of music involved. All this the visitor should be able to see at a glance.

Beyond this, try to come up with a banner, slogan, or catch phrase that describes your music in instantly understandable or at least memorable terms. For example, if you describe your band as delivering "The Loudest Pagan Metal in Seattle," people will get an idea of what you're about. If you describe it as "Warm Strawberry Shortcake for Your Ears," you'll probably get remembered, although with affection or disgust, we couldn't say.

On your home page, present links to the important areas of your site. For example, you might have links to your concert schedule, discography, release dates, artist or band information, lyrics, photos, and so on. You may want to present some of these with a snippet of information (for example, by a link to your concert schedule you might write "November: Shows in Portland, Yreka, and Weed") to draw people in, but don't put too much text on the home page. You want people to see the whole of your home page at once at a screen resolution of 800 × 600, so that they can get an idea of what your site is providing without having to scroll to its nether reaches.

Above all, don't lead with a screed on your political philosophy—90 percent of your visitors won't want to read that first thing. Instead, marshal your most interesting material, and place it (or links to it) front and center on your site. Do include the screed, but put it somewhere that people will access it voluntarily rather than forcibly.

Make Sure the Site Loads Quickly

Next, make sure that your site loads quickly, even across a 28.8kbps modem connection. That means using text with the occasional small graphic rather than a graphics-heavy page.

If your logo is large, you may need to reduce the number of colors in it to get it down to a smaller file size that loads quickly. Most logos look okay at 256 colors; if yours doesn't, consider getting a less complex version of it designed for Web use. Don't take your logo down to 16 colors unless it's deliberately designed with few colors—chances are that it'll look terrible. Besides, if you store the logo as a GIF, you'll get 256 colors whether you want them or not it's a requirement of the file format.

Photographs can greatly increase the appeal of a Web site, so you'll probably want to use them. But use them sensibly. Rather than presenting a gorgeous 1MB picture of you and your ice-blue Stratocaster blowing the audience away at the Fillmore, present a tiny thumbnail with a text description and let people follow a link to the full-sized picture only if they want to. List the size of each linked image and give the approximate download time at either 56kbps or 28.8kbps—for example, "582K, about 2 minutes at 56kpbs." (If you are using FrontPage, insert the picture, and then use the built-in Thumbnail tool to create the pint-sized version and a link to the full-sized picture.)

Above all, don't construct a Flash-only site that alienates most of its visitors. If you must create a Flash site, create a non-Flash version that users with lower bandwidths can enjoy, and use the site's home page to let users choose between the Flash version and the non-Flash version of the site. Don't start people off in the Flash version by default, no matter how proud you are of the effects you've achieved.

Make Sure the Site Is Viewable with Different Browsers

You also need to make sure that your site is adequately viewable with different browsers, preferably on different platforms. It's a fatal mistake to design a complex Web site that looks wonderful on one browser but that won't even load correctly on another.

As you're no doubt aware, the browser field has thinned out a great deal since the early 1990s. At this writing, Internet Explorer has the lion's share of the market, with Netscape Navigator struggling to keep pace. (Netscape 6, due in summer 2000, may do something to redress the balance, especially since it will be available for a wider range of platforms than Internet Explorer.) Other browsers, including the well-regarded Opera from Opera Software, have a much smaller market share.

Given this situation, make sure that each page you create looks okay on both Internet Explorer and Netscape. If you have both a PC and a Macintosh, test each browser on each platform; if you have Linux, test Netscape on that too. Obviously, your site doesn't need to look exactly the same on each browser on each platform, but you want to make sure that no page fails disastrously on any browser on any platform.

You can find plenty of books on effective Web design and cross-browser and cross-platform issues, but the simplest approach is usually to forsake fancy features in favor of tried-and-true standards: text, pictures, and downloadable files.

Structure Your Site for Easy Navigation

Next, structure your site so that it's easy to navigate. It's easy enough to build a Web site by just stacking page on page until something apparently cohesive begins to congeal, but you'll produce a far better result if you deliberately create a structure by which the site is organized. The structure doesn't have to be perfect, just workable. As you know from your use of the Web, the beauty of hyperlinks is that you can have as many of them as you want, so you can link from one extreme of the structure to another as you wish.

> **NOTE**
> If you keep your site's structure relatively shallow, users may be able to download the whole of it for offline browsing by using a Web-whacker utility or even Internet Explorer's offline-Favorites feature.

Beyond structuring your site for easy navigation, develop and maintain a naming convention for the files that make up your Web pages, so that you can easily identify any page if there's a problem. Keep plenty of backups of your site so that you can restore it easily.

Provide Benefits to Your Visitors

To keep visitors coming back to your site, you need to provide things that benefit them. For an artist's Web site, that usually means information and downloads.

We've discussed already some of the information that you can easily add to a site, from your schedule and lyric sheets (annotated or not) to downloadable or streamable MP3 files of tracks recorded live or works in progress. But you may also have extra-value materials that aren't immediately obvious but that will have a strong appeal to your fans. For example, if you have poetry or short stories that you've never had published or to which you retain the distribution rights, you might want to put them up on your site. For best results, release these one at a time rather than all at once, and plug each new release on your home page.

Keep Your Site Updated

Few things are guaranteed to turn fans off more quickly than a Web site that appears to be *resting*, moribund, or comprehensively dead. So keep updating your site regularly—or as regularly as possible. At the very least, publish on your site the details of when you'll next be updating it. Fans will be far happier to read a brief update saying that you'll be in the studio in October and November and that as a result the site won't be updated until Thanksgiving than to visit several times in fruitless search of news about you.

Fitting regular updates to your site into a busy schedule of composing, rehearsing, recording, touring, and doing day work to pay for rent and groceries likely won't be easy, so keep your mind firmly on the benefits you're expecting the site to deliver to both you and your fans.

Above all, maintain a calendar of your performances and release dates, so that your fans know where they'll be able to see you. Because this calendar will rapidly go out of date, you'll need to update it at least once a month—preferably more like once a week. If you can, maintain links to the sites of the venues you'll be playing, so that your fans can find out where a venue is and decide whether they want to go.

To keep the content fresh on your site, put together a list of things that you can add to the site with minimal effort, such as lyrics (or better yet, commented lyrics), memories of how you got started, scanned photos, and so on. If you decide to release live tracks regularly, create an archive to which you can quickly add tracks. Add a teaser to your home page that points visitors to the new tracks: "New tracks available from January gigs in Austin, Phoenix, and Santa Fe."

TIP

If you don't have time to create new content, you may be able to freshen your site by changing the contents of the home page to feature different existing items.

One way of getting around the problem of updating the site yourself is of course to get someone to do it for you. Chances are that among your fans there are at least a few who would jump at the chance to maintain your site for you. You'll need to spend time going over the goals of the site and forging a trusting relationship with your Webmaster, but if you find someone good, even a small investment of time will pay dividends.

Another tactic that you may want to try is getting input from your fans to add content to your Web site. For example, you can build a form that lets fans post reviews of tracks or concerts, or submit reviews for you to post if you approve them.

Add Metatags to Your Site

Next, add metatags to the pages on your site that you want. *x* are keywords that are hidden on a Web page and used by search engines to identify the contents of a page.

At a minimum, you'll want to include metatags for your artist name or band name, the type of music you play, the names of CDs and key tracks, and so on.

Register Your Site with Search Engines

To get the word out about your site, register it with as many search engines as you find reasonable. Target the big search engines, such as Yahoo! (`www.yahoo.com`), InfoSeek (`www.infoseek.com`), Ask Jeeves (`www.askjeeves.com`), and perhaps AltaVista (`www.altavista.com`) first, and then go on to secondary search engines if you have the energy. Alternatively, you can use a registering service such as Web Site Garage (`register-it.netscape.com`) to automatically register your site with a number of search engines.

Starting Your Own Electronic Newsletter

A great way to keep your audience up to date with your music and your movements is to send out an electronic newsletter. How exactly you do this will depend on you, the amenities your ISP provides, and how many people sign up for the newsletter. In a pinch, you can maintain a mailing list in your e-mail program and perform the mailing by simply sending an e-mail with the list of names in the bcc field. (Using the bcc field should prevent each recipient from seeing any e-mail address other than their own.) But if your list grows to a serious size, you'll be better off with custom software that can help automate the process of maintaining an electronic mailing list.

Implement the sign-up mechanism for your newsletter in two ways:

- As a form on your Web site
- As an e-mail mailbox, either automated or manual

Be sure to make unsubscribing from your newsletter as easy as possible by letting people unsubscribe in the same ways—and honor their requests as immediately as possible. In addition to automated sign-up and sign-off mechanisms, you'll need to be able to respond to salvoes of increasingly desperate messages with subject lines such as "REMOVE ME FROM THIS LIST" or "HELP—HOW DO I UNSUBSCRIBE?"

At a minimum, your newsletter should provide news about you or your band, upcoming concerts, and releases. Beyond that, it's limited only by your imagination and resources. Be sure to use the newsletter to bring people to your Web site. In the newsletter, plug any new music files that are available for download from the Web site, and consider including in the newsletter only the beginning paragraphs of any news item or review, pointing people to your Web site to find the rest. Besides bringing people to your site, this technique will keep the newsletter short and more readable—no bad thing in itself.

Commit to sending out the newsletter at regular intervals, preferably once or twice a month. You'll have your work cut out to generate a weekly newsletter with consistently entertaining or interesting material. Any frequency less than monthly is likely to have little effect on your audience because the newsletter will tend to arrive as a surprise, and much of the information in it will be severely out of date. Send out special, off-schedule updates whenever it suits you. For example, if you've suddenly posted a slew of new tracks on your Web site, let people know immediately that they're available.

Up Next

In this chapter, we've suggested some ways of starting to develop a presence on the Web to promote your music. At a minimum, you should put some free tracks up on major MP3 sites so that more people can hear them. Beyond that, you can derive many benefits from creating and maintaining a Web site of your own, and you should think about creating an e-mail newsletter to keep your audience informed about you and your music.

In the next chapter, we'll show you how to go a step further and broadcast your music across the Internet to potential listeners.

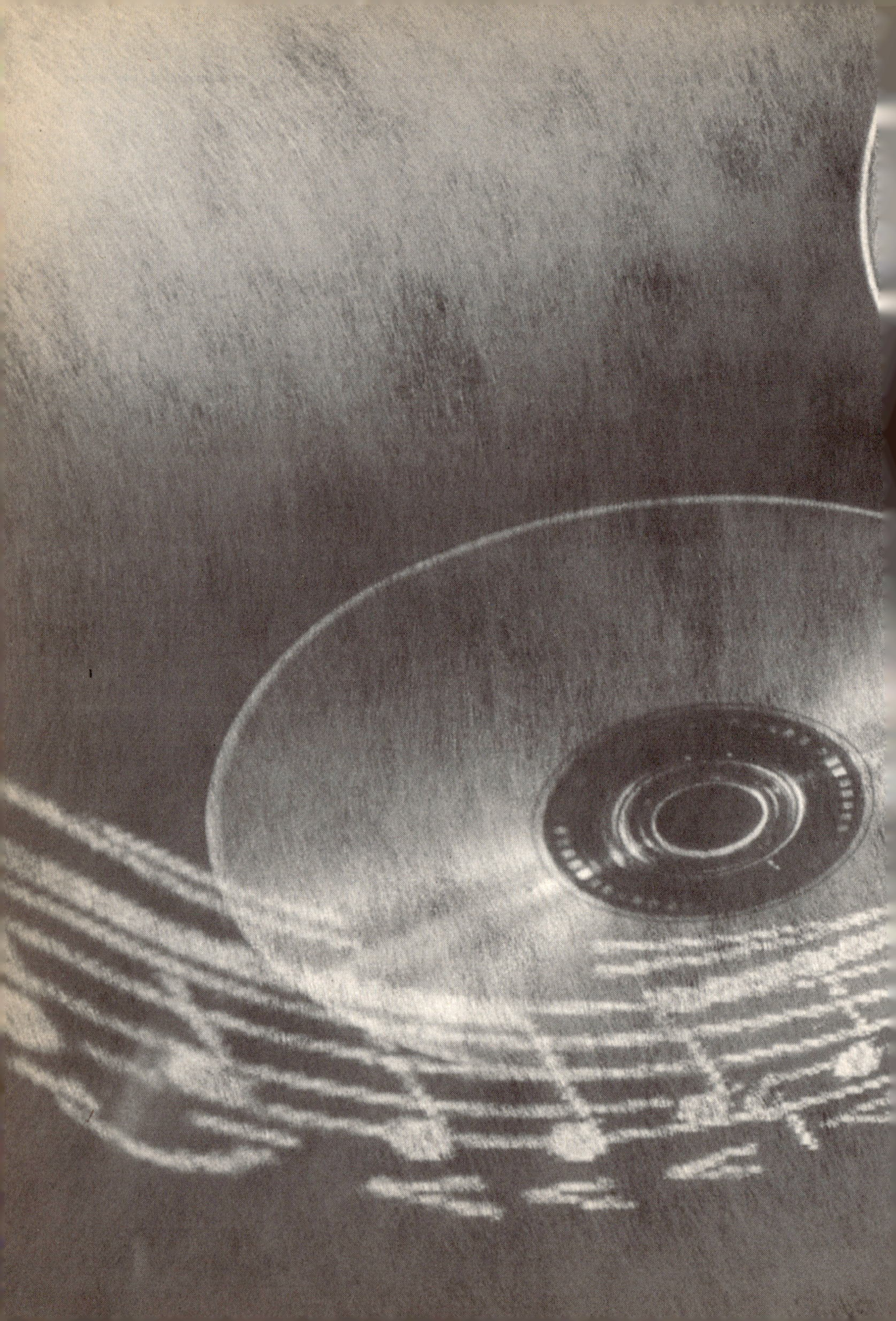

Chapter 18
Broadcasting Your Music across the Internet

FEATURING

- Understanding the rights and wrongs of Internet broadcasting
- Grasping the general principles of Internet broadcasting
- Getting and configuring SHOUTcast
- Broadcasting with SHOUTcast
- Getting and configuring icecast

In this chapter, we'll discuss how you can broadcast your music across the Internet so that anyone on the Internet with a streaming-capable client can tune in and listen to it. Broadcasting can get your music to a wider range of people than posting files on major MP3 sites, so it can be a major tool in your promotional armory.

There are two major technologies for Internet broadcasting: SHOUTcast from Nullsoft (the company that built Winamp before being acquired by America Online) and icecast from the icecast project. Both programs run on a variety of platforms, including Windows and Linux. For variety, we'll show you SHOUTcast on Windows and icecast on Linux; we'll leave you to make the transition to other platforms as necessary.

We'll start by discussing how the law and Internet broadcasting meet and mesh. After that, we'll touch on some of the basics of Internet broadcasting before getting into the specifics of SHOUTcast and icecast.

The Law and Internet Broadcasting

Earlier in this book, we touched on the legal issues concerning ripping music recorded by other people (or music whose rights are held by other people) from CDs or other media. You'll recall that some of the finer legal points there were a little vague or flexible—most people reckon you can legally rip tracks from CDs and encode MP3 files of them the way you can legally tape records or CDs on cassettes, and some people say you can't. Typically, those people who say you can't legally create MP3 files are those with money to lose from your doing so. But even if you rip a ton of CDs and the local law enforcement agencies disagree drastically with your assessment of the copyright laws, it's unlikely (but not impossible) that they'll kick down your door and drag you off if you're ripping the files for nothing more than your own personal use.

When you're distributing music, things tend to be a little more clear-cut. To distribute digital copies of any music, you need the rights to do so. If you created the music yourself and you haven't assigned the rights to anyone, you're most likely in the clear. If you created the music with other people, you need their permission to distribute it. And if you're signed to a record company, chances are that you'll need their consent to distribute any music on your own—even if you made the music yourself in your own studio without the record company being involved in the slightest.

Bottom line: Before you distribute *any* MP3 files, make sure you have the rights to distribute them. Even if you're drawn to the law, intellectual property's an area you really don't want to go spelunking in unless you have time and money to burn.

> **NOTE**
>
> If you're thinking of signing with a record company, make sure that you retain the rights to distribute your music over the Internet. As a promotional tool for artists, MP3 is invaluable—but as we've seen, the record companies are, for the most part, still scared of how it could chew up their profit margins.

By distributing, we mean sending people music files or providing music files for download. If you're broadcasting music (or other audio), the rules are different, and somewhat more in your favor. Basically, you can broadcast, but you're probably going to have to pay for the privilege. Read on.

Until December 1, 1999, you could apply for a *statutory license* that cost a mere $20 and allowed you to broadcast to your heart's content. According to the RIAA's site, you can still go for one of these licenses—which probably means they're arguing about how much more you're going to have to pay. Check the RIAA site (www.riaa.com) for the latest information.

The alternative to getting a statutory license (which may no longer be available when you read this book) is to enter into licensing agreements with individual artists or record companies for the rights to broadcast their music. Unless your station's going to stick to promoting only a few artists, or perhaps just one record label, these licensing agreements will prove such a pain in the seat that you'll run screaming to the RIAA and its cohorts.

The bit of legislation that sets up the hoops for you to jump through on webcasting is the Digital Millennium Copyright Act, or DMCA for short. The DMCA was passed in October 1998 and implements copyright rules set by the World Intellectual Property Organization (WIPO).

If you're going to get heavy into webcasting, you ought to read the U.S. Copyright Office Summary of the DMCA. You'll find this at `lcweb.loc.gov/copyright/legislation/dmca.pdf`. In case you can't be bothered to do that right now, below are the critical points of the DMCA as it applies to webcasting. *Quick disclaimer:* We're paraphrasing here and reducing perhaps beyond the essentials. Also, we're not lawyers.

- ▶ Your ISP isn't responsible for any copyright infringements that you perpetrate using their services—provided they're ready to give your contact information to copyright holders who demand it, and provided that they actively try to prevent you from offending again. Statistics are hard to come by, but anecdotal evidence suggests that many ISPs will not only give an accused subscriber's details to the first copyright holder who complains but they'll also terminate their Internet connection.

- ▶ You're allowed to make an *ephemeral recording* of music. An ephemeral recording is a copy of a recording "to facilitate performance"—for example, an MP3 file that you've created so that you don't need to use the CD. For the MP3 file to qualify as an ephemeral recording, it must be the only copy that you have of the recording, you must be the only person using that copy, you must destroy the copy within six months unless you're keeping it as an archive, and you can only transmit the copy "in the webcaster's local service area." The local service area requirement makes no sense, since everyone on the Internet can receive your broadcast. But the other three requirements are easy enough to comply with.

▶ You're allowed to webcast sound recordings on the Internet, and you're obliged to identify the track, artist, and album, but you can't announce the details of your playlist in advance. This is to prevent you from telling people that you'll be playing a particular track at a given time, because that makes what you're doing too close to providing a digital jukebox for it to be considered a bona fide webcast.

> **NOTE**
>
> SHOUTcast broadcasts artist and track information for you, so you don't need to announce tracks verbally to comply with the identification requirement. icecast can also broadcast this information.

▶ You have to take "steps" not to "induce copying," and you're not supposed to transmit bootlegs.

▶ There are a number of restrictions on what you can and can't play. For example, you can't play more than three tracks from any given album in a three-hour period, and you can't play more than two tracks from any given album consecutively. And if that's not enough, you can't play more than four tracks by any given artist or from any given box set within three hours, and you can't play more than three tracks by any given artist or from any given box set consecutively.

▶ If you loop a program, the loop must be more than three hours long. For a program to differ from another program, you need to make it substantially different—swapping out a couple of songs won't do the trick.

Okay, what about the paying bit? At this writing, exactly how much you'll have to pay isn't clear. Typically, you'll need to get licenses from the following licensing agencies:

ASCAP The American Society of Composers, Authors, and Publishers (www.ascap.com) bills itself as "since 1914 the leader in music licensing" and licenses the rights to "millions of songs created or owned by more than 80,000 of America's and hundreds of thousands of the world's best songwriters, composers, lyricists and publishers." ASCAP's lowest fee is $250 a year.

BMI Broadcast Music, Inc. (www.bmi.com) claims to represent the public performance copyright interest of more than a quarter-million songwriters, composers, and music publishers, giving it a repertoire of more than three million musical works. BMI's fees for webcasting are $250 annually for a site with revenues up to $12,000; $375 annually for a site with revenues up to $18,500; and $500 annually for a site with revenues up to $25,000. (Someone should introduce BMI to the concept of buying in bulk and saving.) If your site pulls in more than $25,000 a year, you're looking at paying BMI a percentage: either 1.75 percent of total site revenues or 2.5 percent of music area revenues. (If your site makes this much money, get your bean-crunchers to work out which option is better for you.)

SESAC SESAC, Inc. (www.sesac.com) describes itself modestly as the "second oldest and most innovative performing rights organization in the U.S." Innovation aside, SESAC seems to us to license the rights to fewer interesting artists than ASCAP and BMI. SESAC's lowest fee is $50 per six-month period.

The Basics of Internet Broadcasting

Now that we've gotten the legalities out of the way, we'll take a look at the basics of Internet broadcasting before getting into the specifics of SHOUTcast and icecast.

How Does It Work?

The basic principles of Internet broadcasting (which is also called *webcasting*) are relatively simple. You need a sound source to produce a source stream and send it to the server software, which then distributes it to whomever is listening. The sound source and the server software can be running on the same computer or on different computers. For example, you might use Winamp (with the appropriate plug-in) running on one computer to create a source stream and send it to another computer running the SHOUTcast server software. That computer then distributes the sound stream to the clients.

Of course, it's more complicated than that—but both SHOUTcast and icecast keep much of the complexity at arm's length. Here are more details:

- The sound source may need to *downsample* the audio signal to decrease its size to something small enough for broadcasting over the Internet. For example, the resultant bitstream from your average 128kbps MP3 file is too dense for most broadcasting, so you'll need to downsample it to a lower bitrate in order to broadcast it successfully. (To avoid downsampling, you can encode MP3 files at the appropriate low bitrate, but it's seldom worth the effort.)

- The sound source identifies the server (typically by IP address and port number), logs in to it, and sends it the sound stream. It also sends the data that needs to be registered on the directory server—the track names, artist names, and so forth.

- ▶ The server relays the source stream and metadata to users connected to the server.
- ▶ The server manages the users connected to it, accepting users up to its specified limit, disconnecting users whose connections are lying fallow.

We'll look at the individual steps in more detail when we discuss each of the packages.

Which Computer Will You Use?

To get broadcasting effectively with SHOUTcast or icecast, you need a computer that can continuously devote CPU cycles to delivering music. You may well want to set up SHOUTcast or icecast on a computer other than your main computer so that you can work (or play) while cranking out the tunes without worrying about interrupting your broadcast.

Neither SHOUTcast nor icecast is a memory- or processor-intensive application, so it's more than possible to broadcast from your one and only computer and still be able to do other things. But remember: Each time you install that new piece of demoware and have to reboot, your server will be down for the count and you'll lose all your listeners.

If anything, the operating system is less of a concern than the hardware. You can run a webcasting server on Windows 95 or 98, Windows NT (Workstation or Server), Windows 2000 (Professional or Server), FreeBSD, BSDi, Linux, IRIX, Solaris, or AIX.

Buying a Microphone

Before you go on the air (or on the wire), make sure that you've got all the hardware you need. The specs for the computer are essentially those we set you up with in Chapter 2, "A Hardware Primer for MP3 and Digital Audio." But if you want to put your voice on the air, you'll need to make sure that your sound card is *full duplex* (able to process both an input and an output stream at the same time). Most sound cards these days are full duplex, but if you've been coasting along with an ancient half-duplex Sound Blaster, now might be the time to upgrade.

You'll need to get a halfway-decent microphone if you want to put your voice on the air. Radio Shack can fix you up with something workable, but we suggest trying your local music store if you're looking for a higher end mike.

It's your choice between a headset mike and a stand-mounted one. Chances are, the latter will make you feel more like a DJ than the former, and you'll be able to stagger off for a bathroom break without accidentally dragging the computer along. That said, headset microphones have the advantage of leaving your hands free to do other things, like open cans or queue up songs. Better yet, you can move away from your computer and still be ready to broadcast voice. With a stand mike, you'll have to get your mouth in front of it before your voice will be picked up properly. Another reason to consider a headset mike is that they tend to reject sounds from directions other than directly in front of the mike element. This helps eliminate the tendency for stray sounds like whirring computer fans or cars honking outside your house to be picked up and broadcast.

For most soundcards, you'll need a mini-plug on the end of the mike's cable rather than a ¼-inch plug. Get an adapter if you need one.

Plug the mike's jack into the Mic input on your sound card, and then configure it as follows:

1. Open the Volume Control window by choosing Start ➢ Programs ➢ Accessories ➢ Entertainment ➢ Volume Control, or by right-clicking the Volume icon in your system tray and choosing Open Volume Controls from the context menu.

2. Choose Options ➢ Properties to display the Properties dialog box.

3. In the Show the Following Volume Controls list box, make sure that the Microphone check box is selected. (Some sound cards call this check box Monitor rather than Microphone.) Click the OK button to close the Properties dialog box.

4. Clear the Mute check box for Microphone (or Monitor) and set the volume to a low level.

5. Choose Options ➢ Properties to display the Properties dialog box again. This time, select the Recording option button.

6. Make sure that the Microphone check box is selected in the Show the Following Volume Controls list box, and click the OK button. You'll see the Recording Control window, an example of which is shown in Figure 18.1. Note that this window will look different depending on the configuration of your computer and the make of your sound card.

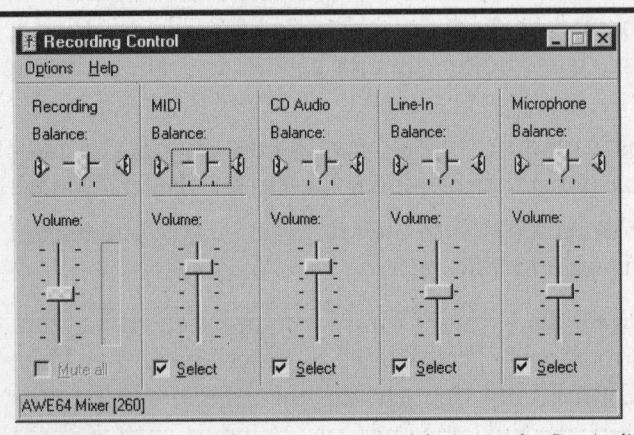

FIGURE 18.1: Configure your microphone in the Recording Control window.

Broadcasting Your Music across the Internet

7. Make sure that the Select check box for the microphone is selected.

8. Set the volume for the microphone to a sensible level—probably pretty low to start with.

9. Close the Recording Control window, or leave it open for the time being if you prefer to have quick access to it.

Is Your Connection Macho Enough?

To have people take your webcast seriously, you'll need a halfway-potent connection to the Internet. We discussed Internet connections in Chapter 2, but at that time we were concerned with the speed with which they delivered information to you. Now the concern is the speed with which you can send data upstream.

The bad news is that a modem won't deliver enough audio for more than about one user at a time. Even the best 56K–modem delivers only 33.6K upstream on the best of lines (that 56K or rather 53K–is downstream only), and that low rate will mangle even ambient music beyond any hope of redemption if you try to broadcast (uh, maybe that should just be *cast*) any wider.

The minimum connection over which you'll be able to deliver to multiple listeners anything worth listening to is an ISDN connection running one channel full—bore preferably two channels.

A DSL connection is typically preferable, but make sure that your upstream speed (from you to your ISP) is high enough. Basic DSL connections may have only 128kbps upstream speeds, which will get you to fewer listeners than you have fingers. If you want to deliver quality audio to double-digit numbers of listeners, you'll need more bandwidth. To get it, you'll probably have to pay for it.

The same caveat goes for a cable modem. As mentioned in Chapter 2, many cable companies implement an *upload cap* that limits your upstream connection, even when there's no bandwidth crunch on the wires you're using. If you're unsure what you're getting, ask the cable company directly, and persist until you get a satisfactory answer. Some of them are reluctant to mention provocative words like "upload cap," preferring to say that they're ensuring 24/7 bandwidth availability to all subscribers and that their cable system is capable of 2Mbps (or whatever) upstream. (It is, but they're not giving you any more than your cap.) Translation: They're limiting your output to make sure that the loser next door can shunt his teen-angst poetry onto the Internet day and night.

Before you ask the cable company how you're supposed to broadcast effectively with an upload cap in place, read your terms of service and make sure that you know what you've agreed not to do. Often the basic home-cable Internet package involves agreeing not to run a Web server. If you've signed an agreement like this, you'll need to claim that you need the speed for something legit like telecommuting.

> **TIP**
>
> If your connection isn't up to snuff, consider webcasting through a relay server. Check www.shoutcast.com for links to servers that provide this service. Some are free; others charge.

Broadcasting with SHOUTcast

This section discusses how to get, configure, and install the software for broadcasting with SHOUTcast. Our example SHOUTcast system consists of a SHOUTcast server that receives an audio stream from the Winamp player via a suitable DSP plug-in.

> **NOTE**
>
> We'll assume that you have Winamp already installed and configured on your computer. If you don't, look back to Chapter 7, "Windows Players."

Broadcasting Your Music across the Internet

The SHOUTcast server software is free if you're using it for non-commercial purposes; for commercial use, you've got to pay $299 after a 14-day trial period.

Collecting the Software

Start by downloading the following software from the SHOUTcast Web site, www.shoutcast.com, as follows:

- The latest version of SHOUTcast Server for the operating system you're using. For example, download the SHOUTcast Win32 Server if you're using Windows.

- The SHOUTcast DSP broadcasting tools. You'll find links to these tools on the SHOUTcast download page. They're wrapped up into a tiny self-extracting file and take only a few seconds to download. Note the filename on this.

- The Microsoft NetShow Server tools. You don't want to run NetShow, but this package contains the *codecs* (coder/decoders) that you need to compress the music you SHOUTcast. You'll find a link to these from the SHOUTcast download page as well, although you can get them from Microsoft if you prefer. The NetShow Server tools are a shade under 4MB, so they'll take a few minutes to download if you're using a modem.

- The SHOUTcast Live Input plug-in, also from the SHOUTcast download page. You need this plug-in to pipe microphone input into SHOUTcast. Even if your microphone is currently a twinkle in the eye of your next paycheck, download this plug-in—it's tiny and takes only a second or two to download.

- The NULL Output plug-in, also from the SHOUTcast download page. This lets you stream audio without it going through your soundcard, so you can broadcast audio without playing it through your sound system. (With this plug-in, you can even broadcast from a computer that doesn't have a sound card—a cool way of reusing that 486 that's serving as a doorstop in the basement.) This plug-in is minuscule, too.

> **NOTE**
>
> You can also download SHOUTcast commercials from the SHOUTcast download page.

Now that you've gathered all that software, install it as described in the following sections.

Unpacking and Installing the NetShow Tools

Double-click the `nstools.exe` file in Windows Explorer to unpack the NetShow Server tools.

NetShow walks you through a mostly standard installation routine in which you get to ponder and accept a license agreement, choose the Complete Installation (the PowerPoint Add-Ins Only installation won't do you much good), and select a suitable directory for the tools files. If you get a NetShow Tools message box telling you that "The NetShow PowerPoint Add-Ins will not be installed as part of this setup. The functionality for these Add-Ins is integrated into the version of PowerPoint on this computer," just click the OK button, and it goes away.

Click the Finish button when NetShow says it's done. You've now got the codecs installed. If you check the bottom of your Start ≻ Programs menu, you'll notice a NetShow Services group with several menu items. Your career as a DJ beckons.

Installing the Plug-Ins

Run the SHOUTcast DSP plug-in self-extracting file by double-clicking it in Explorer and let it extract itself to your \Winamp\ folder, which it auto-detects.

Unzip the SHOUTcast Live Input plug-in, and the NULL Output plug-in (if you chose to get it) to your \Winamp\Plugins\ folder. These two plug-ins are optional, but we think you'll find them useful. Even if you don't end up using them, installing them at this point is unlikely to do you any harm.

To check that all is well, start Winamp (if it's not already running) and choose Options ➤ Preferences from the Main menu to display the Winamp Preferences dialog box. Check the Input, Output, and DSP/Effect Plug-ins categories to make sure that you've installed the plug-ins to the right place.

Installing and Configuring the SHOUTcast Server

Next, install and configure the SHOUTcast server.

First, unzip the SHOUTcast server package into the folder where you want it to live. (There's no installation routine to put the SHOUTcast server in a suitable place for you, so choose wisely.)

Next, configure the server as follows: Double-click the sc_serv.ini initialization file in the \gui\ subfolder of whatever folder you unzipped SHOUTcast to. Windows opens the file in Notepad (or in your default text editor). The settings you'll need will vary depending on your situation, so read the information in the initialization file carefully. The settings that follow are typical for a Windows SHOUTcast server, but you may need to adjust them for your computer.

> **LogFile** Specifies the filename (and path, if used) under which to save the log file. For Windows systems, SHOUTcast Server uses the folder in which the server executable file is stored, which is usually a convenient location.

```
LogFile=sc_serv.log
```

RealTime For Unix and Windows console (non-GUI) systems only. Displays a status line updated every second when set to 1.

ScreenLog For Unix and Windows console systems only. Controls whether SHOUTcast prints logging to the screen.

ShowLastSongs A value between 1 and 20 that specifies the number of tracks to list in the `/played.html` page. The default setting is 10; change it if you wish.

```
ShowLastSongs=20
```

HistoryLog Specifies a filename if you want to log the history of a number of listeners to a file. Leave this setting blank if you don't want to create a file. For Windows systems, SHOUTcast uses the folder in which the server executable is stored, unless you specify a different path.

```
HistoryLog=sc_hist.log
```

HistoryLogTime Specifies the number of seconds between entries created for the history log. The default setting is 30.

```
HistoryLogTime=30
```

PortBase Specifies the TCP/IP port on the server to which listeners tune in to listen. SHOUTcast sends its audio stream to `PortBase+1`, so this port needs to be free, too. Try the default `PortBase` setting, 8000, unless you know you need to use a different port.

```
PortBase=8000
```

SrcIP Specifies the source IP address from which SHOUTcast should receive its source stream. The default setting, ANY, makes SHOUTcast accept a stream from any source. If your SHOUTcast server has multiple network cards, you can specify the IP address of the network card that you want SHOUTcast to use. You can set `SrcIP` to

127.0.0.1 to prevent other computers from broadcasting via your SHOUTcast server.

    SrcIP=ANY

DestIP   Specifies the IP address on which SHOUTcast should listen for clients and contact yp.shoutcast.com. Leave DestIP set to ANY to have SHOUTcast listen on any port. Alternatively, specify the IP address if you have multiple network cards in the computer.

    DestIP=ANY

Yport   Specifies the port that SHOUTcast should use for connecting to yp.shoutcast.com. Leave this setting set to 80 unless that doesn't work for you.

    Yport=80

NameLookups   Set NameLookups to 1 to perform reverse DNS (Domain Name Services) domain-name lookups on people who connect to the server. You'll probably want to start with NameLookups set to its default 0 (zero).

    NameLookups=0

RelayPort and RelayServer   You don't need to specify the RelayPort and RelayServer settings unless your SHOUTcast server is acting as a relay. Leave these lines commented out, with the semicolon at the beginning of the line, or delete them entirely.

    ;RelayPort=8000
    ;RelayServer=

MaxUser   Specifies the maximum number of simultaneous users who can connect to your SHOUTcast server. The maximum setting is 1024 and the default setting is 32, but you'll want to lower this if your connection is slow upstream. Remember that users share the bandwidth, and that if your server is trying to deliver more bandwidth than is available, the music will skip. We've yet to meet anybody who likes skipping—this kind of skipping, that is.

    MaxUser=8

Password Specifies the password for changing the SHOUTcast stream. This password is your protection against someone hijacking your server, so make it good. The default `Password` is changeme, which you'll certainly want to change. Keep the standard password rules in mind:

- Six characters absolute minimum
- Not a recognizable word in any language
- Include letters, numbers, and symbols

This password needs to be the same as the Winamp SHOUTcast DSP plug-in password, which we'll configure in a minute or two.

```
Password=1ndustr!@1N01SE
```

AdminPassword Specifies an administrative password, an additional password that restricts plain old `Password` to controlling broadcasting, taking away its administration tasks (such as kicking off users or banning them). If you're the only person broadcasting on KILZ Rebel Radio, you won't need an `AdminPassword` because `Password` will serve all your needs, so leave the `AdminPassword` line in the file commented out with a semicolon (`;AdminPassword= adminpass`). But if you have an unruly staff, implement an `AdminPassword` by uncommenting the line and specifying the password (for example, `AdminPassword=I@mTheK!ng`).

```
;AdminPassword=adminpass
```

AutoDumpUsers Specifies whether SHOUTcast disconnects users automatically when its source stream disconnects. The default is 0 (zero)—do not automatically disconnect users. (See the entry about `BackupFile` a few blocks south of here.)

```
AutoDumpUsers=0
```

AutoDumpSourceTime Specifies the number of seconds to wait before disconnecting an idle source stream. The default setting is 30; use 0 if you want SHOUTcast to wait indefinitely.

`AutoDumpSourceTime=15`

IntroFile Specifies the MP3 file to stream to listeners when they connect and before they get the live stream. Great for advertising. The intro file must have the same sample rate and channels as the live stream. The default setting is not to have an intro file.

`IntroFile=c:\bc\Hello Cleveland.mp3`

BackupFile Specifies the MP3 file to stream to listeners if and when the source stream fails. To use this feature, set `AutoDumpUsers` to 0 (zero). The backup file loops until the source stream is restored, so choose something either innocuous or extremely long (or both). As with the intro file, the backup file must have the same sample rate and channels as the live stream for it to kick in properly. The default setting is not to use a backup file.

`BackupFile=c:\bc\Tedious Ambient Eno.mp3`

TitleFormat Specifies the title and format to send to the listener. Use %s to include the title of the current track. For example, `Radio Free Cleveland: %s` playing "Billy, Don't Be a Hero" sends the title "Radio Free Cleveland: Billy, Don't Be a Hero." The default setting is not to send a title. Note that this feature doesn't work on relay servers.

`TitleFormat=Radio Free Cleveland: %s`

URLFormat Specifies the URL and format to send to the listener. Again, use %s to include the title of the current track. The default setting is not to send an URL.

PublicServer Specifies whether the server should be publicly available: `Default` (the default setting; publicly available), `Always`, or `Never`.

`PublicServer=Default`

MetaInterval   Specifies how many bytes to leave between sending metadata. The SHOUTcast documentation recommends leaving this setting at its default, 8192.

    MetaInterval=8192

> **NOTE**
>
> In the SHOUTcast initialization file, you can also set options for logging SHOUTcast information in HTML files. Check the information in the initialization file on the `CurrentLog`, `CurrentLogIn`, `CurrentLogOut`, and `CurrentTime` variables for details.

Starting the SHOUTcast Server

Now start the SHOUTcast server by double-clicking the `sc_serv.exe` file in the `\gui\` subfolder of the folder to which you unzipped it. SHOUTcast reads the initialization file and displays the Nullsoft SHOUTcast Server Monitor window (shown in Figure 18.2).

Broadcasting Your Music across the Internet

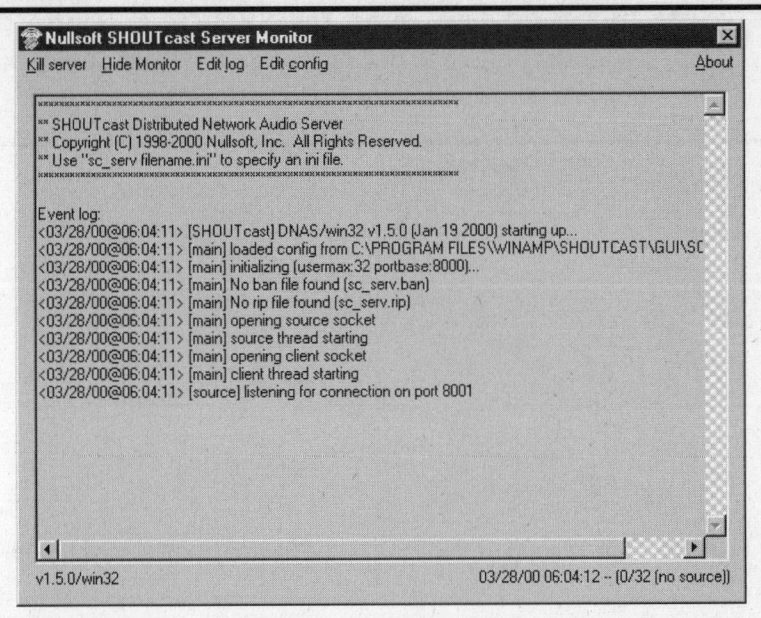

FIGURE 18.2: SHOUTcast up and listening for a connection

Notice that the last line in the figure shows that SHOUTcast server is listening for a connection. Next, you have to give it one. Click the Hide Monitor button on the menu bar to hide the Nullsoft SHOUTcast Server Monitor window for the moment. (To get it back, click the SHOUTcast Server item in the system tray.)

Configuring Winamp to SHOUTcast

Configure Winamp's SHOUTcast plug-in so that it routes its output to the SHOUTcast server. Follow these steps:

1. Start Winamp if it's not running.

2. Press Ctrl+P, or choose Options ➤ Preferences, to display the Winamp Preferences dialog box.

3. In the left-hand panel, select the DSP/Effect item.

4. In the list box, select the SHOUTcast Source for Winamp plug-in to display the SHOUTcast Source dialog box, shown in Figure 18.3 with settings chosen.

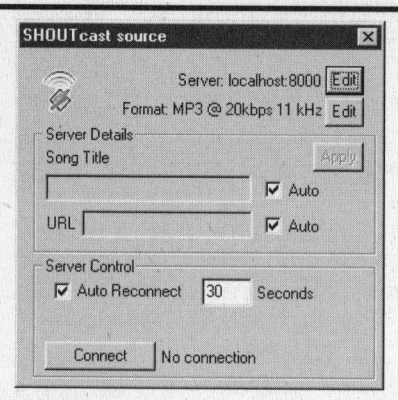

FIGURE 18.3: Configure the SHOUTcast Source for Winamp plug-in.

5. Click the upper Edit button to display the SHOUTcast Server Selection dialog box (shown in Figure 18.4), and choose settings as follows:

SHOUTcast Server Leave the default setting of localhost if you're running the server on the same computer that you're configuring Winamp on. If the server's on a different computer, enter its IP address or host name.

Port Specify the port for listeners to use—the same port as the PortBase setting in the SHOUTcast server initialization file. The default is 8000. Once you've specified the port, Winamp starts piping music to it, so you're on the air.

Password Enter the password for the SHOUTcast server (the password you defined in the initialization file).

List on SHOUTcast.com Select this check box if you want your server to appear in the index at yp.shoutcast.com and fill in the next three text boxes.

Description Enter your name for the station. Keep it short but descriptive.

Genre Enter the genre for the station. Check with shoutcast.com and RadioSpy for the latest list of supported genres. You can enter a new genre of your own if you want, but chances are that people won't find it unless they're browsing all servers.

URL Enter the URL for your station.

IRC Channel If you have an IRC channel associated with the station, enter it here.

ICQ# If you have ICQ information, enter it here.

AIM Name If you have an AIM name associated with the station, enter it here.

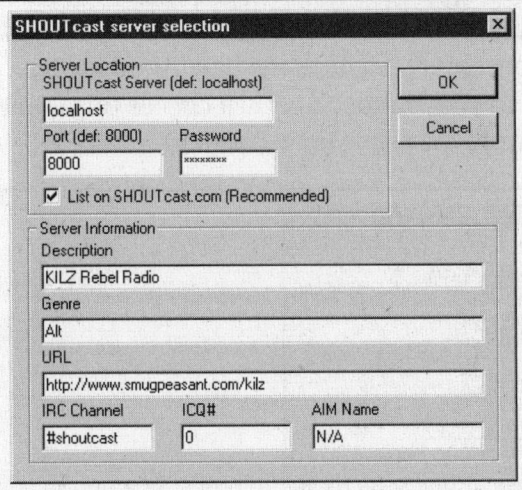

FIGURE 18.4: Choose settings in the SHOUTcast Server Selection dialog box.

6. Click the OK button to close the SHOUTcast Server Selection dialog box and return to the SHOUTcast Source dialog box.

7. Click the lower Edit button to display the Format Selection dialog box (shown in Figure 18.5), and choose settings as follows:

    Format drop-down list Make sure MPEG Layer-3 is selected.

    Attributes drop-down list Select an option that makes sense for the bandwidth you have, the number of users you're trying to serve, and what you're broadcasting. Typically, you'll want to broadcast in stereo at the highest rate your connection supports for your maximum number of users. Usually it's best to use one of the standard sample rates—11,025Hz, 22,050Hz, or 44,100Hz—rather than a nonstandard rate. (The plug-in warns you if you choose a nonstandard rate.)

    Save As button If you want to save this format, click this button, enter a name in the Save As dialog box, and click the OK button. You then choose this format by name from the Name drop-down list.

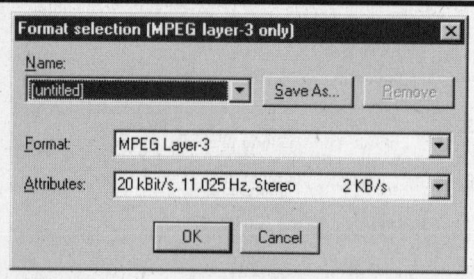

FIGURE 18.5: Choose format settings in the Format Selection dialog box.

8. Click the OK button to close the Format Selection dialog box.

9. Click the Connect button to connect to your SHOUTcast server. You're on the air.

10. To change the title or URL being sent, clear the relevant Auto check box, enter the information you want, and click the Set button.

Now fire up a client (for example, Sonique, Winamp, or RadioSpy) and tune in to your station to make sure everything's working.

Adding Your Voice to the Airwaves

If you've got your mike plugged in and operational, you'll want to know how to get your voice on the air. You can do this in two ways: by adding voice input between tracks, and by adding voice input on top of the music that's playing. The first way is easier, but the second way sounds 10 times more professional, so you should know how to do both.

Adding Voice Input between Tracks

To add voice input between tracks in your playlist, follow these steps:

1. Press Ctrl+L or click the Add button and choose Add URL from the context menu of buttons to display the Open Location dialog box.

2. Enter **linerec://** and click the Open button. The Playlist Editor displays "Line Recording" at that point in the playlist.

3. When the Line Recording item in the playlist comes up, take a deep but silent breath and speak your mind.

4. Click the next item in the playlist to start it playing.

Adding Voice Input on Top of the Music

To add voice input on top of the music, you need to run a second instance of Winamp and use it to pipe the voice in. Here's what to do:

1. Press Ctrl+P or choose Options ➤ Preferences from the Main menu to display the Winamp Preferences dialog box.

2. Click the Options entry in the left-hand panel.

3. Select the Allow Multiple Instances check box.

4. Click the Close button to close the Winamp Preferences dialog box.

5. Start a second instance of Winamp.

6. Press Ctrl+L or click the Add button and choose Add URL from the menu of buttons to display the Open Location dialog box.

7. Enter **linerec://** and click the Open button. The Playlist Editor displays "Line Recording" at that point in the playlist.

8. Set a playlist going in the first instance of Winamp.

9. In the second instance, click the Play button for the Line Recording entry and speak into the mike.

10. Mute the mike when you're not on the air. It's amazing how easy it is to forget you're on the air and embarrass yourself in public. (Ask Dubya.)

Silencing Local Output

Here's how to broadcast without playing at the same time on your own computer:

1. Press Ctrl+P or select Options ➤ Preferences from the Main menu to display the Winamp Preferences dialog box.

2. Click the Output item in the left-hand panel.

3. Select the Nullsoft NULL Output Plug-In in the list box.
4. Click the Close button to close the Preferences dialog box.
5. Exit and restart Winamp.

To restore local playing, display the Preferences dialog box again and select your usual output plug-in, then exit and restart Winamp.

Bringing the Server Down

If you keep feeding your playlist and your Internet connection stays up, you can keep broadcasting until you or your computer drops. Sooner or later, though, you'll need to bring your server down.

To do so, display the Nullsoft SHOUTcast Server Monitor window by clicking the SHOUTcast Server icon in your system tray, then click the Kill Server button. SHOUTcast displays the Shutdown SHOUTcast Server dialog box (see Figure 18.6). Click the Yes button to take yourself off the air.

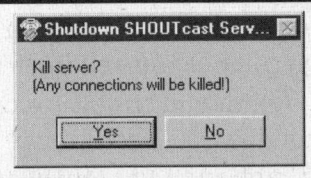

FIGURE 18.6: Taking your radio station off the air

BROADCASTING WITH ICECAST

icecast is an Open Source audio-streaming server created by Jack Moffitt and Barath Raghavan in early 1999. Freeware developed and released under the GNU General Public License (which means that you can tinker with the code if you want and redistribute the results), icecast is designed to be fully compatible with SHOUTcast. icecast can access the directory service at yp.shoutcast.com as well as other directory services. (If you want, you can run your own directory service by running the icedir program with Apache, a MySQL database, and PHP scripting.)

At this writing, icecast is in beta, but relatively stable versions of icecast are available for Linux, Windows 9*x*, and Windows NT. Java, BeOS, and OS/2 versions are in development. In this section, we'll discuss how to get icecast going, using Linux for our examples but mentioning Windows where appropriate.

Getting, Installing, and Configuring icecast

Download the latest release of icecast from the icecast Web site, www.icecast.org.

At this writing, the Windows version of icecast is distributed as a zip file. Unzip the file to the directory where you want to keep icecast—there's no installation routine as such.

If you're running Linux, you'll have the choice of downloading a precompiled binary (for example, an RPM or DEB package, or a tarball) or source code that you'll need to compile yourself (preferably using GNU make) before installing it. You should be able to compile icecast with the default settings by running the ./configure script. (If there isn't a ./configure script, run the ./autogen.sh file instead.) You can also set various configuration options, including

- with-libwrap (for enabling support for Wietse Venema's TCP wrappers)
- with-crypt (for using encrypted passwords)
- without-readline (for excluding readline support).

These options are clearly discussed in the icecast manual included with the distribution.

You can also edit three critical files—the Makefile, `icetypes.h`, and `icecast.h`—to optimize performance and alter icecast's default behavior.

> **NOTE**
>
> If you compile icecast with support for encrypted passwords, compile the `mkpasswd.c` program included with the icecast distribution and use it to create encrypted versions of your passwords.

Once you've downloaded icecast, install it as usual for the distribution of Linux you're using.

Editing the icecast Configuration File

Next, edit the icecast configuration file, `icecast.conf`, to customize various of its parameters to match your setup.

> **NOTE**
>
> If you're feeling impatient, you can go ahead and run icecast with the default configuration by simply issuing the `icecast` command in a terminal window. The default configuration is unlikely to do much for you, but you'll see icecast start up and perhaps give an error message or two. You can then close icecast down again by issuing the `shutdown` command.

Table 18.1 lists the important parameters to set, although icecast supports many more parameters. Read the many helpful lines that `icecast.conf` usually contains to familiarize yourself with the other parameters. (For example, you can use access control lists to explicitly allow and deny people access to your server.)

TABLE 18.1: Important Parameters in `icecast.conf`

Parameter	Explanation
`location`	Part of the meta-information about your server, `location` can be any text string of your choosing.
`rp_email`	Also part of the meta-information about your server, `rp_email` specifies the e-mail address (real or mythical) of the person responsible for your server.
`server_url`	Third and last part of the meta-information about your server, `server_url` provides your server's true or putative URL.
`max_clients`	A number specifying the maximum number of clients for your server.
`max_clients_per_source`	An integer specifying the maximum number of clients per source for your server.
`max_sources`	An integer specifying the maximum number of sources for your server.
`max_admins`	An integer specifying the maximum number of administrators for your server.
`throttle`	A number specifying the maximum bandwidth (in megabits per second) for the server to use. Beyond this number, icecast throttles itself back, not taking on any more clients or sources until bandwidth retreats below the `throttle` threshold. `mount_fallback` 1 or 0, specifying how the server should behave if the stream requested by the user is not found. A value of 1 causes the server to fall back on the default stream; a value of 0 gives the user a "HTTP 404 Stream Not Found" error. By default, the default stream is the oldest stream on the server, but you can change it using the `modify` command.
`encoder_password`	Specifies the encoder password for the server. This password is clear text unless you've compiled icecast with crypt support.
`admin_password`	Specifies the administrator password for the server. This password is clear text unless you've compiled icecast with crypt support.

CONTINUED ➡

TABLE 18.1 continued: Important Parameters in `icecast.conf`

Parameter	Explanation
`open_password`	Specifies the operator password for the server. This password is clear text unless you've compiled icecast with crypt support.
`icydir`	Specifies a directory server on which to list your server—for example, `icydir yp.shoutcast.com`. List multiple directory servers as appropriate.
`touch_freq`	Specifies how often to update the directory server with your server's information. The default value is 5 (minutes).
`hostname`	Specifies the only IP address on which to listen. If you don't specify the host name, icecast listens on all available interfaces.
`port`	Specifies the port on which to listen. By default, all connections use port 8000, so you may not need to change this—but you can add further ports as necessary. Note that icecast binds to the port only when the server is started.
`server_name`	Specifies the host name of your server. This can be either a host name or an IP address. If you use a host name, it must point to your IP address. If you're using a dial-up connection that assigns you an IP address dynamically, you'll probably need to determine your IP address and edit this setting before starting an icecast session.
`console_mode`	Specifies how to start the server. Specify 0 to run the server as an admin console with log file information, 1 to run it as an admin console but without log file information, 2 to run it as a log file window, or 3 to run it as a daemon in the background. (3 isn't available on Win32 platforms.)
`client_timeout`	Specifies how icecast should deal with clients when no encoder is connected. Use 0 to kick the client at once, any negative value to keep the client until they choose to leave, or any positive value to keep them for that number of seconds.
`kick_clients`	Specifies what to do when a client's source has disconnected. Use 1 to kick the client or 0 to move the client to another stream. `kick_clients` applies only if `client_timeout` is 0 or a positive value.
`logfile`	Specifies the location of the icecast log file. The default location is `/var/icecast/`. icecast doesn't automatically truncate this file, so you'll need to empty it from time to time.

Starting icecast

Once you've edited `icecast.conf`, you should be ready to start icecast. Open a console window and start icecast by issuing an `icecast` command.

The `icecast` command takes the following parameters:

Parameter	Meaning	Default
-c	Configuration file to use	`icecast.conf`
-P	Port the server will monitor for client connections	8000
-p	Password for validating encoders	`letmein`
-l	Log file	`icecast.log`
-b	Run icecast in the background	
-d	Specifies the directory containing the configuration files	(none)

For example, the following command starts icecast, specifying the default password for validating encoders:

`icecast -p letmein`

Sending the icecast Server an Audio Stream from an Encoder

Next, you need to send an audio stream to icecast. You can do this in various ways, the simplest of which are

- Use the static streamer shout.
- Use the re-encoding streamer liveice.

This section discusses both briefly.

> **NOTE**
>
> Two quick notes: First, icesource, a next-generation version of shout, is planned to supersede shout and liveice. At this writing, icesource is under development and isn't yet ready for use by any but the most determined users. Second, another tool for streaming MP3 files to an icecast or SHOUTcast server is iceplay, a Perl script that was distributed with earlier versions of icecast. iceplay has been superseded by shout, so there's little point in using it unless you're interested in history.

shout is a *static streamer*, sending the stream at the bitrate at which it is encoded. For example, if you use shout to stream a MP3 file encoded at 128kbps, it streams it at 128kbps. This uses a lot of bandwidth, so unless you have a fat pipe or MP3 files encoded at a low bitrate (for example, 24kbps), it probably won't meet your needs.

You can download shout from the icecast Web site (www.icecast.org) or from various Linux Web sites. shout runs on Linux, BSD, Solaris, Windows 9*x*, and Windows 2000.

You can configure shout by using hard-coded defaults (in the shout.h file), command-line parameters, or the configuration file. Because you need to recompile shout.h after changing it, it's usually easier to use the command-line parameters or the configuration file.

Table 18.2 lists the important command-line parameters for shout, together with their corresponding options in the configuration file (where appropriate). See the README.shout file for further shout options.

TABLE 18.2: Important Command-Line Parameters and Configuration-File Options for shout

Command-Line Parameter	Configuration-File Option and Option Type	Meaning
-C *configuration_file*	N/A	Uses the specified file as the configuration file. The configuration file overrides any options specified before it on the command line, while any options after the configuration file on the command line override it. The default file is shout.conf in /etc/icecast/.
-p *password*	password *text*	Uses the specified password when connecting to the server.
-S		Displays compile-time settings, default settings, and current settings, then exits.
-V	verbose *Boolean*	Turns verbose mode on.
-b	default_bitrate *number*	Uses the specified bitrate. Used only if auto-detection is off.
-e *port*	port *number*	Makes shout connect to the specified port. (The default port is 8000.)
-f	force *Boolean*	Forces shout to skip any files encoded at a bitrate other than the specified default.
-g *genre*	genre *text*	Sends the specified genre to the server.
-l	loop *Boolean*	Loops the playlist until you stop it.
-n *name*	name *text*	Sends the specified name to the server when connecting.
-o	autodetect *Boolean*	Turns off auto-detection of bitrate.
-r	shuffle *Boolean*	Shuffles the playlist when the command is issued. If the playlist is set to loop, reshuffles the playlist at the beginning of each loop through it.

TABLE 18.2 continued: Important Command-Line Parameters and Configuration-File Options for shout

Command-Line Parameter	Configuration-File Option and Option Type	Meaning
-s	public *Boolean*	-s turns off the sending of metadata to the directory server, as does setting public to no.
-t	title_streaming *Boolean*	Turns on streaming of title information to the server.
-F	short_titles *Boolean*	Removes the directory information when sending filenames as part of title streaming.
-u *url*	url *text*	Specifies the URL to use when connecting to the server.
-z	daemon *Boolean*	Launches shout in the background.
-p	playlist *text*	Specifies the playlist to play. Keep your playlists in the etc directory with icecast.

For example, the following command shouts the playlist shout_list_1.m3u to 192.168.1.22, using the password h@ckme!, and specifying the genre alternative and the name Finger Relaxation for You.

```
shout 192.168.1.22 -p h@ckme! -p ~/shout_list_1.m3u
- n "Finger Relaxation for You" -g alternative
```

> **NOTE**
>
> If you're running Windows, you can use Winamp with the SHOUTcast plug-ins to output an audio stream to your icecast server. Alternatively, you can use the Win32 version of shout, although this is limited by comparison. icemaker, a streamer that does live encoding, is in the works at this writing.

Using liveice to Downsample Files for Broadcast

As we mentioned, shout broadcasts files at the bitrate at which they're encoded. This can be a problem because unless you create low-bitrate MP3 files specially for broadcasting, the bitrate of your MP3 files is likely to be too high for effective broadcasting across all but the sturdiest connection.

If you need to downsample your MP3 files before you broadcast them, start with liveice. liveice uses an external MP3 decoder to decode the files and an external encoder to re-encode the files at the specified bitrate. You can also use liveice to mix multiple MP3 files together and to add microphone input to your broadcasting.

Depending on the icecast package you download, liveice may be included. If it's not, download a version of it separately, either from the icecast Web site (www.icecast.org) or from one of the many Linux sites, compile it if necessary, and install it as usual for your distribution of Linux.

You can use liveice with a variety of MP3 encoders, including MP3Enc, LAME, NotLame, and scrEamer, but not with BladeEnc. To use liveice's mixer mode, you'll need mpg123 (discussed in Chapter 12, "Linux Players").

To configure liveice, you can either manually edit the liveice configuration file, liveice.cfg, or use the liveiceconfigure.tk GUI for configuring it graphically. You may want to use the GUI to set most of the parameters in the configuration file, and then open the file manually and set the options for the second channel.

Table 18.3 lists the GUI options and configuration-file equivalents for liveice.

TABLE 18.3: GUI Options and Configuration-File Equivalents for liveice

GUI Option	Configuration-File Equivalent	Explanation
Server	SERVER	Specifies the icecast or SHOUTcast server you'll be connecting to.

CONTINUED ➡

Broadcasting Your Music across the Internet

TABLE 18.3 continued: GUI Options and Configuration-File Equivalents for liveice

GUI Option	Configuration-File Equivalent	Explanation
[Port]	PORT	Specifies the port number you'll be connecting to. Set the port number to one higher than the Listeners port. (For example, if the Listeners port is 8000, set the port to 8001.)
Name	NAME	Specifies the name for your radio station.
Genre	GENRE	Specifies the genre for your radio station.
URL	URL	Specifies the URL for your radio station.
Directory	PUBLIC	Specifies whether to tell the directory server about your broadcast (Public option button, PUBLIC 1) or not (Private option button, PUBLIC 0).
Login Type	ICY_LOGIN or X_AUDIOCAST_LOGIN	Specifies the header format to use: icy (ICY_LOGIN), which is SHOUTcast-compatible, or x-audiocast (X_AUDIOCAST_LOGIN), which lets you use multiple streams on one server.
Password	PASSWORD	Specifies the login password for your icecast server.
PCM Audio Format	SAMPLE_RATE	Specifies the sample rate to use, in hertz (for example, 32000Hz).
[Mono/Stereo]	MONO or STEREO	Specifies the number of channels to use—one (mono) or two (stereo).
Soundcard	SOUNDCARD or NO_SOUNDCARD	Specifies whether the sound card is enabled (Enabled option button, SOUNDCARD) or disabled (Disabled option button, NO_SOUNDCARD).

Part vii

CONTINUED →

TABLE 18.3 continued: GUI Options and Configuration-File Equivalents for liveice

GUI Option	Configuration-File Equivalent	Explanation
Duplex	HALF_DUPLEX *or* FULL-DUPLEX	Specifies whether to use half-duplex (Half-Duplex option button, HALF_DUPLEX) or full-duplex (Full Duplex option button, FULL_DUPLEX). Make sure that your sound card is capable of full duplex before choosing the full-duplex setting.
Encoder	USE_*encoder_name binary*	Specifies the encoder to use. In the configuration file, you can specify both the encoder and the name of the binary if you want. For example, USE_MP3ENC mp3enc specifies to use the MP3Enc encoder.
Bitrate	BITRATE	Specifies the bitrate for encoding the MP3 stream being generated.
VBR Quality	VBR_QUALITY	Specifies the variable bitrate quality to use. (Only some encoders can handle VBR.)
Soundcard Only/ Mp3Mixer Mode	NO_MIXER *or* MIXER	Specifies whether to use only the sound card (Soundcard Only option button, NO_MIXER) or Mp3Mixer mode (Mp3Mixer Mode option button, MIXER).
Playlist File	PLAYLIST	Specifies the filename of the playlist.
Mixer Control	MIX_CONTROL_AUTO *or* MIX_CONTROL_LOGGED *or* MIX_CONTROL_MANUAL	Specifies whether to use automatic (Automatic option button, MIX_CONTROL_AUTO), logged (Logged option button, MIX_CONTROL_LOGGED), or manual (Manual option button, MIX_CONTROL_MANUAL) mixing.

CONTINUED ➜

Broadcasting Your Music across the Internet 731

TABLE 18.3 continued: GUI Options and Configuration-File Equivalents for liveice

GUI Option	Configuration-File Equivalent	Explanation
Command Log	CONTROL_FILE	Specifies the name of the command log.
Track Log	TRACK_LOGFILE	Specifies the name for the log file.

By default, the configuration settings specified in the configuration file apply to the first channel, fed by encoder stream 0. If you'll be running two channels, you'll need to set configuration options for the second channel, fed by encoder stream 1, in the configuration file, by adjusting the settings after the ENCODER_STREAM_SET 1 statement.

Once you have liveice running, you can control it using the keyboard controls listed in Table 18.4.

TABLE 18.4: Keyboard Controls for liveice

Action	Key for Channel 1	Key for Channel 2
Next track	1	A
Previous track	Q	Z
Start/stop	2	S
Reset	W	X
Increase volume	3	D
Decrease volume	E	C
Increase speed	4	F
Decrease speed	R	V
Sticky mode on/Random/Off	5	G
Preview	T	B
Random track	U	M

Shutting Down icecast

To shut down your broadcasting, issue the `shutdown` command in the terminal window from which you ran icecast.

UP NEXT

In this chapter, you've learned the basics of webcasting—broadcasting your own radio station over the Internet so that anybody can tune into you. You've seen how to get SHOUTcast running on Windows and icecast running on Linux.

In the next chapter, we'll discuss how to record CDs—a great means of not only archiving your MP3 files but also taking them with you.

Part VIII
Advanced Digital-Audio Maneuvers

Learn To:

- Record music files onto CDs
- Modify and enhance digital-audio files
- Create skins for Winamp and RealJukebox
- Build a serious music collection
- Understand other digital-audio formats besides MP3

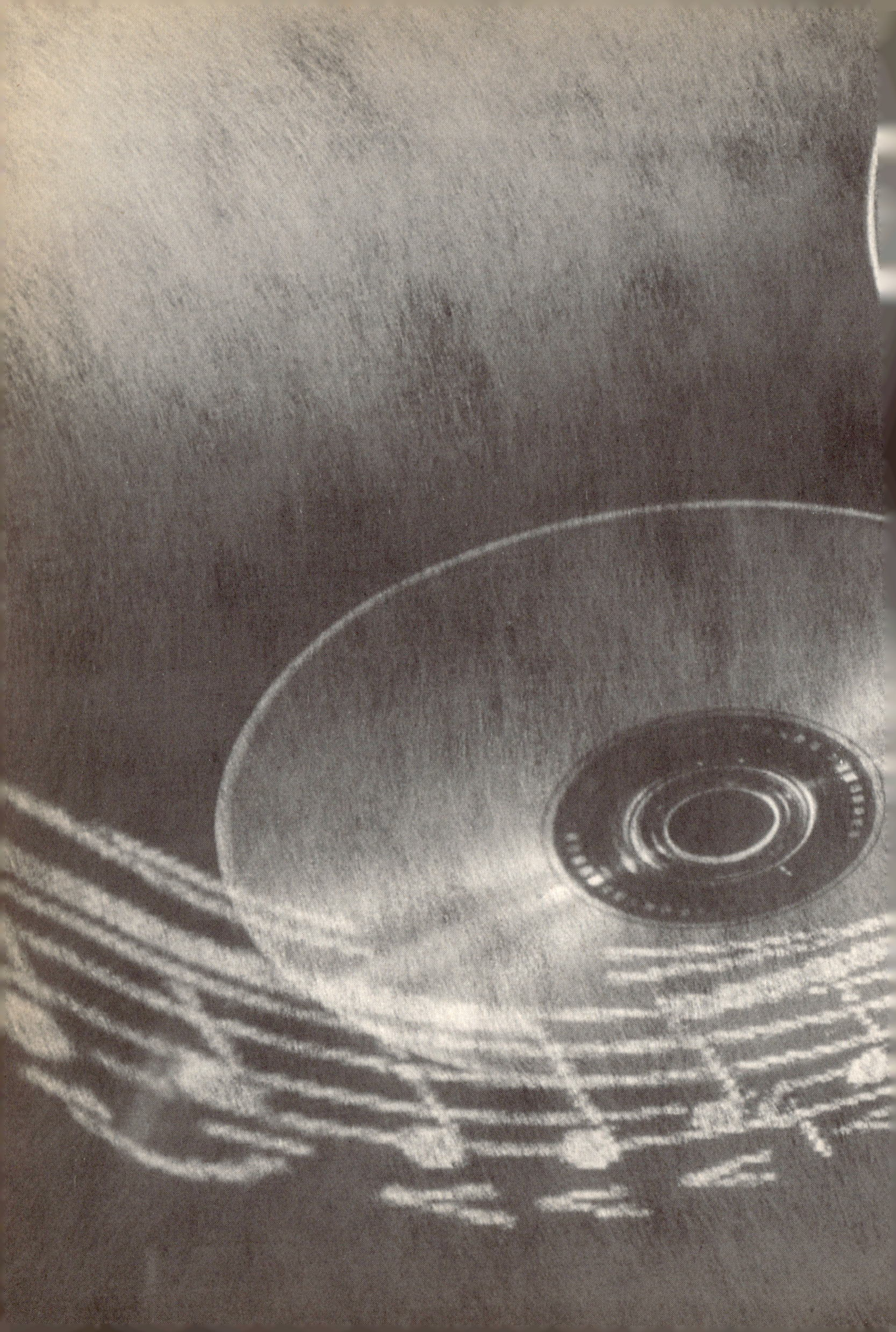

Chapter 19

Recording Music Files onto CDs

FEATURING

- Why burn CDs of music files?
- Data CDs and audio CDs
- Choosing a CD recorder or a CD rewriter
- Understanding CD-R and CD-RW media
- Choosing CD-recording software
- An example: Creating a CD with Easy CD Creator

In this chapter, we'll discuss how to create CDs of (and from) your music files. Most CD-recording software is relatively easy to use, so this chapter will focus on the most important information rather than getting bogged down in a blow-by-blow description of drag-and-drool interfaces. Here's what we'll do:

- Consider why you may want to create CDs containing music files, because some of the choices you'll make later in the chapter depend on this.

- Recap briefly the differences between data CDs and audio CDs, because you'll need to decide which you want to create (probably both).

- Discuss how to choose a CD recorder or CD rewriter.

- Lay out your options for CD-recording software.

- Discuss a few of the CD-recording programs available for Windows, the Macintosh, and Linux.

- Show you an example of creating a CD with Easy CD Creator.

Why Burn CDs of Music Files?

There are several reasons to burn CDs of music that you've downloaded or ripped and encoded. These are the main reasons:

- First, you may want to enjoy the music you've downloaded or received in MP3 format in a more widely playable format. By creating a CD of music you've downloaded, you can play it on many of the hundreds of millions of CD players now in use around the world, from home stereo players though boom boxes and portable players to car CD players.

- Second, you may want to burn backup CDs of your MP3 files or other files in case your hard drive goes belly up.

▶ Third, you may want to burn MP3 files to CDs so that you can play them on another computer or in a custom MP3 CD player (such as the Pine D'music).

Chances are, you won't want to use CDs as your main storage format for music. Recordable CDs are one of the cheapest types of storage media available, rivaled only by hard disks and tape drives, but their limited capacity (650 to 700MB) offsets their advantages of portability and playability. CDs are great for backing up a relatively small number of files, and of course, they're even better for taking music with you, but we bet you won't want to change CDs every half-hour or so when you want to listen to a range of music.

Likewise, tape drives aren't good for data that you'll access daily, because most models are too clumsy for anything but archival storage. So in most cases, it'll make much more sense to keep as many music files as possible on hard drives so that you can access them on a moment's whim. To maximize the amount of hard-disk space that you have available, you may want to have a dedicated server for storing your music files. (Chapter 22, "Building a Serious Music Collection," discusses how to plan and build such a server.)

If your computer is maxed out for storage space (for example, if it's a laptop and you're reluctant to attach external hard drives to it because you're saving for a new laptop), recordable CDs can provide effective stop-gap storage.

Data CDs and Audio CDs

Before we get any further, you need to understand the differences between data CDs and audio CDs.

Audio CDs are CDs with their data written in a format readable by audio CD players, like the "regular" CDs you buy at your local music store. Audio CDs use the PCM (Pulse Code Modulation) format, a standard format for uncompressed audio, with handles (pointers) identifying the tracks. As you'll recall from Chapter 1, "MP3 and Digital Audio," when you list the contents of an audio

CD in a Windows file-management program, you see a list of 1KB CDA files that represent the handles. You can fit about 74 minutes of uncompressed audio in PCM format on an audio CD. Computer CD-ROM drives can also read audio CDs.

To store MP3 files in audio format on CD, you convert them to uncompressed WAV files (on the PC) or AIFF files (on the Mac), which expands their size greatly, and then write the converted tracks to the CD. Many software packages handle this conversion transparently in a single operation, so the package appears to take MP3 files and write them to the CD in CDA format. With other software, you need to convert the tracks to WAV format (or AIFF format) and then write the converted tracks to the CD in a separate step.

The advantage of audio CDs is that you can play them in most audio CD players. (Some players are unable to read CD-R and CD-RW discs properly.) The disadvantage is that you can get relatively little audio on each CD.

Data CDs are CDs whose data is readable by a CD-ROM drive but not by an audio CD player. Historically, CD-ROM drives have been attached to computers, but recently, some manufacturers have launched stand-alone CD players that can read data CDs. One example of this is Pine's D'music portable CD-ROM player, which can play both audio CDs and data CDs. Some manufacturers of car audio systems have also started making data-CD–capable CD players.

The advantage of data CDs is that you can store 10 or 11 hours' worth of compressed audio (at a bitrate of 128kbps) on a single CD. The disadvantage is that you cannot play data CDs on audio CD players. Also, you may need to shorten long filenames (and path names) in order for the CD's file system to be able to store them satisfactorily.

If you're seriously into music, you'll most likely want to be able to create both data CDs and audio CDs. So when you're choosing CD-recording software, make sure it can handle both formats.

Choosing a CD Recorder or CD Rewriter

If you don't have a CD recorder or CD rewriter but want to get one, this section explains what you need to know.

> **NOTE**
>
> For general discussion (for example, of speeds), we'll use the term *CD recorder* to encompass both CD recorders that write only once and CD rewriters.

Get a Fast Recorder

First off, you'll probably want to get one of the fastest CD recorders you can afford. This doesn't necessarily mean the fastest CD recorder available to you, as there are several considerations that you need to keep in mind when choosing your CD recorder.

CD recorder speed is measured by the same rating system as CD drives: 1X, 2X, 4X, and so on. Each X represents 150kbps, so a 4X drive chugs through 600kbps, an 8X drive handles 1200kbps (1.2Mbps), and a 12X drive manages 1800kbps (1.8Mbps).

At this writing, CD recorders that write at 12X are becoming widely available. Writing full bore, a 12X drive can fill a whole CD in six minutes or so. (The speed will vary a bit depending on your system; if your other components are lame, chances are the CD recorder will have to scale back its speed so as not to choke them.) 12X writers are generally much more expensive than slower drives, with external models costing as much as $500 or $600.

6X and 8X CD recorders are much more affordable, with many available between $200 and $400. 4X CD recorders tend to be cheaper still, but with prices on the 6X and 8X recorders dropping, you may want to forego a 4X recorder unless either your primary interest is an incredible bargain or you need a parallel or USB connection. (USB cannot reliably handle transfer speeds of faster than 4X.)

That said, you shouldn't need to put yourself into bankruptcy and buy a 12X drive unless you're burning many CDs or your time is very precious. A 2X drive takes 36 minutes to write a CD, which is far too slow for most people. The 18 minutes that a 4X drive takes is likewise too long for some people; but the difference between the 12 minutes that a 6X drive takes and the 9 minutes that an 8X drive takes is almost negligible, unless you'll be holding your breath watching the CD being burned. Still, we're not denying that it'll be great when some friendly hardware manufacturer comes out with a 96X drive that can spit out a smoking new CD within 30 seconds of your having set it a-burning.

CD recorders almost invariably read data at a faster rate than they write it. Some CD recorders now read up to 32X, making them almost as fast as a dedicated CD drive. Even so, unless you're out of space, look to add a CD recorder to your computer rather than replace your existing CD drive with a CD recorder. That way, you'll be able to duplicate a CD (assuming that you have the right to do so) or install Quake at the same time you're enjoying the cannons in Tchaikovsky's *1812 Overture*.

Check out the range of CD recorders at your local computer superstore or online paradise, and choose a recorder that satisfies both your budget and your temperament.

Internal or External?

Generally speaking, an internal drive costs less than an external drive, but you'll need to have a drive bay free in your computer. An external drive usually costs more, occupies space on your desk, and needs its own power supply. In addition, most external drives are much noisier than internal drives because they contain their own fans. But if your main computer is a laptop, or if you want to be able to move the drive from computer to computer as the fancy strikes you, you'll need an external drive.

Most external drives include a cable (SCSI, parallel, USB, or FireWire) for connecting to your computer—but many external drives don't include an audio cable for connecting their audio output jacks to your sound card's input jacks. Before you go shopping for an external drive, determine what type of connection you'll need at the PC end (typically a ⅛-inch miniplug, but sometimes two RCA jacks). Then check the connection on the CD drive, find out whether the package includes the cable, and buy a cable if necessary.

EIDE drives are all internal. SCSI drives can be internal or external. Because the parallel port, the USB ports, and any FireWire ports are external connections, almost all of these drives are external only. (You can find internal FireWire CD-R drives if you look hard enough.)

EIDE, SCSI, Parallel Port, USB, or FireWire?

The next question is: How will you connect the drive to your computer? If you have a SCSI card in your computer, you'll probably want to get a SCSI CD recorder, because it typically performs better *and* puts much less burden on the processor than an EIDE CD recorder does.

> **WARNING**
>
> There's one restriction you need to know here if you want to copy CDs: Most SCSI CD recorders copy CDs directly only from other SCSI drives, not from EIDE drives. If you have a SCSI CD recorder and an EIDE CD drive, you'll need to copy the CD to the hard disk and then burn it from there.

SCSI drives cost a bit more than EIDE drives of the same speed, but if your computer's already got SCSI, the extra cost is probably worth it. If you don't have a SCSI card, remember to factor in the cost of the card in your cost analysis. Some SCSI CD recorders come with a bundled SCSI card, but most don't, so in most cases you'll have to budget for the card as well. (Check the specifications or the box to make sure you know what you're getting.) If you don't have SCSI, but you want the best, bite the bullet and cough up the cash for a good SCSI card and SCSI CD recorder.

If you don't want to pay for SCSI but you want an internal drive, or if your CD player is EIDE and you want to do a lot of CD-to-CD duplicating, EIDE is the way to go. Before you buy, make sure that you have an EIDE connector available on your computer. If it's already chock-full of drives (most modern machines can take four EIDE devices), you won't be able to add another without sacrificing an existing one.

If you're looking at an external non-SCSI drive, your current choices are a parallel-port drive, a USB drive, or a FireWire drive. The performance of parallel-port drives is miserable because the transfer speed of the parallel port is far less than that of EIDE or SCSI. But they're compatible with most computers ever built, and they get the job done—eventually. USB is much more promising, provided that your computer has USB ports and your operating system supports USB. (If your desktop computer doesn't have USB ports, you can add them via an internal adapter or a PC card.) USB delivers better speed and (in theory) the convenience of being hot-pluggable.

NOTE

Though slow, a parallel-port CD drive can have an additional benefit: If you have a computer without a built-in CD drive, you can use a parallel port CD drive to install an operating system (or to reload it after a fatal crash). Usually, you'll need to install a driver to access the CD drive, but you can install the driver after booting from a Windows 95 or Windows 98 boot diskette—or from DOS, if you still have a copy.

Barreling down the shoulder of the hardware turnpike are FireWire CD recorders. (FireWire, as you'll remember, is the most widespread snappy name for the IEEE 1394 high-performance serial bus. Sony, determined to continue its assaults on the English language, calls it i.LINK instead.) Consider a FireWire CD recorder only if you have a FireWire-capable computer or if you have another compelling reason to add FireWire to your current computer. (For example, you might be feeling a burning need to start editing digital video.)

At this writing, built-in FireWire ports are more or less confined to Macintoshes and Sony computers, meaning that FireWire drives have a select and largely enthusiastic clientele. You can add FireWire to an existing computer via a PCI card (about $100) or a PC Card (about $150), but for most people the expense doesn't justify the relatively meager benefits. As more FireWire peripherals are introduced, though, this will change.

CD-R or CD-RW?

Next, decide whether you want just a CD-recordable drive (CD-R) or a read/write drive (CD-RW). Burning a CD-R disc is essentially a one-time process: Once the data is written to the CD, you can't remove it or change it, although you can read it as many times as you want. (However, see the sidebar on packet writing.) With a CD-RW drive, on the other hand, you can write to the disc multiple times, erasing and changing the data as you see fit. (If you'd like the acronyms, CD-R discs are *Write Once, Read Multiple* media—*WORM* for short—while CD-RW discs are *Write And Read Multiple* (or *WARM*) media.

Needless to say, CD-RW drives are more expensive than CD-R drives, although the gap is shrinking. CD-RW prices have dropped dramatically over the past year or so, and they now cost only a little more than CD-R drives. However, CD-RW blanks are two to three times as expensive as CD-R blanks, which you can get for less than a buck if you buy in bulk and maybe send in coupons.

For most people, the price difference on the drives is negligible, and the benefits of a CD-RW drive over a CD-ROM drive are huge.

CD-RW drives can write both CD-RW discs and CD-ROM discs, making them a good investment.

Because CD-RW discs use a different technology than regular CD-ROMs, they're not as compatible with all CD-ROM drives. If you want to share a CD with someone else, a CD-R disc is a better bet than a CD-RW disc. Likewise, only the most recent audio players can play CD-RW discs, whereas most audio players can play only prerecorded CDs and CD-R discs.

> **PACKET WRITING: FLEXIBILITY FOR CD-R**
>
> Early recorders and CD-R software let you write only once to a disc, making for something of an exciting operation. You would line up all the files you wanted to write to the CD, double-check that they would (in theory) fit, and set the CD burning. You would then be very careful not to interrupt it before it finished, and if you were lucky, the CD would be written correctly. All too often, though, something would go wrong in the course of the burn, and you'd be left with another toasted coaster to add to your collection of AOL beer mats.
>
> If your recorder and operating system support *packet-writing software*, you'll be able to treat a CD-R disc more or less like a giant (and rather shiny) floppy or removable disk—with a couple of differences:
>
> ▶ You can write only once to any given sector of the disk, so you can't reclaim any space by deleting files that you've already written to the CD. The files will be deleted, but the space they occupied will be used.
>
> ▶ Each session that you write also costs you some space on the disc in overhead.
>
> For all but the most demanding uses, these limitations aren't too serious. With 650MB to burn (yes, pun intended) on each CD, you can usually afford to squander a dozen megabytes here and there.

CD-R and CD-RW Media

If you've looked at CD-R or CD-RW discs, you'll know that most of them look very different from prerecorded audio or data CDs (*pressed* CDs). Depending on their make and type, CD-R and CD-RW discs may have a gold, green, or bluish coating on their data side. Typically, this is a polycarbonate substrate over a reflective layer of 24-carat gold (real gold, but real thin) or a silver-colored alloy.

Information is transferred to CD-R and CD-RW discs by a different process than for pressed CDs. While pressed CDs are pressed in a mold from a master CD, CD recorders and CD rewriters use a laser to burn the information onto the CD-R or CD-RW media. Pressed CDs use physically raised areas called *lands* and lowered areas called *pits* to store the encoded data. Recordable CDs have a dye layer in which the laser burns marks that have the same reflective properties as the lands and pits.

Not only do CD-R and CD-RW discs look different than pressed CDs, but they're also less robust. You can damage them more easily with extreme heat and moderate cold, by scratching or gouging them, or by leaving them in direct sunlight. The data is actually stored closer to the label side of the CD than to the business side, so if you're compelled to scratch one side of the CD, go for the business side over the label side.

When buying CD-R and CD-RW discs, you need to balance economy with quality. Beware of cheapo discs, because they may give you skips and errors—you may even lose your precious music or data. If you can, buy a few discs for testing before you drop the dough for a bargain bucket-full.

One way to save some money is to buy CD-R and CD-RW discs without jewel cases. This makes for a good discount, as the jewel cases are relatively expensive to manufacture and bulky to package (and easy to break, as you no doubt know from personal experience). The discs are typically sold on a spindle, which makes for handy storage until you use them—after which you'll have to find safe storage for them on your own. (One possibility to consider is a CD wallet, which can be especially handy if you need to take your CDs with you when you travel.)

Some manufacturers try to sell you special CDs that are supposed to deliver better results at higher writing speeds than less worthy media. We're split on the virtues of these überCDs. On the one hand, you want your dangerously expensive CD recorder to record as fast as possible. But on the other hand, chances are that you're paying enough for regular media anyway. You may want to spend extra on CD-RW discs if you find that those higher quality discs appear to deliver on the performance claim, but you're unlikely to want to spend extra on CD-R discs unless your time is mighty precious.

Choosing CD-Recording Software

At this writing, there are dozens of applications for recording CDs, some with very different features than others. This section discusses how to choose CD-recording software to meet your needs. Along the way, we'll mention a few specific packages, but our primary focus is to make you aware of the possibilities and get you thinking about your needs.

1. Did You Get Any CD-Recording Software with Your Drive?

First, did you get some kind of CD-burning application with your CD recorder drive? Depending on how much you paid for the drive, you may have gotten a lite version of something good (quite likely), or you may have gotten the real thing (less likely, but possible). If you got stuck with a lite version, you may need to get something better before too long, but the lite version may be enough to get you started.

Recording Music Files onto CDs 747

If you haven't already checked out the capabilities of whatever was bundled with your drive, stop reading and go check it out to see if it'll get the job done. There's more than a fair chance that you have a limited version that can copy data files to CDs slowly and clumsily enough to persuade you to pay for an upgrade, but it's worth checking to make sure it's inadequate before you pay good dining-out money for more software.

If you're running Windows, you may well have received a version of Adaptec's DirectCD with your drive. DirectCD lets you format a CD and then use it more or less like a giant floppy, as described earlier in this chapter. A Wizard walks you through the process of initializing and formatting the drive, after which you can add files to it using standard Windows operations such as drag-and-drop or copy-and-paste. Copying the files takes a while, depending on the speed of your CD recorder. Once you've transferred all the files to the CD, you then issue the program's command for making the disc readable by CD drives, and DirectCD converts the CD to the CD file system (CDFS). You then get to choose between closing the CD-writing session but being able to write to the CD again and closing the session and anchoring the CD's contents permanently.

2. Can You Make Do with Your MP3 Player or Jukebox?

If you struck out on the first question, try this one: Does your MP3 player software or MP3 jukebox software offer features for creating CDs?

For example, if you're using Windows, MusicMatch Jukebox is a good place to start, because not only is it free but it includes features for burning both data CDs and audio CDs. (We discussed these capabilities in the section "Burn CDs" in Chapter 9, "Windows Jukeboxes.") If you find that MusicMatch Jukebox agrees with your CD recorder and meets your needs, you may not need to buy any software.

Many MP3 players and jukeboxes can write MP3 files to WAV files or AIFF files. You can then burn these WAV files or AIFF files to CDs using software such as DirectCD or an equivalent. The following sections give examples of creating WAV files or AIFF files with popular software.

Creating WAV Files with Winamp

To create WAV files with Winamp, follow these steps:

1. Press Ctrl+P, or choose Options ➢ Preferences from the main menu, to display the Preferences dialog box.

2. Select the Output category in the Plug-Ins list box.

3. In the Output Plug-Ins list box, select the Nullsoft Disk Writer plug-in entry.

4. Click the Configure button to display the Select Directory dialog box.

5. Select the directory in which you want to store the WAV files. Click the OK button.

6. Click the Close button to close the Preferences dialog box.

To create a WAV file from an MP3 file, open the MP3 file and play it as usual. You won't hear any sound, and you'll see from the time display that Winamp is jerking through the song in bursts at a far greater speed than usual (unless you have a really slow hard drive or really slow computer, that is). When it stops, you'll find that it has created a WAV file of the MP3 file in the directory that you specified.

Creating WAV Files with Sonique

To create WAV files with Sonique, follow these steps:

1. From the Navigation Console, click the Setup Options button to display the Setup Options screen.

2. Make sure the General page is selected. If it's not selected, click the General button at the bottom of the screen.

3. Click the Audio tab on the right-hand side of the screen to display the Audio options.

4. In the Select Output list box, select the .WAV Writer Plugin entry.

5. Click the Configure button to display the .WAV Writer Plugin configuration screen.

6. Double-click in the Select Output Directory list box, and use the resulting Browse for Folder dialog box to select the folder in which you want to store the WAV files. Click the OK button.

You can then create a WAV file from an MP3 file by opening the MP3 file and playing it. Sonique displays a Note dialog box warning you that you are about to write to disk. This is a nice touch if you forget you've set it to write to disk because you'll not only get no output, but you'll be consuming hard-disk space at about 50MB a minute. Not such a nice touch, though, is that Sonique doesn't give you any feedback about how the creation of the WAV file is progressing. So open an Explorer window to the directory you chose and watch the file or files arrive. Press the F5 key periodically to prompt Explorer to update its directory display.

Creating AIFF Files with SoundJam

To create AIFF files from MP3 files with SoundJam, follow these steps:

1. Display the Converter dialog box if it's not already displayed.

2. Add to the Converter dialog box the MP3 files that you want to convert.

3. In the Convert Using drop-down list, choose SoundJam AIFF Encoder.

4. Click the Start Converting button.

Creating WAV Files with xmms

To create WAV files from MP3 files with xmms, follow these steps:

1. Press Ctrl+P, or choose Options ➤ Preferences from the main menu, to display the Preferences dialog box.

2. On the Audio I/O Plugins page of the dialog box, choose the Disk Writer Plugin listing from the Output Plugin drop-down list.

3. Click the Configure button to display the Disk Writer Configuration dialog box.

4. Enter the path in the Path text box (use the Browse button and the resulting dialog box to specify the path if you want), and click the OK button.

5. Click the OK button to apply the changes and close the Preferences dialog box. (Alternatively, click the Apply button to apply the changes, and then close the Preferences dialog box.)

As with Winamp, you can now create a WAV file from an MP3 file by opening the MP3 file and playing it. xmms speeds through the song (if your computer and hard drive are up to it) and won't produce any sound, but writes the WAV file of the MP3 file in the directory you specified in the Disk Writer Configuration dialog box.

3. Do You Want a General-Purpose Package or an MP3-Specific Software Package?

If your drive didn't come with any suitable software, you'll need to get some. You can get either a general-purpose CD-recording package or an MP3-specific (or digital-audio–specific) package that features writing to CD. Which package you want will depend on your needs; you might even want both.

General-purpose CD-recording software will serve you more thoroughly than a more specialized package. For example, if you want to use your CD drive to back up crucial files (or your entire hard drive), you'll do best with general-purpose software. If you want more MP3-specific features, such as a variety of templates for designing CD labels and sleeve inserts, you may do better with a specialized package.

Examples of general-purpose CD-recording software include the following:

- **Windows** Easy CD Creator Deluxe, from Adaptec, is a powerful and effective program. We'll show you how to use Easy CD Creator Deluxe to burn an audio CD from MP3 files a little later in this chapter.

- **Macintosh** Toast, also from Adaptec, is one of the most popular CD-recording applications for the Mac.

- **Linux** As usual with Linux, you can get the job done without opening your wallet. cdrecord is an effective command-line CD-recording program that you can get from the cdrecord Web site (www.fokus.gmd.de/research/cc/glone/employees/joerg.schilling/private/cdrecord.html) and Linux sites such as freshmeat.net. xcdroast is a graphical interface that works with cdrecord.

Examples of MP3-specific CD-recording software include the following, which are all for the Windows platform:

- PTS AudioCD MP3 Studio
- MP3 Wizard from Data Becker
- HyCD Play&Record

An Example: Creating Audio CDs with Easy CD Creator

This section will show you how to create audio CDs with Easy CD Creator from Adaptec. We chose Easy CD Creator because it's one of the most widely available CD-recording applications. Not only is it available from just about every software retail outfit you can think of, but it comes preinstalled on many computers that include CD-R or CD-RW drives.

If you buy Easy CD Creator, you'll find the installation a breeze. We recommend installing Adaptec DirectCD as well if that's an option with the package you get.

Follow these steps to create an audio CD with Easy CD Creator:

1. Choose Start ➤ Programs ➤ Adaptec Easy CD Creator ➤ Create CD, then click the Audio button. (Quick note: The menu choices may vary depending on the version of Easy CD Creator you have.) Easy CD Creator displays the Audio screen shown in Figure 19.1.

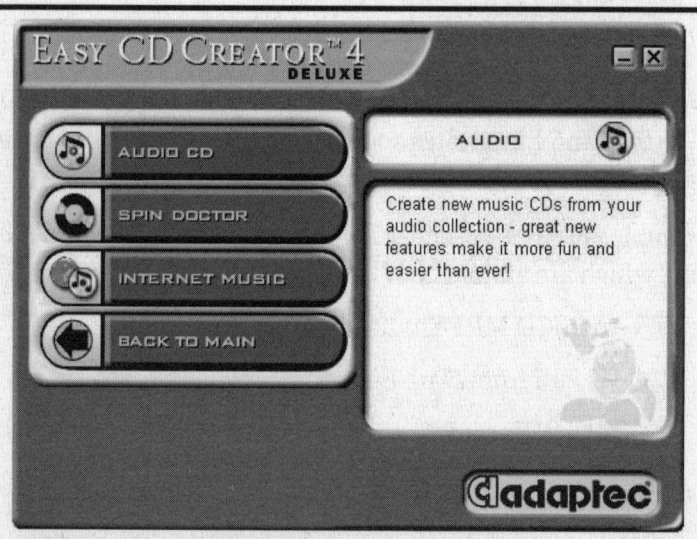

FIGURE 19.1: Getting started on the creation of an audio CD with Easy CD Creator

Recording Music Files onto CDs 753

2. Click the Audio CD button to start Easy CD Creator. You'll see Easy CD Creator, probably as shown in Figure 19.2, with the CD Guide assistant demanding your attention.

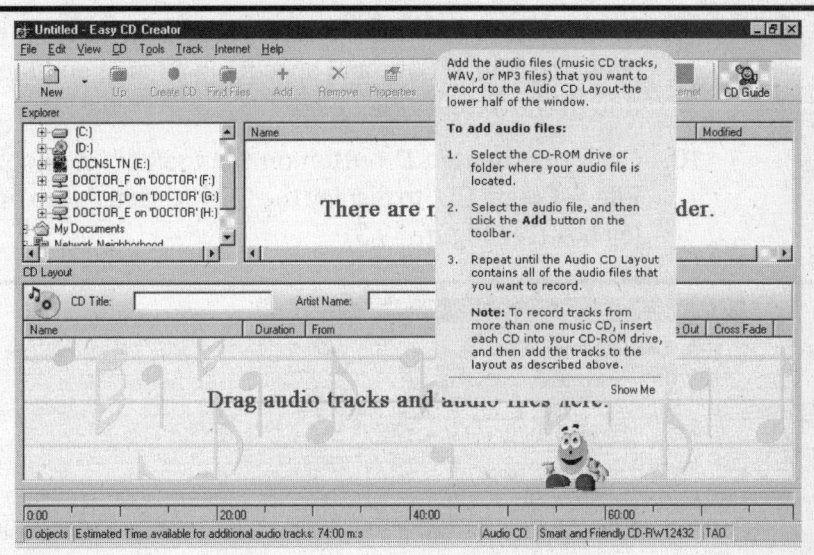

FIGURE 19.2: Easy CD Creator will hit you with the CD Guide assistant. Dismiss it.

3. Dismiss the CD Guide assistant by right-clicking it and choosing Hide from the context menu.

4. Use the tree on the left-hand side of the upper part of the window to navigate to the folder that contains the MP3 files that you want to burn to CD.

5. Drag the tracks from the right-hand side of the upper part of the window to the CD.

6. Repeat steps 4 and 5 until you've added as many tracks to the CD as you want or as many tracks as it will hold. Use the graphical and text readouts at the bottom of the CD to see how much space you've used and how much space you have left.

7. Drag the tracks up and down until they're in the order in which you want them to appear on the CD.

8. Enter the title for the CD in the CD Title text box and the artist's name in the Artist Name text box.

9. If you plan to use this CD layout frequently, save it by choosing File ➤ Save and specifying a name and location in the Save As dialog box.

10. Click the Create CD button on the toolbar, or choose File ➤ Create CD, to display the CD Creation Setup dialog box (see Figure 19.3).

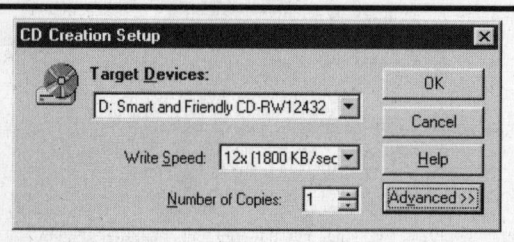

FIGURE 19.3: Choose the basic parameters for recording in the smaller version of the CD Creation Setup dialog box.

11. Make sure that Easy CD Creator has selected the correct CD recorder in the Target Devices drop-down list, an appropriate write speed in the Write Speed drop-down list, and the number of copies you want in the Number of Copies text box.

12. Click the Advanced button to display the hidden section of the CD Creation Setup dialog box (see Figure 19.4) that contains advanced options.

Recording Music Files onto CDs 755

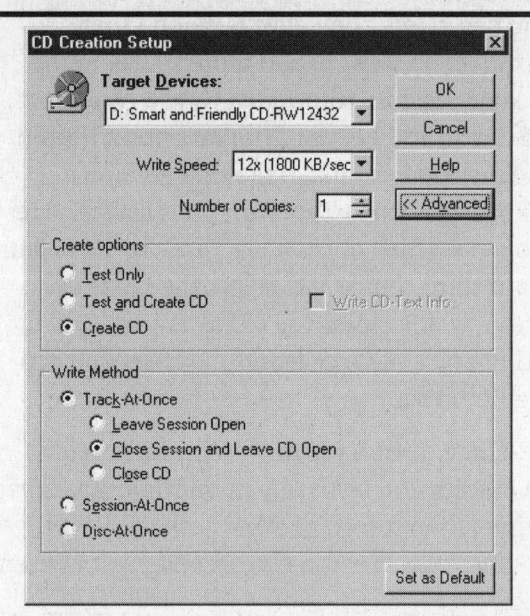

FIGURE 19.4: Set advanced options in the hidden section of the CD Creation Setup dialog box.

13. Choose advanced options as follows:

    Create Options group box In this group box, select the Test Only option button if you want to test the CD-creation process without writing any files to the CD. Select the Test and Create CD option button if you want to perform the test and then write to the CD. Otherwise, leave the Create CD option button selected to create the CD without testing. If your CD drive supports CD-Text information and you use the Disc-at-Once writing method (more on this in a moment), you can select the Write CD-Text Info check box to add the CD title and the artist and track names to the CD.

    Write Method group box In this group box, choose the writing method you want to use for creating the CD:

    Track-at-Once option button This button lets you record one track at a time. If you choose this option button, you can select the Leave Session Open option button if you want to add more tracks to the CD in the same session. Alternatively, you can select the Close Session and Leave CD Open option button to close the session (and make the first session's audio tracks playable on CD players) but leave the rest of the CD open for further sessions. (This is the default setting.) Your third choice is to select the Close CD option button, which closes the CD after writing the track. Writing Track-at-Once leaves a two-second gap between audio tracks.

Session-at-Once option button   This button lets you record one session (typically of multiple tracks) at the same time, then record another session. Writing Session-at-Once also leaves a two-second gap between audio tracks.

Disc-at-Once option button   This button writes and closes the CD in a single operation. This option is good for creating a full CD of music because it lets you eliminate the two-second gap between tracks.

Set As Default button   When you've made your choices, click this button to set them as your defaults.

14. Click the OK button to close the CD Creation Setup dialog box. Easy CD Creator starts creating your CD, keeping you informed of its progress in the CD Creation Process dialog box, shown in Figure 19.5.

15. When Easy CD Creator tells you that the CD was created successfully, either pop it out and get ready to enjoy it, or click the Jewel Case button to use Easy CD Creator's Jewel Case Creator (if you installed it) to create a jewel-case insert for the CD.

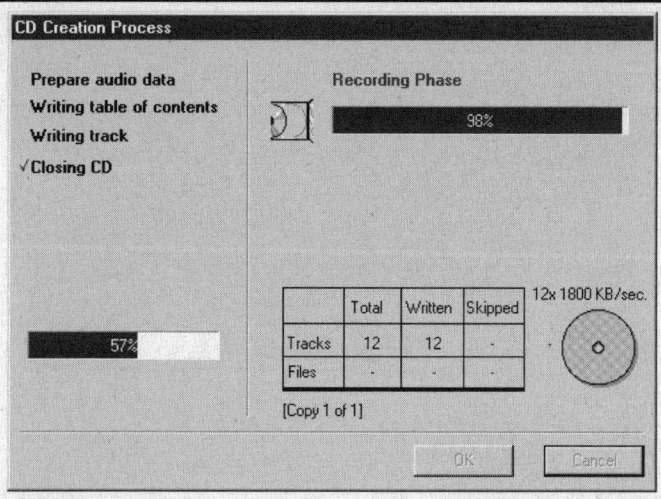

FIGURE 19.5: Easy CD Creator at work creating the CD

Up Next

In this chapter, we've discussed how to go about choosing a CD recorder or CD rewriter, selecting software for it, and putting the two together to create audio CDs and data CDs.

In the next chapter, we'll discuss how to manipulate MP3 files and solve some common problems with them.

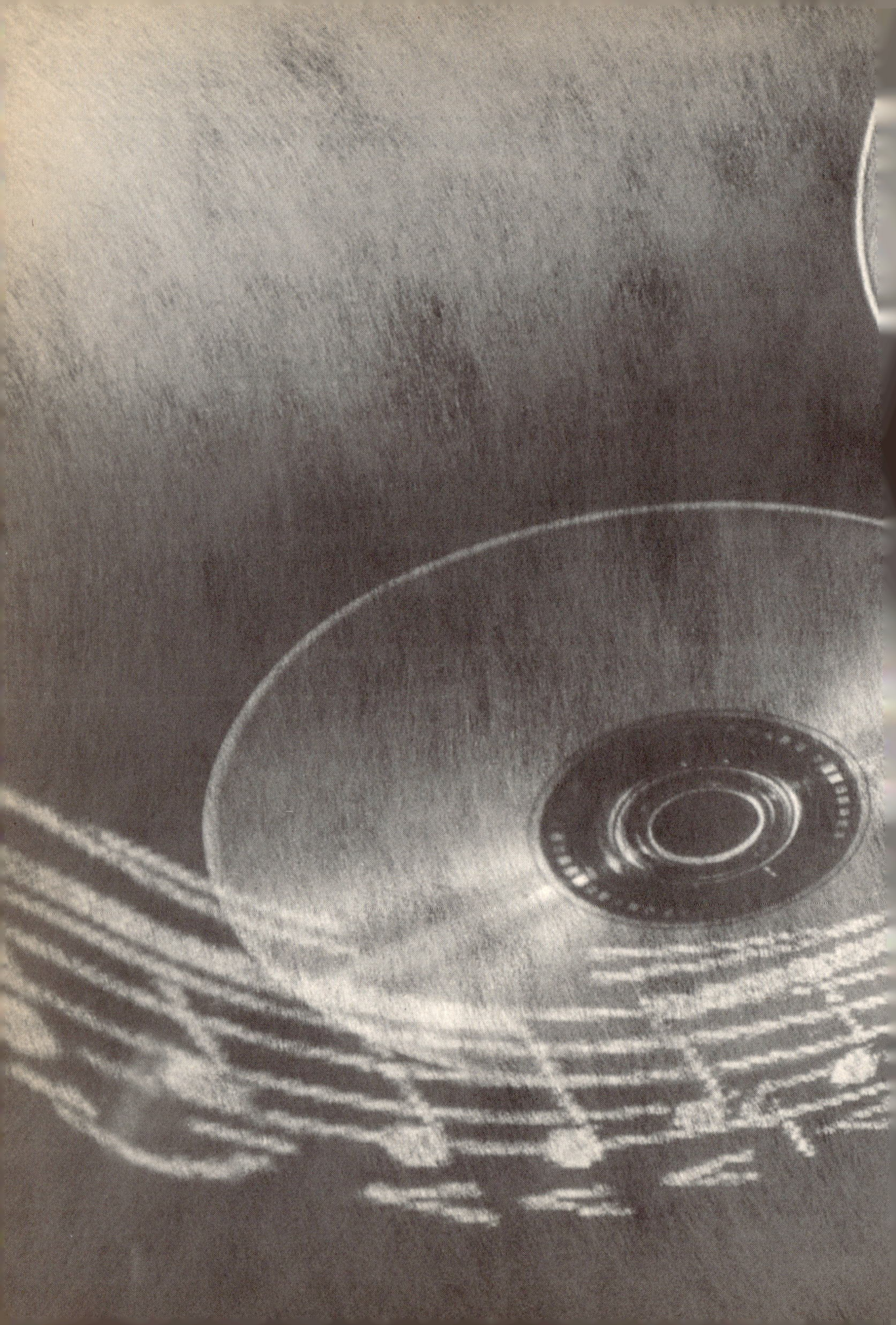

Chapter 20
Working with MP3 Files

FEATURING

- Creating MP3 files of your own music
- Editing ID3 tags
- Renaming MP3 files
- Repairing cooked files
- Editing MP3 files
- Creating executable MP3 files
- Adding information to CDDB

This chapter discusses some of the key maneuvers that you may need to perform on your MP3 files. We'll start by outlining briefly how to create MP3 files from your own music or your recordings. After that, we'll move on to editing ID3 tags, which you'll need to do to keep your music collection in good order—especially if you use jukebox software that uses the ID3 tags to organize your music.

We'll then show you what (perhaps we should say "what little") you can do to clean up grubby files and how you can edit MP3 files. We'll finish by showing you how to create executable MP3 files and enter information in CDDB, the online database of CD information.

Some of these techniques apply to all the platforms covered in this book—Windows, the Macintosh, and Linux. For other techniques, though, the tools are available only on some platforms. We'll indicate in the headings which platform each section refers to.

CREATING MP3 FILES OF YOUR OWN MUSIC (WINDOWS, MAC, LINUX)

If you have an ounce of musical talent in your body, you won't always want to be on the receiving end of the digital music revolution. If you've recorded anything (yes, *anything*) in any medium that's still playable, you can create MP3 files of it and share them with six billion other people in the world. (Note that we said *can*—you don't *have to* post your adolescent poems on the Web. In fact, we'd prefer that you don't. But technically, it's frighteningly feasible, as you'll know if you've read the remainder of this book.)

Once you're sure that you have the rights needed to distribute content, create MP3 files of it. If your content is on CD (or DVD), you'll have no problem ripping it to MP3 files the same way as you rip anyone else's CD. If you've made it far enough to get your CD (or DVD) listed on CDDB—or if you've listed it on CDDB yourself—

you won't even need to add ID3 tags manually, although you'd do well to add comments to your tracks to personalize them. (You might want to add nothing more than a URL to some tracks, while to other tracks you might add a comment as explicit as you can manage in the 30 characters the Comment field can hold.)

If your content is on a different medium than CD or DVD, you'll need to pipe the audio into your computer and record it there. Typically, you'll want to record input as WAV files by using an application such as SoundForge XP or Cool Edit (on Windows), and then convert them into MP3 files.

> **WARNING**
>
> When distributing your music, remember that the lack of security and copy protection that caused you to love MP3 as a consumer can work against you as an artist. If you're ready to embrace the world of open music, go ahead with MP3 files. But if you feel you need to secure the digitally available versions of your creations, you'll need to use another format, such as those we describe in Chapter 23, "Other Digital-Audio Formats." Remember that none of these formats is guaranteed to keep your work from being re-recorded (out through the sound card, back into the same sound card or another sound card) or audio-jacked at the sound card.

EDITING ID3 TAGS (WINDOWS, MAC, LINUX)

Unless you don't use ID3 tags, or you use them but get exceptionally pure information from CDDB, you'll need to edit the ID3 tags on your MP3 files before too long. This section discusses some of the many possibilities for doing so.

Editing ID3 Tags in Windows

Many of the Windows MP3 players and jukeboxes provide tag-editing features. Failing those, you can use a custom tag editor. This section discusses some of each type of tool.

Winamp

In Winamp, use the built-in ID3 tag editor to edit ID3 tags. Select the track and press Alt+3, or choose View File Info from the Main menu to display the MPEG Info Box + ID3 Tag Editor dialog box (see Figure 20.1). Modify the information as appropriate and click the Save button to save the tag, or click the Remove ID3 button to remove the tag from the track.

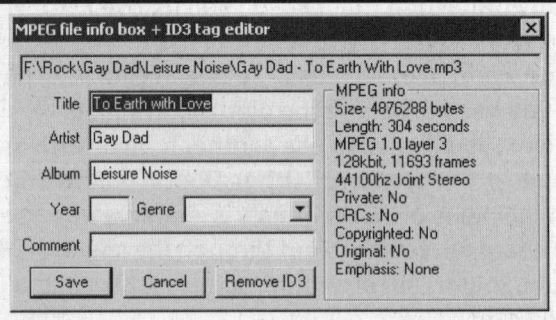

FIGURE 20.1: Winamp's MPEG Info Box + ID3 Tag Editor dialog box provides straightforward tag editing.

MusicMatch Jukebox

In MusicMatch Jukebox, use the built-in ID3 tag editor by selecting the track in the Music Library window and clicking the Tag button to display the Tag Song File dialog box (see Figure 20.2). Add the information, and click the OK button to apply it.

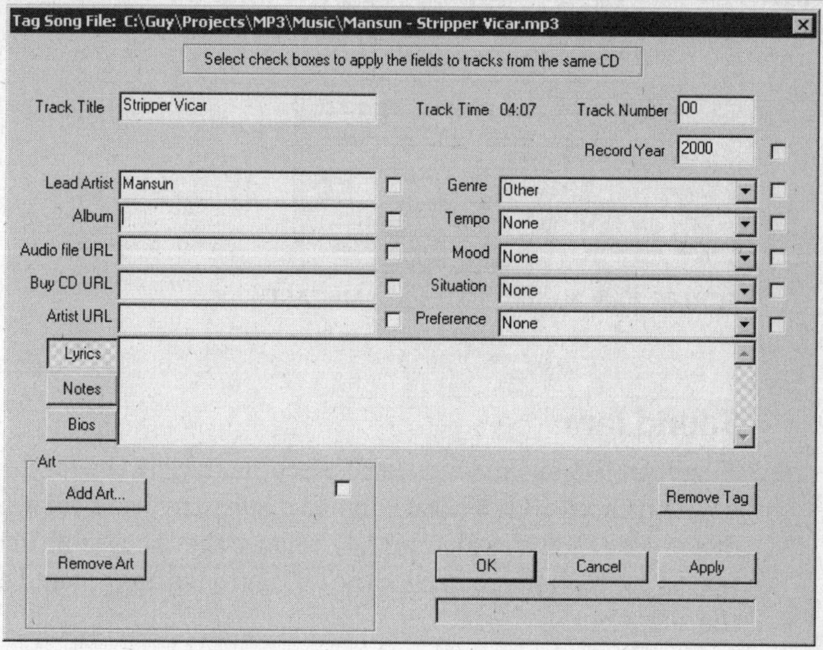

FIGURE 20.2: MusicMatch Jukebox provides comprehensive tag editing.

Editing ID3 Tags on the Mac

As with Windows, some of the most popular MP3 players and jukeboxes for the Mac provide tag-editing features, while others do not. This section touches on the tag-editing features in MACAST and SoundJam and then discusses mp3tool, an ID3 tag editor for the Mac.

MACAST

To edit an ID3 tag in MACAST, select the track in the Playlist window and click the Info button to display the Info dialog box (see Figure 20.3). Change the information as necessary, click the Save button to save it, and close the Info dialog box. To enter the lyrics for a track, click the More Information button to display the lower part of the Info dialog box, select the Lyrics option button, and enter the lyrics in the text box.

FIGURE 20.3: Editing ID3 tags in MACAST

SoundJam

To edit an ID3 tag in SoundJam, select the track in the Playlist window and choose File ≻ Track Info to display the Track Information dialog box (shown in Figure 20.4). Change the changeable information as appropriate, then click the OK button to apply it and close the dialog box.

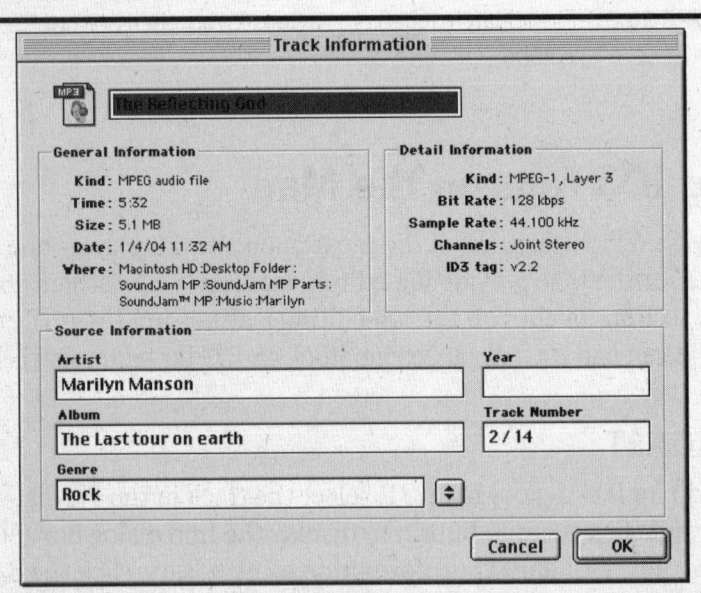

FIGURE 20.4: Use the Track Information dialog box to edit ID3 tags in SoundJam.

MusicMatch Jukebox

Like its Windows counterpart, MusicMatch Jukebox for the Mac provides good tag-editing capabilities. To edit a tag, select the track in the Music Library and click the Tag button to display the MP3 Tag Editor dialog box (see Figure 20.5). Change the information as appropriate, then click the OK button to apply the changes and close the dialog box.

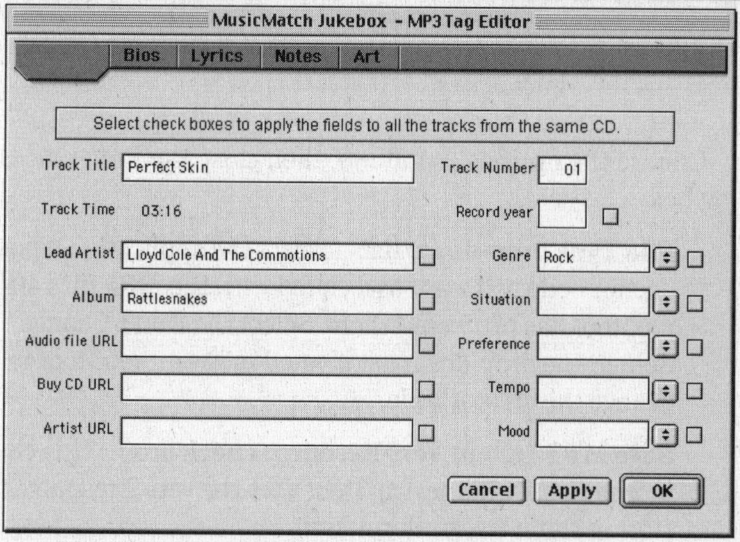

FIGURE 20.5: Editing ID3 tags with MusicMatch Jukebox for the Macintosh

mp3tool

If your MP3 player doesn't provide tag-editing features, you'll need to get a program such as mp3tool, a capable tag editor for the Mac.

Download the latest version of mp3tool from your friendliest Mac software archive and let it unstuff itself. Then run the mp3tool item in the resulting folder to start the program.

The first time you run mp3tool, it displays the mp3tool Preferences dialog box, shown in Figure 20.6.

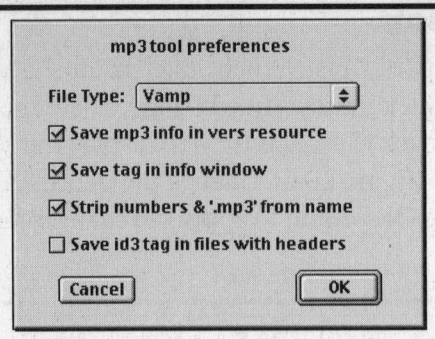

FIGURE 20.6: The first time you run mp3tool, it asks you to declare your preferences.

Choose the options as follows, then close the Preferences dialog box:

File Type drop-down list   Select the application whose creator code you want associated with the MP3 files after mp3tool has processed them. Select the Don't Change item in the drop-down list if you don't want mp3tool to change the creator code.

Save MP3 Info in Vers Resource check box   This check box controls whether mp3tool uses the vers 2 resource for storing static track information.

Save Tag in Info Window check box   This check box controls whether mp3tool saves the tag in the info window.

Strip Numbers & '.mp3' from Name check box   This check box controls whether mp3tool removes track numbers and MP3 extensions from files. Use this feature if you want to use the FN button to apply the filename as the title field in the ID3 tag.

Save ID3 Tag in Files with Headers check box   This check box controls whether mp3tool saves ID3 tag information in files that have headers.

Working with MP3 Files

Once you've chosen your preferences, mp3tool starts up. Choose File ➢ Open MP3 File/Folder to display a dialog box that you can use to open an MP3 file or to open a folder containing MP3 files.

When you open an MP3 file, the mp3tool window displays information for all the ID3 fields, as shown in Figure 20.7.

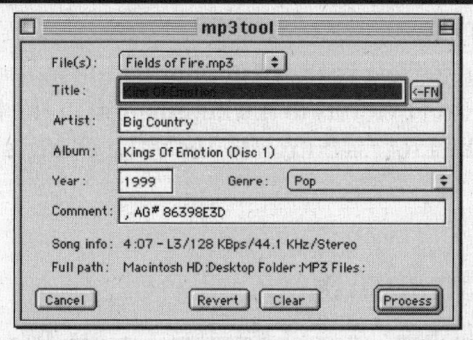

FIGURE 20.7: When you open a single MP3 file, mp3tool displays the information for each ID3 field.

When you open a folder that contains multiple MP3 files, the mp3tool window displays the number of tracks in the File(s) drop-down list and any common information in the appropriate field. For example, in Figure 20.8, each of the three tracks is by Big Country and has the same genre.

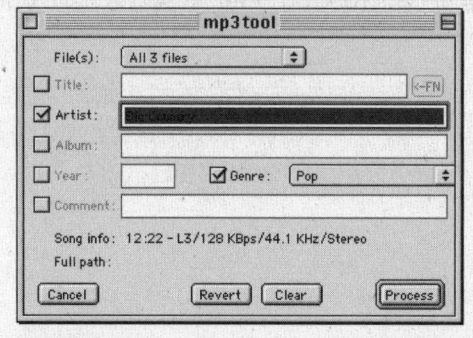

FIGURE 20.8: When you open a folder that contains multiple MP3 files, mp3tool displays the number of tracks and any information that's common to all the tracks.

To enter information in a field that's not common to all the files, select its check box to enable the field. To work with one of the files, select its name in the File(s) drop-down list.

   Click the FN button to apply the filename to the title field of the ID3 tag. This option works best when you have selected the Strip Numbers & '.mp3' from Name check box in the Preferences dialog box, as discussed previously.

   Click the Clear button to clear the current information in the ID3 tag. Click the Revert button to revert to the information in the file's current ID3 tag. Click the Process button to apply the changes to the file or files.

Editing ID3 Tags on Linux

As befits the ultimate hackers' operating system, Linux offers a welter of tools for editing ID3 tags. This section discusses just a few of the many options that are available to you.

xmms

If you're using xmms, start by using the built-in ID3 tag editor for editing tags. Select the track and choose View File Info from the main menu to display the File Info dialog box (see Figure 20.9). Alter the information as necessary, and then click the Save button to save it.

Working with MP3 Files

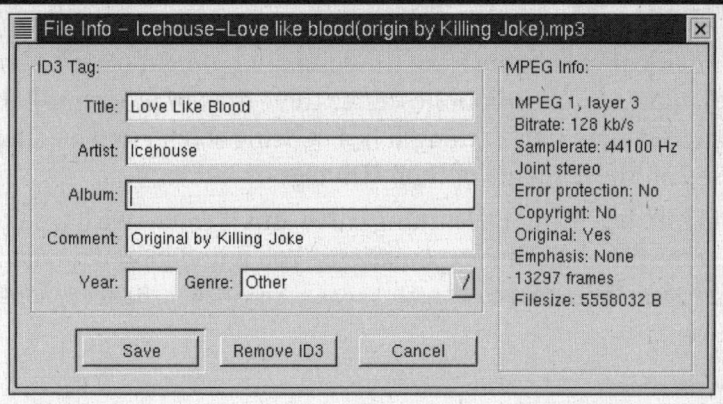

FIGURE 20.9: xmms provides basic tag-editing facilities in the File Info dialog box.

FreeAmp

If you're using FreeAmp as your player, you'll probably want to use its Information Editor for editing ID3 tags. To display the Information Editor dialog box (shown in Figure 20.10), select the track in the My Music window and then click the Edit button. Change the information as desired and then click the OK button to apply it and close the Information Editor dialog box.

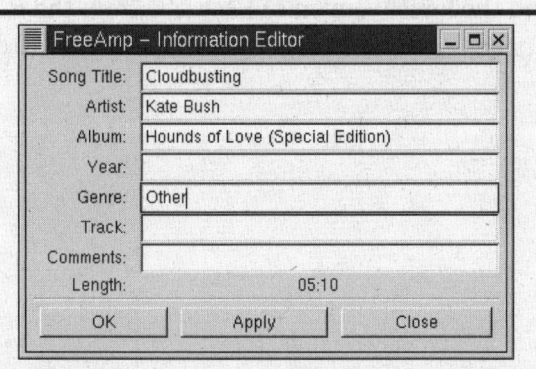

FIGURE 20.10: FreeAmp's Information Editor dialog box provides basic tag editing.

id3ren

For hardcore renaming from the command prompt (or via a batch file), most Linux audiophiles agree there are few programs better than id3ren. id3ren's strength lies in being able to rename files based on the contents of their ID3 tags.

id3ren has a bit of a learning curve, but it comes with a helpful Readme file and other explanations. You'll find id3ren on many Linux resource sites or at www.tscnet.com/pages/badcrc/apps/id3ren/.

> **NOTE**
> id3ren is also available for Windows.

EasyTAG

If your MP3 player doesn't have an ID3 editor, and you'd like something simpler and more graphical than id3ren, EasyTAG may be of interest. EasyTAG has a straightforward interface (see Figure 20.11) and at this writing (September 2000), EasyTAG supports ID3 v1 and v1.1 tags.

You can download the latest version of EasyTAG from the Easy-TAG Project home page (easytag.sourceforge.net/index.htm).

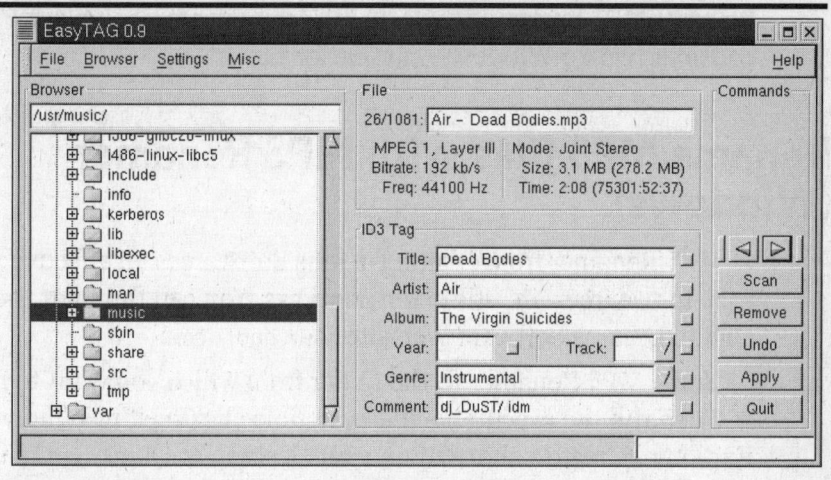

FIGURE 20.11: EasyTAG is a graphical tag editor for Linux.

Renaming MP3 Files (Windows, Linux)

If you download enough MP3 files from the Internet, chances are you'll soon end up with tracks whose names include percent signs or underscores instead of spaces, making them impossible to decipher easily—for example:

    sisters%20of%20mercy-under%20the%20gun.mp3

or

    sisters_of_mercy-under_the_gun.mp3

Also, you'll probably find that some of the people creating the MP3 files that you're downloading suffer from Morbid Phobia of Capital Letters, as in the previous two examples. On special days, you may be lucky enough to run into files that exhibit all three of these characteristics.

You can of course rename these files manually in Windows Explorer or your favorite file-management utility, but there's a better way—MP3-renaming tools. Quite a variety are available; we'll consider two for Windows and one for Linux.

Rename MP3 files with MP3 Renamer (Windows)

MP3 Renamer from Digital Dreams Software is an effective and easy-to-use freeware utility for Windows. You can find it at the Digital Dreams Software Web site, www.dgdr.com.

Unzip MP3 Renamer to the folder from which you want to run it. Then run the executable file by double-clicking it in Windows Explorer. (Create a shortcut on your Desktop or Quick Launch toolbar if you think you'll want to run MP3 Renamer frequently.) You'll see the MP3 Renamer window, as shown in Figure 20.12.

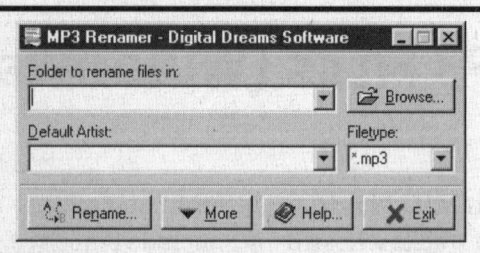

FIGURE 20.12: MP3 Renamer is a MP3-renaming utility for Windows

Using MP3 Renamer is easy. Take the following steps:

1. In the Folder to Rename Files In drop-down list box, specify the folder that contains the MP3 files with offending names. Either type in the folder and path, or select a recently used folder from the drop-down list, or click the Browse button and use the resulting Browse for Folder dialog box to choose the folder.

2. If you want to apply a default artist to MP3 files that appear not to have one, enter the artist's name in the Default Artist text box. For example, if you've been downloading a couple of thousand Grateful Dead

bootlegs into the folder in question, enter **Grateful Dead** in the Default Artist text box.

3. In the Filetype drop-down list, make sure that *.mp3 is selected.

4. Click the More button to display the lower half of the MP3 Renamer window.

5. In the Presets drop-down list, you can choose one of the preset replacements that it specifies. But usually you'll do better to leave the Auto Rename check box selected (as it is by default), in which case MP3 Renamer performs the following operations:

   ▶ Converts each underscore to a space.

   ▶ Converts %20 to a space, %28 to an opening parenthesis, %29 to a closing parenthesis, and %7E to a tilde (~).

   ▶ Makes sure that there is a space on either side of each hyphen and ampersand.

   ▶ Makes sure that there is a space before an opening parenthesis and after a closing parenthesis.

   ▶ Replaces each double space with a single space.

6. Alternatively, choose Custom in the Presets drop-down list and use the Replace and With drop-down list boxes to specify the text to be replaced and the replacement text.

7. Leave the Capitalize Every Word check box selected if you want MP3 Renamer to capitalize every word in the track name. Clear this check box to leave the capitalization as is.

8. Click the Rename button to perform the renaming operation. MP3 Renamer chugs and whirrs for a moment as it works and then displays the Results window (as shown

in Figure 20.13, with the window widened so that you can see all the results).

```
Results
Renamed 'smug_peasant-visions_of_guinevere.mp3' to 'Smug Peasant - Visions Of Guinevere.mp3'
Renamed 'Till%20The%20Furrow%20Straight%20%28Field%20Mix%29.mp3' to 'Smug Peasant - Till The Furrow Straight (Field Mix).mp3'
Renamed 'industrial_sodom-neverneverland.mp3' to 'Industrial Sodom - Neverneverland.mp3'
Renamed 'smug%20peasant-live%20at%20leeds%201.mp3' to 'Smug Peasant - Live At Leeds 1.mp3'
Renaming completed succesfully.

                          [ Close ]
```

FIGURE 20.13: When MP3 Renamer has finished renaming the MP3 files, it displays the Results window.

9. Click the Close button to close the Results window. Then either rename more files or click the Exit button to close MP3 Renamer.

Rename MP3 files with G6 Renamer (Windows)

Another powerful MP3-renamer for Windows is G6 Renamer, a $10 shareware package that you can download from www.gene6.com/renamer/. The demo version of G6 Renamer allows you 15 uses before it times out in order to encourage you to register it. G6 Renamer lets you not only manipulate MP3 filenames and their extensions, but it also lets you rename files based on the contents of their ID3 tags.

Run the `rensetup.exe` distribution executable to extract the G6 Renamer files to a suitable location, then run the resulting `renamer.exe` file to run the application.

Figure 20.14 shows G6 Renamer. As you can see, the upper half of the window is a list box that displays the names and paths of the files you're working with. The lower half of the window is a ten-page control that gives access to the application's different features:

▶ Changing the case of names

Working with MP3 Files

- Changing their extensions (without converting the files)
- Changing their attributes
- Renaming MP3 files and VQF files
- Zipping and unzipping files
- Replacing strings in the names
- Inserting strings
- Numbering tracks
- Deleting characters from track names

The following sections describe some examples of what you can do with G6 Renamer.

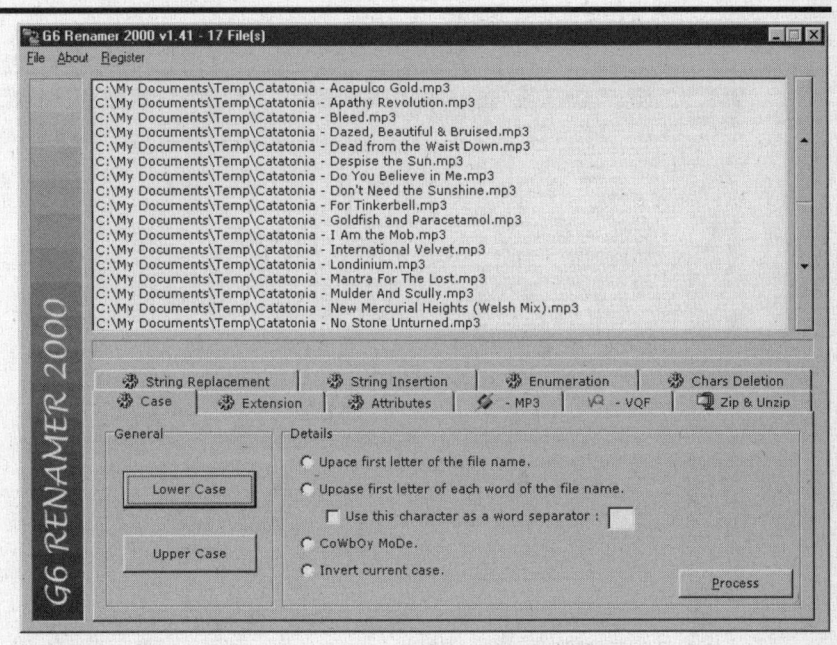

FIGURE 20.14: G6 Renamer provides multiple features in an easy-to-use interface.

Replacing a String in a Filename

The first operation you'll probably want to perform with G6 Renamer is to replace a string in a filename with another string. (A *string* is any number of text characters from 0 upwards. A zero-character string is called an *empty string* or a *blank string*.)

For example, say you've ripped a CD's worth of files with the CD name misspelled (perhaps courtesy of somebody else's mistyping in CDDB). You can fix the CD name by using the String Replacement page of G6 Renamer, shown in Figure 20.15, specifying the string you want to replace in the Replace text box and the replacement text in the By text box. Leave the Ignore Case check box selected (as it is by default) if you don't want to discriminate by case (uppercase or lowercase). Leave the All Occurrences check box selected (as it too is by default) if you want to replace every occurrence of the string.

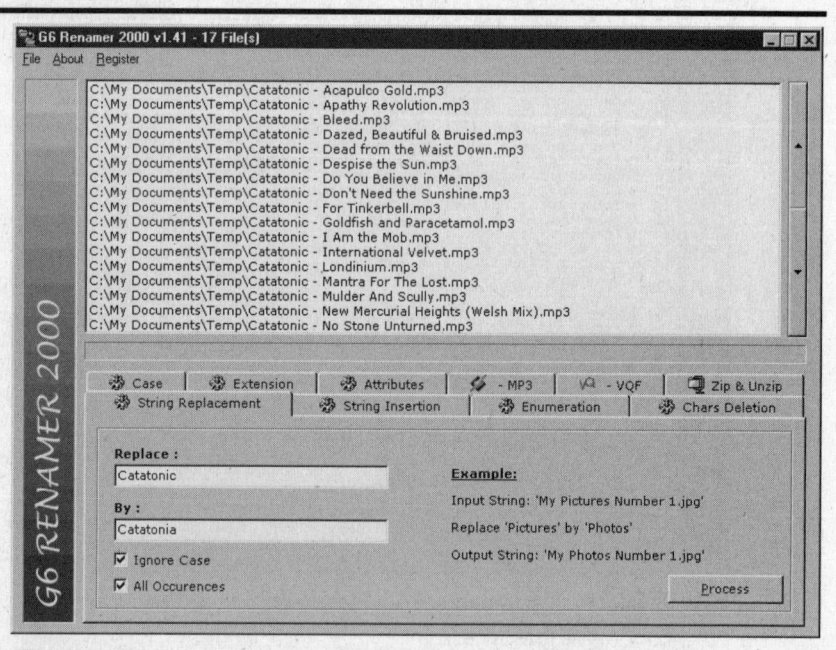

FIGURE 20.15: Use the String Replacement page of G6 Renamer to replace one string of text with another string.

TIP

Two quick tips: First, you can use an empty string as the replacement text to remove the target string. For example, suppose you want to change all instances of "Joan Jett and the Blackhearts" to "Joan Jett" for brevity. You could replace the string "Joan Jett and the Blackhearts" with the string "Joan Jett," but you could also replace the string "and the Blackhearts" with an empty string. Second, remember to include spaces in the strings where appropriate.

Inserting a String in a Filename

Often, you can use the string-replacement feature to insert a string in a filename. (For example, if you wanted to add the album name *Parachutes* to some Coldplay tracks, you could replace the string "Coldplay –" with the string "Coldplay – Parachutes –".)

Other times, you may need to insert a string in a constant position on tracks that do not include constant information in their names for example, if you're inserting information into the names of tracks by different artists on a compilation album. For this task, use the String Insertion page of G6 Renamer, shown in Figure 20.16. Enter the string in the String to Insert text box, then use the Position to Insert text box to specify the character position in which to insert it. Watch the Example area to see the effect of your change.

For example, specify **1** to insert the text at the beginning of the filename. Select the Append Mode check box if you want to append the string to the end of the filename before the extension. When the Append Mode check box is selected, the value in the Position to Insert text box does not apply.

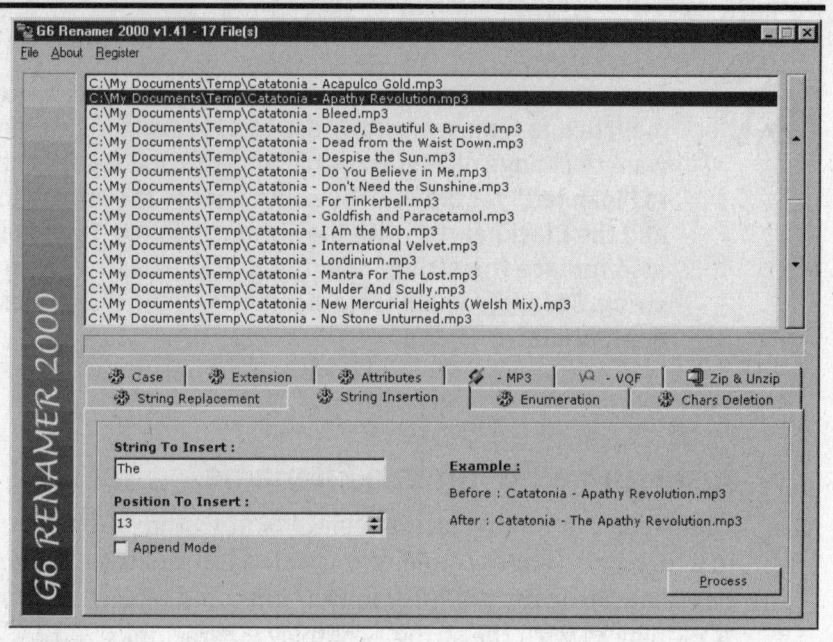

FIGURE 20.16: Use the String Insertion page of G6 Renamer to insert a string of text within the file names.

Renaming MP3 Files or VQF Files by ID3 Tag Information

If you have misnamed but correctly tagged MP3 files or VQF files, the renaming feature implemented on the MP3 page (see Figure 20.17) and the VQF page may be of interest. This feature lets you specify the *mask* (format) that G6 Renamer should use to construct the new name for the file from the tag information. For example, by specifying **%A - %B - %T**, you can find filenames consisting of the artist's name, the album name, and the track title—for instance, *Pink Floyd – The Wall – Goodbye, Blue Sky*.

Working with MP3 Files

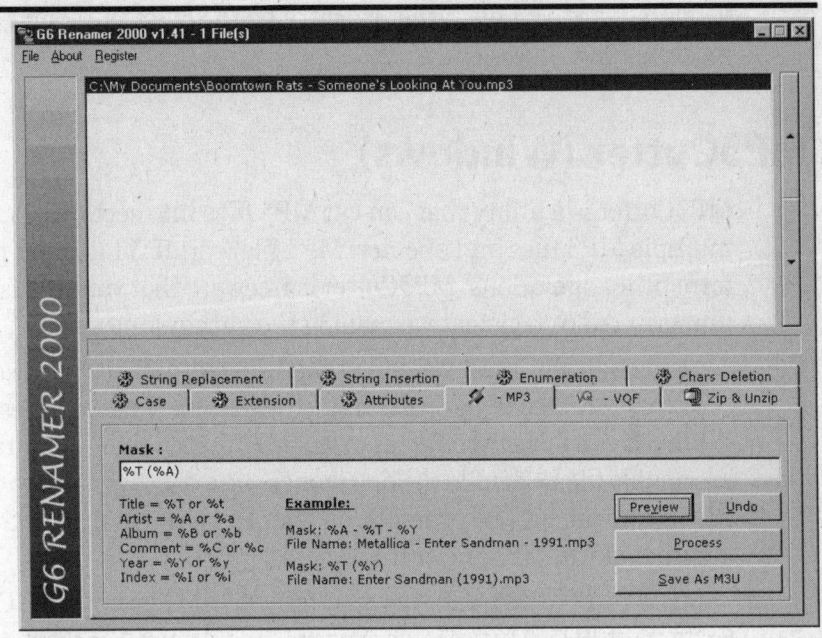

FIGURE 20.17: Use the MP3 page to rename MP3 files by the information included in their tags.

Renaming MP3 files on Linux

id3ren, which we mentioned in the section on editing ID3 tags earlier in this chapter, also offers functions for renaming MP3 files.

Editing MP3 Files (Windows, Linux)

Because MP3 is a compressed format, the files are difficult to edit. To change an MP3 file, you usually need to decode it to PCM audio (for example, WAV format or AIFF format) and edit it there, then convert the result back to MP3. In doing so, you'll lose audio quality, so in most cases, you'll get a better result from encoding a new version of an MP3 file rather than trying to adjust the sound of an existing file.

MP3Cutter (Windows)

MP3Cutter is a utility that can cut MP3 files into sections, paste multiple MP3 files into one new MP3 file, edit ID3 tags, and perform other operations. MP3Cutter is freeware that you can use unregistered or register by e-mailing the author for a serial number.

Download the latest version of MP3Cutter from `members.xoom.com/_XMCM/videoripper/mp3cutter/index.htm`. Unzip the files to the folder from which you want to run MP3Cutter, then either run the executable file by double-clicking it or create a shortcut for it somewhere convenient (for example, on your Desktop or on your Start menu) and run MP3Cutter from there.

MP3Cutter has an easy-to-use interface with seven pages: Cut, Paste, Edit, ID3, MusicMatch, Special, and About. For most operations, you'll want to start by using the Browse button and the resulting Select a File dialog box (see Figure 20.18) to select the file that you want to work with. (For Paste operations, you'll want to select multiple files, as we'll discuss in a bit.) Use the left-hand and center list boxes to select the drive, folder, and file as usual, and use the readout in the bottom part of the dialog box to make sure you've got the correct file and not a near relative. If necessary, you can use the Play button or the Autoplay check box on the right-hand side to play the track for identification. Click the Open button to open the track.

You'll see the Scanning dialog box as MP3Cutter scans the file, then MP3Cutter displays the About page, which boasts the author's photo and registration information. This page won't get you far, so click the tab for the page you want to work on and get down to business.

Figure 20.19 shows the Cut page, which lets you cut from one specified second and frame of a track to another.

Working with MP3 Files 781

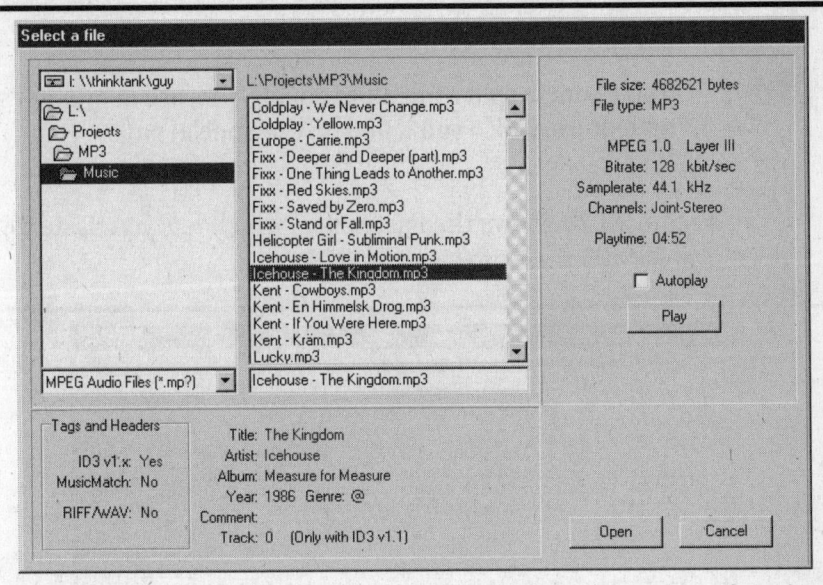

FIGURE 20.18: Use MP3Cutter's Select a File dialog box to identify and select the file you want to manipulate.

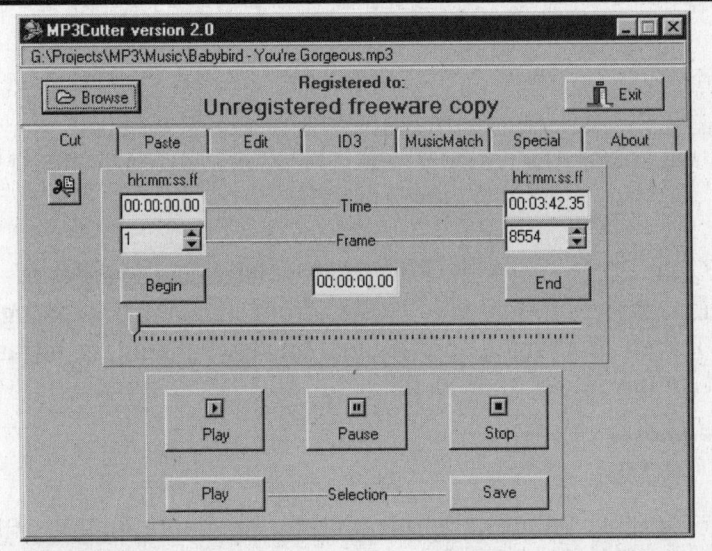

FIGURE 20.19: Use the Cut page of MP3Cutter to cut a track into segments.

> **NOTE**
>
> If you want to split a track into equal parts, use MP3Cutter's Splitter feature, which you'll find on the Special page.

Figure 20.20 shows the Paste page, which lets you paste together multiple MP3 files into a single MP3 file.

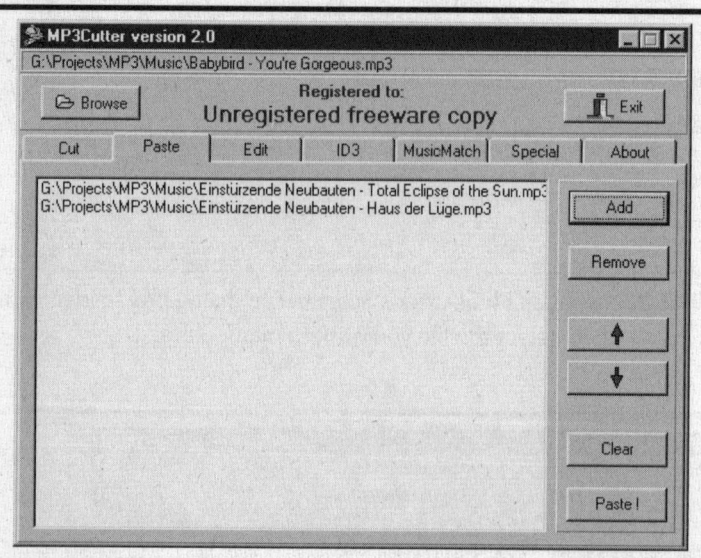

FIGURE 20.20: Use the Paste page of MP3Cutter to paste multiple MP3 files into a single new file.

Figure 20.21 shows the Edit page, which offers a variety of options for manipulating MP3 files, from changing the settings of the Private, Copyright, and Original bits to changing the bitrate and sample rate of an MP3 file.

> **NOTE**
>
> Another Windows application for manipulating MP3 files is mp3Trim (www.logiccell.com/~mp3trim/).

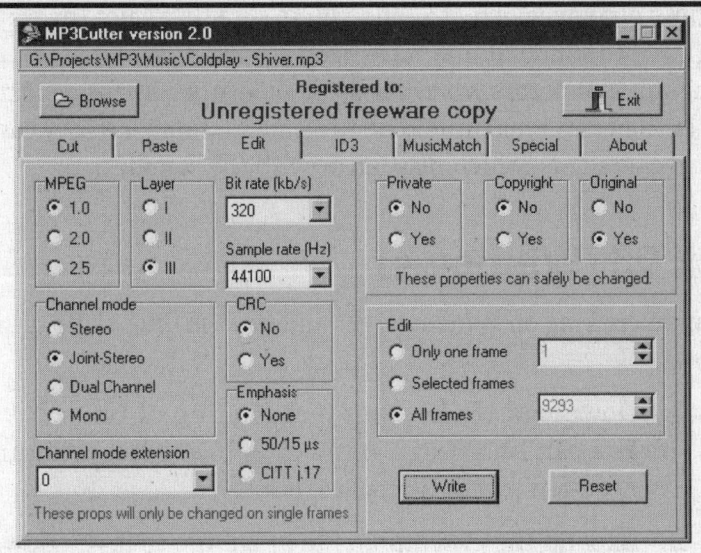

FIGURE 20.21: Use the options on the Edit page to manipulate MP3 files.

mp3asm (Linux)

mp3asm, which you can download from www.ozemail.com.au/~crn/mp3asm.html, is a command-line utility for Linux and Unix. mp3asm performs three main functions:

- Checking MP3 files for damage
- Fixing damaged MP3 files
- Assembling (combining) multiple MP3 files into one MP3 file (whence the name MP3 assemble)

Repairing Cooked Files (Windows, Linux)

If an MP3 file that you've downloaded from the Internet sounds not just bad but truly terrible—for example, it sounds as though it's nothing but squeaky noise—and you're sure that's not the way it's supposed to sound, it may have been *cooked*. *Cooking* is a type of mangling that occurs when a server sends an audio file as text rather than as a binary file. The text includes unnecessary carriage-return characters, which play havoc with the sound.

Uncook 95 (Windows)

To undo cooking on Windows, get and use the Uncook 95 utility as follows:

1. Download the current distribution of Uncook 95. You can find it at a number of locations, including free-music.com/uncook95.htm.

2. Expand the executable file or zip file that you downloaded.

3. Run the resulting executable file. You'll see the Uncook 95 window (see Figure 20.22).

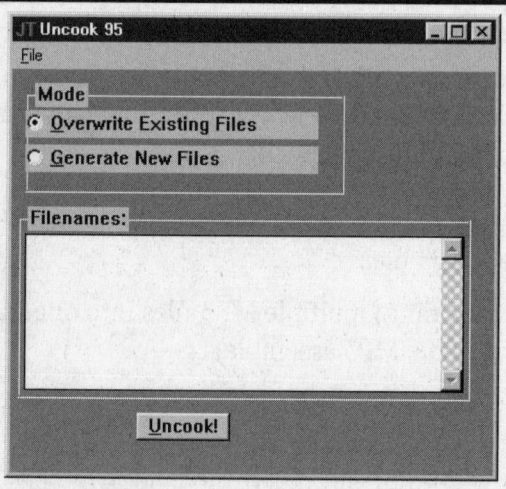

FIGURE 20.22: Uncook 95 is a utility for uncooking cooked MP3 files.

4. Choose File ➢ Open to display the Open dialog box, select the MP3 file or MP3 files you want to uncook, and

Working with MP3 Files

click the Open button. Uncook adds the files to the Filenames text box (see Figure 20.23).

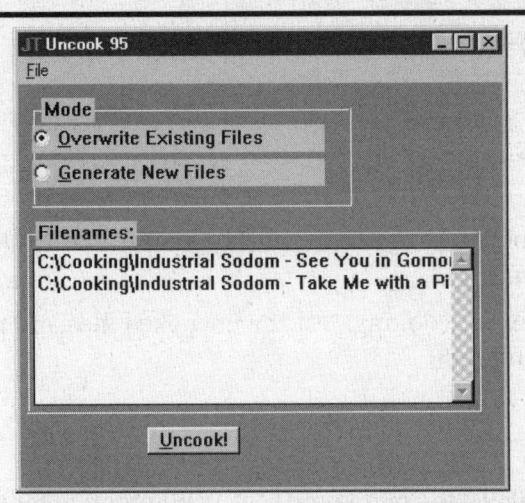

FIGURE 20.23: Uncook 95 with two files ready for uncooking

5. In the Mode group box, make sure that the appropriate option button is selected:

   Overwrite Existing Files option button Select this button only if you're 200 percent sure that the files are cooked and that you want to overwrite the originals with the uncooked versions.

   Generate New Files option button Select this button if there's even the slightest doubt in your mind about the files being cooked. If you use this option, Uncook creates new files named "Copy of *the original filename.*"

6. Click the Uncook button to uncook the files. Uncook displays the Files Are Uncooked message box, shown in Figure 20.24, telling you when the files are uncooked. Note that this message box lists only the first of the files that was uncooked.

FIGURE 20.24: When the files have been uncooked, you'll see the Files Are Uncooked! message box.

7. Uncook more files as necessary, then choose File ➢ Quit to exit Uncook.

When you're done uncooking, test the uncooked files and make sure that they sound right.

> **NOTE**
>
> Another Windows (or, more precisely, DOS) program for removing extra carriage returns from an MP3 file is Detox.

mp3asm (Linux)

mp3asm (discussed in the previous section) includes features for uncooking cooked files.

Creating Playlists (Windows, Mac, Linux)

As you saw in the chapters on MP3 players and jukeboxes, most players and jukeboxes have features for creating playlists. If your player or jukebox doesn't have adequate features for creating playlists, you may want to supplement it with a custom utility. This section presents a few of the many possibilities.

Creating Playlists on Windows

As you saw earlier in this book, you'll have no problem creating playlists with many Windows MP3 players and jukeboxes, including Winamp, Sonique, FreeAmp, MusicMatch Jukebox, and Real-Jukebox. But if your player or jukebox doesn't have playlist features, or if you want a little variety, consider a utility such as Playlist Pro or ShufflePlay, which we'll discuss in the next sections.

Playlist Pro

Playlist Pro is an easy-to-use freeware playlist editor that you can find at many MP3 sites. Download the latest version, unzip the distribution zip file to a temporary folder, and then double-click setup.exe to run the setup routine.

First, tell Playlist Pro which MP3 player to use. Choose Player ➤ Install Player to display the Player Selection dialog box (see Figure 20.25). Choose the MP3 player—at this writing, Playlist Pro supports Winamp, WinPlay3, MaPlay, and Nad—and click the Continue button. When Playlist Pro displays the Location dialog box, navigate to the location of the MP3 player, select the executable file, and click the Open button.

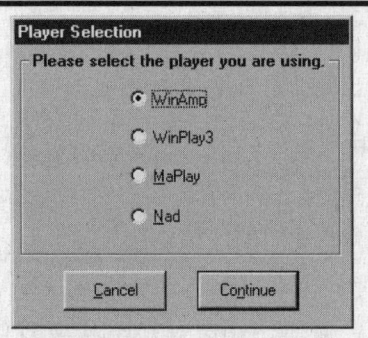

FIGURE 20.25: In the Player Selection dialog box, choose the MP3 player you're using.

Next, add the MP3 files on your system to Playlist Pro's database. Choose File ➤ Search Directories for MP3s to have Playlist Pro find the MP3 files on your system and add them to its database.

Once you've done that, you're ready to create playlists, as shown in Figure 20.26. Select the files in the left-hand list box, then click the Add button to add them to the playlist. Use the Remove button to remove any stray files that sneak into the playlist. Use the Up and Down buttons to rearrange the tracks to your liking, or use the Shuffle button to rearrange them to chance's liking. Then choose File ➤ Save Playlist (or press Ctrl+S) to display the Save Playlist dialog box. Specify the name, location, and file type for the playlist, and click the Save button to save it. Then click the Play button to start the playlist playing.

FIGURE 20.26: Creating a playlist with Playlist Pro

ShufflePlay

For creating playlists in the M3U format, you may want to try ShufflePlay, a shareware playlist editor that you can find at many MP3 sites. You get 14 days to evaluate the software before registering, which costs $10. Download the latest version you can find, unzip the distribution zip file to a convenient temporary folder, and then double-click the `setup.exe` file to run the setup routine.

The first time you run ShufflePlay, you'll see a Welcome message box. When you dismiss it, ShufflePlay displays the Setup dialog box (see Figure 20.27), which you use to configure ShufflePlay to your liking. ShufflePlay has a goodly number of options; we'll mention only the most important options in the following paragraphs.

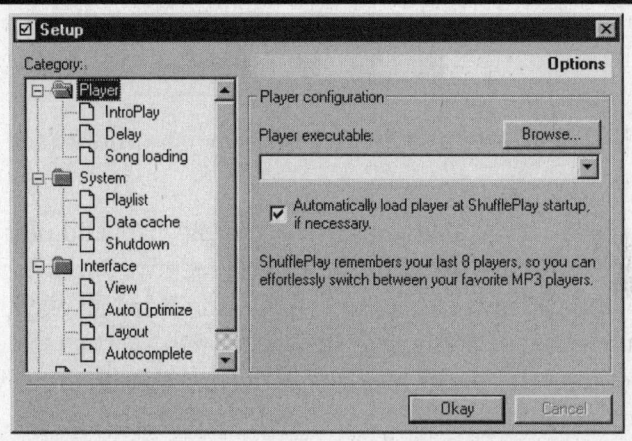

FIGURE 20.27: The first time you run ShufflePlay, it displays the Setup dialog box to encourage you to configure ShufflePlay for your needs.

First, make sure the Player item in the Category list box is selected. Click the Browse button and use the resulting Open dialog box to navigate to and select the executable file for your MP3 player (for example, `Winamp.exe`). Then click the Open button to enter its path and filename into the Player Executable text box. Make sure that the Automatically Load Player at ShufflePlay Startup,

If Necessary check box is selected if you want ShufflePlay to fire up this player as needed. (This is usually a good idea.)

Next, if you're using Winamp or Nad, click the Song Loading item and choose the appropriate mode for loading playlists into the player. Usually you'll want the Fast Snap item in the Loading Mode drop-down list. (If you find that fast snap mode causes problems, drop back to regular snap mode or conventional mode.) In the When Loading More Than NNN Song(s), Use drop-down list, you'll probably want to leave the Conventional item selected, as it is by default, but you may want to increase the number of songs from its default 200.

Click the System item to display the System options and choose the type of shuffle you want: a simple shuffle (a single pass and random allocation) or an enhanced shuffle, in which ShufflePlay reduces the chance that tracks by the same artists will be played one after the other.

Click the Playlist item to display the Playlist options (see Figure 20.28):

- If you want to be able to transfer your playlists and files to other computers, select the Store with Relative Paths check box. ShufflePlay then stores the file details in the playlists with relative paths (shorter paths relative to a certain folder) rather than those with absolute paths that specify the drive, folder, subfolder or subfolders, and filename.

- Select the Remember Last Playlist check box if you want ShufflePlay to save your last playlist automatically at the end of a ShufflePlay session and load it in the next session so that you can pick up where you left off.

- Select the Hide Non-Existent Playlist Entries check box if you want ShufflePlay to hide entries that it can't open. (This

Working with MP3 Files 791

is usually a good idea, but you may be puzzled that some files apparently disappear from your playlists.)

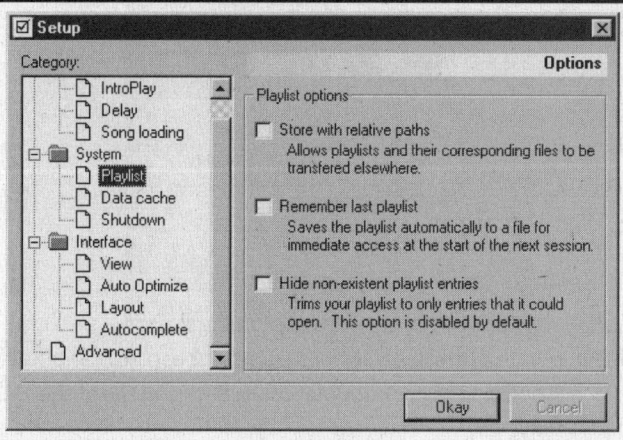

FIGURE 20.28: Choose playlist options on the Playlist page of the Setup Browser dialog box.

By default, ShufflePlay prompts you to save any unsaved changes to your current playlist when you exit the application. If you change your playlists frequently but don't want to save changes to them, you may want to alter this behavior. Click the Shutdown item to display the Shutdown options, then select the Never Ask to Save Playlist at Shutdown option button and choose either the Automatically Save List option button or the Don't Do Anything at All option button.

Click the Interface item to display the Interface options (see Figure 20.29). Choose how you want your double-clicks and your presses of the Delete key to be interpreted in the file selector and the song playlist.

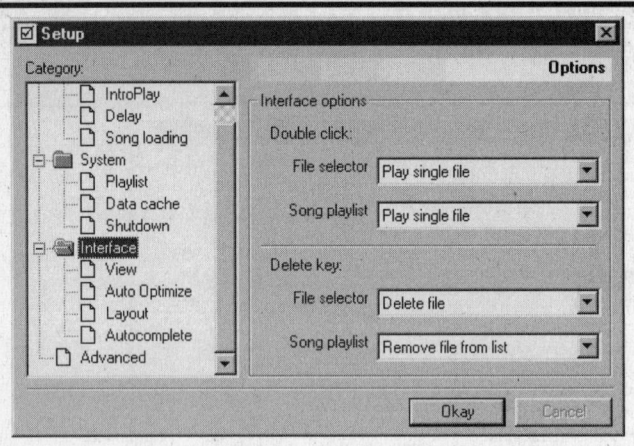

FIGURE 20.29: On the Interface options page, choose how ShufflePlay should interpret double-clicks and presses of the Delete key.

Other options that you may want to investigate on your own time include the following:

- The View options, which let you control how ShufflePlay manifests itself (for example, whether it appears on the Taskbar, in the system tray, or both).
- The Auto Optimize options, which align the columns to display as much information as possible in the available space
- The Layout options, which let you choose between a wider playlist or a taller tree
- The AutoComplete option, which enables automatic completion for fields

Once you've finished choosing options for ShufflePlay, click the Okay button to close the Setup dialog box.

You'll then see the Tip of the Day dialog box. Browse more tips if you like by using the Next Tip button, or clear the Show Tips on Startup check box to prevent ShufflePlay from showing you any more. Then click the Okay button.

Working with MP3 Files 793

Once you've got ShufflePlay running, you can use the tree on the left-hand side to navigate to a folder containing MP3 files (see Figure 20.30). From there, you can drag and drop files into the playlist in the lower portion of the ShufflePlay window, or use commands such as Folder ➢ Add This Folder, Folder ➢ Recurse Folder, or Folder ➢ Recurse Virtual Drives to add or scan specific folders or drives. (Use the Folder ➢ Recurse My Computer command to scan all the drives available to your computer.)

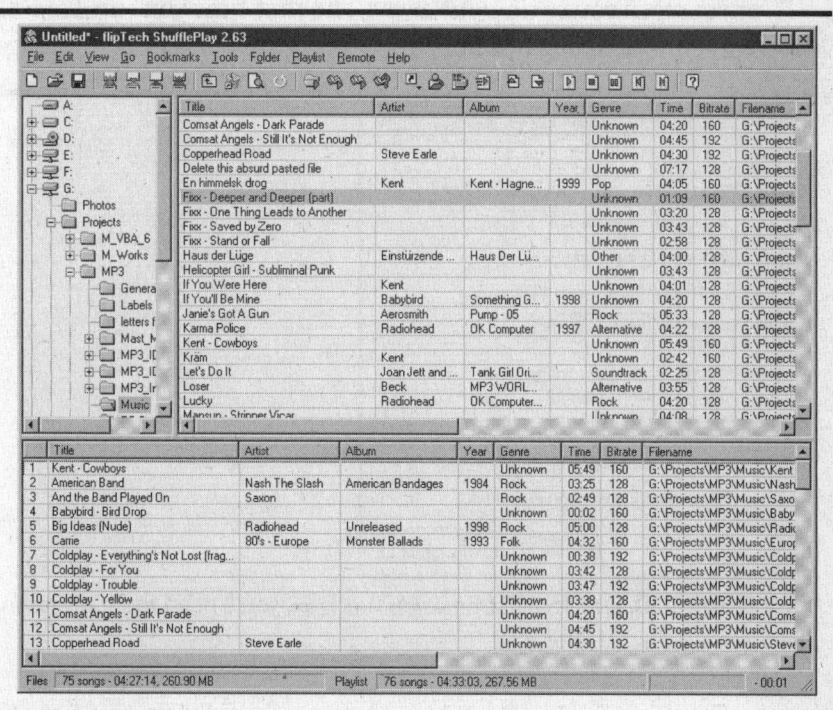

FIGURE 20.30: Creating a playlist with ShufflePlay

Once you've created a playlist, you can save it by issuing a File ➢ Save command, specifying the location and name in the Save dialog box, and clicking the Save button. You can play items on the playlist by using the commands on the Playlist menu and the Remote menu.

Creating Playlists on the Mac

One of our favorite utilities for creating playlists on the Mac is Trax.

You can find Trax at many Mac software archives and at MP3 sites such as MP3.com. Download the latest version of Trax, let it unstuff itself, and double-click the Trax item in the resulting folder to start the application.

Trax is easy to use once you've set your preferences, which it encourages you to do right away: The first time you run Trax, the Preferences dialog box appears (see Figure 20.31).

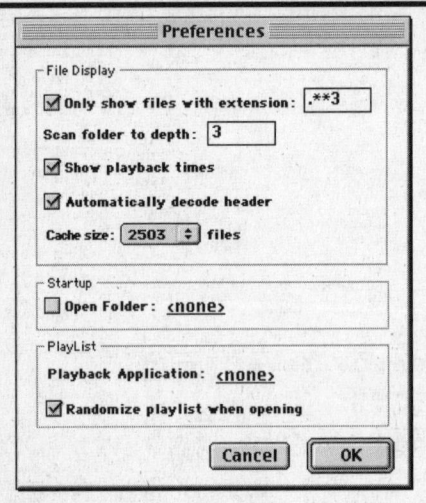

FIGURE 20.31: The first time you run Trax, you'll need to set preferences for it.

The File Display group box contains the following preferences:

Only Show Files with Extension check box and text box   If you want to filter the files displayed, select this check box (it's selected by default) and specify the filter in the text box. The default filter is .**3, which includes files with extensions such as MP3 and MPEG3.

Scan Folder to Depth text box Specify the number of folders deep to scan on your system. The default number is 3, but you'll want to increase this number if you have a deeply nested folder structure.

Show Playback Times check box This check box controls whether Trax displays the track lengths (the "playback times") in the playlist window.

Automatically Decode Header check box This check box controls whether Trax automatically decodes the header on each track. Turning off the decoding of headers speeds up Trax's display of folders that you open, particularly on a slow Mac.

Cache Size drop-down list This drop-down list lets you specify the number of files for Trax to keep in its cache. At this writing, the preset values are 101, 499, 997, 2503, and 4999. The more files you keep in the cache, the more memory Trax will need, but the quicker you'll be able to access them. If you're accessing files on a CD drive, set a high cache size.

The Startup group box contains just one preference:

Open Folder check box If you want to specify the folder that Trax should open on startup, click the link and use the resulting dialog box to select the folder.

The PlayList group box contains these two options:

Playback Application selector Click the link to display a dialog box in which you can select your MP3 player or jukebox.

Randomize Playlist when Opening check box Select this check box if you want Trax to put each playlist into random order when you open it.

When you've made your selections, click the OK button to close the Preferences dialog box. The Trax window appears with an empty playlist titled (so to speak) Untitled.

To create a playlist in Trax, open a *source folder*—a folder that contains music files. You can open your source folder either by dragging the folder over the Trax icon in the Finder or by choosing File ➢ Open Source Folder, selecting the folder in the resulting dialog box, and clicking the Open button. Trax opens a window listing the files. You can then double-click a file to add it to the current playlist or select the files you want and click the Add button (the button with the plus sign on it). Figure 20.32 shows a playlist being created.

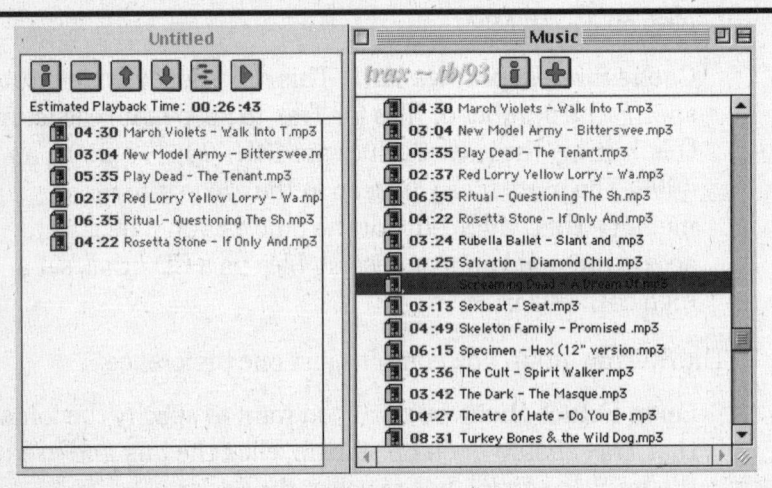

FIGURE 20.32: Adding tracks to a Trax playlist

Once you've added tracks to the playlist, arrange them into the order you want. You can use either the buttons at the top of the playlist window or the keyboard shortcuts listed in Table 20.1.

TABLE 20.1: Keyboard Shortcuts for the Trax Playlist Window

KEYBOARD SHORTCUT	ACTION
Apple+↑	Moves the selected track up one position in the playlist.
Apple+↓	Moves the selected track down one position in the playlist.
Apple+I	Makes Trax read the header information for the selected track.
Return	Deletes the selected file.
Delete	Deletes the selected file.

You can then save the playlist by choosing File ➢ Save and using the resulting dialog box to specify the name and location for the file. You can send the playlist to the MP3 player you designated in the Preferences dialog box by choosing Trax ➢ Send List to Player.

Creating Playlists on Linux

Linux programmers have created an almost frightening wealth of playlist editors for Linux. We won't look at any in depth here, but you might want to start by investigating MP3 Commander and Gm3u.

CREATING EXECUTABLE MP3 FILES WITH MP3 TO EXE (WINDOWS)

As you've seen so far in this book, you need a MP3 player to play MP3 files. Getting an MP3 player is no hardship, but what if someone doesn't want to (or cannot) install a player on their PC, and does not even have Windows Media Player installed? For example, your company's MIS department may restrict employees from installing *any* program—even a screen saver—on company computers. If they catch you with an unauthorized MP3 player on your machine, your career (or at least your friendly relationship with MIS) is over.

Oliver Buschjost's MP3 to EXE converter provides the solution, allowing you to wrap an MP3 file into an executable file.

> **WARNING**
>
> MP3 to EXE is a cool utility, but it's problematic in this wicked world of ours. Because executable files can contain a multitude of sins that no virus checker yet invented can uncover, you may want to send executable MP3 files only to people who already trust you. Anyone else should delete them on sight—if their anti-virus software hasn't done so already.

MP3 to EXE is a $15 shareware product that you can download from www.mp3toexe.com. Unlike some shareware, it's not a crippled version, so you can try it out thoroughly before paying.

Once you've downloaded MP3 to EXE, unzip it and double-click the executable file to run the installation routine. As usual, you get to select a destination directory and Start menu group for it.

Launch MP3 to EXE and you'll see the MP3 to EXE Converter window, shown in Figure 20.33 with a track ready for conversion.

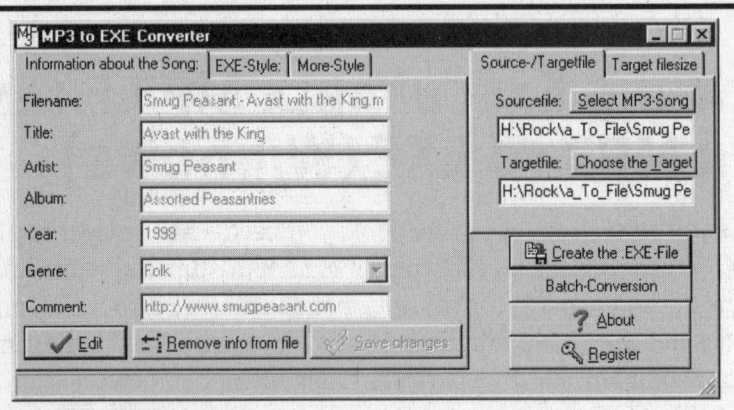

FIGURE 20.33: MP3 to EXE is a utility that packages MP3 files as executable files.

Working with MP3 Files 799

Here's how to use MP3 to EXE:

1. Click the Select MP3-Song button to display the Open dialog box.

2. Select the track and click the Open button. MP3 to EXE displays the track's name in the Sourcefile text box and a suggested EXE name in the Targetfile text box. MP3 to EXE also enters information from the track's filename and tag in the Information About the Song panel.

3. Change the Targetfile name if you want.

4. If you need to edit the track information, click the Edit button to enable the text boxes.

5. To choose options for the EXE file, click the EXE-Style tab to display the EXE-Style page, and make your choices. We recommend going with the standard settings, but if you must, you can do antisocial things like setting a default volume, locking the volume, and looping the track.

6. To choose yet more options, click the More-Style tab to display the More-Style page, shown in Figure 20.34. Here, you can enter a URL and caption to display, and you can choose to make the track expire at a given point in the future.

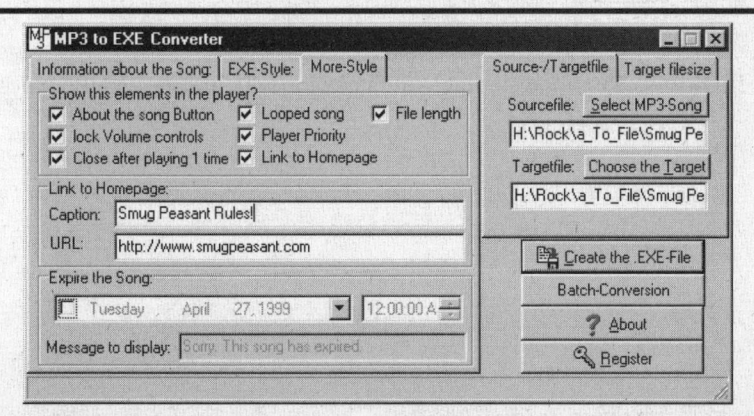

FIGURE 20.34: If necessary, choose more options on the More-Style page of MP3 to EXE Converter window.

7. To split the executable file into several smaller files to make it easier to distribute, click the Target Filesize tab to display the Target Filesize page. Select the Split into Several Files check box, and then specify a maximum file size in the Maximum Filesize group box.

8. Click the Create the .EXE-File button to create the executable. You'll see a progress bar in the lower-right corner of the window as MP3 to EXE builds the executable. When it's done, MP3 to EXE displays the Confirm dialog box offering to execute the file for you.

9. Click the Yes button or the No button as appropriate.

> **NOTE**
>
> To convert multiple MP3 files to EXE files, click the Batch-Conversion button and work in the MP3 to EXE Converter – Batchmode dialog box.

Figure 20.35 shows an executable MP3 file playing.

FIGURE 20.35: An executable MP3 playing with its built-in MP3 player

Entering Information in CDDB (Windows, Mac, Linux)

As you've seen so far in this book, CDDB is a fantastic database of information about CDs, containing artist and track information about an amazing number of CDs. But if you have CDs that are old, new, borrowed, or blues, CDDB may well not have them.

When you run into a CD that CDDB can't identify, it's your chance to give a little back to the online music community by adding the CD's information to the CDDB. Most CDDB-compliant players and rippers provide a mechanism for adding this information.

Here's an example using MusicMatch Jukebox:

1. When MusicMatch Jukebox has queried CDDB and come up empty, open the Recorder window if it's not already open.

2. Enter the album name in the Album text box, the artist's name in the Artist text box, and the names of the tracks in the track list text boxes.

3. Choose Options ➢ Recorder ➢ Send Album Info to CDDB. MusicMatch Jukebox grinds for a moment and then displays the Submit to CDDB dialog box, shown in Figure 20.36. MusicMatch Jukebox has filled in the artist's name, the album name, and the track names from the Recorder window, together with the CDDB DiscID (from the CD).

4. Check the artist, album, and track names. (Any typos or errors in capitalization may result in CDDB users cursing you for years to come.)

5. Select the appropriate genre in the Genre drop-down list.

6. Enter your e-mail address in the Your Email Address text box.

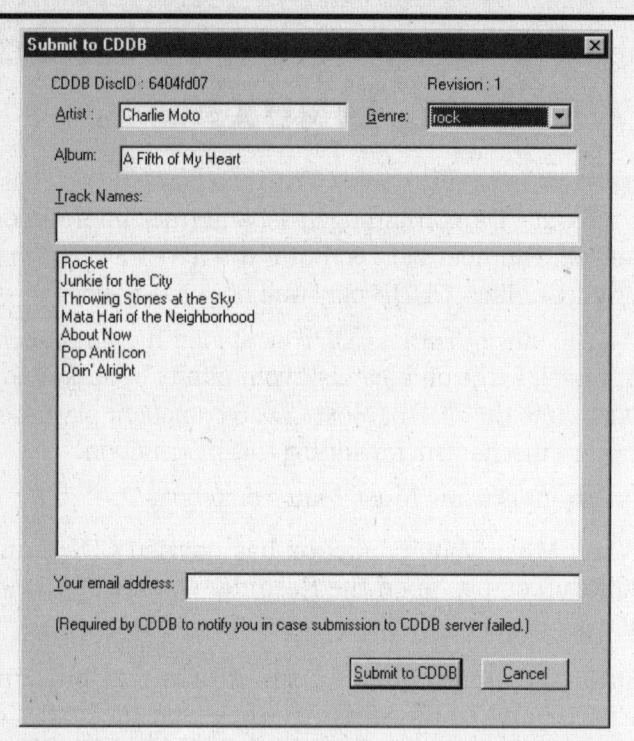

FIGURE 20.36: Use the CDDB dialog box in MusicMatch Jukebox to submit to CDDB information on CDs that CDDB doesn't yet list.

   7. Check everything once again, then click the Submit to CDDB button. MusicMatch Jukebox displays the snappily named MMSITESERV message box shown in Figure 20.37. Wait till the excitement subsides, then click the OK button to dismiss the message box.

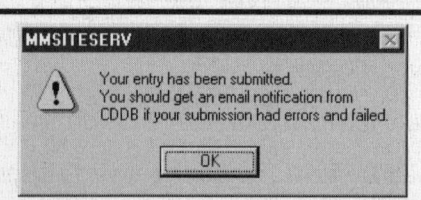

FIGURE 20.37: MusicMatch Jukebox displays the MMSITESERV message box to let you know when it's finished submitting information to CDDB.

If your submission is new, you won't hear anything from CDDB. (To make sure that the information took, visit the CDDB site in a day or two and plug the artist's name and the CD into the search engine.) But if your submission is a duplicate, CDDB may send you an e-mail telling you politely to go climb a medium-sized tree. Do so with joy.

Up Next

In this chapter, you've seen how to perform a half-dozen odd operations with MP3 files. These operations ranged from the frequently needed, such as renaming MP3 files and editing their tags, to operations you'll most likely need to perform only seldom, such as entering CD information in CDDB.

The next chapter focuses on style over substance, discussing how to create your own custom skins for Winamp and RealJukebox.

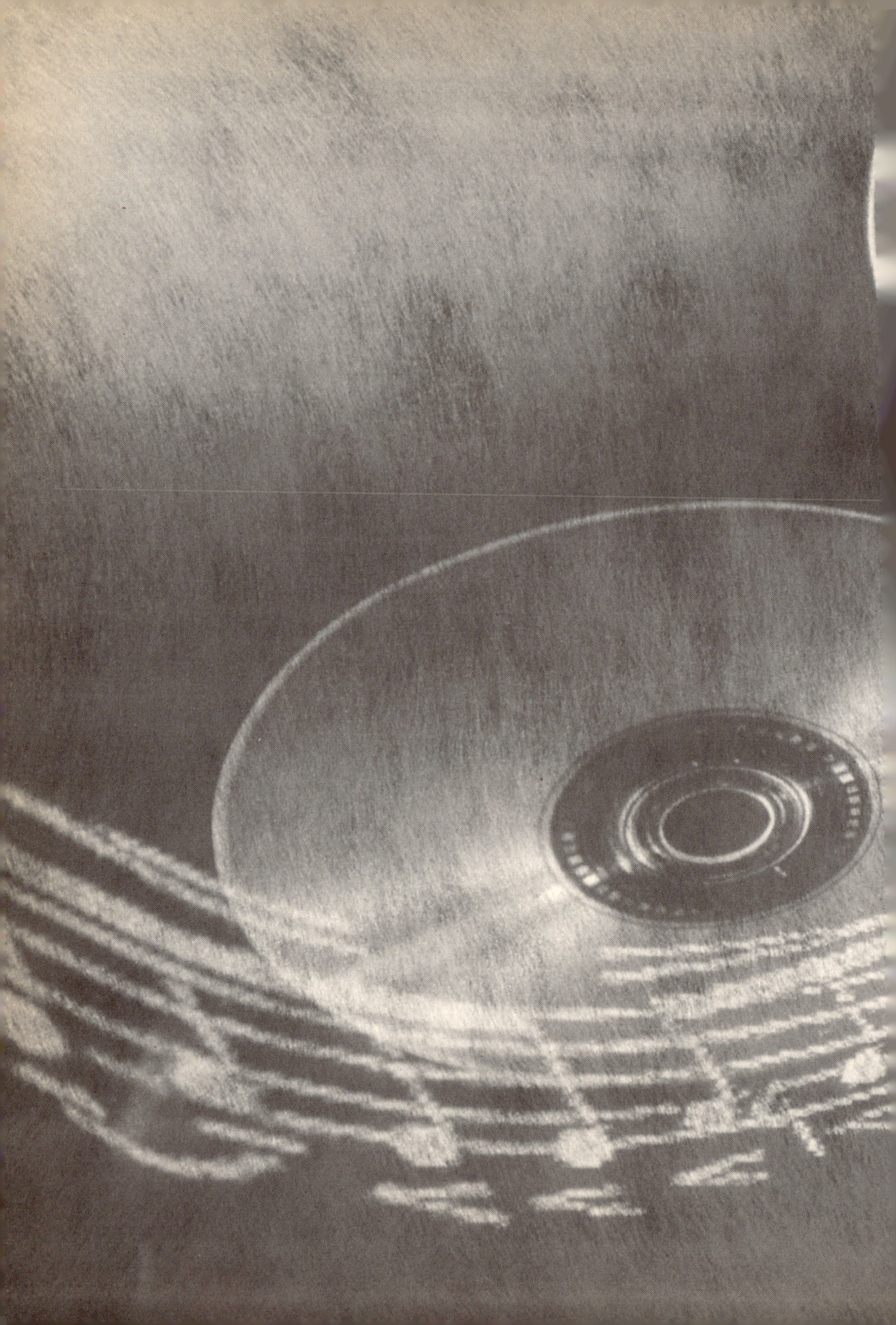

Chapter 21

Creating Skins for Winamp and RealJukebox

Featuring

- Why create skins?
- Creating skins for Winamp
- Creating skins for RealJukebox
- Converting Winamp skins to RealJukebox skins

This chapter discusses how to create skins for two of the most widely used MP3 software packages: the Windows player Winamp and the Windows jukebox RealJukebox. The chapter starts by touching quickly on why you'd want to create skins (that part's simple), and then outlines the process of creating skins for each of the applications.

Why Create Skins?

As you saw earlier in this book, a skin is to an MP3 player or jukebox somewhere between what skin and clothes are to people. A skin provides a different graphical interface for the player, just as a set of clothes provides a different graphical interface for a human. (Graphical? Yes—beneath your 501s or your Armani, you're still a mess of carbon, hydrogen, and questionable opinions.) By applying a new skin, you can completely change the look of your MP3 player or jukebox—for your own visual excitement, to impress your friends, or to confuse your parents.

If skins are like clothes that you can change, why did we say that skins are like human skin? Because you can change your skin by painting, tattooing, or branding it. You can get most paint off easily, but changing tattoos and brands is much harder. (One theory holds that that's why clothing got invented.)

As with clothes (and tattoos; we're divided on brands), skins can be elegant, stylish, garish, offensive, outrageous, or just plain ugly. If you look around, you'll find that people have created skins that comfortably illustrate all those adjectives and more. This is particularly true for Winamp, which at this writing has far more skins available than other skinnable players and jukeboxes. (At this writing, Winamp.com alone has something on the order of 10,000 Winamp skins available for downloading.)

Creating Skins for Winamp

This section discusses how to create skins for the Winamp MP3 player.

Winamp comes with a default skin (shown in Figure 21.1) that's clean, functional, and—by some standards—good-looking. But given the plethora of skins available, most people like to try other skins from time to time. Some people even like to create their own skins. Creating a skin isn't difficult, but it takes a little time—particularly if you want to create something complex.

FIGURE 21.1: Winamp's default skin is clean, functional—and altogether too sober by half for a lot of people.

As we mentioned, there are already thousands of skins available for Winamp. Here are a few samples to give you some idea of the range of skins that people have created already:

- SketchAmp, shown in Figure 21.2, provides a simple and informal look for Winamp.

FIGURE 21.2: SketchAmp gives Winamp a nicely executed informal makeover.

- Tomatoes Go Splat, shown in Figure 21.3, is based on a dramatic and doubtless alluring (for some) image of moist, ripe tomatoes.

FIGURE 21.3: Tomatoes Go Splat gives Winamp a juicy interface.

- Woody Wood Amp (shown in Figure 21.4) is a sleek-looking, wood-grained skin. (You've seen those fancy keyboards, monitors, and mice with a wooden overlay that the catalog firms sell to people with more money than sense? Woody Wood Amp would fit right in—only the price matches your budget, not theirs.)

FIGURE 21.4: Woody Wood Amp shows you how much wood Winamp could chuck if it could chuck wood.

With all the skins available, it might take you a serious while to find the one you want to live on your desktop. The good news comes in two parts: First, browsing for skins may take a while, but it's not exactly work. Second, you can create that perfect skin for yourself by following the techniques described in this section more quickly than browsing for the next best thing. And if your skin is really good, you can even inflict it on other people via Winamp.com or another skin site once you're done with it.

As you'll probably remember from Chapter 7, "Windows Players," skins live in the \skins\ folder under the \Winamp\ folder. The contents of a skin can either be in their own folder under the \skins\ folder or in a zip file there. Usually, you'll find zip files easier, because there's less mess and they take up less space.

Preparing for Skinning

To create a skin, you'll need several programs, as explained in the following sections, and you'll need the Winamp Base Skin.

Painting or Illustration Program

First, you'll need a painting or illustration program (also called a *bitmap editor*) for messing with the images. There's good news here: This is one of the few tasks that Microsoft Paint (which ships with most known versions of Windows) can handle. But many people prefer to use a more powerful program, such as Jasc's Paint Shop Pro. (You can download an evaluation version of Paint Shop Pro from www.jasc.com.)

If you already have Adobe Photoshop, lucky you—that'll more than get the job done. If you don't have Photoshop but feel inclined to try it, mosey your browser on over to www.adobe.com and see what you find. Before you decide to get Photoshop, be ready to invest a little time. Photoshop's not the easiest program in the world to use, but that's the price of power.

Icon Editor

For more advanced skins, you'll want to change the cursor images that go along with the skin. One of the better tools for changing cursor images is the icon editor Microangelo from Impact Software (www.impactsoft.com). You'll find a 30-day evaluation on Impact's Web site, which should see you through your initial burst of skinning. If you get heavily into skins, you'll want to cough up the cash for the registered version of Microangelo, which costs $59.95 at this writing.

Other icon editors include Icon Edit Pro and NeoSoft Icon Editor.

Text Editor

You also need a text editor—an application for creating and editing text files. Odds are that you already have one—just about every known operating system comes with a text editor. Windows is no exception: It provides Notepad, a limited and uninspiring text editor that's competent in what it does.

If Notepad is installed on your computer, you should find it on the Accessories menu (Start ➢ Programs ➢ Accessories). If it's not installed, dig out your Windows CD and install it.

You can also use a word processor such as Microsoft Word or WordPerfect to create and edit the necessary text files.

Winamp Base Skin

Now download the Winamp Base 2.*x* Skin from Winamp.com's Skins DIY area, www.winamp.com/nsdn/winamp2x/dev/skins/base.jhtml. This base skin serves as a template for the skins you create. Unzip the Winamp Base Skin to a new folder somewhere convenient.

> **NOTE**
>
> For other information on making skins for Winamp, check out Winamp.com's Skins DIY area, www.winamp.com/nsdn/winamp2x/dev/skins/base.jhtml.

Open the folder, and you'll find it contains 16 bitmap (BMP), 27 cursor (CUR), and 3 text (TXT) files. For the moment, we're interested in the bitmaps, because they represent the easiest

Creating Skins for Winamp and RealJukebox

parts of the Winamp skin to customize. Later on, we'll discuss the cursor files (which you can change to create your own cursors for the Winamp window) and the text files.

> **SKINNING PROGRAMS FOR WINAMP**
>
> If you don't want to take the time to create each bitmap for a Winamp skin manually, you may want to try one of the skinning programs that aim to take the heavy lifting out of creating skins.
>
> Generally speaking, these skinning programs don't give you the fine control you get when you manipulate the bitmaps by hand, but they can be a great way of getting the main bitmaps of the skin created quickly. After that, of course, you can change each bitmap manually until it looks the way you want it.
>
> Skinning programs include the following:
>
> - Skinmaster is available from `skinmaster.wego.com`.
>
> - Winamp Skin Maker, also known as Skinner, is available from many Internet sites, including the Tucows sites.
>
> - Winamp Trans Trace, which excels in creating transparencies, is available from `www.fortunecity.com/skyscraper/motorola/153/TransTrace.html`.
>
> - Winamp Skin Wizard, known for its button-extracting features, is available from `www.geocities.com/SouthBeach/6857/download.htm`.

The Golden Rules of Skinning

Before you start creating a skin, here are the golden rules you need to keep in mind.

1. The Rule of Intellectual Property

If you're going to base your skin on a picture, and you're going to distribute the skin, you must have the right to use the picture. If the picture's an original of yours, you shouldn't have a problem. If it's in the public domain, you shouldn't have a problem. But if the picture belongs to somebody else, you'll need to get their permission to use it.

> **NOTE**
>
> We're well aware that many people seem to violate intellectual property laws without appearing to suffer any consequences. (Those Heidi Klum amps that use pictures from *Sports Illustrated*—we seriously doubt that anybody got permission to use them.) But remember that these people *are* miserable sinners and will probably get the sharp end of the stick if the copyright holder goes after them.

2. The Rule of Antisocial Distortion

If you're going to use a photo as the basis for your skin, don't stretch it to make it the right size and shape because it'll look horrible. Instead, crop it. If the photo is too small, use your graphics program to add a delicate border to the sides. Or get a bigger photo. *Exception*: For purposes of parody, you can stretch a photo as much as you want.

Figure 21.5 shows Salma Hayek distorted widthwise.

FIGURE 21.5: Don't distort a picture to make it the right size, because the result will look dreadful, as you can see here.

Creating Skins for Winamp and RealJukebox 813

3. The Rule of Disfigurement

If you're using a photo, make sure the controls don't disfigure the photo. We know that this can be a tough order if you're trying to use a large photo but check out how Neve Campbell suffers in Neve Amp 1 (see Figure 21.6). The readouts in her hairline are marginally fetching, but the Vis display on her forehead is unpleasant, and the slider over her left eye is a disaster. And this was done (presumably) by someone who *likes* her...

FIGURE 21.6: Try not to obscure the photo with the controls, as has happened here...

Figure 21.7 shows Shania Twain suffering a similar fate. We bet that don't impress her much.

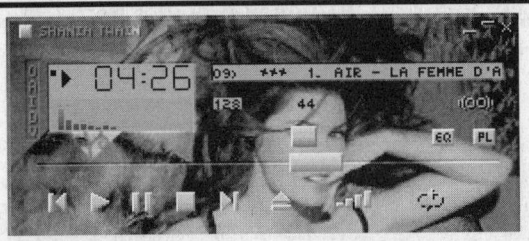

FIGURE 21.7: ...because nobody will like the effect.

By comparison, see how the creator of the Cindy Crawford amp shown in Figure 21.8 has placed her with her face almost entirely clear of disfigurement. To do so, they've suppressed the display of the track name.

FIGURE 21.8: Try to place the photo so that it won't suffer from the controls. If that's not possible, suppress a control or two, as has been done here.

4. The Rule of Accessible Controls

Next, make the controls visible; otherwise, they're not much use to the user. You can achieve a certain delicacy with the controls—they don't have to be outlined with the equivalent of an inch of mascara—but if someone has to guess at where to click to reach a control, you've got a problem with your skin. Do something about it.

Figure 21.9 shows a problem skin, 1914. It could be argued that the Add, Del, Sel, and Opt buttons on the Playlist Editor window are subtle, but the buttons on the Main window are impossible to decipher.

As an example of something with good controls, examine StoneAmp, shown in Figure 21.10, which provides both a great look and buttons that are visually distinct.

Creating Skins for Winamp and RealJukebox 815

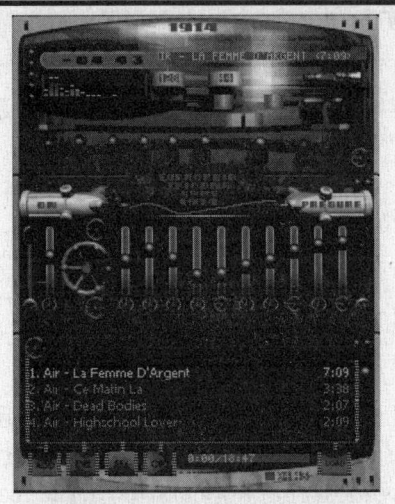

FIGURE 21.9: If you make the controls hard to identify, as they are here, the skin will be hard to use.

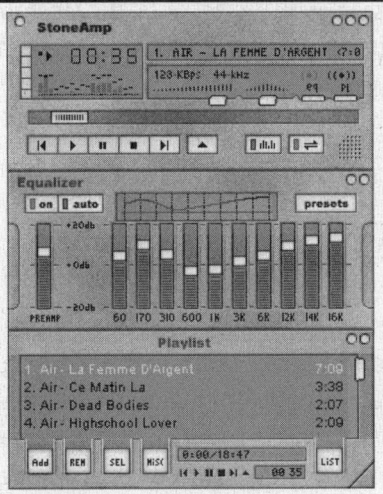

FIGURE 21.10: StoneAmp shows better visual distinction on the controls.

5. The Rule of the Configurable Player

Remember that the user won't always want to have all the Winamp windows open—even if you designed the skin so that it looks good only with two or three of the windows together.

For example, if the Main window contains only the celebrity's face down to the nose (as in the Neve Amp 1 example above), it won't look good without the window that's intended to go below it. In most skins, this will be the Graphical Equalizer window, because its size is fixed. The expandable Playlist Editor window will then appear below that.

Similarly, you should allow the user to resize the Playlist Editor window without ruining the effect. For best results, include the photo in only the part of the window that appears above the playlist. If you have a full-length picture of a loved one (or of a celebrity), you'll probably be tempted to use as much of it as possible. But this is usually a mistake, because many users will want to expand the Playlist Editor window lengthwise, widthwise, or both. Most people, however good-looking in real life, look terrible when you separate their upper body from their lower body by a long playlist.

Creating a Skin

You can create a skin either by painting a new picture or a new design in the appropriate bitmaps or by cutting up (and modifying if necessary) an existing picture file.

If you create a new picture or design of your own, you're creating an original work, and there are no copyright issues to worry about (unless you're directly copying an existing work). You also won't have any concerns about the size of the picture or the file format.

If you're using an existing picture file, you may have to deal with size, format, and copyright issues. The following should be your main considerations when looking for a suitable file:

- ▶ Ultimately, you'll need a Windows bitmap (BMP) file. But any graphics program worth its salt will open files in any

Creating Skins for Winamp and RealJukebox 817

widely used graphics format and then save it in a different format. So if the file you find is in a format other than BMP, you should be fine as long as you have a decent graphics program.

- For conventional effects, you'll want a picture in portrait orientation rather than landscape. Most people create skins on the assumption that the user will have the Winamp windows arranged in a vertical stack, with the Main window at the top, the Graphical Equalizer window second, and the Playlist Editor window third—and the Minibrowser window either not displayed, displayed somewhere else, or ignored. You can of course create a skin that expects the windows to be arranged horizontally (or diagonally, or in a different order), but chances are that you'll confuse people if you distribute it. People put the Graphical Equalizer window second because it has a fixed size (whereas the Playlist Editor window is resizable) and because it has a full background (whereas the Playlist Editor window, as you saw a moment ago, is mostly uncustomizable background).

- If you want to use a photograph or picture of which you have only a hard copy, you'll need to scan it to a graphics file. If you don't have a scanner, chances are you can get the picture scanned at a local photo store.

- There's nothing to stop you from downloading a graphics file from the Web and using that—nothing except copyright law, that is. Remember the basic premise of intellectual property law: If you didn't create it, you need the creator's permission to use it. The fact that someone has posted it to a Web site does *not* constitute permission (unless there's a statement specifically telling you that you can use it). As with creating and possessing illegal MP3 files, chances are that if you use someone else's picture to create a skin for personal use without asking for permission won't bring the copyright police to your door. But if you distribute a skin that uses someone else's copyrighted material, you're exposing yourself to notice and retribution. (At this point, you're probably saying you bet most of the people who created skins using celebrity photos and famous logos didn't get permission. We bet you're right. But they should have—and so should you.)

Once you've got your picture and converted it to BMP format, you'll probably need to resize it. If you're going to use the vertical-stack orientation for your skin (Main window on top of Graphical Equalizer window on top of Playlist Editor window), you'll want a portrait-orientation picture that's 275 pixels wide and some multiple of 116 pixels deep:

- ▶ 116 pixels if you just want to customize the Main window
- ▶ 232 pixels if you want to do the Graphical Equalizer window as well
- ▶ 348 pixels if you want to risk assuming that users will display the Playlist Editor window at the same size as the Main window

Change your picture to fit these dimensions by rotating, resizing, stretching, and cropping it as appropriate. Which commands you use will depend on what the picture is like. For example, if you're using a picture of someone, you probably won't want to rotate it or stretch it, because the result will look strange (at best). You'll do best to crop the picture to get the effect you need (you might also want to add to the sides of the picture if it's too narrow).

> **TIP**
>
> If your picture is the wrong size, but you don't want to crop it, use a resizing command (such as the Image ≻ Resize command in Paint Shop Pro) to resize the image to the size you need. Usually you'll want to maintain the aspect ratio of the picture—otherwise, it'll get distorted. (In Paint Shop Pro, make sure that the **Maintain Aspect Ratio** check box is selected in the Resize dialog box.) Distortion can look good on artistic pictures, but you wouldn't want to do it to any picture that's supposed to be realistic.

Save the picture under a different name, so that you don't overwrite the original. (If you screw up, you'll need the original again.) If the picture isn't a bitmap, save it as one now—it'll save complications later. If you need to keep the file size down, choose 256 colors rather than more colors.

Creating the Bitmaps

Your next step is to create the component bitmaps of the skin. Because of the way Winamp's skins are put together, you don't need to customize every bitmap to create a workable skin—although you'll get a better overall effect if you do customize every bitmap. For example, if you want, you can customize just the Main window, or just some components of the Main window.

This section discusses the bitmaps contained in the Winamp Base Skin in the order in which you'll probably want to customize them. We start with the bitmaps in the Main window, because you'll probably want to finish customizing it before you move along to the Graphical Equalizer window and the Playlist Editor window—if you choose to customize them at all. You can stop anywhere along the way once you've achieved the look you want for your skin.

Main Window

The Main window is where you'll be spending most of your customization efforts. Let's take it from the top.

Main.bmp Main.bmp (see Figure 21.11) contains the faceplate or chassis alone. The black, cut-out areas represent where some of the other bitmaps go. Other bitmaps, such as the button controls, are layered on top of Main.bmp.

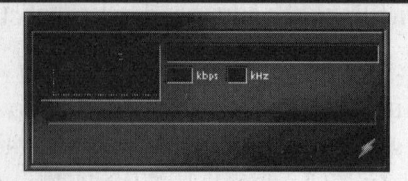

FIGURE 21.11: Main.bmp is the faceplate for the Main window.

Getting Main.bmp right is key to making your skin work, because this one bitmap defines much of the look of the Main window. So once you've got the bitmap into what you feel is a tenable state, save it as Main.bmp in the folder for your new skin (preferably in your \skins\ folder). Then switch to Winamp, display the Skin Browser by pressing Alt+S or choosing Options ≻ Skin Browser from the main menu, and apply your new skin. The Main window takes on the picture you just created. Everything else keeps its default Winamp look for the time being, but don't worry about that—you're on your way.

Titlebar.bmp Titlebar.bmp is perhaps the most daunting of the bitmaps to create or customize because it contains so many elements. Needless to say, these elements make it crucial that you create a good skin.

Figure 21.12 shows the whole of Titlebar.bmp.

FIGURE 21.12: Titlebar.bmp contains the title bar and clutter bar.

Creating Skins for Winamp and RealJukebox 821

First, and most obviously, this bitmap contains the title bar in all its possible modes—the regular mode (with the full Main window displayed), all the Windowshade modes (opened, playing, and scrolling a song title), and the Easter Egg modes. Figure 21.13 shows the title-bar components of `Titlebar.bmp`.

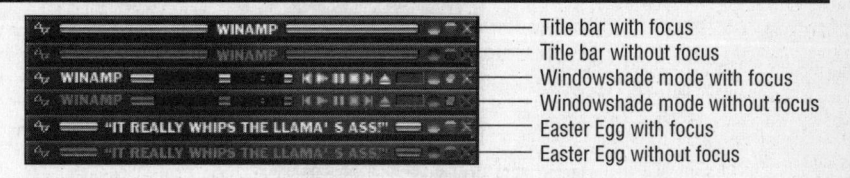

(figure showing title bars labeled:)
- Title bar with focus
- Title bar without focus
- Windowshade mode with focus
- Windowshade mode without focus
- Easter Egg with focus
- Easter Egg without focus

FIGURE 21.13: `Titlebar.bmp` contains six different title bars.

Next, this bitmap contains (in its upper-left corner) the Winamp Menu, Minimize, Toggle Windowshade Mode, and Seeking Bar buttons. Figure 21.4 shows these components.

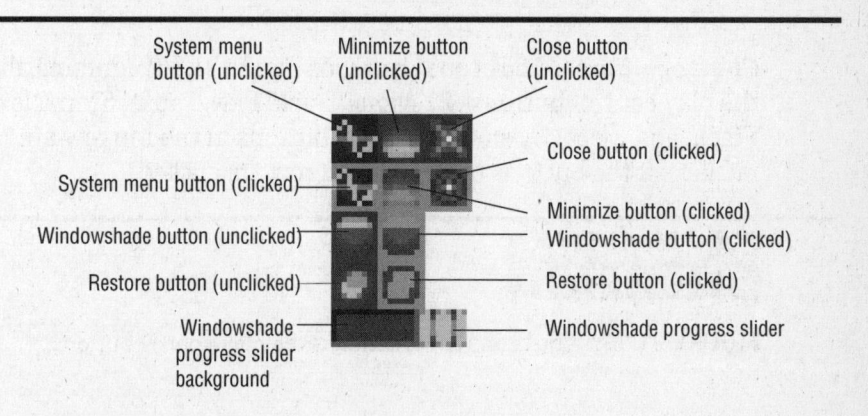

(figure showing buttons labeled:)
- System menu button (unclicked)
- Minimize button (unclicked)
- Close button (unclicked)
- System menu button (clicked)
- Close button (clicked)
- Windowshade button (unclicked)
- Minimize button (clicked)
- Restore button (unclicked)
- Windowshade button (clicked)
- Windowshade progress slider background
- Restore button (clicked)
- Windowshade progress slider

FIGURE 21.14: `Titlebar.bmp` also contains the buttons for the title bar.

Finally, `Titlebar.bmp` also contains the Clutterbar—the five letters O, A, I, D, and V (Options Menu, Toggle Always On Top, File Info Box, Toggle Double Size Mode, and Visualization Menu, respectively) found next to the Main Window visualization section—in all seven of its possible manifestations. Figure 21.15 shows the buttons for the Clutterbar.

822 Chapter Twenty-One

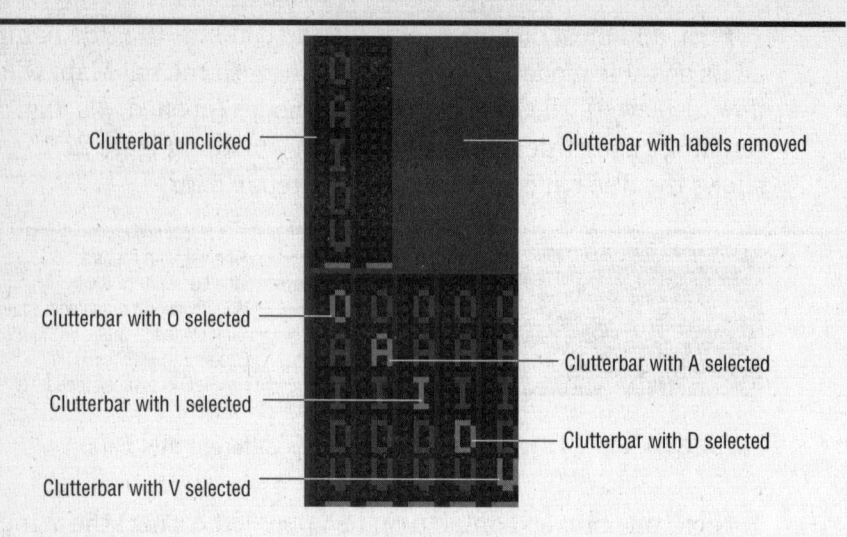

FIGURE 21.15: Last, `Titlebar.bmp` contains the buttons for the Clutterbar.

Cbuttons.bmp Cbuttons.bmp (see Figure 21.16) contains all the play-control buttons—Previous Track, Play, Pause, Stop, Next Track, and Eject (Open file(s)). The buttons in the top row are unclicked; the buttons in the bottom row are clicked.

FIGURE 21.16: Cbuttons.bmp contains the play-control buttons.

Shufrep.bmp Shufrep.bmp (see Figure 21.17) contains the Toggle Shuffle, Toggle Repeat, Toggle Graphical Equalizer, and Toggle Playlist Editor shown activated and not activated.

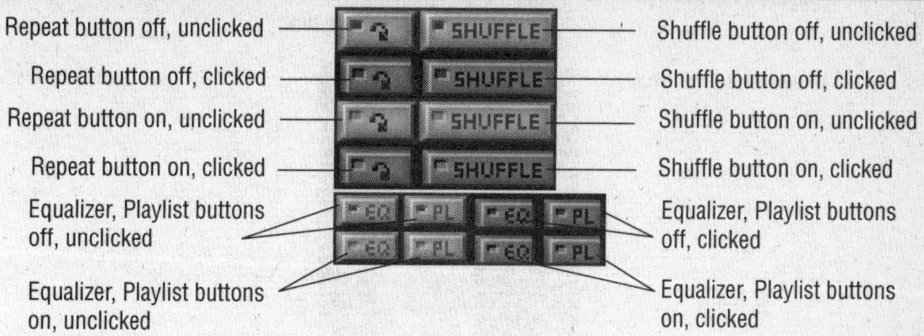

Creating Skins for Winamp and RealJukebox   823

Repeat button off, unclicked	Shuffle button off, unclicked
Repeat button off, clicked	Shuffle button off, clicked
Repeat button on, unclicked	Shuffle button on, unclicked
Repeat button on, clicked	Shuffle button on, clicked
Equalizer, Playlist buttons off, unclicked	Equalizer, Playlist buttons off, clicked
Equalizer, Playlist buttons on, unclicked	Equalizer, Playlist buttons on, clicked

FIGURE 21.17: Shufrep.bmp contains the components of the toggle buttons for Repeat, the Equalizer, and the Playlist Editor.

Volume.bmp* and *Balance.bmp   Volume.bmp is the bitmap for the Volume control slider, clicked and unclicked, and for the color(s) displayed behind it.

Balance.bmp is the bitmap for the bar for adjusting the balance—in Winamp's terminology, the *panning bar*. (Logic says it should be called Panning.bmp, but logic seems to have lost out.) When you click this button and drag it left or right, the song-title display area displays on the sound balance for Winamp's output.

Figure 21.18 shows Volume.bmp on the left and Balance.bmp on the right. As in the base skin, you may want to use the same color scheme for each.

824 Chapter Twenty-One

Volume.bmp — Lowest volume / Highest volume / Slider, clicked / Slider, unclicked

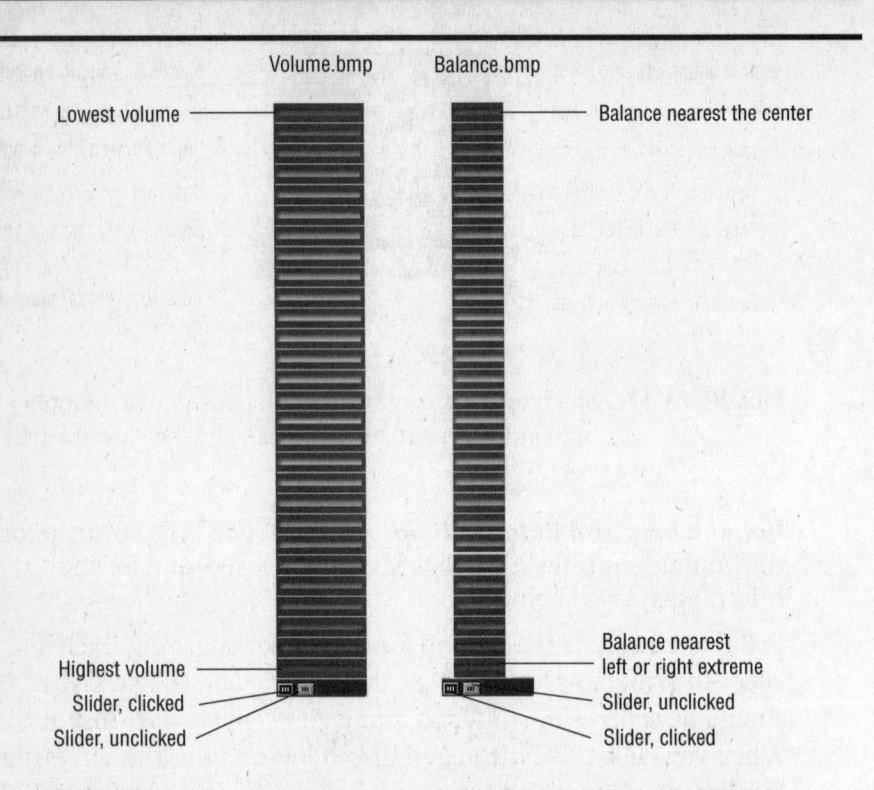

Balance.bmp — Balance nearest the center / Balance nearest left or right extreme / Slider, unclicked / Slider, clicked

FIGURE 21.18: Volume.bmp (on the left) contains the parts of the volume control. Balance.bmp (on the right) contains the parts of the panning bar.

Monoster.bmp (see Figure 21.19) contains the Mono/Stereo indicators. The top row shows the indicators in the on position, and the bottom row shows them in the off position.

FIGURE 21.19: Monoster.bmp contains the Mono/Stereo indicators.

Posbar.bmp Posbar.bmp (see Figure 21.20) contains the seeking bar—the bar you can drag from left to right to move to a different part of the current track.

Creating Skins for Winamp and RealJukebox 825

Background | Position slider, unclicked | Position slider, clicked

FIGURE 21.20: `Posbar.bmp` contains the components of the seeking bar.

Playpaus.bmp `Playpaus.bmp` (see Figure 21.21) contains the buttons that appear in the Visualization Window to show whether a song is playing, paused, or stopped. The right-most icon (which consists of one green dot and one red dot) indicates synchronization, buffering, or a break in transmission on the song being played.

FIGURE 21.21: `Playpaus.bmp` contains the buttons that appear in the Visualization window.

Numbers.bmp

`Numbers.bmp` (see Figure 21.22) contains the numbers shown in the Time Display.

FIGURE 21.22: `Numbers.bmp` contains the numbers shown in the Time Display.

Text.bmp `Text.bmp` (see Figure 21.23) contains the alphanumeric characters used in the song title text and the numbers in the kbps and kHz displays on the Main Window, and in the time display when the Main Window is shaded. These numbers and letters are also used in the Playlist Editor when it is in Windowshade mode, and for the current song duration and complete playlist duration and time displays.

Part viii

As you can see in the illustration, each of the letters, numbers, and symbols is represented as an area of pixels, so you can change the color of each of the letters, numbers, and symbols. To maintain readability, it's best not to stray too far.

FIGURE 21.23: Text.bmp contains the letters and numbers used for the title display and other displays.

Graphical Equalizer Window

After you've finished the Main window (and perhaps taken a goodly break), your next target should be the Graphical Equalizer window. This window shouldn't take nearly as long as the Main window, because it contains only two bitmaps.

Eqmain.bmp Eqmain.bmp contains all aspects of the Graphical Equalizer—active and inactive, and with different buttons shown as pressed. Figure 21.24 shows all of Eqmain.bmp.

FIGURE 21.24: Eqmain.bmp contains all aspects of the Graphical Equalizer.

Creating Skins for Winamp and RealJukebox 827

Figure 21.25 shows the top half of `Eqmain.bmp`.

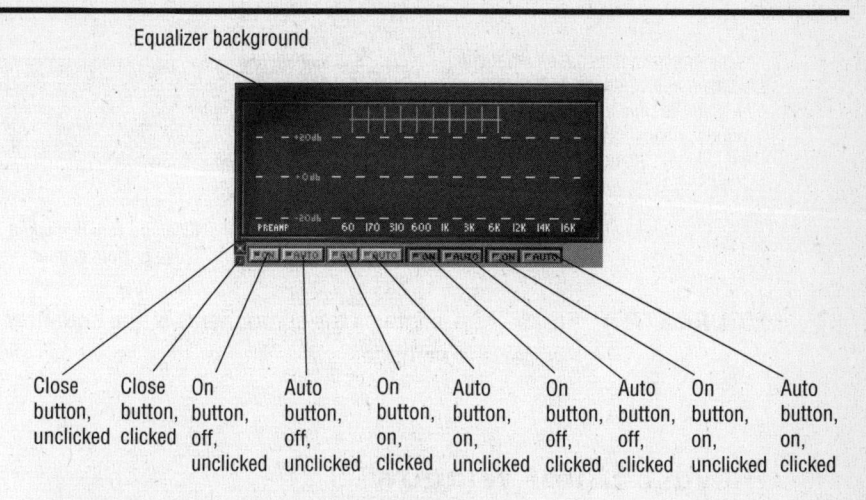

FIGURE 21.25: The top half of `Eqmain.bmp`

Figure 21.26 shows the bottom half of `Eqmain.bmp`.

FIGURE 21.26: The bottom half of `Eqmain.bmp`

Eq_ex.bmp Eq_ex.bmp (see Figure 21.27) contains the Graphical Equalizer in Windowshade mode (both active and inactive) and its buttons and controls.

Chapter Twenty-One

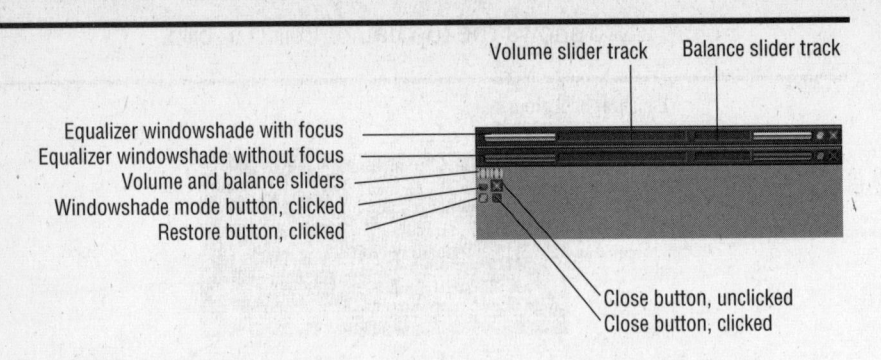

[Figure showing Equalizer components with labels: Equalizer windowshade with focus, Equalizer windowshade without focus, Volume and balance sliders, Windowshade mode button clicked, Restore button clicked, Volume slider track, Balance slider track, Close button unclicked, Close button clicked]

FIGURE 21.27: Eq_ex.bmp contains the components of the Equalizer in Windowshade mode.

Playlist Editor Window

Two windows down, two to go.... If you're up for a little more customization, your next victim should be the Playlist Editor window.

As mentioned earlier, the Playlist Editor window isn't such a good candidate for customization because it's resizable in both dimensions. So while it's quite reasonable to include at the top of the Playlist Editor window the lowest part of a picture that you've already spread across the Main window and the Graphical Equalizer window, it's a mistake to carry the picture through to the sides and bottom of the Playlist Editor window as well. When the user enlarges the window, the sides and bottom are lengthened, and the picture falls apart.

To customize the Playlist Editor window, you work with `Pledit.bmp`, which contains every aspect of the Playlist. As you can see in Figure 21.28, which shows the whole bitmap, the bitmap appears complex. But in fact, it's quite easy to work with once you know what's what. To show you that, we need to break the bitmap down into more manageable pieces.

Creating Skins for Winamp and RealJukebox 829

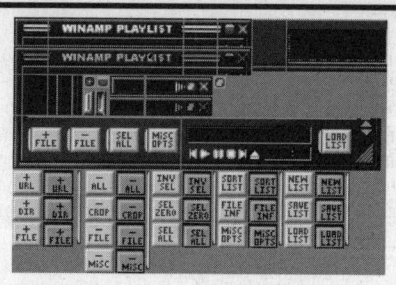

FIGURE 21.28: `Pledit.bmp` contains the different components of the playlist.

Figure 21.29 shows the topmost part of `Pledit.bmp`.

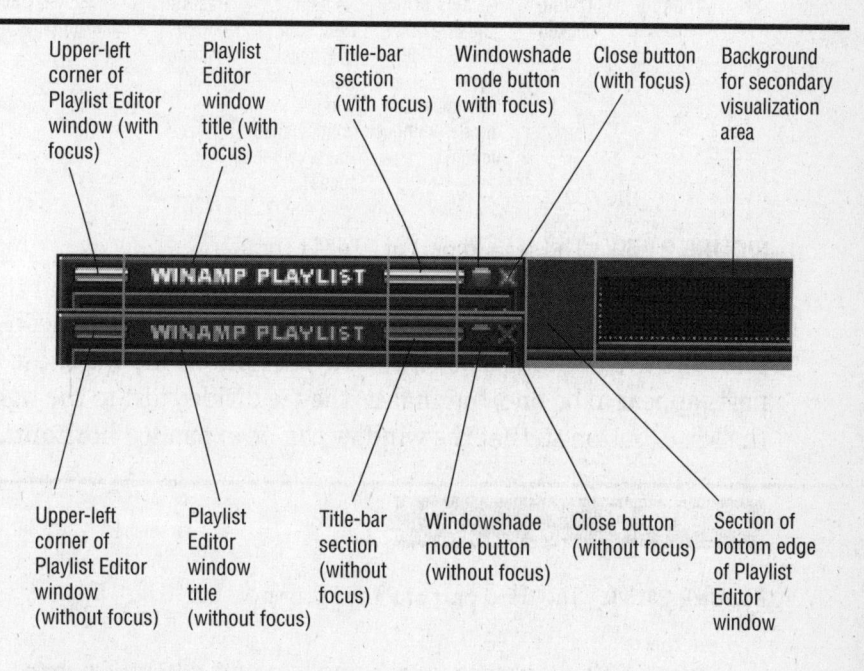

FIGURE 21.29: The top part of `Pledit.bmp`

Figure 21.30 shows the second part of `Pledit.bmp`.

Chapter Twenty-One

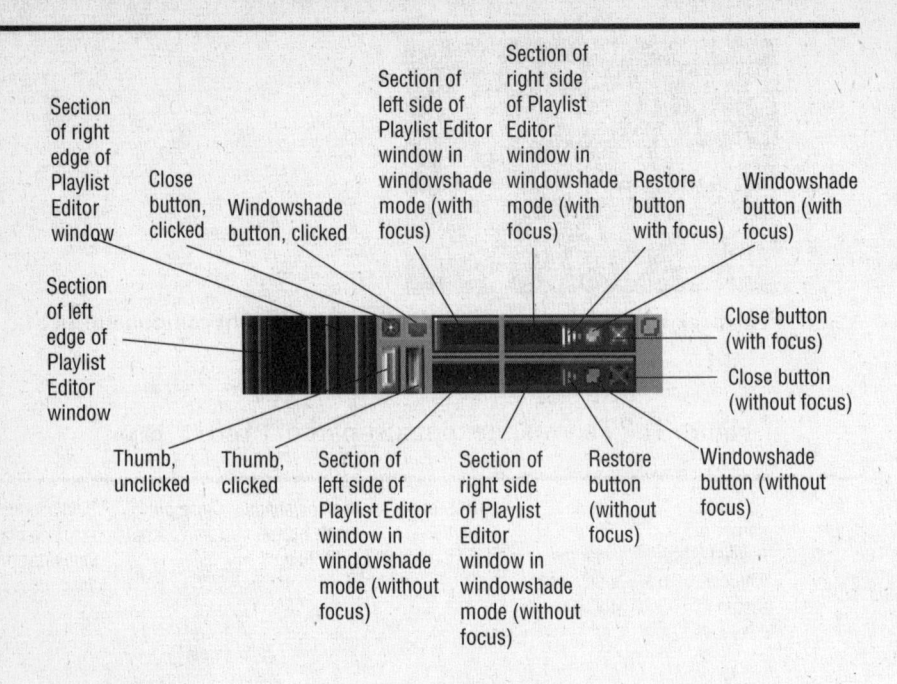

FIGURE 21.30: The second part of `Pledit.bmp`

Figure 21.31 shows the third part of `Pledit.bmp`, which contains the two bottom parts of the Playlist Editor window. These two parts appear to be one, but in fact, they're divided just to the right of the Misc. button so that the window can be expanded horizontally.

FIGURE 21.31: The third part of `Pledit.bmp`

Figure 21.32 shows the fourth and last part of `Pledit.bmp`, which contains the unclicked and clicked versions of the menu buttons. The unclicked versions of the buttons appear to the left of the clicked versions and with a lighter color on their faces.

Creating Skins for Winamp and RealJukebox   831

FIGURE 21.32: The fourth part of Pledit.bmp contains the unclicked and clicked versions of the menu buttons.

Minibrowser Window

Finally, customize the Minibrowser window if you want to.

Because many Winamp users don't use the Minibrowser at all, and because those who do use it tend to put it in different places relative to the other Winamp windows, there are strong arguments for not making the Minibrowser an integral part of your skin. Instead, you may want to do nothing more than adjust its color scheme so that it ties in with the rest of the skin when it's displayed.

Mb.bmp (see Figure 21.33) contains all the components of the Minibrowser, active and inactive.

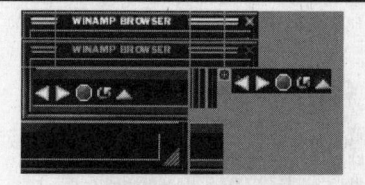

FIGURE 21.33: Mb.bmp contains the various components of the Minibrowser.

Since this is another complex bitmap, we've broken it into two. Figure 21.34 shows the upper part of the Minibrowser.

Part viii

832 Chapter Twenty-One

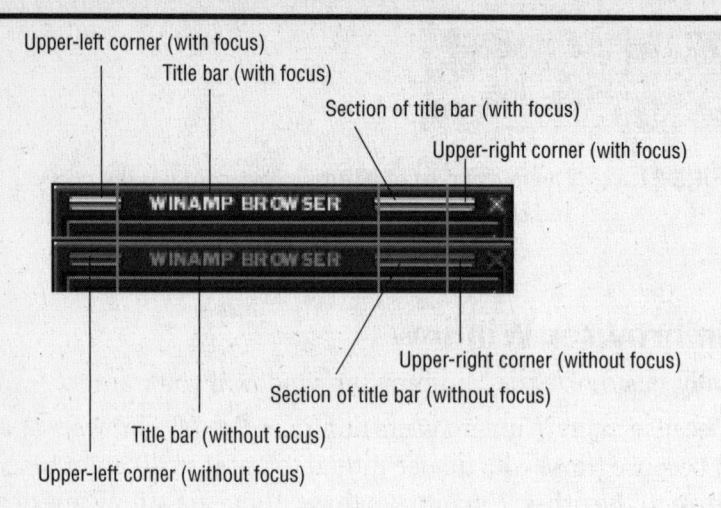

FIGURE 21.34: The upper part of the Minibrowser

Figure 21.35 shows the lower part of the Minibrowser.

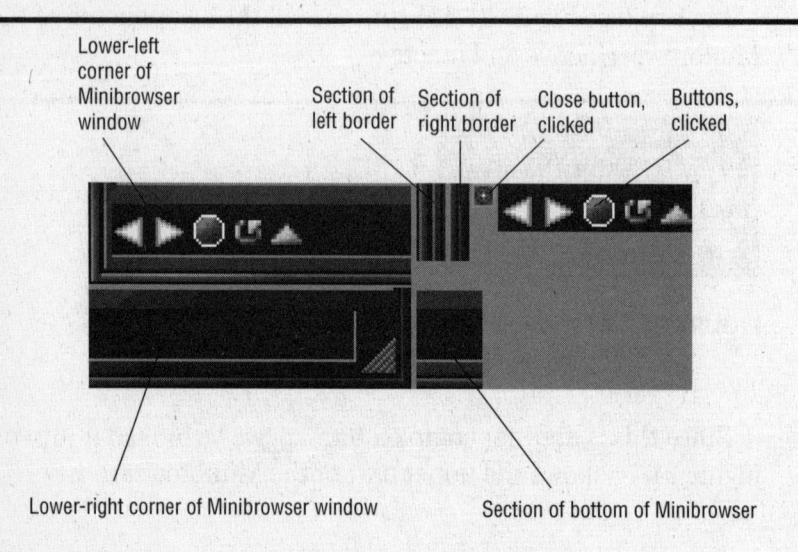

FIGURE 21.35: The lower part of the Minibrowser

Changing the Cursors

Once you've made your skin look like you want it to, you can add different cursors to the skin to personalize it further.

Table 21.1 lists the cursor files that Winamp uses. To adjust a cursor, use an icon editor such as Microangelo to create a new cursor file or to adapt an existing file.

TABLE 21.1: Winamp Cursor Files

FILENAME	REPRESENTS CURSOR OVER
CLOSE.CUR	The Close button
EQCLOSE.CUR	The Close button on the Graphical Equalizer window
EQNORMAL.CUR	The Graphical Equalizer window
EQSLID.CUR	A slider on the Graphical Equalizer window
EQTITLE.CUR	The title bar on the Graphical Equalizer window
MAINMENU.CUR	The main menu
MIN.CUR	The Minimize button
NORMAL.CUR	The Main window
PCLOSE.CUR	The Close button on the Playlist Editor window
PNORMAL.CUR	The Playlist Editor window
POSBAR.CUR	The Seeking bar
PSIZE.CUR	The resizing corner of the Playlist Editor window
PTBAR.CUR	The title bar of the Playlist Editor window
PVSCROLL.CUR	The vertical scroll bar on the Playlist Editor window
PWINBUT.CUR	The Windowshade button on the Playlist Editor window
PWSNORM.CUR	The Playlist Editor window in Windowshade mode
PWSSIZE.CUR	The Restore button on the Playlist Editor window in Windowshade mode
SONGNAME.CUR	The track name display
TITLEBAR.CUR	The title bar of the Main window
VOLBAL.CUR	The Panning bar and the Volume bar
WINBUT.CUR	The Windowshade button on the Main window

CONTINUED ➡

TABLE 21.1 continued: Winamp Cursor Files

Filename	Represents Cursor Over
WSCLOSE.CUR	The Close button on the Main window in Windowshade mode—in theory. (In practice, it doesn't seem to do anything.)
WSMIN.CUR	The Minimize button on the Main window in Windowshade mode—again, in theory.
WSNORMAL.CUR	The Main window in Windowshade mode
WSPOSBAR.CUR	The Position bar in Windowshade mode
WSWINBUT.CUR	The Restore button on the Main window in Windowshade mode—again, in theory.

Editing the Text Files

After you've created new cursors, your skin should be fully functional. But you can customize your skin further by editing the three configuration files that Winamp uses: `pledit.txt`, `region.txt`, and `viscolor.txt`.

Here's what they do:

- `Pledit.txt` defines the font and color for the text in the Playlist Editor window track listing and in the URL display in the Minibrowser.

- `Region.txt` lets you define transparencies for creating skin masks.

- `Viscolor.txt` controls the colors used in the visualization.

You can change any or all of these text files to get the effects you want. You don't need to change all three at once if changing one or two produces those effects.

Pledit.txt

As we mentioned, `Pledit.txt` controls the font and color of the playlist text. Double-click the copy of `Pledit.txt` in the Base Skin to open the file in Notepad or your default text editor. You'll see something like this:

```
[Text]
Normal=#00FF00
Current=#FFFFFF
NormalBG=#000000
SelectedBG=#0000FF
MbFG=#FF8924
MbBG=#1A120A
Font=Arial
```

Here's what these lines control:

- The `Normal` line controls the color of the regular text in the playlist.

- The `Current` line controls the color of the text for the current track in the playlist.

- The `NormalBG` line controls the background for normal text in the playlist.

- The `SelectedBG` line controls the background for the selected track in the playlist.

- The `MbFG` line controls the text color in the status bar in the Minibrowser.

- The `MbBG` line controls the background to the text in the status bar in the Minibrowser.

- The `Font` line specifies the font used in the playlist and Minibrowser. You can use any font that's available to Windows. (If you plan to distribute your skin, use a widely available font so that everyone can use the skin.)

The values for all the lines but the `Font` line are hexadecimal (hex) RGB values—RGB values converted to hexadecimal. To calculate hex values, launch the Calculator (Start ➢ Programs ➢ Accessories ➢ Calculator) and choose View ➢ Scientific to display it in Scientific mode (see Figure 21.36). Make sure the Dec (decimal) option button is selected, enter the number, and then click the Hex option button to convert the number to hexadecimal.

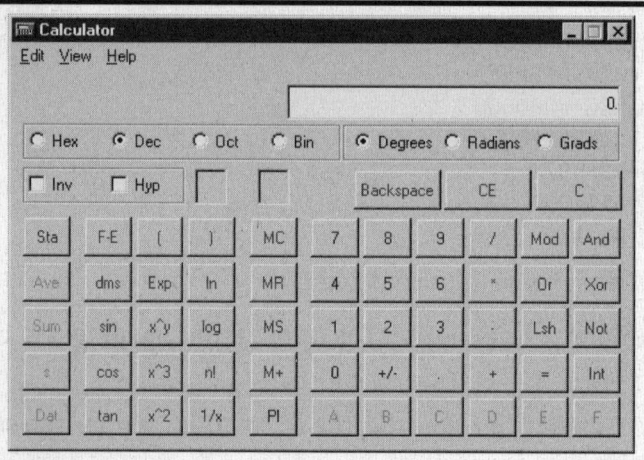

FIGURE 21.36: Use the Windows Calculator in Scientific mode to calculate hex values.

TIP

Another tricky but more roundabout way to get these values is to use a Web page editor such as FrontPage Express (which is included with Windows 98, Windows Me, and Windows 2000). Create a blank HTML page, then right-click it and select Page Properties. Set the Background color using the Color dialog box to a shade that you want to use in Winamp. Now view the page's HTML code and look for the line that sets the BGCOLOR. It has the hex codes for the color that you set as the background color for the page. You can cut and paste these hex codes into the Winamp file.

Viscolor.txt

Viscolor.txt is the configuration file for setting the colors for the Visualization panel. It consists of 24 lines of color values in RGB (red, green, blue) format, for example:

```
0,196,196
0,196,196
0,64,64
0,64,64
```

> **NOTE**
>
> RGB is a method of defining color by specifying a red value, a green value, and a blue value, each on a scale of 0 (none of that color) to 255 (a whole lot of that color). For example, an RGB value of 255, 0, 0 gives pure red—255 red, 0 green, 0 blue. An RGB value of 0, 255, 0 gives pure green; an RGB value of 0, 0, 255 gives pure blue; an RGB value of 48, 23, 91 gives deep purple; and an RGB value of 0, 0, 0 gives black.

Each line can also have a comment, which is denoted by a double forward slash; for example:

```
0,196,196 // this is a comment
0,196,196 // same color again here
0,64,64
0,64,64
```

Here's what these lines control:

- The first line controls the background color in the visualization area.
- The second line controls the color of the dots used in the visualization area.
- The third through eighteenth lines control the colors used in the Spectrum Analyzer. The third line controls the peak value, and the eighteenth line controls the lowest value, with the lines in between controlling the values in between.

- The nineteenth through twenty-third lines control the oscilloscope colors, with the nineteenth line controlling the lowest value and the twenty-third line controlling the highest value.

- The twenty-fourth line controls the color used for the last peak value.

Region.txt

`Region.txt` lets you define skin masks for Winamp. Defining skin masks basically means creating polygons within which you can add your own creative work. The areas that you don't block out for working in remain transparent.

If you'd rather not use this file in your skin, delete it, and Winamp uses its standard settings for keeping itself covered.

The best way to get started defining skin masks is to open the copy of `Region.txt` that came with the Base Skin, examine it, and try uncommenting some of the lines that it contains. A semi-colon denotes that the rest of a line is a comment, and as it comes, most of the file is commented out.

You define each polygon as a series of XY coordinates, moving clockwise around the polygon. Because the fixed-width Winamp windows are 275 pixels wide by 116 pixels high, the X coordinates range from 0 (the left-most pixel) to 275 (the right-most pixel) and the Y coordinates range from 0 (the top-most pixel) to 116 (the bottom-most pixel).

To find out the coordinates of any given point in a bitmap, open the bitmap in an image-editing program, zoom it nice and large, and then move the mouse pointer over the point. Almost all image-editing programs display the coordinates of the mouse pointer, either in a pop-up readout or in the status bar. (For example, Microsoft Paint displays the coordinates in the status bar.)

Creating Skins for Winamp and RealJukebox 839

Each polygon definition starts with a `[Normal]` statement followed by a `NumPoints` statement that gives the number of points in the polygon, for example:

```
[Normal]
NumPoints = 4
```

It's usually a good idea to enter this `NumPoints` statement only after you've defined the polygon. That way, you can double-check that it gives the correct number of points. If you get the number of points wrong, you'll see an error message like that shown in Figure 21.37.

FIGURE 21.37: Make sure that your `NumPoints` statement is correct. Otherwise, users of your skin will see this error.

After the `NumPoints` statement appears the `PointList` statement, which gives the coordinates of the points, pair by pair, separated by commas and spaces. However long it is, the `PointList` statement needs to appear on a single line—don't break it across multiple lines by using carriage returns, although of course it's fine for the statement to wrap from one line to the next in your text editor.

Here's an example of a `PointList` statement:

```
PointList = 11,22, 103,22, 103,64, 11,64
```

To create a mask that has multiple areas, separate the different groups with a comma. The following example creates two polygons, the first with three points (a triangle) and the second with four points (a rectangle):

```
[Normal]
NumPoints = 3, 4
PointList = 0,0, 104,65, 0,116, 104,0, 275,0, 275,116, 104,116
```

Zipping Your Skin for Distribution

Once you've got everything in your skin working to your satisfaction, zip it so that you can distribute it easily and (if you want) post it on the Winamp Skins Web site or another site for public consumption. Use any zipping program (for example, WinZip) to create a regular zip file of the skin, then rename the zip file, changing the extension from ZIP to WSZ.

> **NOTE**
>
> WSZ files are simply renamed ZIP files. The WSZ extension is used to differentiate Winamp skin zip files from regular zip files. By using the WSZ extension, Winamp can have WSZ files associated with it rather than with the zipping program, so that when the user double-clicks a WSZ file, Winamp installs the skin automatically.

Creating Skins for RealJukebox

This section outlines the process for creating skins for RealJukebox. Like Winamp skins, RealJukebox skins consist of bitmaps with a configuration file, `Skin.ini`, telling RealJukebox how to assemble the skin.

Unlike Winamp, though, RealJukebox has a skinning kit supplied by Real. To get started creating skins for RealJukebox, download the latest version of the RealJukebox Skins Toolkit from the RealJukebox Web site, `www.real.com/rjcentral/make_skins/index.html`. Apart from this, you'll need a text editor, such as Notepad or your favorite word processor, and any graphics that you want to use in your skin.

The RealJukebox Skins Toolkit provides a good deal of help in creating skins, but not as much as it might. One area in which it falls noticeably flat is in helping you create the `Skin.ini` configuration file that defines where each of the controls appears on your skin and how each control behaves. As a result, we'll spend a good proportion of this section discussing `Skin.ini`.

The Graphics Files

RealJukebox can use both bitmap (BMP) files and JPEG (JPG) files. JPEG files are typically much smaller than bitmap files, so you can make your skin much easier to distribute by using JPEG files. If you're using transparent regions in your skins, you'll need to use bitmaps, as JPEG images won't always work correctly.

The first file you need is—surprise, surprise—the background. This image forms the basis of your RealJukebox skin, so you'll want to choose it with due care and diligence. Again, remember the basic tenets of intellectual property—if you're using someone else's image, you'll probably need permission to do so. Save this image as `Backgrnd.bmp`.

You can make RealJukebox skins pretty much any shape. Typically, you'll do best to start with a square or rectangle larger than the size you need. You can then make the unwanted pieces of the square or rectangle transparent to give the shape you need.

To make an area of the graphic transparent, set its color to RGB 255, 0, 255. This value gives the color magenta, which is used to denote transparency in RealJukebox. Make sure that your graphics program doesn't dither the magenta areas, because if it does, the colors other than magenta will not be transparent in the skin. (To *dither* is to approximate a color by creating a pattern of pixels of colors that are close to the desired color.)

On top of the background go the controls, such as buttons, sliders, and other elements. For most of the controls, RealJukebox uses four images, one for each state of the control:

- Disabled (not available)
- Mouse-Over (when the user moves the mouse pointer over the control)

- Active (when the control is active)
- Normal (the rest of the time)

The exceptions are the graphics that make up the slider controls for track position and volume. Each of the track components of the slider controls has three images:

- One for the Disabled state
- One for the Non-Filled state (before the thumb—the scroll box—has passed it)
- One for the Filled state (after the thumb has passed it).

The thumb bitmap has only two states: Enabled and Disabled.

For most skins, you'll want to use custom graphics for the controls to give the skin exactly the look you want. However, if you so choose, you can use RealJukebox's standard controls on your skin, either by specifying them explicitly or by not specifying any controls. If you don't supply a graphics file for any control, RealJukebox uses its default control.

Table 21.2 lists the controls and their filenames. By giving a graphic the appropriate filename and including it in the skin, you use it for the control. Note that the two exceptions are the PlayStatus and RecordStatus controls, which are status windows rather than graphical objects and so do not use bitmaps.

TABLE 21.2: RealJukebox Controls and Their Filenames

Control Name	Control Description	Filename
Record	Record button	Record.bmp
Play	Play button	Play.bmp
Pause	Pause button	Pause.bmp
Stop	Stop button	Stop.bmp
Previous	Previous Track button	Previous.bmp
Next	Next Track button	Next.bmp

CONTINUED →

Creating Skins for Winamp and RealJukebox

TABLE 21.2 continued: RealJukebox Controls and Their Filenames

Control Name	Control Description	Filename
Continue	Continuous Play button	Continue.bmp
Shuffle	Shuffle Play button	Shuffle.bmp
Mute	Mute button	Mute.bmp
Exit	Exit button	Exit.bmp
Minimize	Minimize button	Minimize.bmp
Menu	Menu button	Menu.bmp
FullMode	Full Mode button	Fullmode.bmp
Vol	Volume Slider track	Voltrack.bmp
Vol	Volume Slider thumb	Volthumb.bmp
Pos	Track Position Slider track	Postrack.bmp
Pos	Track Position Slider thumb	Posthumb.bmp
Eject	Eject button	Eject.bmp
RealLogo	Real Logo control	RealLogo.bmp
CDInfo	Get CD Info button	Cdinfo.bmp
PlayStatus	Play Status window	—
RecordStatus	Recording Status window	—
RPLaunch	Launch RealPlayer button	rplaunch.bmp

> **NOTE**
>
> `Postrack.bmp` must be the same height as `Posthumb.bmp`, and `Voltrack.bmp` must be the same height as `Volthumb.bmp`.

If the predefined controls don't give you the functionality you want, you can add up to 30 custom controls to a skin. For each custom control, you create a custom bitmap containing four images for the four states (Disabled, Normal, Mouse-Over, and Active) from left to right, then enter commands in the [MAIN] section of the Skin.ini configuration file to identify the image, specify its position, and define what it does.

Each custom control is named Control*n*, where *n* is the next lowest available number above 0: The first control is Control1, the second is Control2, and so on up to Control30 (should you need that many). You can assign to the custom controls a variety of actions such as changing the visualization or displaying a particular URL. We'll cover these actions in the section "Creating the Skin.ini File" later in this chapter.

Finding the Positions for Your Controls

The next step is to determine where you want the controls to appear. This is where the Skins Toolkit could provide a great deal of help, by letting you maneuver the control bitmaps to the positions in which you want them, and by recording those positions automatically. Unfortunately, it doesn't do this, so you have to do it yourself.

Use Windows Explorer to create a copy of your background file, then open the copy in your bitmap editor. (You're creating the copy because you're going to mess it up placing the controls.) Open one of the control graphic files, copy one of the controls, paste it onto the copy of the background, and maneuver it to where you want it to appear. Then position the mouse pointer at the upper-left corner of the control and jot down the coordinates for the control. Rinse and repeat for each of the other controls that you'll use on your skin so that you have a list of each control and the coordinates for its upper-left corner. Then save your mock-up if you want, and close it.

Creating the *Skin.ini* File

Skin.ini is the configuration file that defines how RealJukebox assembles and displays the skin in question. As we mentioned, at this writing you need to create Skin.ini manually, as opposed to

Creating Skins for Winamp and RealJukebox

having the Skins Toolkit create and adjust it for you automagically. This section gives you enough detail to get started with `Skin.ini`, but because it's a complex file, and because Real adds frequently to RealJukebox's capabilities, we suggest checking the RealJukebox Central Web site for further information.

Typically, you'll want to start your `Skin.ini` with comment lines giving the name of the skin, the creator (you), the version, and the date. As in the Winamp skin-configuration files, comments are denoted with a semicolon, so you might start your `Skin.ini` file like this:

```
; Kings of Oblivion Skin
; by Miles Standish
; Version 0.9b
; Released 09-30-2000
```

Then add a [MAIN] section. This section tells RealJukebox whether to display each control and where to display those you choose to display. This section is also where you define custom controls.

Start the [MAIN] section by specifying the application with an `Application` statement and the version with a `Version` statement. The application will always be RealJukebox, and the version will be the version of RealJukebox that the skin is for, as in the following example:

```
[MAIN]
Application=RealJukebox
Version=2.0
```

Then specify the buttons that you want to appear on the skin. Table 21.3 lists the controls available and whether they appear by default.

TABLE 21.3: Buttons for RealJukebox Skins

Control Name	Control	Displayed by Default in Skin Mode?
Record	Record button	Yes
Play	Play button	Yes
Stop	Stop button	Yes

CONTINUED →

TABLE 21.3 continued: Buttons for RealJukebox Skins

Control Name	Control	Displayed by Default in Skin Mode?
Pause	Pause button	Yes
Previous	Previous button	Yes
Next	Next button	Yes
Continue	Continuous Play button	Yes
Shuffle	Shuffle Play button	Yes
Eject	Eject button	No
Menu	Menu button	Yes
Exit	Close button	Yes
Minimize	Minimize button	Yes
FullMode	Full Mode button	Yes
RPLaunch	RealPlayer Launcher button	Yes
Mute	Mute button	Yes
Vol	Volume control	Yes
Pos	Position control	No
PlayStatus	Playing status area	Yes
RecordStatus	Recording status area	Yes
RealLogo	Real logo	Yes

As you can see in Table 21.3, most of the controls are displayed by default in Skin mode, so you don't need to specify those that you want to be displayed, only those that you want not to be displayed. However, you'll probably find it easier to read your Skin.ini file if you include statements for each control.

To specify whether a control is displayed or hidden, you set its Show attribute to the appropriate value or state. Table 21.4 lists the possible values for the Show attribute.

Creating Skins for Winamp and RealJukebox 847

TABLE 21.4: Values for the Show Attribute

Value	Explanation
1	Show the control.
0	Hide the control.
Playing	Show the control when a track or stream is playing.
NotPlaying	Show the control when no track or stream is playing.
Paused	Show the control when a track or stream is paused.
NotPaused	Show the control when no track or stream is paused.
Recording	Show the control when a track is being recorded.
NotRecording	Show the control when no track is being recorded.
CDReady	Show the control when a CD is ready.
NotCDReady	Show the control when no CD is ready.

The Show values give you the flexibility to display the controls appropriate to what the user is doing in RealJukebox. As a simple example, you might choose to display the Play button and the Stop button in the same space, and have the appropriate button displayed at the appropriate time. The following example specifies that the Play button appear when no track is playing and the Stop button appear when a track is playing:

```
PlayShow=NotPlaying
StopShow=Playing
```

You can also specify multiple states for a control by separating the values with commas. This makes more sense for some controls than for others. For example, the following statement displays the Eject button when RealJukebox is not playing, not recording, or when a CD is ready. (The states are interpreted using the Boolean OR—one state OR the next state OR the next state.)

```
EjectShow=NotPlaying,NotRecording,CDReady
```

To specify the position in which a button is to appear, set its `TopLeft` property to specify the XY coordinates for the upper-left corner of the button. For example, the following statement displays the Play button with its upper-left corner 15 pixels across the bitmap and 10 pixels down:

```
PlayTopLeft=15,10
```

Adding Custom Controls

As mentioned earlier in this chapter, in addition to the standard controls with which RealJukebox comes equipped, you can add up to 30 custom controls to serve your own needs. Custom controls are named `Control1` through `Control30`.

You use the `Image` property to specify the bitmap to be used for the control. The following statement specifies that the file `tbc_logo.bmp` be used for Control1:

```
Control1Image=tbc_logo.bmp
```

As with the standard controls, you use the `TopLeft` property to specify the coordinates for the upper-left corner of a custom control, as follows:

```
Control1TopLeft=10,20
```

You use the `IsButton` property to specify whether a control is a button (a value of 1) or not (a value of 0), as follows:

```
Control1IsButton=1
```

To specify the text of a ToolTip for a custom button, you set its `ToolTip` property, as follows:

```
Control1ToolTip=Do not click this button!
```

To make the control take the user to a URL, set the URL property. For example, the following statement makes Control1 take the user to the URL www.acmeheavyindustries.com:

```
Control1URL=www.acmeheavyindustries.com
```

Usually, you'll want to assign an action to a custom button. To do so, assign to its `Action` property one of the actions listed in Table 21.5.

Creating Skins for Winamp and RealJukebox

TABLE 21.5: Actions for Custom Buttons

Action	Explanation
ShowTemplatesMenu	Displays the Track Info Styles menu.
EditTrackInfo	Displays the Track Info Editor dialog box with the information for the current track.
ShowPreferences	Displays the Preferences dialog box.
ShowEqualizer	Displays the Equalizer Settings dialog box.
BrowseML	Displays the Track Browser.
ShowHideTrackInfo	Toggles the track information on and off.
ShowVizPreferences	Displays the Visualization Preferences dialog box.
ShowVizMenu	Displays the menu of visualizations.
NextVisualization	Starts the next visualization.
PrevVisualization	Starts the previous visualization.
ChangeSkin	Changes RealJukebox to the specified skin if it's available.

Adding Status Windows to the Skin

To display information to the user of your skin, you can use status windows—rectangular areas in which you can display your choice of information. Table 21.6 lists the properties for status windows.

TABLE 21.6: Properties for Status Windows

Property	Specifies
Type	The type of data to display. See Table 21.7 for a list of the types of data.
Rect	XY coordinates giving the four corners of the status field.
TextColor	An RGB value specifying the color for text.
BackgroundColor	An RGB value specifying the color for the background.
Justification	The justification of the text: Left, Center, or Right.
FontName	The name of the font for the status window.
FontHeight	The height of the font for the status window, in points.

CONTINUED →

TABLE 21.6 continued: Properties for Status Windows

Property	Specifies
FontBold	Whether the font is bold (1) or not (0).
FontItalic	Whether the font is italic (1) or not (0).
FontUnderline	Whether the font is underlined (1) or not (0).
Show	Whether and when to display the status window. Can be any of the Show values listed in Table 21.4 above.
Transparent	Whether the background is transparent (1) or not (0).

Table 21.7 lists the types of data available for the Type property for status windows.

TABLE 21.7: Data Types for the Type Property for Status Windows

Data Type	Displays
PlayTitle	The name of the current track
PlayArtist	The name of the artist associated with the current track
PlayAlbum	The name of the album associated with the current track
PlayGenre	The genre associated with the current track
PlayTimeElapsed	The amount of time elapsed on the current track
PlayTimeRemaining	The amount of time remaining on the current track
PlayTimeRatio	The elapsed time and the total track time (in "1:44/4:32" format)
PlayTimeTotal	The total time of the current track
PlayBitrate	The bitrate of the current track
PlayFormat	The format of the current track (for example, "MP3" or "RealAudio")
RecordName	The name of the track currently being recorded. (If no track is currently being recorded, this and the next seven data types return an empty string.)
RecordArtist	The name of the artist associated with the track currently being recorded
RecordAlbum	The name of the album associated with the track currently being recorded

CONTINUED ➟

Creating Skins for Winamp and RealJukebox

TABLE 21.7 continued: Data Types for the Type Property for Status Windows

DATA TYPE	DISPLAYS
RecordGentre	The genre of the track currently being recorded
RecordPercent	The percentage of the current track that has been recorded
RecordIndex	The index number (for example, "3 of 10") of the track currently being recorded
RecordSpeed	The current recording speed

> **TIP**
>
> You can use any two of Artist, Album, Title, and Genre together with Play or Record to display more information. For example, PlayArtistTitle displays information such as "Metallica – The Unforgiven."

Specifying Where the Skin Appears on the Screen

To specify where the skin appears on the screen when the user switches RealJukebox to it, set the HorizontalJustification tag to Left, Right, or Center, and the VerticalJustification tag to Top, Center, or Bottom. For example, the following two statements specify that the skin appear in the upper-right corner of the screen:

```
HorizontalJustification=Right
VerticalJustification=Top
```

Packaging and Distributing Your Skin

Once you've finished creating your skin, use a zipping program such as WinZip to create a zip file containing all the files for the skin. You can leave the file with the ZIP extension that the zipping program automatically gives it, but you might want to change the extension (using Explorer) to RJS to make clear that the zip file is a RealJukebox skin file.

Then, copy the skin file into the `\Real\RealJukebox\skins\` folder (probably in your `\Program Files\` folder) and load it to test it. If it works well, consider uploading it to the RealJukebox Central skins Web site so that other people can download it and wonder at your work.

Converting Winamp Skins to RealJukebox Skins

If you have Winamp skins that you like, you can convert them to RealJukebox skins by using the RealJukebox Skin Converter tool, which is available from Calypso Softworks (www.calypsosoftworks.com).

When it converts a skin, RealJukebox Skin Converter essentially creates a RealJukebox skin the size and shape of the Winamp Main window and maps the RealJukebox controls to the positions of the corresponding Winamp controls. The effect is a little peculiar—it's like using Winamp, but in fact, you're using RealJukebox.

Unzip RealJukebox Skin Converter and run `Setup.exe` to start the installation routine. Once it's installed, start it from the Desktop icon or from the Start menu item (Start ➤ Programs ➤ RealJukebox Skin Converter). Then follow the four-step process to convert the skin.

Up Next

In this chapter, you've learned how to create custom skins for Winamp and RealJukebox.

In the next chapter, we'll discuss how to put together a serious collection of MP3 files—including how to plan and build a server to hold them all. Turn the page.

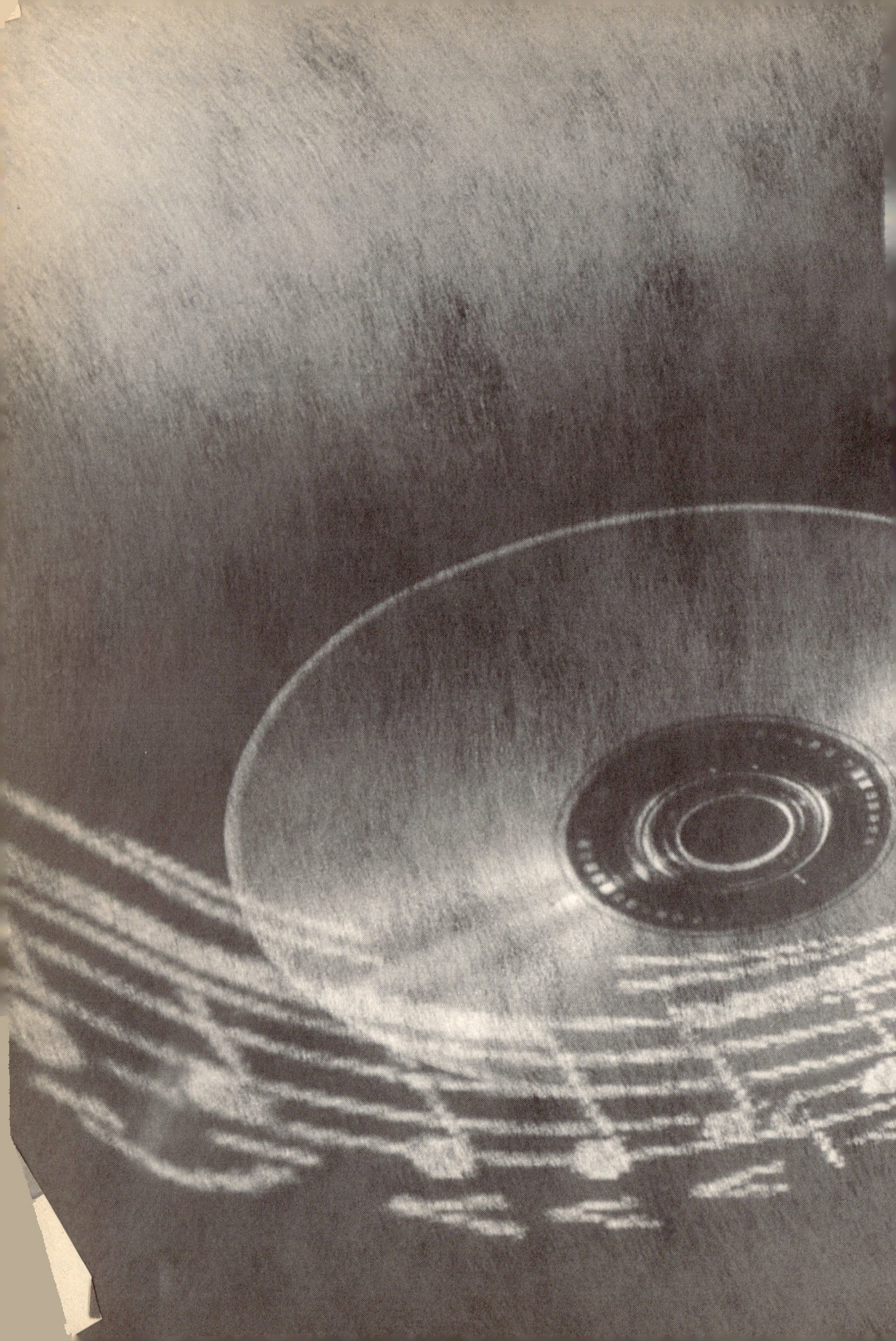

Chapter 22

Building a Serious Music Collection

FEATURING

- Facing up to the specter of bit-rot
- Getting the best music quality possible
- Choosing a naming convention for your MP3 files
- Building an MP3 server
- Backing up your server or music collection

In this chapter, we'll discuss the considerations that should churn through your brain when you're building a serious music collection. If you're reading this book, you're probably heavily into music, and likely to remain so for the foreseeable future. By now, you've found that MP3 (or one of the other digital-audio formats that we discuss in Chapter 23, "Other Digital-Audio Formats") makes a great way of storing, organizing, and enjoying your music. And you're thinking about how you'll use MP3 (or that other format) in the long term.

This chapter offers some suggestions.

We'll start off by briefly kicking around the cheerless topic of bit-rot, how it grieves CDs, and what you might want to do about it. We'll then review how to get the best music quality possible in your MP3 files and how to simplify your life by choosing and using a naming convention for each file you create. After that, we'll suggest how you might want to approach building a server to store your MP3 files and deliver them to all the computers in your building. And we'll close by raking up the tedious but necessary topic of backing up your files before catastrophe strikes.

This chapter is on the short side, which should help you either take it seriously or skip over it. It's your choice.

CDs and Bit-Rot

If you're a serious audiophile and CD collector, you've probably heard of *bit-rot*—the degeneration of the data stored on a CD. If you own CDs and you haven't heard of bit-rot, it's about time you did. Ready? Remember not to shoot the messenger...

Weren't CDs supposed to last forever? In theory, yes. But nobody really knows for sure. At this writing, there's no doubt that some of the CDs produced in the 1980s are no longer playable. Some have been trashed through overplaying and clumsy use. Others have been deliberately destroyed in a valiant effort to preserve the innocence of those people in the world lucky enough not to have experienced the New Romantic movement. The remainder appear perfect—but some of them won't play because they've suffered invisible deterioration.

For anyone who remembers the CD-versus-vinyl demonstrations of the late 1980s, in which CDs were portrayed as virtually indestructible, there's a certain humor in the situation. For example, Guy happened to be living in Japan in late 1987, and bought a CD player from a department store because, in Japan at that time, CDs were no more expensive than cassette tapes (in other words, cassettes in Japan were viciously overpriced).

The Japanese sales clerk demonstrated the robustness of the CD by dropping it on the floor, throwing it to a colleague (who dropped it), and wiping it deliberately across a gritty surface so that it was covered in enough dirt to stop a record-player's stylus dead in its tracks. Then he put it into the CD player that Guy was considering buying, and demonstrated that it played perfectly (which it did).

Such enthusiasm for CDs seemed normal at the time. But these days, now that the CD format is well established as a key standard for long-term storage, people who've heard of bit-rot tend to treat CDs with something more approaching the deference normally accorded to Porsche 969s stashed in rather large safety deposit boxes in Swiss banks because they're too valuable to drive.

REVENGE OF THE LP

Bit-rot threatens to make CDs a more fragile storage medium than the much-maligned vinyl. Many vinyl records from the early 1900s are still playable, provided that you can come up with the right equipment. But there's doubt about the viability of CDs even 10 or 15 years old. Besides, a vinyl LP will play with a scratch or two in it: You'll get unpleasant blips in the sound as the needle bumps through the scratches, but the rest of the music should sound just fine. But if even a few

CONTINUED →

> tracks of a CD lose enough data, a CD drive will be unable to play any of it.
>
> Moreover, audio CDs are much less sensitive to data dropout than data CDs. Most audio CD players have a fair tolerance for scratches and dust. In addition, portable CD players are built to withstand bumps and drops. A blip in the audio stream tends to be no more than annoying, while a few vital bits dropped from a data CD can leave a whole file—or a whole disc—unreadable.

For anyone who hasn't caught it at work on their CD collection, bit-rot is elusive and easily ignored. Depending on whom you believe, the evidence of bit-rot ranges from anecdotal to semi-scientific—but as soon as you find your CDs becoming unplayable for no apparent reason, chances are that you'll look down and see something that looks like a road to Damascus under your feet.

The worst bit (no pun) of it is that once you discover bit-rot in your CDs, you may no longer be able to salvage the CDs. You can't solve it by copying the bit-rotten CDs, as doing so would copy the rotten bits along with the good bits. Your best bet is probably to rip the CDs to WAV files, ripping as slowly as possible, using all the error-correction features that your ripper provides. Use analog extraction where digital extraction fails. That way, you should be able to get a copy, close if not perfect, of each of the tracks from the CD.

So—your CDs are perishable, or may be perishable, or may prove completely stable and faithful till a hundred generations of men pass away. But you need to assume that they may not last, and back up any CDs that you cannot afford to lose. Once you've encountered bit-rot, you'll probably start to consider creating backups of your music CDs to make sure that none of your music becomes unplayable. By making regular backups of your CDs, you can protect yourself against the bit-rot that claims some CDs in the long term.

You can copy a CD to a recordable CD, but because recordable CD media are thought to be less stable than commercially burned CDs, this may not get you far. Perhaps the ultimate protection against bit-rot on CDs is to rip the CD tracks as WAV files and store those on a hard drive. That way, if the CD goes bad, you have a perfect digital copy from which you can cut a new CD.

As you'd imagine, there are several disadvantages to doing this. The first is the amount of space you need: up to 650MB per CD, depending on how full it is, so a monster 60GB drive might hold only 100 or so CDs. Second, the WAV file doesn't have any capacity for tag information, so the filename is the only way of directly identifying a WAV file.

Oh, and third—you'll need to back up the hard drive... and with the quantity of information we're talking about here, that's not going to be easy. We'll discuss a couple of backup solutions later in the chapter, but in short, it ain't going to be fun.

Getting the Best Music Quality

If you're going to be storing all your music digitally, you'll want to make sure as much of it as possible is of as high a quality as possible. This is easy enough to do in theory, but it takes a while in practice.

First, establish your baseline quality for MP3 files that you create. Rig the best setup you can manage at the moment and run some tests to find the quality you want.

What the best setup is for you will depend entirely on your circumstances. If you have a single computer, and you'll be doing everything on it (ripping, encoding, and playing back), you won't have too many variables. If you have multiple computers, test their relative performance. You might want to rip on one computer, encode on another, and play back on a third.

If you'll be piping output from your sound card to your stereo system, test the sound through that. Use quality cables and connectors—don't degrade the signal supplied by a quality sound card to thunderous speakers by running it through an inferior cable. Also, do some listening tests through high-quality headphones. Headphones may reveal some imperfections that your speakers mask—and vice versa, of course.

Once you've established your baseline quality, consider carefully whether to encode your MP3 files at that quality or at a higher quality. The baseline is for your current setup, but if you improve one or more of the components next month or next year, you may expose deficiencies in the quality that you weren't able to hear before. And because MP3 is a lossy compression format, any information you discard during encoding is lost to you for good.

So even if you establish that a bitrate of 128kbps delivers as good sound as you can get on your current setup, you might want to encode at a higher bitrate (160kbps, say, or maybe 192kpbs) so as to keep more information in your MP3 files as insurance against an improvement in your setup. For crucial tracks, such as those on a failing CD or on a rare CD you've (ahem) borrowed, you may want to crank up the bitrate as far as the encoder goes (typically 320kbps) for an archive copy in addition to a copy at your regular bitrate. (You might also store WAV files of the tracks so that you have a lossless version, but as usual, it'll cost you disk space.)

Try a variety of the encoders available for your platform. As mentioned earlier in the book, some encoders are free, some are shareware, and some have demos, but you may well have to pay for others if you want to test them to your satisfaction. (A bunch of 30-second test files may not give you the definitive answer on quality, and some demo versions choose which few tracks on a CD they'll record, perhaps ignoring your designated comparison tracks.) Buying software that you're not sure you want, or that you might end up not using, goes against the grain for most people—but compared to the cost of a handful of CDs (whose contents you may turn out not to like), it's perhaps not so bad.

If you need to adjust the sound balance of any of the music from which you're creating MP3 files, you'll need to do so at the WAV stage. Rip the CD tracks to WAV files, then manipulate them as necessary before encoding them. Because the CD is (in theory) delivering a perfect rendition of the audio, you're essentially disagreeing with the mixing or mastering of the original music. The results you achieve may be disappointing—it's not like taking the clicks, pops, and hisses out of a WAV file derived from a vinyl record. But if someone has really screwed up the mastering on a CD, or if they've dumped an LP onto a CD without cutting the noise, there's no reason you shouldn't try to take care of the problem.

For MP3 files you download, you'll need to be more forgiving of lower quality. The tracks may be available only at a bitrate that's lower than your ideal, or they may have been encoded using an encoder that produces poor results. There's not much you can do about either problem except use your graphic equalizer to take the sting out of anything horrible.

Picking a Naming Convention for Your MP3 Files

Next, you'll need to pick a naming convention for your MP3 files. Do we see you recoil in horror? Yes, a naming convention is stuffy, pretentious, and bureaucratic—that's why you hate the network administrator in the office who makes you use a naming convention for the files that you create every work day—but it works. Well.

Jukebox software such as MusicMatch Jukebox, RealJukebox, and SoundJam can handle much of the organization for you, presenting the contents of many different folders (and, if necessary, different drives) as an apparently seamless database. But you'll want to have an underlying naming and locating scheme so that you can easily locate the files you want on your hard drives.

In order to pick an effective naming convention, decide how you will store your MP3 files. Your options are clear enough:

- You could divide the music into major genres (Alternative, Trance, Rock, Classical, Gospel), with each genre in a different folder. If you do this, you'll have to be consistent about the divisions. For example, should the Chemical Brothers be filed under Techno, or should they really be under Seething Electronic Noise? Is Rainbow actually Heavy Metal, or is it Ancient Rock? Is Britney Spears more of a Tedious Teenage Star or a Bellybutton Superstar? Yes, we're being silly about it—but you get the point.

- You could divide the music by artist, either within the categories or without.

- Within the artist folders, you could divide the tracks by CD or album.

Once you've decided how to store your MP3 files, you should have no problem in deciding how to name each track. At a minimum, you'll probably want the artist's name and the track's name—for example, `Rolling Stones - Brown Sugar.mp3`. If you don't use folders to contain CDs or albums, you may want to include the CD or album name in the title: `Led Zeppelin - IV - Stairway to Heaven.mp3`, and so on. (This can make the filenames uncomfortably long.)

If you include the CD or album name, you may also want to include the track number. If you don't include the CD or album name, the track number helps little. If you do include the track number, be sure it's a double-digit number (01, 02, etc.) if the CD or album contains more than ten tracks, so that the tracks sort properly in an ascending alphabetical sort.

Don't underestimate the value of ID3 tags. We recommend that you tag all your MP3 files as soon as you create them. If your preferred ripper/encoder combination doesn't offer you CDDB features, enter the information manually using a tagger, as discussed in Chapter 20, "Working with MP3 Files."

Most jukebox programs let you view, sort, select, and play songs from their tags. This capability is invaluable if you have a large collection and want to choose tunes by mood (say, all Jazz) or you want to create a playlist of certain artists. And, if your collection is *really* big, it may help you find that elusive song whose title you can't quite remember. Finally, most MP3 jukeboxes and many ID3 utility programs can rename your files using a pre-specified format from their ID3 tags. Get the tags right, and you can automatically get the file names right.

BUILDING AN MP3 SERVER

If you have a serious music collection—let's say, upwards of 500 CDs' worth of MP3 files that you believe you'll want to listen to regularly (or at least be able to access at a moment's notice)—consider building an MP3 server for your household.

Building an MP3 server is less of an undertaking than it might seem. (Having one built for you is even less so.) If you're used to buying adequately performing or supercharged home or business PCs, buying a server can even be a pleasant surprise. You don't need many of the expensive components that are de rigueur for a desktop PC, such as a fast processor, half a ton of RAM, a screaming graphics card, a large monitor, and a DVD drive. Instead, get a modest processor (a midrange Celeron or Duron, perhaps; a K6; a Pentium II; or even a Pentium) and 64MB RAM. Add a suitable backup unit, depending on your taste. (We discuss backup techniques in the last section of this chapter.) Dig out last year's graphics card, and clean off that 14-inch monitor that's been gathering dust and sneers in your basement—you won't need more than a basic display on your server.

> **NOTE**
>
> Another option is to buy a pre-configured server. Almost every computer manufacturer from your local Three Guys and a Goat PCs up to Dell, IBM, HP, and Compaq will sell you a wide variety of servers. The trouble with most of these pre-configured servers is that they're designed for business needs rather than your needs: They'll have more expensive processors and motherboards than you want to pay for, and nothing like enough disk space. You can of course get additional disks fitted (preferably when you buy the server), but you'll pay substantially more for a pre-configured server than for one you spec out yourself.

If you'll be ripping on your desktop PC, you may even be able to dispense with a CD-ROM drive on your server. (You might need access to a CD-ROM drive to load your server's operating system. Or you might decide to put a CD-R or CD-RW drive in your server so that you could easily burn CDs for enjoyment or backup.) Even if you *are* using your server for ripping and encoding, you may be able to dispense with a sound card if your software is able to extract digital audio from the CD drive.

If you use your server to store and deliver files (rather than to play them back), your needs will be storage, connectivity, and reliability. We'll discuss these needs in the following subsections.

Storage

If your server is anything like ours, storage is where most of the money you spend on the server is going to go. These days, you can't be too rich, Kate Moss can't be too thin, and your server can't have too much storage. In bulk, quality MP3 files take up a bunch of space, and in order to satisfy the demands of a voracious appetite for music, you'll need scores of gigabytes of storage. And if you then start collecting video clips, you'll need every byte you can squeeze into your server.

Building a Serious Music Collection

Once you've decided to create a server rather than keep your music on your screaming desktop machine, your first decision should be what kind of drives you'll use in your server: EIDE or SCSI? Usually this question comes down to cost and performance, though there's an element of capacity as well:

Cost Money talks and storage walks. Decide whether you want to pay the extra for a SCSI controller. It'll give you extra flexibility for your server because you can attach more drives and devices to a SCSI bus than to an EIDE bus, but it'll cost you substantially more than a standard EIDE setup. SCSI drives will typically set you back a bit more than EIDE drives as well, but you'll be able to build more storage capacity.

Performance If you're planning to need to bombard your server with requests, SCSI may suit you better than EIDE because a SCSI disk can respond more quickly than an EIDE disk to multiple requests. Under conventional stimulation, though, EIDE disks are more than fast enough, so don't feel that you have to pay the extra for SCSI.

Hard drives keep growing in size, roughly doubling year by year, but if you have a truly impressive collection of MP3 files, you'll be looking at using multiple drives. Under Windows, each drive appears as a separate letter, so each time you go to access a file, you need to remember (or work out) which drive it's on. Under other operating systems, you may be able to span the drives, so that the disks containing your files appear to client computers as just one drive. (If you're using a network—your network administrator almost certainly does this with your major network drives, which you probably call the F: drive or the U: drive.)

Whether you decide to go SCSI or EIDE, don't fill your server to capacity with drives at this point. Leave yourself some room for expansion with a bigger drive or two next year. At this writing, the largest available drives are 73GB, with 100GB drives on the horizon.

The largest *affordable* drives are in the 60GB range. A couple of these will give you a good amount of storage space to get started, and you'll be able to add a 120GB drive next year and a 250GB drive the year after that...you get the idea.

Connectivity

The second element in your server is connectivity. In order to be of any use, your server needs to be able to deliver in short order the files it contains to the clients that demand them.

Usually, this means giving your server the nicest network card that makes sense. If your network is limited to 10Mbps, it may make sense to reuse an old 10BaseT network card, but if you're buying a new card, get one that can handle Fast Ethernet speeds (100Mbps) as well. Get a parallel-tasking card if you're expecting the server to be putting a lot of bits on the wire in a short time.

If you're cabling your house, apartment, or dorm for the first time, your first choice network should be Fast Ethernet, because it'll give you the speed that you'll need in the future. You can get away with 10Mbps Ethernet for the time being if that's what you already have installed, but at this writing, it's a mistake to buy 10Mbps equipment, because 100Mbps equipment costs only a little more.

> **NOTE**
> Wireless, phone-line, and power-line networks aren't great for connecting to a music server. If they're your only options, so be it. But if you have the choice, go with a regular wired network. Phone-line and power-line networks deliver less speed than regular wires, and wireless network cards tend to get unhappy when fed a constant diet of music files.

Reliability

Storage is vital, and connectivity is key—but reliability may well outclass them both.

When building your server, don't use any ancient components that might compromise the server's reliability. In particular, don't use a motherboard, a processor, RAM, or drives that you even suspect might be flaky. You may be able to get away with older items for less-vital components such as the graphics card and network card, but don't use any component that might damage your data.

Choose a suitable operating system (as discussed in the next subsection), and burn in your system for at least 72 hours before committing any files to it. Once you've got files on it that you value, make regular backups (as discussed at the end of this chapter).

Operating System

Your server doesn't need to use any of the traditional "server" operating systems—it can use any reliable operating system that'll deliver the results you need. Above all, don't imagine for a moment that you need to buy a copy of NetWare or Windows 2000 Server for your MP3 server. You don't need to spend anything like that amount of dough.

Unless you're majorly strapped, it's probably going to be a mistake to use Windows 9*x* or Windows Me for your server. Despite the best efforts of Microsoft's Windows technicians, none of these operating systems is suitable for providing reliable services to even the smallest network of computers. If you're a Windows 98 regular, you may recall the minuscule amount of surprise that greeted the belated revelation of the bug that caused Windows 98 to crash after 47 days of nonstop operation. There was little surprise because few users had reached anything like that length of uptime without a crash, and those who *had* reached 47 days didn't find anything odd with their computer crashing at that point.

If you're a Windows regular, get Windows NT 4 Workstation. You can pick up a copy of Windows NT 4 Workstation cheap these days if you cruise some of the less trendy sections of the Web. Windows 2000 Professional is about $150 after rebates if you're upgrading from Windows 9x. Either of these operating systems can run on a computer with 64MB RAM and deliver good enough uptime between restarts—anything up to three or four months if you avoid bogging it down with memory-eating services.

If you have even a nodding familiarity with Linux or one of the free Unix operating systems, you'd do well to use that for your server's operating system. Linux in particular scores highly because of its low cost, its stability, its performance on modest or even disappointing hardware, and its rapid development cycle. Better yet, the Linux community has demonstrated a strong interest in digital music, and, as you saw earlier in this book, great players and encoders are available for Linux.

> **BUYING A COMPONENT SERVER**
>
> Instead of planning and building a custom server, you may want to buy a component server such as a Cobalt Qube (from Cobalt Networks). Component servers have the great advantage of ease of use—they come as a sealed unit with the operating system installed, so installing the server takes little more than plugging it into electricity and Ethernet and configuring a few simple parameters. They also offer features such as RAID (Redundant Array of Inexpensive Disks), which can help prevent your losing data.
>
> The disadvantage is that they cost far more than custom servers that contain the same amount (or more) of storage space. For example, a Qube server with 120GB capacity costs around $2999 at this writing, while you could put together a custom server with 120GB of disk space for less than half that.

Backing Up Your Server

If you build or buy an MP3 server, you'll need to back it up regularly to protect yourself against data loss when something untoward happens.

Again, backing up is a businesslike, bureaucratic, and boring thing to suggest, but if you've invested anything like as much time as we have in building a collection of MP3 files, no way do you want to lose it. As a computer owner, you're probably already familiar with the range of threats to your data, from power outages and nearby lightning strikes (do you live in Virginia, Florida, or Colorado, by any chance?) to viruses, software mishaps, user error (such as formatting the wrong drive), and theft or vandalism. If the worst comes to the worst, you'll be looking at a good few months' worth of ripping and downloading—and that's if you can devote yourself to it full time.

So plan a backup strategy from the start, and follow it consistently. Choose a suitable backup device, attach it to your server, and use it regularly.

Recordable CDs typically provide the least expensive form of backup—but unless you have a smallish collection or are very determined, they may not prove a satisfactory backup medium, because you'll need scores or even hundreds of them to back up all the files on your server. However, you may be able to manage a workable solution by creating incremental backups. Since most of the files on the server will not change once you've encoded them, tagged them, and put them in the right folder, an incremental backup will back up only the files that you've added to the server since your last backup. But restoring the server from a multitude of CDs still won't be any fun.

High-capacity removable disks, such as the Iomega Jaz and the Castlewood Orb, offer 2GB or more per disk. Recordable DVDs provide better capacity (up to 5.2GB) but are far more expensive than CD-R disks. Digital tape provides better capacity—50GB tapes are relatively affordable—but the drives themselves set you back several hundred dollars.

> **AN ALTERNATIVE: CREATING AN AUDIO SERVER**
>
> If you have multiple PCs distributed around your dwelling, having a file server and playing the music on the client PCs is usually the easiest way of getting audio to multiple locations. But it's not the only way.
>
> Another way to send MP3 music around your household is to have a central PC acting as an audio server. You can get higher-end sound cards that support multiple sets of WAV drivers and multiple outputs. You can then set up multiple copies of your favorite MP3 player, each attached to a different WAV driver that pipes audio to a particular location in the house: the living room, the master bedroom, the kitchen, the den, and so on.
>
> The disadvantage to this kind of setup is that you need to command the central PC to control the MP3 software. So if the PC is in the den, you'll need to go into the den to set music playing in the kitchen or bedroom. You can get around this problem by using remote-control software (for Windows or the Mac), remote login (for Linux or Unix), or special remote mice.
>
> If you're interested in remote-control software for Windows, start with Microsoft's NetMeeting, which is included with Windows 9x, Windows NT, Windows 2000, and Windows Me. (Usually it's a good idea to download the latest version of NetMeeting from the Microsoft Web site, www.microsoft.com.) For the Macintosh, various remote-control packages are available, including Timbuktu Pro from Netopia (www.netopia.com).

Up Next

In this chapter, we've discussed some of the important considerations for building a serious music collection based on MP3: protecting yourself against bit-rot; getting quality files; naming and storing them consistently; building a server to keep them on; and backing up your server or your collection.

It's time for a change of focus. In the next chapter, we'll round off the book by discussing the other digital-audio formats that are trying to challenge MP3.

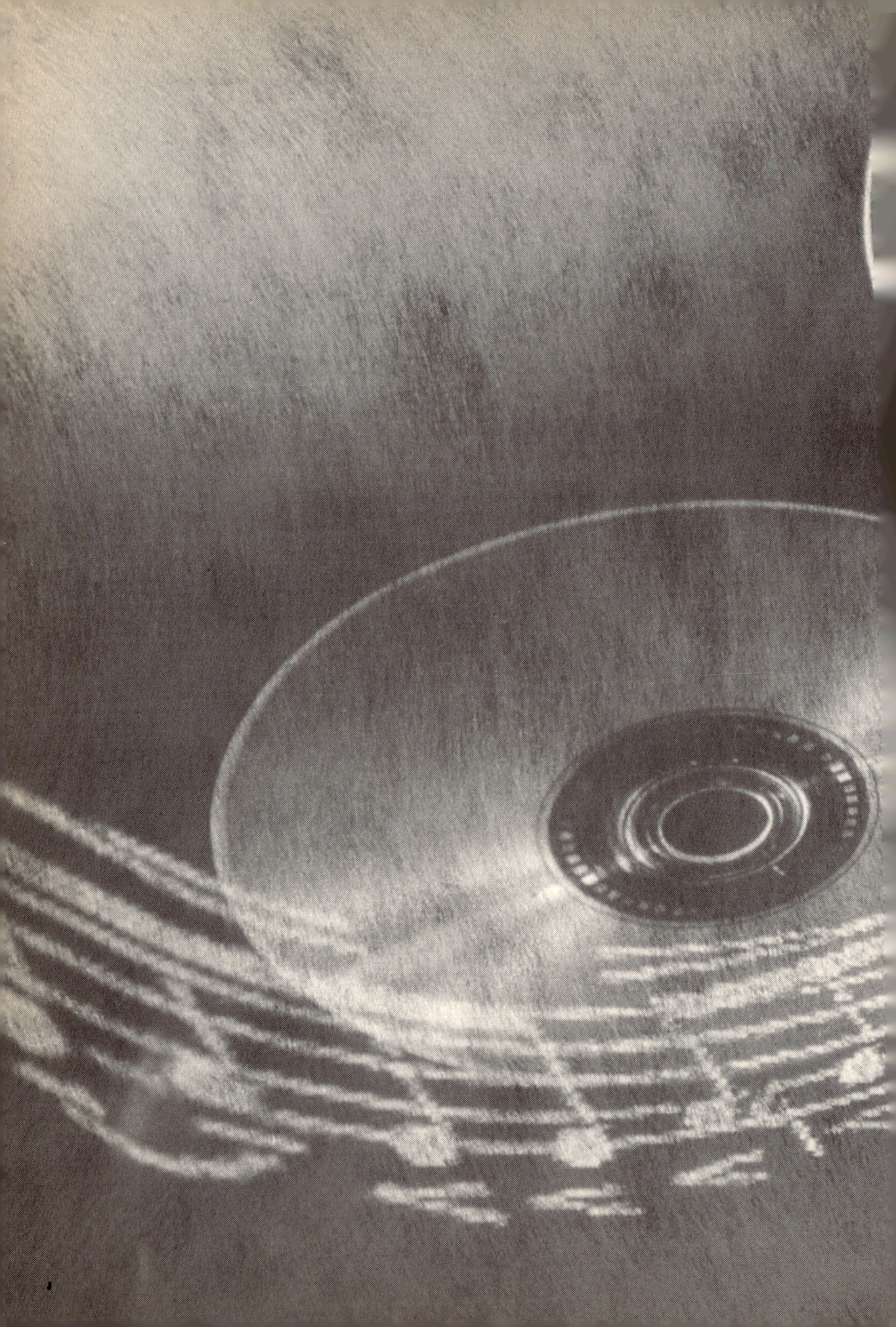

Chapter 23

Other Digital-Audio Formats

Featuring

- Why consider using other digital-audio formats?
- AAC
- A2B
- ATRAC3
- Liquid Audio
- QDesign
- MS Audio and Windows Media Technologies
- TwinVQ
- RealAudio
- QuickTime

In this chapter, we'll discuss some of the other digital-audio formats that compete with or (perhaps more accurately) provide alternatives to MP3.

We'll start by asking the $64,000 question: Why should you even consider using a digital-audio format other than MP3? As you'll see, there are a number of good reasons, but they only hold water for some people.

We'll then move on and examine the alternative digital-audio formats. There are quite a few of these, and we'll concentrate on the ones that appear to be most viable at this writing, not necessarily the ones that provide the best quality or are technologically the most advanced.

Why Consider Using Other Digital-Audio Formats?

There are various reasons to consider using digital-audio formats other than MP3. Depending on who you are, some of the reasons are almost compelling, while others are trivial. But to put it in a nutshell, if MP3 is giving everything you need in digital audio, you'll probably find little reason to investigate these other formats, let alone switch to one of them.

Better Technology

Some of the other digital-audio formats claim to have better technology than MP3. (In some cases, "better" simply means "newer," but we'll leave that aside.) Where this is true, it's more or less irrelevant. What matters are the features that the technology delivers, and the features that the other digital-audio formats need to beat MP3 on the features that matter to the consumer.

Better Audio Quality

Some of the other digital-audio formats claim better audio quality than MP3. Some of these claims seem to be true; others are more debatable. But for most listeners, the quality of MP3 files is high enough, so they have no need for a higher quality format.

Better Security

Most of the other digital-audio formats offer built-in security features that give the creator (or distributor) of the file more control over its distribution and usage. For example, some digital-audio formats essentially lock the file to the computer on which it's downloaded or first used so that you can't play it on any other computer. Others let you create a file that expires on a certain date or after a certain number of plays.

These security features tend to be a selling point for artists, record companies, and other creators and publishers of audio content. They tend to have no detectable appeal to most consumers— which is a significant part of the reason why none of these formats has become popular yet. If consumers were screaming for a digital-audio format that would prevent them from transferring an audio file they've purchased from one computer they owned to another, no doubt the market would take off vertically.

Greater Compression Ratios

As we've mentioned, MP3 offers an impressive compression ratio of around 10:1 (at the 128kbps bitrate) while retaining near-CD quality. Some of the other digital-audio formats manage better compression ratios than this while retaining about the same audio quality. But in most cases, the improvement isn't enough to drive people to a new format.

For example, a2b files typically run about a third smaller than MP3 files. A three-minute a2b file would be about 2.25MB compared to an MP3 file's 3MB. This means you can wedge more files into the same amount of disk space or memory, but the difference isn't enough to overcome people's resistance to secure formats or the inertia that MP3 has accumulated.

...and the Disadvantages

Most of the competing digital-audio formats have some or all of these disadvantages:

- There's not much audio content available in these digital-audio formats.

- There are restrictions on what you can do with the files that you download or create. For example, several of the formats lock a file to a particular PC.

- Many of the file formats require a proprietary player.

- Many of the file formats do not work with portable audio hardware (such as portable MP3 players).

- It can be expensive, difficult, or even impossible to create your own files in these formats. If a format is designed for secure distribution of music, it's not surprising if the company behind it doesn't provide an encoder so that you can rip your CD collection and encode it in this format—but it certainly lessens the appeal of the format vis-à-vis MP3.

AAC

AAC, the Advanced Audio Codec, is a powerful codec that by all accounts produces terrific sound and technologically out-muscles all the other formats. However, there's no effective widespread ISO-compliant implementation of AAC.

Developed by engineers at a number of the major players in the digital-audio business—including heavy hitters like Fraunhofer, AT&T, Lucent, Dolby, and Sony—AAC supports up to 48 channels, far outclassing the simple mono/stereo to which MP3 is limited. To give the engineers a free hand, AAC was built *not* to be backwards compatible with MP3, which means that you can't play AAC files on MP3 players that don't specifically have support for AAC. (You can find AAC plug-ins for a variety of MP3 players, including Winamp.)

At this writing, you can find several AAC implementations, some ISO-compliant (such as the K+K AAC Encoder) and others not (such as Liquid Audio's Liquifier Pro). AT&T's a2b (which is discussed later in this chapter) implements some parts of AAC.

> **NOTE**
> AAC will be one of the components of the MPEG-4 specification.

QDESIGN'S QDMC AND MVP

The QDesign Music Codec (QDMC for short) is a promising codec that appears to be making faster headway than many of its peers—even if it has a long way to go before it challenges MP3 for the public's hearts and minds.

Created by Canada-based QDesign Corporation, the QDMC is optimized for low bitrates and gives acceptable quality at compression ratios of 50:1 or lower. To achieve quality at high compression ratios, QDMC creates custom audio filters on the fly for each signal encoded instead of using a standardized set of filters. This makes for a slower encoding process than for MP3, but it produces more accurate results—even at low bitrates.

Unlike some of its competitors, QDesign seems to be making good progress at getting its technology into the marketplace:

- ▶ QDesign provides a proprietary encoder, the QDesign Music Encoder Professional, that runs on the Macintosh G4 and on Windows and costs $399.
- ▶ Tonos, Inc., which describes itself as a "music insider's network," has licensed QDesign's compression technology for its Tonocorder product, which lets users record, mix, and create custom tracks on the Tonos Web site, adding vocals directly from their own computer.
- ▶ PortalPlayer, Inc. has partnered with QDesign to extend the storage capacity on digital music players.
- ▶ SpinRecords.com, a large online-music site, is using MVP (described shortly) as a cross-platform solution.
- ▶ InterTrust Technologies Corporation and the MetaTrust Utility have partnered with QDesign to use the QDMC in MetaTrust-certified audio applications to deliver digital-rights management–enabled streaming audio.

At the same time, QDesign is also delivering an effective end-user solution. It provides an encoder and player called MVP for both the Mac and Windows platforms. MVP plays MP3 files and QDesign files and encodes in both formats, storing QDesign files in the QuickTime MOV file format. (You can play the QDesign files back using QuickTime if you like; Apple is using the QDMC as part of the audio component for QuickTime 4.)

You can download a free version of MVP from the MVP site (www.mvpsite.com). MVP requires QuickTime, which the MVP site supplies as part of the download if you don't have it. Together, MVP and QuickTime make a hefty download of just under 10MB. If you download QuickTime, the MVP installation routine runs the QuickTime installation routine for you.

The free version of MVP provides a 30-day trial of MP3 and MP2 encoding. After that, it plays all tracks but records only in QDesign

Other Digital-Audio Formats

format. After the trial period, you'll need the $19.99 version of MVP, which can record unlimited numbers of tracks in MP3 and MP2 format. You can upgrade the free version of MVP to the paid version by paying and entering a serial number.

Figure 23.1 shows the MVP player for Windows.

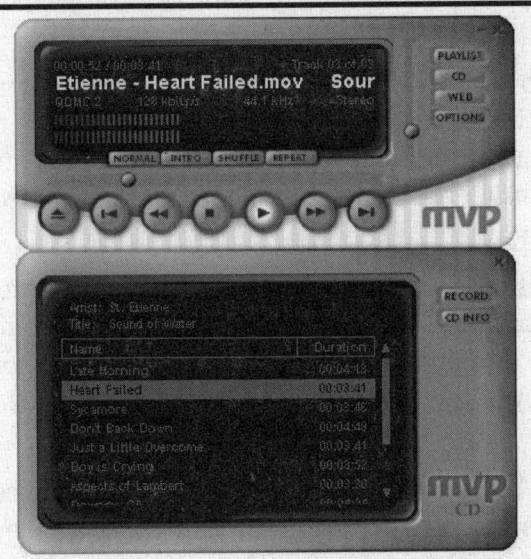

FIGURE 23.1: QDesign's MVP player can play MP3 files and QDesign files.

If you're interested in checking out the QDMC, download the demo encoder from the QDesign Web site (www.qdesign.com).

A2B

a2b is a proprietary music format created by AT&T Labs. Using the AAC codec and proprietary AT&T compression algorithms, a2b claims better audio performance than MP3 (which seems to be true), and a compression ratio of up to 20:1 without a "perceptual loss of quality," which we doubt. (We feel that at this compression ratio, you start to lose music quality. At lesser compression ratios, a2b sounds very good.)

a2b Components

a2b provides (in theory) tight security by using four components as follows:

- The CryptoLib Security Library is used to encrypt music in a track while it's being transmitted across the Internet. (This is primarily to prevent the audio stream from being hijacked in transit.) The track is then stored in an encrypted format.

- A digital signature is used to identify the user, or (more precisely) their computer. The a2b player checks that the computer's digital signature matches that of the computer for which the copy of the track has been licensed. No match, no audio.

- A unique song key is used to identify each track, so that once you've purchased a copy of a track, only your player can play that copy of the track.

- The PolicyMaker electronic licensing system lets the licensor specify how the user can use a track: whether the user can copy the track, how many times they can play it, what the "timeframe" is for the track (whether the track is set to expire at a certain date), and whether the user can sell the track to another person. PolicyMaker kicks in when you try to start a track playing. It checks the track license against your digital signature and sets the track playing if all is in order. If it is not, PolicyMaker prevents you from playing the track.

These four components notwithstanding, any halfway-determined pirate can hijack the sound signal either at the sound card or at the output, just as they can with any other audio signal.

Advantages and Disadvantages of a2b

The advantages and disadvantages of a2b are clear:

- a2b provides better audio quality than MP3 at about the same compression ratio, or similar quality with smaller file sizes. This is good for both audio content producers and consumers.

- a2b provides strong but not foolproof security features, making it interesting to audio content providers but less interesting to consumers.

- As yet, very little audio content is available in a2b format. Unless the consumer's primary motivation is audio quality (rather than content), there's little reason to use a2b.

- The consumer can't easily create a2b files they way they can MP3 files. This means you can't rip all your CDs and transition all your music to a2b format.

- You can only download a track using the computer on which you will play it. For example, you can't download a track on a friend's computer that has a fast Internet connection, then transfer the track to your computer and play it. This is a significant disadvantage for consumers.

- The a2b MES file format lets the creator of the file include a track's lyrics, credits, a message, and a graphic (for example, the CD cover). These features are good for artist, record company, and consumer.

Getting and Installing the a2b music player

The a2b music player is available for the Windows and Macintosh platforms. The Windows player requires a minimum of a Pentium-120 with 16MB RAM, a halfway recent version of Netscape (version 3.1 or above) or Internet Explorer (version 3 or above), and a Sound Blaster–compatible sound card. For streaming audio, you also need RealPlayer. The Mac player requires a 120MHz PowerPC chip, 32MB RAM, System 8 or better, and a browser of the same caliber as for the PC.

Download the a2b music player from www.a2bmusic.com and double-click the distribution file to start the installation.

On the PC, close Netscape and RealPlayer before running the setup routine. (If you have the Control Panel open, close that too.) On the Mac, the setup routine asks your permission to forcibly quit all other running applications so that they cannot interfere with it.

On the PC, the a2b music player uses a standardized InstallShield routine. On the Mac, it uses a straightforward VISE routine. In each case, the main excitement is creating a digital ID, which you do in the Create Digital ID dialog box, the PC version of which is shown in Figure 23.2.

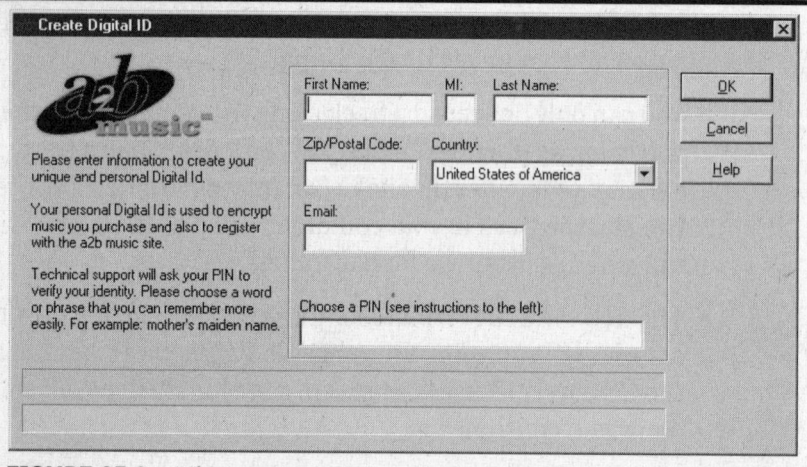

FIGURE 23.2: When setting up the a2b music player, you need to create a digital ID.

Once the digital ID has been created, a process that takes 30 to 60 seconds, the a2b music player is displayed. You can then download tracks (for example, from the a2b Music Web site, which has a number of free tracks and many others that you can purchase) and play them. When you start downloading a track, the download mechanism checks that you have the a2b music player set up on

Other Digital-Audio Formats 883

your computer and that your license key is appropriate for playing the track. It then starts the download.

> **TIP**
>
> If you get the message "Error retrieving keys" when trying to download an a2b track, you may need to reconfigure your proxy settings on the Connection page of the a2b music Preferences dialog box (Options ➢ Preferences). If the Netscape proxy or the Internet Explorer proxy seem not to be working, you can configure the proxy manually (if you know the settings) or choose to disable the HTTP proxy.

By default, the a2b music player automatically plays the file when the download ends. To disable this, clear the Play Song When Download Is Finished check box in the download dialog box. Figure 23.3 shows the a2b music player for Windows playing a Chely Wright track.

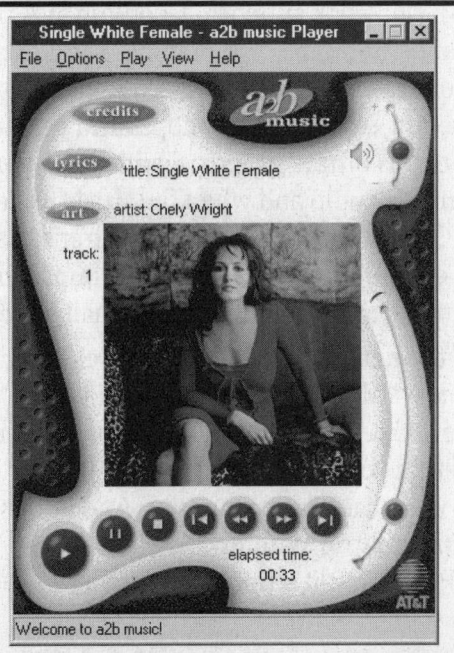

FIGURE 23.3: The a2b music player can display pictures, lyrics, and more.

OpenMG and ATRAC3

OpenMG is a proprietary Sony Corporation copyright-protection technology that uses the secure ATRAC3 format (the same format used for MiniDiscs). OpenMG is SDMI-compliant, conforming to the Portable Device Specification version 1.0.

Unlike some of the other digital-audio formats, OpenMG has been implemented to allow the end user to

- Download files securely (with an Electronic Music Distribution key).

- Create files easily enough—at this writing, typically by using Sony's OpenMG Jukebox software.

- Lend (or "check out") copies of files to SDMI-compliant portable hardware. (At this writing, that mostly means Sony's VAIO Music Clip and Memory Stick Walkman products, though others may yet emerge.)

At this writing, OpenMG Jukebox supports recording in ATRAC3 format at bitrates of 132kbps, 105kpbs, and 66kbps. The 105kbps bitrate sounds (to us) about the same quality as 128kbps MP3 files encoded with a good encoding setup. The 132kbps bitrate sounds appreciably better. The 66kbps bitrate sounds significantly worse, and is best used for non-music audio and when file size is more important than quality. (Given that you can't usefully transfer ATRAC3 files to another computer, file size should be important only if you're trying to squeeze a lot of music onto a small drive.)

Despite the "open" in the name, OpenMG files are closed in all conventional senses of the word. OpenMG files are stored in encrypted format and are locked to the computer on which they were created. Any copies that you check out to a portable device need to be checked back in on the same computer. And at this writing, OpenMG Jukebox runs only on Windows 98. Sony has announced an ATRAC3 Player, but it's not yet available.

Worse, at this writing, there's no way to restore OpenMG files from backup, so if your hard drive goes south, so does your music collection, and all the time and money you've invested in it. This dangerous and customer-unfriendly restriction makes it hard to recommend the OpenMG format to anybody except those who feel compelled to use Sony portable audio players.

Liquid Audio

One of the longer-lasting contenders in the digital-audio business, Liquid Audio has long been used as the format for IUMA, the Internet Underground Musical Archive ("the granddaddy of all music Web sites").

Liquid Audio offers high-quality audio (they claim true CD quality, which we'd say is an exaggeration) and impressive security features, which include registration both for downloading and playing tracks on one computer and downloading and playing tracks on multiple computers. Liquid Audio tracks include a significant amount of information, including a graphic of the album cover, credit information, liner notes, and lyrics. A track can also include a Genuine Music logo (if it's genuine) that contains information on "the origin and authenticity of the music file."

To play Liquid Audio files, you need the Liquid Audio player, which is called Liquid Player and is available for Windows and the Macintosh. Liquid Player plays both Liquid Audio tracks and MP3 files, giving you good flexibility. As you'd hope, you can mix the two in Liquid Player playlists as you wish.

Liquid Player supports a modest variety of CD burners from several manufacturers, including (at this writing):

- The Creative Labs CDR-4210
- The HP CD Writer 6020

- Assorted Plextor PlexWriter models
- The Philips CDD2400 Omniwriter
- A half-dozen Yamaha models

If you have one of the PlexWriters, a Yamaha, or another make, check the Liquid Audio Web site (www.liquidaudio.com) for the latest list.

> **TIP**
> If you're using RealPlayer G2, you can add to it a Liquid plug-in for listening to streaming audio.

Getting and Installing Liquid Player

The PC version of Liquid Player requires a 166MHz Pentium or better processor, 32MB RAM, and any full 32-bit version of Windows: Windows 95, Windows 98, Windows ME, Windows NT 4, or Windows 2000. The Macintosh version requires a 150MHz PowerPC processor (a G3 processor is recommended), 32MB RAM, and MacOS 7.6.1 or later.

Download the latest version of Liquid Player from www.liquidaudio.com or from one of the MP3 software sites, and double-click the distribution file to start the setup routine.

Both the Windows and Mac setup routines are unremarkable. The only thing worth mentioning is the Choose Data Streaming Rate dialog box (the Windows version of which is shown in Figure 23.4), in which you specify the speed of your Internet connection. At this writing, the choice is a bit limited, offering you nothing between two-channel ISDN and a T1 or greater line. If you have cable or DSL, you'll probably do better to choose the ISDN 2 Channel option rather than the T1, even if you typically get several hundred kilobits of throughput from your connection. At the end of the installation, you'll need to reboot your computer before you can run Liquid Player.

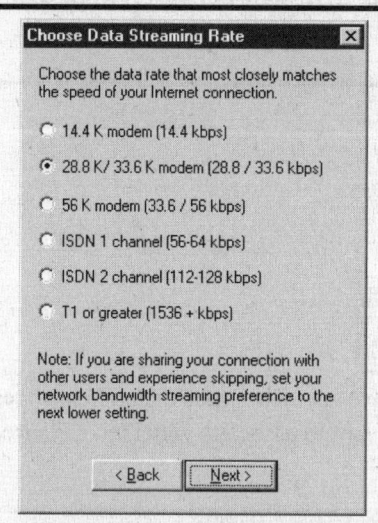

FIGURE 23.4: In the Choose Data Streaming Rate dialog box, choose something approximating the speed of your Internet connection.

The first time you run Liquid Player, you may need to select a proxy in the Liquid Player Proxy Settings dialog box. After that, you'll see the Liquid Player Music File Types dialog box, shown in Figure 23.5. Select the check boxes for the file types you want to associate with Liquid Player, and clear the others. If you want Liquid Player to automatically reclaim any file type that another player or ripper steals, select the Automatically Reclaim Audio File Types check box. Then click the OK button.

Liquid Player then encourages you to register, as shown in Figure 23.6 (again, this is the Windows version). You can choose to register either with FastTrack Security, which allows you to download and play the music only on the computer you're currently using, or with Passport, which allows you to download and play the music on multiple computers, but for which you need a credit card. In either case, you need to have an Internet connection up. If you don't register, you won't be able to download and purchase any songs.

FIGURE 23.5: In the Liquid Player Music File Types dialog box, choose the file types you want to associate with Liquid Player.

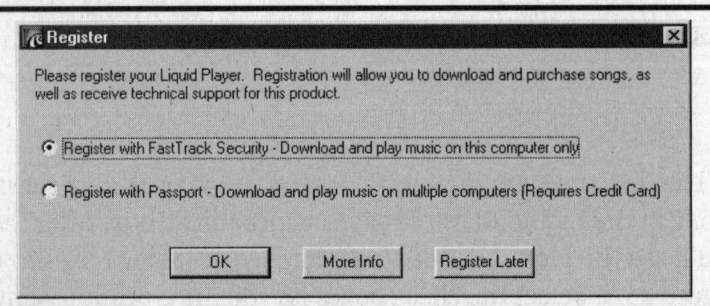

FIGURE 23.6: You'll need to register Liquid Audio before you can do anything much useful with it.

If you have a credit card and you trust secure Internet sites, the Liquid Audio Passport is probably a better bet than FastTrack Security, since it gives you the option to use any Liquid Audio tracks that you download or purchase on multiple computers. Your credit card is used to check your identity; it doesn't accrue any charge.

If you choose the Passport option in the Register dialog box, Liquid Player fires up your browser and points it at the liquid operations center, `https://loc.liquidaudio.com`. (If your connection fails, point your browser to this URL manually.) Fill in the form, including the exact postal address that your credit card uses (you need to get this address letter perfect), and submit it. If all goes well, you're issued your Passport, which is stored in a file named `passport.lqp` on your hard drive

If you choose to register with FastTrack Security, the Passport Registration dialog box shown in Figure 23.7 appears. Enter the requested information, click the Submit button, and you're on your way.

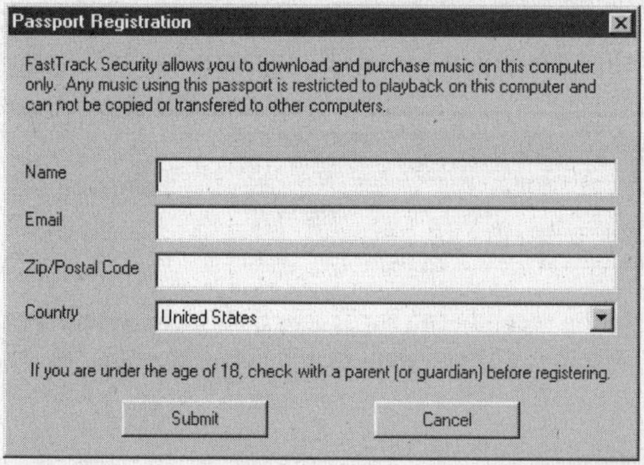

FIGURE 23.7: Registering for Liquid Audio via FastTrack Security involves surrendering the minimum amount of information but gives you less flexibility than registering with Passport.

Once you're registered, Liquid Player then displays the first Scan For Tracks dialog box (shown in Figure 23.8), offering to scan your computer for Liquid Audio tracks. If you have Liquid Audio tracks already, you'll probably want to choose the Yes button.

FIGURE 23.8: Liquid Player offers to scan your computer for Liquid Audio tracks.

If you choose Yes, Liquid Player displays the second Scan For Tracks dialog box, shown in Figure 23.9. Either choose a drive in the Scan Directory drop-down list, or click the Browse button to display the Browse For Folder dialog box, navigate to and select the directory, and click the OK button. Click the Scan button. The Scanning Drives dialog box appears while Liquid Player performs the scan, and then the main Liquid Player window is displayed.

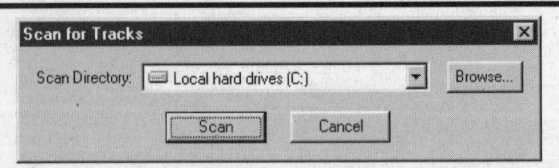

FIGURE 23.9: In the second Scan For Tracks dialog box, select the drive or folder that you want Liquid Player to scan.

TIP

You can also scan for tracks or playlists at your convenience by choosing View ➢ Track Pool to display the Music Organizer dialog box, then clicking the Scan button on the Track Pool page (to scan for tracks) or the Scan button on the Track Lists page (to scan for playlists). To import a track list manually, choose File ➢ Import Track List and use the resulting Open dialog box to identify the track list.

Other Digital-Audio Formats 891

Figure 23.10 shows Liquid Player playing a track.

FIGURE 23.10: Liquid Player can display album art, promotional information, notes, lyrics, or credits associated with the track.

Getting Liquid Audio Tracks

You can download a variety of Liquid Audio tracks from various sites on the Internet, including (naturally) the Liquid Audio Web site and the Internet Underground Musical Archive (www.iuma.org).

Depending on where you look, you'll find some free promotional tracks, but for most artists, the attraction of Liquid Audio is that, unlike with MP3, you can successfully charge people for tracks—so you'll also find more tracks for sale. Be warned that some Liquid

Audio sites implement *territory restrictions*, which mean that certain tracks are designated as being available only to certain geographical areas. For example, if you're in the U.K. and you want to download a track whose territory restrictions specify North America and Canada only, you're straight out of luck unless you can do some fancy redirection of your IP packets.

If a track that you're downloading uses a faceplate that's not currently installed on your system, Liquid Player displays the Download Faceplate dialog box, shown in Figure 23.11, asking whether you want to download the faceplate. Choose the Yes button or the No button as appropriate. If you don't want Liquid Player to harass you about faceplates again, select the Disable Faceplate Downloading check box before you dismiss the Download Faceplate dialog box.

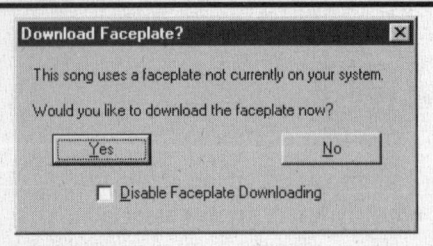

FIGURE 23.11: If you're downloading a track that uses a faceplate you don't have, Liquid Player invites you to download it.

You can also create your own Liquid Audio tracks by using the Liquifier Pro software that's available from Liquid Audio. Liquifier Pro is available under various pricing schemes, most of which seem too expensive for your average music fan. The pricing schemes are geared to bands that want to produce their own Liquid Audio tracks for secure distribution. (Liquid Audio also offers a service that creates Liquid Audio tracks for you.)

If you want to digitize your existing music collection, you'll do better to use MP3 than Liquid Audio. Given that the Liquid Player plays MP3 files with no problem, you can then mix your purchased (or free) Liquid Audio tracks with your homegrown MP3 files into playlists that meet your needs.

Windows Media Technologies

To nobody's surprise, Microsoft is eager to play in the digital-audio arena—and (as usual) they're using Windows to help them do so.

Microsoft's entry in this field is the Windows Media Audio (WMA) file format, which is part of Microsoft's Windows Media Technologies. Windows Media Technologies includes video compression as well as audio compression. The main tool for creating, managing, and playing WMA files is Windows Media Player, which comes included in every version of Windows except NT Embedded.

WMA files actually use the Advanced Streaming Format (ASF). As Microsoft explains it, WMA files are ASF audio files compressed with the Windows Media Audio codec. This is a fine distinction that doesn't seem worth making, and not surprisingly, many people regard WMA files as ASF files and name them accordingly, with ASF extensions. So you'll find a lot of audio-only ASF files on the Internet.

Equally unsurprisingly, Microsoft claims great things for the Windows Media codec, among them better sound quality than MP3 at similar bitrates. Even less surprisingly, many digital audiophiles take Microsoft's claims with anything from a grain to a pillar of salt. That said, WMA/audio ASF files encoded at a decent bitrate sound pretty good—and you can play them on a wide variety of MP3 players (including Winamp and Sonique) and jukeboxes (including MusicMatch Jukebox and Siren Jukebox).

WMA files have digital rights management features that include copyright protection—but these, like all other security features, can be cracked without much difficulty. (One cracking product, unfuck, was unleashed the day after Microsoft released MS Audio 4.0.)

The easiest way to create WMA files (without any renaming) is to use Windows Media Player version 7, which comes with Windows Me and is available for download for other Windows platforms from the Windows Media pages on the Microsoft Web site, `www.microsoft.com/windows/windowsmedia/en/default.asp`. Windows Media Player version 7 lets you "copy" a CD to your hard disk; this "copying" is actually ripping the tracks from the CD and encoding them in the WMA format.

Before you start "copying," choose Tools ➢ Options to display the Options dialog box, select the CD Audio page (see Figure 23.12), and choose the following settings:

- ▶ Select the Digital Playback check box and the Digital Copying check box for digital audio rather than for analog audio.

- ▶ Select the two Use Error Correction check boxes only if you find you're not getting good results without error correction. Error correction on "copying" slows down the process, and error correction on playback requires more processing power.

- ▶ Select either the third notch or the fourth notch on the Copy Music at This Quality slider—either the Best Quality setting (which encodes at 160kpbs) or the setting to its left (which encodes at 128kbps).

- ▶ Clear the Enable Personal Rights Management check box if you don't want to use Microsoft's personal rights management software.

- ▶ Use the Change button and the resulting Browse for Folder dialog box to select the folder in which you want to archive your music.

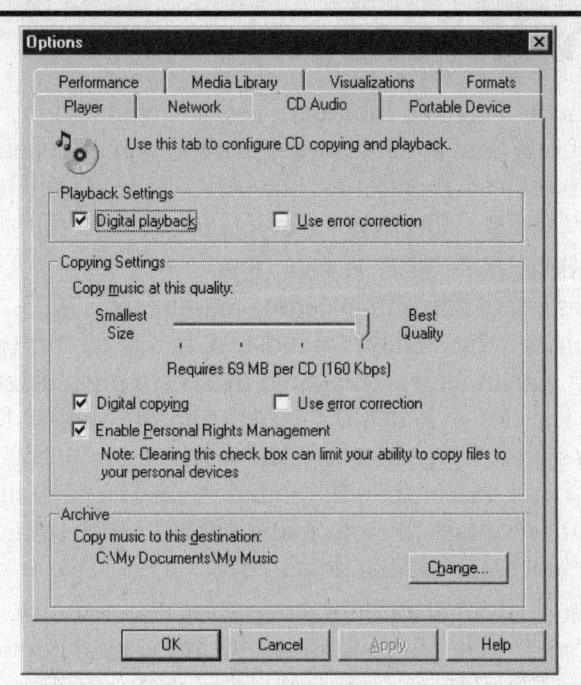

FIGURE 23.12: Choose application settings on the CD Audio page of the Options dialog box before you start "copying" music with Windows Media Player.

> **NOTE**
>
> Another possibility is to download the Windows Media Tools toolkit from the Microsoft Web site. At this writing, you can find the toolkit at www.microsoft.com/windows/windowsmedia/en/default.asp. Files that you create with the Windows Media Tools will be in ASF format, but you can rename them with the WMA extension if you want to make it clear that these are audio files rather than video files.

TwinVQ (VQF Format)

Transform-domain Weighted Interleave Vector Quantization (TwinVQ for short) is an audio-compression format developed by NTT Human Interface Laboratories. Like AAC, TwinVQ will be part of the MPEG-4 specification. TwinVQ files use the VQF extension and are usually referred to as *VQF files*.

TwinVQ uses a very different encoding method than MP3. TwinVQ combines individual bits of music data into *vectors* (pattern segments). Each vector is compared to a list of pre-built standard patterns, the closest match is selected, and the number for that pattern is stored. In crude terms, the VQF file contains a recipe for the sound, rather than the sound itself. This is similar to the way MIDI files contain the information about which sounds to play, except in much, much finer detail.

Reading a reductio-ad-absurdum description like that may make you feel that TwinVQ couldn't sound even halfway good if it was extremely lucky. What's surprising is that TwinVQ actually sounds pretty good to most people, and at very low bitrates, it tends to produce a more faithful result than MP3.

At higher bitrates, TwinVQ tends to suffer. Where MP3 encoding introduces small compression artifacts in the sound, TwinVQ loses detail. As a result, VQF files tend to sound softer or less precise than MP3 files of around the same quality; they also sometimes suffer from pre-echo and spatialization (in which the sound seems to be further away than in the original).

Generally speaking, TwinVQ needs much more CPU power for its encoding than MP3 does, and as a result, encoding VQF files at higher quality can be very slow. This is because TwinVQ was designed for use on higher powered processors than were in most PCs. However, thanks to the efforts of Intel and AMD, processors have more or less caught up to the required power. By contrast, TwinVQ decoding was designed to work on lower powered processors, and you can get good results on a (by today's standards) relatively slow PC such as a Pentium 166.

Other Digital-Audio Formats 897

From the consumer's perspective, the biggest strike against TwinVQ is that (at this writing) very few people are using it, nobody much appears to be championing it, and as a result, it's very hard to find tracks in VQF format.

Playing VQF Files

There are several possibilities for playing VQF files:

- Use the Yamaha SoundVQ Player, a 90-day trial version of which is available from the TwinVQ area on the Yamaha Web site (www.yamaha-xg.com/english/xg/SoundVQ/). Figure 23.13 shows the SoundVQ Player in action.

FIGURE 23.13: The Yamaha SoundVQ Player

- If you have Winamp, you can download a Winamp plug-in to play the tracks. The Winamp VQF plug-in is available from a number of sources, including www.mp3hotlist.com/vqf.htm.

- Use the MP3 player K-jofol, which also is available from a variety of sources.

- Use the Yamaha SoundVQ Encoder or the TwinVQ Encoder, both of which can play TwinVQ files as well as create them.

> **TIP**
>
> For more information on the VQF format, visit www.vqf.com. You'll also find a good list of links to TwinVQ utilities at www.mp3hotlist.com/vqf.htm.

Creating VQF Files

To create VQF files, rip tracks from a CD to WAV files using a ripper (as discussed in Chapter 8, "Windows Rippers and Encoders"), then encode them using a TwinVQ encoder:

- Get the Yamaha SoundVQ Encoder (at this writing, a 90-day beta version) from the TwinVQ area on the Yamaha Web site (www.yamaha-xg.com/english/xg/SoundVQ/). Figure 23.14 shows the SoundVQ Encoder.

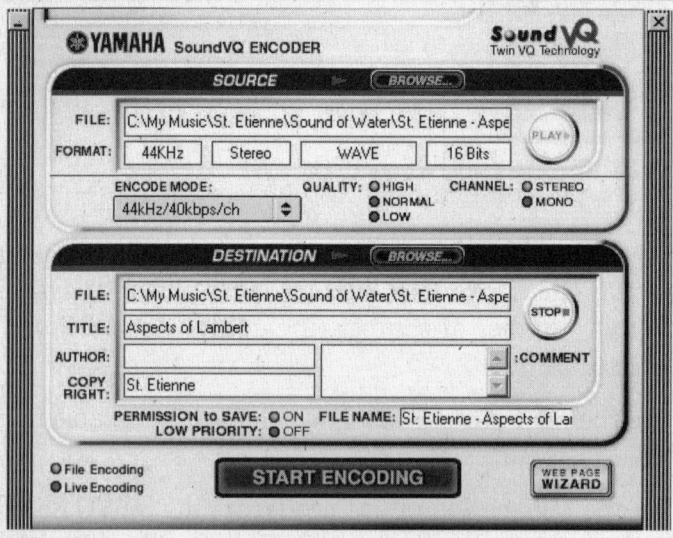

FIGURE 23.14: The Yamaha SoundVQ Encoder

Other Digital-Audio Formats 899

- Get the TwinVQ Encoder (which is available from a variety of sources, including www.idcomm.com/personal/eas22/vqf/twinvqencoder211e.zip). This encoder, shown in Figure 23.15, could hardly be simpler to use. As you might guess, choose the High setting in the Quality drop-down list for best results.

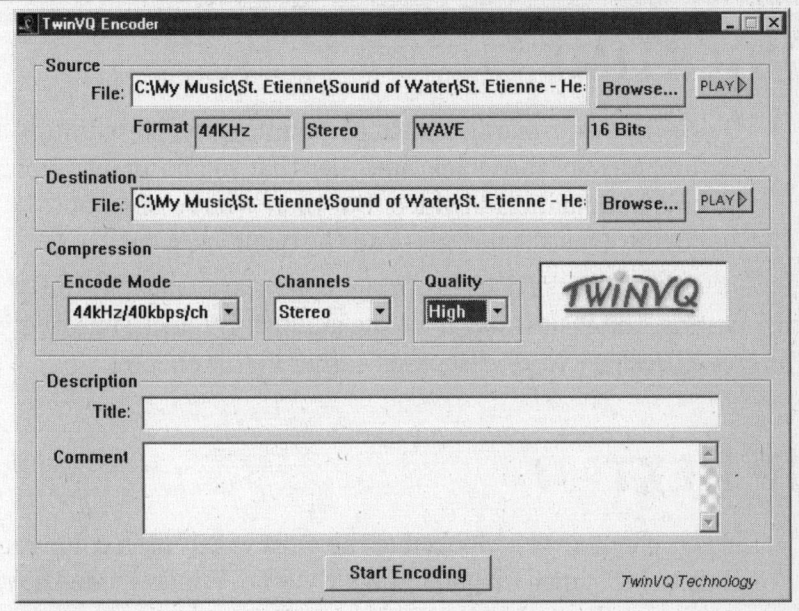

FIGURE 23.15: The TwinVQ Encoder produces quality TwinVQ files.

RealAudio

RealAudio, best known as a streaming audio solution, is also a viable format for storing compressed audio on your hard drive. RealAudio tracks provide high-quality sound at lower bitrates than MP3 files, so they take up less storage space.

RealJukebox (discussed in Chapter 9, "Windows Jukeboxes") can encode tracks as either MP3 files or as RealAudio files (at up to 96kbps) and can mix the two formats in playlists. To specify the format in which you want to encode, choose Tools ➢ Preferences to display the Preferences dialog box, select the Audio Quality page, and make your choice in the Select a Format list box.

QuickTime

QuickTime is primarily known as a multimedia presentation architecture. Most of the QuickTime files that you'll run into typically include both audio and video. But there's no reason not to create audio-only QuickTime files—and the quality is good.

Various QuickTime-authoring toolkits are available, but at this writing, the easiest way to create audio-only QuickTime files is to use QDesign's MVP, discussed earlier in this chapter.

Up Next

In this chapter, we've looked at the most widely used competing formats to MP3, including a2b, Liquid Audio, Windows Media Audio, and TwinVQ, touching on their advantages and disadvantages.

As we mentioned at the beginning of this chapter, at this point none of the competing formats is anywhere near displacing MP3 as the dominant format, because MP3 gives the consumer what they need: good-enough to high music quality, a small-enough file size, the freedom to create and distribute files as they will, and an abundance of MP3 tracks available on the Internet. So from the consumer's point of view, there's little motivation to move from MP3 unless another format is released that can do all the things that MP3 can do—and do them significantly better. Content creators, on the other hand, have strong motivation for using a format that's more secure than MP3 and that enables them to protect their intellectual property against piracy.

That's the end of the book, except for the glossary, which starts on the next page.

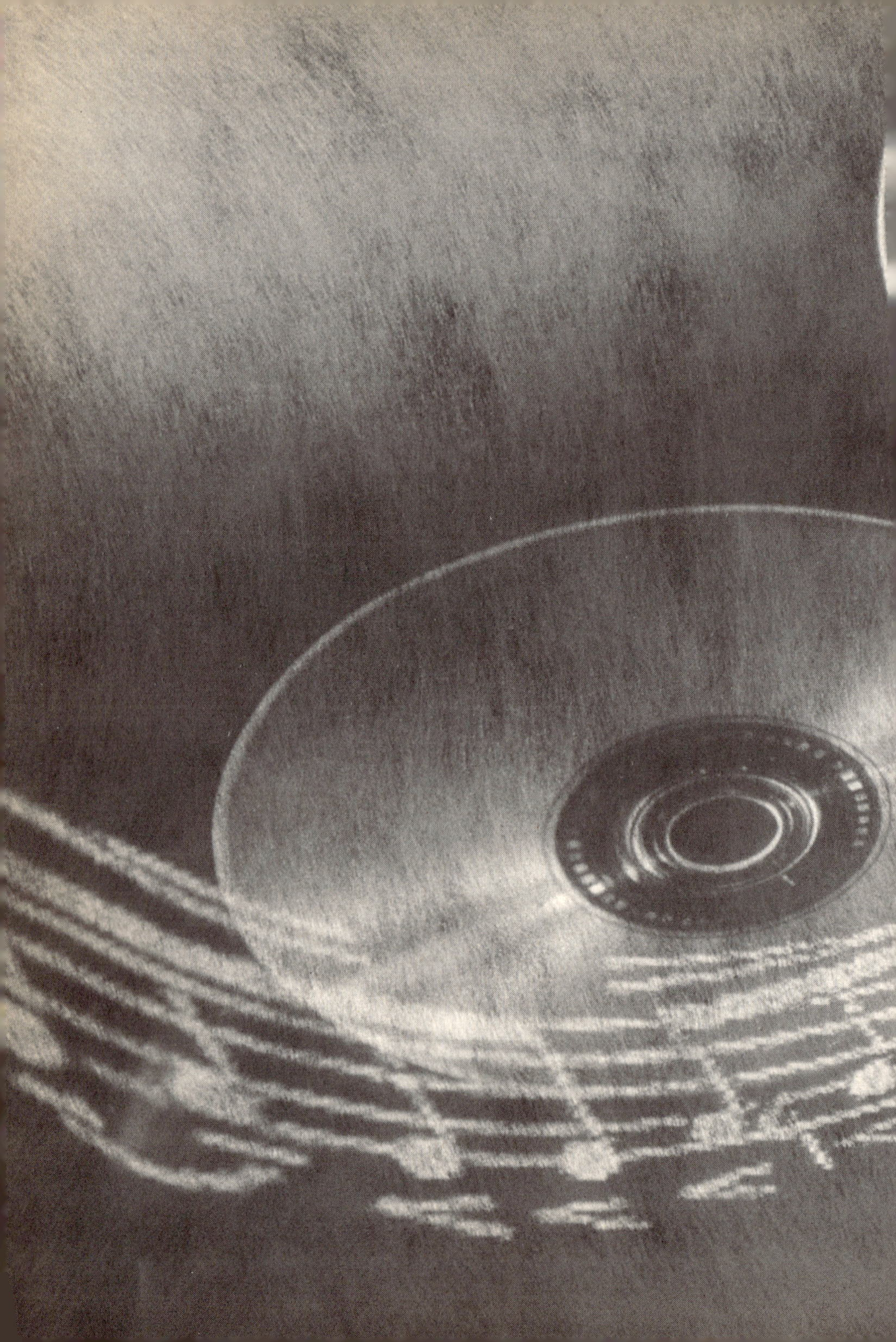

Glossary

Words that appear in **boldface** are defined elsewhere in this glossary.

a2b

A proprietary, encrypted, and secure format for compressed audio. a2b was created by AT&T and claims better compression and sound quality than **MP3**.

AAC

The abbreviation for **Advanced Audio Codec**.

ADC

The abbreviation for **analog-to-digital converter**.

Advanced Audio Codec

A powerful **codec** that produces great sound and supports up to 48 channels—but that is not yet widely available in an ISO-compliant implementation. Abbreviated to AAC.

AIFF

A standard format for uncompressed **PCM** audio. AIFF is typically used on the Macintosh.

Amiga

An early personal computer with multimedia capabilities.

amplified speakers

Speakers that contain their own amplifier or amplifiers. Usually, only one speaker in the set contains the amplifier.

analog signal

A continuously variable waveform.

analog-to-digital converter

Sound circuitry that converts an analog signal into a digital signal. For example, a sound card converts the input from an analog source (such as a microphone or a record player) to a digital signal in order to record it as an **MP3** file.

ATRAC3

Adaptive Transform Acoustic Coding. A secure and encrypted format for compressed audio created by Sony. ATRAC3 is used in MiniDisc players and Sony portable players such as the VAIO Music Clip and the Memory Stick Walkman.

bandwidth

The amount of data that a communications channel (for example, a phone line or a **cable modem**) can transmit per second.

bitrate

The number of bits per second used to store encoded information.

Bitrates are measured in kilobits per second (kbps). A bitrate of 128kbps is generally considered to provide almost-CD-quality sound. Most **MP3 encoders** can encode at either a **constant bitrate** (CBR) or a **variable bitrate** (VBR).

bit-rot

The degeneration of the data stored on a CD. Bit-rot can render an audio CD unplayable and a data CD unreadable.

broadcast streaming audio

Streaming audio broadcast across a network or the Internet in real time. Also known as *Internet radio*.

cable modem

A device that receives and transmits data through the cabling of a cable TV system. Technically, a cable modem is not a modem (because it does not modulate and demodulate the signal), but the name was catchy enough to stick.

CBR

The abbreviation for **constant bitrate**.

CD

Compact disc. A digital audio format designed primarily for audio distribution. Audio CDs contain uncompressed digital audio recorded at 44.1kHz.

CDDB

The Compact Disc Database, an online database of CD information (including artist name, CD name, and track names). By submitting the unique CD ID number to CDDB, a ripper, player, or jukebox can retrieve the information associated with the CD.

CD-quality audio

Audio sampled at a sampling rate of 44.1kHz and a sampling precision of 16 bits. CD-quality audio is considered perfect for human hearing because the amount of information it provides is enough that most people cannot hear anything missing from the audio.

CD-ROM

The abbreviation for CD read-only memory.

CIR

The abbreviation for **committed information rate**.

circumaural headphones

Headphones that completely enclose the ear. Circumaural headphones may be **open headphones** or **sealed headphones**.

Glossary

clipping
A form of audio distortion that can occur if you overload your sound card's audio circuits.

codec
Software or hardware for encoding and decoding an audio signal. (This term is condensed from the term *coder/decoder*.)

committed information rate
The minimum data rate guaranteed to be available on a connection such as a **cable modem** or a frame relay circuit. Abbreviated to *CIR*.

cone
A speaker component that produces sound. Also sometimes called a *driver*.

constant bitrate
One method of encoding **MP3** files, by using the same **bitrate** throughout the file rather than varying the bitrate to optimize the sound. Abbreviated to *CBR*. Compare to **variable bitrate** (VBR).

DAC
The acronym for **digital-to-analog converter**.

DAT
The abbreviation (or, to some, the acronym) for digital audio tape.

digital audio
Audio that is stored in a digitized format rather than in an analog format.

digital signal processor
A category of chip for manipulating and altering sound. Abbreviated to *DSP*.

digital subscriber line
A technology for high-speed transmission of data over standard copper telephone lines. Abbreviated to *DSL*.

digital-to-analog converter
Sound circuitry that converts a digital signal into an analog signal. For example, a sound card typically converts an **MP3** file (which is digital) to an analog signal for outputting through speakers or headphones. The acronym is *DAC*.

downsample
To decrease the **bitrate** (and thus the size) of an audio signal.

driver
In speakers, another term for **cone**.

DSL

The abbreviation for **digital subscriber line**.

DSP

The abbreviation for **digital signal processor**.

dual-line modem

A modem that can bond two telephone lines together to produce a faster aggregate connection. Also called a *shotgun modem*.

DVD

The abbreviation for digital versatile disc or digital video disc, depending on whom you believe. A DVD can store up to 2.3GB on each of its two sides, giving a total capacity of 4.6GB.

DVD-RAM

A writable form of **DVD**.

ear-bud headphones

Headphones whose earpieces are buds that poke or wedge into the ear.

encoder

Hardware or software for creating an **MP3** file from an audio stream.

fair access policy

A policy by which some Internet access providers, typically satellite services, reserve the right to throttle back a user's download speed if the user continuously runs it at capacity. Most users affected by fair access policies consider them poorly named. The acronym for fair access policy is *FAP*.

fair use

A provision in the Copyright Act that lets you use a portion of a copyrighted work "for purposes such as criticism, comment, news reporting, teaching (including multiple copies for classroom use), scholarship, or research" without infringing copyright. Fair use does not allow the unauthorized sharing of copyrighted intellectual property (for example, **MP3** files).

FAP

The acronym for **fair access policy**.

Fraunhofer

Fraunhofer Institute for Integrated Circuits IIS-A. The German company that created the **MP3** encoding method.

handle
On an audio CD, an electronic pointer to the audio.

home theater
A sound setup that produces **surround sound** by using a 5.1 setup (five satellite speakers with a powered subwoofer) or a 7.1 setup (seven satellite speakers with a powered subwoofer) to deliver realistic sound effects and positional audio.

icecast
A server for **streaming audio**.

IFPI
The abbreviation for the International Federation of Phonographic Industries.

Internet broadcasting
Broadcasting an audio stream across the Internet. Also called *webcasting*.

Internet radio
Another term for **broadcast streaming audio**.

ISDN
The abbreviation for *Integrated Services Digital Network*, a digital line that's not as fast as a **DSL** but can be implemented over longer distances from the telephone company's central office.

jukebox
An application for organizing and playing **MP3** and other audio files.

line-level output signal
A signal output by a line-out jack (for example, on a sound card) that is compatible with standard line-level inputs such as those on a home stereo amplifier or cassette deck.

Liquid Audio
A digital-audio format used by a number of sites, including the Internet Underground Musical Archive.

lossless compression
Compression that does not remove information from the source. The opposite of lossless compression is **lossy compression**.

lossy compression
Compression that removes information from the source in order to reduce its size. The opposite of lossy compression is **lossless compression**.

MiniDisc
A digital audio storage medium designed to provide optimum quality with extreme portability. MiniDiscs use the proprietary **ATRAC3** compression format to store compressed audio.

Mjuice
An encrypted **MP3** format that provides the same audio quality as MP3 but lets the creator create a copy-protected version of a track that can be played back any number of times on a registered user's player but not at all on an unregistered player. Mjuice files can also contain an expiration date.

MP3
A file format for storing compressed digital audio on computers. The name refers to MPEG-1 Layer III compression and MPEG-2 Layer III compression.

MP3.com
One of the major Web sites for MP3 music, software, and information.

MP3z
Illegal MP3 files. Compare to **warez**.

MP4
The informal abbreviation for the MP4 Structured Audio Format, a successor to MP3 that's currently under development.

MPEG
The Moving Picture Experts Group, a working group of the International Standards Organization (ISO) and the International Engineering Consortium (IEC) that develops "international standards for compression, decompression, processing, and coded representation of moving pictures, audio, and their combination." Pronounced *em-peg*.

normalization
The process of maximizing the volume of the digital audio data without adding any distortion. Usually when ripping and encoding from CD, normalization isn't needed, but it can be valuable when the source material is too quiet. If you normalize everything you encode, it all plays back in the same relative volume range.

on-demand streaming audio
An audio stream that the listener can start and stop at his or her convenience. Compare to **broadcast streaming audio**.

open headphones
Circumaural headphones that expose the back of the headphone diaphragm to the air, providing better sound but admitting more ambient noise. Contrast to **sealed headphones**.

OpenMG
A proprietary copyright-protection technology developed by Sony Corporation. OpenMG is **SDMI**-compliant and conforms to the Portable Device Specification version 1.0.

OpenMG MP3
A proprietary secure audio format developed by Sony. Despite the name, OpenMG MP3 files are not open.

passive speakers
Unpowered speakers, typically used with an amplifier.

PCM
The abbreviation for **pulse code modulation**.

PDA
The abbreviation for *personal digital assistant*, a small (typically hand-held) electronic device for storing and organizing information.

peak output
The maximum wattage that an audio component (such as an amplifier or speakers) can deliver momentarily. Also known as *peak power*. Contrast with **root mean square watts**.

personal use
A provision of the Audio Home Recording Act (AHRA) of 1992 that allows users of digital audio recording devices to make copies of copyrighted works on other media. For example, if you buy a CD, you can record it onto cassette so that you can listen to it in your Walkman.

ping time
The amount of time that it takes for a packet of information to get from your computer to the host computer and back. A longer ping time usually means there are more hops (stages) in the connection between your computer and the host. The more hops in a connection, the more Internet resources are involved, and the slower the connection will typically be.

playlist
A file that contains the names (and, if necessary, paths) of a list of audio files. You can use playlists

to organize groups of tracks that you want to treat as single units. Playlists are text files (so you can create them using a simple text editor such as Notepad in Windows) saved under an extension such as M3U or PLS. Most **MP3** players, **jukeboxes**, and organizers include playlist-editing capabilities.

plug-in
An add-in component that provides additional features for a software application.

pressed CD
A prerecorded audio or data CD (as opposed to a recordable CD).

proxy server
A computer that relays information, stores frequently accessed information in its cache, and applies filters to requests. Proxy servers are typically used to connect a network (for example, a company network or a college network) to the Internet or to another network.

psychoacoustics
The study of what people can and can't hear. In this case, "hear" means not that the ear can pick up the sound but that the brain can identify it as a separate sound.

pulse code modulation
A standard format for uncompressed audio, used (among other uses) for data stored on audio CDs. Abbreviated to *PCM*.

QDesign
A digital-audio format created by QDesign Corporation. To create QDesign files, you use the QDesign Music Codec (QDMC). Unlike **MP3 codecs**, which apply a standardized set of audio filters to the audio they encode, the QDMC creates custom audio filters on the fly for each signal encoded. This makes for a slower encoding process than for MP3, but it produces more accurate results, even at low bitrates. The QDesign encoder can create both QDesign files and MP3 files, and it stores its native files in **QuickTime** format.

QuickTime
Best known as a video format, QuickTime is also an effective format for audio-only files. The easiest way to create QuickTime files is to use the **QDesign** codec.

ratio site
An Internet site (usually an FTP site) that lets you download files only after you've uploaded some files to the site. Typically, a ratio

site allows you to download files in some ratio to the number of files you upload.

RealAudio

A digital-audio format created by RealNetworks. Though best-known and most widely used for streaming audio, RealAudio is also a viable audio-storage format, providing near-**CD-quality audio** at **bitrates** lower than **MP3** requires.

RF modulator

A device that you may be able to use to patch a portable **MP3** player into you car stereo. (*RF* stands for *radio frequency*.)

RIAA

The abbreviation for the *Recording Industry Association of America*, a trade association that represents the interests of record companies and the artists signed to them. In fighting music piracy, the RIAA has sued Napster, Inc. and MP3.com.

Rio

A series of portable **MP3** players developed by Diamond Multimedia.

ripper

A program that extracts the audio data from the CD.

ripper/player/jukebox

An application that combines a **ripper**, an **encoder**, a player, and **jukebox** capabilities. Examples of ripper/player/jukeboxes include MusicMatch Jukebox (for Windows and the Macintosh), RealJukebox (for Windows), and SoundJam MP (for the Macintosh).

RMS watts

The abbreviation for **root mean square watts**.

root mean square watts

The wattage that an audio component (such as an amplifier or speakers) can deliver continuously. Abbreviated to *RMS watts*. Contrast with **peak output**.

sampling

The process of examining the patterns of a sound to determine its characteristics and to record it from an analog format into a digital format. Sampling creates a pattern of data points for the audio that are saved to a digital file. The more data points there

Glossary

are, the closer the audio sounds to its original.

sampling precision

The amount of information about the individual sample that is saved to the audio file. CDs use a **sampling** precision of 16 bits (2 bytes) per second; most people encoding MP3 files use this sampling precision as well. Also known as *sampling resolution*.

sampling rate

The frequency with which sound is examined in **sampling**. The sampling rate is measured in kilohertz (kHz).

sampling resolution

Another term for **sampling precision**.

SDMI

The abbreviation for **Secure Digital Music Initiative**.

sealed headphones

Circumaural headphones that do not expose the back of the headphone diaphragm to the air, insulating the listener from outside sound. Contrast with **open headphones**.

Secure Digital Music Initiative

A forum of more than 180 companies and organizations interested in developing a framework for "a voluntary, open framework for playing, storing, and distributing digital music in a protected form." The companies and organizations involved include the recording industry, agencies, distributors and retailers, consumer electronics companies, information technology companies, computer hardware manufacturers, and **MP3** hardware and software companies. Abbreviated to *SDMI*.

shotgun modem

Another term for **dual-line modem**.

SHOUTcast

A server for **streaming audio**.

skin

A graphical look that you can apply to an MP3 player or **jukebox**.

sound pressure level

Speaker volume. Abbreviated to *SPL*.

SPL

The abbreviation for **sound pressure level**.

streaming audio

An audio-delivery technique in which playback occurs while the audio is being downloaded rather than after the download is complete. Typically, streaming audio files are not saved to disk after being played. This makes streaming audio analogous to broadcasting the audio rather than distributing copies of it, thus avoiding many legal issues.

subwoofer

A speaker whose **cones** are designed to produce bass and very-low-frequency sounds. A subwoofer is usually designed for placement on the floor.

supra-aural headphones

Headphones that sit on the ears (as opposed to enclosing the ears). Also called *on-the-ear headphones*.

surround sound

A sound setup that uses four or five speakers to produce the effect of the listener's being surrounded by the sound source.

T1

A fast dedicated phone line typically used for business. A T1 delivers a constant 1.5 million bits per second (Mbps).

T3

A very fast dedicated phone line used for business. A T3 delivers a constant 45 million bits per second (Mbps).

tag

A container in an **MP3** file (or another digital-audio file) with various slots to hold pieces of information about the MP3 files, such as the artist's name and the track title.

tweeter

The **cone** in a speaker that plays treble (high-frequency) sounds.

TwinVQ

The acronym for Transform-domain Weighted Interleave Vector Quantization Format, a digital-audio format that provides better compression and equal or greater sound quality to **MP3**.

upload cap

An artificially imposed limitation to the upload speed on a connection such as a cable modem. The limitation is artificial in that it is imposed by the service provider to prevent a user from hogging bandwidth rather than by a limitation of the connection. Also referred to as *upload speed cap*.

variable bitrate

A method of encoding information to an MP3 file by varying the bitrate to optimize the sound. Abbreviated to *VBR*. Compare to **constant bitrate** (CBR).

VBR

The abbreviation for **variable bitrate**.

visualization

A graphical display in a **MP3** player or **jukebox**, in which the graphics are triggered by the audio being played.

VQF

The file extension for **TwinVQ** files and, by association, the generic term for those files.

warez

Pirated software. See also **MP3z**.

WAV

A standard format for uncompressed **PCM** audio. Most WAV files are PCM files with a WAV header.

webcasting

Another term for **Internet broadcasting**.

Windows Media Technologies

A digital-audio format developed by Microsoft. Windows Media Technologies 4 has a secure compression scheme called MS Audio that claims to surpass **MP3** in both compression and music quality. The main player for Windows Media Architecture files is Windows Media Player, which is included with every version of Windows for the PC and some versions of Windows for PDA and hand-held devices.

WMA

The abbreviation and file-format extension for Windows Media Architecture, which is part of the **Windows Media Technologies** family. WMA files use the Advanced Streaming Format file format.

woofer

The **cone** in a speaker that plays bass (low-frequency) sounds.

INDEX

Note to the Reader: Throughout this index **boldfaced** page numbers indicate primary discussions of a topic or definitions of terms. *Italicized* page numbers indicate illustrations.

A

a2b digital-audio format, *See also* digital-audio formats
- advantages, 881
- compression ratios, 876, 879–880
- defined, **34–35**, **904**
- disadvantages, 881
- installing players for, 881–883, *882–883*
- MES file feature, 881
- security components, 880

AAC (Advanced Audio Codec), 48, **876–877**, **904**

Adaptec software
- Direct CD, **747**
- Easy CD Creator, *752–755*, **752–756**, 757
- Toast, **751**

Adobe Photoshop, **809**

AIFF files, **749–750**, **904**

Altec Lansing subwoofer system, **53**

amplified speakers, **51**, **904**

amplifiers, headphone, 58

analog audio, **4–5**, 12, **904**

Apple QuickTime MP3 player, **476–477**, *477*

artists, *See also* promoting your music on the Web
- creating MP3 files of own music, 760–761
- legal issues and, 80, 761
- MP3 pros and cons for, 23–25

ASCAP (American Society of Composers, Authors, and Publishers), **698**

ASF (Advanced Streaming Format), **893**, 895

asynchronous IO, **524**

ATRAC3 digital-audio format, **35**, **884–885**, **904**

audio, *See also* digital audio; sound

audio cassettes, levies on, 28

audio CDs, *See also* burning CDs; CDs
- advantage, 738
- burning with Easy CD Creator, 752–756, *752–755*, *757*
- burning with MusicMatch Jukebox, 443–448, *445*, *447*
- defined, **737–738**
- disadvantage, 738
- overview of, 21
- pressed CDs, 745, 911

Audio Manager software, RioPort, *See also* portable MP3 players
- editing song information, 630, *630*
- loading songs onto portable players, 630, *631*
- monitoring music files, 628–629, *629*
- reviewing new songs, 629–630, *629*

audio watermarks, 662

Audioactive Player, *See also* Windows MP3 players
- downloading, 374
- editing ID3 tags, 376, *377*
- installing, 375
- options, 376, *376*
- overview of, 374–375, *375*
- Playlist Editor, *375*

Audioactive Production Studio ripper/encoder, *See also* Windows rippers and encoders
- downloading, 410
- encoding WAV files to MP3 files, 412–413, *412–413*
- installing, 410–411
- interface, 411, *411*
- overview of, 409–410
- ripping from CDS, 414–415, *414*
- warning, 411

AudioCatalyst ripper/encoder for the Mac, *See also* Macintosh ripper/encoders
- buying, 516
- CDDB/ID preferences, 519–520, *520*
- configuring preferences, 517–520, *517–520*
- Encoder preferences, 518, *518*
- General preferences, 517, *517*
- limitations, 516
- Normalization preferences, 519, *519*
- overview of, 516

AudioCatalyst ripper/encoder for Windows, *See also* Windows rippers and encoders
- CDDB Disk Submit Wizard, 398
- CDDB Settings, 394–395, *395*
- downloading, 389
- encoding MP3 files from WAV files, 398
- General Settings, 390–392, *390*
- installing, 389–390
- MP3 Playback Settings, 396
- Normalizing Settings, 395–396, *396*
- overview of, 389
- ripping/encoding with, 396–397, *397–398*
- XingMP3 Encoder Settings, 392–394, *393*

Audiogalaxy search engine, **114**

audioGnome, **217–231**, *See also* MP3 files, finding
- browsing user libraries, 229–230, *230*
- configuring options, 219–223, *223*
- connecting to servers, 224–225, *224*
- defined, **217**
- downloading files, 227–229, *227*
- finding music via, 225–227, *225*
- installing, 217–218, *218*
- multipage interface, 218, *219*
- sharing files, 230–231, *231*
- stopping sharing, 219, *220*

Auto Update option in iMesh, 257, **257**
Auto-Join properties in Gnapster, 195, *195*
Auto-Play feature in Sonique, **350**
AutoDJ feature in MusicMatch Jukebox, 439, *439*, 562–563, *563*
automobile. *See* car
AutoPlaylist feature in RealJukebox, 464
AutoSleep feature in MACAST, 508, **508**
AutoStart option in RealJukebox, 453

B

backing up
- CDs, **858–859**
- MP3 servers, **869–870**

batteries in portable players, **622–623**
Beam-it feature, **30**, 102
bit-rot, **856–858**, **905**
bitmap editors, **809**, *See also* skins, creating
bitrates, **12–13**, **426–427**, **904–905**, *See also* encoding rates
bits, 12
BladeEnc encoder, **409**, **605**
blank strings, **776**
BMI (Broadcast Music, Inc.), **698**
bookmarking tracks in Winamp, 328, *329*
bootlegs of live shows, **664–665**
Brandenburg, Dr. Karlheinz, 11
BRI (basic rate interface), **64**

broadcast streaming audio, 281, 282, **905**,
  See also Internet broadcasting; Internet
  radio
Bubble Blues skin, 363, *364*
burner support in Liquid Player, CD, 885–886
burning CDs of Liquid Audio files, 35, 892
burning CDs of MP3 files, **736–757**
  audio CDs
    advantage, 738
    defined, **737–738**
    disadvantage, 738
    using Easy CD Creator, 752–756,
      752–755, 757
    using MusicMatch Jukebox,
      443–448, *445, 447*
    overview of, 21
    pressed CDs, 745, 911
  using CD-R or CD-RW drives, **739–746**
    comparing disc media, 745–746
    comparing drives, 743–744
    comparing ports, 741–742
    defined, **743**
    EIDE ports, 741–742
    external drives, 740–741
    FireWire ports, 742–743
    internal drives, 740–741
    overview of, 59–60, 739
    packet-writing software and, 744
    parallel ports, 742
    SCSI ports, 741–742
    speed of, 739–740
    USB ports, 742
    warning, 741
  CD-ROM drives and, 738, 743–744
  copying CDs and, 741
  data CDs
    advantage, 738
    defined, **738**
    disadvantage, 738
    using MusicMatch Jukebox, 444,
      445, 747
  overview of, 21
  pressed CDs, 745, 911
  file storage formats and, 737
  overview of, 21, 736
  pressed versus recordable CDs,
    745–746, 911
  reasons for, 736–737
  software for, **746–757**
    bundled with drives, 746–747
    creating AIFF files, 749–750
    creating WAV files, 748–750
    Direct CD, 747
    Easy CD Creator, 752–756,
      752–755, 757
    general-purpose software, 750–751
    on Linux, 751
    on Macintosh, 751
    in MP3 players/jukeboxes, 747–750
    MP3-specific software, 750–751
    MusicMatch Jukebox, **443–448**,
      445, 447, 747
    Sonique, 748–749
    SoundJam, 749–750
    Winamp, 748
    on Windows, 751
    xmms, 750
  warning, 741
Buschjost, Oliver, 798

C

cable modems, **63**, **703–704**, **905**
calculating hex values, **835–836**, *836*
car MP3 players, *See also* MP3 players
  defined, **611**
  empeg car in-dash player, 649–653,
    651–652
  in-car jukeboxes, 647–649, 653
  in-dash players, 647–649, 653
  overview of, 645

portable players as, 646–647
Web site, 648
cassettes, audio, levies on, 28
CBR (constant bitrate), 13, **427**, **906**
CD-R or CD-RW drives. *See* burning CDs of MP3 files
CD-ROM drives, 738, 743–744, 864, **905**
CDDB (Compact Disk DataBase)
    adding CD information to, 801–803, *802*
    defined, **553**, **801**, **905**
cdparanoia ripper, *See also* Linux rippers and encoders
    command-line options, 588
    defined, **587**
    downloading, 587
    overview of, 578, 591
    ripping with, 588–590, *590*
    testing, 588, *589*
cdrecord software, **751**
CDs, *See also* burning CDs
    backing up, 858–859
    bit-rot in, 856–858, 905
    CD-quality audio
        defined, **7**, **905**
        versus MP3 audio quality, 22
        overview of, 5, 11, 12–13
    CDA files on, **8**
    compilation CDs, 102
    DAM CDs, **101**
    defined, **905**
    digital audio and, 5–8
    drive requirements, 44
    durability of, 856–858
    history of, 5–7
    MiniDiscs and, 6, **909**
    playing with Winamp, 324
    recordable CDs, **745–746**, 859, 869
    ripping audio files from, 8
    sampling and, 12–13

    transferring CD files, 7–8
    versus vinyl records, 857
chatting
    in Gnapster, 204–207, *205–206*
    in Macster, 188–190, *188–191*
    in Napster, 139–140, *140*, 158–164, *158–161*, *163*
    in RadioSpy, 284, *285*
children, Web sites and, 684
Children's Net Privacy Law (COPPA), 236, *237*
chip requirements, **42–43**
CIR (committed information rate), 64, **906**
circumaural headphones, **55–56**, **905**, **910**, **913**
Climax plug-in for Winamp, *343–346*, **343–346**
clipping, 543, **906**
Cobalt Qube server, 868
codec, 705, **906**
collections. *See* music collections
CompactFlash cards, 636, 637, 640
component servers, **868**
compressing digital audio, 8–9, 15
compression ratios, 875–876
computer requirements, *See also* hardware
    CD drives, 44
    chips, 42–43
    DVD drives, 44, 907
    overview of, 40
    RAM, 43
    sound cards, 44–49, 701
    upgrading versus buying, 40–42
    warning, 49
cones, **50**, **906**
cooked files. *See* repairing cooked MP3 files
Copah CD-Reader plug-in, **365**
COPPA (Children's Net Privacy Law), 236, *237*
copyright, *See also* legal issues
    copying digital audio, 83

copyright notices, 75–76
defined, **74–75**
distributing digital audio, 83–85, 761
fair use provision, 77–78
First Sale Doctrine, 84–85
granting to others, 77
overview of, 73
registering, 76
webcasting and, 696–697
what is not copyrightable, 74
Creative Labs MicroWorks subwoofer system, **53**
CryptoLib Security Library in a2b, **880**
CuteFTP, 112, **115**
CuteMX (Cute Media eXchange), **231–232**, *233*

D

DAM CDs, **101**
DAT (digital audio tape), 29, **906**
data CDs, *See also* burning CDs
   advantage, 738
   burning with MusicMatch Jukebox, 444, *445*, 747
   defined, **738**
   disadvantage, 738
   overview of, 21
   pressed CDs, 745, 911
decibels (dB), 52
DeFX plug-in for Winamp, *347–348*, **347–349**
Desktop Theater 5.1, **54–55**
Detox software, 786
Diamond Monster Sound MX400 card, 49
Diamond Rio portable player, 613
Digital Age theme, 563, *564*
digital audio, *See also* legal issues; sound
   versus analog audio, 4–5, 12, 904
   CDs and, 5–8
   compressing, 8–9, 15

defined, **4**, **906**
MP3 and, 8–10
recording studios and, 4–6
spoken audio
   literature online, 104
   sampling and, 14
   storing on portable players, 615
digital signal processor (DSP), **340**, **906**
digital signatures, **880**
Digital Subscriber Line (DSL), **63–64**, 703–704, **906**
digital-audio formats, **874–901**, *See also* CDs; MP3
   a2b format
      advantages, 881
      compression ratios, 876, 879–880
      defined, **34–35**, **904**
      disadvantages, 881
      installing players for, 881–883, *882–883*
      MES file feature, 881
      security components, 880
   AAC format, 48, **876–877**, **904**
   advantages, 34, 661, 874–876
   ATRAC3 format, 35, **884–885**, 904
   audio quality, 875
   channels, 48
   choosing for Web sites, 668–669
   comparing with MP3, 33–34, 661, 874–876, 900–901
   compression ratios, 875–876
   disadvantages, 33–34, 661–662, 876
   Liquid Audio format, *See also* Liquid Player
      burning CDs in, 35, 892
      defined, **35**, **885**, **908**
      Liquid Player for, 35, 885–893
      MP3 files and, 892–893
      territory restrictions, 892
      Web sites, 886, 889

Direct CD software—editing ID3 tags 921

Liquid Player, **885–893**
    associating file types with, 887, *888*
    CD burner support, 885–886
    choosing data streaming rates, 886–887, *887*
    creating tracks, 35, 892
    defined, **35**, **885**
    downloading, 886
    downloading tracks, 891–892, *892*
    FastTrack Security option, 887–888, 889, *889*
    hardware requirements, 886
    installing, 886–887, *887*
    Passport option, 888–889, *888*
    playing tracks, 891, *891*
    registering, 887–889, *888–889*
    scanning for tracks, 889–890, *890*
Mjuice format, **36**, **909**
MOD format, 105
MS Audio format, 35–36
    overview of, 874, 900
    versus physical media, 669
QDesign Music Codec format, 36–37, **877–879**, *879*, **911**
QuickTime format, 37, 900, 911
RealAudio format
    adding to Winamp, *342*, **342–343**
    defined, **37**, **899**, **912**
    in RealJukebox, 454, *454*, 468, 469, 900
secure formats, 661–662, 663, 668, 875
TwinVQ/VQF format
    CPU power and, 896
    creating VQF files, 898–899, *898–899*
    decoding method, 896
    defined, **36**, **896**, **914**
    disadvantage, 897
    encoding method, 896
    versus MP3, 896
    playing VQF files, 897, *897*
    renaming VQF files, 778, *779*
    sound quality, 896
    Web sites, 898
    WMA format, 639, **893–895**, *895*, **915**
Direct CD software, **747**
distributing digital audio
    legal issues in, 83–87, 695, 761
    as MP3 files, 20, 23–25, 668–669
dithering, **841**
DJs, software for
    in MusicMatch Jukebox for the Mac, 562–563, *563*
    in MusicMatch Jukebox for Windows, 439, *439*
    Visiosonic, 471–472
DMCA (Digital Millennium Copyright Act), **696**
D'Music portable CD-ROM player, **738**
domain names, **667**
downsampling, **699**, **906**
downsampling MP3 files in icecast, **727–731**
DSL (Digital Subscriber Line), **63–64**, 703–704, **906**
DSP (digital signal processor), 340, **906**
dual-line modems, 66, **907**
DVD drives, 44, **907**
DVD-RAM drives, 59–60, **907**

E

e-mailing MP3 files, 89
ear-bud headphones, **56–57**, 625, **907**
Easy CD Creator software, *752–755*, **752–756**, *757*
EasyTAG editor, **770**, *771*
eatsleepmusic.com, **104–105**
editing ID3 tags, **761–771**
    on Linux
        with EasyTAG, 770, *771*
        with id3ren, 770

overview of, 768
in xmms, 768, 769
overview of, 761
tags, defined, **15**, **914**
on the Mac
in MACAST, 763, *764*
with mp3tool, 765–768, *766–767*
in MusicMatch Jukebox, 556–557, *556*, 765, *765*
overview of, 763
in SoundJam, 541–542, *541*, 764, *764*
on Windows
in Audioactive Player, 376, *377*
in FreeAmp, 769, *769*
in MusicMatch Jukebox, 430–432, *431*, 762, *763*
overview of, 762
in Sonique, 358–359, *359*
in Winamp, 333, *333*, 762, *762*
editing MP3 files
in Linux with mp3asm, 783
overview of, 779–780
in Windows with MP3Cutter, 780–782, *781–783*
in Windows with mp3Trim, 782
eGo portable MP3 player, 617, 624
EIDE drives, **741–742**, **865**
Eiger MPMan MP3 player, 613
electronic newsletters, starting, 690–691
empeg car in-dash player, **649–653**, *651–652*
emplode software, *651*, **651**
empty strings, **776**
EMusic.com, **102–103**, 573
encode, **387**
encoders, **907**, *See also* Linux rippers and encoders; Macintosh ripper/encoders; Windows rippers and encoders
encoding rates, **16–19**, *See also* bitrates
ephemeral recordings, **696–697**

equalization controls in portable MP3 players, 632
equalizers. *See* graphic equalizers
executable MP3 files. *See* MP3 to EXE
external drives, **740–741**

F

Fanning, Shawn, 128
FAP (fair access policy), **65**, **907**
FastEnc encoder, 400
finding files in Freenet, 275, *See also* MP3 files, finding
Finger information, 160, *161*, 162–163
firewall settings in Napster on Windows, **135–137**, *136*, 166
Firewall/Proxy options in RadioSpy, 285
firewalls, 62
FireWire ports, 61, **742–743**
First Sale Doctrine in Copyright Act, **84–85**
FNC (FreenetCentre), 274, *275*
Forté Free Agent newsreader, 120
Franke, Norman, 478
Fraunhofer Institute, 11, 399, 539, **907**
Free Music Archive, **105**
Free Tracks links, 102
FreeAmp on Linux, *See also* Linux MP3 players
defined, **568**, **571**
Download Manager feature, 573
downloading, 571
interface, 571, *571*
My Music window, 572, *572*
preferences, 573–574
saving SHOUTcast/icecast streams, 573
Search for Music feature, 572, *573*
FreeAmp on Windows, *See also* Windows MP3 players
disadvantage, 368
editing ID3 tags, 769, *769*

features, 368
installation options, 369
interface, 369, *369*
My Music window, 370, *370*
overview of, 368
FreeDrive.com, 60
FreeMem Professional, **449**
Freenet, **272–275**, *275*
FreenetGUI, 274
FTP, Cute, 112, **115**
FTP sites for MP3 files, **98**
full duplex sound cards, **701**

G

G6 Renamer software, **774–778**, *775–776, 778–779*
gnap software, 191–192
Gnapster. *See* Napster on Linux
GNOME-Napster software, 191, 192
GNU General Public License, **369**, **719**
gnutella, **209–216**, *See also* MP3 files, finding
    closing, 216
    configuring, 211–212, *213*
    connecting to gnutellaNet, 212–214, *214*
    defined, **210**
    downloading files, 215, *216*
    installation options, 210, *210*
    interface, 211, *211*
    Napster and, 209–210
    overview of, 93
    searching for files, 214, *214*
    transferring files, 216
GOGO-no-coda encoder, *See also* Linux rippers and encoders
    command-line options, 604
    defined, **603**
    downloading, 603
    versus LAME encoder, 603

Go!Zilla search utility, **117–118**
graphic equalizers
    in MACAST, 506–507, *506*
    in MusicMatch Jukebox for Windows, 440–441, *440*
    in portable MP3 players, 632
    in SoundJam, 542–543, *543*
    in Unreal Player MAX, 382
    in Winamp, 319–321, *319–320*, 329–332, *330, 332*
graphics. *See* skins; visualizations
GrayAMP player, *See also* Macintosh MP3 players
    downloading, 509–510
    features, 509
    interface, 510, *510–512*, 512
    limitations, 509
    overview of, 509
    preferences, 510–512, *511–512*
Grip ripper/encoder, **578–586**, *See also* Linux rippers and encoders
    CDDB options, 586
    configuring options, 580–586
    downloading, 579
    ID3 tag options, 585
    main window, 579, *580*
    Misc options, 586
    MP3 encoder options, 583–585, *584–585*
    overview of, 578, 579
    Proxy options, 586
    Rip options, 581–582, *581, 583*
    ripping/encoding with, 586–587, *587*

H

hand-held PCs. *See* portable MP3 players
handles, 8, **387**, **908**
Handspring Visor device, **612**, **641**

HanGo Personal Jukebox player, 617, 626
hard drives, storing audio files on, 16–17, 58–59
hardware requirements, **40–67**
   computers
      CD drives, 44
      chips, 42–43
      DVD drives, 44, **907**
      for Internet broadcasting, 700–701
      overview of, 40
      RAM, 43
      sound cards, 44–49, 701
      upgrading versus buying, 40–42
      warning, 49
   headphones
      amplifiers for, 58
      circumaural headphones, 55–56, 905
      ear-bud headphones, 56–57, 625
      overview of, 55
      for portable MP3 players, 625–626
      supra-aural headphones, 56, 914
      wireless headphones, 58
   for Internet broadcasting, 700–703, *702*
   Internet connections
      cable modems, 63, 905
      DSL, 63–64
      ISDN, 64, 908
      modems, 65–66
      overview of, 62
      satellite, 65
      security of, 62
   microphones, 701–703, *702*
   overview of, 40, 67
   ports, 60–62
   speakers
      amplified speakers, 51, 904
      cheap speakers, 50
      components of, 50–51
      home theater systems, 54–55, 908
      matching to needs, 53–54
      measuring loudness, 51–53
      overview of, 49
      passive speakers, 51, 910
      surround sound, 54, 914
      trying out, 55
   storage, 58–60
headphones, *See also* hardware requirements
   amplifiers for, 58
   circumaural headphones, 55–56, 905
   ear-bud headphones, 56–57, 625
   overview of, 55
   for portable MP3 players, 625–626
   supra-aural headphones, 56, 914
   wireless headphones, 58
hertz (Hz), **329**
hex values, calculating, **835–836**, *836*
home stereos as MP3 players, *See also* MP3 players
   by connecting PCs to, 642–643
   by connecting portable players to, 641
   using dedicated components
      AudioReQuest component, 644
      defined, **611**
      overview of, 643–644
      SongBank component, 644, 645
      warning, 645
   overview of, 22, 641
home theater systems, **54–55**, **908**
hops, **147**
Hum software, **638**, **640**

I

icecast broadcasts, **719–731**, *See also* promoting your music on the Web
   configuring liveice, 727–730
   configuring shout, 724–726
   defined, **280**, **719**, **908**
   downloading, 719–720

icemaker—Internet broadcasting

downsampling MP3 files, 727-731
editing parameters, 720-723
liveice keyboard controls, 730-731
saving streams in FreeAmp, 573
sending audio streams to, 724-727
shutting down, 731
starting, 723-724
icemaker, **727**
iceplay, **724**
icesource, **724**
icon editors, **809-810**
icons, smiley-face, 160, *160*
iCrunch Web site, **103**
ID3 tags. *See* editing ID3 tags
id3ren software, **770**, 779
IEC (International Engineering Consortium), 10
IEEE1394. *See* FireWire
IFPI (International Federation of Phonographic Industries), 6, 908
i.LINK. *See* FireWire
iMesh search tool, **233-271**, *See also* MP3 files, finding
    configuring options, **245-258**
        About page, 257, *258*
        Appearance options, 240-244, *241-244*, 254-255, *255*
        Auto Update option, 257, *257*
        Connection page, 254, *254*
        Contacts options, 255-256, *256*
        Download options, 250-251, *251*
        General options, 245-246, *246*
        Locations page, 246, *247*
        My Details page, 249, *249*
        Search options, 249, *250*
        Security options, 247-248, *248*
        Share options, 252-253, *253*
        Upload options, 251-252, *252*
    contacts
        deleting, 268
        ignoring, 256, *256*, 268-269

        renaming, 270
        sending file links to, 270-271, *271*
        sending messages to, 270, *270*
        viewing files of, 269, *269*
    defined, **233**
    downloading, 234
    downloading tracks, 262-264, *262-263*
    exiting, 271
    forwarding tracks to friends, 261, *261*, *263*, 264
    home page, *234*
    installing
        Additional Details, 236-238, *237*
        Connection Settings, 238, *239*
        Location Details, 235-236, *236*
        Personal Details, 235, *235*
    opening downloaded files, *263*, 264
    recommending tracks to friends, 264, *264*
    searching with, 258-260, *259-260*
    Share Wizard, 239-240, *239-240*
    sharing files, 265-266, *265*
    stopping sharing, 238
    uploading files, 266, *267*
    warnings, 233, 266
    window, 244-245, *245*
intellectual property, **72-73**, 695, **812**, 817
internal drives, **740-741**
Internet broadcasting, **694-731**, *See also* Internet radio; promoting your music on the Web
    buying microphones, 701
    computer hardware for, 700-701
    configuring microphones, 701-703, *702*
    connection power for, 703-704
    defined, **908**
    getting licenses, 698
    how it works, 699-700
    with icecast, **719-731**
        configuring liveice, 727-730

configuring shout, 724–726
defined, **719**, **908**
downloading, 719–720
downsampling MP3 files, 727–731
editing parameters, 720–723
liveice keyboard controls, 730–731
saving streams in FreeAmp, 573
sending audio streams to, 724–727
shutting down, 731
starting, 723–724
legal issues and, 694–697, 761
overview of, 694
with SHOUTcast, **704–719**
adding your voice, 716–718
configuring servers, 707–712
configuring Winamp to, 713–716, *713*, *715–716*
downloading software support, 705–706
installing NetShow Server tools, 706
installing plug-ins, 707
installing servers, 707
overview of, 280, 694, 704–705
saving streams in FreeAmp, 573
shutting servers down, 718, *719*
silencing local output, 718
starting servers, 712–713, *712*
Internet connections, *See also* hardware requirements
cable modems, 63, 905
DSL, 63–64
ISDN, 64, 908
modems, 65–66
overview of, 62
satellite, 65
security of, 62
Internet radio, *See also* Internet broadcasting
defined, **908**

finding MP3 music via RadioSpy, **279–293**
Chat options, 284, *285*
configuration options, 282–285, *284–285*
connecting to stations, 291–292, *291*
defined, **280**
downloading, 282
Favorites list, 293
Firewall/Proxy options, 285
General options, 282–283, *284*
installing, 282
interface, 285–291, *286–287*
overview of, 293
Skins options, 285
streaming audio and, 280–282
Web site, 280
playing in MusicMatch Jukebox, 442–443, *442–443*
iQfx audio enhancement product, **449**
ISDN (Integrated Subscriber Digital Network), 64, 703–704, **908**
ISO (International Standards Organization), 10, **82**
ISPs, choosing, **678–679**
IUMA (Internet Underground Musical Archive), 35, **885**, 891

J

Jansson, Tord, 409, 605
Jasc's Paint Shop Pro, **809**, 819
Jaz drives, **59**
JPEG graphic files, 841
JRE (Java 2 Runtime Environment), 273
jukeboxes, *See also* Macintosh ripper/player/jukeboxes; Windows ripper/player/jukeboxes
defined, **21**, **908**
in-car jukeboxes, **647–649**, 653

K

K-jofol VQF player, 36, 897
karaoke site, 104–105
kbps (kilobits), **12**
key servers in Freenet, **275**
keyboard shortcuts
    in MACAST, 503–504
    in Sonique, 355–357, 365–367
    for Trax playlists, 797
    in Winamp, 328, 335–338
keys in Freenet, **275**
keys, song, in a2b, **880**
kilohertz (kHz), **12**, **329**
knapster software, 191

L

LAME encoder, *See also* Windows rippers and encoders
    versus BladeEnc encoder, 409
    downloading, 405
    encoding files, 408–409, *408*
    versus GOGO-no-coda encoder, 603
    versus MP3Enc encoder, 601
    NotLame encoder and, 601
    overview of, 405
    running from command lines, 405
    running from LameBatch GUI, 406–409, *406*, *408*
    setting options, 406–408, *406*
lands, **745**
legal issues, **70–94**, *See also* piracy
    artists and, 80, 761
    Beam-it feature and, 102
    copyright
        copying digital audio, 83
        copyright notices, 75–76
        defined, **74–75**
        distributing digital audio, 83–85, 761
        DMCA and, 696–697
        ephemeral recordings and, 696–697
        fair use provision, 77–78
        First Sale Doctrine, 84–85
        granting to others, 77
        ISPs and infringements of, 696
        overview of, 73
        registering, 76
        webcasting and, 696–697
        what is not copyrightable, 74
    in creating digital audio, 83, 694
    detecting legal digital audio, 87–88
    in distributing digital audio, 83–87, 695
    gnutella and, 209, 694
    intellectual property, **72–73**, 695, **812**, 817
    in Internet broadcasting, 694–698, 761
    MP3 and, 22–23, 82, 694–695
    music consumers and, 80
    Napster and, 88–93, 127, 129, 157
    overview of, 70–71, 94
    personal use, 79, 694, 910
    pirate sites and, 107
    record companies and, 81
    retail industry and, 81–82
    RIAA and, 81, 127, 912
    SDMI and, 85–87
    and what's really happening, 88–90
Levi ICD+ clothing collection, **624–625**
levies on audio cassettes, 28
licenses for Internet broadcasting, 698
licenses, statutory, 695
line-level output signals, **622**, **908**
line-out jacks, **621–622**
Linux MP3 players, **568–575**, *See also* Macintosh; MP3 players; Windows
    FreeAmp

defined, **568**, **571**
Download Manager feature, 573
downloading, 571
interface, 571, *571*
My Music window, 572, *572*
preferences, 573–574
saving SHOUTcast/icecast streams, 573
Search for Music feature, 572, *573*
mpg123
defined, **568**, **574**
downloading, 574
playing music, 574
in verbose mode, 575, *575*
overview of, 568, 575
xmms
applying skins, 569
in burning CDs, 750
converting MP3 files to WAV, 750
defined, **568**
downloading, 569
interface, 569, *569*
plug-ins, 571
preferences, 570, *570*
versus Winamp, 569–571, *570*
Linux rippers and encoders, **578–606**
BladeEnc encoder, **409**, **605**
cdparanoia ripper
command-line options, 588
defined, **587**
downloading, 587
overview of, 578, 591
ripping with, 588–590, *590*
testing, 588, *589*
GOGO-no-coda encoder
command-line options, 604
defined, **603**
downloading, 603
versus LAME encoder, 603

Grip ripper/encoder
CDDB options, 586
configuring options, 580–586
downloading, 579
ID3 tag options, 585
main window, 579, *580*
Misc options, 586
MP3 encoder options, 583–585, *584–585*
overview of, 578, 579
Proxy options, 586
Rip options, 581–582, *581*, *583*
ripping/encoding with, 586–587, *587*
MP3Enc encoder
defined, **399**, **605**
downloading, 399, 605
encoding with, 400
versus LAME encoder, 601
testing demo versions, 399
NotLame encoder
command-line options, 601–602
downloading, 601
encoding with, 603, *603*
LAME encoder and, 601
overview of, 601
overview of, 578, 606
ripperX ripper/encoder
CDDB options, 596–597, *597*
configuring options, 592–599
defined, **591**
downloading, 591
Files options, 597–599, *598*
General options, 592–593, *593*
MP3 encoder options, 595, *595*
overview of, 578
Players options, 595–596, *596*
ripping/encoding with, 599, *600*
running, 591, *591–592*
Wav ripper options, 594, *594*

Linux systems, *See also* Napster on Linux
    building MP3 servers on, 868
    CD burners supported by, 751
    creating MP3 playlists on, 797
    distributions of, 568
    editing ID3 tags on
        with EasyTAG, 770, *771*
        with id3ren, 770
        overview of, 768
        in xmms, 768, *769*
    editing MP3 files on, 783
    renaming MP3 files on, 779
    repairing cooked MP3 files on, 786
    sound cards and, 49
    Winamp, xmms, and, 314
Liquid Audio format, *See also* digital-audio formats; Liquid Player
    burning CDs in, 35, 892
    defined, **35**, **885**, **908**
    MP3 files and, 892–893
    territory restrictions and, 892
    Web sites, 886, 889
Liquid Player, **885–893**
    associating file types with, 887, *888*
    CD burner support, 885–886
    choosing data streaming rates, 886–887, *887*
    creating tracks, 35, 892
    defined, **35**, **885**
    downloading, 886
    downloading tracks, 891–892, *892*
    FastTrack Security option, 887–888, 889, *889*
    hardware requirements, 886
    installing, 886–887, *887*
    Passport option, 888–889, *888*
    playing tracks, 891, *891*
    registering, 887–889, *888–889*
    scanning for tracks, 889–890, *890*

Liquifier Pro software, **35**, **892**
Listen.com, **103**
literature on audio, 104
live show bootlegs, 664–665
liveice software, **727–731**
looping programs, legality of, 697
lossy/lossless compression, **15**, **908**
Lycos search engine, **114**
Lydstrom Web site, 644, 645

M

M3U format, creating playlists in, 789–793, *789*, *791–793*
MACAST. *See* Macintosh MP3 players
Macintosh MP3 players, **476–513**, *See also* Linux; MP3 players; Windows
    GrayAMP
        downloading, 509–510
        features, 509
        interface, 510, *510–512*, 512
        limitations, 509
        overview of, 509
        preferences, 510–512, *511–512*
    MACAST, **501–508**
        applying skins, 507, *507*
        AutoSleep feature, 508, *508*
        defined, **501–502**
        downloading, 502
        editing ID3 tags, 763, *764*
        graphic equalizer, 506–507, *506*
        installing, 502–503, *502*
        interface, 503–504, *503–504*
        keyboard shortcuts, 503–504
        playlists, 504–506, *505*
        visualizations, 507
    MACAST Lite, 513
    MVP, **878–879**, *879*
    overview of, 513
    QuickAmp, **491–501**

adding information to tracks, 499, 500

Advanced settings, 498–499, *499*

Appearance settings, 497, *497*

applying skins to, 500–501, *500–501*

downloading, 491

enlarged format, 492, *492*

General settings, 494–496, *494–495*

minimized format, 491, *491*

overview of, 491

Playlist settings, 496–497, *496*

playlists, 492–494, *492–493*

Timer settings, 497–498, *498*

warning, 494

QuickTime, **476–477**, *477*

RealPlayer Basic, 476, 478, *478*

SoundApp, **478–490**

    CD Audio preferences, 488–489, *488–489*

    CDDB Host Selection box, 489, *489*

    Controls window, 479, *479*

    Convert preferences, 486–487, *487*

    defined, **478**

    disadvantage, 478

    downloading, 479

    General preferences, 482–484, *483*

    Keys preferences, 489–490, *490*

    overview of, 481–482

    Play preferences, 484–485, *485*

    playing music, 479, *479*, 480

    playlists, 480–481, *480*

    Status window, 479, *479*

    viewing file information, 481, *481*

Macintosh ripper/encoders, **516–527**

    AudioCatalyst

        buying, 516

        CDDB/ID preferences, 519–520, *520*

        configuring preferences, 517–520, *517–520*

        Encoder preferences, 518, *518*

        General preferences, 517, *517*

        limitations, 516

        Normalization preferences, 519, *519*

        overview of, 516

        ripping/encoding with, 521, *521*

    MPegger

        Asynchronous IO option, 524

        downloading, 522

        Encoding options, 522–524, *523*

        encoding WAV files to MP3, *523*, 527

        I/O & Systems options, 524, *524*

        overview of, 522, *523*

        selecting tracks to encode, 525, *526*

        Tag/Filename/CDDB options, 525, *526*

    overview of, 516, 564

Macintosh ripper/player/jukeboxes, **527–564**

    defined, **912**

    MusicMatch Jukebox for the Mac, **545–564**

        adding tracks to libraries, 558

        applying themes, 563, *564*

        AutoDJ feature, 562–563, *563*

        CDDB preferences, 553–555, *554*

        changing sampling rates, 553

        clearing libraries, 559, *560*

        configuring preferences, 549–555

        creating libraries, 557–558

        downloading, 546

        editing ID3 tags, 556–557, *556*, 765, *765*

        finding songs with, 546, *547*

        finding tracks in libraries, 560–561, *561*

        Full view, *548*, 549

        General preferences, 550–551, *550*

        installing, 546, *546*

Main window, 547–549, *548*
Music Library window, 547–549, *548*
opening music libraries, 560
overview of, 545–546
Player preferences, 551, *551*
playlists, 561–563, *563*
Recorder preferences, 552–553, *552*
Recorder window, 555–556, *555*
registering, 549
removing tracks from libraries, 558–559, *559*
ripping and encoding with, 555–556, *555*
Small view, 549, *549*
Welcome Tips box, 547
windows, manipulating, 547, 549
overview of, 516, 564
SoundJam, **527–545**
    adding missing ID3 tags, 542
    Advanced preferences, 537–538, *538*
    applying skins, 545, *545*
    burning CDs, 749–750
    CD Lookup preferences, 534, *534*
    Converter preferences, 535–537, *536*
    Converter window, 539–541, *540*
    converting MP3 files to AIFF, 749–750
    editing ID3 tags, 541–542, *541*, 764, *764*
    features, 527
    Files preferences, 531–533, *532*
    General preferences, 529–531, *530*
    graphic equalizer, 542–543, *543*
    ID3 Tags preferences, 533–534, *533*
    installing, 527–529, *528–529*
    navigating interface, 538–539, *539*
    overview of, 527
    Player window, 538, *539*
    playlists, 542

Plugins preferences, 535, *535*
ripping/encoding with, 539–541, *540*
virtual memory and, 528, *528*
visualizations, 544, *544*
windows, 538–539, *539*
Macintosh systems, *See also* Linux; Windows
    a2b players for, 881–883, *882–883*
    CD burning software, 751
    creating playlists on, 794–797, *794*, *796*
    editing ID3 tags on
        in MACAST, 763, *764*
        with mp3tool, 765–768, *766–767*
        in MusicMatch Jukebox, 430–432, *431*, *762*, *763*, *765*
        overview of, 763
        in SoundJam, 541–542, *541*, 764, *764*
Macster. *See* Napster for Macintosh
masks, 778
Melt-O-Rama visualization, 544, *544*
memory, *See also* RAM; storing
memory capacity of portable MP3 players, **615–617**
memory, virtual, SoundJam and, 528, *528*
metatags, adding to Web sites, 689
Microangelo software, **809–810**
microphones, **701–703**, *702*
Microsoft, *See also* Windows
    NetMeeting, **870**
    NetShow Server tools, **705**
    Web sites, 870, 894, 895
MicroWorks subwoofer system, **53**
MiniDisc players, 617
MiniDiscs, 6, **909**
MiniJam MP3 Player, 641
Mjuice digital-audio format, **36**, **909**
Mobile Audio Player software, **639**
MOD digital-audio format, 105

modems
- cable modems, **63**, **703–704**, **905**
- Internet broadcasting and, 703
- optimizing connections, **65–66**

Moffitt, Jack, 719

moving pictures. *See* visualizations

MP3, **4–37**, *See also* digital audio
- advantages, 20–21, 23–24, 25–26
- artists and, 23–25, 659–661
- Beam-it feature, 30
- CD-quality audio and, 11, 12–13, 22
- codecs, 911
- defined, **9–10**, **12**, **909**
- digital audio and, 8–10
- disadvantages, 22–23, 25, 27–32
- future of, 32–33
- how it works, 12–16
- legal issues, 22–23, 82, 694–695
- MPEG and, 10–11
- music enthusiasts and, 20–23, 31
- piracy and, 25, 27, 28–32, 660–661
- portability, 20–21
- psychoacoustics and, 14, 911
- record companies and, 24, 25–32
- sampling and, 12–14
- Web site, 19

MP3 Enc, 578, **605**

MP3 Encoder for Linux, 578

MP3 Fiend, 117

MP3 files, **760–803**, *See also* burning CDs
- choosing encoding rates, 16–19
- comparing with other formats, 33–34, 661
- converting
  - to AIFF files, 749–750
  - to WAV files, 748–750
  - to WMA files, 639
- converting with MP3 to EXE
  - batch conversions, 800
  - choosing options, 799, *799*
  - downloading, 798
  - overview of, 797–798, *798*
  - using, 799–800, *800*
  - warning, 798
- creating of own music, 760–761
- creating playlists of, **786–797**
  - on Linux, 797
  - overview of, 786
  - on the Mac with Trax, 794–797, *794*, *796*
  - in Windows, overview of, 787
  - in Windows with Playlist Pro, 787–788, *787–788*
  - in Windows with ShufflePlay, 789–793, *789*, *791–793*
- distributing, 20, 23–25, 668–669
- downloading, 19, 21
- downsampling in icecast, 727–731
- e-mailing, 89
- editing
  - in Linux with mp3asm, 783
  - overview of, 779–780
  - in Windows with MP3Cutter, 780–782, *781–783*
  - in Windows with mp3Trim, 782
- editing ID3 tags, **761–771**
  - with EasyTAG, 770, *771*
  - in FreeAmp, 769, *769*
  - with id3ren, 770
  - on Linux, 768–770, *769*, *771*
  - in MACAST, 763, *764*
  - with mp3tool, 765–768, *766–767*
  - in MusicMatch Jukebox for the Mac, 556–557, *556*, 765, *765*
  - in MusicMatch Jukebox for Windows, 430–432, *431*, 762, *763*
  - overview of, 761
  - in SoundJam, 764, *764*
  - on the Mac, 763–768, *764–767*
  - in Winamp, 762, *762*
  - in Windows, 762, *762–763*

in xmms, 768, *769*
encoding from WAV files, 398
encoding WAV files to, *523*, 527
FTP sites for, 98
Liquid Audio format and, 892-893
versus other formats, 33-34, 661, 874-876, 900-901
overview of, 760
publishing, 20, 23-25, 668-669
renaming
    on Linux with id3ren, 779
    overview of, 771-772
    in Windows with G6 Renamer, 774-778, *775-776, 778-779*
    in Windows with MP3 Renamer, 772-774, *772, 774*
repairing cooked files
    defined, **783-784**
    in DOS with Detox, 786
    in Linux with mp3asm, 786
    in Windows with Uncook 95, 784-786, *784-786*
sharing, 21, 31-32
sorting, 15-16
sound quality and, 16-19, 22
storing, 16-17, 58-60
transferring, 15, 17, 21
MP3 files, finding, **98-293**, *See also* Napster
    using audioGnome, **217-231**
        browsing user libraries, 229-230, *230*
        configuring options, 219-223, *223*
        connecting to servers, 224-225, *224*
        defined, **217**
        downloading files, 227-229, *227*
        finding music via, 225-227, *225*
        installing, 217-218, *218*
        multipage interface, 218, *219*
        sharing files, 230-231, *231*
        stopping sharing, 219, *220*

using CuteMX, 231-232, *233*
using Freenet, 272-275, *275*
using gnutella, **209-216**
    closing, 216
    configuring, 211-212, *213*
    connecting to gnutellaNet, 212-214, *214*
    defined, **210**
    downloading, 210
    downloading files, 215, *216*
    installing, 210, *210*
    interface, 211, *211*
    Napster and, 209-210
    overview of, 93
    searching for files, 214, *214*
    transferring files, 216
using iMesh, **233-271**
    About page, 257, *258*
    Additional Details box, 236-238, *237*
    Appearance options, 240-244, *241-244*, 254-255, *255*
    Auto Update option, 257, *257*
    configuring options, 245-258
    Connection page, 254, *254*
    Connection Settings box, 238, *239*
    contacts, managing, 267-271
    Contacts options, 255-256, *256*
    defined, **233**
    deleting contacts, 268
    Download options, 250-251, *251*
    downloading, 234
    downloading tracks, 262-264, *262-263*
    exiting, 271
    forwarding tracks to friends, 261, *261, 263*, 264
    General options, 245-246, *246*
    home page, *234*
    ignoring contacts, 256, *256*, 268-269

iMesh window, 244–245, *245*
installing, 234–239, *235–237, 239*
Location Details box, 235–236, *236*
Locations page, 246, *247*
My Details page, 249, *249*
opening downloaded files, *263*, 264
Personal Details box, 235, *235*
recommending tracks to friends, 264, *264*
Registration Wizard, **234–239**, *235–237, 239*
renaming contacts, 270
Search options, 249, *250*
searching with, 258–260, *259–260*
Security options, 247–248, *248*
sending file links to contacts, 270–271, *271*
sending messages to contacts, 270, *270*
Share options, 252–253, *253*
Share Wizard, 239–240, *239–240*
sharing files, 265–266, *265*
stopping sharing, 238
Upload options, 251–252, *252*
uploading files, 266, *267*
viewing contact files, 269, *269*
warnings, 233, 266
on Internet radio via RadioSpy, **279–293**
Chat options, 284, *285*
configuring options, 282–285, *284–285*
connecting to stations, 291–292, *291*
defined, **280**
downloading, 282
Favorites list, 293
Firewall/Proxy options, 285
General options, 282–283, *284*
installing, 282
interface, 285–291, *286–287*
overview of, 293
Skins options, 285

streaming audio and, 280–282
Web site, 280
using MusicMatch Jukebox for the Mac, 546, *547*
on newsgroups, 119–122, *121*
overview of, 122–123
using search engines
    Audiogalaxy, 114
    Lycos, 114
    Musicseek, 114
    Oth.Net, 114
    overview of, 111
    ratio sites and, 112–113, 911–912
    Scour, 114–115
using search utilities
    Go!Zilla, 117–118
    MP3 Star Search, 115–117, *116*
using SpinFrenzy, 275–276, *276*
on Web sites, **98–111**
    and downloading or not, 99
    eatsleepmusic.com, 104–105
    EMusic.com, 102–103, 573
    Free Music Archive, 105
    FTP sites, 98
    iCrunch, 103
    Listen.com, 103
    MP3 Place, 105
    MP3.com, 101–102
    MP3Lit.com, 104
    overview of, 98–99
    pirate sites, 107–111
    porn sites and, 108–111
    record company sites, 106–107
    Riffage.com, 100–101
    RioPort, 106
    songs.com, 103
    Spinfrenzy.com, 104
    WorldWideBands, 106
using Wrapster, 207–209, *209*
MP3 Place Web site, **105**

MP3 players, *See also* Linux; Macintosh; portable MP3 players; Windows
  car players
    defined, **611**
    empeg car in-dash player, 649–653, *651–652*
    in-car jukeboxes, 647–649, 653
    in-dash players, 647–649, 653
    overview of, 645
    portable players as, 646–647
    Web site, 648
  home stereos as
    by connecting to PCs, 642–643
    by connecting to portable players, 641
    using dedicated components, 22, 611, 643–645
  overview of, 610–611, 636

MP3 Producer/Producer Professional encoders, *See also* Windows rippers and encoders
  batch processing, 403–405, *404*
  buying, 401
  disadvantages, 400–401
  encoding with, 402–405, *402*, *404*
  installing, 401–402, *401*
  overview of, 400

MP3 Renamer, 772, **772–774**, *774*

MP3 servers, *See also* music collections
  backing up, 869–870
  component servers as, 868
  network connectivity, 866
  operating systems, 867–868
  overview of, 863–864
  using PCs as, 870
  reliability, 867
  storage drives, 864–866

MP3 Star Search utility, **115–117**, *116*

MP3 to EXE software
  batch conversions, 800

  choosing options, 799, *799*
  downloading, 798
  overview of, 797–798, *798*
  using, 799–800, *800*
  warning, 798

mp3Agent software, **627**, *628*

mp3asm software
  editing MP3 files, 783
  repairing cooked MP3 files, 786

MP3.com
  defined, **909**
  finding MP3 files on, 101–102
  getting own music onto, 673, 674–675

MP3Cutter software, **780–782**, *781–783*

MP3Enc (MPEG Layer-3 Commandline Encoder)
  defined, **399**, **605**
  downloading, 399, 605
  encoding with, 400
  versus LAME encoder, 601
  testing demo versions, 399

MP3Lit.com, **104**

mp3tool tag editor, **765–768**, *766–767*

mp3Trim editor, **782**

MP3z files, **88**, 107, **909**

MP4, 33, **909**

MPDJ software, **626**, *627*

MPEG (Moving Picture Experts Group), 10–11, **909**

MPegger ripper/encoder, *See also* Macintosh ripper/encoders
  Asynchronous IO option, 524
  downloading, 522
  Encoding options, 522–524, *523*
  encoding WAV files to MP3, *523*, 527
  I/O & Systems options, 524, *524*
  overview of, 522, *523*
  selecting tracks to encode, 525, *526*
  Tag/Filename/CDDB options, 525, *526*

mpg123 player, *See also* Linux MP3 players
    defined, **568**, **574**
    downloading, 574
    playing music, 574
    in verbose mode, 575, *575*
MS Audio format, **35–36**
MTU Speed Pro utility, **66**
Müller, Sergej, 343
music collections, **856–871**
    backing up CDs, 858–859
    building MP3 servers for
        and backing up, 869–870
        network connectivity, 866
        operating systems, 867–868
        or buying component servers, 868
        or using PCs as audio servers, 870
        overview of, 863–864
        reliability, 867
        storage drives, 864–866
    CDs, bit-rot, and, 856–858, 905
    getting best music quality, 859–861
    overview of, 856, 871
    picking naming conventions, 861–863
music consumers
    legal issues and, 80
    MP3 pros and cons for, 20–23, 31
musicians. *See* artists; promoting your music on the Web
MusicMatch Jukebox for the Mac, **545–564**, *See also* Macintosh ripper/player/jukeboxes
    applying themes, 563, *564*
    AutoDJ feature, 562–563, *563*
    changing sampling rates, 553
    configuring preferences
        CDDB, 553–555, *554*
        General, 550–551, *550*
        overview of, 549
        Player, 551, *551*
        Recorder, 552–553, *552*

downloading, 546
editing ID3 tags, 556–557, *556*, 765, *765*
finding songs with, 546, *547*
Full view, *548*, 549
installing, 546, *546*
music libraries
    adding tracks to, 558
    clearing, 559, *560*
    creating, 557–558
    finding tracks in, 560–561, *561*
    opening, 560
    removing tracks from, 558–559, *559*
    window, 547–549, *548*
overview of, 545–546
playlists, 561–563, *563*
registering, 549
ripping/encoding with, 555–556, *555*
Small view, 549, *549*
Welcome Tips box, 547
windows
    Main, 547–549, *548*
    manipulating, 547, 549
    Music Library, 547–549, *548*
    Recorder, 555–556, *555*
MusicMatch Jukebox for Windows, **418–448**, *See also* Windows ripper/player/jukeboxes
    accessing music on Internet, 441, *441*
    adding CD information to CDDB, 801–803, *802*
    AutoDJ feature, 439, *439*
    burning CDs, 443–448, *445*, *447*
    Confirm Association box, 422
    downloading, 419
    editing ID3 tags, 430–432, *431*, 762, *763*
    Filetype Registration box, 420–421, *421*
    graphic equalizer, 440–441, *440*
    installing, 419–421, *420–421*
    Jukebox File Associations box, 421

music libraries
    adding tracks to, 434–435, *435*
    creating, 432, 434
    deleting tracks from, 435–436, *436*
    finding tracks in, 437, *437*
    opening, 435–436, *436*
    settings for, 433–434, *433*
    sharing, 436–437
    window, 422–424, *423*
Net Music feature, 441, *441*
Net Radio feature, 442–443, *442–443*
overview of, 418
Personalize Net Music box, 419–420, *420*
playing Internet radio, 442–443, *442–443*
Playlist window, 423–424, *423*, 438
using playlists, 438–439, *439*
previewing tracks, 438
registering, 424
ripping CDs, 429–430, *429–430*
searching for music, 422, *422*
settings for
    CDDB/Connectivity, 424–425, *425*
    Music Library, 433–434, *433*
    New Songs Directory, 427–428, *427*
    Recorder, 425–429, *426–427*
User Registration Info box, 419
warning, 436
windows
    Jukebox Recorder, 429–430, *429*
    Main, 422–424, *423*
    manipulating, 423–424
    Music Library, 422–424, *423*
    overview of, 422
    Playlist, 423–424, *423*, 438
Musicseek search engine, **114**
MVP encoder/player, **878–879**, *879*
MyMP3.com, **102**
myplay.com, 60

N

naming conventions for music collections, **861–863**
naming. *See* renaming
Napster, **126–207**, *See also* MP3 files, finding
    defined, **126**, **128**
    getting own music played on, 675
    legal issues, 88–93, 127, 129, 157, 209
    overview of, 126, 128–129, 277
    piracy and, 30–31
    RIAA versus, 127
    sharing MP3 files via, 30–31, 157
    sharing non-MP3 files, 207
    warning, 129
    Web sites, 126, 127
    Wrapster and, 207–209, *209*
Napster for Macintosh
    Macster, **168–191**
        Account Information box, 170, *170*
        browsing user libraries, 185–186, *185–186*
        canceling transfers, 184
        chat rooms, 189–190, *189–191*
        chats, private, 188, *188*
        Download Folder box, 171, *171*
        downloading, 169
        downloading tracks, 183–184, *183*
        finding music via, 180–182, *181–182*
        if setup crashes, 173
        Network Options box, 171–172, *172*
        overview of, 168–169
        panel buttons, 173–175, *174*
        preferences
        Account, 176–177, *177*
        General, 175–176, *176*
        Network, 178, *178*
        Personal, 170, *171*
        Transfers, 179–180, *180*

Proxy Server box, 172, *172*
receiving messages, 187, *187*
Registration box, 173, *173*
replying to messages, 188, *188*
sending private messages, 187, *187*
setting up, **169–173**
viewing user information, 186–187, *186*
Web site address, 169
Rapster, 168
Napster on Linux, **191–207**
gnap, 191–192
Gnapster, **191–207**
Auto-Join properties, 195, *195*
browsing user MP3 files, 202–203, *203*
chat rooms, 204–207, *205–206*
connecting to servers, 196–197, *196–197*
Display properties, 194, *195*
downloading, 192
downloading MP3 files, 200–202, *201*
exiting, 207
getting user information, 203
multipage interface, 198, *199*
Options properties, 193–194, *194*
overview of, 191
searching for MP3 files, 198, 199, *200*
setting properties, 192–195, *193–195*
sharing MP3 files, 204
User Information properties, 192–193, *193*, 197, *198*
GNOME-Napster, 191, 192
knapster, 191
overview of, 191–192
Napster on Windows, **129–167**
canceling transfers, 167
chatting on, 158–164, *158–161*, *163*
connection speeds and, 147–148, 150, *150*
deleting tracks, 157
downloading, 129
downloading tracks, 151–156, *152*, *154*
etiquette, 164
exiting, 167–168
finding music with, 146–151, *146*, *150*
firewall settings, 135–137, *136*
firewalls and, 166
Home page, 137, *138*
ignoring/unignoring users, 162, *163*
installing
Connection Information, 130–131, *130*
File Server Settings, 135, *136*, 137
Napster Configuration, 132–133, *133*
New File Repository, 135, *136*
Optional Information, 133, *134*
Proxy Setup, 131–132, *132*
Scan for files?, 133, *134*
Shared Folders, 134, *135*
maintaining hot lists, 164–166, *165–166*
playing music, 156–157, *156*
preferences
Chat, 139–140, *140*
Downloading, 142–144, *144*
Personal, 138, *139*
Proxy, 144–145, *145*
Schemes, 141, *141*
Sharing, 141–142, *142*
sending private messages, 161–162, *161*
sharing music via, 166–168, *167*
swear filter, 164
viewing user information, 160, *161*, 162–163
warnings, 157, 168
NetMeeting software, **870**
NetShow Server tools, **705**, **706**

newsgroups, finding MP3 files on, **119–122**, *121*
newsletters, electronic, starting, **690–691**
No Electronic Theft (NET) Act of 1997, **84**
normalization, **395**, **909**
Notepad, **810**
NotLame encoder, *See also* Linux rippers and encoders
    command-line options, 601–602
    downloading, 601
    encoding with, 603, *603*
    LAME encoder and, 601
    overview of, 601
NULL Output plug-in, **705–706**

O

Oliphant, Mike, 579
on-demand streaming audio, **280–281**, **909**
online storage drives, 60
open headphones, **55**, **910**
OpenMG technology, 35, 85, **884–885**, **910**
Oscilloscope options, *334*, **334–335**
Oth.Net search engine, 114
Oxygen theme, 563

P

packet-writing software, 744, **744**
Paint Shop Pro software, **809**, 819
Palm-size PCs. *See* portable MP3 players
parallel ports, **61**, **742**
passive speakers, **51**, **910**
passwords, Web sites and, 676
PCM (Pulse Code Modulation) format, **737**, **911**
PDAs, **910**, *See also* Handspring Visor; portable MP3 players
peak output/power, **52**, **910**
personal use, **79**, 694, **910**

photographs
    in creating skins, 812–814, *812–814*, 816–819
    in Web sites, 685
Photoshop, **809**
pictures. *See* skins; visualizations
Pine's D'Music portable CD-ROM player, **738**
ping time, **147**, **910**
piracy, *See also* legal issues
    using as an advantage, 664
    audio cassette levies and, 28
    digital audio tape and, 29
    ease of, 29–30
    encouraging live show bootlegs, 664–665
    MP3 and, 25, 27, 28–32, 660–661
    Napster and, 30–31
    recording companies and, 25, 27, 28–32
    releasing free lo-fi tracks, 662–663
    releasing no music, 663
    releasing secure format tracks, 661–662, 663
    tolerable levels of, 28, 32
pirate sites, **107–111**
pits, **745**
players. *See* Linux; Macintosh; MP3 players; Windows
playing CDs with Winamp, 324
playing Liquid Audio tracks, 891, *891*
Playlist Editors
    in Audioactive Player, *375*
    in Unreal Player MAX, 382
    in Winamp, 318, *319–320*, 320–321, 828–830, *829–831*
    in XingMP3 Player, 371, *372*
playlists of MP3 files, **786–797**
    changing font/color, 834–836, *836*
    on Linux, 797
    overview of, 786
    playlists, defined, **910–911**
    on the Mac

in MACAST, 504–506, *505*
in MusicMatch Jukebox, 561–563, *563*
in QuickAmp, 492–494, *492–493*, 496–497, *496*
in SoundApp, 480–481, *480*
in SoundJam, 542
with Trax, 794–797, *794*, *796*
on Windows
in MusicMatch Jukebox, 423–424, *423*, 438–439, *439*
overview of, 787
with Playlist Pro, 787–788, *787–788*
in RealJukebox, 463–464, *463*
with ShufflePlay, 789–793, *789*, *791–793*
in Sonique, 357–358, *358*
in Unreal Player MAX, 381–382, *381*
in Winamp, 324–328, *324*, *327*, 337–338
in Windows Media Player, 304, *304*, 307, *307*
Pledit.txt files, **834–836**, *836*
plug-ins
Copah CD-Reader plug-in, **365**
defined, **911**
for SHOUTcast
DSP, **705**, 707
Live Input, **705**, 707
NULL Output, **705–706**, 707
smpeg-xmms plug-in, **571**
for Sonique, 365
Web sites for, 341, 365
for Winamp
Climax, *343–346*, **343–346**
DeFX, *347–348*, **347–349**
overview of, 340–341
RealAudio, *342*, **342–343**
VQF, 897
for xmms, 571

Plugins preferences in SoundJam, 535, *535*
Pocket PCs, **611–612**, 636, *See also* portable MP3 players
PolicyMaker in a2b, **880**
POPs (points of presence), **679**
porn sites, escaping from, **108–111**
port requirements, **60–62**
portable MP3 players, **610–641**, *See also* MP3 players
CompactFlash cards for, 636, 637, 640
connecting to car stereos, 646–647
connecting to home stereos, 641
considerations in choosing, **615–633**
batteries, 622–623
carrying methods, 623–624
ease of use, 621
equalization controls, 632
headphones, 625–626
line-out jacks, 621–622
looks, 633
memory/storage needs, 615–617
music file formats, 620
operating system support, 618
recording capability, 620
size, 621
software functionality, 626–631, *627–631*
sound quality, 619
tuners, 621
defined, **611**
Diamond Rio player, 613
hand-held PCs as
defined, **639–640**
Hum software for, 640
overview of, 611–612, 640
Handspring Visor as, 612, 641
marketability limitations
computer dependency, 614
expense, 614
quality, 614
size, 613

overview of, 610
Palm-size PCs as
    criteria for, 636–637
    defined, **611**
    Hum for CE player for, 638
    Mobile Audio Player for, 639
    overview of, 611–612, 636
    Windows Media Player for, 637–638
Pocket PCs as, 611–612, 636
using RealJukebox with, 464–467, 465–466
software for
    Audio Manager, 628–630, *629–631*
    mp3Agent, 627, *628*
    MPDJ, 626, *627*
    overview of, 626, 628
ultraportable players, **610–611**
upgrade cards, 616
pressed CDs, **745**, **911**
privacy policies for Web sites, 683
promoting your music on the Web, **658–731**
    advantages of, 659–661
    building Web sites, **675–689**
        adding interactive features, 679–684
        adding metatags, 689
        advantage of, 676
        caution, 680
        children and, 684
        choosing domain names, 667
        choosing ISPs, 678–679
        collecting visitor information, 681–684
        developing privacy policies, 683
        disadvantage of, 676
        with easy navigation, 686–687
        ensuring browser viewability, 686
        ensuring quick load speed, 685–686
        information to include, 676–678, 687
        overview of, 667, 675, 687
        passwords and, 676
        photographs in, 685
        presenting clear focus, 684–685
        providing visitor benefits, 687
        registering with search engines, 689
        and updating, 688–689
        warning, 684
    developing strategies, 666–668
    digital-audio formats for
        advantages, 659–661
        choosing, 668–669
        disadvantages, 660–662
        MP3 format, 659–661, 668–669
        versus physical media, 669
        secure formats, 661–662, 663, 668
    disadvantages of, 660–662
    establishing goals, 665–666
    getting tracks onto music sites
        MP3.com, 673, 674–675
        Napster, 675
        overview of, 672–674
        Riffage.com, 673, 674
    via icecast broadcasts, **719–731**
        configuring liveice, 727–730
        configuring shout, 724–726
        defined, **280**, **719**, **908**
        downloading, 719–720
        downsampling MP3 files, 727–731
        editing parameters, 720–723
        liveice keyboard controls, 730–731
        saving streams in FreeAmp, 573
        sending audio streams to, 724–727
        shutting down, 731
        starting, 723–724
    via Internet broadcasting, **694–731**
        buying microphones, 701
        computer hardware for, 700–701

configuring microphones, 701–703, *702*

connection power for, 703–704

getting licenses, 698

how it works, 699–700

with icecast, 719–731

legal issues and, 694–697, 761

overview of, 694

with SHOUTcast, 704–719

overview of, 658–659, 669, 672, 691

piracy and

    using as an advantage, 664

    encouraging live show bootlegs, 664–665

    using MP3 format, 660–661

    releasing free lo-fi tracks, 662–663

    releasing no music, 663

    releasing secure format tracks, 661–662, 663

via SHOUTcast broadcasts, **704–719**

    adding your voice, 716–718

    configuring servers, 707–712

    configuring Winamp to, 713–716, *713*, *715–716*

    downloading software support, 705–706

    installing NetShow Server tools, 706

    installing plug-ins, 707

    installing servers, 707

    overview of, 280, 694, 704–705

    shutting servers down, 718, *719*

    silencing local output, 718

    starting servers, 712–713, *712*

starting electronic newsletters, 690–691

warning, 666

proxy servers, **132**, **911**

psychoacoustics, **14**

publishing MP3 files, 20, 23–25, 668–669, *See also* promoting

Pure MP3 site, **111**

Q

QDesign Music Codec format, **36–37**, **877–879**, *879*, **911**

Qube server, 868

QuickAmp, **491–501**, *See also* Macintosh MP3 players

    adding information to tracks, 499, *500*

    applying skins to, 500–501, *500–501*

    choosing settings

        Advanced, 498–499, *499*

        Appearance, 497, *497*

        General, 494–496, *494–495*

        Playlist, 496–497, *496*

        Timer, 497–498, *498*

    downloading, 491

    enlarged format, 492, *492*

    minimized format, 491, *491*

    overview of, 491

    playlists, 492–494, *492–493*

    warning, 494

QuickTime digital-audio format, **37**, **900**, **911**

QuickTime MP3 player for the Mac, **476–477**, *477*

R

radio broadcasting. *See* Internet broadcasting

RadioSpy, **279–293**, *See also* MP3 files, finding

    Chat options, 284, *285*

    configuring options, 282–285, *284–285*

    connecting to stations, 291–292, *291*

    defined, **280**

    downloading, 282

    Favorites list, 293

    Firewall/Proxy options, 285

    General options, 282–283, *284*

    installing, 282

    interface, 285–291, *286–287*

    overview of, 293

Skins options, 285
streaming audio and, 280-282
Web site, 280
Raghavan, Barath, 719
RAID (Redundant Array of Inexpensive Disks), 868
RAM requirements, **43**, *See also* memory
Rapster for Macintosh, **168**
ratio sites, **112-113**, **911-912**
Real Entertainment Center, **448-449**, 450-451
RealAudio format, *See also* digital-audio formats
    adding to Winamp, *342*, **342-343**
    defined, **37**, **899**, **912**
    in RealJukebox, 454, *454*, 468, *469*, 900
RealJukebox, **448-469**, *See also* skins; Windows ripper/player/jukeboxes
    AutoPlaylist feature, 464
    changing skins, 467-468, *467*
    configuration options
        Audio Playback, 452-453
        AutoStart, 453
        CD Recording, 454, *454*
        Find Music, 453
        Internet, 455
        Music File Location, 453
        re-running, 456
        Recording, 455
        Security Feature, 453-454
    configuring portable players, 465, *466*
    converting track formats, 468, *469*
    creating playlists, 463-464, *463*
    downloading, 450-451
    Driver Problem Detected box, 465, *465*
    Full Mode, 459, *459*
    identifying portable players to, 464-465, *465*
    installing, 451-452
    interface, 459-460, *459-460*
    loading portable players, 466
    overview of, 418, 448-449
    playing music, 462-464, *463*
    using with portable MP3 players, 464-467, *465-466*
    preferences
        Audio Quality, 457, 900
        General, 456
        Music Files, 457-458, *458*
        Recording, 456, *457*
    RealAudio format in, 454, *454*, 468, *469*, 900
    RealNetworks and, 449-450
    removing portable players from, 466-467
    ripping CDs, 461-462, *461*
    Skin Mode, 460, *460*
    starting, 459
    viewing music libraries, 462-463
    warning, 451
RealJukebox Plus, 389, 448, 451-452, 454, 455
RealJukebox Skin Converter tool, **852**
RealNetworks, **448-450**, 516
RealPlayer Basic for Macintosh, **476**, *478*, **478**
rebates for computers, 41-42
recordable CDs, **745-746**, 859, 869, *See also* burning CDs
recording artists. *See* artists
recording companies
    digital audio and, 4-6
    legal issues and, 81, 695
    MP3 pros and cons for, 24, 25-32
    piracy and, 25, 27, 28-32
    signing with, 695
    sites, for MP3 files, 106-107
Region.txt files, **834**, **838-839**, *839*
registering
    copyrights, 76
    Web sites with search engines, 689
remote-control software, 870

renaming MP3 files
- on Linux with id3ren, 779
- overview of, 771–772
- in Windows with G6 Renamer, 774–778, *775–776, 778–779*
- in Windows with MP3 Renamer, 772–774, *772, 774*

repairing cooked MP3 files
- defined, **783–784**
- in DOS with Detox, 786
- in Linux with mp3asm, 786
- in Windows with Uncook 95, 784–786, *784–786*

retail industry, legal issues and, 81–82
RF modulators, 646, **912**
RGB (red green blue) format, **837**
RIAA (Recording Industry Association of America)
- defined, **81**, **912**
- versus Napster, 127
- Web site address, 695

Richardson, Eileen, 93
Riffage.com
- finding MP3 files on, 100–101
- getting own music played on, 673, 674

RioPort Audio Manager software
- editing song information, 630, *630*
- loading songs onto portable players, 630, *631*
- monitoring music files, 628–629, *629*
- reviewing new songs, 629–630, *629*

RioPort Web site, **106**
rip, **387**
rippers, **8**, **912**, *See also* Macintosh ripper; Windows ripper
ripperX ripper/encoder, *See also* Linux rippers and encoders
- CDDB options, 596–597, *597*
- configuring options, 592–599
- defined, **591**
- downloading, 591
- Files options, 597–599, *598*
- General options, 592–593, *593*
- MP3 encoder options, 595, *595*
- overview of, 578
- Players options, 595–596, *596*
- ripping/encoding with, 599, *600*
- running, 591, *591–592*
- Wav ripper options, 594, *594*

RJS file extensions, 852
Route 66 software, **653**

S

sampling, **12–14**, **912–913**
sampling precision, **12**, **913**
sampling rate, **12**, **913**
satellite connections, **65**
Scour search engine, **114–115**
SCSI drives, **741–742**, **865**
SDMI (Secure Digital Music Initiative), **85–87**, 913
sealed headphones, **55–56**, **913**
search engines, *See also* MP3 files, finding
- Audiogalaxy, 114
- Lycos, 114
- Musicseek, 114
- Oth.Net, 114
- overview of, 111
- ratio sites and, 112–113, 911–912
- registering Web sites with, 689
- Scour, 114–115

search utilities
- Go!Zilla, 117–118
- MP3 Star Search, 115–117, *116*

Secure Digital Music Initiative (SDMI), **85–87**, 913
security
- in a2b digital-audio format, 880

SESAC, Inc.—skins, creating for RealJukebox 945

    in digital-audio formats, 661–662, 663, 668, 875
    in iMesh search tool, 247–248, *248*
    in Liquid Player, 887–889, *888–889*
    of Internet connections, 62
    in RealJukebox, 453–454
SESAC, Inc., **698**
shotgun modems, **66**, **913**
shout, configuring, 724–726
SHOUTcast broadcasts, **704–719**, *See also* promoting your music on the Web
    adding your voice, 716–718
    configuring servers, 707–712
    configuring Winamp to, 713–716, *713*, *715–716*
    downloading software support, 705–706
    installing NetShow Server tools, 706
    installing plug-ins, 707
    installing servers, 707
    overview of, 280, 694, 704–705
    saving streams in FreeAmp, 573
    shutting servers down, 718, *719*
    silencing local output, 718
    starting servers, 712–713, *712*
SHOUTcast DSP broadcasting tools, 705
SHOUTcast Live Input plug-in, **705**
ShufflePlay for Windows, 789, **789–793**, *791–793*
Siren Jukebox, **469–470**, *471*
SketchAmp skin, *339*, **339**, *807*, **807**
Skinmaster software, 811
Skinner software, 811
skins, **806–853**
    Bubble Blues skin, 363, *364*
    defined, **339**, **806**, **913**
    for MACAST, 507, *507*
    for QuickAmp, 500–501, *500–501*
    for RadioSpy, 285
    for RealJukebox

    applying, 467–468
    creating, 840–852
    downloading, 467, 468
    Skin Mode and, 460, *460*
    Stainless Steel, *460*
    Wood and Water, *467*
for Sonique, 363–364, *364*
for SoundJam, 545, *545*
subrad skin, *507*
Thunderstorm skin, *501*
Web site addresses, 339, 364
for Winamp
    1914, 814, *815*
    applying, 339–340
    creating, 807–840
    default skin, 807, *807*
    downloading, 339, 806
    SketchAmp, 339, *339*, 807, *807*
    StoneAmp, 814, *815*
    Tomatoes Go Splat, 808, *808*
    Woody Wood Amp, 808, *808*
WonderJelly skin, *545*
for xmms, 569
skins, creating for RealJukebox, **840–852**
    adding status windows, 849–851
    background graphics, 841
    using bitmap files, 841
    controls
        adding custom controls, 843–844, 848–849
        default controls, 842–843, 845–846
        filenames of, 842–843
        graphic images for, 841–842, 843
        positioning, 844, 848
        Show attribute of, 846–847
    by converting Winamp skins, 852
    creating Skin.ini files, 844–848
    using JPEG files, 841
    overview of, 840–841

using Skins Toolkit, 840–841
specifying screen location, 851
storing in folders, 852
zipping for distribution, 851–852
skins, creating for Winamp, **807–840**
  using bitmap files, 816–817, 818, 819
  changing
    cursors, 833–834
    playlist font/color, 834–836, *836*
    skin masks, 834, 838–839, *839*
    visualization colors, 834, 837–838
  and converting to RealJukebox, 852
  customizing bitmaps, **819–832**
    in Graphical Equalizer window, 826–827, *826–828*
    in Main window, 820–826, *820–826*
    in Minibrowser window, 831, *831–832*
    overview of, 819
    in Playlist Editor window, 828–830, *829–831*
  editing text files
    overview of, 834
    Pledit.txt, 835–836, *836*
    Region.txt, 838–839, *839*
    Viscolor.txt, 837–838
  using existing picture files, 816–819
  finding bitmap coordinates, 838
  golden rules in
    accessible controls rule, 814, *815*
    antisocial distortion rule, 812, *812*
    configurable player rule, 816
    disfigurement rule, 813–814, *813–814*
    intellectual property rule, 812, 817
  methods for, 816
  overview of, 808–809
  programs needed
    bitmap editors, 809
    icon editors, 809–810
    paint programs, 809
    text editors, 810
    Winamp Base Skin, 810–811
  resizing pictures, 812, *812*, 818–819
  using skinning programs, 811
  storing in folders, 809
  Web site on, 810
  zipping for distribution, 840
smiley-face icons, 160, *160*
smpeg-xmms plug-in, **571**
song keys in a2b, **880**
songs.com, **103**
Sonique, **349–367**, *See also* Windows MP3 players
  adding plug-ins, 365
  Audio Enhancement Control, 359–361, *360–361*
  Auto-Play feature, 350
  burning CDs, 748–749
  changing skins, 363–364, *364*
  converting MP3 files to WAV, 748–749
  creating playlists, 357–358, *358*
  defined, **349**
  downloading, 349
  editing ID3 tags, 358–359, *359*
  installing, 349–351, *350–351*
  interface, 352–356, *353–355*
  keyboard shortcuts, 355–357, 365–367
  launching, 352
  overview of, 298
  playing music, 356–357
  visualizations, 361–363, *362*
Sony
  ATRAC3 format, 35, **884–885**
  OpenMG technology, 35, 85, **884–885**, **910**
  SDMI-compliant software, 86–87
  VAIO Music Clip, **27**
sorting MP3 files, 15–16

sound cards–static streamers   947

sound cards
    for Internet broadcasting, 701
    for MP3 and digital audio, **44–49**
    Sound Blaster, **48**
sound quality
    MP3 and, 16–19, 22
    music collections and, 859–861
    of digital-audio formats, 875
    in portable MP3 players, 619
    on telephones, 14
    in TwinVQ/VQF audio format, 896
SoundApp, **478–490**, *See also* Macintosh MP3 players
    CDDB Host Selection box, 489, *489*
    choosing preferences
        CD Audio, 488–489, *488–489*
        Convert, 486–487, *487*
        General, 482–484, *483*
        Keys, 489–490, *490*
        overview of, 481–482
        Play, 484–485, *485*
    Controls window, 479, *479*
    defined, **478**
    disadvantage, 478
    downloading, 479
    playing music, 479, *479*, 480
    playlists, 480–481, *480*
    Status window, 479, *479*
    viewing file information, 481, *481*
SoundJam ripper/player/jukebox, **527–545**, *See also* Macintosh ripper/player/jukeboxes
    adding missing ID3 tags, 542
    applying skins, 545, *545*
    burning CDs, 749–750
    Converter window, 539–541, *540*
    converting MP3 files to AIFF, 749–750
    editing ID3 tags, 541–542, *541*, 764, *764*
    features, 527
    graphic equalizer, 542–543, *543*

    installing, 527–529, *528–529*
    interface, 538–539, *539*
    overview of, 527
    Player window, 538, *539*
    playlists, 542
    preferences
        Advanced, 537–538, *538*
        CD Lookup, 534, *534*
        Converter, 535–537, *536*
        Files, 531–533, *532*
        General, 529–531, *530*
        ID3 Tags, 533–534, *533*
        Plugins, 535, *535*
    ripping/encoding with, 539–541, *540*
    virtual memory and, 528, *528*
    visualizations, 544, *544*
    windows, 538–539, *539*
source folders, **796**
speakers, *See also* hardware requirements
    amplified speakers, 51, 904
    cheap speakers, 50
    components of, 50–51
    home theater systems, 54–55, 908
    matching to needs, 53–54
    measuring loudness, 51–53
    overview of, 49
    passive speakers, 51, 910
    surround sound, 54, 914
    trying out, 55
Spectrum analyzer options, *334*, **334–335**
Spinfrenzy.com, **104**, **275–276**, *276*
SpinRecords.com, 878
SPL (sound pressure level), 52, **913**
spoken digital audio, *See also* digital audio
    literature online, 104
    sampling and, 14
    storing on portable players, 615
Springboard modules, 612
static streamers, **724**

statutory licenses, 695
stereos. *See* car MP3 players; home stereos
StoneAmp skin, **814**, *815*
storing audio files
    on floppy disks, 59
    on hard drives, 16–17, 58–59
    on MP3 servers, 864–866
    on online drives, 60
    on portable MP3 players, 17, 615–617
    in RealAudio format, 37, 899, 912
    on removable media, 59
    requirements for, 58–60
streaming audio, **280–281**, **914**, *See also* Internet broadcasting; Internet radio; RealAudio
strings, **776**
subrad skin, *507*
subwoofers, **50**, **914**
supra-aural headphones, **56**, **914**
surround sound, **54**, **914**

T

T1 line connections, **130**, **914**
T3 line connections, **130–131**, **914**
tags, **15**, **914**, *See also* editing ID3 tags
telephone audio quality, 14
territory restrictions, **892**
text editors, **810**
themes, **563**, *564*
Thunderstorm skin, *501*
Timbukto Pro software, **870**
Toast software, **751**
Tomatoes Go Splat skin, *808*, **808**
Tonocorder software, **878**
transferring audio files
    CD files, 7–8
    MP3 files, 15, 17, 21
Trax software, *794*, **794–797**, *796*

TTL (time to live) settings, **212**
tuners for portable players, **621**
Turtle Beach Montego II Quadzilla sound card, **49**
TweakDUN utility, **66**
tweeters, **50**, **914**
TwinVQ Encoder, 897, 899, *899*
TwinVQ/VQF format, *See also* digital-audio formats
    CPU power and, 896
    creating VQF files, 898–899, *898–899*
    defined, **36**, **896**, **914**
    disadvantage, 897
    encoding method, 896
    versus MP3, 896
    playing VQF files, 36, 897, *897*
    renaming VQF files, 778, 779
    sound quality, 896
    Web sites, 898

U

UltraPlayer, *See also* Windows MP3 players
    ad flashing in, 378
    downloading, 378
    features, 377–378
    installing, 378
    interface, 378, *379*
    overview of, 377
ultraportable players, **610–611**
Uncook 95 software, *784–786*, **784–786**
Unreal Player MAX, *See also* Windows MP3 players
    configuring options, 381, *382*
    DJ Console feature, 382–383, *383*
    Download Component box, 380, *381*
    downloading, 379
    graphic equalizer, 382
    installing, 379
    interface, 381

Online Update box, 380
overview of, 379
playing music, 381, *381*
playlist editor, 382
Select Your Processor box, 379, *380*
updating Web sites, 688–689
upgrading
computers, 40–42
portable MP3 players, 616
upload speed caps, **63**, **703–704**, **914**
U.S. Copyright Office Summary of DMCA, 696–697
USB ports, **61**, **742**
UtopiaSoft Hum software, 638, 640

V

VAIO Music Clip, **27**
VBR (variable bitrate), 13, **426–427**, **915**
virtual memory, SoundJam and, 528, *528*
viruses, 107–108, 208
Viscolor.txt files, **834**, **837–838**
Visiosonic PCDJ ripper/player/jukebox, **471–472**
Visto.com, 60
visualizations
changing colors in Winamp, 834, **837–838**
Climax for Winamp plug-in, 343–346, *343–346*
defined, **21**, **915**
in MACAST, 507
in Sonique, 361–363, *362*
in SoundJam, 544, *544*
in Winamp, 334–335, *334*, 336
in Windows Media Player, 312, *313*
VQF files. *See* TwinVQ/VQF format

W

warez software, **88**, **915**
wattage of speakers, 52–53
WAV files
converting MP3 files to, 748–750
defined, **915**
encoding MP3 files from, 398
encoding to MP3 files, 412–413, *412–413*, *523*, 527
Web site addresses
Adobe Photoshop, 809
for analysis of LAME versus MP3Enc, 601
Apple QuickTime, 477
ASCAP, 698
Audioactive Player, 374
audioGnome, 217
Beyond.com, 389, 516
BladeEnc, 409, 605
BMI, 698
for buying computers, 41
Calypso Softworks, 852
for CD recorders, 444
cdparanoia, 587
cdrecord, 751
Copah CD-Reader, 365
CuteFTP, 115
CuteMX, 232
Digital Dreams Software, 772
Digital Thoughts, 509
for domain names, 667
for download-scheduling utilities, 66
EasyTAG, 770
Empeg Ltd., 649
for firewalls, 62
Forté Free Agent, 120
Fraunhofer Institute, 11, 399
FreeAmp, 368

Freenet, 274
G6 Renamer, 774
Gnapster, 192
gnutella, 210
GOGO-no-coda, 603
Go!Zilla, 117
Grip, 579
icecast, 719, 724, 727
id3ren, 770
iMesh, 234
Impact Software, 809
Innogear, 641
Internal Corporation, 379
IUMA, 891
Joker.com, 667
LAME encoder, 405
LameBatch, 406
Liquid Audio, 886, 889
Lydstrom, 644, 645
MACAST, 502
MACAST Lite, 513
Macster, 169
Maximum PC, **653**
Microangelo, 809
Microsoft, 870, 894, 895
MP3, 19
MP3 Fiend, 117
MP3 Star Search, 115
MP3 to EXE, 798
mp3asm, 783
MP3Cutter, 780
MP3Enc, 605
mp3Trim, 782
MP4, 33
MPEG, 11
mpg123, 574
MusicMatch, 419, 444, 546
MVP encoder/player, 878

Napster, 126, 127, 675
Netopia, 870
Network Solutions, Inc., 667
NotLame, 601
for online storage drives, 60
Paint Shop Pro, 809
for plug-ins, 341, 365
Proteron, 522
Pure MP3, 111
QDesign, 879
QuickAmp, 491
RadioSpy, 280
RealJukebox Skins Toolkit, 840
RealNetworks, 450, 478, 516
Red Hat Software, 49
for relay servers, 704
Request, Inc., 644
RIAA, 695
Route 66, **653**
SDMI, 87
for search engines, 689
SESAC, Inc., 698
SHOUTcast, 705, 719
on skin creation, 810
for skinning programs, 811
for skins, 339, 364, 806
smpeg-xmms, 571
SongBank, 644
Sonic Foundry, 470
Sonique, 349
SoundApp, 479
SoundJam, 527
SpinFrenzy, 276
Sun Java, 273
TwinVQ/VQF format, 898
UltraPlayer, 378
Uncook 95, 784
Unreal Player MAX, 379

Web sites—Windows Media Technologies 951

UtopiaSoft, 638, 640
Visiosonic, 471, 472
Web Site Garage, 689
Winamp, 314, 806, 810
Winamp VQF, 897
Windows Media Players, 637, 894
Wrapster, 208
Xing Technologies, 89
XingMP3 Player, 371
Xiphophorus, 587
xmms, 569
Yamaha, 897, 898

Web sites
    building, **675–689**
        adding interactive features, 679–684
        adding metatags, 689
        advantage of, 676
        caution, 680
        children and, 684
        choosing domain names, 667
        choosing ISPs, 678–679
        collecting visitor information, 681–684
        developing privacy policies, 683
        disadvantage of, 676
        with easy navigation, 686–687
        ensuring browser viewability, 686
        ensuring quick load speed, 685–686
        information to include, 676–678, 687
        overview of, 667, 675, 687
        passwords and, 676
        photographs in, 685
        presenting clear focus, 684–685
        providing visitor benefits, 687
        registering with search engines, 689
        and updating, 688–689
        warning, 684

for finding MP3 files, **98–111**
    and downloading or not, 99
    eatsleepmusic.com, 104–105
    EMusic.com, 102–103, 573
    Free Music Archive, 105
    FTP sites, 98
    iCrunch, 103
    Listen.com, 103
    MP3 Place, 105
    MP3.com, 101–102
    MP3Lit.com, 104
    overview of, 98–99
    pirate sites, 107–111
    porn sites and, 108–111
    record company sites, 106–107
    Riffage.com, 100–101
    RioPort, 106
    songs.com, 103
    Spinfrenzy.com, 104
    WorldWideBands, 106

getting own music onto
    MP3.com, 673, 674–675
    Napster, 675
    overview of, 672–674
    Riffage.com, 673, 674

webcasting. *See* Internet broadcasting
Winamp. *See* Windows MP3 players
Windows Media Player. *See* Windows MP3 players
Windows Media Technologies
    ASF audio files and, 893, 895
    defined, **915**
    MS Audio format, 35–36
    Windows Media Player, 301–313, 893–895, *895*
    Windows Media Player for Palm-size PCs, 637–638
    Windows Media Tools toolkit, 895
    WMA file format, 639, 893–895, *895*

Windows MP3 players, **298-383**, *See also* Linux; Macintosh; MP3 players
    Audioactive Player
        downloading, 374
        editing ID3 tags, 376, *377*
        installing, 375
        options, 376, *376*
        overview of, 374-375, *375*
        Playlist Editor, *375*
    choosing, 299-301
    FreeAmp
        disadvantage, 368
        editing ID3 tags, 769, *769*
        features, 368
        installing, 369
        interface, 369, *369*
        My Music window, 370, *370*
        overview of, 368
    MVP, **878-879**, *879*
    overview of, 298-299, 367, 383
    Sonique, **349-367**
        adding plug-ins, 365
        Audio Enhancement Control, 359-361, *360-361*
        Auto-Play feature, 350
        burning CDs, 748-749
        changing skins, 363-364, *364*
        converting MP3 files to WAV, 748-749
        creating playlists, 357-358, *358*
        defined, **349**
        downloading, 349
        editing ID3 tags, 358-359, *359*
        installing, 349-351, *350-351*
        interface, 352-356, *353-355*
        keyboard shortcuts, 355-357, 365-367
        launching, 352
        overview of, 298
        playing music, 356-357

        visualizations, 361-363, *362*
    UltraPlayer
        ad flashing in, 378
        downloading, 378
        features, 377-378
        installing, 378
        interface, 378, *379*
        overview of, 377
    Unreal Player MAX
        configuring options, 381, *382*
        DJ Console feature, 382-383, *383*
        Download Component box, 380, *381*
        downloading, 379
        graphic equalizer, 382
        installing, 379
        interface, 381
        Online Update box, 380
        overview of, 379
        playing music, 381, *381*
        playlist editor, 382
        Select Your Processor box, 379, *380*
    Winamp, **314-349**, *See also* skins
        adding plug-ins, **340-349**
        adding RealAudio, 342-343, *342*
        adding sound effects, 347-349, *347-348*
        adding visual effects, 343-346, *343-346*
        applying skins, 339-340, *340*
        arranging windows, 318-321, *319-320*, 336
        bookmarking tracks, 328, *329*
        browser shortcut keys, 338
        Browser window, 319-321, *319-320*
        burning CDs, 748
        configuring to SHOUTcast, 713-716, *713*, *715-716*
        converting MP3 files to WAV, 748
        defined, **314**

downloading, 314
editing ID3 tags, 333, *333*, 762, *762*
exiting, 321
Graphical Equalizer, 319–321, *319–320*, 329–332, *330*, *332*
installing, 314–318, *315*
keyboard shortcuts, 328, 335–338
Linux and, 314
Main window, 318, *319–320*, 320–323, *322*
overview of, 298
playing music, 321–324, *322*, 336–337
Playlist Editor, 318, *319–320*, 320–321
playlists, managing, 324–326, *324*, 337–338
playlists, navigating, 327–328, *327*, 338
setting options, 315–317, *315*, 334, *334*
tweaking sound, 329–332, *330*, *332*, 338
User Information box, 317–318
visualizations, 334–335, *334*, 336
Web site, 314
windowshade mode, 320, *320*
versus xmms player for Linux, 569–571, *570*

Windows Media Player, **301–313**
    CD Audio options, 309–310, *310*
    Compact mode, 305, *306*
    configuring options, 307–313
    creating playlists, 304, *304*, 307, *307*
    Formats options, 312, *313*
    Full mode, 305, *305*
    Media Library options, 312, *312*
    Media Library page, 307, *307*
    Network options, 309, *309*
    overview of, 301–302
    Performance options, 310, *311*
    Player options, 308, *308*
    Portable Device options, 310, *311*
    Search for Media tool, 306–307, *306*
    starting, 302, 305, *305*, *306*
    switching playlists, 307
    version 7, 304–313, 893–895, *895*
    versions before 7, 302–304, *303*
    Visualizations options, 312, *313*
    WMA files and, 893–895, *895*
Windows Media Player for Palm-size PCs, **637–638**
XingMP3 Player
    bug in, 373, *373*
    downloading, 371
    interface, 371–373, *372*
    overview of, 370–371, 389
    Play List Editor, 371, *372*
    Properties/Settings, 373–374
    starting, 371
Windows Notepad, **810**
Windows ripper/player/jukeboxes, **418–472**
    defined, **912**
    MusicMatch Jukebox, **418–448**
        accessing music on Internet, 441, *441*
        adding tracks to libraries, 434–435, *435*
        AutoDJ feature, 439, *439*
        burning CDs, 443–448, *445*, *447*
        CDDB/Connectivity settings, 424–425, *425*
        Confirm Association box, 422
        creating music libraries, 432, 434
        creating playlists, 438
        deleting tracks from libraries, 435–436, *436*
        downloading, 419
        editing ID3 tags, 430–432, *431*, 762, *763*

Filetype Registration box, 420–421, *421*
finding tracks in libraries, 437, *437*
graphic equalizer, 440–441, *440*
installing, 419–421, *420–421*
Jukebox File Associations box, 421
Jukebox Recorder window, 429–430, *429*
Main window, 422–424, *423*
Music Library settings, 433–434, *433*
Music Library window, 422–424, *423*
Net Music feature, 441, *441*
Net Radio feature, 442–443, *442–443*
New Songs Directory box, 427–428, *427*
opening music libraries, 435–436, *436*
opening playlists, 438
overview of, 418
Personalize Net Music box, 419–420, *420*
playing Internet radio, 442–443, *442–443*
Playlist window, 423–424, *423*, 438
using playlists, 438–439, *439*
previewing tracks, 438
Recorder settings, 425–499, *426–427*, *428–429*
registering, 424
ripping CDs, 429–430, *429–430*
saving playlists, 438
Search for Music box, 422, *422*
setting options, 424–429
sharing libraries, 436–437
User Registration Info box, 419
warning, 436
windows, manipulating, 422–424, *423*
overview of, 418, 472

RealJukebox, **448–469**, *See also* skins
Audio Playback options, 452–453
Audio Quality preferences, 457, 900
AutoPlaylist feature, 464
AutoStart options, 453
CD Recording options, 454, *454*
changing skins, 467–468, *467*
configuring options, 452–456
configuring portable players, 465, *466*
converting track formats, 468, *469*
creating playlists, 463–464, *463*
downloading, 450–451
Driver Problem Detected box, 465, *465*
Find Music options, 453
Full Mode, 459, *459*
General preferences, 456
identifying portable players to, 464–465, *465*
installing, 451–452
interface, 459–460, *459–460*
Internet options, 455
loading portable players, 466
Music File Location options, 453
Music Files preferences, 457–458, *458*
overview of, 418, 448–449
playing music, 462–464, *463*
using with portable MP3 players, 464–467, *465–466*
preferences, 456–458
RealAudio format in, 454, *454*, 468, *469*, 900
RealNetworks and, 449–450
Recording options, 455
Recording preferences, 456, *457*
removing portable players from, 466–467
ripping CDs, 461–462, *461*
Security options, 453–454

Windows rippers and encoders—Windows systems 955

Skin Mode, 460, *460*
starting, 459
viewing libraries, 462–463
warning, 451
versus rippers and encoders, 386–388
Siren Jukebox, 469–470, *471*
Visiosonic PCDJ, 471–472
Windows rippers and encoders, **386–415**
   Audioactive Production Studio ripper/encoder
      downloading, 410
      encoding WAV files to MP3, 412–413, *412–413*
      installing, 410–411
      interface, 411, *411*
      overview of, 409–410
      ripping from CDS, 414–415, *414*
      warning, 411
   AudioCatalyst ripper/encoder
      CDDB Disk Submit Wizard, 398
      CDDB Settings, 394–395, *395*
      downloading, 389
      encoding MP3 files from WAV, 398
      General Settings, 390–392, *390*
      installing, 389–390
      MP3 Playback Settings, 396
      Normalizing Settings, 395–396, *396*
      overview of, 389
      ripping/encoding with, 396–397, *397–398*
      XingMP3 Encoder Settings, 392–394, *393*
   BladeEnc encoder, 409, **605**
   determining need for, 386–388
   encoders, defined, **387**
   LAME encoder
      versus BladeEnc encoder, 409
      downloading, 405
      encoding files, 408–409, *408*
      versus GOGO-no-coda encoder, 603
      versus MP3Enc encoder, 601
      NotLame encoder and, 601
      overview of, 405
      running from command lines, 405
      running from LameBatch GUI, 406–409, *406*, *408*
      setting options, 406–408, *406*
   MP3 Producer/Producer Professional encoders
      batch processing, 403–405, *404*
      buying, 401
      disadvantages, 400–401
      encoding with, 402–405, *402*, *404*
      installing, 401–402, *401*
      overview of, 400
   MP3Enc encoder
      defined, **399**, **605**
      downloading, 399, 605
      encoding with, 400
      versus LAME encoder, 601
      testing demo versions, 399
   overview of, 386, 415
   versus ripper/player/jukeboxes, 386–388
   rippers, defined, **387**
Windows systems, *See also* Napster on Windows
   a2b music players for, 881–883, *882–883*
   building MP3 servers on, 867–868
   CD burning software, 751
   creating playlists in
      overview of, 787
      with Playlist Pro, 787–788, *787–788*
      with ShufflePlay, 789–793, *789*, *791–793*
   editing ID3 tags on
      in Audioactive Player, 376, *377*
      in FreeAmp, 769, *769*
      in MusicMatch Jukebox, 430–432, *431*, *762*, *763*
      overview of, 762

in Sonique, 358–359, *359*
in Winamp, 333, *333*, 762, *762*
editing MP3 files on, 780–782, *781–783*
renaming MP3 files on, 772–778, *772*, *774–776*, *778–779*
repairing cooked MP3 files on, 784–786, *784–786*
windowshade mode in Winamp, *320*, **320**
Winshade VU options, *334*, **334–335**
WIPO (World Intellectual Property Organization), 696
wireless headphones, 58
WMA (Windows Media Audio) files, 639, **893–895**, *895*, **915**
WonderJelly skin, *545*
Woody Wood Amp skin, *808*, **808**
woofers, **50**, **915**
WorldWideBands Web site, **106**
Wrapster software, **207–209**, *209*
Wrist Audio Player, 624
WSZ file extensions, **840**

X

XingMP3 Player, *See also* Windows MP3 players
bug in, 373, *373*
downloading, 371
interface, 371–373, *372*

overview of, 370–371, 389
Play List Editor, 371, *372*
Properties/Settings, 373–374
starting, 371
xmms player, *See also* Linux MP3 players
applying skins, 569
in burning CDs, 750
converting MP3 files to WAV, 750
defined, **568**
downloading, 569
editing ID3 tags, 768, *769*
interface, 569, *569*
overview of, 314
plug-ins, 571
preferences, 570, *570*
versus Winamp, 569–571, *570*

Y

Yahoo!, 60
Yamaha SoundVQ Encoder, 897, 898, *898*
Yamaha SoundVQ Player, 897, *897*

Z

Zip drives, **59**
zipping files, **59**

Evolve to a Higher Level!

"I Didn't Know You Could Do That™....," is a new Sybex™ series for beginners through intermediate users. Each book covers a popular subject certain to appeal to the general consumer. Written in a light, conversational style, well-known authors teach users cool, fun, immediately useful tips and secrets. Each companion CD is loaded with valuable software and utilities.

MP3!
$19.99
ISBN: 0-7821-2653-7

Internet!
$19.99
ISBN: 0-7821-2587-5

PalmPilot!
(and Palm Organizers)
$19.99
ISBN: 0-7821-2588-3

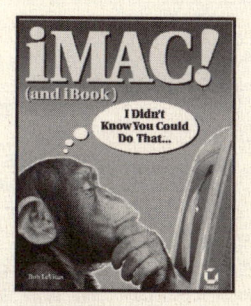

iMac™!
$19.99
ISBN: 0-7821-2589-1

Home Networking!
$19.99
ISBN: 0-7821-2631-6

Linux!
$19.99
ISBN: 0-7821-2612-x

SYBEX®
www.sybex.com

Topics Covered	Page #
Maximize your **modem speed**	65
Encode with **MP3 Producer Professional** on Windows	400
Build an **MP3 server**	863
Encode with **MP3Enc** on Windows	399
Encode with **MP3Enc** on Linux	605
Rip and encode with **MPegger** on the Macintosh	522
Play MP3 files with **mpg123** on Linux	574
Rip, encode, and play MP3 files with **MusicMatch Jukebox** on the Macintosh	555
Rip, encode, and play MP3 files with **MusicMatch Jukebox** on Windows	429
Use a **naming convention** for your MP3 collection	861
Use Gnapster—**Napster for Linux**	192
Use Macster—**Napster for the Macintosh**	168
Use **Napster on Windows**	129
Encode with **NotLame** on Linux	601
Learn about the **OpenMG** digital-audio format	884
Get an **overview of Napster**	128
Understand **personal use**	79
Use **piracy** to promote your music	663
Be realistic about **piracy of your own music**	662
Create **playlists on Linux**	797
Create **playlists on the Macintosh**	794
Create **playlists on Windows**	787
Play MP3 files on a **Pocket PC or Palm-Size PC**	636
Choose the right **portable MP3 player** for your needs	615
Post your own music on online sites	671
Assess the **promises and threats of digital audio for artists**	659
Develop a **promotional strategy** for your own music	666
Use the **QDMC** codec	877
Play MP3 files with **QuickAmp** on the Macintosh	491
Play MP3 files with **QuickTime** on the Macintosh	477
Use **QuickTime** for digital audio	900
Listen to Internet radio with **RadioSpy**	291
Learn about **RealAudio**	889
Rip, encode, and play MP3 files with **RealJukebox** on Windows	46